CAMBRIDGE GREEK TESTAMENT COMMENTARY

GENERAL EDITOR

C. F. D. MOULE

*Lady Margaret's Professor of Divinity in the
University of Cambridge*

THE GOSPEL
ACCORDING TO
SAINT MARK

IN THIS SERIES

The Epistles of Paul the Apostle to the Colossians
and to Philemon.   By C. F. D. MOULE

THE GOSPEL
ACCORDING TO
SAINT MARK

AN INTRODUCTION AND
COMMENTARY BY

C. E. B. CRANFIELD

Reader in Theology, University of Durham

FOURTH IMPRESSION
WITH REVISED ADDITIONAL SUPPLEMENTARY NOTES

CAMBRIDGE
AT THE UNIVERSITY PRESS
1972

Published by the Syndics of the Cambridge University Press
Bentley House, 200 Euston Road, London NW1 2DB
American Branch: 32 East 57th Street, New York, N.Y.10022

ISBNS:
0 521 04253 4 clothbound
0 521 09204 3 paperback

First edition 1959
Reprinted with supplementary notes 1963
Reprinted with additional supplementary notes 1966
Reprinted with revised additional supplementary notes 1972

Printed in Great Britain at the University Printing House, Cambridge
(Brooke Crutchley, University Printer)

PREFACE

BY THE GENERAL EDITOR

The last fifty years have seen a considerable shift in emphasis within New Testament scholarship. When the primary task was to establish the text and to discuss the authenticity of the documents, linguistic and historical considerations were foremost. But gradually, as these foundation-tasks were done, it became possible to devote increasing attention to the elucidation of the theological and religious contents of the New Testament, and to see it in the setting of the life and worship of Christian communities.

To be sure, no scholarship worthy of the name had at any time neglected this aspect of New Testament studies; still less can this aspect be examined without the linguistic and historical: that would be to build on sand. Nor can the primary tasks ever be taken as completed once and for all. Foundations need continual re-examination and reinforcement.

Nevertheless, it is for the sake of the superstructure that foundations exist: and it is the superstructure which now rightly claims its due attention. Accordingly, the time seems ripe for a revision of the New Testament volumes of a long-established series of Cambridge biblical commentaries.

Not that the intention is—as yet, at any rate—to replace all the old volumes; still less to belittle those which are selected for replacement. It would be folly to despise a series begun under the editorship of J. J. S. Perowne with a galaxy of eminent collaborators, and maintained at a high standard ever since.

But it is believed that the new series, in a more attractive format and written with contemporary trends in view and with the advantage of such new material as has come to light, will meet a need.

The series began, in 1877, with *The Cambridge Bible for Schools* (on the English text) and, shortly afterwards, with *The Cambridge Greek Testament for Schools and Colleges.* At the present time, however, it seems better not to use titles suggesting any definition of the readers. There are many beyond school age who will welcome a commentary without Greek; and there are some outside the Universities who will use one on the Greek text. The new series—confining itself for the time being to the Greek Testament—will therefore be called simply the *Cambridge Greek Testament Commentary.*

The first General Editor of this new series was Professor A. M. Ramsey; and it was under him that the first contributors, including the present General Editor, were enrolled. Professor Ramsey's elevation to the See of Durham, however, led to his resignation; and at about the same time one of the pledged collaborators, the Rev. R. G. Heard, Dean of Peterhouse, was removed by death.

It falls to the new General Editor to take up the midwifery, and this he is proud to attempt—although, like his predecessors, he does not accept responsibility for all the views expressed by the children, but only for their general character and conduct.

> *et sit splendor Domini Dei nostri super nos!*
> *et opus manuum nostrarum dirige.*
>
> *Amen.*

C. F. D. M

CAMBRIDGE
1955

CONTENTS

CONTENTS

NOTES

LIST OF ABBREVIATIONS

References to books and articles cited more than once are by abbreviated titles; commentaries on Mark are cited by the author's name alone. The details are given below. Details of books and articles cited only once are given at the citation.

COMMENTARIES

ALLEN, W. C., *The Gospel according to St Mark* (London, 1915).

BACON, B. W., *The Beginnings of Gospel Story* (New Haven, 1909).

BARTLET, J. V., *St Mark* (Century Bible, Edinburgh, 1922).

BEDE, *In Marci Evangelium Expositio* (in J. P. Migne, *Patrologia Latina*, XCII, columns 131–302).

BENGEL, J. A., *Gnomon Novi Testamenti* (Tübingen, 1742).

BLUNT, A. W. F., *The Gospel according to St Mark* (Clarendon Bible, Oxford, 1929).

BRANSCOMB, B. H., *The Gospel of Mark* (London, 1937).

CALVIN, J., *Commentary on a Harmony of the Evangelists, Matthew, Mark, and Luke* (Latin, 1555; Eng. tr. by W. Pringle, Edinburgh, 1845, reprinted Grand Rapids, U.S.A., 1949).

EUTHYMIUS ZIGABENUS, Ἑρμηνεία τοῦ κατὰ Μᾶρκον εὐαγγελίου (in J. P. Migne, *Patrologia Graeca*, CXXIX, columns 765–852).

HAUCK, F., *Das Evangelium des Markus* (Theologischer Handkommentar zum N.T., Leipzig, 1931).

HUNTER, A. M., *The Gospel according to St Mark* (Torch Bible Commentaries, London, 1948).

LAGRANGE, M.-J., *Évangile selon Saint Marc* (Paris, 1910; 4th (revised) ed. 1929).

LOHMEYER, E., *Das Evangelium des Markus* (Kritisch-exegetischer Kommentar über das N.T., Göttingen, 1937; new ed. revised by G. Sass, 1951).

LOWRIE, W., *Jesus according to St Mark* (London, 1929).

PLUMMER, A., *The Gospel according to St Mark* (Cambridge Greek Testament for Schools and Colleges, Cambridge, 1914).

RAWLINSON, A. E. J., *The Gospel according to St Mark* (Westminster Commentaries, London, 1925).

SCHLATTER, A., *Die Evangelien nach Markus und Lukas* (Stuttgart, reprinted 1947).

SCHNIEWIND, J., *Das Evangelium nach Markus* (Das N.T. Deutsch, Göttingen, 1934).

SWETE, H. B., *The Gospel according to St Mark* (Macmillan N.T. Commentaries, London, 1898; 3rd ed. 1909).

† TAYLOR, V., *The Gospel according to St Mark* (Macmillan N.T. Commentaries, London, 1952).

THEOPHYLACT, Ἑρμηνεία εἰς τὸ κατὰ Μᾶρκον εὐαγγέλιον (in J. P. Migne, *Patrologia Graeca*, CXXIII, columns 487–682).

TURNER, C. H., *The Gospel according to St Mark* (reprinted from *A New Commentary on Holy Scripture*, ed. C. Gore, H. L. Goudge, A. Guillaume; London, 1928).

VICTOR OF ANTIOCH, in P. Possinus, *Catena Graecorum Patrum in Evangelium secundum Marcum* (Rome, 1673).

WELLHAUSEN, J., *Das Evangelium Marci* (Berlin, 1903; 2nd ed.
* 1909).

OTHER BOOKS AND ARTICLES

ABRAHAMS, *Studies*: I. ABRAHAMS, *Studies in Pharisaism and the Gospels* (Cambridge, I, 1917; II, 1924).

A.D.P.B.: *The Authorised Daily Prayer Book of the United Hebrew Congregations of the British Empire with a new translation by the late Rev. S. Singer* (London, 23rd ed. 1954).

BACON, *Gospel of Mark*: B. W. BACON, *The Gospel of Mark: its Composition and Date* (New Haven, U.S.A., 1925).

BARRETT, *H.S.G.T.*: C. K. BARRETT, *The Holy Spirit and the Gospel Tradition* (London, 1947).

BARRETT, *John*: C. K. BARRETT, *The Gospel according to St John* (London, 1955).

BARTH, *Credo*: K. BARTH, *Credo* (1935; Eng. tr. by J. S. McNab, London, 1936).

BARTH, *K.D.*: K. BARTH, *Die Kirchliche Dogmatik* (Zollikon, 1932–).

BARTH, *C.D.*: K. BARTH, *Church Dogmatics* (being the Eng. tr. of the above) (Edinburgh, 1936–).

BAUER: W. BAUER, *Griechisch-Deutsches Wörterbuch zu den Schriften des Neuen Testamentes und der übrigen urchristlichen Literatur* (Berlin, 4th (revised) ed. 1952). An English translation and adaptation of this under the title *A Greek–English Lexicon of the New Testament and other Early Christian Literature* by W. F. Arndt and F. W. Gingrich was published by the Cambridge University Press in 1957. (A 5th ed. of Bauer has now been published (1958).)

B.D.B.: F. Brown, S. R. Driver and C. A. Briggs, *A Hebrew and English Lexicon of the Old Testament* (Oxford, 1907; corrected impr. 1952).

Beasley-Murray, *Jesus and the Future*: G. R. Beasley-Murray, *Jesus and the Future* (London, 1954).

Beasley-Murray, *Mark xiii*: G. R. Beasley-Murray, *A Commentary on Mark Thirteen* (London, 1957).

B.G.U.: *Ägyptische Urkunden aus den Museen zu Berlin: Griechische Urkunden*, I–VIII (1895–1933).

Bieneck, *Sohn Gottes*: J. Bieneck, *Sohn Gottes als Christusbezeichnung der Synoptiker* (Zürich, 1951).

Bishop, *Jesus of Pal.*: E. F. F. Bishop, *Jesus of Palestine* (London, 1955).

Black: M. Black, *An Aramaic Approach to the Gospels and Acts* (Oxford, 2nd (revised) ed. 1954).

Boobyer, *Transfig.*: G. H. Boobyer, *St Mark and the Transfiguration Story* (Edinburgh, 1942).

Bultmann, *G.S.T.*: R. Bultmann, *Die Geschichte der synoptischen Tradition* (Göttingen, 2nd ed. 1931).

Bultmann, *Theology*: R. Bultmann, *Theology of the New Testament*, I (1948; Eng. tr. by K. Grobel, London, 1952).

Burrows, *D.S.S.*: M. Burrows, *The Dead Sea Scrolls* (London, 1956).

C.N.: *Coniectanea Neotestamentica* XI *in honorem A. Fridrichsen* (Lund, 1947).

Cullmann, *Baptism*: O. Cullmann, *Baptism in the New Testament* (Eng. tr. by J. K. S. Reid, London, 1950).

Dalman, *S.S.W.*: G. Dalman, *Sacred Sites and Ways* (Eng. tr. by P. P. Levertoff, London, 1935).

D.-B.: A. Debrunner, *Friedrich Blass' Grammatik des neutestamentlichen Griechisch* (Göttingen, 9th ed. 1954).

Dodd, 'Appearances': C. H. Dodd, 'The Appearances of the Risen Christ: An Essay in Form-Criticism of the Gospels', in *Studies in the Gospels: Essays in Memory of R. H. Lightfoot*, ed. D. E. Nineham (Oxford, 1955), pp. 9–35.

Dodd, *Parables*: C. H. Dodd, *The Parables of the Kingdom* (London, 1935; revised ed. 1936).

Farrer, *St Mark*: A. M. Farrer, *A Study in St Mark* (London, 1951).

Field: F. Field, *Notes on the Translation of the New Testament* (Cambridge, 1899).

FLEMINGTON, *Baptism*: W. F. FLEMINGTON, *The New Testament Doctrine of Baptism* (London, 1948).

HUCK: A. HUCK, *Synopsis of the First Three Gospels* (Eng. ed. by F. L. Cross, Oxford, 1949).

† JEREMIAS, *E.W.*: J. JEREMIAS, *The Eucharistic Words of Jesus* (Eng. tr. by A. Ehrhardt from the 2nd German ed. (1949), Oxford, 1955).

JEREMIAS, *Parables*: J. JEREMIAS, *The Parables of Jesus* (Eng. tr. by S. H. Hooke from the 3rd German ed. (1954), London, 1954).

KILPATRICK, 'Gentile Mission': G. D. KILPATRICK, 'The Gentile Mission in Mark and Mark xiii. 9–11', in *Studies in the Gospels: Essays in Memory of R. H. Lightfoot*, ed. D. E. Nineham (Oxford, 1955), pp. 145–58.

KNOX, *Sources*, I: W. L. KNOX, *The Sources of the Synoptic Gospels*, I, *St Mark* (edited by H. Chadwick, Cambridge, 1953).

KÜMMEL, *P. and F.*: W. G. KÜMMEL, *Promise and Fulfilment* (Eng. tr. from the 3rd German ed. (1956), London, 1957).

LAMPE, *Seal*: G. W. H. LAMPE, *The Seal of the Spirit* (London, 1951).

L. & S.: H. G. LIDDELL & R. SCOTT, *A Greek-English Lexicon* (revised and augmented by H. Stuart Jones and R. McKenzie, Oxford, 1940).

LIGHTFOOT, *Gospel Message*: R. H. LIGHTFOOT, *The Gospel Message of St Mark* (Oxford, 1950).

LUTHER, W.A.: M. LUTHER, *Werke* (Weimarer Ausgabe).

MANSON, 'Cleansing': T. W. MANSON, 'The Cleansing of the Temple', in *B.J.R.L.* XXXIII (1951), pp. 271–82.

MANSON, *Jesus the Messiah*: Wm. MANSON, *Jesus the Messiah* (London, 1943).

MANSON, *Sayings*: T. W. MANSON, *The Sayings of Jesus* (London, 1949).

MANSON, *S.-M.*: T. W. MANSON, *The Servant-Messiah* (Cambridge, 1953).

MANSON, *Teaching*: T. W. MANSON, *The Teaching of Jesus* (Cambridge, 1931; 2nd ed. 1935).

M.H.: J. H. MOULTON & W. F. HOWARD, *A Grammar of New Testament Greek*, II (Edinburgh, 1929).

MICHAELIS, *Verheissung*: W. MICHAELIS, *Der Herr verzieht nicht die Verheissung* (Berne, 1942).

M.M.: J. H. MOULTON & G. MILLIGAN, *The Vocabulary of the Greek Testament* (London, 1930).

MOULE: C. F. D. MOULE, *An Idiom-Book of New Testament Greek* (Cambridge, 1953).

MOULE, *Colossians*: C. F. D. MOULE, *The Epistles to the Colossians and to Philemon* (Cambridge, 1957).

MOULTON, *Proleg.*: J. H. MOULTON, *A Grammar of New Testament Greek*, I, *Prolegomena* (Edinburgh, 1908).

NINEHAM, 'Order of Events': D. E. NINEHAM, 'The Order of Events in St Mark's Gospel—an examination of Dr Dodd's Hypothesis', in *Studies in the Gospels: Essays in Memory of R. H. Lightfoot*, ed. D. E. Nineham (Oxford, 1955), pp. 223–39.

NUNN, *Elements*: H. P. V. NUNN, *The Elements of New Testament Greek* (Cambridge, 8th ed. 1945).

P.Flor.: G. VITELLI & D. COMPARETTI, *Papiri Fiorentini*, I–III (Milan, 1906–15).

P.Grenf.: B. P. GRENFELL & A. S. HUNT, *New Classical Fragments and other Greek and Latin papyri* (Oxford, 1897).

P.Oxy.: B. P. GRENFELL & A. S. HUNT, *Oxyrhynchus Papyri* (London, 1898–).

PREISS, *F. de l'H.*: T. PREISS, *Le Fils de l'Homme* (Montpellier, I, 1951; II, 1953).

RAMSEY, *Resurrection*: A. M. RAMSEY, *The Resurrection of Christ* (London, 2nd ed. 1946).

RENGSTORF, *Apostleship*: K. H. RENGSTORF, *Apostleship* (Eng. tr. by J. R. Coates of article in *T.W.N.T.*, London, 1952).

RICHARDSON, *Miracles*: A. RICHARDSON, *The Miracle Stories of the Gospels* (London, 1941).

ROUX, *L'Évang. du Royaume*: H. ROUX, *L'Évangile du Royaume: Commentaire sur l'Évangile de Matthieu* (Paris, 1942).

S.–B.: H. L. STRACK & P. BILLERBECK, *Kommentar zum Neuen Testament aus Talmud und Midrasch*, I–IV (Munich, 1922–8).

SCHLATTER, *Evang. Matt.*: A. SCHLATTER, *Der Evangelist Matthäus* (Stuttgart, 1929).

SCHMIDT, *Rahmen*: K. L. SCHMIDT, *Der Rahmen der Geschichte Jesu* (Berlin, 1919).

SMITH, *Hist. Geog.*: G. A. SMITH, *The Historical Geography of the Holy Land* (London, 11th ed. 1904).

STREETER, *Four Gospels*: B. H. STREETER, *The Four Gospels: A Study of Origins* (London, 1924).

TURNER, *J.T.S.*: C. H. TURNER, articles on 'Marcan Usage' in *J.T.S.* XXV–XXIX (1924–8).

T.W.B.: A. RICHARDSON (ed.), *A Theological Word Book of the Bible* (London, 1950).

T.W.N.T.: G. Kittel (ed.), continued by G. Friedrich (ed.), *Theologisches Wörterbuch zum Neuen Testament* (Stuttgart, 1933–).

WHITEHOUSE, *C.F.S.A.*: W. A. WHITEHOUSE, *Christian Faith and the Scientific Attitude* (Edinburgh, 1952).

ZIMMERLI & JEREMIAS, *Servant*: W. ZIMMERLI & J. JEREMIAS, *The Servant of God* (Eng. tr. of the article on παῖς Θεοῦ in *T.W.N.T.*
* London, 1957).

JOURNALS

B.J.R.L.: *Bulletin of the John Rylands Library*, Manchester.

B.S.N.T.S.: *Bulletin of the Studiorum Novi Testamenti Societas*, I–III (1950–2, Oxford).

E.T.: *The Expository Times*, Edinburgh.

Ev. Theol.: *Evangelische Theologie*, Munich.

Exp.: *The Expositor*, London.

H.T.R.: *The Harvard Theological Review*, Cambridge, Massachusetts.

Interp.: *Interpretation*, Richmond, Virginia.

J.T.S.: *Journal of Theological Studies*, Oxford.

N.T.S.: *New Testament Studies*, Cambridge.

S.J.T.: *Scottish Journal of Theology*, Edinburgh.

S.T.: *Studia Theologica*, Lund.

T.T.: *Theology Today*, Princeton.

T.Z.: *Theologische Zeitschrift*, Basel.

Z.N.T.W.: *Zeitschrift für die neutestamentliche Wissenschaft*, Giessen.

RABBINIC LITERATURE

Tractates of the Mishnah, Talmud and Tosephta are cited by the abbreviations listed in H. Danby, *The Mishnah, Translated from the Hebrew with Introduction and Brief Explanatory Notes* (Oxford, 1933), p. 806. Where the reference is to the Mishnah, the abbreviated title is preceded by (*M*), where to the Talmud by *j* or *b* (according as the Jerusalem or Babylonian Talmud is meant), where to the Tosephta by *t*. Other Rabbinic writings referred to are cited by unabbreviated titles. They are all Midrashim, i.e. biblical expositions (see Strack, *Introduction to the Talmud and Midrash* (Philadelphia, 1945), pp. 199–234), with the exception of the Targums, which are Aramaic paraphrases of Scripture, and *Sopherim*, which is an extra-canonical tractate attached to the Babylonian Talmud (see Strack, *op. cit.* p. 73).

OTHER CITATIONS

The pseudepigraphical literature of the Old Testament is most
easily accessible in vol. II of R. H. Charles, *The Apocrypha and
Pseudepigrapha of the Old Testament in English* (Oxford, 1913);
the apocryphal literature of the New Testament in M. R.
James, *The Apocryphal New Testament* (Oxford, 1924). A
translation of the Qumran sect's scriptures is to be found in
T. H. Gaster, *The Scriptures of the Dead Sea Sect* (London,
1957). For a general account of the Dead Sea Scrolls the
reader should refer to Burrows, *D.S.S.*: specially valuable is
the sober discussion of the contribution of the Dead Sea
Scrolls to the study of Judaism and Christianity on pp. 326–45.   *

Josephus is cited by the sections of Niese's edition which are used in
the Loeb Classical Library edition.

TEXTS

Nestle: *Novum Testamentum Graece*, ed. E. Nestle (Stuttgart, 22nd
(revised) ed. 1956).

Souter: *Novum Testamentum Graece*, ed. A. Souter (Oxford, 2nd
(revised) ed. 1947).

W.H.: *The New Testament in Greek*, ed. B. F. Westcott & F. J. A.
Hort (*editio maior*, two vols., Cambridge and London, 1881;
editio minor, one vol. without introduction, etc., 1895).

The commentary is based on the British and Foreign Bible Society's
text (second edition, of which the proofs were made available
by the courtesy of Professor G. D. Kilpatrick), and the *sigla* of
the apparatus of that edition (referred to as 'the Bible Society')
are mainly used. Thus D, L, etc. in the textual notes $= D_1$, L_1,   *
etc. alluded to on p. 24.

OTHER ABBREVIATIONS

LXX: The 'Septuagint' version of the Old Testament.
M.T.: The Masoretic text of the Hebrew Old Testament.
R.V.: The English Revised Version.
R.S.V.: The American Revised Standard Version.
v.l.: *varia lectio*. (*v.ll.*: *variae lectiones*.)

Hebrew words are transliterated in accordance with the table in
H. H. Rowley (ed.), *The Old Testament and Modern Study* (Oxford,
1951), p. xiii.

ACKNOWLEDGEMENTS

The author gratefully acknowledges his indebtedness to his many predecessors, in particular to the Rev. Dr Vincent Taylor, to whose invaluable commentary he is specially indebted and whose generous personal encouragement he will not forget; and to his former teachers, the Rev. Dr R. Newton Flew and the Rev. W. F. Flemington, who first introduced him to the serious study of the New Testament. His gratitude is also due to the Rev. Professor C. F. D. Moule, the General Editor of this series, but for whose patient and thorough criticism this book would have been far more inadequate than it is; to the Rev. J. N. Sanders for contributing the fourth chapter of the Introduction; to the editors of the *Scottish Journal of Theology* and of *Interpretation* for permission to include material already published in their journals; to Mr A. L. Moore, of Cranmer Hall, Durham, for compiling the index; and above all to his wife, who has been his unfailing helper at every stage of the work.

NOTE ON THE SECOND, THIRD AND FOURTH IMPRESSIONS

While only a few minor corrections have been made in the body of the commentary, a number of supplementary notes have been added. Those added at the second impression will be found on pp. 477 ff.; attention is drawn to individual notes by an asterisk in the margin of the text. In the third and fourth impressions a dagger is used to draw attention to the additional supplementary notes on pp. 490 ff.

C.E.B.C.

INTRODUCTION

I. AUTHORSHIP, DATE AND PLACE OF WRITING

1. EARLY TRADITION

The earliest extant statement about the Gospel according to St Mark is a quotation in Eusebius (*H.E.* III. 39) from a lost exposition of the Lord's sayings written by Papias, bishop of Hierapolis, about A.D. 140. It may be translated as follows:

> This also the Elder said: Mark, who became Peter's interpreter, wrote accurately, though not in order, all that he remembered of the things said or done by the Lord. For he had neither heard the Lord nor been one of His followers, but afterwards, as I said, he had followed Peter, who used to compose his discourses with a view to the needs [of his hearers], but not as if he were composing a systematic account of the Lord's sayings. So Mark did nothing blameworthy in thus writing some things just as he remembered them; for he was careful of this one thing, to omit none of the things he had heard and to make no untrue statement therein.[1]

The first sentence at any rate—and this is the vital one— is a quotation within a quotation and gives us the testimony of an older contemporary of Papias who is probably to be identified with the Elder John mentioned by him in another passage which Eusebius has just quoted. It is thus evidence of what was believed in the province of Asia at the beginning of the second century. It represents Mark as closely associated with Peter and testifies to his accuracy, while at the same time drawing attention to a certain lack of order in his gospel (whether the reference is to chronological order or to systematic arrangement and comprehensiveness is not clear). The exact meaning of ἑρμηνευτὴς Πέτρου γενόμενος is problematical—perhaps that Mark acted as interpreter when

[1] The Greek is given in Huck, p. vii.

3

Peter was teaching, translating his Aramaic into Greek, or perhaps that by writing down Peter's reminiscences he made them available to more people. The second and third sentences are probably not part of the quotation, but they probably gloss it correctly. They explain the lack of order as due to Mark's not having been himself a first-hand witness but having derived his information from Peter's discourses, and underline the Elder's testimony to Mark's accuracy.

Justin Martyr's reference to Peter's[1] 'memoirs' (*Dial.* 106) is probably a reference to Mark; for the words he quotes occur only in Mark. If so, it is another testimony (before 161) to the close connection between this gospel and Peter.

The 'Anti-Marcionite Prologue' to Mark is perhaps to be dated as early as 160–80 (though some would date it much later). The beginning is lost. What remains may be translated as follows:

> ...Mark declared, who is called 'Stump-fingered' because he had short fingers in comparison with the size of the rest of his body. He was Peter's interpreter. After the death of Peter himself he wrote down this same gospel in the regions of Italy.[2]

This contains two significant details not given by Papias: that the gospel was written after Peter's death and that it was written in Italy.

Irenaeus (about 180) agrees with the 'Anti-Marcionite Prologue' in dating Mark after Peter's death: 'And after their [i.e. Peter's and Paul's] deaths Mark, the disciple and interpreter of Peter, himself also handed down to us in writing the things preached by Peter' (*adv. Haer.* III. i. 1).[3]

The first line of what has been preserved of the Muratorian Canon (about A.D. 200) reads: '...at which he was present, and so wrote them down'.[4] From what follows it is

---

[1] αὐτοῦ is ambiguous, but more probably refers to Peter than to Christ.
[2] The Latin is given in Huck, p. viii.
[3] The Greek is given in Huck, p. viii.
[4] The Latin is given in Huck, p. ix.

clear that the subject of the verbs must be Mark. It is highly probable that the relative refers to Peter's discourses.

The tradition of the gospel's connection with Peter is repeated by later writers, the tendency being to heighten it—Clement of Alexandria, for example, represents the gospel as having been written during Peter's lifetime and, while in one place he says that Peter 'neither actively hindered nor encouraged the undertaking' (Eusebius, *H.E.* VI. 14),[1] in another place he actually asserts that the apostle 'ratified the writing for reading in the churches' (*ibid.* II. 15).

The testimony of early tradition to Mark's authorship and to the gospel's connection with Peter is thus clear and constant from the beginning of the second century onwards. The support for dating the composition of the gospel after Peter's death is early and reliable. That the place of writing was Rome is probably implied.

2. AUTHORSHIP

The unanimous tradition of the early Church that the author of the gospel was Mark, the associate of Peter, is not open to serious doubt. While the gospel provides no direct internal evidence in support of the tradition, it contains nothing which is incompatible with it and a good deal that points to a connection with Peter.

But is this Mark, who is presumably also the person referred to in I Pet. v. 13, further to be identified with the Mark of Acts xii. 12, 25, (xiii. 13), xv. 37–9, Col. iv. 10, II Tim. iv. 11 and Philem. 24? Objections have been raised to this identification, but they are unconvincing. The objection that the gospel contains blunders concerning Palestinian conditions which would hardly have been made by someone who had grown up in Jerusalem loses its impressiveness when it is realized that the most significant of

[1] The Greek is given in Huck, p. ix.

these alleged blunders, the Markan dating of the Passion in relation to the Passover, is probably not a blunder at all (see the notes on xiv. 12). The explanation of the failure of writers earlier than Jerome to make this identification explicitly is probably that they took it for granted and assumed that their readers would do so too. As to the indirect form of Jerome's statement in his commentary on Philemon with reference to the Mark of Philem. 24 (*Marcum...quem puto evangelii conditorem*), it is perhaps due to the fact that he had not found the identification explicitly made by earlier writers: it can hardly be pressed as a reason for doubting the truth of the identification. We may take it as virtually certain that the Mark who is the associate of Peter and the author of the gospel and the Mark of Acts and the Pauline epistles are one and the same person.

3. THE PRIORITY OF MARK

It is now very widely agreed that Mark was the first gospel to be written. The arguments for the priority of Mark may be stated briefly as follows:

(i) The substance of over 90 per cent of Mark's verses is contained in Matthew, of over 50 per cent in Luke.

(ii) Where the same matter is found in all three Synoptic gospels, usually more than 50 per cent of Mark's actual words will be found either in both Matthew and Luke or in one of them; and, while there is often agreement in sentence structure and collocation of words between both Matthew and Luke and Mark or between one of them and Mark, it hardly ever happens that Matthew and Luke agree together against Mark, except in some instances covered by (iv) below.

(iii) Usually all three Synoptists agree as to the order in which they arrange their common material: where either Matthew or Luke differs from Mark, the other usually agrees with him.

(iv) Often, where the language of Matthew and/or Luke differs from that of Mark, it will be seen that it represents a grammatical or stylistic improvement.

(v) Things in Mark which could offend or perplex are sometimes either omitted or presented in a less provocative form in Matthew and/or Luke (e.g. xv. 34, omitted by Luke; iv. 38b, contrast Matt. viii. 25, Luke viii. 24; x. 17f., contrast Matt. xix. 16f.).

(vi) The disciples' pre-Resurrection way of addressing Jesus as Rabbi or Teacher is faithfully reflected in Mark, whereas Matthew and Luke represent Jesus as being addressed by the title 'Lord', thus reflecting the usage of the post-Resurrection Church.

Against the hypothesis that Matthew was written first and used by Mark, which has recently been stoutly championed by Abbot Butler, two further points must be mentioned:

(vii) That Matthew, whose style is much more succinct than Mark's, should have omitted superfluous words and phrases which he found in Mark in order to make room for additional matter is understandable: the opposite process of omitting valuable material in order to make room for diffuseness, which the theory of Matthaean priority presupposes, is incomprehensible.

(viii) On a number of occasions when Matthew's order differs from Mark's, it appears to be secondary (see, for example, the Matthew parallels to Mark ii. 1–iii. 6 and vi. 6b–33).

On the subject of this section see further: Streeter, *Four Gospels*, pp. 157–69; B. C. Butler, *The Originality of St Matthew* (Cambridge, 1951), pp. 62–171; H. G. Wood, 'The Priority of Mark', in *E.T.* LXV (1953–4), pp. 17–19. The discussion has been reopened by W. R. Farmer, *The Synoptic Problem* (New York, 1964; also London).

4. DATE

That Mark wrote his gospel after Peter's death is actually
stated in the 'Anti-Marcionite Prologue' and by Irenaeus,
and is probably implied by Papias (note the two references
to remembering). It is confirmed by the internal evidence
of the gospel, the relentlessness with which the apostle's
failures are recorded being most easily understandable on
the assumption that he had already died a martyr's death by
the time Mark was writing: Mark's frankness, which earlier
would have seemed malicious, would after Peter's martyrdom
be welcomed as underlining the encouragement it afforded
to weak disciples. This gives us A.D. 65 as our *terminus a quo*,
for it is fairly certain that Peter died in the Neronian persecution of 64–5. The use of Mark by the later Synoptists
makes a date later than A.D. 70 unlikely. We may date the
gospel between 65 and 70, and probably, since chapter xiii
is not coloured by any awareness of the actual events of the
Jewish War of 66–70 (contrast Lk. xxi. 20–4), we should
date it before the later stages of the war—so within the
* narrower period 65–7.

5. PLACE OF WRITING

The fact that Mark supplies translations of Aramaic expressions (iii. 17, v. 41, vii. 11, 34, xv. 22) and explanations of
Jewish customs (vii. 3f., xv. 42) suggests that he wrote for
Gentiles. The 'Anti-Marcionite Prologue' states that he
wrote the gospel in Italy. Clement of Alexandria implies
that he wrote it in Rome.

Some support for Rome is afforded by I Pet. v. 13; for, if
the epistle is Petrine, the verse is direct evidence that Mark
was in Rome ('Babylon' clearly stands for Rome) shortly
before Peter's martyrdom, and, even if the epistle is
pseudonymous and to be dated as late as 112, it is evidence

of the existence of a tradition to that effect at the beginning of the second century. It is possible that Mk xv. 21 also points to Rome; for the fact that Simon's sons are mentioned by name suggests that they were known to the church for which Mark was writing, and it is reasonably likely that Simon's son Rufus is to be identified with the Rufus named by Paul (Rom. xvi. 13) in a series of greetings which were probably (in spite of the doubts of some scholars) addressed to the church in Rome. The rapid and wide dissemination of the gospel, of which the use made of it by the later Synoptists and probably also the Fourth Evangelist is evidence, suggests that it had behind it the authority of an important church: such a church the one in Rome certainly was—though of course there were others. The prominence given by Mark to sayings about persecution and martyrdom (e.g. viii. 34–8, xiii. 9–13) might perhaps be regarded as a pointer to Rome: at least it would be very understandable, if the gospel was written there soon after the Neronian persecution.

The arguments in favour of Rome are not conclusive, but they are much stronger than those put forward in support of any other place. Antioch, which has been preferred by a few modern scholars, has perhaps the next best claim; but the explanation of the two mites as equivalent to a *quadrans*, a coin that was not in circulation in the east,[1] in xii. 42 and the presence of a considerable number of other Latin loan-words and of some possible Latinisms of idiom tell in favour of a western rather than an eastern origin.

The statement of Chrysostom that Mark wrote the gospel in Egypt is doubtless a mistake: it probably rests on a misunderstanding of a statement in Eusebius' *History* (II. 16).

[1] See W. M. Ramsay in *E.T.* x (1898–9), pp. 232, 336.

II. THE CHARACTER OF
THE GOSPEL

After exercising an extensive influence for a time, during which it was used by the writers of the First and Third Gospels, and probably also the Fourth, St Mark's Gospel suffered relative neglect for centuries. That this was so is hardly surprising; for, when compared with the other gospels, Mark was clearly at a disadvantage. It contained very little that was not also to be found in Matthew, while Matthew contained much additional matter of great value. Its roughness of style made it less suitable than the other gospels for liturgical use; and both for liturgical and for catechetical purposes its arrangement was less satisfactory than that of Matthew and Luke. It was not the work of an apostle, as Matthew and John were both thought to be. The fact that it was the first gospel to be written was soon forgotten. Irenaeus dates its composition after that of Matthew (*adv. Haer.* III. i. 1), while Augustine actually speaks of Mark having followed Matthew *tamquam pedisequus et breviator eius* (*de Cons. Evang.* I. ii. 4); and until the nineteenth century, during the course of which the hypothesis of the priority of Mark established itself, this view prevailed unchallenged. Not unnaturally Mark was the least read and least commented on of all the gospels.

But the discovery of Mark's priority transformed the situation. Since the end of last century its importance as the earliest gospel and the primary source of information about the ministry of Jesus, the study of which is fundamental to the study of the other gospels, has been widely acknowledged. The vast amount of work done during the last sixty or seventy years on St Mark's Gospel has gone a considerable way to compensate for the neglect of centuries. As a result of it the importance of St Mark's witness to Christ has become more and more apparent.

2. CONTENTS AND SOURCES

It is possible to distinguish four different kinds of narrative material in the gospel:

(i) Narratives the wealth of detail and vividness of which suggest direct derivation from the reminiscence of an eye-witness. Many of these record incidents in which Peter played a prominent part, or which must have had a special interest for him, or which only a few people (including Peter) witnessed: e.g. i. 16–20, i. 29–31, i. 35–8, v. 21–4, 35–43 (see *vv.* 37 and 40), ix. 2–8, xiv. 27–31, 54, 66–72, xiv. 32–42, while in ix. 14–27 the story is told from the point of view of those who returned with Jesus, of whom Peter was one. With regard to most narratives of this sort we may with considerable confidence accept the tradition of Mark's dependence on the reminiscences of Peter.

(ii) Narratives which by their rounded form and lack of vivid details give the impression of being units of oral tradition which have been worn smooth by frequent repetition. Many of these narratives are pronouncement-stories (e.g. ii. 18–20, ii. 23–6, iii. 31–5)—to use a convenient technical term for a narrative which has for its climax and *raison d'être* a saying of Jesus.

(iii) Narratives which, though based on tradition, do not seem to be actual units of oral tradition, but rather to have been constructed by Mark himself: e.g. iii. 13–19, vi. 6b–13, vi. 30–3, vi. 53–6. Dr Taylor calls them 'Markan constructions'. They lack vivid details and are rather vague.

(iv) Brief summary statements indicating in general terms what was happening during a certain period: e.g. i. 14f.,

iii. 7–12, iv. 33 f. These form to a large extent the framework of the gospel (see further pp. 17 f. below).

A good deal of sayings material also is to be found in Mark. Some of it is contained in narratives which we may regard as Petrine (class (i) above): for example, the sayings of Jesus contained in ix. 14–27, x. 17–27. Other sayings have come to the evangelist by way of oral tradition, some of them along with narrative-settings (the pronouncement-stories—see (ii) above) and others as isolated sayings, preserved as independent tradition-units, the circumstances in which they had been uttered having been forgotten. It seems that collections of dominical sayings were made in the different churches for use in catechetical teaching. Mark will probably have derived some of his sayings material from such a collection in use in Rome.

It seems likely that some of the groupings of material in the gospel go back beyond Mark to his sources. In the sayings collections the sayings would naturally tend to be arranged by topics or in some other way that would aid the memory. The arrangement according to catchwords to be seen in ix. 37–50 (see the introduction to ix. 41–50) is particularly interesting: it was probably taken over by Mark from his source. Some groupings of narrative material are probably also pre-Markan. In some cases the grouping may well be historical, going back to the memory of an eye-witness (e.g. i. 21–38, iv. 35–v. 43); in others it would appear to be simply topical. The series of conflict-stories, ii. 1–iii. 6, is probably of the latter sort. As far as the Passion is concerned, it is fairly certain that a continuous narrative was traditional. Most likely it was brief; and Mark's narrative may well be such a traditional narrative supplemented by material drawn from the reminiscences of an eye-witness or of eye-witnesses.

Two questions fall to be mentioned here: (i) How far, if at all, were the sources to which reference has been made above written sources? and (ii) Was there an intermediate stage (or perhaps stages) between sources of this sort and the actual compilation of the gospel we now possess? It is difficult to see how (i) can be answered with any confidence. With regard to (ii), various suggestions have been made: for instance, that there was an earlier 'edition' of Mark (an *Ur-Markus*) which was without those passages which both Matthew and Luke lack and which was used by Matthew and Luke, or one which was without vi. 45–viii. 26, and used by Luke; or that there was an original form of the gospel, used by Luke, which was expanded by a Galilean redactor into the form used by Matthew, and that our Mark is this expanded form further edited by a Roman editor;[1] or that the evangelist combined a 'Twelve-source' and a 'disciple-source';[2] or that he used three sources, an Aramaic gospel written in Palestine, a gospel of the Dispersion written by Mark himself, and a Gentile gospel written for the Pauline mission.[3] But none of these suggestions has commanded general assent. (On these two questions see further: Streeter, *Four Gospels*, pp. 168–81; Taylor, pp. 67–77; Knox, *Sources*, 1.)

3. STRUCTURE

The gospel falls naturally into two parts. The second of these, which opens with the narrative of Peter's confession of Jesus as the Messiah and the first prediction of the Passion (viii. 27–33), itself falls naturally into four main divisions. The main divisions of the first part, apart from the introduction (i. 1–13), are not so easily defined, and commentators differ as to what they are; but, on the whole, it seems best to recognize three main divisions beginning respectively

---

[1] W. Bussmann, *Synoptische Studien*, I–III (Halle, 1925–31).

[2] E. Meyer, *Ursprung und Anfänge des Christentums*, I–III (Stuttgart and Berlin, 1921–3).

[3] A. T. Cadoux, *The Sources of the Second Gospel* (London, 1935).

at i. 14, iii. 7 and vi. 14. The resultant scheme is as follows:

That the story of the Passion and Resurrection is the climax of the book and that it dominates divisions V–VIII is apparent at once from the above scheme; but a further analysis of the structure of Mark makes it abundantly clear that not only the second half but the whole of the gospel is dominated by its climax. Thus as early as i. 14 the reference to the arrest of John the Baptist points forward to the arrest of him whose forerunner he was; the mounting opposition to Jesus indicated in ii. 1–iii. 6 culminates in a plot to compass his death; the rejection of Jesus by his home town (vi. 1–6a) foreshadows his rejection by his people as a whole; and the account of Herod's fears in vi. 14–16 and the grim narrative of the forerunner's execution which is inserted in order to explain them (vi. 17–29) carry unmistakable implications. From the time of Peter's confession the references to the approaching Passion and Resurrection become increasingly plain—see viii. 31, ix. 9–13, 31, x. 32–4, 38f., 45.

4. PURPOSE

The very first verse of Mark provides a clear indication of the writer's purpose. It was to set forth 'the good news', to bear witness to Jesus as the Messiah and the Son of God. But this general purpose is common to all four gospels. The purposes which are special to Mark would seem to be to supply the catechetical and liturgical needs of the church in Rome, to support its faith in face of the threat of martyrdom and to provide material for missionary preachers. *

5. HISTORICAL RELIABILITY

We have still to consider a question which is clearly of the very greatest importance—the question of the historical reliability of the gospel.

We may begin by asking about Mark's treatment of his sources. Here there are several things to be said:

(i) The presence in this gospel of a number of features which must have been liable to offend or perplex and which are either omitted or modified in Matthew and/or Luke suggests that Mark made no attempt to smooth away the difficulties he found, but reproduced his sources with remarkable frankness. (To the examples mentioned in I. 3 (v) above others may be added: for instance, x. 35–7, contrast Matt. xx. 20 f.; xiv. 33, omitted by Luke, softened in Matt. xxvi. 37; xiv. 37, the addition of ἀπὸ τῆς λύπης in Luke xxii. 45 spares the disciples; xiv. 71, contrast the much less offensive words of Luke xxii. 60; xv. 34, omitted by Luke.)

(ii) The fact that the Church's use of the title 'Lord' with reference to Jesus is not reflected in this gospel as it is in Matthew and Luke is also significant.

(iii) The striking contrast between the lack of vivid details in the Markan constructions (see 2 (iii) above) and the vividness and wealth of detail characteristic of the passages which may plausibly be regarded as Petrine suggests that, where Mark did not find vivid details in his sources, he refrained from creating them.

(iv) The same self-restraint may be discerned in the linking together of the different sections. Apparently, when Mark had received a tradition-unit in isolation and had no reliable information as to its historical context, he refrained from creating suitable geographical and temporal details to link it with the context in which he decided to place it, preferring to join it to the previous section by means of a simple καί.

(v) Self-restraint and respect for his sources seem to be indicated also by the way Mark has left intact groups of units which he had received as such, even when the grouping was clearly not historical but topical.

The evidence points to Mark's being not a creative literary artist but an extremely honest and conscientious compiler. One's immediate reaction to this description might perhaps be, 'How dull and uninspired!' But one does not have to think very long to realize that an honest and conscientious compiler is precisely what an intelligent Christian must want the earliest evangelist to have been. As far as Mark's own part is concerned it would seem that a very great confidence in the gospel's reliability is justified.

But what of the sources which he used? It is well known that the more sceptical of the Form Critics regard much of the narrative material as legend and ideal construction and many of the sayings attributed to Jesus as the creation of the primitive Church.[1] According to this view the material which Mark received was evidence of what Jesus had come to mean for Christian faith rather than of what he had actually been in his historical life; of the latter it was only indirectly evidence. Many things can be said in reply to this thorough-going scepticism. It will be enough here to list some of them.

(i) There is good reason, as we saw above, to think that a considerable amount of the material in Mark was derived directly from Peter.

(ii) As far as the rest of the material is concerned, the material which has come through the processes and pressures

[1] See, for example, Bultmann, *G.S.T.*

16

of oral tradition, it is important to remember that eye-witnesses, hostile as well as believing, survived through the period of oral tradition and their survival must have set limits to the community's freedom to invent and embellish.

(iii) The prominence in the New Testament of the μάρτυς group of words suggests that the early Church had a strong sense of responsibility for the truthfulness of its tradition.

(iv) The fact that it was within a community possessed of its own long-established and carefully preserved oral tradition that the early Church grew up is important.

(v) The fact that the perplexing and offensive material, already mentioned in connection with the question of Mark's own reliability, was preserved at all and reached Mark says much for the general reliability of the sources used by him.

(vi) The presence of Semitisms both in many of the sayings of Jesus and also in many of the narratives, while it cannot of course guarantee the historical reliability of the material, at least tells strongly against any theory alleging the corruption of the tradition by Hellenistic influences.

These considerations would seem to justify us in rejecting the radical scepticism of Bultmann and in believing that a substantially reliable picture of the historical Jesus was preserved in the sources available to Mark.[1]

Some special questions remain to be mentioned. One is the question of the Markan outline, about which opinions differ widely. While there are still some who have very great confidence in it, others regard it as purely artificial (apart from the Passion narrative and possibly one or two complexes like i. 21–38).[2] A middle view has been expressed by

[1] On the subject of this paragraph see further: V. Taylor, *The Formation of the Gospel Tradition* (London, 1935); E. B. Redlich, *Form Criticism: its Value and Limitations* (London, 1939); Manson, *Jesus the Messiah*; C. H. Dodd, *About the Gospels* (Cambridge, 1950).

[2] See especially Schmidt, *Rahmen*.

C. H. Dodd[1] and has been widely accepted. According to him, while 'it is hazardous to argue from the precise sequence of the narrative in detail...there is good reason to believe that in broad lines the Marcan order does represent a genuine succession of events, within which movement and development can be traced'. So much is highly probable; but his suggestion that the summary statements (see pp. 11 f. above) are fragments of a traditional outline of the ministry of Jesus seems less likely than the view that they were composed by Mark on the basis of a general knowledge of the course of the ministry possessed by him as a result of his association with Peter. (A very brief outline may well have been traditional, but hardly such a detailed outline as Dodd seems to envisage.) That Peter is likely to have remembered not only particular incidents but also the general course of the ministry must surely be granted. There is then no need to dismiss the Markan framework as merely artificial. At the same time it must of course be remembered that a considerable amount of Mark's material seems to have reached him in the form of independent tradition-units which carried no indication of their historical contexts, while in some cases several units had already been grouped together for topical, not historical reasons. The relation of each particular unit to the outline has therefore to be considered on its merits.

There are a number of other special questions which need not be discussed here since the reader may be referred to the relevant sections of the commentary. On the miracles of Jesus see on i. 31; on the sequel to the Baptism and on the Transfiguration see on i. 10f. and the discussion following the note on ix. 8; on the Empty Tomb see on xvi. 6; on the references to angels, Satan and demons see on xvi. 5, i. 13, and i. 23, respectively; on the alleged distortion of some of

* [1] In *E.T.* XLIII (1932), pp. 396–400. For a criticism of it see Nineham, 'Order of Events'; also in *J.T.S.* n.s. IX (1958), pp. 13–25, 242–52.

18

the teaching of Jesus through the preoccupation of the early Church and of Mark himself with apocalyptic hopes see on xiii; and on the alleged colouring of the material by a theory of messianic secrecy see on i. 25, iv. 11f.

One other matter should at least be mentioned here—the contention of Rudolf Bultmann[1] that the New Testament contains a mythological element which modern man cannot be expected to accept and which therefore needs to be 'demythologized'. It has of course long been recognized that the New Testament sometimes makes use of picture-language and that this picture-language should not be taken literally (e.g. Calvin comments on the imagery of the Son sitting at the right hand of the Father: 'A similitude borrowed from princes', and explains that 'the subject here considered is not the posture of His body, but the majesty of His empire'). But what Bultmann proposes to treat as myth and to reinterpret anthropologically in terms of man's understanding of his own existence includes much more than the features which in the past have been recognized as picture-language: it includes, for example, not merely the picture-language which is made use of in Mark xvi. 19 ($\dot{\epsilon}\kappa\dot{\alpha}\theta\iota\sigma\epsilon\nu$ and $\dot{\epsilon}\kappa$ $\delta\epsilon\xi\iota\hat{\omega}\nu$) but also the Ascension itself; it includes the Incarnation and the Resurrection. The historical reliability of the statements that the pre-existent Son of God assumed human nature (implicit in the $\upsilon\dot{\iota}o\hat{\upsilon}$ $\Theta\epsilon o\hat{\upsilon}$ of i. 1), that Jesus was raised from the dead ($\dot{\eta}\gamma\dot{\epsilon}\rho\theta\eta$, xvi. 6), that he was exalted to heaven (xvi. 19), cannot be proved by the ordinary methods of historical science. The Incarnation, Resurrection and Ascension are not historical events in the sense of being of the same texture as ordinary historical events. But, *pace* Bultmann and his followers, the belief that the Incarnation, Resurrection and Ascension are historical in the sense of having actually happened at particular times

[1] In his essay, 'New Testament and Mythology', reprinted in H. W. Bartsch (ed.), *Kerygma and Myth* (Eng. tr., London, 1953).

2-2

in the past is vital to Christian faith. The demythologized gospel, in which the historicity (in this latter sense) of the Incarnation, Resurrection and Ascension and also of the Parousia (in the sense that it will actually happen at a particular time in the future) is called in question, is in our view, whether it proves attractive to modern man or not, an example of ἕτερον εὐαγγέλιον, ὃ οὐκ ἔστιν ἄλλο.[1]

6. STYLE

The style of the gospel is unpretentious and close to the everyday spoken Greek of the time, making up for its lack of the elegances of literary Greek by its simplicity and directness.

Characteristic of Mark are the following:

(i) The use of periphrastic tenses (e.g. ii. 6, 18, iv. 38).

(ii) The use of the historic present (J. C. Hawkins lists 151 instances, of which nearly half are λέγει or λέγουσι).[2]

(iii) The use of the indefinite plural (e.g. i. 22, 30, 32, 45).

(iv) The use of the aorist of ἄρχομαι as a redundant auxiliary verb (e.g. i. 45, ii. 23, vi. 7).

(v) The use of parataxis in preference to subordinate clauses.

(vi) The use of asyndeton, i.e. the placing of one sentence after another without any connecting particle or conjunction (e.g. iii. 35, iv. 28, v. 39b, xiv. 3b, 6c, 8).

(vii) The use of Latin loanwords—these are more numerous in Mark than in the other gospels and some occur in the New Testament only in Mark.

(viii) The frequent use of εὐθύς (41 times).

(ix) The use of diminutives (e.g. θυγάτριον in v. 23, vii. 25, πλοιάριον in iii. 9, ὠτάριον in xiv. 47).

(x) A certain diffuseness of expression (e.g. ὀψίας δὲ

---

* [1] For a penetrating criticism of Bultmann's position see Karl Barth, *Rudolf Bultmann: ein Versuch, ihn zu verstehen* (Zollikon, 2nd ed. 1953).

[2] *Horae Synopticae* (Oxford, 2nd ed. 1909), pp. 143ff.

γενομένης, ὅτε ἔδυσεν ὁ ἥλιος in i. 32, ἀπὸ τοῦ ὄχλου κατ᾽ ἰδίαν in vii. 33, κατ᾽ ἰδίαν μόνους in ix. 2, ἐσιώπα καὶ οὐκ ἀπεκρίνατο οὐδέν in xiv. 61)—though in fairness it should be noted that this is seldom a matter of mere pointless redundancy (as has sometimes been alleged), the second element in Mark's double expressions usually adding something in the way of precision or dramatic effect or emphasis.

The Semitic flavour of the Greek of the gospel is unmistakable. Of the characteristics mentioned above (i), (iii), (iv), (v), (vi), and, in some cases, (x) are probably due to the influence of Aramaic. In addition to these there are a considerable number of other features which reflect Aramaic influence: e.g. the insertion of a resumptive pronoun after a relative as in i. 7 (οὗ οὐκ εἰμὶ ἱκανὸς κύψας λῦσαι τὸν ἱμάντα τῶν ὑποδημάτων αὐτοῦ), the use of the positive for the comparative or superlative of adjectives as in ix. 43, 45, 47, and the use of the proleptic pronoun as in vi. 17 (αὐτὸς γὰρ ὁ Ἡρῴδης).[1]

III. THE THEOLOGY OF THE GOSPEL

As considerable space is given to theological exposition in the body of the commentary, we shall here do no more than indicate the main references where discussion of some of the more important theological topics will be found.

Kingdom of God	i. 15
Gospel	i. 1
The name Jesus	i. 1
Christ, Messiah	viii. 29
Son of Man	viii. 31

[1] On the Aramaic background see further Taylor, pp. 55–66; also Black; and Moule, pp. 171–91.

Son of God	i. 1, 11, xiii. 32, xiv. 61, xv. 39 (other references at i. 1)
Servant of the Lord	i. 9, 11, ii. 20, iii. 27, viii. 31, ix. 12 x. 45, xiv. 24
Lord	i. 3
Baptism of Jesus	i. 9–11
'Messianic secret', messianic veiledness	i. 25, iv. 11 f.; also iv. 21 f., 26–32, viii. 31 (Son of Man (iv) (d)), the concluding note on xi. 1–11, xiv. 61 f.
Miracles	The concluding note on i. 29–31
Transfiguration	ix. 2–8
Last Supper, Eucharist	xiv. 22–5
Death of Christ	viii. 31, ix. 31, x. 38 f., 45, xiv. 24, 33 f., 36, xv. 21, 34, 38
His Resurrection	xvi. 1–8
His Exaltation	xvi. 19; also xiv. 62
His Parousia, eschatology	viii. 38, xiii, xiv. 62; also i. 15, iv. 21 f., 26–32
Law of God	i. 41, 44, vii. 1–23, x. 1–12, 19–21, xii. 28–34
Future life	xii. 18–27
Angels	xvi. 5
Satan and the demons	i. 13, 23, 26, iii. 22–7, xiv. 34

On the theology of the gospel see further the author's article, 'Mark, Gospel of', § 9, in *The Interpreter's Dictionary* * *of the Bible* (New York, 1962).

IV. TEXTUAL CRITICISM OF THE GOSPELS[1]

Since exegesis must go hand in hand with textual criticism, the student of the interpretation of the New Testament needs to have some acquaintance both with the materials for the establishment of the text of the New Testament, and

[1] This chapter is kindly contributed by the Rev. J. N. Sanders, Dean of Peterhouse.

with the principles governing their use for that purpose. The present note is designed as an introduction to the art of textual criticism, so far as it is concerned with the gospels. A good popular account is given by Sir Frederic Kenyon's *Our Bible and the Ancient Manuscripts* (4th ed., London, 1939); for more advanced study *The Textual Criticism of the New Testament* by the same author may be recommended and A. H. McNeile and C. S. C. Williams' *Introduction to the New Testament* (Oxford, 1953), and A. Souter's *The Text and Canon of the New Testament* (London, 1913, 2nd ed., revised by C. S. C. Williams, 1954). The *Introduction* to Westcott and Hort's edition of the New Testament in Greek (1881) and Streeter, *Four Gospels*, are still valuable. †

I. MATERIALS

The materials for the establishment of the text of the Gospels consist of (*a*) Greek manuscripts; (*b*) ancient translations; and (*c*) quotations in the writings of early Christian authors.

(*a*) Manuscripts are either on papyrus or vellum, the papyri being on the whole earlier. The earliest extant manuscript of any part of the New Testament is $\mathfrak{p}^{52}$, a scrap of papyrus of the first half of the second century in the John Rylands Library, Manchester, with John xviii. 31–4 on one side, and 37–8 on the other (which shows that it comes, not from a roll, but from a *codex*—the modern book-form).

Other noteworthy early codices, both of the same period, about A.D. 200, are $\mathfrak{p}^{45}$, the Chester Beatty Papyrus, containing fragments of all four gospels, and $\mathfrak{p}^{66}$, the Bodmer Papyrus II, containing the bulk of St John's Gospel.

Of the manuscripts written on vellum, the earlier are written in uncials (separated capitals), the later in minuscules (small letters, which could be written continuously). Uncial manuscripts are denoted by capital letters or by arabic numerals beginning with o (o1, etc.), minuscules by arabic numerals (1, 2, etc.).

The earliest extant uncial manuscripts are two third-century fragments, one (o212) being in the form of a harmony of the four gospels. But complete manuscripts of the gospels are extant only from the fourth century.

ℵ, C(odex) Sinaiticus (fourth century), A, C. Alexandrinus (fifth century), B, C. Vaticanus (fourth century), and C, C. Ephraemi Rescriptus (fifth century), a palimpsest (a manuscript washed or scraped and then reused for a different text, but with substantial portions of all four gospels still decipherable), all include the four gospels, and originally contained the whole Bible.

Other manuscripts either of the four gospels, or including them with other books of the New Testament, are: D_1, C. Bezae (fifth century), including Matthew, John, Luke, Mark (in that order) with a Latin version (d_1) facing the Greek; L_1, C. Regius (eighth century), of the four gospels, with the double ending to Mark; W, the Washington C. (fifth century), of Matthew, John, Luke, Mark, with a unique interpolation in the longer ending of Mark, and exhibiting a text varying in type from 'Syrian' in Matthew to 'Neutral' in Jn v. 12–Lk viii. 12, 'Syrian' again in the rest of Luke, 'Western' in Mk i–v. 30, and 'Caesarean' for the rest of Mark; Δ, C. Sangallensis (ninth or tenth century), of the four gospels, with an interlinear Latin version; Θ, the Koridethi C. (ninth century), including the four gospels; Φ, C. Beratinus (sixth century), of Matthew and Mark (with lacunae), written in gold and silver letters on purple vellum; and Ψ, C. Laurensis (eighth century), of Mk ix. 5–end, Luke, and John, with the double ending to Mark.

Minuscules are much more numerous, but usually much less important than papyri and uncials, though they occasionally supply valuable evidence for the text, having been copied, or corrected, from manuscripts of an earlier period.

Such, for example, are the two groups of minuscules known respectively as 'family 1' and 'family 13', from their leading manuscripts, both of about the thirteenth century. The former group has Jn vii. 53–viii. 11 as an appendix to the gospel, the latter places it after Lk. xxi. 38. Again, 33, though of the ninth or tenth century, has a text often identical with that of the early uncials ℵ and B.

(b) Of the ancient translations, the most important are the Latin, Egyptian, and Syriac.

(i) There are two forms of the Latin, the 'Old Latin', made before the time of St Jerome, and St Jerome's Vulgate, issued in A.D. 383–4. The Old Latin again exists in two forms, 'African' and 'European', the African most probably being the earlier, made in the second century. The manuscripts of the Old Latin, though often very ancient, are usually also very imperfectly preserved. African manuscripts include e (fifth century), of parts of all four gospels; and k (fourth century), containing the latter half of Mark and less than half of Matthew, and with the shorter ending to Mark; European a (fourth century); b (fifth or sixth century); ff² (fifth century); n (fourth or fifth century); and q (seventh century)

Vulgate manuscripts exist in great abundance, many of them being more or less 'contaminated' with Old Latin readings. A critical edition was published by Wordsworth and White in 1912.

(ii) Egyptian translations of the complete New Testament are extant in the two chief Coptic dialects, Sahidic and Bohairic. Both were made probably in the third century, the Sahidic being the earlier of the two. Fragments also exist of versions in other Coptic dialects.

(iii) The earliest form in which the gospels appeared in Syriac was in Tatian's *Diatessaron*, a harmony of the four gospels made in Greek about A.D. 170, and translated into Syriac by its compiler. A version of the 'Separated' gospels was also made at an early date, though it failed to supersede the *Diatessaron*. It is however represented by two more or less imperfect manuscripts, one a palimpsest, the 'Sinaitic Syriac' (fourth century), the other the 'Curetonian Syriac' (fifth century).

The Syriac equivalent of the Latin Vulgate, the *Peshitta*, was probably made in the late fourth or early fifth century. Though this became the standard Syriac version, others were also made. Of the 'Philoxenian' version, made in A.D. 506, nothing now remains of the gospels, and of the 'Palestinian', the date of which is disputed, but which probably is to be assigned to the sixth century, there are only fragments. In A.D. 616 Thomas of Harkel made a revision of the *Peshitta* with the aid of ancient Greek manuscripts at Alexandria, and his version, the 'Harklean', contains some important readings, both in the text and in the Syriac and Greek variants which he noted in the margin.

(iv) Translations of the gospels into other ancient languages also exist, of which the Gothic, Armenian, Georgian, Ethiopic, and Arabic are occasionally important.

(c) Quotations of scripture in early Christian writings are important as enabling us to identify the type of text current in a particular church at a particular time, often much earlier than our earliest manuscripts. Particularly important are Marcion (for Luke), Tatian, Irenaeus, Tertullian, and Origen.

2. PRINCIPLES

A considerable period elapsed between the actual composition of the gospels and the earliest extant manuscripts, and, though it was not by any means as long as that between the autographs and extant manuscripts of the Greek and Latin classical authors, it was sufficient to allow many variations to appear in the texts of the gospels. During the whole period of manuscript tradition errors gradually accumulated, and though efforts were made to produce a standard text, they were not made on sound critical principles. When Westcott and Hort compiled their justly celebrated text of the New Testament, published in 1881, they relied in the main upon the most ancient manuscripts then known, ℵ and B. Their *Introduction* gives a classic formulation of the principles which the critic should follow in the elimination of corruptions from his text, and, if their results do indeed often need modification, it is not because their principles were unsound, but because much fresh evidence has come to light since their time.

Briefly, their principles are that where different readings exist, the authorities exhibiting them must not simply be counted, but weighed and classified. They must be weighed according to the relative probability of the readings which they contain, and that probability is of two kinds, 'intrinsic' and 'transcriptional'. Intrinsic probability is by itself untrustworthy, since it depends on the individual critic's subjective judgement that one reading is preferable to, and so more probable than, another. It must therefore be reinforced, or modified, by considering transcriptional probability, i.e. by considering which reading best accounts for the existing variants. It is, for example, transcriptional probability which led Westcott and Hort to prefer a shorter to a longer reading, on the assumption that copyists are more likely to have inserted glosses, or paraphrased obscure passages, than to have made omissions from the text of scripture.

Applying these principles, Westcott and Hort distinguished between the mass of later manuscripts (which they called 'Syrian', but which are also named 'Byzantine') and two smaller groups of manuscripts, on the whole much earlier in date, which shared certain characteristics distinct from each other and from the 'Syrian' manuscripts, and which they called 'Neutral' and 'Western' respectively. The 'Syrian' text is found in A in the gospels, in the majority of minuscules and in some later uncials, and, in an early form, in the *Peshitta*. The 'Neutral' text, which they so named because they believed it substantially free from corruption, they found in its purest form in B, ℵ and 33, and, in an inferior, 'Alexandrian' form, in C L and the Egyptian versions. Their 'Western' text, so called from its supposed area of origin, they found chiefly in D and the Old Latin. They regarded it as ancient, but corrupt in comparison with the Neutral.

Subsequent study, and discoveries of fresh evidence, have led to the realization that both 'Neutral' and 'Western' are misnomers. The 'Neutral' appears to have been the result of deliberate emendation by scholars whose conception of 'intrinsic probability' resembled Westcott and Hort's: it is an Egyptian text, and not the first that existed in Egypt. Also the 'Western' text was far more extensively used in ancient times than Westcott and Hort realized. It is rather a group of texts more ancient than the revisions which produced the 'Neutral' and 'Syrian' texts, and attested from many parts of the ancient Christian world, including Egypt. It has also come to be realized that the 'Syrian' text may contain genuinely ancient readings.

The non-'Neutral', non-'Syrian' texts are by no means homogeneous. Some are geographically Western, like the African Old Latin. Others were associated with other ancient churches, the Sinaitic Syriac, for example, with Antioch. In particular, a distinctive type of text found in the gospels in Θ and part of W, and also less clearly in Φ, families 1 and 13 and other manuscripts, has been isolated and named 'Caesarean' from its supposed origin in Caesarea. But again, subsequent study has shown that this text was more widespread than its name suggests. The earlier one penetrates, the more confusing the picture becomes, for the newly-discovered early evidence (of $\mathfrak{p}^{45}$

and $\mathfrak{p}^{66}$ for example) does not fit neatly into any previous classifications.

Exclusive reliance on the 'Neutral' text, or on any single form of text, is no longer possible. When the authorities have been classified, on whatever principle, the necessity of informed and responsible choice between readings still lies upon the critic.

NOTES

I. THE BEGINNING

(i. 1–13)

The first main division, which is made up of three little sections closely joined together, relates those events which immediately preceded the opening of the public ministry of Jesus and at the same time serves as a prologue to the gospel, providing the reader with essential clues to the understanding of what follows. It tells of John the Baptist, underlining his Elijah role as the forerunner of Messiah in accordance with O.T. prophecy and indicating his twofold message, the summons to repent and the pointing to one coming after him; it introduces Jesus of Nazareth as the one to whom John had pointed, recording his submission to the baptism of repentance, the messianic gift of the Spirit, and the declaration of divine Sonship, thus putting the reader in the way to know the secret of his person—the Servant, the Messiah, the Son of God; and lastly it tells of his going forth as the Spirit-impelled champion to meet the enemy of God and man, this preliminary encounter pointing forward to the warfare which the whole gospel will relate and the ministration of the angels providing an anticipatory hint of the final victory of chapter xvi.

1. THE MINISTRY OF JOHN THE BAPTIST (i. 1–8)
(Mt. iii. 1–12; Lk. iii. 1–18)

In this section Mark has used existing tradition, selecting those details which would best serve his purpose to indicate briefly but clearly the true significance of John as the forerunner of Jesus the Messiah. The historical value of the section is beyond serious question. The picture of the Baptist which emerges from it and from the rather fuller accounts

33

in Matt. iii and Luke iii is self-consistent and intrinsically probable, and is well borne out by Josephus when one makes allowance for that writer's known peculiarities.

1. The relation of *v.* 1 to what follows has been variously explained.

(i) The whole verse is a gloss. But this would more probably have been inserted at the beginning of Matthew or have included the words τοῦ κατὰ Μᾶρκον.

(ii) ἀρχή stands for ἄρχεται ('here begins': cf. Lat. *incipit*), the title of the book being τὸ εὐαγγέλιον etc. and the whole verse by Mark.

(iii) ἀρχή is a gloss, which has forced an original τὸ εὐαγγέλιον into the genitive; this has some support in the reading of sy[pal] which omits ἀρχή and has the equivalent of τὸ εὐαγγέλιον.

(iv) The whole verse is the title of the book, Mark meaning that all that he is going to record is the beginning of the gospel, the Church's mission being its continuation. Acts i. 1, Heb. ii. 3 are cited in support, but probably wrongly.

(v) The whole verse is the title, but ἀρχή means 'origin'— Mark is going to relate the historic basis of the Church's message.

(vi) The whole verse is the title, but ἀρχή means 'summary', i.e. a summary for use in the instruction of catechumens; Ecclus xxix. 21, Heb. v. 12, vi. 1 are cited in support of this meaning—very questionably.

(vii) Taking *v.* 1 with *vv.* 2–3 and supplying ἦν, the meaning is then that the beginning of the gospel was in accordance with prophecy.

(viii) Others take *v.* 1 with *v.* 4 (*vv.* 2–3 being in parenthesis), and consider *v.* 4 as the predicate of *v.* 1.

(ix) Others understand the passage as in the previous explanation, but reverse subject and predicate.

(x) Yet others take *v.* 1 to refer to the things related in *vv.* 2–13 (or, less probably, *vv.* 2–8), but as a sort of title for the content of those verses, rather than as forming one sentence with what follows.

Of these the last seems, on the whole, the most satisfactory. Cf. LXX Hos. i. 2: Ἀρχὴ λόγου Κυρίου ἐν Ὡσηέ· * καὶ εἶπε Κύριος πρὸς Ὡσηέ, Βάδιζε, λάβε σεαυτῷ γυναῖκα πορνείας.... For the thought of the ministry of John as in some sense the ἀρχὴ τοῦ εὐαγγελίου compare Acts i. 21 f., x. 37 (perhaps also Lk. iii. 1 f., 23, Jn xv. 27, xvi. 4).

τοῦ εὐαγγελίου. For the right understanding of εὐαγγέλιον in the N.T. the use of the Hebrew root *bśr* in the O.T. is of fundamental importance. The noun occurs only six times (twice meaning 'reward for bringing good news'); but the verb in the Pi'el occurs often (nearly always represented in LXX by the middle of εὐαγγελίζω) and means 'to announce good news' (e.g. I Kgs i. 42, Jer. xx. 15), especially of victory (e.g. I Sam. xxxi. 9). Of special importance are the following: Isa. xl. 9, xli. 27, lii. 7, lx. 6, lxi. 1, Nah. i. 15, Ps. xl. 9 (R.V.: 'publish'), xcvi. 2 (R.V.: 'shew forth'). Here the content of the good news is the in-breaking of God's kingly rule, the advent of his salvation, vengeance, vindication (e.g. Isa. lii. 7: 'Thy God reigneth'). In this expectation of the great victory of Yahweh the herald who is to announce it has a prominent part, and the participle *mᵉbaśśēr* becomes a religious technical term. In later Palestinian Judaism *bśr* is mainly a religious term. The figure of the *mᵉbaśśēr* of Second Isaiah is frequently referred to, and is sometimes an unnamed person, sometimes a number of people together, sometimes the Messiah himself, sometimes Elijah. When the herald appears and announces his news, those who hear him themselves become heralds too (cf. Lk. ix. 6). The content of the message is still the advent of God's kingly rule (the substantival 'kingdom of heaven' now taking the place of the verbal 'thy God reigneth').

That Jesus regarded himself as fulfilling the role of the *mᵉbaśśēr* is indicated by Mt. xi. 5 = Lk. vii. 22, Lk. iv. 17–21, and also perhaps by Mt. v. 3 = Lk. vi. 20. That Mark thinks of Jesus' preaching (on which he lays great emphasis) against this background seems clear from i. 14 f. We take it therefore that the basic idea in εὐαγγέλιον here is that of the announcement of good news by Jesus ('Ιησοῦ Χριστοῦ subjective genitive). But Jesus was not only the herald of good tidings; he was also himself the content of the good tidings he announced, as every section of Mark is eloquent to proclaim. Jesus' own consciousness of being the content, as well as the announcer, of the gospel is indicated by a number of his sayings, as we shall see. Mark certainly regarded him as the content of the gospel, and this thought is also present here as a powerful undertone. 'Ιησοῦ Χριστοῦ is best explained as a subjective genitive; but an objective genitive is in fact implicit here.

It remains to point out that εὐαγγέλιον has also a pagan background, and for the inhabitants of the Roman Empire it had special associations with the Emperor-cult, the announcements of the birth of an heir to the throne, of his coming-of-age, or his accession, being εὐαγγέλια. In the Christian use of the word, determined as it is by the O.T. and centred in the word and work and person of Jesus, there is therefore also a contact with contemporary pagan usage and an implied contrast between the one true εὐαγγέλιον and these other εὐαγγέλια, between the kingdom of God and the kingdom of those who falsely claimed to be gods.[1]

The events referred to in vv. 2–13 are, then, the ἀρχὴ τοῦ εὐαγγελίου 'Ιησοῦ Χριστοῦ in the sense that they are the immediate prelude to the public announcement of the good news by Jesus Christ, to his coming forward as the herald of the kingdom of God, and also, since he is himself the content of his message, the immediate prelude to the *publication* of the good news *of* Jesus Christ. The words do not, of course, mean that these events are the beginning of the gospel, in

[1] On εὐαγγέλιον see further G. Friedrich in *T.W.N.T.* II, pp. 705 ff.

the sense that they are the beginning of that saving act of God which is the content of the good news; for Jesus' life prior to his public ministry is also part of the gospel.

'Iησοῦ. 'Iησοῦς is the Greek form of the Hebrew *Yēšûaʿ*, the post-exilic form of *Yᵉhôšuaʿ* (Joshua, the son of Nun, is *Yᵉhôšuaʿ* in the Pentateuch and in Joshua, but in Neh. viii. 17 he is called *Yēšûaʿ*). The name was borne by a number of men in the O.T. In the N.T. 'Iησοῦς is used of Joshua, son of Nun, of someone in the genealogy of Jesus (Lk. iii. 29), of Barabbas (in some MSS.), in the name Bar-jesus, and of Jesus Justus. Till the beginning of the second century A.D. it was a very common name among Jews. Josephus mentions some twenty bearers of it, of whom ten are contemporary with Jesus. Both the Hebrew and the Greek forms are found in ossuary inscriptions from the early imperial period. Thus our Lord's name was a common one among his people. (From the beginning of the second century A.D. it disappears among both Jews and Christians, Jews avoiding it out of hatred for Jesus, and Christians avoiding it as a common name out of reverence for him.) According to Mt. i. 21, Lk. i. 31, ii. 21, the name was not chosen for him haphazard, but on the ground of a divine promise. It means 'Yahweh * is salvation' or 'salvation of Yahweh', and is so explained by Philo: ἑρμηνεύεται...'Iησοῦς...σωτηρία Κυρίου; though Mt. i. 21 suggests that in the shorter form only the verb *yāšaʿ* was felt—unless αὐτός could refer to God, as has been suggested. Apart from Mt. i. 21 there is no direct play on the meaning of the name in the N.T.

Χριστοῦ. *Pace* Taylor (*Names of Jesus*, p. 18: 'Here the name is personal, the Messianic reference being contained (and transcended) in the phrase, "Son of God"'), it is probable that Mark intends his readers to understand the full titular sense; for in this verse he is indicating the theme of his whole book, in the course of which the title Χριστός will be taken up (viii. 29, xiv. 61, xv. 32, and also where the name is not used but the idea is present—e.g. in the Baptism and the Anointing in Bethany). For a discussion of the word see on viii. 29.

After Χριστοῦ read Υἱοῦ Θεοῦ. The words are omitted by ℵ* Θ 28 255 1555* sy^pal geo^1 arm (some MSS.), and there is considerable Patristic support for the omission. W.H., Nestle, etc. accept it. But, while it may be argued that a scribe is more likely to have added than omitted the phrase, there are very strong reasons for regarding it as original. (i) The attestation is very strong. (ii) The Patristic evidence for omission is not as weighty as at first it seems, for an ecclesiastical writer's omission of words that are not relevant to the point he is making does not prove that they were omitted by the text he knew. (Both Irenaeus and Epiphanius can also omit the words Ἰησοῦ Χριστοῦ here!) (iii) The phrase could easily be omitted by homoioteleuton. (iv) 'Son of God' is a theme of this gospel (see i. 11, iii. 11, viii. 38, ix. 7, xii. 6, xiii. 32, xiv. 36, 61, xv. 39) and it is intrinsically probable that it would be found in this first verse (compare what was said above on Χριστοῦ). (v) It has been suggested that at a time when the divine Sonship of Jesus was taken for granted the phrase could have been omitted on stylistic grounds in order to reduce the ugly piling up of genitives. On the significance of 'Son of God' see further on i. 11, and the other passages just referred to.

2. γέγραπται (the perfect denoting a past action the results of which remain) is regularly used to introduce quotations from scripture.

τῷ Ἠσαΐᾳ τῷ προφήτῃ. The v.l. τοῖς προφήταις is no doubt an attempt to remove a difficulty, the first quotation not being from Isaiah.

Ἰδοὺ ἀποστέλλω...τὴν ὁδόν σου seems to be a combination of Mal. iii. 1 a and Exod. xxiii. 20. It is not included in the parallels, but does appear in the same form (with the addition of ἔμπροσθέν σου) in Mt. xi. 10 and Lk. vii. 27. In view of this and the fact that it separates the reference to

Isaiah from the Isaiah quotation in *v.* 3, it has been argued that it is an early gloss. But, while this is possible, it is probably wiser to regard it as part of what Mark wrote, in the absence of more conclusive contrary evidence and in view of the fact that there is no textual support for its omission. The former part of the quotation agrees with the LXX of Exod. xxiii. 20, the latter part with the M.T. of Mal. iii. 1, except that 'the way before me' becomes 'thy way', the change to the second person expressing the messianic interpretation of the passage. It is probable that 'my messenger' (cf. 'the messenger of the covenant' later in the verse) in Mal. iii. 1 meant originally 'the angel of Yahweh', as in Exod. xxiii. 20 (cf. Exod. xxxii. 34, xxxiii. 2, etc.), but Mal. iv. 5 f. would suggest the identification of this figure with Elijah. Mal. iii. 1 ff., iv. 5 f., combined with II Kgs ii. 11, gave rise to lively speculation about Elijah in Judaism, and this is reflected in Mk vi. 15, viii. 28, ix. 11–13. Three distinct forms of the expectation of Elijah's return may be traced. In Mal. and in Ecclus xlviii. 10 (more clearly in the Hebrew version) and in the view of some Rabbis he is a messianic figure preparing the way for God himself and restoring Israel. According to another view which is more widely spread he is the forerunner not of God but of the Messiah. It is this view that is behind Mk i. 2. (Cf. the ancient prayer preserved in *Sopherim* xix. 9: 'May Elijah the prophet come to us soon; and King Messiah come forth in our days.') According to the third view Elijah belongs to the tribe of Levi and is the High Priest of the messianic age. For the identification of John the Baptist with Elijah cf. i. 6, vi. 15, ix. 11–13, Lk. i. 16f., Jn i. 21, 25 (in the Jn passages the identification is rejected by the Baptist himself).

3. The second quotation (from Isa. xl. 3) agrees with the LXX apart from one significant variation—the substitution of αὐτοῦ for τοῦ θεοῦ ἡμῶν, which has the effect of making possible, though not necessitating, the identification of the

Κύριος with Jesus. Though Mark avoids the use of Κύριος as
a title of Jesus, truly reflecting pre-Resurrection usage (cf. on
vii. 28 and xi. 3), it is probable that he had here this possibility in mind. By the time he was writing, of course, Κύριος
was a regular title for Jesus, and O.T. passages in which
Κύριος represents the Tetragrammaton were being referred
to Jesus (e.g. Joel ii. 32 in Rom. x. 13).

The M.T. connects 'in the wilderness' with 'prepare ye';
but the LXX (though the order of the words is actually the
same as in the M.T.) is naturally understood to be coupling
ἐν τῇ ἐρήμῳ with βοῶντος—which makes easy the reference
of the verse to John preaching in the wilderness.

4. Take closely with *vv.* 2–3, putting a comma at the end
of *v.* 3 (John's ministry occurs in accordance with God's
purpose revealed in scripture). The words between Ἰωάννης
and κηρύσσων vary slightly in the MSS.: (i) B and a few
others have ὁ βαπτίζων ἐν τῇ ἐρήμῳ; (ii) ℵ C L etc., followed
by the R.V., have the same +καί after ἐρήμῳ; (iii) W f1
f13 ς have the same as (ii) with ὁ omitted; (iv) D Θ 28,
supported by lat syᵖ, have ἐν τῇ ἐρήμῳ βαπτίζων καί. The
translation varies according to which of these we read and
how we take ἐγένετο. On the whole, (i) is to be preferred,
the other readings being explainable as alterations for the
sake of smoothness; it may be rendered either: 'John the
Baptist appeared, preaching in the wilderness' (taking
ἐγένετο as standing alone, as in Jn i. 6, I Jn ii. 18—a
Semitism); or 'John the Baptist was (or 'appeared') in the
wilderness, preaching' (cf. Rev. i. 9); or 'John the Baptist
was preaching in the wilderness' (taking ἐγένετο with
κηρύσσων as a periphrastic tense). Of these the last is
perhaps the least likely because of the word-order. There is
little to choose between the other two.

For ὁ βαπτίζων meaning 'the Baptist' or 'the Baptizer'
cf. vi. 14, 24; in vi. 25, viii. 28 he is called ὁ βαπτιστής.

On John the Baptist reference should be made to

Barrett, *H.S.G.T.* pp. 25–34; Flemington, *Baptism*, pp. 3–24; Lampe, *Seal*, pp. 19–32; Manson, *S.-M.* pp. 36–49, and 'John the Baptist' in *B.J.R.L.* xxxvi, pp. 395–412; and, on the possibility of a connection between John and the Qumran sect, Burrows, *D.S.S.* pp. 328f.[1] There are only two primary sources of information about John: the N.T. and Josephus, *Ant.* xviii. 116–19. The Mandaean literature, though containing many references to him, is not a primary source. Josephus describes John as 'a good man who bade the Jews cultivate virtue by justice towards one another and piety towards God, and (so) come together for baptism (βαπτισμῷ συνιέναι): for immersion, he said, would appear acceptable to God only if practised, not as an expiation for specific offences, but for the purification of the body, when the soul had already been thoroughly cleansed by righteousness'. He also testifies to the strength of John's influence with the people.

ἐν τῇ ἐρήμῳ. Mt. iii. 1 adds τῆς 'Ιουδαίας. But it seems unlikely that Judea can have been the main centre of John's activity, as the gospels and Josephus agree that it was Herod Antipas who put him to death, and Judea was not under his jurisdiction. Lk. iii. 3 says John came εἰς πᾶσαν τὴν περίχωρον τοῦ 'Ιορδάνου and Jn i. 28 sets his activity on the east side of the Jordan. This suggests that his main centre may have been Peraea, which was in Herod's territory. Moreover Machaerus, where according to Josephus John was killed, was in Peraea.

John's choice of the wilderness as the scene of his preaching was probably due to the associations it had come to have in the thought of his people. Israel's sojourn in the wilderness was remembered both as a time of Israel's disobedience and also as a time of grace, of God's mighty acts. As the latter aspect was emphasized there was a tendency to ascribe everything good to this period and also to see in it a

[1] Also J. A. T. Robinson in *H.T.R.* l (1957), pp. 175ff.   *

foreshadowing of the messianic end-time. Already in Hos. ii. 14 (cf. xii. 9) the idea of a second wilderness period is found, and this verse was influential. The idea grew up that the final eschatological salvation would have its beginning in the wilderness—the Messiah would appear there. Hence the tendency of revolutionary messianic movements to be attracted to the wilderness (e.g. Acts xxi. 38, Josephus, *B.J.* ii. 259, 261, vi. 351, vii. 438; cf. Mt. xxiv. 26). Compare also the settlement of the Qumran sectarians in the wilderness of Judea. It was probably, then, because he was announcing the kingdom of God and the coming of the Messiah that John gathered the people around him ἐν τῇ ἐρήμῳ. Whether the Messiah would appear in the wilderness of Judea or in the wilderness of Sihon and Og (to the east of Jordan) was apparently a subject of dispute: it is possible that the Mt. addition of τῆς Ἰουδαίας is connected with the expectation of some that it would be in the wilderness of Judea.

κηρύσσων. The verb κηρύσσω, derived from κῆρυξ, 'a herald', means 'to announce in a loud voice'. It occurs thirty-three times in the LXX, in eighteen places representing ḳārā'. Surprisingly, it is not often used of prophetic preaching, though it is used in Isa. lxi. 1 (κηρῦξαι αἰχμαλώτοις ἄφεσιν), in Joel ii. 1, and also with reference to the preaching of Jonah. Isa. lxi. 1 and Joel ii. 1 are specially significant because of their eschatological associations, the former being the passage which Jesus regarded as fulfilled by himself (Lk. iv. 21), the latter a demand for the alarm to be sounded, 'for the day of the LORD cometh, for it is nigh at hand'. Similar are the associations of Zeph. iii. 14, Zech. ix. 9, where the verb denotes the joyful shout of the redeemed. In the N.T. it is regularly used of the preaching of Jesus and the apostles and of John the Baptist. The use of this verb of John's preaching underlines the close connection between his preaching and that of Jesus and the apostles (cf. Lk. iii. * 18, where it is actually said that John εὐηγγελίζετο τὸν λαόν) and should make us wary of exaggerating the contrast between John and Jesus as Manson does (*S.-M.* p. 49).

The object of κηρύσσων is βάπτισμα μετανοίας εἰς ἄφεσιν ἁμαρτιῶν: John was announcing a baptism of repentance with a view to the forgiveness of sins. This singling out of baptism as the most characteristic element of his preaching has the support of Josephus, who says that John was called ὁ βαπτιστής, and so, in spite of his apparent desire to minimize the importance of this aspect of John's ministry, betrays the fact that this was the most notable thing about him. To look for the origin of John's baptism outside Judaism is quite perverse in view of the fact that, as Manson points out, 'the rest of John's thought moves on orthodox Jewish lines'.[1] Rather should we recognize as its background the many ritual washings laid down in the O.T. law (e.g. Lev. xv. 5, 8, 13, 16), the frequent O.T. use of the imagery of washing in connection with repentance (e.g. Isa. i. 16), and above all Jewish proselyte-baptism.[2] That proselyte-baptism was established by this time is now generally agreed. It is inconceivable that the Jews should have taken on the custom *after* the rise of the Christian Church, of which baptism was characteristic. If this view that John's baptism was derived from proselyte-baptism is granted, then it follows that the implication of his baptism was that Jews did not have a right to membership in the people of God by the mere fact that they were Jews (cf. Mt. iii. 9, Lk. iii. 8): by their sins they had become as Gentiles and now they needed as radical a repentance as did Gentiles, if they were to have any part in God's salvation. John was seeking to awaken his compatriots out of their false sense of security. It would also seem to be implied that he thought of himself as the instrument by which the true Israel was being brought together,

---

[1] *S.-M.* p. 43.

[2] For the ablutions of the Qumran sect see *Manual of Discipline*, iii. 4f., 9, iv. 21, v. 13, and *Zadokite Fragment*, xii (in Gaster, x. 10–13).

those who submitted to his baptism being incorporated into the true people of God. Cf. Lk. i. 17: ἑτοιμάσαι Κυρίῳ λαὸν κατεσκευασμένον. (Whether or not the curious phrase of Josephus, βαπτισμῷ συνιέναι, lends any support to this is not certain: if it means 'come together by means of baptism', then it would seem to; but it may well mean merely 'come together for baptism'.)

μετανοίας. Proselyte-baptism seems to have had some ethical significance, though it was no doubt primarily a means of ritual cleansing. In the case of John's baptism the ethical significance is clear. Implied by μετανοίας here, it is made very clear by Mt. iii. 7–10 = Lk. iii. 7–9, and by Lk. iii. 10–14, and borne out by Josephus' account which strongly emphasizes the moral aspect of John's work.

In classical Greek μετανοῶ means to notice or recognize afterwards (with the idea of being too late), change one's mind or disposition, be sorry, regret; and the substantive μετάνοια means change of mind, regret, remorse. But the clue to the meaning of μετανοῶ and μετάνοια in the N.T. is rather to be found in the O.T. In the LXX in fifteen out of a total of about twenty occurrences in the canonical books μετανοῶ represents niḥam, which means to be sorry about something, and so, to change one's intention out of pity (e.g. I Sam. xv. 29, Jer. xviii. 8, Amos vii. 3, 6). In Jer. viii. 6, xxxi. 19 niḥam is used to denote sorrow for sin committed. Often this verb is used in close association with another, šûḇ (translated in LXX by ἐπιστρέφω, ἀποστρέφω): see e.g. Jer. iv. 28, Exod. xxxii. 12 and 14. In fact niḥam and šûḇ can be used as synonyms. Thus, while šûḇ is never represented in the canonical books in the LXX by μετανοῶ (apart from the possible exception of Isa. xlvi. 8), the way was open for the subsequent appropriation of μετανοῶ as the regular equivalent of šûḇ. So it is to the meaning of šûḇ in the O.T. and among the Rabbis that we must look for the real background of μετανοίας here.

Šûb means 'to turn back', 'return'. Used over 1000 times in the O.T., it has a religious significance in about 120 occurrences. It occurs twenty-eight times in Jer.—the largest number in a single book. This 'returning' as it is preached by the prophets is, basically, 'a matter of returning to Yahweh with one's whole being and in all decisions taking Him absolutely seriously as Israel's God'.[1] It is realized in obedience to his will; it involves trusting absolutely in him and ceasing to rely on such human helps as foreign alliances or on false gods; it includes a new attitude to everything, which expresses itself negatively as a turning away from all evil; and it is something which in the last resort comes not from man but from God.

In Rabbinic Judaism the idea of repentance still plays an important part, but the noun *tešûbāh* is more prominent than the verb, and the expression 'to do repentance' ('*āśāh tešûbāh*) tends to replace the simple verb. 'Great is repentance' is a saying that occurs often in Rabbinic literature. In (*M*) *Ab*. iv. 17 we find: 'Better is one hour of repentance and good works in this world than the whole life of the world to come; and better is one hour of bliss in the world to come than the whole life of this world.' Repentance is still a turning away from evil, a turning to God, and involves obedience to God's laws; and the consciousness that God must work it is still present, as in the fifth petition in the '*Shemoneh Esreh*' (Palestinian version): 'Bring us back to Thee, O Lord, so that we may repent.' But there is a tendency to a legalistic understanding of repentance.

The *tešûbāh* that was the key-note of John's preaching was then something familiar enough to his hearers; and yet in his preaching it gains a new significance, for the summons to repentance on his lips is more urgent than it had been on the lips of earlier prophets, since it is under the pressure of the imminence of the eschatological event. This eschatological

[1] E. Würthwein in *T.W.N.T.* IV, p. 981.

motive, about which more will have to be said in connection with *vv.* 7f., is already implied by εἰς ἄφεσιν ἁμαρτιῶν. The baptism of repentance had for its goal forgiveness of sins, salvation in the approaching judgement.

ἄφεσιν. The verb ἀφίημι is used in the LXX to translate several Hebrew verbs meaning 'to let go', 'release', etc., and also several verbs of forgiving. The latter use involves a certain modification of meaning, since, while these Hebrew verbs of forgiving are originally cultic, ἀφίημι is forensic. The substantive ἄφεσις only once in the LXX has the meaning 'forgiveness'. It is used in Lev. xxv and xxvii to render *yôbēl* (R.V.: 'jubile'). The fact that John's baptism of repentance was with a view to forgiveness of sins implies that there was an element of gospel in his message, of the good news of the hope of forgiveness and of eschatological salvation, and should make us hesitate to accept an estimate of him that overstresses the contrast between his message and that of Jesus.

Exactly how John regarded the connection between his baptism and the forgiveness of sins it is difficult to be sure. That he did not think of baptism as effecting automatically a man's acceptance before God, but held that it needed to be accompanied by obedience, is indicated by Mt. iii. 8 = Lk. iii. 8a. But it is probable that he thought of it as having some real effectiveness towards forgiveness, and as in some measure at any rate a pledge of it.

Note that this phrase εἰς ἄφεσιν ἁμαρτιῶν strikes at the very outset of Mark's gospel a note which is to be a main theme throughout. It will next become explicit again in ii. 5, but in the intervening verses it will be hinted at more than once.

5. πᾶσα and πάντες are doubtless an exaggeration; but that John made a deep impression is confirmed by Josephus, *Ant.* xviii. 118: 'Now, as many flocked to him, for they were greatly moved by hearing his words, Herod, fearing that the

great influence John had over the people might lead to some rebellion, (for the people seemed likely to do anything he should advise,) thought it far best, by putting him to death, to prevent any mischief he might cause.' The authentic voice of prophecy had for a long time been silent (see Ps. lxxiv. 9, Lam. ii. 9, I Macc. iv. 46, ix. 27, xiv. 41): now once again men heard it in the message of the Baptist.

ἐξομολογούμενοι τὰς ἁμαρτίας αὐτῶν. Their submission to baptism was itself a confession of sinfulness. Cf. above on v. 4. It is possible that a spoken confession of sin preceded the actual baptism.

6. ἦν with the perfect participle ἐνδεδυμένος and the present participle ἔσθων (ἔσθω is an older form of ἐσθίω)—a double example of the use of periphrastic tenses, which is specially common in Mk. The force of the imperfect here is to indicate habitual action. The accusatives τρίχας, ζώνην, are normal after the passive of ἐνδύω, since the active verb takes a double accusative (both of the person clothed and of the garment). Cf. ἐνδιδύσκω in xv. 17.

By τρίχας καμήλου Mark probably means a garment woven of camel's hair. The v.l. δέρριν ('skin'), found in D, supported by a (pellem), is accepted by C. H. Turner. It is possible that it should be read, but on the whole more probable that it is a corruption due to the influence of Zech. xiii. 4, where the word occurs in the LXX. Zech. xiii. 4 is evidence that the 'hairy mantle' was the sign of a prophet in Israel. The description of John here is no doubt meant to suggest the identification with Elijah (cf. II Kgs i. 8).

ἀκρίδας. According to Lev. xi. 22 it is permissible to eat locusts. The Bedouin are said to eat them either salted or roasted.

μέλι ἄγριον. 'Either the honey found in rocks or possibly the sap of certain trees' (Taylor).

7. The eschatological motivation of John's baptism, already implied in v. 4, becomes explicit in this and the next

verse. Of the approaching judgement nothing is said directly, it is true (though see on *v.* 8)—only that one mightier than John (i.e. the Messiah) is coming after him. But the things mentioned in Mt. and Lk. ('the wrath to come', 'the axe laid unto the root of the trees', and the separation of the wheat and the chaff) are implied here too. It is in view of approaching judgement *and also* the approaching redemption of the true Israel that John calls his contemporaries to repent and be baptized.

Ἔρχεται. Cf. Mt. xi. 3=Lk. vii. 19.

ἰσχυρότερος. See note on iii. 27.

μου. John is apparently conscious 'of standing at the beginning of the unfolding of the eschatological drama' (Taylor); and so to compare the coming one with himself is natural. He feels himself to be closely associated with him as his herald and forerunner.

So John's preaching includes a messianic preaching. Josephus does not mention this, but by omitting it he has made his account obscure—for he leaves Herod's destruction of John unexplained. It was the eschatological-messianic element in John's message which was likely to seem dangerous to Herod. And of this stronger one John says ἔρχεται. It is an announcement of the imminent approach of the Messiah.

οὗ οὐκ εἰμί...αὐτοῦ. To carry someone's shoes after him or to take them off his feet was the work of a slave. A Hebrew slave was not obliged to do it (*Mekilta* on Exod. xxi. 2). Rabbi Joshua b. Levi is quoted as saying: 'All services which a slave does for his master a pupil should do for his teacher, with the exception of undoing his shoes' (*b Ket.* 96 a).

The redundant αὐτοῦ after οὗ is a characteristic Semitic construction. In Hebrew the pronoun is not redundant but necessary, since the relative pronoun is indeclinable.

8. ἐγώ and αὐτός are both emphatic, stressing the contrast.

ἐβάπτισα. The aorist is best explained as representing a

Semitic perfect with present meaning (the Mt. and Lk. parallels have βαπτίζω here).

Πνεύματι. ἐν is inserted before Πνεύματι by almost all MSS., but is probably rightly omitted by W.H., Nestle, etc., following B L b vg. The omission of the article before Πνεύματι is probably not significant (cf. Mt. i. 18, Lk. i. 15, 35, ii. 25). (See further Moule, pp. 106–17, esp. 112f.)

What Mark understands by this sentence is fairly clear. It is a confession by John of the vast superiority of the coming one over himself. While John administers the eschatological sacrament of baptism, the coming one will actually bestow the eschatological gift of the Spirit. Mark may have thought of Pentecost. He may also, since the early Church closely connected the gift of the Spirit with baptism, have had in mind the fact that now that Christ has died, risen and ascended, those who receive baptism in his name can receive *at once* the ἀπαρχή of the Spirit. But the contrast is primarily between the persons of John and Jesus, not between John's baptism and Christian baptism. Theologically, it is important here not to make the mistake of turning this into a simple contrast between John's and Christian baptism, as though the meaning were that the former is merely a matter of water, while the latter is both water-baptism and also a baptism with the Spirit; for, on the one hand, the Christian minister needs to make precisely the same confession with regard to the baptism he administers (all that *he* does is to baptize with water; the gift of the Spirit is the gift not of the celebrant but of Christ), and, on the other hand, there is a real continuity between John's baptism and Christian baptism, to overlook which is to rob the Baptism of our Lord of a great part of its significance.[1]

But we have to ask also about the historical foundation for Mark's words. What did John the Baptist mean? Here it is important to notice that the saying has come down to us in

---

[1] Cf. Calvin, I, pp. 180f., 197f., and see further on *v.* 9.

two forms—that in Mk (cf. Jn i. 33, Acts i. 5) and that in
Mt. and Lk., according to which the words καὶ πυρί are
added. From Acts ii. 3 ('tongues...like as of fire') it seems
likely that Luke at least thought of the fire as the fire of the
Holy Spirit. The suggestion on the basis of this connection
between fire and Spirit that we have here a Synoptic
reference to the Spirit that has its origin in Hellenistic
religion is rightly rejected by Barrett (*H.S.G.T.* p. 126).
Another explanation—one that has become popular—is
that originally the contrast was simply between John's
baptism with water and the messianic baptism with the fire
of judgement, the reference to the Holy Spirit being an early
Christian interpretative addition transforming the original
meaning of 'fire'. In support of this view it is pointed out
that both Mt. iii. 10 = Lk. iii. 9 and Mt. iii. 12 = Lk. iii. 17
contain references to fire of judgement. A further explanation (giving a similar significance) was suggested by Eisler
and has been accepted by Barrett: that the original reference
was to wind and fire, both being used as symbols of judgement. (Πνεῦμα and its Hebrew and Aramaic equivalents
can mean both wind and spirit.) The word Ἁγίῳ would
then be a Christian interpretative addition. This gives a
highly plausible connection with Mt. iii. 12 = Lk. iii. 17—
the wind carrying away the chaff. But, as there is evidence
that a general bestowal of the Spirit was expected as a
feature of the last days (see esp. Joel ii. 28f.; also Isa. xxxii.
15, xliv. 3, Ezek. xxxvi. 25–7, xxxvii. 14, xxxix. 29), and also
some evidence, though not much, that the Messiah was
expected, not only to be equipped with the Spirit, but
actually himself to bestow the Spirit (Test. Levi xviii. 11), it
seems more probable that the original saying of John did
contain a reference to the bestowal of the Spirit.[1] If the

[1] Manson's appeal to Acts xix. 1–6 as evidence against John's having
foretold a baptism with the Holy Spirit (*Sayings*, p. 41) falls to the ground,
if the R.V. translation of Acts xix. 2b is justified.

Mt./Lk. form is original, then the meaning would be that the coming one would bring the eschatological outpouring of the Spirit and also the eschatological judgement.

2. THE BAPTISM OF JESUS (i. 9–11)
(Mt. iii. 13–17; Lk. iii. 21 f.)

That Jesus was baptized by John can scarcely be doubted. The fact that his submission to a baptism of repentance embarrassed the early Church (cf. Mt. iii. 14, the passages from the Gospel of the Ebionites and the Gospel according to the Hebrews quoted in Huck with reference to Mt. iii. 13–17, and perhaps also the omission of Mark's phrase βάπτισμα μετανοίας εἰς ἄφεσιν ἁμαρτιῶν in Mt. iii. 1) makes it unlikely that the Church would ever have invented the incident. The sequel may perhaps be interpreted as a visionary experience. That Jesus should at this point have experienced a vision is intrinsically quite probable, and we may suppose that the account of it derives ultimately from himself. The ideas and the matter-of-factness of the narrative stamp the section as based on primitive tradition.

9. Both the construction Καὶ ἐγένετο...ἦλθεν and the phrase ἐν ἐκείναις ταῖς ἡμέραις (neither of which is frequent in Mk) have an O.T. ring (cf. e.g. Exod. ii. 11). Was Mark perhaps, consciously or unconsciously, feeling after a special dignity at the point where he was introducing Jesus for the first time?

Ναζαρεθ. See Smith, *Hist. Geog.* pp. 432f., Dalman, *S.S.W.* pp. 57–78. That Jesus should have spent most of his life in an obscure village which had no proud history and is never mentioned in the O.T., Josephus, or the Talmud (see also Jn i. 46) is congruous with the messianic veiledness (on which see further at iv. 11).

ἐβαπτίσθη. To the question concerning Jesus' motive in submitting to baptism various answers have been given,

including the suggestion that he was conscious of sin. The true answer, however, is suggested by the fact that *v.* 11 contains an echo of Isa. xlii. 1, which speaks of that Servant of the Lord whose mission is further described in Isa. lii. 13–liii. 12. Jesus' submission to John's baptism of repentance was his mature self-dedication to his mission of self-identification with sinners which in due course would involve the Cross. In his baptism he became for men's sake and in their
* place 'the one great Sinner who repents'—to use Barth's daring phrase. That Jesus later in his ministry associated baptism with death seems to be indicated by Mk x. 38, Lk. xii. 50, and it is by no means unlikely that already at the Jordan he was aware that his baptism by John foreshadowed another baptism, more bitter, without which his Mission could not be completed.

A further reason for his baptism (hardly perhaps a conscious motive of Jesus at the time, but a reason in the divine plan) is indicated by Calvin's words: 'that He might consecrate baptism in His own body, that we might have it in common with Him'. Our Lord's submission to baptism by John is the fundamental dominical institution of the Christian sacrament of baptism.

εἰς here, as often in Hellenistic Greek, is used instead of ἐν.

ὑπὸ 'Ιωάννου. Apparently John actually administered the baptism, whereas proselyte-baptism seems to have been self-administered before witnesses.

10. εὐθύς. A favourite adverb in Mk, occurring over forty times. Here it has its proper meaning, 'straightway', 'immediately'.

The subject of εἶδεν is Jesus, and there is nothing in Mark's account that necessarily implies that anyone else saw the heavens opened and the Spirit descending, or heard the voice. It seems likely that Mark intended to record not externally objective phenomena but a vision—albeit a vision that was no empty dream but a real communication from God. (Luke seems to objectify the elements of the vision by his ἐγένετο... ἀνεῳχθῆναι... καταβῆναι... γενέσθαι and perhaps further by inserting σωματικῷ εἴδει (unless possibly that should be taken closely with ὡς περιστεράν rather than with καταβῆναι?). The form of Matthew's account seems to imply the same objectification (the order ἰδοὺ ἠνεῴχθησαν οἱ οὐρανοί, καὶ εἶδεν... and, still more, the use of the third person in v. 17 suggesting that the voice was heard by others); but it is possible that in Mt. this objectification has occurred in the transmission of the text rather than in the original, as one v.l. inserts αὐτῷ after ἠνεῴχθησαν and another has the second person in v. 17.)

σχιζομένους τοὺς οὐρανούς. Cf. Isa. lxiv. 1, Ezek. i. 1, Jn i. 51, Acts vii. 56, x. 11, Test. Levi ii. 6, v. 1, and esp. xviii. 6 and II Bar. xxii. 1, where the opening of the heavens is associated with the hearing of a voice, and Test. Jud. xxiv. 2f., where it is associated with the pouring out of the Spirit (as it is also in Test. Levi xviii. 6f.). This imagery, though it also occurs in pagan sources, is thoroughly Jewish. Here the opening of the heavens is the natural prelude (in the imagery of a vision) to a divine communication. The present participle indicates action actually in progress.

τὸ Πνεῦμα...καταβαῖνον εἰς αὐτόν. In view of the evidence for the expectation that the Messiah would be specially endowed with the Spirit of God and would actually bestow the Spirit (see on v. 8) it is reasonable to suppose that the early Church saw a messianic significance in the descent of the Spirit on Jesus—and also that Jesus himself did so.

If Mark is describing a vision, the question arises whether these words indicate simply a divine assurance to Jesus of a truth about himself by means of the symbolism of a vision, or whether there really was a special outpouring of the Spirit on Jesus at the time of his baptism. It may be suggested that there was, and that this was an invisible event (just as the gift of the Spirit in Christian baptism is invisible), but that at the same time Jesus experienced a supernatural vision, the symbolism of which was an assurance of the reality of the unseen event.

ὡς περιστεράν. That the imagery of the vision should be derived from the O.T. and Judaism is natural. The comparison of the Spirit to a dove seems to go back to Gen. i. 2, where the Hebrew *m^eraḥepeṭ* suggests the brooding of a bird. There is Rabbinic evidence that on the basis of that text the Holy Spirit was sometimes likened to a dove.

11. φωνὴ [ἐγένετο] ἐκ τῶν οὐρανῶν. ἐγένετο should clearly be omitted. Cf. ix. 7 and parrs., Jn xii. 28; also Test. Levi xviii. 6, II Bar. xiii. 1, xxii. 2, Josephus, *Ant.* XIII. 282f., and the various passages in Rabbinic lit. which speak of a *baṭ-ḳôl*. The *baṭ-ḳôl* (= 'daughter of the voice', i.e. an echo of a heavenly voice) is in Jewish thought an inferior substitute for the Word of God given directly to the prophets by the Holy Spirit ('When Haggai, Zechariah and Malachi, the last prophets, died, the Holy Spirit vanished from Israel; but they were allowed to hear the *baṭ-ḳôl*'—*t Soṭ.* xiii. 2). Apparently Mark was thinking in terms of a *baṭ-ḳôl*, and we may assume that Jesus had thought of the message he had received in that way too. During his earthly life his intercourse with the Father was subject to human conditions and limitations.

The words of the *baṭ-ḳôl* are reminiscent of Isa. xlii. 1 (cf. the form in which it is quoted in Mt. xii. 18 which includes the words ὁ ἀγαπητός μου ὃν εὐδόκησεν ἡ ψυχή μου), a passage which speaks of the gift of God's Spirit to the Servant. But the suggestion that we should therefore recognize behind ὁ Υἱός μου an earlier ambiguous ὁ Παῖς μου (representing Hebrew *'abdî* = 'my servant'), which has been changed by Greek-speaking Christians, who regarded it as too humble a term, to ὁ Υἱός μου at an earlier stage than the composition of Mk, is probably not to be accepted; for the presence in the Temptation narratives in Mt. and Lk.

of the twice repeated and by its order very emphatic εἰ
Υἱὸς εἶ τοῦ Θεοῦ, in which (in view of the close connection in
all three Synoptics between the Baptism and the Temptation) it is natural to see a reference back to the words of the
voice, and also the presence in the Synoptic Gospels of a
number of passages that reflect Jesus' filial consciousness,
make it probable that the original words of the bat-kôl
contained some reference to sonship.

It is now increasingly recognized that the Western reading
in Lk. iii. 22 (accepted in Huck, 9th ed.), which is an exact
quotation of Ps. ii. 7 (LXX), should be rejected; but the
question still remains, whether the bat-kôl contains an echo
of Ps. ii. 7 as well as Isa. xlii. 1. To this it may be replied
that, if Mark himself had thought that the first part of the
bat-kôl was an echo of Ps. ii. 7, we should on the whole have
expected him to have reproduced the LXX order υἱός μου
εἶ σύ as is done elsewhere in the N.T. when Ps. ii. 7 is quoted.

'Son of God' here is not to be explained as merely a
messianic title (the evidence of its use as a messianic title in
pre-Christian Palestinian Judaism is scanty and doubtful).[1]
The voice does not proclaim Jesus' newly established status
of sonship consequent upon his installation as Messiah;
rather it confirms his already existing filial consciousness.
In response to his self-dedication to the mission of the
Servant, made in his submission to baptism, he is given a
confirmation of his own consciousness of being the Son of
God, that is at the same time a confirmation of his Servant-
vocation. (On the title 'Son of God' reference should be
made to Bieneck, *Sohn Gottes*.)   †

ὁ ἀγαπητός can, of course, be taken with ὁ Υἱός μου—'my
beloved son' or, since ἀγαπητός can signify 'only' (e.g. LXX
Gen. xxii. 2, etc.), 'my only son'; but in view of Mt. xii. 18
it is perhaps better to take it as a separate designation, an
echo of beḥîrî in Isa. xlii. 1, 'my son, my (or 'the') beloved'.

[1] Cf. Jeremias, *Parables*, p. 57.

55

εὐδόκησα may be explained as a timeless aorist.

On the Baptism of Jesus see further: Barth, *The Teaching of the Church regarding Baptism* (Eng. tr., London, 1948), pp. 17–19; Barrett, *H.S.G.T.* pp. 25–45; Flemington, *Baptism*, pp. 25–33; Cullmann, *Baptism*, pp. 9–22; Lampe, *Seal*, * pp. 33–45; Cranfield in *S.J.T.* VIII, pp. 53–63.

3. THE TEMPTATION (i. 12–13)
(Mt. iv. 1–11; Lk. iv. 1–13)

The accounts of the Temptation probably go back ultimately to Jesus himself, who may well have told his disciples about it after their recognition of him as the Messiah. On the whole, it seems more likely that we have two independent accounts—that represented by Mt. and Lk. and that given by Mk—than that Mark is here giving an abbreviated version of the account given more fully by the other two.

12. In view of Mark's excessive use of εὐθύς we cannot press it; but all three Synoptists place this incident and the Baptism in immediate juxtaposition, and there is no reason to doubt that the one followed the other closely.

τὸ Πνεῦμα αὐτὸν ἐκβάλλει. He goes not by chance, nor by his own fancy, but by the leading of that Spirit who had come upon him in special fulness at his baptism—in obedience to God and in fulfilment of his mission. In view of Mark's usage ἐκβάλλει probably does have the sense of strong compulsion, though often in Hellenistic Greek it has a quite weak sense. But it is quite unnecessary to think of an 'ecstatic condition', and the citation of I Kgs xviii. 12, II Kgs ii. 16, Ezek. iii. 12, 14, viii. 3, Acts viii. 39, in this connection is probably inapposite. Rather should we think of a moral compulsion by which the Spirit made it clear to Jesus that the acceptance of his Servant-vocation must lead him by way of this encounter.

εἰς τὴν ἔρημον. Probably not because the solitude

would be conducive to meditation and prayer, but rather because the wilderness was specially associated with demons (cf. Lk. viii. 29, xi. 24, Mt. xii. 43, and S.-B. IV, pp. 515f.). Whereas other men must avoid temptation in so far as they can (cf. Mt. vi. 13), this man must voluntarily seek it out and take the offensive (cf. the final πειρασθῆναι in the Matthew parallel).

13. ἦν . . . πειραζόμενος could be a periphrastic imperfect, but it is probably better to take πειραζόμενος . . . Σατανᾶ as a separate participial clause.

τεσσεράκοντα ἡμέρας. It is quite likely that Mark would be conscious of the parallel with the forty days' and nights' fasts of Moses, the type of Messiah (Exod. xxxiv. 28, Deut. ix. 9, 18), and Elijah, the forerunner of the Messiah (I Kgs xix. 8); but perhaps the differences here are more significant than the similarities. As to the often made suggestion that Mark had in mind the forty years of Israel's wanderings in the desert, it should be noted that years are not days, that in the O.T. the association of the wilderness sojourn with Israel's being tested (Deut. viii. 2, 16) is much less common than its association either with Israel's putting God to the test by its disobedience or with God's graciousness toward Israel, and finally that forty is a common round number in the Bible.

Mark says nothing of fasting (Mt. iv. 2, Lk. iv. 2). That this element of the tradition was unknown to him is hardly likely. Perhaps he thought its mention unnecessary for his purpose or (more probably) that it was sufficiently clearly implied by ἐν τῇ ἐρήμῳ. The most probable explanation of Jesus' fast is that it is connected with his submission to a baptism of repentance in self-identification with men; for 'fasting brings to expression man's recognition of his unworthiness to live longer . . . and so the radical nature of his repentance'.[1] In support of this cf. Joel ii. 12, I Sam. vii. 6, Neh. ix. 1, Dan. ix. 3.

[1] Barth, K.D. IV/1, p. 286 (C.D. IV/1, p. 260).

πειραζόμενος. Mark's language suggests that Jesus was tempted during the forty days (cf. Lk. iv. 2); but Mt. iv. 2f. seems to imply that the temptation was subsequent to the forty days' fast. The verb πειράζω is used in the LXX to render Hebrew *nissāh*. The two verbs correspond closely. Both mean 'to make trial of' a thing, to 'attempt' to do something, and to 'test' or 'prove' a person. In the O.T. the words are used in this last sense of God proving men (e.g. Gen. xxii. 1, Exod. xvi. 4, xx. 20, Deut. viii. 2, Ps. xxvi. 2) and of men putting God to the test (e.g. Exod. xvii. 2, Num. xiv. 22, Deut. vi. 16). But there is no instance in the O.T. of their being used in the modern sense of 'tempt', i.e. 'entice to sin'. On the strength of this some would explain πειραζόμενος here as meaning simply 'tested' (God testing Jesus by means of Satan and also Satan putting God to the test). But this will hardly do; for it does not do justice to post-O.T. Jewish thought about Satan or to the Mt./Lk. narrative, which depicts the devil as seeking to draw Jesus away from the mission to which he has dedicated himself. Moreover, πειράζω is quite definitely used sometimes in the N.T. in the sense of enticing to sin (e.g. James i. 13f., I Cor. vii. 5, Gal. vi. 1, I Thess. iii. 5; cf. I Tim. vi. 9). And in the O.T., though the verbs *nissāh*/πειράζω are not used to express it, the idea of enticing to sin is present and connected with the serpent in Gen. iii. So we take it that πειραζόμενος here means not just 'being tested', but being tempted to turn aside from his appointed path.

ὑπὸ τοῦ Σατανᾶ. The Hebrew *śāṭān* means 'adversary', and is used e.g. of men whom God raised up as adversaries of Solomon (I Kgs xi. 14, etc.). Then it is used with the definite article of the superhuman adversary (*haśśāṭān*, Job i and ii, Zech. iii. 1f.), who is a sort of heavenly public prosecutor, not demonic but belonging among the 'sons of God'. In I Chr. xxi. 1 the word is used without an article as a proper name. Here Satan is apparently a spirit who

entices to sin. Outside the O.T. there was a great development of the idea of Satan in Judaism, and he comes to be
thought of as 'that one who seeks to destroy the relationship
between God and men, especially between God and Israel'.[1]
But legalism prevented the full development of the idea of
Satan in Judaism, and it is not till we turn to the N.T. that
we find the fully developed conception of Satan as the ruler
of an organized empire of evil, the prince of this world, from
whose control men are totally unable to free themselves.

According to the N.T. it was in order to overcome the
kingdom of Satan and to set men free from his thraldom
that the Son of God became man: 'To this end was the Son
of God manifested, that he might destroy the works of the
devil' (I Jn iii. 8). The gospel is the record of the great
encounter. Jesus' exorcisms, his healing of the sick and
raising the dead, his self-identification with sinners, his
refusal to adopt any other methods but those ordained by
his Father—all these are the offensive of the Son of God
against the power of Satan; and the climax of the encounter
is of course the Passion. Here at the very beginning of the
ministry the devil attempts to win a decisive victory by
diverting his opponent from the path of the Servant to some
less costly way.

On Satan and the demons see further W. Manson,
'Principalities and Powers', in *B.S.N.T.S.* iii, pp. 7–17; *
Barth, *K.D.* iii/3, pp. 327–425, 608–23; and for a magni- *
ficent exposition of the content of the temptation *C.D.* iv/i,
pp. 261–4.

καὶ ἦν μετὰ τῶν θηρίων. A detail peculiar to Mk,
included most probably in order to emphasize the loneliness
of the place and the absence of human help. That the idea
of wild beasts being in some way associates of Satan and the
demons (cf. Lk. x. 19, Test. Benj. v. 2, Test. Naph. viii. 4,
Test. Iss. vii. 7) was also in mind is conceivable. That the

[1] W. Foerster in *T.W.N.T.* ii, p. 75.

thought is of Jesus after his victory being revered by the beasts, as Adam had once been revered by the beasts in Paradise, is less likely.

οἱ ἄγγελοι. On the angels see on xvi. 5.

With regard to διηκόνουν there are two interrelated problems, concerning the time and the nature of the action signified. The structure of the verse suggests that the time of the angelic ministration coincided with that of our Lord's being with the beasts (which it seems preferable to regard as coincident with the period of temptation rather than as coming after it). On the other hand, Mark's style is not so strict as to forbid us to think of the ministration as taking place after the temptation was over, as in Mt. iv. 11. The imperfect in itself would be no obstacle to this interpretation here any more than it is in Mt. iv. 11; for it would be expressing continued or linear action in past time (in Mt. iv. 11 the imperfect is perhaps inceptive). The verb may have its special sense, 'wait at table', and so the meaning be that the angels supplied Jesus with food (cf. I Kgs xix. 5–8, Ps. lxxviii. 23–5); but it can equally well denote any service, and even in Mt. iv. 11 it is separated by several verses from the mention of Jesus' hunger. If we insist on taking it to refer to a ministration lasting throughout the period of temptation, then we should probably have to understand Mark to mean that the angels attended him in the sense that they were witnesses of his encounter with Satan. But it is probably better to think of a special assurance of the divine presence granted to Jesus after the temptation had been overcome.

II. BEGINNINGS OF THE
GALILEAN MINISTRY
(i. 14–iii. 6)

The second main division includes two complexes along with some other material. The first complex is i. 21–38, a closely articulated group of four narratives, probably all Petrine in origin, concerned with the ministry of Jesus in and around Capernaum. The second is ii. 1–iii. 6, a topical complex (probably pre-Markan) of conflict stories arranged to show the development of hostility to Jesus: in ii. 6f. the questioning is unspoken, in ii. 16 the disciples of Jesus are approached, in ii. 18 Jesus himself is questioned, in ii. 24 he is actually rebuked, in iii. 2 his adversaries watch him with malicious intent, and in iii. 6 they plot his death.

4. THE BEGINNING OF THE GALILEAN MINISTRY
(i. 14–15)
(Mt. iv. 12–17; Lk. iv. 14f.)

The first of the summary statements (see pp. 11f.). It is apparently meant to cover the whole of the main division i. 14–iii. 6.

14. Καὶ μετὰ (the *v.l.* Μετὰ δέ is preferred by C. H. Turner) τὸ παραδοθῆναι τὸν Ἰωάννην. While according to Jn the ministries of John and Jesus overlapped, the Synoptic Gospels date the beginning of Jesus' Galilean ministry after John's imprisonment. Mark's statement, however, does not altogether rule out the possibility of an earlier activity of Jesus alongside that of John, room for which could be found between i. 13 and i. 14.

The use of παραδίδωμι as a technical term in police and law-court jargon for 'deliver up as a prisoner' is attested in papyri and inscriptions; but, since it simply means 'to hand over' and can be used in a wide variety of connections, in Greek usage generally it is normal to make clear by additional words in what particular sense it is being used. Mark's lack of explicitness here is possibly just careless writing, but more probably it is intentional. Either one or both of two possible considerations may have influenced him. On the one hand, the use here of a general term without any addition to make it explicit might suggest the parallel between the delivering up of John and the subsequent delivering up of Jesus, whereas the addition of εἰς φυλακήν would only have obscured this, as Jesus was never imprisoned. On the other hand, the use of the general term, particularly in the passive, could suggest that behind the schemes and actions of men in relation to John *God's* purposing and doing were to be recognized. On παραδίδωμι see further at ix. 31; and on John's imprisonment and subsequent execution at vi. 17 ff.

ἦλθεν. Mark does not say whence. Was it straight from the scene of the Temptation? Or did some activity in Judea precede the Galilean ministry?

On κηρύσσων see on i. 4; on εὐαγγέλιον on i. 1. But note that εὐαγγέλιον is used in a slightly different sense here. Whereas in i. 1 it meant the publication of the good news, here it means rather the content of the good news, the message.

τοῦ Θεοῦ. Variously explained as subjective or objective genitive (i.e. 'from God' or 'about God'). The former is probably to be preferred. That which Jesus was preaching was God's message of good news. (Cf. II Cor. xi. 7, I Thess. ii. 2, 8, 9, I Pet. iv. 17.)

15. ὅτι here is *recitativum*, i.e. it introduces a quotation, so is equivalent to inverted commas.

Πεπλήρωται. Cf. Gen. xxv. 24, xxix. 21, etc. in the LXX, where the same verb is used, and Gal. iv. 4, and also Lk. i. 57, ii. 6, where a different verb meaning 'fill', 'fulfil', is used. The form of expression is common in the O.T., the Hebrew verb being *mālē*'. The idea is that of 'the completion of a fixed period of time': where we think of the point of time at which a particular event is to happen, 'the Hebrews thought of the space of time which must elapse before something happened'.[1] So the meaning here is that the καιρός has come.   *

ὁ καιρός. In ordinary Greek the word denotes the favourable time for a particular undertaking, so 'opportunity'. In the LXX it most often represents Hebrew '*ēt*, and the idea of the right time or decisive time being determined by God is prominent. So in Dan. vii. 22 the LXX has καὶ ὁ καιρὸς ἐδόθη (*sc.* by God). In Ezek. vii. 12 (and often elsewhere) it is the time of God's judgement. In the N.T. use of the word the thought of determination by God is more than ever important. It is God's decision that makes a particular moment or period of time into a καιρός, a time filled with significance. So here the meaning of the sentence is that the time appointed by God for the fulfilment of his promises, the time to which the O.T. was pointing, the eschatological time, has come. Cf. Lk. iv. 21. The exact nuance of καιρός here is given by the words which follow. See further O. Cullmann, *Christ and Time* (Eng. tr., London, 1951), pp. 39–44, and also the articles on 'time' and 'fulfil' in *T.W.B.*   *

ἤγγικεν will be more conveniently discussed after the next phrase.

ἡ βασιλεία τοῦ Θεοῦ. When Jesus preached about the kingdom of God, he did not have to begin by telling his hearers that there was such a thing. He could assume that they had already heard about it. 'Kingdom of God' in the teaching of Jesus has an O.T. and Rabbinic background.

The kingship (root *mlk*) of God is thought of in two main ways in the O.T.: (i) God is thought of as being even now the King of Israel (e.g. I Sam. xii. 12, Isa. xli. 21, xliii. 15, Jer. viii. 19) and of the whole world (e.g. Jer. x. 7, Mal. i. 14,

[1] J. Y. Campbell in *T.W.B.* p. 88.

Ps. cxlv. 11–13, I Chr. xxix. 11 f.). But the men of the O.T. were conscious of very many things which seemed to contradict the statement that God was king. Even his rule over his own people Israel was called in question by their disobedience and disloyalty. So we get (ii) the other main class of passages, in which the divine kingship is referred to in terms of expectation and hope, as something yet to be realized (e.g. Isa. xxiv. 23, lii. 7, Obad. 21, Zeph. iii. 15, Zech. xiv. 9).

But these two ways of thinking are, of course, not mutually exclusive watertight compartments. Nor can we put every reference into one or the other class securely. Rather the two ways of thinking about God's kingship intermingle and now one, now the other, predominates. When the Hebrew thought in the second way he was after all looking forward to the time when God would make manifest and unambiguous that kingship which he knew was all the time a reality. But it was natural, especially in times of frustration and suffering, that attention should be directed increasingly to this future manifestation of God's rule (which was, besides, the more exciting thought), and that there should be a tendency to understand in a more and more eschatological way passages in which the eschatological way of thinking had not originally been predominant.

When we turn to the Rabbinic background, while the general picture is the same, there are some special features that are important for our present purpose:

(i) The use of the expression 'kingdom of heaven' (Heb. *malkût šāmayim*; Aram. *malkûtā' dišmayyā'*). About this two things are to be noted. First, that 'heaven' is used to avoid mentioning the divine Name; so in the gospels the Matthaean 'kingdom of heaven' is the more Jewish form, and therefore likely to be what Jesus used. Secondly, that 'kingdom' here reflects the tendency in late Judaism to avoid using verbal expressions of God and to use abstract nouns instead (so the

Targum of Onkelos substitutes for 'the LORD shall reign' in
Exod. xv. 18, 'God's kingdom stands firm'). So the phrase
βασιλεία τοῦ Θεοῦ in the Gospels means not the area or the
people over which God reigns, but simply God's rule, his
acting as king.

(ii) The references to the kingdom's 'being revealed'
(Aram. *gly*, *gl'*), which express vividly the meaning of the
eschatological thought of the kingship of God. At present
God's rule is in a real sense hidden; but it is to become manifest and unambiguous (cf. Lk. xix. 11: ἀναφαίνεσθαι).

(iii) The references to 'receiving' (and 'throwing off')
'the kingdom' (or 'the yoke of the kingdom') 'of heaven'.
It is because God's rule is at present hidden that men are in
a position to decide whether they will receive or reject it; and
the fact that the day is coming when it will be made manifest makes that decision a matter of urgency.

Jesus shares with the O.T. and with later Judaism the
conviction that God is even now 'the great King' (Mt. v.
35), the 'Lord of heaven and earth' (Mt. xi. 25), without
whom not even a sparrow can fall to the ground (Mt. x. 29);
but, when he preaches about the kingdom of God, it is to the
eschatological *malkût šāmayim*, the kingdom of God in the
sense of the decisive manifestation of God's kingship, that he
refers. We may now indicate briefly some of the main points
about the kingdom which emerge from Jesus' teaching.

(i) It has come near (in this verse ἤγγικεν, on which see
below); it has come upon those to whom he is speaking
(Mt. xii. 28 = Lk. xi. 20); it is in their midst (Lk. xvii. 21).
That which for the O.T. was in the future, the object of hope,
is now present.

(ii) Yet, paradoxically, Jesus can still speak about it as
future. His disciples are to pray, 'Thy kingdom come'
(Mt. vi. 10); he 'will not drink from henceforth of the fruit
of the vine, until the kingdom of God shall come' (Lk. xxii.
18).

(iii) It is intimately connected with his own person. It is in his activity that it has come upon his contemporaries (Mt. xii. 28 = Lk. xi. 20); it is because he is in their midst that it is in their midst (Lk. xvii. 21). It is in his words and works and person that the kingdom has come. In fact, we may actually go so far as to say that the kingdom of God *is* Jesus and that he *is* the kingdom. (Cf. Marcion's saying, recorded in Tertullian, *adv. Marc.* iv. 33: 'In evangelio est Dei regnum Christus ipse'; and the words of Origen, *Comment. in Matt.* Tom. xiv. 7, on Mt. xviii. 23: 'As he is the wisdom itself and the righteousness itself and the truth itself, so maybe he is also the kingdom itself (αὐτοβασιλεία)...and, if you ask how the kingdom of heaven is theirs, you can say that Christ is theirs.') He is himself the fulfilment of God's promises, God's royal intervention in judgement and mercy. The fact that the kingdom of God is, for the evangelists, identical with Jesus himself is indicated by the way in which a reference to Jesus may be parallel to a reference to the kingdom (e.g. Mk. x. 29 = Mt. xix. 29 = Lk. xviii. 29; Mk. ix. 1 = Mt. xvi. 28). Here we have the key to the problem how (i) and (ii) can be reconciled. The kingdom has both come and is still to come, because Jesus has come and is to come again. The prayer of Mt. vi. 10 is equivalent to 'Marana tha' (I Cor. xvi. 22) and 'Come, Lord Jesus' (Rev. xxii. 20).

(iv) If what has just been said is true, then we must be chary of explaining the contrast between the kingdom already come with Jesus and the kingdom still to come in terms of a contrast between partial and complete. It is rather a contrast between veiled and manifest. The kingdom in its fulness came in Christ, for he came really and fully. What the Church now awaits is not something more complete than Christ himself, but rather Christ manifest and in glory. But this contrast between hidden and revealed is not the same as that which we have already seen above between the two senses of God's kingship in the O.T. and Judaism; for in

Christ God did manifest his kingdom, did intervene decisively, but it was a 'veiled manifestation'; he revealed his
kingdom, not in such a way as to make assent unavoidable,
but in a way that still left room for men to make a personal
decision. (On this see further on iv. 11f. and iv. 21.)

(v) The future coming of the kingdom is (in some sense)
imminent. On this see further on xiii. 28 ff.

(vi) From what has already been said it should be plain
that the identification of the kingdom of God with the
Church made by Augustine, which has become deeply
rooted in Christian thinking, is not true to the teaching of
Jesus.

(vii) Finally, it is instructive to notice the variety of terms
by which men's relation to the kingdom is indicated. It is
first of all God's gift (Lk. xii. 32, Mt. xxi. 43). Of men it is
said that they receive it (Mk. x. 15 = Lk. xviii. 17), wait for it
(Mk. xv. 43 = Lk. xxiii. 51), inherit it (Mt. xxv. 34), enter it
(Mt. v. 20, vii. 21, xviii. 3 par., xix. 23 f. par., xxiii. 13,
Mk. ix. 47, Mt. xxi. 31). It is also said that the kingdom
belongs to certain people (Mt. v. 3, 10, Mk. x. 14). Men are
summoned to seek it (Lk. xii. 31 = Mt. vi. 33), to strive to
enter it (Lk. xiii. 24: cf. Mt. vii. 14 which speaks of the gate
and the way to life, a synonym for the kingdom); the rich
young ruler is told to sell all and give to the poor in order to
enter it (Mk. x. 17 ff.). No sacrifice is too costly in order to win
it (Mt. xiii. 44-6, Mk. ix. 47). †

The meaning of ἤγγικεν has been much discussed (see
R. H. Fuller, *The Mission and Message of Jesus* (London,
1954), pp. 20-5; Kümmel, *P. and F.* pp. 22-5). The linguistic
objections to Dodd's proposal to translate it 'has come' are
strong. It is better to translate 'has come near'. But it does
not follow that we must therefore understand this in the
sense of 'is imminent'. Fuller notes that of the thirty-five
times that ἐγγίζω occurs in the N.T. (apart from the times it
refers to the kingdom of God) it is used twenty-four times in

a spatial sense. He then says: 'It is the remaining occurrences referring to time which interest us here.' But it is unwise to brush aside the majority of the occurrences in this way. In both the other occurrences of the verb in Mk. (xi. 1, xiv. 42) it is strictly spatial; and it is better here too to understand 'has come near' in a spatial rather than a temporal sense. The kingdom of God has come close to men in the person of Jesus, and in his person it actually confronts them. (Cf. xii. 34.) Thus the verb is given its natural meaning, 'come near', and at the same time full justice is done to the theological truth which Dodd's translation expresses.

μετανοεῖτε. See on μετανοίας in v. 4.

πιστεύετε ἐν τῷ εὐαγγελίῳ. The only clear example of πιστεύειν ἐν in the N.T. (Jn iii. 15, Eph. i. 13 are probably to be explained otherwise). Probably a Semitism. It occurs in the LXX (though in nearly every place there is a *v.l.* omitting the ἐν) and there it is clearly imitation of the Hebrew *he᾽emîn be*.—They are to believe the good news that the hoped for kingdom of God has come near.

5. THE CALL OF THE FIRST DISCIPLES (i. 16–20)
(Mt. iv. 18–22; cf. Lk. v. 1–11)

The presence of such details as ἀμφιβάλλοντας ἐν τῇ θαλάσσῃ and καταρτίζοντας τὰ δίκτυα and the mention of Zebedee and the hired servants, the fact that Peter is himself directly concerned, and the improbability that the metaphor of fishing for men would be used in the sense it has here except in close connection with the actual occupation of those who were called—all these things encourage us to believe that here we have a Petrine story and are near to an actual eye-witness account. The suggestion of Bultmann that this is an 'ideal scene' spun out of the metaphor 'fishers of men' is extremely unlikely. What Taylor calls 'the somewhat schematic character' of the narratives of these two calls and that related in ii. 14 may well reflect constant repetition in preaching, and the emphasis on the decisiveness of the break in the repeated ἀφέντες may also be due to the use of the story in preaching and catechizing, for which this material was obviously valuable.

In this section we have the first of a series of incidents that illustrate the authority of Jesus. His word lays hold on men's lives and asserts his right to their whole-hearted and total allegiance, a right that takes priority even over the claims of kinship. In other sections we shall see how this same authoritative word of Jesus casts out the demons, heals the sick, quells the tempest, raises the dead. In this pericope the good news (i. 1, 15) is veiled under the outward form of stern and total demand, but it is nonetheless present; for the section points to the mystery of the person of this man who thus disturbs men's lives.

16. παράγων παρά is odd. Lohmeyer may well be right in thinking that παρὰ τὴν θάλασσαν τῆς Γαλιλαίας is Mark's interpolation into his source, which merely spoke of Jesus 'passing by'.

θάλασσαν. Lk. more correctly uses λίμνη of the Lake of Galilee; but the use of θάλασσα in the sense of λίμνη is thoroughly Semitic.

Σίμων was a common Greek name, at any rate since the fifth to fourth century B.C. Being a near-sounding name, it was apparently used as a Greek equivalent of the Hebrew Šim‘ôn, which is represented in the canonical books of the LXX by Συμεών. In Acts xv. 14 and II Pet. i. 1 Simon Peter is called Συμεών.

Ἀνδρέας was a Greek name, but it also occurs in the Talmud.

ἀμφιβάλλω occurs only here in the N.T. Here it is used absolutely of casting a net.

ἐν used where classical Greek would use εἰς. Cf. on v. 9.

17. On the meaning of Δεῦτε ὀπίσω μου, and also

ἀκολουθεῖν in the next verse, and ἀπέρχεσθαι ὀπίσω in *v.* 20, see on viii. 34 ff. What following Jesus means will become plain as the Gospel proceeds. It is interesting to compare the narrative in I Kgs xix. 19–21.

ποιήσω ὑμᾶς γενέσθαι. For ποιεῖν + accusative and infinitive meaning 'to cause someone to do something' cf. vii. 37, Mt. v. 32, etc. The usage is good Greek.

ἁλεεῖς ἀνθρώπων. The metaphor is used in the O.T. in a bad sense only (Jer. xvi. 16; cf. Ezek. xxix. 4 f., Amos iv. 2, Hab. i. 14–17), and similarly in Rabbinic literature. So it would hardly have been used in the sense it has here, if it had not been suggested by what the two men were actually doing.

18. εὐθύς has here its full value—their response is immediate. Mark does not tell us whether they had had any contact with Jesus before. Cf. Jn i. 35–42, and also Lk. v. 1–11. Mark's account emphasizes the divine compulsion of Jesus' word; cf. the part played by his word in the miracle stories.

ἀφέντες. Ἀφίημι, a verb with a wide variety of meanings, here means 'leave'.

19. Ἰάκωβος is the Greek form of Hebrew *Ya‘ᵃḳōb* (LXX: Ἰακώβ).

Ζεβεδαῖος represents Hebrew *Zabday* or *Zᵉbadyāh*. LXX has various forms.

Ἰωάννης represents Hebrew *Yôḥānān* or *Yᵉhôḥānān*. LXX has various forms, but B has Ἰωάνης in II Chr. xxviii. 12, I Esdr. viii. 38.

From Lk. v. 10 we learn that James and John were 'partners to Simon'.

καὶ αὐτοὺς ἐν τῷ πλοίῳ καταρτίζοντας.... We may translate: 'He saw James and John also in their boat mending...', understanding the force of καὶ αὐτούς to be that, just as Jesus had seen Simon and Andrew in their boat, so now he saw this second pair also in a boat. Cf. Lk. i. 36, Acts xv. 27, 32. On the other hand, it is possible that Mark's sentence reflects an Aram. circumstantial clause ('Now they were mending...'), though, if this is so, he has brought it inside the grammatical structure of the Greek sentence by using the accusative instead of the nominative. Cf. Black, p. 63.

καταρτίζοντας. The verb means 'put in order', 'render ἄρτιος'. Used with reference to nets it would include not only mending, but also cleaning and folding—making ready for another night's fishing.

20. ἐκάλεσεν. The words καλῶ, κλῆσις, κλητός are rich in theological significance in the Bible. See, e.g., Prov. i. 24, Isa. xli. 9, xlii. 6, xliii. 1, xlv. 3, xlvi. 11, xlviii. 12, 15, l. 2, li. 2, lxv. 12, Rom. viii. 30, ix. 11, 24, I Cor. i. 9, 26, vii. 15 ff., I Pet. i. 15, ii. 21, v. 10.

Discipleship comes into being through the call of Jesus. 'The disciple does not hurry along to Jesus, but rather is chosen and called by Him' (Schlatter).

6. IN THE SYNAGOGUE AT CAPERNAUM (i. 21-8)
(Lk. iv. 31-7; with vv. 21 f. cf. Mt. vii. 28 f.)

To try to force this section into conformity with the specifications of a form-critic's ideal miracle-story by the use of Procrustean methods is doctrinaire. The truth is that we have here a story more primitive than the rounded form of the common miracle-story—a piece of very direct and authentic tradition, which is best regarded as Petrine material. (So Taylor.) The suggestion that v. 21 a belongs properly to the preceding narrative is improbable.

21. Καφαρναουμ. One of the few place-names in Mk. Like Nazareth it is not mentioned in the O.T. It is almost certainly to be identified with Tell Ḥum on the N.W. shore of the lake about two miles west of the place where the Jordan flows into it. See further Dalman, S.S.W. pp. 128f., 138 ff.

σάββασιν. Σάββατον regularly has this third declension

form in the dative plural in the N.T. The plural is used with a singular meaning, as is the case with festivals (e.g. τὰ ἄζυμα, τὰ ἐνκαίνια), though occasionally σάββατα is a true plural, as in Acts xvii. 2.

εἰσελθών is omitted and ἐδίδασκεν placed before εἰς τὴν συναγωγήν in ℵ C L f13 and some other authorities; and this form of the text is probably to be preferred. εἰσελθών looks like an insertion to improve the grammar, and the transposition of ἐδίδασκεν would be explicable as connected with the insertion. εἰς would then be equivalent to ἐν, as in i. 9, etc.

ἐδίδασκεν. Inceptive: 'He began to teach.' The verb διδάσκω occurs seventeen times in Mk (sixteen times with Jesus as subject), and the noun διδάσκαλος eleven times (in every case used of Jesus). Though, compared with the other evangelists, Mark does not give much of the actual teaching of Jesus, he does, like them, lay very great stress on Jesus' teaching ministry. Both in form and matter his teaching was thoroughly in the Rabbinic tradition. Fundamental for him as for the Rabbis was the conviction that the will of God is revealed in the scriptures alone and especially in the Law. Where he differed from them was partly in the seriousness and consistency with which he followed out their own basic presuppositions, but above all in his consciousness of personal authority. That he was recognized as a Rabbi not only by his own disciples and by the common people, but even by the learned themselves, is suggested by the fact that in Mk xii. 14 and 32 he is addressed as 'Teacher' by them (cf. x. 17 and xii. 19). His unquestionable competence compelled their serious consideration, in spite of the fact that he did not possess the conventional qualifications (cf. Jn vii. 15, and also Mk vi. 2f.)—though he may well have had more than elementary Rabbinic education—and was without official authorization to teach. (See further K. H. Rengstorf, in T.W.N.T. II, pp. 138–68, and also Manson, *Teaching*, pp. 46–50.)

22. ἐξεπλήσσοντο. Indefinite plural (frequent in Mk). The passive of ἐκπλήσσω is used five times in Mk—here and in vi. 2, xi. 18, of the effect of Jesus' teaching on the people, in x. 26 of its effect on the disciples, in vii. 37 of the effect of a miracle on the people present. When we add to these the following occurrences of other words expressive of amazement: θαυμάζω: v. 20, xv. 5, 44; ἐκθαυμάζω: xii. 17; θαμβοῦμαι: i. 27, x. 24, 32; ἐκθαμβοῦμαι: ix. 15 (xvi. 5f.); ἐξίστημι: ii. 12, v. 42, vi. 51 (cf. the use of φοβοῦμαι in iv. 41, v. 15, 33, 36, vi. 50, ix. 32, x. 32, xi. 18 (xvi. 8), and of ἔκφοβος in ix. 6), it becomes clear that references to the amazement occasioned by Jesus are a striking feature of the gospel. G. Bertram seeks to explain them as being, not historical reminiscence of the impression actually made by Jesus on people at the time, but rather Mark's method of underlining for his readers the revelation-content of what he is recording.[1] But it is much more probable surely that they are genuine historical reminiscence, evidence, not merely of the theology of the early Church, but of the impression made by Jesus in his lifetime,[2] though it is, of course, possible that *sometimes* this feature may have been added even where there was no factual basis for it, in accordance with the natural tendency toward assimilation to a characteristic pattern. The amazement or wonder which these words denote is something which may prove to be the 'first step towards faith' (Wohlenberg), or it may turn into a σκανδαλίζεσθαι—a 'being offended'.

διδαχῇ includes both content and manner.

The latter half of the verse gives the reason for the people's astonishment. It has been suggested by D. Daube[3] that ἐξουσία here represents Hebrew rᵉšûṯ in the sense of the autho-

[1] *T.W.N.T.* III, pp. 5f.
[2] I am here reversing the opinion concerning Bertram's explanation which I expressed in *S.J.T.* III, p. 58, n. 1.
[3] 'Exousia in Mark i. 22 and 27', in *J.T.S.* XXXIX (1938), pp. 45–59.

rity of a properly ordained Rabbi as opposed to the inferior
sort of teachers, and that γραμματεῖς here denotes these
inferior teachers. He thinks that at this time a Rabbi with
rᵉšût̠ would be quite rare in Galilee. On this view the reason
for the people's surprise is that Jesus does not teach as one of
the inferior, not properly authorized, teachers they were
most accustomed to, but in an authoritative way as though
he were an ordained Rabbi like the learned Rabbis in
Jerusalem. But, though ἐξουσία is certainly equivalent to
rᵉšût̠, it seems unlikely that Daube's suggestion is right. It is
more probable that the rᵉšût̠ referred to here is such authority as the prophets had had, the authority of a direct commission from God, and that the γραμματεῖς with whom Jesus
is contrasted are not the inferior teachers, but the properly
ordained Rabbis. Even these did not claim an immediate
authority; they were rather the exponents of a tradition
handed down to them. The people sensed in the way Jesus
taught the implicit claim to an authority superior to that of
Rabbinic ordination. The word γραμματεύς in the N.T. is the
equivalent of the Hebrew sôp̠ēr. This was the word used for
the ordained theologians in the oldest Rabbinic tradition.
(After the time of Christ the contemporary Rabbis ceased
to be called sôp̠ᵉrîm, and were known as h̬ᵃk̠āmîm.)

23. ἐν here is a Semitism—Luke improves the Greek by
substituting ἔχων πνεῦμα. . . .

πνεύματι ἀκαθάρτῳ is a thoroughly Jewish expression, rûah̬
t̬ûm'āh being a specially common way of denoting demons in
Rabbinic literature. On the subject of demons, in addition
to the literature already referred to in connection with
Σατανᾶ in i. 13, the article on δαίμων etc. in *T.W.N.T.* II,
pp. 1–21 by W. Foerster should be consulted. In comparison
with the Pseudepigrapha, Rabbinic literature, and also the
contemporary non-Jewish world, the N.T. rarely mentions
the demons except in connection with exorcisms. This reti-
cence and abstention from speculation on the subject are due,

on the one hand, to the fact that in the N.T. the demons are no longer thought of as more or less independent individualities but rather as altogether subordinate to Satan, and, on the other hand, to the fact that the writers, knowing that the demons have met their master, no longer find them of fascinating interest. But this is far from meaning that the demons are not taken seriously. On the contrary, the victory of Christ over the powers of darkness is a central feature of the gospels. (This is as true of the fourth as of the first three gospels, in spite of the fact that it includes no exorcism narrative.)

Here we are up against something that presents many difficulties to the modern mind, which is apt to dismiss the whole subject as outgrown superstition. It is important to approach it with as open a mind as possible. To suggest that there may be more truth here in the N.T. picture than has sometimes been allowed is not to wish to turn the clock back on scientific progress or to open the flood-gates to obscurantism. The question whether the spread of a confident certainty of the demons' non-existence has not been their greatest triumph gets tragic urgency from such twentieth-century features as Nazism, McCarthyism, and Apartheid. And lest we should be prejudiced by the memory of such horrors as the burning of witches, it must be said that they were due, not to taking the N.T. too seriously, but to failing to take it seriously enough.

ἀνέκραξεν indicates strong emotion: cf. vi. 49.

24. Τί ἡμῖν καὶ σοί; Similar expressions occur in the O.T. (e.g. Josh. xxii. 24, Judg. xi. 12, II Sam. xvi. 10, xix. 22, I Kgs xvii. 18) and also in classical Greek (for examples see L. & S., under εἰμί (sum), C.III.2). The meaning is: 'What have we and you in common?', so 'Why do you interfere with us?' or 'Mind your own business!' Cf. v. 7, Jn ii. 4.

ἡμῖν. Cf. ἡμᾶς immediately below. The man's personality

has been so disabled that the demon, usurping the place of the self, speaks through him—the plural denoting the demons as a class.

Ναζαρηνέ. Ναζαρηνός occurs four times in Mk, twice in Lk.; otherwise Ναζωραῖος is used (Mt. twice, Lk. once, Jn three times, Acts seven times). On the discussion these two words have caused and the various derivations which have been suggested see the full discussion by H. H. Schaeder in *T.W.N.T.* IV, pp. 879–84, or the short note in Taylor, pp. 177f. *Pace* Black, pp. 143–6, we may accept Schaeder's conclusion that both forms mean 'of Nazareth', being two different graecizings of Aramaic *nāṣrāyā*' formed from Aramaic *nāṣrat*–Nazareth.

ἦλθες [*sc.* into the world: cf. on i. 38, iv. 21] ἀπολέσαι [the infinitive of purpose is specially common in N.T. after verbs of motion] ἡμᾶς can be read as a question (so W.H., A.V., R.V., R.S.V.) or as a statement (so Nestle, Huck, Taylor). In either case it expresses a mixture of fear and defiance. The demon's foreboding is due to his recognition of the identity of Jesus. The destruction of the evil spirits was expected in the last days.

οἶδά σε τίς εἶ, ὁ "Αγιος τοῦ Θεοῦ. Note the hyperbaton. The pronoun which should be the subject of the subordinate clause is brought forward into the main clause, where it becomes the object. This is much more common in Aramaic than in Greek. Cf. vii. 2, xi. 32, xii. 34, Mt. xxv. 24, etc. Against the view that the recognition of Jesus by the demoniacs is simply part of an invented theory by which the early Church sought to get over the embarrassing fact that there was no evidence that Jesus had claimed to be the Messiah or his disciples recognized him as such during his life, it has been rightly pointed out that the early Church is not likely to have invented a feature which, far from having apologetic value, would be likely to occasion mockery (iii. 22 suggests how readily a pretext for accusing Jesus of being in league with the demons would be seized). There is therefore very good reason for believing that the possessed did actually recognize Jesus.

It is often assumed that ὁ Ἅγιος τοῦ Θεοῦ must be used as a messianic title; but it is not a known messianic title, and in the only other place in the N.T. where it occurs (apart from the Lk. parallel to this verse), Jn vi. 69, it is not used as a messianic title but rather (as Bultmann points out)[1] to designate Jesus as from beyond this world and belonging to God, and is to be connected with Jn x. 36. We may compare Lk. i. 35 b, where ἅγιος is closely associated with Υἱὸς Θεοῦ and with the miraculous birth of Jesus. So it is better here to understand ὁ Ἅγιος τοῦ Θεοῦ as in line with ὁ Υἱὸς τοῦ Θεοῦ in iii. 11 and Υἱὲ τοῦ Θεοῦ τοῦ Ὑψίστου in v. 7. It is as the divine Son of God rather than as Messiah that the demoniacs address Jesus. (Cf. Bieneck, pp. 46–8.) Had 'son of God' been intended as a messianic title merely, we should have expected them sometimes to have used a more common messianic title.

These 'confessions' (here and in iii. 11, v. 7) can hardly be explained as testimonies wrested from the demons against their will. More probably they are to be understood as desperate attempts to get control of Jesus or to make him harmless, in accordance with the common idea of the time that by using the exactly correct name of a spirit one could gain the mastery over him.

25. ἐπετίμησεν. In LXX ἐπιτιμῶ, ἐπιτίμησις represent the Hebrew root g'r, which denotes the divine word of rebuke (e.g. II Sam. xxii. 16, Job xxvi. 11, Ps. lxxx. 16, civ. 7, cvi. 9, Zech. iii. 2), the counterpart to the divine creating word (br'). When used in the gospels of Jesus (with this example cf. iv. 39, viii. 30, 33, Lk. iv. 39, ix. 55) the verb perhaps carries with it an overtone of divine authority.

αὐτῷ. I.e. the unclean spirit, as the following words show.

[1] *Das Evangelium des Johannes* (Göttingen, 1941), p. 344.

Φιμώθητι. Φιμοῦν means properly 'to muzzle' (so I Cor. ix. 9), but is also used in the sense of 'to silence' (e.g. Mt. xxii. 12, 34). The word was apparently used as a technical term in magic for binding a person with a spell, and it has been suggested that there is some such idea here; but the meaning 'be silent!' is more probable. Cf. iv. 39.

Attention was drawn by W. Wrede in 1901, in *Das Messiasgeheimnis in den Evangelien* (for useful accounts and criticisms of which see W. Sanday, *The Life of Christ in Recent Research* (1907) and V. Taylor, 'The Messianic Secret in Mark' in *E.T.* LIX, pp. 146–51), to the presence in Mk of numerous injunctions to secrecy. In this verse and i. 34, iii. 12, the demons are silenced; in i. 44, v. 43, vii. 36, viii. 26, silence is enjoined after miracles; in viii. 30, ix. 9, the disciples are bound to secrecy. With these Wrede connected the withdrawals of vii. 24, ix. 30, the frequent references to private instruction of the disciples, and also the stress on the disciples' dullness. Wrede concluded that Jesus neither claimed to be Messiah nor was recognized as such by his disciples during his life, but that after the disciples had come to regard him as Messiah on the basis of the Resurrection (he specially stressed ix. 9), there was a natural tendency to read messiahship back into his life. The conception of a messianic secret is, according to Wrede, a transitional conception resulting from the tension between this natural tendency and the continuing influence of an earlier idea of the messiahship of Jesus as beginning from the Resurrection, evidence of which he saw in Acts ii. 36.

Though Wrede's theory is to be rejected (for—to mention only two obvious objections—it is unlikely that the Resurrection would have sufficed to convince the disciples of Jesus' Messiahship, had they not already had some idea of it before his death; and moreover it is undeniable that it was as a messianic pretender that he was actually condemned to death), it has made a valuable contribution to our under-

standing of the gospels by calling attention to elements in
them which had tended to be overlooked. And Wrede's
term 'Messianic Secret'—though there is much to be said
for preferring Bieneck's term *Sohnesgeheimnis* ('Son of God
Secret'), particularly in connection with the demons' 'confessions' (cf. on ὁ Ἅγιος τοῦ Θεοῦ above)—has proved a
useful and suggestive way of referring to these elements,
which are to be regarded not, as Wrede regarded them, as
part of an hypothesis imposed on the tradition by Mark or
by the early Church, but (with Schniewind, Taylor *et al.*) as
an integral element of the history itself. We shall have to
return to this subject in connection with iv. 11 f. At this point
it will be enough to suggest that the reasons for this secrecy
are to be sought in the very nature and purpose of Jesus'
ministry and of the Incarnation itself. To have allowed the
demons' disclosure of his divine Sonship to go unrebuked
would have been to compromise that indirectness or veiledness which was an essential characteristic of God's merciful
self-revelation.

ἔξελθε ἐξ αὐτοῦ. The exorcism is effected by Jesus' word
of command.

26. σπαράξαν αὐτόν. Cf. ix. 20, where συνσπαράσσω is
used in a similar context. In classical Greek σπαράσσω
means 'to tear', 'rend'; here perhaps 'convulse'. Luke
keeps the συνεσπάραξεν of Mk ix. 20, but here he changes
Mark's wording to ῥῖψαν αὐτὸν...εἰς τὸ μέσον, and adds
μηδὲν βλάψαν αὐτόν—perhaps in order to underline the
completeness of the demon's defeat. (Was the omission of
this exorcism in Mt. perhaps suggested by the presence of
this detail? The fact that the man was convulsed after Jesus
had ordered the demon to come out may have been distaste-
ful to the author of Mt. Cf. the omission by Mt. of Mk vii.
31–7, viii. 22–6—both miracles that seem to be wrought
with some difficulty.)

τὸ πνεῦμα τὸ ἀκάθαρτον...ἐξῆλθεν ἐξ αὐτοῦ. That Jesus

healed a large number of people who were regarded at the
time as demon-possessed (though modern medical science
would describe their condition in a different way) is hardly
open to doubt. For Jesus himself and for the early Church
these exorcisms were signs of the in-breaking of the kingdom
of God (Mt. xii. 28 = Lk. xi. 20): the strong one had been
bound and those whom he had held in bondage were being
set free. The exorcisms were an integral and important part
of the work of him, the purpose of whose coming was 'that
he might destroy the works of the devil' (I Jn iii. 8).

It remains to draw attention to the fact—at first sight
disturbing—that the exorcisms of Jesus are outwardly
strikingly similar to those recorded of others, both Jewish
and Gentile, in the ancient world. Barrett has listed six
features of the gospel exorcism narratives which can be
closely paralleled: the giving of details to prove the demoniac's grievous state; the recognition by the demons of
the one who is going to exorcize them; the exorcist's addressing the demon; the expulsion by a word of command (the
very word ἔξελθε, used here and in v. 8, ix. 25, can be
paralleled); the giving of unmistakable evidence of the
expulsion; the astonishment of the spectators.[1] The true
significance of the existence of these parallels is recognized
when we see it as part of the indirectness or veiledness of
revelation (see on v. 25, iv. 11).

27. ἐθαμβήθησαν. Cf. on ἐξεπλήσσοντο (v. 22).

Τί ἐστιν τοῦτο; διδαχὴ καινὴ κατ' ἐξουσίαν· καί...is
almost certainly the correct text, the v.ll. being due to the
desire for smoothness and perhaps assimilation to Lk. which
would seem itself to be a smoother version of Mk here. But
the punctuation is doubtful. R.V. and R.S.V. follow W.H.
in placing a stop after καινή and taking κατ' ἐξουσίαν with
the following words; but, in view of the connection between
ἐξουσία and teaching in v. 22 and also of the fact that κατ'

[1] *H.S.G.T.* pp. 55–7.

ἐξουσίαν hardly adds anything to the words that follow, as they anyway include the statement that the demons ὑπακούουσιν αὐτῷ, it is probably better to punctuate as the Bible Society does, placing the colon after ἐξουσίαν instead of after καινή. The meaning then is: 'What is this? A new teaching with authority! He commands even....'

καινή. '"New" in respect of quality, as distinct from νέος, "new" as regards time' (Taylor).

ὑπακούουσιν. Attic Greek strictly adheres to the rule of singular verb with neuter plural subject. In the N.T., as also in the LXX, there is much wavering in the matter.

28. **ἀκοή** here as in xiii. 7 means 'report', 'rumour'; in vii. 35 it means 'ear'.

αὐτοῦ, 'concerning him'.

ὅλην τὴν περίχωρον τῆς Γαλιλαίας could mean (i) 'all the country around Galilee', i.e. including a bigger area than Galilee (cf. Mt. iv. 24); (ii) 'throughout Galilee' (τῆς Γαλιλαίας being an epexegetic genitive explaining περίχωρον); (iii) 'all that part of Galilee which is around (Capernaum)', i.e. an area less than the whole of Galilee. Taylor favours the last, which is perhaps supported by the Lk. parallel.

7. THE HEALING OF PETER'S MOTHER-IN-LAW
(i. 29–31)
(Mt. viii. 14 f.; Lk. iv. 38 f.)

A narrative that may be confidently described as Petrine. The story is told from Peter's viewpoint. Significantly the detail concerns not the sickness and its cure, but rather unimportant matters which would nevertheless be of special interest to the people involved. The incident is precisely located.

29. **Καὶ εὐθύς** might mean 'So then', but it is probably better to give εὐθύς here its proper meaning 'immediately', 'straightway'. The following words anyway connect this incident closely with the preceding. It would seem to be implied that the healing of Peter's mother-in-law (as also the exorcism related in the last section) took place on the sabbath (cf. *v.* 21).

ἐξελθόντες ἦλθον. The singular ἐξελθὼν ἦλθεν has strong support in B D W Θ f1 f13 it, and should probably be read.

εἰς τὴν οἰκίαν Σίμωνος καὶ Ἀνδρέου. Apparently the two brothers shared a house in Capernaum. It appears to have been the rendezvous of Jesus and his disciples during this period of the ministry in Capernaum.

30. Peter's wife is mentioned in I Cor. ix. 5.

πυρέσσουσα. Luke takes it to have been 'a high fever', according to the ancient distinction between μέγας and μικρὸς πυρετός.

31. κρατήσας. Κρατεῖν here means 'take hold of'.

τῆς χειρός. Partitive genitive, as is usual after verbs of touching. Cf. v. 41, ix. 27.

ἀφῆκεν: 'left'; cf. *v.* 18.

διηκόνει: 'she began to wait'.

As this is Mark's first account of a healing miracle, it will be well to say something at this point about Jesus' miracles in general. They may be divided into four classes: exorcisms, healing miracles, raisings of the dead, nature miracles. About the first of these we have already said something (i. 23–8). The importance of the miracles for Mark is indicated by the fact that 47 per cent of the verses of the first ten chapters deal directly or indirectly with them.

In the Synoptists they are characteristically referred to both in narrative and on the lips of Jesus as δυνάμεις (e.g. vi. 2, 5, Mt. xi. 20, 21, 23). These 'mighty works' reflect the might of him who is 'mightier' (ἰσχυρότερος) than John the Baptist (i. 7). His exorcisms are evidence that he is 'stronger' (ἰσχυρότερος, Lk. xi. 22) than the strong one Satan (iii. 27 = Mt. xii. 29 = Lk. xi. 21 f.). The disciples on the way to Emmaus speak of him as having been 'a prophet mighty (δυνατός) in deed and word...' (Lk. xxiv. 19).

According to Jesus himself his miracles are the activity of God, wrought by God's Spirit or 'finger', and the manifestation of God's kingdom (Mt. xii. 28 = Lk. xi. 20). They are inspired by God's Spirit (Lk. iv. 18f.), the fulfilment of O.T. eschatological prophecies (Lk. iv. 18, Mt. xi. 4f. = Lk. vii. 22: cf. Isa. xxix. 18f., xxxv. 5f., lxi. 1) and evidence that Jesus is the promised Coming One (Mt. xi. 2–6 = Lk. vii. 18–23). They signify that Satan has been bound (iii. 27): those whom Satan has kept bound are being loosed (Lk. xiii. 16—which indicates that, while all disease is not demon-possession, it is all Satan's work). In the case of one miracle at least Jesus expressly indicates that his motive is compassion (viii. 2); he also indicates that his miracles are the expression of God's own pity (v. 19).

At the same time the miracles are not compelling proofs. The cities of Chorazin, Bethsaida and Capernaum do not repent (Mt. xi. 20–4 = Lk. x. 13–15), and even the disciples can misunderstand them (vi. 52). Their true significance is recognizable only by faith. They are, as it were, chinks in the curtain of the Son of God's hiddenness. The light let through the chinks is real light (the miracles do reveal, they are an effective manifestation of Christ's glory for those who believe (cf. Jn ii. 11), and failure to discern their meaning and to respond to the summons to repentance which they constitute is without excuse (Mt. xi. 20–4 = Lk. x. 13–15)); but the light is not so direct as to be compelling. There are several reasons why it is not. For one thing, the amazement which the miracles cause is offset by the apparent weakness and unimpressiveness of him who works them (e.g. vi. 1–6a). For another, other people were credited with miracles. Jesus himself refers to Jewish exorcisms (Mt. xii. 27 = Lk. xi. 19) and reckons with false messiahs and false prophets working miracles in the future (xiii. 22). The O.T. records numerous miracles and even attributes miracles to heathen magicians (Exod. vii. 11, etc.), and in the contemporary Gentile world people certainly were credulous about miracles (the healings attributed to Vespasian a little later are well known). Moreover, there are striking external similarities between many of Jesus' healing miracles and those attributed to others (those in the case of the exorcisms have already been mentioned):[1] for example, his use of material means such as spittle (vii. 33, viii. 23) and his touching the sufferer. Thus other explanations lay close to hand besides that of faith: another prophet, another Rabbi, or even just another wonder-worker. Again, the amazing authority manifest in miracles wrought by a word only was strangely offset by other occasions when Jesus apparently effected a cure only gradually and with difficulty (vii. 31 ff., viii. 22 ff.). And even the things which were specially characteristic of Jesus' miracles were not the sort of things to render them compelling proofs for unbelievers: his dependence on God (e.g. vi. 41 (see note *in loc.*), vii. 34 (cf. Jn v. 36, x. 32, xiv. 10): in this cf. O.T. miracles—e.g. I Kgs xvii. 20–2, xviii. 36f.); his valuing preaching above miracle (i. 37f.); his effort to conceal his miracles (e.g. i. 44); his demand for faith—a faith which is no mere openness to suggestion, but involves a real decision with regard to his person (e.g. ii. 5, iv. 40, v. 34, 36, ix. 23f., x. 52).

So the miracles are not inconsistent with the general veiledness or indirectness of God's self-disclosure in Jesus, nor is there any real inconsistency between Jesus' appeal to his miracles in Mt. xi. 4–6 and his refusal to give a compelling proof in Mk viii. 11f.

About the significance of the miracles a further point may be made. For the evangelists and the tradition behind them the miracles are not only signs of the kingdom of God in the sense that the fact of their occurrence is evidence of its

[1] P. 80.

presence; they are also signs of it in the sense that they are eloquent symbols of it, picturing it forth. So, for instance, the healing miracles are signs of the forgiveness of sins, not only because, there being a real connection between sin and disease, the release from disease is a pledge of divine forgiveness (ii. 1 ff.), but also because they are pictures of forgiveness and salvation, there being not only a connection but also a resemblance between sin and disease. That this way of thinking about the miracles is present in the Fourth Gospel is clear; it is also present already in the Synoptists (see esp. on vii. 31–7, viii. 22–6, and also iv. 35–41, vi. 45–51, etc.). But this symbolic significance was always something additional and secondary. To suggest that the evangelists thought of the miracles as 'symbolical acts' conveying 'in a dramatized form essential Christological teaching' and to belittle their significance as the response of Christ's compassion to particular concrete need[1] is to give a seriously wrong impression.

But did the miracles really happen? It would be fairly widely agreed today that to reject them out of hand as simply impossible would be too rigid and doctrinaire to be truly scientific. 'The so-called "laws"', says Taylor, 'summarize what is observable in the world of nature under normal conditions…they do not preclude the emergence of unusual phenomena, granted the presence of a sufficient cause….' If, then, we believe that God was present and active in Jesus in a unique way, we certainly shall not assume from the start that the answer must be 'No'.

As far as the healing miracles are concerned it is not so very difficult for the modern man to answer 'Yes'. For one thing, the fact that modern partial parallels have been well authenticated enables us to approach them with a more open mind. The third and fourth classes are more difficult. Here two serious theological objections are raised: (i) Would

[1] As Richardson, *Miracles*, p. 57, does.

not such signal demonstrations of supernatural power be compelling proofs of the sort Jesus refused to give? But since both raisings of the dead and nature miracles were attributed to O.T. figures, these things could not be to Jews of the first century compelling proofs of divinity, but at the most proofs of prophetic status. With regard to the other closely related objection: (ii) Do not the nature miracles call the full reality of the Incarnation in question and involve a docetic Christology? the following points, though not as they stand an adequate reply, should be taken into consideration: (i) *If* the historicity of any O.T. nature miracles be granted, then those of Jesus do not lift him above *human* conditions; (ii) Jesus is represented as working these miracles for the sake of other people out of compassion, and resolutely refusing to work miracles in order to make the fulfilment of his own mission any less costly (e.g. contrast Mk viii. 2 with Mt. iv. 4); (iii) the possibility of the tempta- tion to work miracles for selfish ends actually aggravated rather than eased the difficulty of his way.

Since these two theological objections do not seem in- superable, and since we have good reason to suppose that the gospel tradition is derived from honest and not unintelli- gent people, and since there is—for the most part at any rate—a notable reserve about the miracles ascribed to Jesus (contrast the apocryphal gospels!), which would hardly be compatible with whole classes of Jesus' miracles being an invention, it does not seem unreasonable to believe that miracles of all four classes occurred. This does not, however, mean that we need not examine the historical evidence critically in each case.

See further Manson, *Jesus the Messiah*, pp. 33–50 (esp. 43–6); Whitehouse, *C.F.S.A.* pp. 73–7; Richardson, *Miracles*.

8. THE SICK AND POSSESSED HEALED AT EVENING
(i. 32–4)
(Mt. viii. 16f.; Lk. iv. 40f.)

Probably Petrine. Connected with the preceding by the references to the time and to the door (of Simon's house). The news of the synagogue exorcism and perhaps also of the healing of Peter's mother-in-law has spread through the town. This is not a 'summary statement', though at first it looks like one; it is a 'story about Jesus connected with a particular time and place' (Taylor).

32. 'Οψίας. The feminine of the adjective ὄψιος (= 'late') is used in N.T. as a noun, the noun ὥρα being omitted. Cf. ἡ ἔρημος (χώρα). It denotes the late afternoon and evening.

ὅτε ἔδυσεν ὁ ἥλιος indicates the time more exactly and so is not really tautologous after the preceding phrase. After sunset the Sabbath was over, and the sick could therefore be brought without any breaking of the Law.

ἔφερον, indefinite plural, 'people were bringing'.

33. Note the vividness of the sentence. For the exaggeration of ὅλη ἡ πόλις cf. i. 5. The mention of the door connects this episode with the previous one, the door being presumably that of Peter's and Andrew's house, and indicates that this story also is told from Peter's point of view.

34. ἐθεράπευσεν. The verb means 'to serve', 'attend', and is used in classical Greek of attending medically. It then comes to be used in the sense of 'heal', as here.

πολλούς. Mark is probably not using πολλούς exclusively, in contrast with πάντας in v. 32 (which would mean that Jesus healed only some of the sick who had been brought), but inclusively (= 'all'). Cf. Mt. viii. 16, where Mk's πάντας in v. 32 and πολλούς in v. 34 have been transposed, and Lk. iv. 40: ἑνὶ ἑκάστῳ. This inclusive use of πολλοί is a Semitism. (Cf. Jeremias, *E.W.* pp. 123–5.)

δαιμόνια. Δαιμόνιον, the neuter of the adjective δαιμόνιος used as a noun, is equivalent to the more Jewish expression πνεῦμα ἀκάθαρτον (v. 23).

ἤφιεν. Ἀφίημι here means 'allow'.

ὅτι: 'because'.

ᾔδεισαν αὐτόν. Cf. on i. 24.

The v.l. which adds Χριστὸν εἶναι after αὐτόν is 'a clear example of assimilation [cf. Lk. iv. 41], to which most of our Alexandrian authorities, even the best, have succumbed' (C. H. Turner).

9. JESUS' DEPARTURE FROM CAPERNAUM AND PREACHING IN GALILEE (i. 35–9)
(Lk. iv. 42–4; with v. 39 cf. Mt. iv. 23)

The connection between vv. 35–8 and vv. 21–34 is probably factual and not merely editorial; for this section is not self-contained, but needs a context like the preceding sections on which to lean. This does not mean, however, that the night referred to here was necessarily the night following the Sabbath about which vv. 21–34 have told; it is possible that there was a period of activity in Capernaum between i. 34 and i. 35. Probably vv. 35–8 are Petrine; v. 39 appears to be a summary statement to conclude the complex i. 21 ff.

35. The odd but vivid πρωῒ ἔννυχα λίαν perhaps reflects Peter's recalling of the reactions of those who discovered that Jesus had gone. Contrast Luke's staid expression. ἔννυχα is an accusative plural neuter of an adjective used adverbially.

The double phrase ἐξῆλθεν καὶ ἀπῆλθεν is very much in Mark's manner and should be retained, though some authorities omit ἐξῆλθεν καί and others καὶ ἀπῆλθεν.

ἔρημον. Here used adjectivally. It need not mean 'desert': as the country round Capernaum was cultivated at this time, it is better to translate 'lonely' or 'quiet'.

προσηύχετο. Cf. vi. 46, xiv. 32 ff. 'Only here at the

beginning, in the middle (vi. 46) and again at the end, in
Gethsemane, is Jesus' praying mentioned; and each time it
is at dead of night' (Lohmeyer). Luke mentions it more
often, but strangely omits this reference.

36. κατεδίωξεν. The *v.l.* κατεδίωξαν is probably a grammatical improvement. The verb probably is no stronger
than 'sought after' or 'searched for'. There is a natural
tendency for the sense of a word to be weakened: cf. σκύλλεις
in v. 35 and the way βάλλω is often used in the N.T. So it is
unwise to build on the use of this verb here, as Lightfoot
does,[1] though the word may well reflect the memory of their
anxiety to find Jesus.

οἱ μετ' αὐτοῦ: presumably Andrew, James and John.
Cf. i. 29.

37. ὅτι is *recitativum*, as in *v.* 15.

Πάντες ζητοῦσίν σε testifies to the considerable impression Jesus had made in Capernaum.

38. ἀλλαχοῦ (only here in Greek Bible) means 'elsewhere',
'elsewhither'.

ἐχομένας: present participle middle of ἔχω used in the
sense of 'next', 'neighbouring', as often in LXX and also in
classical Greek.

The word κωμόπολις is used by Strabo and often by Byzantine writers to denote a small town having only the status
of a village.

κηρύξω. The disciples apparently wanted Jesus to make
the most of the opportunity to become a popular miracle-
worker; but Jesus rejected it, regarding preaching more
highly than miracles. Miracles were 'appendages' to the
Word (Calvin): the relation was not to be reversed.

εἰς τοῦτο γὰρ ἐξῆλθον. Does this mean (i) that Jesus had
left Capernaum in order to exercise a wider preaching
ministry in the neighbourhood; or (ii) more generally, that
he had undertaken his mission with a wider preaching

[1] *Gospel Message*, pp. 23f.

ministry in view; or (iii) that it was for the sake of this
preaching ministry that he had come forth from God? The
fact that ἐξέρχεσθαι has just been used in *v*. 35 of his leaving
the house in Capernaum supports (i). On the other hand,
Luke's substitution of ἀπεστάλην is support for (iii), and
Jesus frequently uses 'come' of his mission (see on ii. 17).
Perhaps the ambiguity was intentional—a *veiled* reference to
his coming from God?

39. ἦλθεν. ἦν (the reading of A C D W and the great
majority of MSS.) is probably to be preferred. It is supported by the Lk. parallel; the periphrastic imperfect is
characteristic of Mk; and ἦλθεν looks like a grammatical
improvement due to εἰς (which, if ἦν is read, is equivalent
to ἐν).

10. A LEPER HEALED (i. 40-5)
(Mt. viii. 1-4; Lk. v. 12-16)

The connection of this section with its present context is
loose: it is joined to what precedes by simple καί, and again
what follows is introduced by καί. It serves as a link between
i. 21-39 and ii. 1-iii. 6, two groups of units which apparently
already existed as groups before the gospel was written.
Taylor with good reason regards it as derived from the
earliest tradition at a stage 'before the process of oral
attrition had reduced it to a rounded form'. It may well be
Petrine, though this is not certain.

40. λεπρός. The Hebrew word which is translated
'leprosy' in Lev. xiii–xiv (*ṣāra'aṯ*) covered various skin
diseases, not just what is called leprosy today; and it is quite
likely that this man was suffering from one of these other
diseases. But persons suffering from any of the diseases
covered by the term *ṣāra'aṯ* had to keep away from their
fellows: they were forbidden by the law to enter a dwelling,
and, if anyone approached, they had to cry 'Unclean,
unclean!' as a warning (Lev. xiii. 45 f.).

καὶ γονυπετῶν, though omitted by B D W *al* it^pt sa, is strongly attested (א L Θ f1, *pm* it^pt vg bo, etc.) and supported by the parallels (Mt.: προσεκύνει αὐτῷ; Lk.: πεσὼν ἐπὶ πρόσωπον), and should be read.

According to Lohmeyer the fact that the leper is represented as kneeling to Jesus means that he is represented as knowing already that Jesus is more than a mere man. (He argues similarly with reference to v. 22 and x. 17.) But, while it is true that among the Hebrews kneeling is characteristically the mark of man's humility before God (both in O.T. and N.T.), it is also an act of homage to a king (I Chr. xxix. 20 (LXX)), and a posture of supplication before a man of God (II Kgs i. 13). So here it expresses earnest entreaty and respect, not more—though, no doubt, Mark and his readers may have seen a special appropriateness in his kneeling before the one whom *they* knew to be the Son of God.

The word κύριε is read before ὅτι by B, in place of ὅτι by C L W Θ *c e ff*² vg^codd, and after θέλῃς by a few MSS.; but in spite of the strong attestation it is unlikely that it belongs to the original text, since it is not characteristic of Mk, and is explicable as assimilation to Mt. or Lk.

Ἐὰν θέλῃς δύνασαί με καθαρίσαι. The leper is sure that Jesus is able to heal him, if he is willing to do so. The stress no doubt is more on δύνασαι than on θέλῃς: this is more an expression of confidence in Jesus' ability than of doubt about his willingness. But nevertheless it is an entreaty (perhaps approaching 'Do cleanse me, for thou canst!') and the section directs attention here and in the next verse to Jesus' will to heal. With the believing δύνασαι contrast the εἴ τι δύνῃ of ix. 22f. Καθαρίζειν in this section must mean 'make clean', so 'heal', as is clear from *v.* 42 (ἀπῆλθεν ἀπ᾽ αὐτοῦ ἡ λέπρα), and not 'pronounce clean' in the sense in which it is used in Lev. xiiif. The suggestion that the original story was of a recovered leper who wanted Jesus, instead of a priest, to pronounce him clean is fanciful. The use of καθαρίζειν to denote the healing of leprosy is natural, since the disease rendered the sufferer ritually unclean.

41. σπλαγχνισθείς. Read ὀργισθείς with D *a d ff*² *r*¹* Tatian. It is easy to see why an original ὀργισθείς should have been altered to σπλαγχνισθείς, but not why an original σπλαγχνισθείς should have been changed to ὀργισθείς. Moreover, neither Mt. nor Lk. has σπλαγχνισθείς here, which would be surprising if it was original in Mk.

Why was Jesus angry? Was it (i) because the leper was breaking the Law (Lev. xiii. 45 f.) by approaching him, perhaps even coming into the house—ἐξέβαλεν; or (ii) because of the interruption of his preaching ministry; or (iii) because of the implied doubt about his will to heal (so Ephraem: 'Quia dixit: "Si vis", iratus est'; but it was surely right for the man to recognize Jesus' freedom and not take his response for granted—see Mt. vi. 10 b, Mk xiv. 36 c); or (iv) was his anger in a general way his reaction to the foul disease; or (v) was it anger with Satan at his disfigurement of God's creature? The last seems the most likely. Not only demon-possession but all disease was the devil's work (cf. Lk. xiii. 16); and in his healing miracles Jesus was waging war on Satan's power.

ἐκτείνας τὴν χεῖρα αὐτοῦ. Lagrange compares Exod. vii. 19 and comments, 'a gesture of authority'; but it is better to regard the action simply as the necessary preliminary to touching him.

ἥψατο. αὐτοῦ quite probably should be read after ἥψατο as well as before it: so D it vg. But anyway the sense is the same. According to the Law, to touch a leper was to incur defilement. (The Rabbis took extraordinary precautions to avoid even the remotest possibility of such defiling contact.) So Jesus' action is in line with his ἐγὼ δὲ λέγω ὑμῖν (Mt. v. 22, etc.). But, as in Mt. v the ἐγὼ δὲ λέγω ὑμῖν is counter-balanced by *vv.* 17–19, so here his action is followed by the command of *v.* 44 b. His touching the leper does not imply disrespect for the Law, but rather reflects his consciousness of being the Son. Penetratingly Victor comments: 'But why does He touch the leper instead of effecting the cure by a word?...because defilement naturally does not touch the Saviour...and because He is Lord of His own Law.' His action expresses compassion. 'By His word alone He might have healed the leper,' says Calvin, 'but He applied...the touch of His hand, to express the feeling of compassion.' For Jesus' touching sufferers cf. vii. 33, viii. 22, and for their touching him iii. 10, v. 27 f., 30 f., vi. 56.

καθαρίσθητι. Cf. II Kgs v. 13 (the LXX has the same form exactly). When the priest pronounced a recovered leper clean, he used a similar expression, *ṭāhartā* (= κεκαθάρισαι) (*Tanhuma*, *ḥukkaṭ* 26). (Is there here a hint of the idea of Christ as priest?)

42. εὐθύς indicates the instantaneousness of the cure.

ἐκαθερίσθη. Cf. II Kgs v. 14. (For the spelling see Moulton, *Proleg.* p. 56.) On the miracle see the concluding note on i. 29–31.

43. ἐμβριμησάμενος. The simple verb βριμάομαι is used rarely in classical Greek with the meaning 'be enraged with'. The compound ἐμβριμάομαι is used by Aeschylus of horses snorting and in the LXX (Dan. xi. 30; cf. Lam. ii. 6) of anger. By derivation (ἐν + βρίμη, 'strength') it should denote strong feeling within oneself. In Jn xi. 33, 38 'groan' is a possible translation. In the other three places where it occurs in the N.T. (xiv. 5, Mt. ix. 30 and here) it has an indirect object. In xiv. 5 the meaning is perhaps 'upbraid'. The present instance and Mt. ix. 30 are more difficult. There is a close similarity between them. In both the verb is used of Jesus and the indirect object is someone whom he has healed. Some have seen here a reference to Jesus' anger at the leper's infringement of the Law; others a reference to the deep emotion he felt toward the leper (perhaps to be

connected with his warfare with Satan and reflecting the
great strain of the conflict and the costliness of the miracle);
others connect the word closely with the injunction to
silence. Perhaps the last is the most probable. The word
would then refer to the stern and urgent admonition with
which Jesus drove home the seriousness of his request for
secrecy. The maintenance of his messianic veiledness was
indeed an urgent matter.

εὐθὺς ἐξέβαλεν αὐτόν. It is often maintained that
ἐκβάλλειν here must mean something like 'thrust out',
'drive out', and it is sometimes suggested that the meaning
is that Jesus thrust the man out of the house, which as a
leper he should never have entered. But ἐκβάλλειν is sometimes used in the N.T. without any suggestion of force (e.g.
Mt. vii. 4f., xii. 35, xiii. 52), and in Jas ii. 25 it probably
means simply 'send away'. So here it should probably be
translated 'sent away', 'dismissed'. Some idea of urgency
is however present in εὐθύς, and this haste is probably to be
connected with Jesus' desire to avoid unnecessary publicity
for his miracles.

44. Ὅρα. For this use of the present imperative of
ὁρᾶν followed asyndetically by a command or prohibition
cf. viii. 15, Mt. viii. 4, ix. 30, xviii. 10, xxiv. 6, I Thess.
v. 15.

μηδενὶ μηδέν. In Greek two or more negatives of the
same kind regularly strengthen one another provided the
last is a compound, as here. For the command to tell no
one see on i. 25.

With σεαυτὸν δεῖξον τῷ ἱερεῖ cf. Lev. xiv. 2f., and with
προσένεγκε κ.τ.λ. cf. Lev. xiv. 4–32. Notice Jesus' attitude
to the Law. Even the ritual Law is for him holy and to be
respected. (On Jesus' attitude to the Law see further on
vii. 1–23, x. 1–12, 19–21.)

περί here means 'in respect of'.

καθαρισμοῦ here is better understood (*pace* Taylor) not of

Jesus' cleansing (i.e. healing) the leper, but rather of the ritual cleansing prescribed in Lev. xiv. 1-32.

εἰς here indicates purpose.

μαρτύριον αὐτοῖς. Various interpretations have been suggested.

(i) If εἰς μαρτύριον αὐτοῖς is taken closely with προσέταξεν Μωϋσῆς, the possibilities are: (a) a statute for Israel; cf. Ps. lxxxi. 5 (M.T.: lxxxi. 6; LXX: lxxx. 5), where μαρτύριον renders 'ēḏûṯ which is parallel with ḥōḳ (R.V.: 'statute') in the previous verse; (b) a testimony to Israel (the real purpose of Moses' ordinances being to point to Christ; cf. Jn v. 45 f.).

(ii) If εἰς μαρτύριον αὐτοῖς is taken with the whole sentence from σεαυτόν or προσένεγκε down to Μωϋσῆς, the interpretations are: (c) evidence for the priests or people in general that Jesus respects the Law; (d) evidence for the priests or people in general of the true significance of the one who has healed the leper; (e) evidence that will be used against the people in the final judgement as a damning proof of their unbelief; (f) evidence for the priests or the people generally of the fact of the cure. Of these the last is perhaps the most likely. On μαρτύριον see further at xiii. 9.

45. It has been suggested that the subject of ἤρξατο is Jesus (there has been no indication of a change of subject since λέγει in v. 44) and that τὸν λόγον means the gospel (cf. vv. 14 f.); but it is better to take the subject of ἤρξατο to be the leper (in spite of the awkward change of subject this involves at αὐτόν in the middle of the verse) and τὸν λόγον to refer to the news of the cure.

The redundant ἤρξατο is perhaps a Semitism.

πολλά is used adverbially.

μηκέτι...δύνασθαι. I.e. he could not, if he was to fulfil his ministry according to his own plan.

πόλιν. 'A town', rather than 'the town'.

ἤρχοντο. Indefinite plural: 'people came'.

11. A PARALYTIC HEALED (ii. 1–12)
(Mt. ix. 1–8; Lk. v. 17–26)

The suggestion of Bultmann, Taylor and others that we have here a composite unit (*vv.* 1–5a, 10b–12, being a miracle story, with which *vv.* 5b–10a have been combined) seems to result from failure to recognize the real and close connection between the healing of sickness and the forgiveness of sins. When this connection is seen, there is no need to make any such suggestion, the whole section holding together as an intelligible whole except for *v.* 10a, which is best explained as Mark's own comment in parenthesis. Quite probably Petrine. (Those who regard the section as composite differ in their evaluation of *vv.* 5b–10a, some regarding them as *Gemeindetheologie*, a product of the early community's theological reflection, others (including Taylor) recognizing in them historical testimony.)

1. Either ἠκούσθη is impersonal ('it was heard') and εἰσελθών (agreeing with ὁ Ἰησοῦς understood) is left hanging by anacoluthon, or, just possibly, ἠκούσθη is personal (cf. I Cor. xv. 12 (κηρύσσεσθαι), II Cor. iii. 3, I Jn ii. 19 (φανεροῦσθαι)).

δι' ἡμερῶν: 'after some days' (cf. classical διὰ χρόνου = 'after some time'). Better taken with εἰσελθών than with ἠκούσθη.

ὅτι. Here either *recitativum*, or introducing indirect speech (the original tense of the direct speech being correctly retained).

ἐν οἴκῳ: 'at home', i.e. presumably in Peter's and Andrew's house. Perhaps this reflects Peter's point of view.

2. ὥστε...θύραν. Either 'so that there was no longer room for them even about the door' (χωρεῖν, impersonal; τὰ πρὸς τὴν θύραν = accusative of respect), or 'so that not even the space about the door could any longer contain them' (τὰ πρὸς τὴν θύραν=subject of χωρεῖν, in accusative after ὥστε). Of these the former is perhaps more natural.

τὸν λόγον. I.e. the gospel. Cf. τὸ εὐαγγέλιον τοῦ θεοῦ in i. 14. ὁ λόγος is used again in this way in iv. 14–20, 33.

3. ἔρχονται. Indefinite plural.

Φέρειν here means 'bring', αἴρειν 'carry'.

4. προσενέγκαι αὐτῷ: supply αὐτόν. Προσφέρειν here means 'bring to'. The widely spread v.l. προσεγγίσαι is probably due to the absence of a direct object after προσενέγκαι.

ἀπεστέγασαν...ἐξορύξαντες. 'The roof was probably formed by beams and rafters across which matting, branches and twigs, covered by earth trodden hard, were laid' (Taylor). Most probably the house was only one storey. The ascent to the roof would be by means of an outside staircase.

κράβαττον. The word denotes a poor man's pallet or mattress. It was condemned as not being Attic Greek. It is not used in Mt. and Lk., but occurs in Jn and Acts.

5. τὴν πίστιν αὐτῶν. Does αὐτῶν refer only to the four men who carry the paralytic or to them and the paralytic himself? Most modern interpreters prefer the latter explanation.

On the place of faith in Jesus' miracles and its significance see the concluding general note on i. 29–31.

Τέκνον is simply an affectionate form of address.

ἀφίενται is an 'aoristic' or punctiliar present (see Moule, p. 7): 'are this moment forgiven' (Taylor). The perfect ἀφέωνται is widely attested here, but the present should be read. This authoritative declaration of forgiveness comes at the point where we might expect a command like καθαρίσθητι in i. 41 or an action like that in i. 31. Taylor explains this psychologically: Jesus perceives that this particular man's illness is due to his sin. But it is wiser to refrain from reading into the passage more than the words really justify. We should not assume that this man's illness

was specially a punishment, that it was of the hysterical or
nervous sort or that he was specially oppressed by a sense of
guilt or had a particularly sensitive conscience. The explanation is rather that Jesus recognizes an organic connection
between disease and sin—though not in the sense that a man
suffers in exact proportion to his sinfulness (Job and Ps. lxxiii,
and above all Jesus' own words in Lk. xiii. 1 ff., Jn ix. 2 f.,
deny this). Because there is this organic connection between
sin and disease and Jesus makes war on both, the healing
of disease is a sign and token of the forgiveness of sins.
Jesus' healing miracles are sacraments of forgiveness. The
declaration of forgiveness here is therefore not surprising
after all.

6. Their complaint, though Mark puts it into words in
the next verse, is unspoken: no doubt their faces expressed it.
This is the first hint of Jewish opposition to Jesus.

7. Τί. Perhaps we should rather read Ὅτι with B Θ 482.
Mark has this ὅτι = τί elsewhere (ii. 16, ix. 11, 28), and the
tendency of copyists was to substitute the more ordinary τί
or διὰ τί. (See Moule, p. 159.)

οὗτος. Contemptuous: 'this fellow'.

οὕτως λαλεῖ. It is Jesus' declaration of forgiveness that
angers the scribes.

βλασφημεῖ. The words βλασφημ-εῖν, -ία, -ος in LXX
represent several Hebrew roots (gdp, n's, ykh). Whereas in
classical Greek they can refer to slandering a man, in the
LXX they always refer to something directed against God.
In the N.T. 'blasphemy' generally denotes, as in the O.T.,
an affront to the majesty of God. As the punishment prescribed in Lev. xxiv. 15 f. for blasphemy was death by
stoning, the implication is that the scribes were already
contemplating Jesus' destruction. According to (M) Sanh.
vii. 5 'The blasphemer is not culpable unless he pronounces
the Name [i.e. the Tetragrammaton] itself', but it is likely
that in N.T. times the term was understood more widely,

so that to usurp God's prerogative would be blasphemy. See further on xiv. 64.

τίς δύναται ἀφιέναι ἁμαρτίας εἰ μὴ εἷς ὁ Θεός; We must distinguish of course between forgiveness in the absolute sense, which is God's prerogative (Exod. xxxiv. 6f., Ps. ciii. 3, cxxx. 4, Isa. xliii. 25, xliv. 22, xlviii. 11, Dan. ix. 9), and forgiveness in a relative sense, i.e. a man's forgiving one who has wronged him (Gen. l. 17, I Sam. xxv. 28, 35). This relative forgiveness is not in question here. But as far as the absolute forgiveness is concerned there is a further distinction to be made: only God can forgive in this sense, but a man may be in a position to announce God's forgiveness (e.g. II Sam. xii. 13). Jesus' declaration ἀφίενταί σου αἱ ἁμαρτίαι (v. 5) is ambiguous: it could mean simply 'God has forgiven your sins' (a prophetic announcement of forgiveness, the passive being a way of reverently avoiding the divine Name) or it could imply that Jesus is himself forgiving the man. This ambiguity is in line with the indirectness of revelation to which reference has more than once been made: Jesus exercises the divine prerogative, but in a veiled way. The reaction of the scribes is not the result of a direct and unambiguous claim on Jesus' part but rather of their eagerness to find an occasion against him. For Mark and his Christian readers the scribes' unspoken thought that none but God himself could forgive sins expressed the truth of which those who thought it were unaware—namely, that he who did forgive men with divine authority must be God.

εἷς ὁ Θεός. 'One, that is, God': cf. x. 18.

8. For Jesus' discernment of men's thoughts cf. xii. 15, Jn ii. 24f.

9. Jesus answers their unspoken questioning by a counter-question. He hardly wants a definite answer. Rather he wants to stimulate reflection by leaving them with a question which is not easy to answer. Could they but recognize the truth, they would know that both his forgiving sins and his

healings equally signify the presence of God's reign and the fulfilment of the promises (on the one hand, Isa. liii. 5f., Jer. xxxi. 34, Ezek. xxxvi. 25–7, Mic. vii. 18, Zech. xiii. 1; on the other hand, Isa. xxix. 18, xxxv. 4–6, lxi. 1).

10. ἵνα...γῆς is usually understood to be part of what Jesus says to the scribes; λέγει τῷ παραλυτικῷ is then a parenthesis of Mark's to show that the following words are addressed not to them but to the paralytic. Jesus would presumably have made clear this change of the persons addressed by a gesture. But according to this explanation the verse is very clumsy. A second explanation takes ἵνα εἰδῆτε as a command (a possible construction: cf. Moule, pp. 144f.); but this still leaves the verse clumsy. A much more satisfactory explanation surely is to take ἵνα...γῆς as Mark's own comment addressed to the readers of the gospel (cf. καθαρίζων πάντα τὰ βρώματα in vii. 19), indicating the significance of the healing miracle. The fact that Jesus heals the paralytic is for the eye of faith a sign that he also can and does forgive sinners. The miracle is a visible sign— to use Calvin's phraseology—confirming and sealing for faith Christ's authority to forgive.

On ὁ Υἱὸς τοῦ ἀνθρώπου see further at viii. 31. If the above explanation of the verse is correct, then we have here an instance of 'Son of Man' being used as a title of Jesus by the Church. If, however, ἵνα...γῆς is held to be part of what Jesus says, then the whole question of what Jesus meant by 'Son of Man' is raised here. But consideration of this is reserved till viii. 31.

Various explanations of ἐπὶ τῆς γῆς have been offered:

(i) It contrasts authority to forgive sins on earth with 'the divine prerogative exercised *in heaven*' (Taylor).

(ii) It denotes the period of Christ's earthly life—even before his death and resurrection he has this authority (if the whole clause is understood as Mark's comment, then on this view of ἐπὶ τῆς γῆς, ἔχει would be a sort of homiletic historic present).

(iii) It stresses the fact that he who can forgive sins has appeared on earth—so that forgiveness is no longer something far away, but something to be accepted here on earth (so Calvin, Schlatter, Schniewind).

(iv) It has the effect of qualifying ἁμαρτίας—so 'done upon earth' or 'among men' (cf. ix. 3). Of these the last seems the simplest and should probably be accepted.

12. ἐξίστασθαι. See on i. 22. It is apparently the miracle that causes the amazement, not what has been said about forgiveness.

12. THE CALL OF LEVI AND THE MEAL IN HIS HOUSE (ii. 13–17)
(Mt. ix. 9–13; Lk. v. 27–32)

The section falls into two parts (*vv.* 13 f. and *vv.* 15–17), but is probably a single unit of tradition. Whether the relevance of the latter part to the controversy in the early Church about table-fellowship (Acts xi. 3, Gal. ii. 12) was noticed at the time we do not know: possibly it was. It is also possible that its significance as a picture of the Eucharist as the feast for sinners was recognized.

While this section is one of the complex of conflict-stories (ii. 1–iii. 6), it also forms (whether intentionally or not) a fitting temporary climax to the series of sections dealing with the healing of sickness and so pointing (in the light of ii. 5 ff.) to the forgiveness of sins, the salvation of sinners (i. 21–ii. 17).

13. On ὄχλος see on vi. 34.

The imperfects ἤρχετο and ἐδίδασκεν 'indicate the coming and going of successive groups of hearers' (Taylor).

14. Λευείν. Levi (Hebrew *Lēwî*) is only mentioned here and in the Lk. parallel passage. The Mt. parallel has 'Matthew' instead. In the list of the Twelve (iii. 16 ff.) Mk includes Matthew but not Levi, while Mt. underlines the identity of the Matthew who is a member of the Twelve with the Matthew mentioned in the parallel to this passage by describing him as ὁ τελώνης. In Mark's list of the Twelve there is a James who is described like Levi here as 'son of Alphaeus'. Various solutions of the problem have been suggested: (i) Levi and Matthew are two names of the same person; (ii) Ἰάκωβον should be read here with D Θ f13 (exc. 346) it Tatian (cf. Origen, *contra Cels*. I. 62); (iii) James and Levi are two names of the same person; (iv) by the time Mk was written there was some confusion about the exact composition of the Twelve. Of these (iv) is perhaps the most likely and then (i). The reading of D etc. looks like a very early attempt to get over the difficulty, while (iii) is pure conjecture. If (iv) is right, then, if Mark thought that Levi was one of the Twelve (as a comparison of this verse with i. 16–20 certainly suggests) but knew that his name was not in the list of the Twelve that he used, it is highly significant that he did not alter his sources. The conclusion to be drawn is that his positive statements should be received with very considerable respect.

ἐπί. Here used with accusative to indicate position, 'at': see Moule, pp. 49f.

τελώνιον: 'custom office', 'toll house'. Capernaum was the first important place in Herod Antipas' territory that travellers from Herod Philip's territory or Decapolis would pass through, coming round the north end of the lake. Levi was presumably in the service of Herod Antipas.

For the call and the response cf. i. 16–20.

15. γίνεται κατακεῖσθαι αὐτόν. This construction, γίνεσθαι used impersonally with following accusative and infinitive, is found fairly often in N.T. (e.g. ii. 23, Lk. iii. 21, xvi. 22, Acts iv. 5, ix. 3, etc.) and also in the papyri.

To whom do αὐτόν and αὐτοῦ refer? Most commentators take both to refer to Levi; others take both to refer to Jesus and understand that it was he who was the host and that the meal was either in his own house or in that of Simon and Andrew. Another possibility is that αὐτόν refers to Jesus and αὐτοῦ to Levi, and this in spite of its clumsiness is perhaps to be preferred. Lk. v. 29 states explicitly that Levi was the host.

κατακεῖσθαι. It is often assumed that reclining was the normal posture at meals among the Jews in Jesus' time, but this does not seem to have been the case as far as simple people and ordinary meals were concerned, though at solemn festival meals and when guests were being entertained in style reclining was the rule.[1] The meal described here was such an entertainment: hence κατακεῖσθαι. Reclining at meals was a Gentile practice. Divans, covered with rugs, were placed around the table, and the guests reclined on them, supporting themselves on their left elbows.

τελῶναι. Contempt for tax-collectors was general on account of their rapacity and can be illustrated from Greek and Latin authors, as well as from Jewish sources. The Jews had additional patriotic and religious reasons for despising men whose work brought them into frequent contact with Gentiles. In Judea and Samaria the taxes and customs were for the Roman treasury, in Galilee and Peraea for Herod. Those who served the Romans and grew rich thereby were naturally regarded as 'quislings', but the τελῶναι of this passage would presumably be Herod's officials. In the gospels tax-collectors are frequently associated with 'sinners' as here.

ἁμαρτωλοί. Ἁμαρτωλός is an adjective (so used in viii. 38), but is often, as here, used as a noun. In this context the term probably denotes not simply all those who did not live according to Pharisaic principles (on Pharisees see below), but rather those who on account of their way of life were shunned not only by Pharisees but also by ordinarily respectable people. (Cf. Lk. vii. 37, 39.)

[1] Cf. Jeremias, *E.W.* pp. 20f.

μαθηταῖς. The word is here used for the first time in Mk, and the 'disciples' of Jesus are abruptly introduced. The term can denote a circle wider than the Twelve, though often it seems to be the Twelve who are meant. The Hebrew equivalent (*talmîd̲*) was used of the pupils of a Rabbi.

ἦσαν γὰρ πολλοί, καὶ ἠκολούθουν αὐτῷ is best understood as a parenthesis explaining τοῖς μαθηταῖς αὐτοῦ, no previous indication having been given of the existence of 'many' disciples of Jesus. This is much better than either to take both ἦσαν πολλοί and ἠκολούθουν αὐτῷ to refer to the τελῶναι καὶ ἁμαρτωλοί, or to take ἦσαν πολλοί to refer to the τελῶναι καὶ ἁμαρτωλοί and to join ἠκολούθουν αὐτῷ with what follows, reading καί before ἰδόντες in v. 16 with ℵ L Δ 33 b r1. The two sentences are joined together in Semitic fashion by 'and', but we may translate 'for there were many (by this time) who followed him'.

16. οἱ γραμματεῖς τῶν Φαρισαίων: i.e. scribes who belonged to the Pharisaic party; cf. Acts xxiii. 9. The name 'Pharisee' is commonly thought to be derived from the Hebrew and Aramaic root *prš* ('divide', 'separate'), and this explanation was given by the Pharisees themselves: they were 'Separatists' in the sense that they separated themselves from all that was impure in God's sight. Some have suggested that the name meant originally 'interpreters' (the Hebrew *pāraš* has the meaning, 'declare distinctly', 'explain'), and others have suggested 'seceders' or 'expelled'. Recently T. W. Manson has proposed another explanation: that originally the name was a nickname given to them by their opponents on account of the foreign elements in their beliefs, Φαρισαῖος being the Graecized form of the Aramaic *parsā'āh* = 'Persian', to which they themselves later gave a more 'edifying etymology'.[1] At any rate, the Pharisees were the spiritual heirs of the *ḥᵃsîdîm* or 'pious ones' of Maccabaean times. They observed the oral as equally binding with

[1] *B.J.R.L.* xxii (1938), pp. 153–9; *S.-M.* pp. 19f.

the written Law. Though they were only a small minority of the population, probably for the most part concentrated in Jerusalem, their community organization gave them an influence in social and political life out of all proportion to their numbers. Only a minority of them were 'scribes' (see on i. 22). In the N.T. the Pharisees appear in the worst possible light, the faults resulting from their legalism standing out with striking clarity. But it is important to recognize their real relative goodness. In the time of Jesus they were the real spiritual leaders of the nation, and their ideals were to prove decisive for the future character of Judaism. Jesus sides with them against the Sadducees in xii. 18 ff. and certainly had more in common with them than with the Sadducees; and much of their theology is taken for granted in the N.T. (See further L. Finkelstein, *The Pharisees* (2nd ed., 1940); Manson, *S.-M.* pp. 16 ff.)

ἐσθίει. The tense 'of the original perception' (Taylor). The idea of eating with such people was to the Pharisees particularly offensive on account of their scrupulousness about ritual purity in connection with food (see on vii. 1 ff.).

ἔλεγον. The imperfect is either inceptive ('began to say') or possibly indicates that the charge was repeatedly made. Their purpose was perhaps to shake the disciples' loyalty to Jesus.

The second ὅτι may be either *recitativum* or more probably (cf. διὰ τί in parallels) used in the sense of τί (cf. ix. 11, 28, and perhaps ii. 7).

17. ἀκούσας could mean either that he heard them himself or that what they had said was reported to him.

ὅτι is only read by B Δ Θ and two cursives. If retained, it is *recitativum*.

Οὐ χρείαν ἔχουσιν... ἔχοντες. Similar proverbial sayings about the doctor and the sick and the healthy are found in pagan literature, but the idea is so obvious that there is no need to think of borrowing. Mark's use of the rather less natural ἰσχύοντες instead of ὑγιαίνοντες which Luke has substituted is perhaps due to the influence of Aramaic *bᵉrî'ā* which means both 'healthy' and 'strong'.

ἦλθον. Cf. on i. 38, iv. 21. And besides these cf. x. 45, Mt. v. 17, x. 34f., Lk. xii. 49, Mt. xi. 19=Lk. vii. 34, Lk. xix. 10; and also Mk i. 24, Mt. viii. 29. The verb ἔρχεσθαι is often used of Jesus, particularly by himself, and expresses his consciousness of his mission. His use of it is perhaps a pointer to his consciousness of pre-existence (cf. Lagrange *in loc.*).

καλέσαι. Probably not in the specific sense 'invite' (had Jesus and not Levi been the host in *v.* 15, it might perhaps have been difficult here not to take it in this sense), but, as Luke who adds εἰς μετάνοιαν understands it, in a more general sense (cf. Isa. lxvi. 4, Jer. vii. 13, 27, etc.).

To discuss whether δικαίους is an 'ironical admission' (cf. Lk. xv. 7, xviii. 9) or whether it denotes non-ironically the relatively righteous, the respectable, is really beside the point. In *v.* 17a the real point is that it is not surprising to find a doctor among the sick; the negative statement merely supports the positive. Similarly in the application it is the positive statement that has the emphasis. Jesus is not at the moment concerned either to affirm that some people are relatively righteous or to deny that any are so righteous as not to need to repent; he is simply concerned to defend his right to associate with the disreputable. The dilemma propounded by Dodd,[1] that, if δικαίους is used ironically, it does not fit the ἰσχύοντες of *v.* 17a, while if it denotes the respectable, then the implication is that the respectable are excluded from Jesus' call, is therefore unreal.

There is no need to deny the authenticity of *v.* 17b and to regard it as a doctrinal addition by the Church, with Bultmann, Dibelius, Dodd, and others. It is not an unapt 'moral', but fits its context well. Moreover, it expresses

[1] *Parables*, pp. 117f.

what we know from other passages was characteristic of
Jesus' attitude (cf. Mt. xi. 19 = Lk. vii. 34, Mt. xviii. 12–14 =
Lk. xv. 1–7, Lk. vii. 36–50, xv. 8–32, xix. 1–10). (The use of
the Pauline word δίκαιος tells in favour of authenticity
rather than against it, as Taylor notes, for it is clearly not
used in its Pauline sense.)

The point of the whole verse may be summed up: For
Jesus to refuse to have dealings with the disreputable would
be as absurd as for a doctor to refuse to have to do with the
sick; he has come on purpose to call sinners, and the disreputable people he is associating with are obvious members
of that class.

[handwritten marginal note: Further Disclosure of Messianic Secret]

13. THE QUESTION ABOUT FASTING (ii. 18–22)
(Mt. ix. 14–17; Lk. v. 33–9)

Luke connects this closely with the preceding: but Mark,
probably rightly, makes no such connection. It is probable
that *vv.* 18–20 and *vv.* 21 f. are independent units which have
been brought together in the course of the transmission of the
tradition. The significance of the twin parables in *vv.* 21 f.
seems wider than the question at issue in *vv.* 18–20. The fact
that Mark refrains from placing any link at the beginning of
v. 21 perhaps indicates his awareness that the two parables
are not in their historical context. But it is better to take
vv. 18–22 together as being a single Markan section; for Mark
clearly intends this. He may have found the two parables
already attached to the pronouncement-story about fasting
and included in the group of conflict stories, or he may himself have inserted them in what seemed a suitable context.

The story in *vv.* 18–20 has lost in the course of transmission
all details of time and place, apart from the information in
v. 18a. On the question whether *vv.* 19b–20 are authentic
words of Jesus or not see the notes. Jesus' attitude to fasting
would naturally be a matter of interest to the early Church.

The parables of *vv.* 21 f. may well have seemed relevant at the time of the struggle about the relation of the Church to Jewish law: that they are a product of it is most unlikely, for the accent is surely that of Jesus.

18. οἱ μαθηταὶ Ἰωάννου. Cf. vi. 29 = Mt. xiv. 12, Mt. xi. 2 = Lk. vii. 18, Lk. xi. 1, Jn i. 35, 37, iii. 25.

The *v.l.* οἱ τῶν Φαρισαίων for οἱ Φαρισαῖοι is simply an assimilation to οἱ μαθηταὶ τῶν Φαρισαίων later in the verse, where other MSS. have another *v.l.* which is an assimilation in the opposite direction.

Some have suggested that both οἱ Φαρισαῖοι and οἱ μαθηταὶ τῶν Φαρισαίων are secondary, being introduced at a stage earlier than the composition of the gospel because the story was included in a group of conflict-stories. Though this is possible, the arguments in favour of it are by no means conclusive. It is true that οἱ μαθηταὶ τῶν Φαρισαίων is rather odd, but there is a parallel to it in Mt. xxii. 16 (τοὺς μαθητὰς αὐτῶν, where αὐτῶν refers back to the Pharisees), and perhaps also in the phrase οἱ υἱοὶ ὑμῶν in Mt. xii. 27 = Lk. xi. 19. And, if what follows suggests that John's disciples were fasting in mourning for their master, there is no reason why we must take the text to imply that the Pharisees were observing the same fast. That the Pharisees fasted frequently we know (cf. Lk. xviii. 12); but these fasts were not enjoined by the Law (the only fast commanded by the Law was the Day of Atonement (Lev. xvi. 29)).

ἔρχονται. Indefinite plural: 'people come'. The connection with the last section is not close enough for it to be legitimate to make the scribes of *v.* 16 the subject of the verb.

If John's disciples were fasting for mourning, we may compare Judith viii. 6 for this association between fasting and mourning. (But it is not absolutely necessary to suppose that it was such a fast; it is likely that they also fasted during John's life.)

19. Jesus replies with a parable. It consists of a question (expecting the answer, 'No'—so μή), to which he provides the answer himself.

οἱ υἱοὶ τοῦ νυμφῶνος, 'wedding-guests' (cf. Hebrew *bᵉnê haḥuppāh*). The form of expression is Semitic: cf. iii. 17, Lk. x. 6, etc., and in O.T. e.g. Deut. xiii. 13 (see R.V. marg.), II Sam. vii. 10.

According to one view (Dodd,[1] Jeremias[2]) the point of *v.* 19a is simply that to expect the disciples to fast now that the new age has come is as unreasonable as to expect wedding-guests to fast during a wedding. It is a simple parable, to which any allegorical identification of the bridegroom with Jesus is alien, but it has been turned into an allegory by the addition of *vv.* 19b–20. But it is doubtful whether this interpretation exactly fits *v.* 19a; for ἐν ᾧ ('so long as', 'while') seems rather to anticipate the end of the wedding-celebration than to concentrate attention on the fact that it has begun. And is even *v.* 19a by itself free from allegory? The words ἐν ᾧ ὁ νυμφίος μετ' αὐτῶν ἐστιν are odd in connection with an ordinary wedding, for they seem to imply that the celebrations are ended by the bridegroom's departure, whereas actually it was the guests who left the bridegroom; but they are appropriate, if the presence of allegory is admitted. It seems a more likely explanation that Jesus was adapting (hence the oddness of expression) what was perhaps a current proverb to indicate the inappropriate (fasting at a wedding!) in order to suggest the contrast between the circumstances of John's disciples and his own. It was appropriate for John's disciples to fast, for their master had been taken from them (whether or not that was actually the motive of their fast); for his own disciples it was inappropriate, for he was still with them.

If there is then an element of allegory in *v.* 19a, we may ask further whether in using this particular image in connection

---

[1] *Parables*, pp. 115f.
[2] *Parables*, p. 42, n. 82; *T.W.N.T.* iv, pp. 1095f.

with himself he saw in it any special significance beyond the general one of his importance for his disciples. It is very often assumed that he was using it with a messianic significance. If so, it seems rather that he was giving it such a significance by using it with reference to himself than that he used it because it already had any such significance; for neither in the O.T. nor in Judaism was the Bridegroom a figure of the Messiah. The O.T. evidence suggests a more august significance (e.g. Hos. *passim*, Isa. l. 1, liv. 5, lxii. 4 f., Jer. ii. 2, 32 f., iii. 1, 14, xxxi. 32, Ezek. xvi. 8); and it is possible that his use of the figure reflects his consciousness of being the Son of God, though no such significance would be suggested to his hearers.

(For the Bridegroom figure elsewhere in the N.T. cf. Mt. xxii. 1–14, xxv. 1–13, Jn iii. 29, II Cor. xi. 2, Eph. v. 22–32, Rev. xix. 7, 9, xxi. 2, 9, xxii. 17.)

The latter half of the verse has no parallel in Mt. and Lk. They probably omitted it because it really adds nothing to *v.* 19a. Its omission by some Greek and some Old Latin MSS. of Mk may be due to homoioteleuton (νηστεύειν–νηστεύειν). The redundancy of expression is characteristic of Mk.

The reason why *v.* 19b is rejected as unauthentic by some is that ὅσον χρόνον inescapably means 'so long as': though ἐν ᾧ, as we have suggested above, also means that, there is some plausibility in suggesting that the original meaning behind it was 'now that' rather than 'so long as', but with ὅσον χρόνον that is ruled out.

20. ἐλεύσονται... ἡμέραι ὅταν. For the form of expression cf. Lk. xvii. 22, xix. 43, xxi. 6, xxiii. 29, and in the O.T. I Sam. ii. 31, Amos iv. 2, etc.

ἀπαρθῇ. The simple verb αἴρω is used twice in Isa. liii. 8 (LXX), for *lākaḥ* (R.V.: 'take away') and *gāzar* (R.V.: 'cut off'). It seems likely that this verse is echoed here and that Jesus is applying (or else is represented as applying) something said of the Servant in Isa. liii to himself. Certainly, if that is so, and most probably even if it is not, there is here a reference to a violent death.

By many scholars *vv.* 19b–20 are held to be the creation of the early Church. It is urged that (i) they reflect the tendency to turn parable into allegory; (ii) they involve a prediction of the Passion at too early a stage in the ministry to be probable and are to be explained as a prophecy after the event; (iii) the attitude to fasting reflected in *v.* 20 is inconsistent with that in *v.* 19a, and *vv.* 19b–20 are an addition by the community to justify its own custom of fasting. But it may be pointed out in reply to (i) that to insist that anything with a hint of allegory must be un-authentic is much too doctrinaire (cf. on iv. 13–20), and that anyway it seems likely, as we have already seen, that *v.* 19a itself is not free from allegory; and to (ii) that this incident is not dated and may well belong to a later stage in the ministry than its place in Mk might suggest, and that anyway, if our understanding of the Baptism was right, Jesus saw his mission as that of the Suffering Servant from the very beginning of his ministry; and to (iii) that *v.* 19a does not rule out fasting in all circumstances but only during Jesus' presence with his disciples; and that, as we have no definite evidence of any custom of regular fasting in the Church before post-apostolic times, the assumption that we have here a construction of the early Church is highly doubtful. Taylor further appeals to the poetic structure of the two verses (the parallelism between *v.* 19a and *v.* 19b, and the contrast between *v.* 19a and *v.* 20a and between *v.* 19b and *v.* 20b) as evidence in support of authenticity.

We take it then that this section contains the first hint of the Passion on the lips of Jesus in Mk. What has happened to the forerunner will be repeated in the case of him who comes after him. When that happens, the disciples will have good reason to fast and mourn.

21. Note the absence of any link with the preceding.

ἐπίβλημα here means 'patch' and ῥάκος 'a piece of cloth' (as in later Greek).

ἀγνάφου: 'unfulled'—so probably here it means (as in the papyri) 'new'; cf. καινόν below.

ἱμάτιον denotes the outer garment (as opposed to χιτών, the under garment).

εἰ δὲ μή: 'otherwise' (also found in classical Greek).

αἴρει. The patch, being of unshrunk material, when it is washed shrinks and so tears the old cloth: translate perhaps 'tears away'.

πλήρωμα here 'that which fills', so 'the patch'; it is used simply as a synonym for ἐπίβλημα.

τὸ καινὸν τοῦ παλαιοῦ is a little clumsy, τὸ καινόν standing in apposition to τὸ πλήρωμα, and τοῦ παλαιοῦ to αὐτοῦ. (This is a simpler explanation than to suppose it to mean 'the new part of the old garment', i.e. the patch, and to regard the whole phrase as in apposition to τὸ πλήρωμα.) But when the phrase is explained in this way there is no need to suggest that it is an explanatory gloss—a rather unlikely suggestion in view of the fact that only one MS. omits it.

χεῖρον σχίσμα γίνεται. Though R.V.: 'a worse rent is made' correctly translates the Greek as Greek, A.V.: 'the rent is made worse' might perhaps be justified on the basis of the Aramaic behind the Greek, there being no clear formal distinction between the definite and the indefinite in Aramaic (see Black, p. 69).

For interpretation see below on v. 22, the two parables being a pair.

22. βάλλει: 'puts'. (For the weakened sense of βάλλειν cf., e.g., Jn v. 7.)

On the distinction between νέος and καινός see on i. 27.

ἀλλὰ οἶνον νέον εἰς ἀσκοὺς καινούς is omitted by D it, and W.H. and Nestle enclose it in square brackets; but it could easily have been omitted accidentally in D (cf. Streeter, p. 311). It seems to be presupposed by Mt. and Lk. The accusative οἶνον νέον is to be explained as the object of βάλλει, the words εἰ δὲ μή...οἱ ἀσκοί being in a way parenthetic. But Taylor points out that the words in question spoil the parallelism between the two parables, there being nothing in *v.* 21 to correspond with them. It is possible, as he says, that the words, though part of the original text of Mk, are not an original part of the parable but an exegetical addition. It is, however, perhaps also possible that Jesus himself purposely went beyond the limit of the poetic form he was using in order to sum up positively and emphatically the burden of the pair of parables.

That directly or indirectly, in one way or another, these twin parables bear on the newness of that which has come into the world with Jesus is fairly certain; but about their exact original application we cannot be sure. Were they a defence of the disciples against those who, failing to recognize this newness, wanted to confine them within the strait jacket of contemporary pious conventions; or a reference to the incompatibility of John's disciples' use of pious practices of Pharisaic pattern with their recognition of the new situation indicated by their insistence on repentance? Or is the point that the kingdom of God cannot be confined within the limits of Judaism, and the coming of the new must bring with it the dissolution of the old? Or did these parables drive home the need for rebirth (cf. Jn iii. 3, and perhaps Mk x. 15)—the impossibility of receiving the new apart from a miracle of new creation (cf. Hilary's comment: 'Atque ideo et Pharisaeos et discipulos Johannis nova non accepturos esse nisi novi fierent'), or the uselessness of half measures, of trying to mend one's old life with a patch of new?

14. PLUCKING CORN ON THE SABBATH (ii. 23–8)
(Mt. xii. 1–8; Lk. vi. 1–5)

In form a pronouncement-story, this is an isolated narrative without details of time or place. Comparison with the parallels shows how Mark has been content to pass on the tradition he had received without inventing links with the context or attempting to make it a more satisfying story by filling it out. On the question of the relation of *vv.* 27 f. to *vv.* 23–6 see notes.

For other stories of conflict about the Sabbath see iii. 1–6, Lk. xiii. 10–17, xiv. 1–6, Jn v. 1–18, ix. 1–41. They would be of special interest in the early Church as it had to face the issue of its relation to the Sabbath.

23. ἐγένετο αὐτὸν . . . παραπορεύεσθαι. For the construction see on ii. 15.

ἐν τοῖς σάββασιν. See on i. 21.

παραπορεύεσθαι. διαπορεύεσθαι is read by B C D *c e ff*² *r*¹, and is accepted by W.H.; but the widely attested παρα-πορεύεσθαι should be preferred; for the change to δια- can be easily explained as a change to the more accurate expression or as assimilation to Lk., while δια- would not be likely to be altered to παρα-.

ὁδὸν ποιεῖν τίλλοντες. ὁδὸν ποιεῖν, which properly means 'to make a road', is here used in the sense of the middle ὁδὸν ποιεῖσθαι, which is used in classical Greek in the sense 'to journey'. Cf. Lat. *iter facere*, but, as the active occurs in the LXX in Judg. xvii. 8 in this sense, the expression can hardly be claimed as a Latinism. (The *v.l.* ὁδοποιεῖν, which is not likely to be original, also means properly 'to build a road', 'make a way for oneself'.) The meaning would have been more clearly expressed had Mark written ὁδὸν ποιοῦντες τίλλειν.

A Jew was allowed to pluck corn that did not belong to him, so long as he used only his hands (Deut. xxiii. 25).

The reference to standing corn here is 'the only clear indication in the Synoptic Gospels that the Ministry covered at least a year' (Taylor). The incident must have occurred not later than the beginning of June.

24. ὃ οὐκ ἔξεστιν. The Pharisees regarded what the disciples were doing as work, which was not permissible on the Sabbath. According to (M) *Shab*. vii. 2 there are 'forty save one' main classes of work: of these the third is reaping. According to (M) *Sanh*. vii. 4 violation of the Sabbath was punishable by stoning; but vii. 8 distinguishes different degrees of guilt, and stoning is prescribed only if the offender has been previously warned. The words οὐκ ἔξεστιν are perhaps intended as a warning (cf. Jn v. 10). Cf. on βλασφημεῖ in ii. 7.

25. For the use of a counter-question including an appeal to scripture (characteristic of Rabbinic arguments) cf. xii. 10, 26. For the incident referred to see I Sam. xxi. 1–6.

χρείαν ἔσχεν καὶ ἐπείνασεν αὐτὸς καὶ οἱ μετ' αὐτοῦ is an inference from the text of I Sam. It would be a wrong interpretation to take this to imply that Jesus excused David on the ground that he was compelled by necessity. It is unlikely that Jesus any more than the Pharisees would admit that any necessity could excuse the breaking of God's law. Rather, the drift of the argument is that the fact that scripture does not condemn David for his action shows that the rigidity with which the Pharisees interpreted the ritual law was not in accordance with scripture, and so was not a proper understanding of the Law itself.

It is sometimes maintained that this appeal to David's example was a veiled messianic claim; but, though the reader may rightly recognize a certain fittingness in the Messiah's appealing to the example of David, it seems unlikely that Jesus cited the case of David for this reason, if what has just been said is true.

26. τὸν οἶκον τοῦ Θεοῦ. The name by which the tent or

shrine where the Ark was kept in Shiloh is referred to, for instance in Judg. xviii. 31. Cf. 'the house of the LORD' e.g. Judg. xix. 18. In I Sam. xxi David comes to Ahimelech the priest at Nob, but there is no reference in the passage to any house of God.

ἐπὶ Ἀβιαθαρ ἀρχιερέως must mean 'when Abiathar was High Priest'. In I Sam. xxi 'the priest' is Ahimelech. Abiathar was that one of Ahimelech's sons who escaped the massacre by Doeg the Edomite. A C Θ and a good many other MSS. insert τοῦ before ἀρχιερέως. The phrase then means 'in the days of Abiathar the High Priest', which need not imply that he was actually High Priest at the time. The variant is probably due to a sense of the historical difficulty. The fact that D W it sy^s omit the phrase altogether—as do Mt. and Lk.—makes the suggestion that the whole phrase is a misguided gloss not unreasonable. But it is perhaps more likely that Jesus himself or possibly Mark mentioned Abiathar as the High Priest particularly associated with David, forgetting that at the time of the incident he was not yet High Priest. It may be that there is some confusion between Ahimelech and Abiathar in the O.T. itself—cf. I Sam. xxii. 20 with II Sam. viii. 17, I Chr. xviii. 16, xxiv. 6.

τοὺς ἄρτους τῆς προθέσεως. I.e. the shewbread or 'bread of the presence' (Hebrew leḥem pānîm), which the Chronicler prefers to call 'bread of arrangement' (leḥem hammaʿareket). For the regulations about it see Lev. xxiv. 5–9; also Exod. xxv. 23–30, Heb. ix. 2. I Sam. xxi is the earliest mention of it.

οὓς οὐκ ἔξεστιν φαγεῖν εἰ μὴ τοὺς ἱερεῖς. Cf. Lev. xxiv. 9. The accusative (τοὺς ἱερεῖς) is less usual than the dative with the infinitive after ἔξεστιν, but it is found also in classical Greek.

27. καὶ ἔλεγεν αὐτοῖς is sometimes used by Mark as a formula for introducing an independent saying (so probably iv. 21, 24) and it is perhaps probable that this saying was originally independent of vv. 23–6—but not certain, since v. 27

is a suitable climax to *vv.* 23–6 and καὶ ἔλεγεν αὐτοῖς could be inserted into a continuous speech in order to mark a new stage in the argument. D W it read λέγω δὲ ὑμῖν instead.

The saying **Τὸ σάββατον**... **διὰ τὸ σάββατον** together with the following ὥστε, though omitted by D it (which also read λέγω δὲ ὑμῖν in place of καὶ ἔλεγεν αὐτοῖς) and also by Mt. and Lk., should probably be read. With the saying cf. the opinion of Rabbi Simeon b. Menasya (*c.* A.D. 180) in *Mekilta* 109b on Exod. xxxi. 14: 'The Sabbath is delivered unto you, and ye are not delivered to the Sabbath', which is perhaps to be traced back to Mattathias, the father of the Maccabees (see I Macc. ii. 39–41). But this Rabbinic principle would only mean that where life was at stake, things might be done on the Sabbath which otherwise would be forbidden. If *v.* 27 is closely connected with *vv.* 23–6, what Jesus is saying has a much more general application, for there is no indication that the disciples were in danger of dying of starvation. If, however, it is independent of *vv.* 23–6, it may originally have been connected with a healing (for Jesus' attitude to healing on the Sabbath see on iii. 1–6).

It has been suggested by T. W. Manson[1] that τὸν ἄνθρωπον and ὁ ἄνθρωπος here should be translated 'the Son of Man' (the underlying Aramaic *bar-nāšā*' having been misunderstood; see further at viii. 31), and that Jesus *and* his disciples are meant. In support of this suggestion Manson argues that according to Jewish thought the Sabbath was for Israel only (cf. *Mekilta* quoted above, and Jub. ii. 31); that in *v.* 23 it is the disciples who infringe the Sabbath law; that Jesus and his disciples regard the claims of the kingdom of God as taking priority over Sabbath observances; and that this interpretation makes the following verse's interpretation easy. But, as we shall see in connection with viii. 31, Manson's view of the corporate significance of 'Son of

[1] *C.N.* xi, pp. 138–46.

Man' is hardly satisfactory. Here it is best to take the
meaning to be simply 'man'.

28. For ὥστε + the indicative meaning 'So...' cf. x. 8.

The suggestion that ὁ Υἱὸς τοῦ ἀνθρώπου in this verse is a
mistranslation of *bar-nāšā*, which here means 'man', is
extremely unlikely. Rawlinson's words: 'Our Lord would
not have been likely to say that "man" was "lord of the
sabbath", which had been instituted by God' are fully
justified. If the verse is Jesus' words, then the meaning will
be as Taylor explains it: 'since the Sabbath was made for
man, He who is man's Lord and Representative has
authority to determine its laws and use'. But there are
difficulties in taking 'Son of Man' to be a self-designation on
the lips of Jesus here. If the term was a recognizable
messianic title (see further at viii. 31), would Jesus have used
it thus openly at this stage of his ministry and in conversation with his opponents (even if *vv.* 27f. is not to be closely
connected with *vv.* 23–6, *v.* 27 would seem more likely to be
addressed to opponents than to disciples)? The most probable
explanation seems to be that this verse is a Christian comment—either Mark's own or an exegetical comment already
attached to *v.* 27 in the tradition he used. Cf. ii. 10. The ὥστε
then introduces the conclusion to be drawn from Jesus'
saying. The insight to which the comment gives expression
would of course have been of the greatest importance to the
* early Church (see Rom. xiv. 5f., Gal. iv. 10, Col. ii. 16).

15. THE HEALING OF THE MAN WITH THE
WITHERED HAND (iii. 1–6)
(Mt. xii. 9–14; Lk. vi. 6–11)

The last of the group of conflict-stories. Bultmann and
others maintain that *v.* 6 is redactional, being added to
round off the complex of conflict-stories; Schmidt and
Taylor are more probably right in thinking that it was an

original part of the tradition-unit and that it determined the place of the unit in the complex. As Taylor points out, *v.* 2 prepares the way for *v.* 6.

The vividness of παρετήρουν in *v.* 2, of the detail of *v.* 3 that is not absolutely necessary to the story, and of the references to Jesus' looking round on his opponents and to his anger and grief in *v.* 5, suggests reminiscence. The unit may well be Petrine. The incident was remembered both as showing clearly the attitude of Jesus to the Sabbath and also as showing the development of opposition.

1. πάλιν may refer back to i. 21; if so, it was presumably added by Mark when he fitted the complex ii. 1–iii. 6 into his gospel. Or possibly it was already a feature of the story, its point being to indicate that Jesus was a regular attender of the synagogue on sabbath days.

ἐξηραμμένην. Some sort of paralysis is apparently meant. To suggest that the participle must imply that the paralysis was not from birth is to put more weight on it than it can carry. Its meaning is probably indistinguishable from that of the adjective used by Mt. and Lk. and by Mark himself in *v.* 3.

ἔχων does not go with ἦν to form a periphrastic tense, but is descriptive.

2. παρετήρουν. Not an indefinite plural, as it is not just equivalent to a passive. Definite people are in mind, though it is not till *v.* 6 that their identity is indicated.

θεραπεύσει. The question in their minds was 'Will he heal?' The tense of the original direct speech is correctly retained in the indirect. The use of an indirect question here suggests that Jesus read their thoughts: Lk. vi. 8 makes this explicit.

According to the Rabbis the sick or injured were to be treated on the Sabbath day, if life was actually in danger (cf. (*M*) *Yom.* viii. 6: 'Whenever there is doubt whether life is in danger this overrides the Sabbath'); but if there was no danger to life, then treatment was not permissible. (For illustrative material see S.-B. I, pp. 623–9.) Since the withered hand did not constitute a danger to the man's life, to heal it on the Sabbath would be in the Pharisees' view an infringement of the Sabbath and punishable as such.

3. In reply to the unspoken challenge Jesus bids the man 'Rise (and come) [the construction is pregnant] into the midst', i.e. where he can the better be seen (cf. xiv. 60). In this case the need for secrecy (see on i. 25, iv. 11f.) is apparently outweighed by other motives.

4. ἀγαθὸν ποιῆσαι. So ℵ W; D has τι ἀγαθὸν ποιῆσαι. Better to read ἀγαθοποιῆσαι with B and the great majority of MSS. The compound verb is used in LXX and later Greek (including N.T.); it was formed on the analogy of κακοποιεῖν which is classical.

Jesus' question is often explained as a challenge to the Pharisees to decide which of two actions is lawful on the Sabbath: that which he is about to do, which can be described as preserving life (cf. the use of σώζω in connection with healing, e.g. v. 28, 34, vi. 56, x. 52), or that which they are actually engaged in, namely, watching him with intent to compass his death—planning murder. (So Taylor.) More probable is the interpretation which takes κακοποιῆσαι and ἀποκτεῖναι to refer to the other course open to Jesus, namely to refrain from healing. To omit to do the good which one could do to someone in need is to do evil. It is to break the Sixth Commandment. 'There is little difference', says Calvin, 'between manslaughter and the conduct of him who does not concern himself about relieving a person in distress.'

οἱ δὲ ἐσιώπων. For they were unwilling to give the true answer, that to do good is allowed and to do evil forbidden, and so admit the falseness of their piety; and they dared not give the other answer, for that would have been to suggest that God had appointed one day in seven on which to do good was forbidden and to do evil allowed.

5. περιβλεψάμενος. Περιβλέπομαι (only used in the middle in N.T.) means 'to look round (upon)', and is used sometimes with a direct object, as here, and sometimes absolutely. In the N.T. it occurs seven times—six times with Jesus as subject (here, iii. 34, v. 32, x. 23, xi. 11, Lk. vi. 10). Cf. the use of ἐμβλέπω in x. 21, 27, Lk. xx. 17, xxii. 61.

μετ' ὀργῆς. For Jesus' anger cf. i. 41 (reading ὀργισθείς), x. 14 (ἠγανάκτησεν). His anger here is often referred to his humanity simply (e.g. Calvin, Taylor). Is it perhaps better to think here of the oneness of his person and to regard his anger as that of the whole Christ, God and Man—and similarly with his grief (συνλυπούμενος)? In Mt. and Lk. this reference to Jesus' anger and grief is omitted.

συνλυπούμενος. Συνλυπεῖσθαι properly means 'to mourn with', 'sympathize': this is the only known instance of its use simply as a strengthened form of λυπεῖσθαι. It is possible that the influence of Latin should be recognized in this use of συν- as an intensive (cf. contristari).

πωρώσει. Πώρωσις occurs in the N.T. in Rom. xi. 25, Eph. iv. 18, and here; πωρῶ in vi. 52, viii. 17, Jn xii. 40, Rom. xi. 7, II Cor. iii. 14. Probably in the N.T. the idea is rather of blindness than hardness. This is suggested by the contexts †
and borne out by ancient versions and commentaries, and by the fact that πήρωσις, πηρῶ are often found as variant readings. (For full discussion see J. A. Robinson, *St Paul's Epistle to the Ephesians* (London, 1903), pp. 264–74.)

ἀπεκατεστάθη. Note the double augment, as in viii. 25. (See M.H. II, p. 189.)

In this miracle Jesus does not touch the sufferer (as in i. 41, vii. 33, viii. 23, 25) or use material means (as in vii. 33, viii. 23), but commands the man to do something with the affected limb. In this case it was something he could do before he was healed (unless Lohmeyer's suggestion that χείρ in this section means 'arm', as in modern Greek, is right); in ii. 11, Jn v. 8, it was something which would only be possible when he was healed. On miracles generally see on i. 31.

6. On the Pharisees see on ii. 16.

This verse implies that the subject of παρετήρουν in v. 2 was the Pharisees.

τῶν 'Ηρῳδιανῶν, i.e. the friends and supporters of Herod Antipas. Cf. xii. 13. Taylor in illustration aptly quotes Josephus, *Ant.* xiv. 450: τοὺς τὰ 'Ηρῴδου φρονοῦντας, which refers to those who were favourable to Herod the Great in Galilee before he became master of the country. (See further H. H. Rowley in *J.T.S.* xli, pp. 14–27.) As Jesus was Herod's subject, it was important to get Herod turned against him. The Herodians would care little or nothing for Pharisaic ideals. So the Pharisees in seeking their help were acting somewhat unscrupulously.

συμβούλιον ἐδίδουν. Συμβούλιον is also used in xv. 1, Mt. xii. 14, xxii. 15, xxvii. 1, 7, xxviii. 12, Acts xxv. 12, once in LXX (IV Macc. xvii. 17), in Plutarch, Josephus, Ignatius, and papyri. Its use in the sense 'counsel' (rather than 'council') is perhaps a Latinism. (But it is dangerous to argue that the presence of two possible Latinisms in this pericope is evidence that this story had passed into Latin before being taken over by Mark.[1]) The use of διδόναι with it is strange. Mt. substitutes λαμβάνειν (cf. Lat. *consilium capere*).

ὅπως αὐτὸν ἀπολέσωσιν. The first *explicit* reference to the intention of Jesus' adversaries to compass his death: there have been hints before (see on ii. 7, 24). The complex of conflict-stories (ii. 1–iii. 6) illustrates the growth of opposition. That this incident is placed in its correct chronological position in the ministry we cannot, of course, be sure; but it is intrinsically likely that the intention of his opponents to bring about his death developed quite early in the course of it.

[1] *Pace* Knox, *Sources*, I, p. 9, n. 2.

III. LATER STAGES OF THE
GALILEAN MINISTRY

(iii. 7–vi. 13)

The accounts of the great crowds following Jesus (iii. 7–12) and of the appointment of the Twelve (iii. 13–19), with which this division opens, are followed by three complexes, iii. 20–35, iv. 1–34 and iv. 35–v. 43. The division closes with the narratives of the rejection at Nazareth (vi. 1–6a) and the mission of the Twelve (vi. 6b–13).

The first complex consists of three sections, iii. 20f., iii. 22–30 (on the unity of this section see below) and iii. 31–5, the last of these being most naturally understood as the sequel of the first. Whether the connection between *vv.* 22–30 and *vv.* 20f., 31–5 is historical is not certain. It seems quite probable that it is—though it is also possible that Mark wanted to insert something between *vv.* 20f. and *vv.* 31 ff. in order to suggest the interval between the setting out of Jesus' family and their arrival, and chose *vv.* 22–30 on account of its topical appropriateness (cf. ἐξέστη in *v.* 21 with Βεεζεβοὺλ ἔχει, κ.τ.λ. in *v.* 22). As the complex stands, it draws attention to the similarity between the attitude of Jesus' family to him and that of the scribes.

The second complex is the collection of parabolic teaching (iv. 1–34): on this see below.

The third complex consists of four miracle stories, which stand out by reason of the great vividness with which they are told.

16. CROWDS BY THE LAKE (iii. 7–12)
(Mt. xii. 15–21; Lk. vi. 17–19)

An editorial summary statement by the evangelist. It has
no connecting links with what precedes, but looks forward,
the references to the crowds and the boat, to the demon-
possessed, and to the anxiety of the sick to touch Jesus,
anticipating iv. 1 ff., iii. 27, v. 1–20, v. 25–34, vi. 56.

The vividness of *vv.* 9 f. suggests strongly that this summary
statement has drawn on the reminiscence of an eye-witness.

7. ἀνεχώρησεν: 'withdrew'; but there is no need to
understand that the motive was to escape from danger (at
any rate as far as Mk is concerned—the addition of γνούς and
ἐκεῖθεν in Mt. xii. 15 does suggest that Jesus' awareness of
the Pharisees' intention was the reason for his withdrawal;
but it is probably due to the desire for a more connected
narrative rather than to the possession of independent
historical knowledge), and it seems that Mark is thinking in
this and the next verse of an extension of the ministry of
Jesus (cf. this list with i. 28) rather than of a retreat. Jesus
leaves 'the towns and synagogues to continue His ministry
in the open air by the lakeside among the crowds from
Galilee and adjacent districts' (Taylor).

For **πρός** we should perhaps read εἰς with D H P *al*; εἰς
would be more likely to be changed into πρός here than the
other way round. The meaning would be 'to', 'to the
neighbourhood of': cf. vii. 31. Taylor is probably right in
preferring the reading πολὺς ὄχλος of D lat to **πολὺ πλῆθος**
and thinking that πλῆθος πολύ in the following verse should
probably be omitted with W *a b c* sy[s] (its presence being
perhaps due to assimilation to Lk. (apart from these two
verses Mark never uses πλῆθος)); and also in omitting
ἠκολούθησεν with D W 28 it sy[s] bo. The effect of the omission of ἠκολούθησεν is to do away with the distinction between
two different crowds and the unlikely break in the series of

ἀπό phrases; there would then be either no punctuation or else just a comma after Γαλιλαίας.

'Ιουδαίας. The first time that Judea is mentioned in connection with the ministry of Jesus.

8. 'Ιδουμαίας. During the sixth to fifth centuries B.C. the Edomites had occupied the Negeb, being pushed out of their former territory by Arab tribes. The new Edom or Idumaea included Bethsura, according to I Macc. iv. 29, about twenty miles S.W. of Jerusalem. Since the time of John Hyrcanus (reigned 134–104 B.C.) Idumaea had been Jewish. Northern Idumaea was part of the Roman province of Judea.

πέραν τοῦ 'Ιορδάνου: i.e. Peraea, part of the territory of Herod Antipas.

Τύρον καὶ Σιδῶνα. Tyre and Sidon were in the Roman province of Syria.

ὅσα ποιεῖ: i.e. his miracles.

9. ἵνα is here used to introduce the substance of a command. Cf. iii. 12, vi. 8, 12, viii. 30, ix. 18. This usage is common only in later Greek; normal classical Greek would be the infinitive after the verb of command.

πλοιάριον. Diminutive in form, but probably not to be distinguished from πλοῖον in iv. 1, 36. Mark often uses diminutives—a colloquial tendency.

10. πολλούς. Cf. on i. 34. Both Mt. xii. 15 and Lk. vi. 19 have πάντας.

ἐπιπίπτειν αὐτῷ. Commentators quote in illustration Thucydides, VII. 84: ἐπέπιπτόν τε ἀλλήλοις καὶ κατεπάτουν.

αὐτοῦ ἅψωνται. Cf. v. 27 ff., vi. 56.

μάστιγας. Cf. v. 29, 34, Lk. vii. 21. The word is used in classical Greek as well as in the N.T. for diseases. The use originated of course in the idea that disease was a divine chastisement.

11. For **ὅταν** followed by indicative (not in classical prose, but occurs in Homer) cf. xi. 19, 25, Rev. iv. 9, viii. 1. It occurs also in the LXX and in late Greek.

ἐθεώρουν, προσέπιπτον... ἔκραζον. What the possessed do is attributed to the spirits possessing them.

ὅτι. *Recitativum*, introducing direct speech.

Σὺ εἶ ὁ Υἱὸς τοῦ Θεοῦ. For the recognition of Jesus by the demons see on i. 24, and for the title 'Son of God' see on i. 1, 11, 24.

12. πολλά is adverbial: 'much'; cf. i. 45.

For the injunction to silence see on i. 25 and also on iv. 11.

17. THE APPOINTMENT OF THE TWELVE (iii. 13–19)
(Mt. x. 1–4; Lk. vi. 12–16)

A narrative constructed by Mark on the basis of tradition. Not having received any vivid details such as are characteristic of an eye-witness's reminiscence, Mark, as usual, refrains from inventing them. The list of the Twelve is clearly traditional; a free creation would not have contained so many difficulties. On the historicity of their appointment see below.

13. εἰς τὸ ὄρος: to escape the crowds. τὸ ὄρος is vague; perhaps the hill country north of the lake is meant.

προσκαλεῖται (the verb is often used in Mk of Jesus with the disciples or the crowd as object: cf. iii. 23, vi. 7, vii. 14, viii. 1, 34, x. 42, xii. 43) οὓς ἤθελεν αὐτός stresses the initiative of Jesus, to which alone the group of Jesus' disciples owed its origin. It is not made clear whether those referred to here are simply the Twelve or a larger company from whom the Twelve are then chosen: in Mt. x. 1 the object of προσκαλεσάμενος is simply τοὺς δώδεκα μαθητὰς αὐτοῦ, but Lk. vi. 13 definitely refers to a larger number from which the Twelve are chosen.

καὶ ἀπῆλθον πρὸς αὐτόν. As in i. 18, 20, ii. 14, 'the response is immediate' (Taylor).

14. ἐποίησεν: 'appointed'; not a classical meaning of the verb, but one that it sometimes has in the LXX (e.g.

I Sam. xii. 6, I Kgs xii. 31, where it represents Hebrew '*āśāh*). In the N.T. cf. Heb. iii. 2.

δώδεκα. It seems likely that the number twelve was deliberately chosen with the tribes of Israel in mind. If it was, then it would seem to be evidence that Jesus thought of himself as beginning to gather together an obedient people of God (of which the Twelve were to be the nucleus) —though it does not, of course, necessarily imply that he envisaged a church continuing under the conditions of history through many centuries.

That the appointment of the Twelve by Jesus is historical is beyond serious doubt; for the existence of a group of twelve apostles in the early Church is scarcely to be accounted for on any other assumption than that its origin goes back to the action of Jesus during his lifetime.

(i) Why otherwise only twelve, when the number of disciples had been greater during his ministry, and when more than twelve had seen the risen Lord?

(ii) How otherwise would Judas have come to be spoken of as one of the Twelve?

(iii) The tradition of 'the Eleven' (Mt. xxviii. 16, Mk xvi. 14, Lk. xxiv. 9, 33, Acts i. 26) and of the choice of Matthias (Acts i. 15 ff.) would otherwise be incomprehensible.

(iv) The N.T. provides no clear indication at all that at any time the Twelve as a group played a special part in the leadership of the Church either in Jerusalem or outside it —a fact which tells decisively against the suggestion that the origin of the group is to be sought after the Resurrection. (See further K. H. Rengstorf in *T.W.N.T.* II, pp. 325–8.)

After δώδεκα א B C* Δ Θ f 13 *al* sy[h mg] sa bo[pl] eth geo[1] insert οὓς καὶ ἀποστόλους ὠνόμασεν (W inserts it after αὐτοῦ); but this is probably an assimilation to Lk. vi. 13, and should almost certainly not be read. It is omitted by A C[c] D L f 1 *pl* latt sy[s,p,h] geo[2] arm.

The purpose of Jesus (ἵνα) according to this and the next

verse was twofold. First, they were to be with him. They had to learn from him before they could be sent out by him —to hear before they could speak for him (cf. vii. 31–7). As Taylor notes, it is not till vi. 7 that they are actually sent out. Secondly, he would give them a mission—a mission which itself was twofold: to preach and to have authority to cast out the demons. The two ἵνα-clauses indicate not only the limited function of the Twelve during the ministry of Jesus, but also their permanent function in the Church. They are to be witnesses to him—at first hand. And in that both their being with him and their being sent out by him are necessarily involved. They must be with him, if they are to be his authoritative first-hand witnesses. So in Acts i. 21 f. the person who is to take Judas' place must not only have been an eye-witness of the Resurrection but also have been with Jesus during his ministry. Their being with him then is not just for the sake of the mission during his ministry; it is much more for the sake of their mission after the Resurrection. In the course of the gospel we shall see the Twelve being with Jesus and Jesus concentrating more and more on their instruction. He appointed them also that he might send them out (see further the note on ἀπόστολος in vi. 30) to preach. In that κηρύσσειν are included both the limited preaching of vi. 7–13, 30 and also their post-Resurrection preaching which remains for us permanently in the N.T. scriptures.

15. καὶ ἔχειν ἐξουσίαν ἐκβάλλειν τὰ δαιμόνια. As Jesus himself had come in order 'that he might destroy the works of the devil', the authority given to the Twelve to cast out the demons was part of the signs of the presence of the kingdom of God in Jesus.

The words θεραπεύειν τὰς νόσους καί are added after ἐξουσίαν by a great many Greek MSS., by lat and other versions; but should probably not be included. They are omitted by ℵ B C* L Δ 565 892 sa bo^{pl}, and are probably to be explained as assimilation to Mt. x. 1. As there is a close connection between healing miracles generally and exorcisms (the former as well as the latter being associated with the breaking of Satan's power), there is perhaps no material difference of meaning involved.

16. The words καὶ ἐποίησεν τοὺς δώδεκα, though read by ℵ B C* Δ 565 579, should probably be omitted with A Cᶜ D L W Θ and other uncials, all minuscules other than those just mentioned, lat sy sa bo. They are probably to be explained either as dittography of καὶ ἐποίησεν δώδεκα in v. 14, or as added in order to make a smoother text, as they pick up the thread after the ἵνα-clauses.

καὶ ἐπέθηκεν ὄνομα τῷ Σίμωνι Πέτρον. This is certainly an awkward beginning to the list. One would expect Simon to be mentioned before this explanatory note is given. But the reading of f13 543 sa (the insertion of πρῶτον Σίμωνα before this sentence), tempting though it is, can hardly be accepted: it is perhaps an assimilation to Mt. x. 2, or else simply an improvement of the awkward text. καὶ ἐπέθηκεν... coming immediately after v. 15 is rough, but the roughness would seem to be Mark's own.

Ἐπιτιθέναι ὄνομα, 'to give a name', is classical and LXX.

Σίμωνι. Mentioned already i. 16, 29 f., 36.

Generally πέτρος means a boulder or stone, while πέτρα means rather the living rock; but in Greek usage the distinction is not always observed, and in Aramaic *kēp̲ā'*, which has only the one form (the final s of the transliterated form is added to give it a Greek ending), does for both meanings, and it is of course *kēp̲ā'* that lies behind Πέτρος here. Here the word πέτρα would have been the more accurate translation, but the masculine πέτρος was probably preferred since the reference was to a man. Neither the Aramaic nor the Greek word is a proper name. The occasion of this giving the name 'Rock' to Simon by Jesus is not certain. Mark here rather suggests, though he does not

explicitly affirm, that it was at the time of the appointment
of the Twelve. Mt. xvi seems to put it at the time of the
Confession of Jesus as the Christ (though this could be
rather the reaffirming of a name given on an earlier occasion). Jn i. 42 places it even earlier than Mk does. Apparently the early Church was not certain about the occasion,
and each evangelist mentions the naming in the context that
seems to him most suitable. Cullmann has suggested that
the logion recorded in Mt. xvi. 17–19, which he accepts as
authentic, belongs historically to the context indicated by
Lk. xxii. 31–3.[1]

The attempt to explain the name psychologically as
describing Simon's character is mistaken; for rock-like firm-
ness is not a feature of the N.T. picture of Simon Peter—not
even after Pentecost (see Gal. ii). The name rather denotes
the part which was to be played by him, during the lifetime
of Jesus, as the spokesman and representative of the chosen
Twelve, and then for a short period, after the Resurrection
and Pentecost, as the acknowledged leader of the Primitive
Church. As the representative of that nucleus and the leader
during its first expansion, he is historically the beginning,
the foundation-rock (next to Christ himself) on which the
Church is built. The reason why he in particular was chosen
by Jesus for this role is best recognized as a mystery of
divine election.

On the name 'Peter' and on the subject of the apostle
Peter generally see further O. Cullmann, *Peter, Disciple,
Apostle and Martyr* (Eng. tr., London, 1953).

17. Ἰάκωβον...Ἰωάννην. Already mentioned in i. 19f.,
29. The accusatives in this and the following verses are after
ἐποίησεν in *v.* 14 (or *v.* 16).

Βοανηργες. W (omitting καὶ Ἰάκωβον...τοῦ Ἰακώβου,
instead of καὶ ἐπέθηκεν...ὄνομα reading κοινῶς δὲ αὐτοὺς
ἐκάλεσεν, and for *v.* 18 reading ἦσαν δὲ οὗτοι Σίμων καὶ

[1] For reference see below.

'Ανδρέας, 'Ιάκωβος καὶ 'Ιωάννης...) refers the name to all
the Twelve, and b c e q provide some support for this; but
the attestation is too weak for this to be at all likely. The
word is doubtless a corrupt transliteration of an Aramaic or
Hebrew phrase. Βοανη- presumably represents bᵉnê—'sons
of'. For -ργες various suggestions have been made: Hebrew
rōgez = 'agitation', 'excitement', 'raging'—used in Job
xxxvii. 2 of thunder, but not an ordinary word for thunder;
Aramaic rᵉgaz = 'anger'; Hebrew regeš means 'throng' in
Ps. lv. 14 (M.T.: 15), but in later Hebrew 'commotion',
'vibration' (while the related Aramaic rigšā' = 'noise'). Of
these the last is probably the best explanation. Though this
word is not used in the sense of thunder in Hebrew or
Aramaic texts, the related Arabic word is used for thunder.

The reason for the name is most probably to be found in
such outbursts as are related in ix. 38, Lk. ix. 54. A more
complimentary explanation (going back to the early Church)
is that the name is a promise (like the name 'Rock') and the
meaning that their witness to Jesus will be as mighty as
thunder. Much less likely is the suggestion of J. Rendel
Harris that the reference is to their being twins.[1]

18. 'Ανδρέαν. Here, as in xiii. 3, Acts i. 13, he is
mentioned after James and John. In Mt. and Lk. he is
named next to his brother Simon. The Mk order is no
doubt due to the desire to group the three leading disciples
together. He has already been mentioned i. 16, 29.

Φίλιππον. A Greek name, but it occurs in the Talmud in
various Hebraized forms.

Βαρθολομαῖον. A patronymic: son of Talmai (a name that
occurs in II Sam. iii. 3, xiii. 37 and that Josephus gives in the
form Θολομαῖος). He probably had another name as well.
Sometimes he is identified with Nathanael, who is also
associated with Philip (Jn i. 45).

[1] In *Exp.* 7 Ser. III) (1907), pp. 146ff., and *E.T.* xxxvi (1924–5),
p. 139.

Μαθθαῖον. Abbreviated form of O.T. Mattathias. See on Λενείν in ii. 14.

Θωμᾶν. Mentioned, in addition to the Mt. and Lk. parallels to this verse and the Acts i list, in Jn xi. 16, xiv. 5, xx. 24, 26 f., 28, xxi. 2. The name means 'twin' (Aramaic *tᵉ'ômā'*).

'Ιάκωβον τὸν τοῦ 'Αλφαίου. Mentioned only in the lists. Sometimes identified with James the Less (xv. 40) or with Levi (see on ii. 14). He may be the brother of Levi, who is also called 'the son of Alphaeus'. 'Αλφαῖος is often identified with Clopas (Jn xix. 25) and Cleopas (Lk. xxiv. 18), but this is quite uncertain.

Θαδδαῖον. Lk. and Acts have 'Ιούδας 'Ιακώβου at this point, while D it have Λεββαῖον here, and D 122 *k* Origen have it in Mt. x. 3. Possibly Judas is the correct name, and Thaddaeus or Lebbaeus an additional name or nickname (cf. Jn xiv. 22—'Judas (not Iscariot)').

τὸν Καναναῖον. So too Mt.: Lk. and Acts have τὸν καλούμενον Ζηλωτήν and ὁ Ζηλωτής respectively. Καναναῖος = *kan'ānā'*, which is correctly rendered by Ζηλωτής. Although the Zealots belong to a later date, there were already extreme nationalists, to whom the name might be applied.

19. Ἰσκαριωθ. Usually explained as *'îš kᵉriyyôt*, i.e. 'man of Kerioth' (cf. "Ιστωβος in Josephus, *Ant.* VII. 121: 'man of Tob'), and Kerioth is identified either with Kerioth-Hezron (Josh. xv. 25) twelve miles south of Hebron or with Kerioth in Moab (Jer. xlviii. 24, where LXX has Καριώθ). The *v.l.* ἀπὸ Καρυώτου occurring several times in Jn shows that at any rate in early times it was understood to contain a place-name; and the objection that *'îš* was not in use in the Aramaic of Jesus' time falls, as names would probably not change with the changes of the language. The alternative suggestion that behind Ἰσκαριωθ is the Latin word *sicarius* ('assassin') is unlikely.

ὃς καὶ παρέδωκεν αὐτόν. On παραδιδόναι see note on i. 14
† and fuller note on ix. 31.

18. THE INTENTION OF JESUS' FAMILY TO
RESTRAIN HIM (iii. 20–1)
(Mk only)

Taylor notes the historic present ἔρχεται, the use of πάλιν, and the double negative, and also the absence of vivid detail as indications that the narrative is Mark's own construction, but regards it as undoubtedly 'based on the best historical tradition'. The primitive Church would certainly never have invented such a thing. The omission of the section in Mt. and Lk. is not surprising: both reverence for Jesus and desire to spare his family would suggest it. Mark's frankness is impressive.

20. οἶκον. Perhaps that of Simon and Andrew in Capernaum (cf. i. 29, ii. 1).

αὐτούς. Presumably Jesus and his disciples (perhaps more than the Twelve, cf. iv. 10; or perhaps only some of them).

ἄρτον φαγεῖν. A Semitic expression for taking food of any sort (cf. e.g. Gen. iii. 19).

For Jesus and his disciples not having time even to eat, cf. vi. 31.

21. οἱ παρ' αὐτοῦ. In Thucydides VII. 10 οἱ παρὰ τοῦ Νικίου = 'the envoys of Nicias', and this is the usual classical significance of οἱ παρά τινος; but οἱ παρά + dative = 'those of someone's household', and rarely in classical Greek οἱ παρά + the genitive denotes someone's 'friends' or 'dependants' (e.g. Xenophon, *Anab.* I. 1. 5). The use of οἱ παρά + genitive for those closely connected with someone is quite common in the Koiné: e.g. Prov. xxxi. 21, I Macc. xi. 73, xii. 27, *P. Grenf.* 36. 9. Here in Mk. iii. 21 it must mean 'his family'; not 'his disciples'—described as οἱ περὶ αὐτόν in iv. 10—for some of them at any rate are actually in the house already. The natural assumption is that οἱ παρ' αὐτοῦ here denotes the same people as are mentioned in *v.* 31, and so includes the mother of Jesus. (The readings of D W it in this verse need not concern us, though they are an interesting indication of the embarrassment of the early Church in face of this verse.)

ἐξῆλθον: 'set out', presumably from their home in Nazareth.

κρατῆσαι. The verb is used in vi. 17, xii. 12, xiv. 1, 44, 46, 49, 51 of 'arresting': here the meaning is similar. His family want to take him into their custody, 'to take control of His actions' (Taylor).

ἔλεγον γὰρ ὅτι ἐξέστη states the reason (γάρ) for their intention. Some explain ἔλεγον as an indefinite plural ('people were saying', 'it was being said'). If that were right, ἐξέστη would be an opinion that was being expressed which was reported to Jesus' family, rather than their own conclusion. But a plural verb can hardly be understood as indefinite when the immediate context contains an obvious plural subject. It is much more likely that the subject is οἱ παρ' αὐτοῦ. ὅτι is better taken as *recitativum*.

ἐξέστη: 'he is beside himself'. The passive and middle and also the second aorist, perfect and pluperfect active of ἐξίστημι are used intransitively, and they are sometimes used both in classical and later Greek (either with some such additional phrase as τῶν φρενῶν or absolutely) in the sense 'to be out of one's mind'. So, e.g., Aristotle has the combination ἐξίσταται καὶ μαίνεται. Cf. II Cor. v. 13.

That Jesus' family should declare him to be out of his mind and should set out from their home with the intention of getting him under their control and restraint (even if there was some element of conscious exaggeration in their ἐξέστη, as there may be in our use of the word 'mad') indicates at least deep misunderstanding of him on their part, and is a striking evidence of that 'hiddenness' or 'veiledness' of the Messiah to which reference has already been made (see on i. 25). It is not necessary, of course, to assume that the dark suspicion reflected in the word ἐξέστη must have originated

in Mary's mind; but at least it is implied that her faith in
Jesus was not strong enough to withstand the determination
of her sons. For their unbelief cf. Jn vii. 5.

19. THE BEELZEBUL CONTROVERSY (iii. 22–30)
(Mt. xii. 22–32, cf. ix. 34; Lk. xi. 14–23, xii. 10)

Taylor divides into two sections: *vv.* 22–6 and 27–30; but
even if *vv.* 27 and 28f. are to be regarded as separate
sayings, it is clear from *v.* 30 that *vv.* 22–30 are at any rate a
single section in Mark's intention. But there is good reason
for regarding *vv.* 27 and 28f. as in their right historical
context (see below).

Mt. and Lk. here follow a different tradition from that
represented by Mk. They both give as the occasion of the
dispute Jesus' healing of a dumb demoniac, which may well
be historically correct. They also insert between the divided
kingdom and house argument and the parable of the strong
man two further sayings: the argument from Jewish
exorcisms (Mt. xii. 27 = Lk. xi. 19) and a saying which
really makes the same point as Mk. iii. 27, though more
directly (Mt. xii. 28 = Lk. xi. 20). And finally they both
give a different form of the saying about the unforgivable
sin from that in Mk.

The whole Markan section seems clearly to be based on
reliable tradition.

22. οἱ γραμματεῖς οἱ ἀπὸ Ἱεροσολύμων καταβάντες. Cf.
the similar expression in vii. 1. They would have greater
prestige and authority than the provincial scribes, from
whom Mark is here clearly distinguishing them. (On
γραμματεῖς see further at i. 22.) It is perhaps implied that
they had come down on purpose to observe the new movement connected with Jesus, which would mean that the
authorities in Jerusalem were already concerned about what
was happening. Καταβαίνω is regularly used in biblical

Greek of journeying from, and ἀναβαίνω of journeying to, Jerusalem or Palestine (e.g. Lk. ii. 51, Acts xxv. 7, 9).

After ἔλεγον Mark gives two charges which they were repeating. (Again ὅτι is better taken in each case as *recitativum*.) The first is that Jesus himself is possessed. With **Βεεζεβουλ ἔχει** cf. πνεῦμα ἀκάθαρτον ἔχει in *v.* 30, and cf. also for the use of ἔχειν in this connection v. 15, vii. 25, ix. 17, Lk. iv. 33, vii. 33, etc., and for the charge of demon-possession made against Jesus Jn vii. 20, viii. 48, 52, x. 20. The name Βεεζεβουλ appears in various forms in Greek MSS. and in the Versions: Βεεζεβουλ in B here and in B and א in Mt. and Lk., Βεελζεβουλ in other Greek MSS., and *Beelzebub* in vg and sy^{s, p}. Of these Βεελζεβουλ must be regarded as the regular form (Βεεζεβουλ being perhaps the common Palestinian pronunciation of it or else due to the strangeness of λζ in Greek, and *Beelzebub* deriving probably from II Kgs i. 2). The most likely explanation of Βεελζεβουλ is that it means 'Lord of the dwelling' (*ba'al* [Aramaic *b^e'ēl*] *z^ebul*), which is supported by the use of the word οἰκοδεσπότης in Mt. x. 25 and perhaps too by the references to οἰκία in Mk iii. 25 and 27 (such punning would be characteristically Semitic). A less probable suggestion is that it is a derisive corruption of the name of the god of Ekron (II Kgs i. 2), 'Lord of dung' (late Hebrew *zibbûl* = 'dung'). Lk. xi. 15 makes Beelzebul 'the prince of the demons', and so probably does the Mt. parallel, xii. 24 (though here the anarthrous ἄρχοντι could mean '*a* prince'); and cf. Mt. xii. 27, Lk. xi. 18f. But perhaps this is due to the merging into one of what in Mk appear as two charges. At any rate, on the lips of the scribes Beelzebul probably signifies simply *a* demon-prince. This is confirmed by the way Mark represents the charge in *v.* 30 and by the fact that Satan is nowhere called Beelzebul in Jewish literature. On Beelzebul see further *T.W.N.T.* I, pp. 605f. (Foerster).

The second charge is that Jesus' exorcisms are effected by

the power of the prince of the demons. For ἐν here cf.
Jn iii. 21 and also Mt. xii. 28; it probably includes the
meanings: 'by the help of', 'in the name of', 'under the
authority of'. The same charge is also reported in Mt. ix.
34, as well as in the parallels to this present verse.

23a. ἐν παραβολαῖς. Παραβολή is here used with
reference to 'the picturesque and allusive maxims which
follow and by which the charge of acting under the power
of the ruler of the demons is rebutted' (Taylor). For
παραβολή see on iv. 2.

23b–27. The argument seems to be as follows: (If I really
cast out demons by the power of the prince of demons, then
it must mean that Satan is actually casting out Satan. But)
how can Satan cast out Satan? [Σαταναν: the demons
represent Satan; they are elements of the corporate personality of Satan.] (To suggest that he does is absurd.) For
[καί at the beginning of *v.* 24 is probably to be explained as
Semitic. It should be translated 'For'. Cf. Hebrew *wᵉ*, e.g.
Gen. xxvi. 27 (R.V.: 'seeing'), Amos ix. 5 (R.V.: 'For'),
Isa. li. 15 (R.V.: 'For'), and see B.D.B. p. 253] a kingdom or
a household divided against itself cannot stand. And if
Satan has really risen up against himself and is divided, then
he cannot stand, but is finished! But (this is obviously not
so—on the contrary Satan is clearly still strong. Therefore
the suggestion that I cast out demons by the power of the
prince of the demons must be false. A quite different conclusion should have been drawn. You should have realized
that) no one can enter the strong one's house and spoil his
goods, unless he first bind the strong one: only when he has
done that will he spoil his house. (The right conclusion to be
drawn from the fact that I cast out the demons is that a
stronger than Satan has come and has bound him.) [There is
a paradox in this argument, the paradox of the strong man
bound by a stronger, yet still strong, to which we shall
return presently.]

In *vv.* 24–6 no distinction of meaning is intended between σταθῆναι and στῆναι.

The argument of *vv.* 23b–27 is suggestive rather than direct—it is indeed ἐν παραβολαῖς. This is particularly true of *v.* 27, where the real point of the parable is only hinted at in a veiled way. It is not a direct claim. With *v.* 27 Isa. xlix. 24f. and liii. 12 should be compared. Had Jesus one or other or both of them in mind? If reminiscence of Isa. liii. 12 is reflected here, then it would be a trace of Jesus' consciousness of being the Servant of the Lord. (Note that the same verse speaks of the Servant's death.) The presence οι allegory in this parable cannot be denied. The ἰσχυρός represents Satan who has taken possession of men and τὰ σκεύη αὐτοῦ represent the hapless victims of his usurping rule, whom he has kept as his chattels (cf. Lk. iv. 18 (αἰχμαλώτοις), xiii. 16). In the figure of the stronger one which is only hinted at in Mk, but explicitly mentioned in the Lk. parallel, the same good news as was announced in i. 15 (ἤγγικεν ἡ βασιλεία τοῦ Θεοῦ) is suggested in a veiled way.

The implication of ἐὰν μὴ πρῶτον τὸν ἰσχυρὸν δήσῃ is, since Jesus is freeing Satan's thralls, that Jesus has already bound Satan. But there is a tension between *vv.* 27 and 23b–26. Jesus has already won a decisive victory (most notably in the Temptation). But this does not mean that Satan's power is finished; on the contrary, the point of *vv.* 23b–26 is precisely that it is still strong. Even after the Cross and Resurrection and Ascension have completed the victory, the power of Satan, though broken, will still be strong. It is the tension between ἔφθασεν ἐφ' ὑμᾶς ἡ βασιλεία τοῦ Θεοῦ (Mt. xii. 28) and ἐλθάτω ἡ βασιλεία σου (Mt. vi. 10), the paradox of Heb. ii. 8. Not till the Parousia will it be resolved.

In the above explanation of *vv.* 22–7 we have treated *v.* 27 as belonging properly to this context. This view of *v.* 27 has however been questioned. So Taylor regards it as originally an independent saying which has been connected with those recorded in *vv.* 22–6 at a very early date (the same association being found both in Mk and in the source used by Mt. and Lk.). But the only real reason for thus separating *v.* 27 from *vv.* 22–6 seems to be that 'the argument is new' (that the theme is the same, Taylor agrees); and this is not at all convincing, for there is no reason why a new argument should not have been used on the same occasion, and, if the explanation above is right, the new argument comes in aptly enough.

28. This and the following verse are often regarded as a separate saying from a different context, since Lk. xii. 10 is placed in a different context. But against this view the following points may be urged: (i) Mt., which appears to reproduce the substance of Mk iii. 28f. in xii. 31, and then in xii. 32 combines that with what looks like a variant tradition of the same saying, anyway supports Mk in connecting this saying with the charge of casting out demons by the prince of demons. (ii) Lk. xii. 10 (i.e. the Lk. parallel to Mt. xii. 32: Lk. has no parallel to Mt. xii. 31) does not seem particularly appropriate in its context. (iii) The appropriateness of Mk iii. 28f. to the context of the scribes' charge that Jesus casts out demons by the prince of demons is clear enough. (iv) Mark, whose general restraint in the matter of connecting links gives him the right to consideration when he makes a definite connection, does connect *vv.* 28f. with *vv.* 22 ff. by the statement of *v.* 30. We are inclined therefore to regard *vv.* 28f. as in its proper historical context.

Αμην. The Hebrew *'āmēn* is used in the O.T. to express (i) acceptance of a commission from a man in the consciousness that it cannot be discharged without God's help (I Kgs i. 36); (ii) acknowledgement of the validity of a threat or curse affecting oneself (Num. v. 22, Deut. xxvii. 15 ff., Neh. v. 13, Jer. xi. 5); (iii) one's will to be associated

with a doxology that has been spoken (I Chr. xvi. 36,
Neh. viii. 6, Pss. xli. 13, lxxii. 19, lxxxix. 52, cvi. 48); and
(iv) as a description of God (Isa. lxv. 16 twice). In uses (i),
(ii) and (iii) it is an adverb meaning 'truly', and in each
case expresses acknowledgement of a word spoken as being
firm and binding. In (iv) it is treated as a noun meaning
'truth', 'faithfulness'. It is from the root *'mn* ('confirm',
'support') from which the words for 'truth', 'faithfulness',
'believe' derive. In Judaism the word *'āmēn* came to be
used a great deal and to have great importance. In the
gospels αμην occurs only on the lips of Jesus (apart from
Mk xvi. 20): Mt., thirty times; Mk, thirteen; Lk., six (Luke
occasionally translates Jesus' *'āmēn* by ἀληθῶς, ἐπ' ἀληθείας);
Jn, twenty-five (always doubled). So it is a highly significant
characteristic of Jesus' speech. It is always followed by λέγω
ὑμῖν (σοι). By its use he solemnly guarantees the truth of
what he is about to say. Jerome, commenting on one
instance of the αμην-formula, says aptly: 'Christ swears: we
ought to believe Christ swearing. For "Amen, amen, I say
unto you" in the New Testament is the equivalent of "As I
live, saith the Lord" in the Old Testament.' See further
H. Schlier in *T.W.N.T.* I, pp. 339–42, who concludes his
discussion suggestively: '...in the ἀμήν before the λέγω ὑμῖν
of Jesus all Christology is contained in a nutshell: He, who
sets up His word as something true (that is, permanent), is
at the same time the One, who acknowledges it and confirms it in His life, and so in turn makes it, once it has been
fulfilled, a demand upon others.'

τοῖς υἱοῖς τῶν ἀνθρώπων: 'men' (cf. Mt. xii. 31: τοῖς
ἀνθρώποις). On the use of the phrase see further at viii. 31.

ἐάν. Here used, as frequently, for ἄν.

The meaning of the verse is clear enough as it stands. No
sin or blasphemy is unforgivable—with the exception of that
which is going to be mentioned in the next verse. (The
suggestion that the original saying had 'son of man' in the

singular, intended generically, i.e. in the same sense as the plural actually has, and that this was by some people misunderstood as the title Son of Man, the mistake giving rise to the version contained in Mt. xii. 32a, Lk. xii. 10a, and by others altered to the plural to avoid misunderstanding, need not concern us here, as anyway it would not involve a different sense from that in Mk.)

29. ὃς δ' ἂν βλασφημήσῃ εἰς τὸ Πνεῦμα τὸ Ἅγιον. What is meant by blasphemy against the Holy Spirit here in this context is plain enough up to a point—and we have seen that there is good reason for thinking it probable that *vv.* 28f. are in their right context: the scribes are blaspheming against the Holy Spirit in that they are attributing to the agency of Satan exorcisms wrought by Jesus in the power of the Holy Spirit. But we must discuss this further in the light of the rest of the verse.

οὐκ... εἰς τὸν αἰῶνα: 'never'; cf. xi. 14.

D W Θ f1ᵖᵗ 22 28 it omit εἰς τὸν αἰῶνα; but it should probably be read—even if it were not, the sense would scarcely be altered in view of the rest of the verse.

ἔνοχος + genitive can mean (i) 'in the power of', 'addicted to' (e.g. Ecclus, Prologue, R.V.: 'addicted to', Heb. ii. 15); (ii) 'guilty of' (e.g. II Macc. xiii. 6, ἱεροσυλίας: classical); (iii) 'liable to' (e.g. xiv. 64, θανάτου). If ἁμάρτημα here means 'sin', we must choose (i) or (ii). But 'eternal sin' is an odd expression—it must mean presumably sin that is so serious as to have eternal consequences—and it is possible that ἁμάρτημα is a mistranslation of an Aramaic word which should have been rendered κατάκριμα (= 'condemnation') (the Aramaic ḥûḇ can mean both 'sin' and 'condemn'). Some support for this explanation is perhaps to be found in the reading κρίσεως in A Cᶜ f1 vg syᵖ,ʰ ς, and it should perhaps be accepted. If so, ἔνοχος will have meaning (iii), and the words can then be translated, 'is liable to eternal damnation'.

The difficulty of this saying, which in the course of church history has been the occasion of untold anguish for many souls, is obvious and our exposition of it cannot be more than tentative.

(i) Attempts to whittle down the severity of the latter part of the verse (οὐκ ἔχει...ἁμαρτήματος), e.g. by suggesting that it is simply hyperbole, are not wise: the note of solemn warning in the teaching of Jesus is too persistent (e.g. ix. 42–8, Mt. xxv. 41–6).

(ii) The distinction between blasphemy against the Son of Man and blasphemy against the Holy Spirit introduced in the Mt. and Lk. forms of the saying should probably be
* interpreted in the light of Heb. vi. 4–8, x. 26–9, I Jn v. 16; but it seems to reflect the loosening of the saying from its original historical context and its application to the problems confronting the early Church, and need not concern us here.

(iii) It is a matter of great importance pastorally that we can say with absolute confidence to anyone who is overwhelmed by the fear that he has committed this sin, that the fact that he is so troubled is itself a sure proof that he has not committed it.

(iv) What is here referred to is not just the uttering of a sentence (the imperfect ἔλεγον in *vv.* 22 and 30 implies at least repetition), but a fixed attitude of mind. (Cf. Calvin: 'Christ did not pronounce this decision on the mere words they uttered, but on their base and wicked thought.')

(v) It is not said that the scribes have actually committed this sin already, and it may be that Jesus' saying is a warning of what they stand in imminent danger of, rather than a pronouncement about a sin of which they are already
† guilty (cf. Taylor).

(vi) At first sight it is not easy to distinguish between the position of the scribes in *v.* 22 and that of Jesus' family in *v.* 21 (the implications of ἐξέστη). We might perhaps look for the difference in the degree of obstinacy with which the attitudes were sustained; but perhaps a more likely clue is to be found in the official position of the scribes. Whereas Jesus' family were ordinary simple people, the scribes were the duly accredited theological teachers of God's people. That Jesus took their position seriously is indicated, e.g., by Mt. xxiii. 2f. As those whose daily business was in the scriptures they were in immediate contact with the living Word of God and therefore with the Holy Spirit (see, e.g., xii. 36, Heb. iii. 7). Moreover, their contact with the Spirit was presumably not purely external; it was not just contact with his work in scripture; for, since the new Israel was not yet separated from the old, they were the leaders of the true people of God, and we may assume that God had not altogether withdrawn the gift of his Spirit from the leaders of his people.

(vii) If in what has just been said we have been following the right clue, then it means that those who most particularly should heed the warning of this verse today are the theological teachers and the official leaders of the churches.

30. Mark's explanatory comment pointing back to *v.* 22.

20. CHRIST'S TRUE KINSFOLK (iii. 31–5)
(Mt. xii. 46–50; Lk. viii. 19–21)

The section has the form of a pronouncement-story. It is most naturally taken to be the sequel to *vv.* 20f. The suggestion of Bultmann that *vv.* 31–4 is an 'ideal scene' invented as a setting for the saying in *v.* 35 is needlessly sceptical. The lack of circumstantial detail is probably due to the interest in the early Church in Jesus' saying about his true kinsfolk and the consequent frequent repetition of the tradition.

31. ἡ μήτηρ αὐτοῦ. The only mention of Mary in Mk apart from vi. 3, though she is probably included in οἱ παρ' αὐτοῦ in *v.* 21. The fact that Joseph is not mentioned here or in vi. 3 probably means that he was dead by this time: his latest appearance in the gospels is Lk. ii. 41 ff.

οἱ ἀδελφοὶ αὐτοῦ. Of the three main explanations of the significance of ἀδελφοί in this connection, (i) the *Helvidian* (Helvidius, *c*. A.D. 380), that they were sons of Joseph and Mary; (ii) the *Epiphanian* (Epiphanius, *c*. A.D. 382), that they were sons of Joseph by a former wife; and (iii) the *Hieronymian* (Jerome, *c*. A.D. 383), that they were cousins of Jesus, sons of Mary's sister, the first is the most simple and probable. The other two are due to the idea of Mary's perpetual virginity. The Helvidian view was held by Tertullian (*adv. Marc.* IV. 29; *de carn. Christi*, 7), and he does not seem to be in any way conscious of departing from the Catholic view in this matter. It is, of course, quite compatible with the doctrine of the Virgin Birth.

ἔξω could perhaps mean on the outskirts of the crowd surrounding Jesus, but more probably means outside the house mentioned in *v.* 20. As the house (perhaps only a one-room cottage) was apparently full of people, the obvious thing to do would be to wait outside and send a message to ask Jesus to come out to speak with them.

στήκοντες: from στήκω, a present formed from the perfect of ἵστημι, and first found in the N.T. (in the LXX it is only an unlikely variant). It occurs again in xi. 25.

32. ὄχλος. Swete notes the absence of the article. This crowd consists at any rate mainly of friendly hearers if not disciples (cf. *v.* 34).

καὶ αἱ ἀδελφαί σου should most probably be omitted with ℵ B C W Θ f1 f13 vg ς. Perhaps an assimilation to *v.* 35 or vi. 3.

33. ἀποκριθεὶς λέγει. This construction occurs for the first time in Mk here. It is due to Semitic usage either directly or as reflected in the LXX. (See further Taylor, p. 63.)

The question Τίς ἐστιν ἡ μήτηρ μου καὶ οἱ ἀδελφοί; prepares the way for the answer which Jesus himself is about to give. It may possibly reflect his disappointment at their lack of sympathy and understanding, as Taylor thinks; but by no means necessarily—for, unless we assume an instance of supernatural knowledge on the part of Jesus, he probably did not yet know at this point what was their purpose in coming. Perhaps it is more likely that his question and the following saying are simply a mild reproof of the too great urgency of those who had brought the message. They are to learn that there is a closer relationship to him than that of kinship.

However, that there was a lack of understanding on the part of Jesus' family is of course not to be disputed: if οἱ παρ' αὐτοῦ in v. 21 means them, that verse is evidence enough. And if these verses are the sequel to vv. 20f., then their purpose in seeking to speak with him reflected their failure to understand him. Taylor argues that this evidence of their lack of understanding is a reason for doubting the truth of the Virgin Birth. But this is not convincing. The brothers would quite likely not have known the peculiar circumstances of Jesus' birth (the knowledge that incredulity would find it only too easy to suggest another—and dishonourable—explanation would probably have led Mary and Joseph to keep that secret to themselves if they possibly could); and, had they heard, they would probably have been incredulous. And the fact of Mary's failure to understand her son is no reason for doubting the truth of his Virgin Birth, which is a pointer to *his* uniqueness, but does not mean that she was not a sinner. We have no grounds for expecting it to have made her for the rest of her life exempt from the possibility of unbelief.

34. περιβλεψάμενος. See on iii. 5.

κύκλῳ. The dative of the noun used as an adverb.

Ἴδε and ἰδού are used by Mark without distinction and about equally often.

35. ὃς ἂν ποιήσῃ τὸ θέλημα τοῦ Θεοῦ brings out clearly the decisive thing. Obedience to God rather than physical relationship binds men close to Jesus. It is not of course that his disciples are perfectly obedient; but they are at least open to God's Word in Jesus; there is in them a beginning of faith and obedience. 'He does not mean', says Calvin, 'that they fulfil, in a perfect manner, the whole righteousness of the law; for in that sense the name *brother*, which is here given by Him to His disciples, would not apply to any man. But His design is to bestow the highest commendation on faith, which is the source and origin of holy obedience....' For this stress on obedience cf. Mt. vii. 21, 24–7 = Lk. vi. 46–9, Lk. xi. 28 (τηροῦντες), Jn xiv. 15, 21, xv. 10, 14, Jas i. 22–7.

οὗτος ἀδελφός μου καὶ ἀδελφὴ καὶ μήτηρ ἐστίν. Christ 'admits all His disciples and all believers to the same honourable rank, as if they were His nearest relatives, or rather He places them in the room of His mother and brethren' (Calvin). Cf. Jn i. 12f., Gal. iii. 26, etc.

It will be convenient to say something at this point by way of introduction to the complex, iv. 1–34, as a whole. That this large block of teaching is composite is fairly certain. For one thing, though *vv.* 10–20 presuppose a different setting from that indicated in *v.* 1, in *v.* 36 Jesus is apparently still in the boat. Moreover, the people addressed in *vv.* 11–20 are 'they that were about him with the twelve' (*v.* 10), i.e. the Twelve plus a wider circle of disciples, but not the multitude; but *vv.* 33f. imply that the preceding parables were addressed to the multitude—though there is no indication of a change of hearers between *vv.* 11 and 33. Again, most of *vv.* 21–5 occurs also in Mt. and Lk. dispersed in other contexts. So it seems probable that we have here a number of originally independent units of tradition which have been brought together in several stages to form a composite discourse.

The initial summary statement (*vv.* 1 f.) provides a setting for the parable of the various soils (*vv.* 3–8), to which a short saying (*v.* 9) is appended. Verses 10–20, which belong to a different setting, seem themselves to be a composite piece. As they stand, *vv.* 11–20 give a double answer to the disciples' question in *v.* 10. Verse 13 (with the singular 'this parable') presupposes a question about the meaning of the particular parable. It looks as if it originally followed *v.* 10. Possibly an original singular 'this parable' in *v.* 10 was altered to the plural in order to facilitate the insertion of *vv.* 11 f. If *vv.* 11 f. were an independent unit of oral tradition, which Mark has inserted into the conversation of Jesus and the disciples about the parable of the various soils, then they may originally have had a wider reference than the parabolic teaching.

Verses 10–20 are followed by a composite section, *vv.* 21–5, made up of two trilogies of sayings, both introduced by the link, 'And he said unto them'. The last saying of the first trilogy is the same summons to attentive hearing as was appended to the parable of the soils (though not in exactly the same form), and the first saying of the second trilogy is similar: 'Take heed what ye hear.' The remaining two sayings in each trilogy are coupled together by the word 'for'; but we must not assume on that account that they were necessarily spoken together originally (they actually occur in Mt. and Lk. in different contexts). The remainder of the complex consists of two more parables (*vv.* 26–9 and *vv.* 30–2) and a summary statement on Jesus' use of parables.

It seems probable that Mark, knowing that there had been an occasion on which Jesus had taught the crowds from a boat on the lake and also that Jesus was in the habit of using parables in his public teaching, decided to mention at this point Jesus' teaching from the boat and at the same time to introduce a collection of representative parables (not only *vv.* 3–8, 26–9 and 30–2, but also *vv.* 21, 22, 24b and 25, are parables in the biblical sense of the word). It is possible that he knew that the parable of the soils had been told on this occasion. Apparently he also knew a tradition of an explanation of that particular parable by Jesus, and decided to insert it (at the same time combining *vv.* 11f. with it) immediately after *vv.* 2–9, thus disturbing (perhaps inadvertently) the unity of scene between *vv.* 1 and 36.

21. THE PARABLE OF THE VARIOUS SOILS (iv. 1–9)
(Mt. xiii. 1–9; Lk. viii. 4–8)

1. πάλιν looks back to iii. 7 and perhaps ii. 13.

πλοῖον. Cf. iii. 9.

ἦσαν. Plural *ad sensum*. The singular (as συνάγεται) would have been more strictly correct.

2. ἐν παραβολαῖς. Translate here 'in parables'. The key to the understanding of παραβολή in the Synoptic Gospels is the use of the Hebrew word *māšāl* in the O.T. and (together with its Aramaic equivalent *mᵉtal, matlā'*) in Rabbinic literature. (In twenty-eight out of the thirty-three times that παραβολή occurs in the canonical books in the LXX it represents *māšāl*.) The term *māšāl* covers a wide range of meanings including the ethical maxim, the short sentence of popular wisdom, proverbs generally, by-word, taunt-song, oracle, riddle, comparison, allegory, fable, in addition to what is meant by 'parable' in the strict sense. Παραβολή in the Synoptic Gospels is simply *māšāl/matlā'* in Greek dress, and discussion of the proper Greek meaning of the word and preconceptions based on the use of the word in classical Greek or of 'parable' in English are irrelevant to the understanding of the gospel usage and positively misleading. Though the word παραβολή has only once before been used in Mk (iii. 23), we have had a number of examples of *mᵉšālîm/παραβολαί*: ii. 17a, 19f., 21, 22, iii. 24, 25, 27. We

shall have more to say about the word itself in connection
with iv. 11, and various points about the parables of Jesus
will have to be discussed in the course of the commentary on
this complex (iv. 1–34). Some suggestions for further reading on the subject of the parables may be mentioned here:
Jeremias, *Parables*, the most important recent book, contains
a full bibliography; Dodd, *Parables*; for a fuller discussion of
Mk iv. 1–20, Cranfield, 'St Mark iv. 1–34' in *S.J.T.* iv,
pp. 398–414, v, pp. 49–66, and of Mk iv. 21–32, 'Message
of Hope' in *Interp.* ix, pp. 150–64.   *

πολλά: 'many things'; here not adverbial.

ἐν τῇ διδαχῇ αὐτοῦ: 'in the course of his teaching'.

3. Ἀκούετε is a request for careful attention. A similar
summons to attentive hearing occurs in vii. 14. With these
cf. the solemn opening of Israel's daily-recited creed, the
Shema (Deut. vi. 4). Another form of challenge to hear,
which is both an appeal to hear aright and at the same time
a solemn warning of the possibility of a wrong hearing,
occurs in *v.* 9 and in *v.* 23, and also [vii. 16]. The fact that the
following parable is both introduced and concluded by an
appeal to hear marks it out as specially important.

σπεῖραι. Infinitive of purpose: cf. on i. 24.

4. For ἐγένετο...ἔπεσεν cf. i. 9.

ἐν τῷ σπείρειν. Cf. Heb. *bᵉ* +infinitive (Moule, p. 174).

ὃ μέν. Ὃς μέν is here used as a demonstrative pronoun
(Moule, p. 125): 'a part', 'some'.

παρά ('by') is perhaps a mistranslation of an ambiguous
Aramaic *'al* which here should have been rendered by ἐπί
('on'). (Cf. Black, p. 120.)

κατέφαγεν. The force of the κατα- is intensive.

5. τὸ πετρῶδες: i.e. the patches where the soil is thin and
the underlying rock near the surface.

7. καρπὸν οὐκ ἔδωκεν. A Semitism (perhaps by way of
LXX, which uses καρπὸν διδόναι to render *nāṯan pᵉrî*). The
ordinary Greek would be καρποφορεῖν or καρπὸν φέρειν.

8. ἄλλα. In the previous verses the seed was thought of collectively, but here the plural directs attention to the individual seeds.

The best explanation of the variants ἄλλο, αὐξανόμενον, αὐξάνοντα, is that first ἄλλα was altered to ἄλλο by assimilation to the previous verses, and that then ἀναβαίνοντα was taken as masculine singular referring to καρπόν, and αὐξανόμενα altered to the singular accordingly.

εἰς…ἐν…ἐν. So B. Textual variants include: εἰς three times (ℵ 28 700), ἓν three times (D f 13ᵖᵗ 565 latt saᵖᵐ ς), ἐν three times (f1 ᵖᵐ). If we read εἰς, ἐν, ἐν, with the Bible Society, we should probably explain the ἐν as ἐν of ratio, and the εἰς as an example of the blurring of the distinction between εἰς and ἐν. On the other hand, it is tempting to read ἓν three times and explain as due to the Aramaic use of ḥaḏ ('one') with multiples (see Black, p. 90; Moule, p. 187).

9. Cf. on *v.* 3.

In view of the doubts entertained by many scholars about the authenticity of the explanation of this parable given in *vv.* 13–20, it is proper to try in the first place to consider the parable by itself without reference to this explanation. Various suggestions have been made about its original purpose. For many the abundance of the harvest in spite of losses is the significant feature; so the parable was told to encourage the disciples in their work of preaching—in spite of the many failures they would have enough success to make their toil abundantly worth while. Others take the point to be that in spite of all present failure and disappointment God's kingdom would certainly come, bringing with it a harvest beyond all expectation. Or the parable is explained in accordance with the theory of 'realized eschatology', according to which the distinctive feature of Jesus' teaching about the kingdom of God was the declaration that it had already come and was present among men in his ministry and the thought of the kingdom of God as something still to come is virtually excluded. On this theory, the parable was intended to counter an objection to the assertion that the kingdom of God had come; to the objection that even the work of the Baptist had not effected that 'restoration of all things' that was expected to precede the Day of the Lord, Jesus replies in effect that one must not allow the presence of some bare patches in the field to blind one to the fact that there is a bumper harvest ready to be reaped.[1] According to another view the key feature is the preponderance of failure over success and the purpose of the parable is to drive home the truth that in this world the Word of God is not generally welcomed.[2] For others the differences of soil are the significant feature, and the parable is a parable about hearing the Word of God.[3]

The last suggestion is surely the most natural. The feature which is emphasized is the fact of the differences of soil. This is the point at which the hearers are challenged to take action: they are summoned to ask themselves which sort of ground they are. The parable indicates the situation of the hearers in the face of the message of the kingdom of God and challenges them to hear the message aright. It is a parable about hearing the Word of God. That is why it is given such prominence—put first in the collection of parables and framed by appeals to attentive hearing. It is in a sense basic to all the other parables, as *v.* 13 hints. On this interpretation the parable was addressed to the multitude.

[1] Dodd, *Parables*, pp. 182f.   [2] So Schniewind.
[3] So A. M. Hunter.

22. THE MYSTERY OF THE KINGDOM OF GOD
(iv. 10–12)
(Mt. xiii. 10–15; Lk. viii. 9f.)

10. See pp. 146–8.

οἱ περὶ αὐτὸν σὺν τοῖς δώδεκα. οἱ περὶ αὐτόν is a phrase Mark uses only here. It could of course by itself denote either the Twelve or the wider circle of disciples. The words σὺν τοῖς δώδεκα are added to make it clear that the subject of ἠρώτων is the larger group.

τὰς παραβολάς. The accusative of the thing about which a question is asked is also found in classical Greek, e.g. Plato, *Rep.* 508A: τὸν ἥλιον γὰρ δῆλον ὅτι ἐρωτᾷς, and *Hipp. Maj.* 289C: ἐρωτηθεὶς τὸ καλόν ('asked about beauty').

11. On the relation of *vv.* 11f. to its context see pp. 146–8.

τὸ μυστήριον. It is often assumed that the use of μυστήριον here is evidence of the influence of Hellenistic religious ideas on the formation of this saying: μυστήριον, it is argued, must mean a mystery which only the initiated are intended to understand, as in the contemporary pagan mystery cults. The saying is then declared to be not an authentic saying of Jesus, but a piece of apostolic teaching. But in the Pauline Epistles the word is used to denote, not something that must not be divulged to the uninitiated, but something that could not be known by men except by divine revelation but that, though once hidden, has now been revealed in Christ and is to be proclaimed so that all who have ears may hear it; and behind Paul's use of it and also its use here we may recognize the O.T. idea of God's *sôd* or 'secret' (e.g. Amos iii. 7, Ps. xxv. 14, Prov. iii. 32, Job xv. 8). The word *sôd* is never translated by μυστήριον in the LXX. In fact μυστήριον is not used in the canonical books in the LXX except in Dan. ii, where it occurs eight times and represents the Aramaic *rāz*. It is however used in the Apocrypha: of a king's secret plan (Tob. xii. 7, 11, Judith ii. 2), of a friend's secret which it is shameful to divulge (Ecclus xxii. 22, xxvii. 16, etc.), of a military secret (II Macc. xiii. 21), and of God's mysteries (Wisd. ii. 22; in xiv. 15, 23 the word is used of heathen religious practices in association with 'solemn rites', a use that clearly reflects the pagan use of the word); and in the other Greek versions of the O.T. it is sometimes used to render *sôd* (e.g. both Symmachus and Theodotion use it for *sôd* in Job xv. 8). It seems as if the earlier translators purposely avoided μυστήριον on account of its pagan religious associations, but that after it had passed into common usage in a neutral sense the later translators came to use it quite freely. (Perhaps this is the explanation of the curious fact that while the LXX does not use μυστήριον in Amos iii. 7, the word is used in the quotation of that verse in Rev. x. 7.) In Rabbinic literature μυστήριον is used as a loanword (*misṭêrîn* or *mistêrîn*).

In view of the above there is no need to appeal to the influence of the mystery cults to explain the presence of μυστήριον here. The idea that God's thoughts and ways are not men's, but that they are his secret, which is not obvious to human wisdom but which he may reveal to those whom he chooses, was familiar to everyone who listened attentively in the synagogue. There was an Aramaic word at hand to express it—the word used in Daniel—and it is probable that that word *rāz* is behind μυστήριον here. * Moreover, the idea is expressed elsewhere in the teaching of Jesus—most obviously in Mt. xi. 25 = Lk. x. 21. (On μυστήριον see also Moule, *Colossians*, pp. 80–3.)

What then is the μυστήριον here? It is the secret that the kingdom of God has come in the person and words and works of Jesus. That is a secret because God has chosen to reveal himself indirectly and in a veiled way. The incarnate Word is not obvious. Only faith could recognize the Son of God in the lowly figure of Jesus of Nazareth. The secret of the kingdom of God is the secret of the person of Jesus.

δέδοται. The passive is a circumlocution to avoid using the divine Name. The meaning is that God has given. The secret of the person of Jesus is not something which men discover by their own insight: it can only be known by God's revelation. Cf. Mt. xvi. 17.

ἐκείνοις... τοῖς ἔξω. Contrasted with the disciples to whom God has given the secret are 'those that are without'. This expression has been held to support the theory of the influence of ideas connected with the mystery cults; but, although οἱ ἔξω is used in classical Greek quite often, no instance of its use to denote 'the uninitiated' has been produced; for that purpose several words are regularly used (ἀμύητος, ἀτέλεστος, ἀβάκχευτος, βέβηλος). It is possible that the phrase may mean quite literally 'those outside (the house in which the disciples are at the moment)'; for 'the house' occurs often in Mk (ii. 1, iii. 20, vii. 17, ix. 28, 33, x. 10) and is the scene of private conversation between Jesus and his disciples. Or it may mean 'those outside the number of the disciples'. The fact that οἱ ἔξω only occurs here in the gospels but occurs four times in Paul (and cf. also οἱ ἔξωθεν in I Tim. iii. 7) is hardly evidence enough to warrant the conclusion that there must be Pauline influence here.

ἐν παραβολαῖς τὰ πάντα γίνεται. This is usually taken as a statement that Jesus uses parables in teaching 'those that are without'; and, if we take vv. 11 f. closely with their context that must be the meaning. But if the saying is treated as independent, παραβολή here can be understood in the sense of 'riddle' (cf., e.g., Pss. xlix. 4, lxxviii. 2, Prov. i. 6, Ezek. xvii. 2, in all of which māšāl (LXX: παραβολή) is clearly synonymous with ḥîdāh = 'riddle', 'dark saying'). We may then translate with Jeremias,[1] 'all things are obscure' (γίνεται being equivalent to ἐστιν, and ἐν παραβολαῖς to an adjective); and the saying ceases to refer particularly to Jesus' parables. The fact that this interpretation gives us a

[1] *Parables*, p. 14.

clear contrasting parallelism between the two parts of *v.* 11 suggests that this probably was the original meaning of the saying. Jeremias' conclusion that the saying was concerned 'with His preaching in general' is supported by λαλῶ in Mt. xiii. 13. But there is nothing in Mk or Lk. to limit the reference to preaching. A wider reference—to Jesus' ministry as a whole—fits the parallelism of the two halves of *v.* 11 better; for the secret of the kingdom of God in the first half is the secret of Jesus' person, works and words, not just of his words. The fact that seeing is mentioned in the quotation in *v.* 12, as well as hearing, is possibly also some support for the wider reference.

12. This verse is dependent on the second member of the antithesis in *v.* 11, and a comma (as in the Bible Society) is required at the end of *v.* 11 rather than a colon (as in R.V.). Isa. vi. 9f. is quoted, in full or in part, not only here and in the Mt. and Lk. parallels but also in Jn xii. 40 and Acts xxviii. 26f. Mk agrees with the Targum of Isa. against both M.T. and LXX in having (i) the third instead of second person plural in Isa. vi. 9; (ii) the verb 'forgive' in place of the verb 'heal' in Isa. vi. 10; and (iii) the passive 'it should be forgiven' (R.V. has passive in Isa. vi. 10, but the M.T. does not). This agreement tells strongly in favour of the authenticity of the saying. Mt. xiii. 14f. reproduces the LXX text. The main difference between Mk iv. 12 and Mt. xiii. 13 is that Mk's ἵνα is replaced by ὅτι. Thus in Mt. the people's spiritual blindness is the reason for Jesus' speaking ἐν παραβολαῖς. Lk. retains the ἵνα of Mk, but greatly abbreviates the quotation.

The stumbling-block here is of course the ἵνα. Various ways of removing it have been suggested. But, though it is true that in the N.T. ἵνα is sometimes equivalent to ὥστε (e.g. Jn ix. 2), that in Rev. xxii. 14 it probably has the force of ὅτι, and that the Aramaic *dᵉ* can serve both as a final conjunction and as a relative pronoun, it is probably wise to

resist the temptation to soften the final clause into a con-
secutive or a causal or a relative. For even if we were to get
rid of the final clause, we should still be up against the
δέδοται in *v.* 11, which implies a corresponding οὐ δέδοται
(in Mt. xiii. 11 it is explicit). Moreover, the ἵνα here is not
a solitary erratic boulder; on the contrary, it reflects the
teleological thinking which is characteristic of the whole of
the Bible, including the Synoptic Gospels.[1] If then the ἵνα
is given its proper final force, its significance is that the fact
that the secret of the kingdom of God, in accordance with
O.T. prophecy, remains hidden from many is something
that is within the purpose of God.

In the last clause μήποτε may be explained in several
ways.

(i) As meaning 'lest' and introducing a further negative
purpose clause dependent on the subjunctives after ἵνα. The
problem then is the same as that involved in the preceding
ἵνα (though possibly it might seem to be raised in a rather
harsher form). 'Lest' is certainly the meaning of the Hebrew
pen in Isa. vi. 10.

(ii) As meaning 'unless', since the Aramaic *dîlᵉmā'*,
which may be presumed to underlie it, can have this
meaning. So Jeremias, who thinks that the *dîlᵉmā'* in the
Targum of Isa. vi. 10 is meant in this sense.[2]

(iii) As meaning 'perhaps', a sense that both *dîlᵉmā'* and
μήποτε can have (μήποτε has this sense as early as Aristotle,
Eth. Nic. 1172 a 33; in the N.T. cf. II Tim. ii. 25). In this
case we should punctuate with a dash or a full stop after
συνιῶσιν. As the reminiscence of Isa. vi. 9f. is anyway free,
this twist to the original meaning is not impossible. If (iii) or
even (ii) is accepted, there is a hint here of a gracious purpose of God beyond the purpose indicated by the ἵνα-clause.

What then is the significance of iv. 11f. as a whole; first,

---

[1] Cf. E. Stauffer in *T.W.N.T.* III, pp. 324 ff.
[2] *Parables*, p. 15.

as an independent saying not specially connected with the parables, and secondly, as set by Mark in its present context?

(i) God's kingly intervention in the person, works and words of Jesus is a secret ($\mu\nu\sigma\tau\acute{\eta}\rho\iota\upsilon\nu$) in the sense that it can only be recognized by a God-given faith ($\delta\acute{\epsilon}\delta\upsilon\tau\alpha\iota$). This secret of the kingdom of God is the secret of Jesus' Messiahship and the secret of his divine Sonship. God's self-revelation is indirect and veiled. (While the eye of faith sees through the veil and grasps the secret, for the unbeliever, so long as he remains an unbeliever, the veil is unpenetrated, and everything is still simply $\dot{\epsilon}\nu\ \pi\alpha\rho\alpha\beta\upsilon\lambda\alpha\hat{\iota}\varsigma$.) No outwardly compelling evidence of divine glory illumines the ministry of Jesus. It is a necessary part of the gracious self-abasement of the Incarnation that the Son of God should submit to conditions under which his claim to authority cannot but appear altogether problematic and paradoxical. In the last hours of his life his incognito deepens until in the helplessness, nakedness and agony of the Cross, abandoned by God and man, he becomes the absolute antithesis of everything that the world understands by divinity and by kingship. But this veiledness is not simply designed to prevent men from recognizing the truth. God's self-revelation is truly revelation; it is precisely *veiled revelation*. Throughout the ministry we can see these two motives (revealing and veiling) at work. On the one hand, Jesus gathers the crowds about him and teaches them, sends out the Twelve to preach, and reveals the power and compassion of God by his miracles. God's self-revelation is not to be accomplished in a corner. On the other hand, Jesus teaches the crowds indirectly by means of parables, seeks to conceal his miracles, and forbids the demoniacs to declare his identity. The two motives, both of which are necessary to the divine purpose, are constantly in tension—a fact which explains some apparent inconsistencies (e.g. between the command $\check{\epsilon}\gamma\epsilon\iota\rho\epsilon\ \epsilon\iota\varsigma\ \tau\dot{\upsilon}\ \mu\acute{\epsilon}\sigma\upsilon\nu$ in iii. 3 and the frequent injunctions to silence).

By this veiled revelation men are placed in a situation of crisis, a separation between faith and unbelief is brought about, and the blindness and sinfulness of men are shown up for what they are. That this judgement (cf. Jn ix. 39) is part of the divine purpose is indicated by the ἵνα in *v.* 12; but it is not the whole purpose of God. His ultimate purpose is salvation, and the latter part of *v.* 12 (μήποτε ἐπιστρέψωσιν καὶ ἀφεθῇ αὐτοῖς) is perhaps to be interpreted, as was suggested above, as hinting at this. God's self-revelation is veiled, in order that men may be left sufficient room in which to make a personal decision. A real turning to God or repentance (ἐπιστρέφειν) is made possible by the inward divine enabling of the Holy Spirit (δέδοται), but would be rendered impossible by the external compulsion of a manifestation of the unveiled divine majesty. The revelation is veiled for the sake of man's freedom to believe.

(ii) Mark by introducing this saying at this point has connected it particularly with the parabolic teaching. The original reference of the saying may well have been much wider, as we have suggested above; but at any rate it is clear that the teaching in parables comes within its scope. While in the case of those who already in some measure believe directness in teaching is appropriate, those who do not yet believe must be taught in an indirect way. (On this see further on *v.* 33.)

23. THE INTERPRETATION OF THE PARABLE OF THE VARIOUS SOILS (iv. 13–20)
(Mt. xiii. 18–23; Lk. viii. 11–15)

Many scholars regard the case against the authenticity of *vv.* 14–20 (i.e. as coming from Jesus himself) as established beyond doubt. It is urged:

(i) That the interpretation allegorizes the parable. Certainly A. Jülicher's attack on the long-established custom of treating the parables as allegories to be interpreted detail by detail[1] marked a real step forward. It effected a liberation from much that was fantastic, for which we must be thankful. It is true, generally speaking, that in a parable of Jesus we have to look for the significant feature that is the point of comparison and that the other details are often put in simply to make the picture life-like. But it is a mistake to make this into a hard and fast rule. To maintain a rigid distinction between parable and allegory is quite impossible in dealing with material originating in Hebrew or Aramaic, languages which have only one word to denote both things. It is true too that there was a strong tendency in the early Church toward allegorization (e.g. Mt. xxii. 1–14 compared with Lk. xiv. 16–24); but it is not safe to assume therefore that all allegorizing must be the work of the early Church. The interpretation cannot be pronounced unauthentic simply on this ground.

(ii) That a parable is meant to illustrate and make plain and therefore cannot itself require an explanation. Jesus' parables, it is said, were all at the time clear enough, but later, partly because, when the original context was forgotten, the parables would seem difficult, partly because of the tendency to allegorize, and partly through the influence of Hellenistic religious ideas, there grew up the idea that they were 'mysteries' needing interpretation and that the interpretation was a matter of esoteric teaching. But the assumption that all Jesus' parables must originally have been obvious takes account neither of the fact that *māšāl/matlā'* can mean a dark, perplexing saying that is meant to stimulate hard thinking; nor of the fact that his parables were not told as illustrations of general ethical principles, as Jülicher imagined, but to point to the significance of the divine act of the kingdom of God, i.e. of his own person and ministry, and of men's situation in face of it. As the truth to which the

[1] In *Die Gleichnisreden Jesu*, I (Tübingen, 1888, 2nd ed. 1899), II (1899).

parables were to bear witness was something that could only be recognized by faith, we should not be surprised to find that they were themselves perplexing even when first uttered. There is nothing improbable in the suggestion that sometimes the disciples asked for, and Jesus gave, an explanation. As a matter of fact, there are only two parables which have an extended interpretation appended (this and the parable of the tares); but Jesus does indicate the interpretation on other occasions (e.g. ii. 17, Mt. vi. 24, vii. 9–11, 24–7, xi. 16–19). Actually Rabbinic parables also sometimes have explanations appended.

(iii) That the interpretation is not consistent and does not fit the parable. It is true that there is a certain looseness of form. In *vv.* 16, 18, 20, the seed is identified with the hearers, though *v.* 14 says expressly that the seed is the word. Jeremias suggests that two distinct ideas—that God's Word is seed (cf. IV Ezra ix. 31) and that men are seed sown by God (cf. IV Ezra viii. 41)—have been mixed together. But it is more likely that what we have here is simply a certain clumsiness or carelessness of expression, for which there are parallels in Rabbinic parables. Cf. Col. i. 6 and Moule's note *in loc.*

(iv) That the concentration on the losses destroys the balance of the parable. It is true that a rather larger proportion of the interpretation than of the parable is given to the losses; but the harvest, being mentioned last, has still most emphasis.

(v) That the interpretation reflects, not Jesus', but the early Church's experience. But the argument that during Jesus' ministry 'there had not yet been time to note the gradual effect of the choking of the seeds by weeds, or even the effect of the scorching sun'[1] is not convincing: the weeds did not require such a long time: we hear in Jn of disciples who walked no more with Jesus and of those who

[1] Lowrie, p. 197.

loved the glory of men above the glory of God (Jn vi. 66, xii. 43). And Jesus seems elsewhere clearly to reckon with the probability of his followers having to face persecution (e.g. viii. 34, 38, Mt. v. 10–12, x. 22f.).

(vi) That the language is not that of Jesus, but of the early Church. Jeremias has an impressive list of words or uses of words which occur nowhere else in the Synoptic Gospels or nowhere in sayings of Jesus, but are common in the rest of the N.T. But the metaphorical use of σπείρειν, ῥίζα, ἄκαρπος, καρποφορεῖν, is natural enough in an explanation of *this* parable; and it is doubtful whether much weight should be placed on the fact that the absolute use of λόγος for the gospel or Word of God is found in sayings of Jesus only here. For other words objected to see below.

(vii) That the interpretation misses the eschatological point of the parable and shifts the stress from the eschatological to the psychological and paraenetic. But this is surely to misunderstand *vv.* 14–20; for the harvest of *v.* 20 is eschatological, not psychological, and the implication of *vv.* 14–20 as a whole is that the seriousness of the question how the Word is received derives from the fact that it is the Word of the kingdom of God that has come near to men in Jesus, and that their final destiny depends on their reception of it.

In view of the above it would seem that, while it would be unwise to claim that the authenticity of *vv.* 14–20 has been proved, it would be equally unwise to assume that the unauthenticity of these verses is an assured result of modern criticism.

13. Οὐκ οἴδατε τὴν παραβολὴν ταύτην may be either a statement or a question. On the singular (contrast the plural τὰς παραβολάς in *v.* 10) see above, p. 147.

καὶ πῶς: 'How then...?' suggests that the parable of the soils is in some sense the key to all the parables.

14. τὸν λόγον. Cf. i. 45, ii. 2, iv. 33. Only in this section is Jesus represented as using 'the Word' absolutely, and here he uses it eight times according to Mk. It is possible that Jesus used some other expression, e.g. 'the gospel' (cf. i. 15, viii. 35) or 'my words' (cf. viii. 38, Mt. vii. 24) or 'the Word of God' (cf. Lk. xi. 28), and that the early Church substituted the later familiar 'the Word'; or that the absolute use did originate with Jesus.

15. In *vv*. 16, 18, 20, the hearers are identified with the seed clearly, while in *v.* 14 the word is identified with the seed: here both identifications are present.

οὗτοι... εἰσιν. Cf. the way in which the parable of Judg. ix. 8 ff. is explained in *Tanhuma*, *wayyērā* 29: 'The trees, these are Israel; the olive, this is Othniel,....'

ὁ Σατανᾶς. See on i. 13.

16. ὁμοίως. 'Similarly'—i.e. by the same principle of interpretation. This is better than the suggestion that it is to be taken like ὡς in iv. 31.

17. πρόσκαιροι. One of the words in this section which are not found elsewhere in the Synoptic Gospels (it occurs elsewhere in the N.T. only in II Cor. and Heb.). According to Jeremias it is a Hellenism for which there is no corresponding Aramaic adjective;[1] but as there is a Syriac adjective *zabnaya* = 'temporary', 'transient',[2] there may perhaps have been a similar adjective in Aramaic. So the presence of πρόσκαιρος does not seem a strong piece of evidence against the authenticity of the interpretation.

θλίψεως... διωγμοῦ. Διωγμός occurs elsewhere in the Synoptic Gospels only in the Mt. parallel and in Mk x. 30; θλῖψις elsewhere in the Synoptic Gospels only in the Mt. parallel and twice in Mk xiii and three times in Mt. xxiv.

διὰ τὸν λόγον is to be taken with γενομένης.

σκανδαλίζονται. The verb σκανδαλίζειν occurs only in biblical Greek and literature influenced by it. It is derived

---

[1] *Parables*, p. 61.
[2] I am indebted to Professor James Barr for pointing this out to me.

from σκάνδαλον, a later form of σκανδάληθρον = 'the stick of a trap on which the bait is set'. The verb occurs only once in LXX in the canonical books (Dan. xi. 41) and there represents the passive (Niph.) of kāšal 'to stumble', 'stagger'. The noun σκάνδαλον in LXX sometimes represents the Hebrew noun mikšôl derived from kāšal—so 'stumbling-block'; but more frequently môkēš (= 'bait', 'lure', and so 'snare'). Σκανδαλίζειν is only used metaphorically, and nearly always means 'to cause to sin', 'lead astray to sin'; occasionally 'to anger', 'provoke'. Here the meaning will be that they allow themselves to be led astray into sin when persecution comes to them on account of the gospel. On σκανδαλίζειν see further Allen, pp. 199-202.

19. The noun μέριμνα occurs only once elsewhere in the gospels—Lk. xxi. 34—apart from the parallels to this verse; ἀπάτη and πλοῦτος occur in the gospels only here and in the parallels. Ἐπιθυμία in the bad sense 'lust' occurs only here in the gospels.

20. παραδέχονται. Perhaps rather stronger than λαμβάνειν, used above in v. 16. Those who are good soil welcome the message and, instead of keeping it on the surface, allow it right into their hearts and lives. Mt. xiii. 23 represents Mark's παραδέχονται by συνιείς ('understand'); Lk. represents it by ἐν καρδίᾳ καλῇ καὶ ἀγαθῇ...κατέχουσιν. Cf. Jas i. 21: δέξασθε τὸν ἔμφυτον λόγον, where the same metaphor is used; also Jn xii. 48 (λαμβάνειν); and Lk. xi. 28 (φυλάσσειν).

ἐν...ἐν...ἐν. See on v. 8. ἐν three times is read here by f1 f13 latt co 𝔖 and is accepted by Taylor.   †

24. THE PARABLE OF THE LAMP AND OTHER
SAYINGS (iv. 21-5)
(Lk. viii. 16-18; with *v*. 25 cf. Mt. xiii. 12)

On the composite nature of this section see above, pp. 146-8.

21. Mt. omits this saying here: both Mt. and Lk. have it elsewhere (Mt. v. 15, Lk. xi. 33). The meaning which the author of Mt. saw in the saying is indicated by the context in which he has placed it; cf. v. 16. Mark has drawn special attention to this saying and the next by his insertion after them of the challenge to hear aright (*v*. 23: cf. *v*. 9): this is probably an indication that he regarded *vv*. 21 and 22, not as proverbial wisdom or moral exhortation, but as containing the mystery of the kingdom of God. The fact that he has placed the saying in this general context points in the same direction. It seems likely then that for Mark the parable had reference to the ministry of Jesus. And it is intrinsically probable that this was also the original reference. (If ἔρχεται belongs to the original form of the parable (at least the Mk form is more primitive than either of the Lk. forms), then perhaps it affords some support for this view; for its use in connection with a lamp is odd, and this suggests the possibility that we should see in its use here an indication that Jesus was thinking of himself and his mission (cf. on ii. 17). If, on the other hand, ἔρχεται is due to Mark, it might at least be a further indication that he understood the parable this way.)

The significant feature of the parable is clearly the contrast between ὑπὸ τὸν μόδιον...ἢ ὑπὸ τὴν κλίνην and ἐπὶ τὴν λυχνίαν. Perhaps the most likely interpretation is: No one in his senses would carry a lighted lamp into a house simply in order to hide it; the intention would rather be to set it on the lampstand. No more must it be supposed that God's whole purpose in sending Jesus is that he should be concealed. He must indeed be rejected and killed, and even after the Resurrection his disciples will have to 'walk by faith, not by sight'; but this painful veiledness will not be for ever, for God's ultimate purpose is that he should be manifest to all. It is on this interpretation a parable of the contrast between 'now' and 'then'. If it was addressed, not just to the disciples, but to the multitude as well, as *vv.* 23 and 33f. suggest that Mark thought, then probably he actually spoke of the kingdom of God, though the veiled reference would still be to himself.

22. It is best to read οὐ γάρ ἐστιν κρυπτόν, and to explain the variants οὐ γάρ ἐστίν τι κρυπτόν and οὐδὲν γάρ ἐστιν κρυπτόν as stylistic improvements. The meaning must anyway be 'for there is nothing hid'. That Mark intended *v.* 22 to be understood closely with *v.* 21 is indicated by γάρ. So, if we were right about the meaning he saw in *v.* 21, the way he interpreted this saying is clear enough. It repeats the idea of *v.* 21, but with the significant difference that, whereas it was not actually indicated there that the lamp is for a while hidden, in this saying there is explicit reference to a period of hiddenness. So this verse serves to correct a possible false impression and to make easier the application of the parable of the lamp to Jesus himself. For a while the kingdom of God is a mystery, concealed under apparent weakness, and this hiddenness (or indirectness of revelation) must not be laid aside before the time. But the present costly hiddenness is for the express purpose of the kingdom's future glorious manifestation.

Note Mark's emphasis on the idea of purpose here—ἵνα four times in two verses, while in Lk. viii. 16f. it only occurs once. What looks like the same saying is also given in two other contexts and with two different meanings in Mt. x. 26 and Lk. xii. 2.

23. Cf. *v.* 9, and note on *v.* 3. In this context it points to the connection between the indirectness of revelation and the fact that faith is only possible where room is left for personal decision. The kingdom is concealed, the revelation indirect, in order to give this room and to make faith possible. This saying seeks to elicit faith. At the same time it presupposes that the possession of the hearing ear is a divine gift.

24. The next saying—Βλέπετε τί ἀκούετε—is also an appeal for spiritual perception. Perhaps a challenge to penetrate beyond the outward forms of what Jesus says— e.g. parables as mere stories—to the message they are meant to impart? (To substitute πῶς for τί, as Lk. viii. 18 does, does not materially alter the sense; for the right way to hear Jesus' teaching is to hear what he means to say.) And, if one hears the Word and recognizes it as such, then one's hearing cannot stop short at hearing, but must become a response of faith and obedience and gratitude.

The next saying (the rest of *v.* 24) is omitted in the Lk. parallel, but is given both in Mt. and Lk. elsewhere. In its Mk context it is natural to understand it in connection with hearing. So perhaps: According to the measure of your response to the Word, so will be the blessing which you will receive from God—or rather God in his generosity will give you a blessing disproportionately large (cf. Lk. vi. 38, and καὶ περισσευθήσεται in Mt. xiii. 12, xxv. 29). The first part of the saying occurs also in Mt. vii. 2, Lk. vi. 38; and the significance it has in Mt. and Lk. is perhaps more probably its original significance: i.e. that in the Judgement God will deal with us according to the way that we have dealt with our fellow men.

25. Given in the same context in Lk. viii. 18. In Mt. xiii. 12 it is placed immediately after the Mt. parallel to iv. 11. It also occurs again in Mt. xxv. 29, Lk. xix. 26. The fact that it is thus present in both of what seem to be different versions of the same parable perhaps indicates at least that it was connected with this parable at an early stage. That may well be its original context, though it might easily have been spoken by Jesus on more than one occasion. Here in Mk its meaning seems to be that to the man who hears the Word, and lets it into his heart and life, an ever-increasing knowledge of the secret of the kingdom will be given; but the man who fails thus to lay hold on the Word will one day lose it altogether. With the first half of the verse cf. *v.* 20, with the latter half *vv.* 15–19.

25. SEEDTIME AND HARVEST (iv. 26–9)
(Mk only)

The suggestion that Mt. xiii. 24–30 is an expansion of this Mk parable has little to commend it. We do not know the historical setting of the parable nor have we any specific indication of its application—only the general formula 'So is the kingdom of God, as if...'. The various interpretations suggested may be roughly classified according as they: (i) take the parable as an allegory, or (ii) direct attention primarily (*a*) to the seed, (*b*) to the period of growth, (*c*) to the harvest, or (*d*) to the contrast between sowing and harvest. Of these lines of interpretation ii (*b*) and ii (*d*) seem most natural. In favour of ii (*b*) it may be said that two out of the four verses are devoted to the period of growth, and each statement of *vv.* 27f. increases the impression that during the period between sowing and reaping the farmer does nothing to help the seed. Taking this line of interpretation, a likely meaning would be that it is without men's assistance that God brings his kingdom. But perhaps ii (*d*) is rather more probable. The fact that this brings the parable into the same pattern of thought as *vv.* 21f. and *vv.* 30–2 is perhaps an indication that Mark at least understood it in this way. And the reminiscence of Joel iii. 13 in *v.* 29 suggests that the harvest is significant for the interpretation, for it lends a certain solemnity to this detail and so serves to emphasize it—and perhaps also hints at the

O.T. associations of harvest. To the development of detail in
vv. 27 f. a delight in dwelling on the pre-eminence of God's
part in the processes of nature may have contributed, as well
as the usual artistic motives which normally led Jesus to fill
out his parables with details not necessary to his actual
purpose. The parable then we take to be a parable of
contrast. As seedtime is followed in due time by harvest, so
will the present hiddenness and ambiguousness of the kingdom of God be succeeded by its glorious manifestation.

26. ὡς. The addition of ἐάν in the Byzantine text is an
obvious grammatical improvement.

βάλῃ. Moule, p. 23, calls this 'a parabolic Subjunctive'
and compares Lk. xi. 5, 6. Bauer (under ὡς, II. 4. c)
regards the construction as intolerable, and suspects that an
ἄν = ἐάν has been lost by accident before ἄνθρωπος. The use
of the aorist here and the present in *v.* 27 is perhaps to be
explained as indicating that, when once the seed has been
sown, the man goes on with his daily routine.

27. νύκτα καὶ ἡμέραν. The order is perhaps Semitic; the
Jewish day begins at sunset. Otherwise it may be explained
as due to the fact that καθεύδῃ has already been put first.

βλαστᾷ: probably subjunctive (βλαστῶ is a by-form of
βλαστάνω).

ὡς here means 'how'.

28. αὐτομάτη. The adjective is here used almost as an
adverb. It occurs only once more in the N.T., in the LXX
six times; in classical Greek it is not specially uncommon.

εἶτεν. The Ionic form of εἶτα, found only here in N.T.,
but not uncommon in the papyri.

πλήρης σῖτος. Perhaps with Taylor we should accept the
reading πλήρης σῖτον as original, as it accounts for the other
readings. Examples of πλήρης treated as indeclinable go
back to the second century B.C.

29. παραδοῖ. A vernacular subjunctive form: cf. δοῖ
(viii. 37), γνοῖ (v. 43). The verb παραδίδωμι is here apparently

used in the sense 'permit', which it sometimes has in classical Greek. It seems hardly necessary to suspect a mistranslation of Aramaic here, as some do.

The last part of the verse is a reminiscence of Joel iii. 13. παρέστηκεν: 'is here'.

26. THE PARABLE OF THE MUSTARD
SEED (iv. 30–2)
(Mt. xiii. 31f.; Lk. xiii. 18f.)

The Mt. parallel seems to be a conflation of the Mk version with that reproduced in Lk. Dodd argues that 'the emphasis on the smallness of the seed is in Mark alone, and is probably intrusive',[1] Mark having interpolated μικρότερον...γῆς in order to indicate the sense in which he understood the parable (according to Dodd, 'the Church is a small affair in its beginnings, but it is the germ of the universal Kingdom of God'[2]). So he proposes to neglect it, and urges that both in Mk and Lk. 'the prevailing idea is that of growth up to a point at which the tree can shelter the birds'. For him then the parable means that 'the time has come when the blessings of the Reign of God are available for all men.... That multitudes of the outcast and neglected in Israel, perhaps even of the Gentiles, are hearing the call, is a sign that the process of obscure development is at an end. The Kingdom of God is here....'[3] But the contrast between the smallness of the seed and the largeness of the plant cannot so easily be pushed aside. Quite apart from the additional words in Mk the idea is present, for mustard seed was proverbial for its smallness (cf. Mt. xvii. 20, Lk. xvii. 6; and see further S.–B. I, p. 669). Moreover in Lk. the hyperbolic δένδρον adequately emphasizes the contrast. This contrast is surely the key feature. This is another parable of contrast. The contrast is not, as is sometimes thought, between the

[1] *Parables*, p. 190.   [2] *Ibid.* n. 1.   [3] *Ibid.* p. 191.

Church's insignificant beginnings and the widely-spread, powerful organization it was to become: it is rather between the present veiledness of the kingdom of God and its future glorious manifestation in the Parousia. To the objection that after all the parable depicts a process of growth Jeremias' answer is sufficient: he points out that, in contrast with modern western man, the men of the Bible did not regard the process of growth by which the seed develops into the mature plant, but rather saw one condition replaced by another by a miracle of divine power; and appeals to I Cor. xv. 35–8, Jn xii. 24, and I Clem. xxiv. 4 f. in support of his statement.[1]

30. Πῶς ὁμοιώσωμεν..., ἢ ἐν τίνι...παραβολῇ θῶμεν; ὡς.... Cf. the opening formulae of Rabbinic parables (given in S.–B. II, pp. 7 f.), especially: 'I will tell you a parable. With what is...to be compared? With (Hebrew *l*ᵉ)....' The subjunctives are deliberative.

31. μικρότερον. Comparative used for superlative, as is common in Koiné Greek.

The parenthesis μικρότερον...γῆς is rather awkward, and may well be Mark's explanatory addition; but even without it the idea of the smallness of the seed is present (see above). The neuter ὄν is due to the connection with σπερμάτων, though properly the participle should rather have been masculine agreeing with ὅς and κόκκῳ. The variant readings are attempts to improve Mark's awkward grammar. The repetition of ὅταν σπαρῇ after the parenthesis is resumptive.

32. ὑπὸ τὴν σκιὰν αὐτοῦ τὰ πετεινὰ τοῦ οὐρανοῦ κατασκηνοῖν. Cf. Ezek. xvii. 23, xxxi. 6, Dan. iv. 12, 14, 21. When at last he comes in his glory, who is himself the kingdom (cf. on i. 15), he will be not only the Judge of all men, but also the one under whose shadow all who have truly trusted in him will find shelter.

κατασκηνοῖν (so spelt in B: other MSS. have -οῦν) means

[1] *Parables*, pp. 90 f.

probably not 'perch', but 'nest' (cf. W. Michaelis, 'Zelt und Hütte im biblischen Denken' in *Ev. Theol.* xiv, pp. 29–49). So in Mt. viii. 20 = Lk. ix. 58 κατασκηνώσεις means 'nests'.

27. SUMMARY STATEMENT ON THE USE OF PARABLES (iv. 33 f.)

(Mt. xiii. 34 f.)

33. τοιαύταις παραβολαῖς πολλαῖς. Mark gives only a small selection of the parabolic teaching.

ἐλάλει. . τὸν λόγον. See on ii. 2.

αὐτοῖς: i.e. to the multitudes (cf. Mt. xiii. 34: τοῖς ὄχλοις). The disciples would also hear, as 34b suggests.

καθὼς ἠδύναντο ἀκούειν. Calvin commenting speaks of Christ 'accommodating Himself to their capacity' and adopting 'a method of teaching which was proper and suitable to hearers, whom He knew to be not yet sufficiently prepared to receive instruction', and then goes on to suggest that his purpose in employing parables was 'to keep the attention of His hearers awake till a more convenient time', in the meantime allowing them 'to remain in a state of suspense'. Had he spoken to the crowds in a direct way, he would have forced them to make a final decision at once, and that decision could only have been a decision of unbelief and rejection. Instead he spoke to them in an indirect way, thus engaging and maintaining their interest, and summoning them to decision without compelling them to make a final decision immediately. The parabolic teaching was at once a judgement pronounced upon their unpreparedness for the kingdom of God and also the expression of divine mercy that desires to spare and save. (See further T. F. Torrance, 'A Study in New Testament Communication' in *S.J.T.* iii, pp. 298–313; A. Schlatter, *Die Evangelien nach Markus und Lukas* (Stuttgart, 1947), p. 45.)

34. χωρίς. . .παραβολῆς οὐκ ἐλάλει αὐτοῖς does not mean

that Jesus never spoke to the crowds except in parables like that of the mustard seed or the good Samaritan; but that what he addressed to them was consistently indirect and veiled.

κατ' ἰδίαν: 'privately'. Cf. vi. 31, 32, vii. 33, ix. 2, 28, xiii. 3; and also iv. 10.

ἐπέλυεν. 'Επιλύω means primarily 'to loose', 'untie'. It only occurs once more in the N.T.—in Acts xix. 39, where R.V. translates: 'settle'. The noun ἐπίλυσις occurs in II Pet. i. 20, and there means 'interpretation' or 'explanation'. So here the verb means 'expound'. The crowds would understand that Jesus was talking about the kingdom of God: what they would not grasp would be the relation of the kingdom of God to his person (cf. on v. 11).

28. THE STORM ON THE LAKE (iv. 35-41)
(Mt. viii. 23-7; Lk. viii. 22-5)

The narrative is probably Petrine. The details 'at once vivid and artless' (Taylor) suggest the reminiscence of an eyewitness: the precise statement of time, the expression ὡς ἦν, the reference to other boats, the mention of the cushion, the disciples' rough question, and Jesus' severe rebuke of them. Suggestions that the story is to be traced to the influence of Ps. lxxxix. 9 or cvi. 9 or Jonah are, in the face of this evidence, improbable. It is surely clear that the narrative reflects the actual memory of something that happened and the significance that the disciples at the time saw in it. Whether we accept as historical their interpretation or prefer a rationalistic explanation (e.g. that the ceasing of the storm just after Jesus' words was a coincidence) will depend on our attitude to the miracles generally. For a general discussion of the miracles see the concluding note on i. 29-31.

35. ἐν ἐκείνῃ τῇ ἡμέρᾳ ὀψίας γενομένης. Since it is not characteristic of Mark to add such details, it seems likely that they were contained in his source.

Διέλθωμεν. The verb normally means 'to pass through' (of journeys on land). In I Cor. x. 1 it is used of passing through the sea in the sense of passing between the walls of water. Here 'cross over'. The subjunctive is hortatory: the initiative is taken by Jesus. Possibly his purpose was to escape the pressure of the crowds, or to find a new sphere of ministry.

εἰς τὸ πέραν: i.e. to the eastern side of the lake.

36. ἀφέντες. Perhaps with Taylor we should follow D W Θ 𝔭⁴⁵ f 13 it sy^p sa in reading ἀφίουσιν and inserting καί before παραλαμβάνουσιν, and explaining ἀφέντες as a stylistic correction of an original Semitic parataxis.

παραλαμβάνουσιν. In vii. 4 the verb is used of receiving tradition (cf. I Cor. xi. 23, xv. 1, etc.); here, as in v. 40, ix. 2, x. 32, xiv. 33, of taking someone with one.

ὡς ἦν—'as he was'—perhaps means 'without going ashore'. Cf. iv. 1.

καὶ ἄλλα πλοῖα ἦν μετ' αὐτοῦ: '...we hear no more of them. This detail, so unnecessary to the story, is probably a genuine reminiscence' (Taylor).

37. The Lake of Galilee is notorious for its sudden storms. See further Smith, *Hist. Geog.* pp. 441 f.

ἐπέβαλλεν. The intransitive use of the active of ἐπιβάλλω is found in classical as well as later Greek.

That εἰς here means 'into' is indicated by the following clause.

38. ἦν and καθεύδων are better taken together as a periphrastic tense than as in the R.V. Apparently Jesus is weary after a day's teaching. For his weariness cf. Jn iv. 6.

ἐν τῇ πρύμνῃ ἐπὶ τὸ προσκεφάλαιον. Only in Mk. It suggests the vivid reminiscence of an eye-witness. For ἐπί + accusative of place where, without any idea of movement, cf. Jn xii. 15, II Cor. iii. 15, etc. It is found also in classical Greek. The προσκεφάλαιον is perhaps a rower's cushion, but the article rather suggests that it is the only one on board— perhaps a cushion kept for the seat of honour in the stern.

Διδάσκαλε. See on i. 21 (ἐδίδασκεν).

οὐ μέλει σοι ὅτι ἀπολλύμεθα; A definite reproach, softened in Mt. into a prayer, in Lk. into a statement implying a request for help (though this form of reproach does occur in Lk. x. 40). The rudeness of the Mk form, which is no doubt more original, is an eloquent pointer to the messianic veiledness—the Son of God subject to the rudeness of men.

39. διεγερθείς. R.V.: 'he awoke, and' is correct, as against the A.V.: 'he arose, and'.

ἐπετίμησεν. See on i. 25. In Ps. cvi. 9 (cf. civ. 7), Isa. l. 2, Nah. i. 4, the Hebrew root *g'r* is used of God rebuking the sea. So Jesus is here said to rebuke the wind. There is no need to infer that either Jesus or Mark thought of a demon of the wind.

καὶ εἶπεν τῇ θαλάσσῃ. Calvin comments: 'not that the lake had any perception, but to show that the power of his voice reached the elements, which were devoid of feeling'. So too in xi. 14 he is represented as addressing the fig tree. Cf. the divine Word in creation (Gen. i).

πεφίμωσο. The perfect imperative passive (which is rarer) is more emphatic than the aorist used in i. 25: so 'be silent and remain so'. For the verb see on i. 25.

καὶ ἐκόπασεν ὁ ἄνεμος, καὶ ἐγένετο γαλήνη μεγάλη. That this was regarded by the disciples as the direct result of Jesus' rebuking the wind and commanding the sea to be silent is clear from *v.* 41.

40. πῶς οὐκ (probably we should rather read οὔπω with ℵ B D L Θ f1 f13 *al* lat co) ἔχετε πίστιν; As in ii. 5, πίστις here means faith in God's helping power present and active in Jesus. It is misleading to contrast, as Taylor does, 'faith in God' and 'confidence in the wonder-working power of Jesus'; for the faith in God here referred to is not to be separated from the person of Jesus. Schniewind is nearer the truth when he says in commenting on this verse: 'Thus faith in Jesus coincides with faith in God', and compares

Jn xiv. 1. The force of οὔπω (or πῶς οὐκ) here is that they should by this time have learned something of the secret of the kingdom of God (iv. 11), which is the secret that the kingdom is come in the person and work of Jesus. (However, if by 'wonder-working power' Taylor means the power to do all sorts of things independently of God, then of course it is true that faith in such a power is not referred to here; for the N.T. nowhere suggests that Jesus' miracles were wrought independently of God.)

This is the first of the series of rebukes of the disciples by Jesus for their lack of faith and understanding (cf. vii. 18, viii. 17f., 21, 32f., ix. 19).

41. ἐφοβήθησαν φόβον μέγαν. See on i. 22 (ἐξεπλήσσοντο).

ἔλεγον: 'they began to say'. They have an inkling of the secret of the kingdom of God. For those who are beginning to have faith—though it is still exiguous—the miracle is an effective pointer in the direction of the truth. In ὑπακούει there is the idea of the ἐξουσία of Jesus (cf. i. 27).

In addition to the miracle's significance as a pointer to the secret of Jesus' person Mark probably saw in it, and meant his readers to see, a symbolic significance (see on i. 31). The parallel between the situation of the disciples on the lake and that of the Church in the midst of persecution would naturally suggest itself. (Very early a ship was a symbol of the Church in Christian art.) In the midst of persecution and all manner of perils, if Jesus be truly with his Church, then, even though his help may not at once be felt, his own must never doubt him, and need have no fear.

29. THE GERASENE DEMONIAC (v. 1–20)
(Mt. viii. 28–34; Lk. viii. 26–39)

The vividness of the narrative and the amount of detail suggest that here we are close to an eye-witness account. Quite probably derived from Peter.

1. **Γερασηνῶν.** So ℵ* B D latt sa. There are two variants: ℵᶜ L Θ f1 28 33 *al* syˢ bo, etc. have Γεργεσηνῶν; A C f13 *pm* ς have Γαδαρηνῶν. In all three Synoptic Gospels the MSS. and versions vary between these three readings, Γερασηνῶν being the best attested in Mk and Lk., Γαδαρηνῶν in Mt. Here in Mk it is clear that Γαδαρηνῶν is an assimilation to Mt., while Γεργεσηνῶν is apparently a Caesarean correction traceable to Origen. The most likely explanation seems to be that Mark wrote 'Gerasenes' with reference to a town by the lake (whose name may be preserved in the modern Kersa or Koursi on the eastern shore), but that early readers mistook this for a reference to the well-known Gerasa. Since this Gerasa was some thirty miles from the lake, it was natural that improvements should be attempted: hence the variants. Gadara was a not unreasonable guess, but, being six miles from the shores of the lake, is hardly likely (though it was near enough for the land between it and the lake to be called 'the country of the Gadarenes'). Origen was right in seeking a site by the lake but wrong in connecting it with the Girgashites mentioned in the O.T. At Kersa the shore is level, but about a mile further south there is a fairly steep slope within about forty yards of the shore. (See further Lagrange, pp. 132–6; Dalman, *S.S.W.* pp. 177–9.)

2. **ἐξελθόντος αὐτοῦ...αὐτῷ.** A clumsy use of the genitive absolute with reference to a person otherwise mentioned in the sentence, such as is common in late Greek but is not classical. Luke correctly puts the participle into the dative in agreement with αὐτῷ.

εὐθύς should perhaps be omitted with B W it syˢ⋅ ᵖ.

For ἐν πνεύματι ἀκαθάρτῳ see on i. 23.

3. This and the next two verses (for the most part peculiar to Mk) vividly suggest the man's wretchedness and the brutal treatment he had suffered.

ὃς τὴν κατοίκησιν εἶχεν ἐν τοῖς μνήμασιν. For the use

of tombs as dwellings cf. the LXX version of Ps. lxviii. 6 (LXX: lxvii. 6). Often in Palestine tombs were caves, which would afford shelter. (Cf. also Job xxx. 6, Heb. xi. 38.) For Jews tombs were of course unclean, but this man was probably a Gentile, as *v.* 20, and the fact that the people of the place kept pigs, suggest.

4. For διὰ τό+infinitive cf. iv. 5; but here the construction indicates not the reason for something, but circumstances mentioned by way of explanation; γάρ+indicative would have been more natural.

The string of perfect infinitives vividly suggests the explanations given by the townsfolk.

5. διὰ παντός: 'continually' (χρόνου understood) is found in classical Greek, and is 'common in papyri as in biblical Greek in place of the obsolescent ἀεί' (M.M., p. 146).

On the order νυκτὸς καὶ ἡμέρας see on iv. 27.

6. Picks up the story that has been interrupted by *vv.* 3–5. What was there baldly summed up in ὑπήντησεν is now related in more detail. To see any inconsistency between *vv.* 2 and 6 is unnecessary.

προσεκύνησεν. Here 'fell on his knees before': cf. προσέπιπτον in iii. 11, and also γονυπετῶν in i. 40.

7. Τί ἐμοὶ καὶ σοί; See on i. 24.

Υἱὲ τοῦ Θεοῦ. See on i. 24 and iii. 11.

Ὕψιστος (= Hebrew *'elyôn*) is used in the O.T. mainly by non-Israelites to denote the God of Israel (e.g. Gen. xiv. 18ff., Num. xxiv. 16, Isa. xiv. 14, Dan. iii. 26, iv. 2; cf. I Esdras ii. 3, and in N.T. Acts xvi. 17). (See further J. A. Montgomery, *Daniel* (Edinburgh, 1927), pp. 215f.)

ὁρκίζω σε τὸν Θεόν. 'I adjure thee by God.' Omitted in Mt. and softened in Lk.

μή με βασανίσῃς. For the demon's fear of punishment cf. i. 24. The punishment referred to is probably eschatological—so Mt. viii. 29 (πρὸ καιροῦ) understands it.

8. Apparently Mark's own explanatory insertion. Cf. vi.

52. The imperfect ἔλεγεν is probably best explained as equivalent to a pluperfect: cf. v. 28, vi. 18, and most clearly Acts ix. 39. It is implied that the demon was not compelled to obey Jesus at once.

τὸ πνεῦμα τὸ ἀκάθαρτον. The nominative is used instead of the vocative: cf. *v.* 41, Lk. xviii. 11, etc. (Moule, pp. 31 f.).

9. Cf. Gen. xxxii. 27, 29. In the ancient world it was considered of the utmost importance to know the correct name of an adversary. In exorcizing it was thought that knowledge of the true name of the demon gave one power over it. If it is the demon's name that Jesus is asking, then this sort of idea would presumably be present. (On the other hand, it is just possible that he is asking the man's name with the purpose of recalling him to a consciousness of his own identity in distinction from that of the demon or demons inhabiting him; but this is hardly likely.)

Λεγιών. The Latin word *legio* found its way into Hellenistic Greek and into Aramaic. A Roman legion numbered from 4000 to 6000 men. Does the answer express the man's sense of being possessed by a whole host of demons (the name being suggested perhaps by the memory of having seen a Roman legion on the march)—a pathetic indication of his loss of all sense of his own identity? Or is it an evasive answer—the demons wishing to conceal their true names?

10. It is better to take the subject of παρεκάλει to be the man rather than the demons; for, while it is true that the neuter δαιμόνια (understood) could take a singular verb, Mark uses the plural with reference to them in *vv.* 12 f. (cf. ἐσμεν in *v.* 9), and similarly plural verbs are used in iii. 11 (in [xvi. 9] a singular verb is used with δαιμόνια, as is usual in Lk.). But in any case it is the man who actually speaks, though he is regarded as the mouthpiece of the demons.

πολλά. Adverbial, as in i. 45.

ἵνα: giving substance of command or request (cf. iii. 9).

ἔξω τῆς χώρας. The belief that demons were associated with particular districts was widespread.

11. πρὸς τῷ ὄρει: 'on the hill'. πρός+dative used of locality should indicate proximity, but here it can hardly mean anything but 'on'. It is very rare in the N.T. (see Moule, p. 54).

χοίρων. The presence of pigs indicates that the area was mainly pagan.

12. παρεκάλεσαν. Swete comments perhaps rightly: 'The spirits at length dissociate themselves from the man, for they know that their hold over him is at an end, and the plural is consequently used.' The aorist is used here to indicate a particular request in contrast with the repeated request (παρεκάλει) in v. 10.

ἵνα εἰς αὐτοὺς εἰσέλθωμεν. It is probably better to regard this simply as an example of redundancy of style than to explain it as an instance of the imperatival use of ἵνα (for which reference may be made to Moule, pp. 144f.).

That they should actually ask to be sent into the swine may perhaps be a sign of their brokenness. Calvin suggests tentatively that their purpose may have been 'to excite the inhabitants of that country to curse God on account of the loss of the swine'.

13. The verse bristles with difficulties. Some would be rid of them by regarding the story as a piece of Palestinian folk-magic that has been fathered on to Jesus, an unedifying legendary accretion. Others rationalize it in various ways: e.g. the man in the paroxysm accompanying his cure rushed at the swine and frightened them, or they were startled by the approach of strangers. The fact that the actions indicated by ἐξελθόντα and εἰσῆλθον were not seen, but inferred, makes such rationalizing tempting. We should not care to rule out dogmatically the possibility that a measure of sober rationalizing might be in place here. But, supposing we are right (see on i. 23) in suggesting that there may be more in

the N.T. view of the demons than has for some time been
generally allowed, we must then take seriously the possibility that Jesus permitted real demons to enter the herd of
swine, and the question 'Why?' becomes pressing. One
might possibly suppose that he did not foresee the destruction of the swine, but this seems hardly likely. What then if
he did foresee it? It is wise with Calvin to acknowledge that
we cannot know with certainty why Jesus consented; but it
might well have been for the sake of reassuring the man, that
he allowed the demons to enter the swine and to carry out
their malicious prank (for which cf. ix. 22). If Jesus judged
that to grant their request was the most effective way of
assuring the man of the reality of his liberation, then we
may suppose that, even if he knew what would become of
the swine, he would—although none of God's creatures is
to be destroyed needlessly or thoughtlessly—count one man
as of more value than many swine.

14. εἰς τὴν πόλιν. See above on *v.* 1.

ἀγρούς: here and in vi. 36, 56 'hamlets' (for other
examples see Bauer, *s.v.*).

ἦλθον: indefinite plural.

15. τὸν δαιμονιζόμενον. The description, no longer true,
reflects the townsfolk's point of view. Contrast the perfect
participle used later in the verse.

'The three participles, καθήμενον, ἱματισμένον, and
σωφρονοῦντα describe features which must immediately have
struck the attention of the beholders' (Taylor). Previously
even chains had not been able to control his demonic energy
and restlessness; now he sits at rest. He had been naked like
a beast; now his human characteristics are restored. It is
likely that Mark saw in the contrast a vivid picture of conversion. Cf. Calvin: 'Though we are not tormented by the
devil, yet he holds us as his slaves, till the Son of God
delivers us from his tyranny. Naked, torn, and disfigured,
we wander about, till He restores us to soundness of mind.'

ἐσχηκότα. To be explained as an aoristic perfect (see further M.H. i, pp. 143 ff.), but rendered in English by the pluperfect—'who had had'—as the aorist participle δαιμονισθείς in *v.* 18 should also be. (See also Moule, pp. 13-16.)

ἐφοβήθησαν. See on i. 22 (ἐξεπλήσσοντο).

17. The pathos of their request no doubt struck Mark and would be meant to strike his readers. Offended, it seems, by the loss of their property, they ask Jesus to leave them.

18. ἐμβαίνοντος αὐτοῦ...αὐτόν. See on *v.* 2.

ἵνα. See on *v.* 10.

With ἵνα μετ᾽ αὐτοῦ ᾖ cf. ἵνα ὦσιν μετ᾽ αὐτοῦ (iii. 14). He would accompany Jesus. The desire was natural—the result of gratitude and also perhaps of reluctance to remain where his past was known.

19. τοὺς σούς. 'A circle wider than the man's family is indicated' (Taylor).

ἀπάγγειλον. Contrast with i. 25, 44, iii. 12, v. 43, vii. 36, viii. 26 (see on i. 25). Was it because the man was a Gentile and would be among Gentiles that there was not the same need to damp down the effect of the miracle as among Jews, among whom he was working continuously? (The explanation of Wrede that the command to go home and tell his own people what God (not Jesus) had done for him was tantamount to a command to secrecy about Jesus, and that the man was disobeying Jesus by proclaiming publicly through Decapolis what Jesus (rather than God) had done, is unconvincing.)

ὁ Κύριος: i.e. God (cf. Lk. viii. 39: ὁ Θεός). Jesus' miracle is the expression of God's pity.

Strict grammar would require ὡς before ἠλέησεν, but Mark makes ἠλέησεν loosely dependent on ὅσα.

The perfect πεποίηκεν denotes action the effects of which remain; but whether the aorist ἠλέησεν really has a different nuance (as Lagrange and Taylor, following M.H. i, p. 143, maintain) is perhaps doubtful in view of the fact that no occurrence of a perfect active of ἐλεῶ seems to be known.

For many of the Gospel's readers from the early days onward Jesus' command to the restored demoniac has been a summons to their own difficult and costly vocation.

20. κηρύσσειν. See on i. 4.

τῇ Δεκαπόλει. Decapolis was the territory of a league of free Greek cities, originally at any rate ten in number, under the protection of the Roman governor of Syria. According to Pliny the Elder the cities were Damascus, Raphana, Dion, Canatha, Scythopolis, Gadara, Hippos, Pella, Gerasa and Philadelphia.

ὁ Ἰησοῦς: instead of ὁ Κύριος, i.e. the God of Israel, as Jesus had commanded (v. 19).

καὶ πάντες ἐθαύμαζον. See on i. 22 (ἐξεπλήσσοντο).

30. JAIRUS' DAUGHTER AND THE WOMAN
WITH AN ISSUE OF BLOOD (V. 21–43)
(Mt. ix. 18–26; Lk. viii. 40–56)

The combination of the two narratives is probably not an artificial intercalation of one narrative into another in order to indicate the lapse of time, but due to historical recollection. In view of Mark's restraint with regard to connecting-links, the preparation for vv. 25–34 in v. 24 and the backward link in v. 35 must be taken seriously. Both narratives read like first-hand accounts, and it is reasonable to suppose that both are Petrine.

21. On the grammar of διαπεράσαντος τοῦ Ἰησοῦ...ἐπ' αὐτόν see on v. 2.

ἐν τῷ πλοίῳ. Possibly we should omit with 𝔓⁴⁵ D Θ f1 28 it syˢ.

πάλιν is placed immediately before συνήχθη in ℵ* D 565 700 and also in 𝔓⁴⁵, which omits εἰς τὸ πέραν. This has the

effect of connecting πάλιν with συνήχθη rather than διαπεράσαντος, and is accepted by Lagrange, Taylor.

εἰς τὸ πέραν here presumably means to the west side of
the lake, perhaps to the neighbourhood of Capernaum on
the N.W. shore.

22. On εἷς = τις see Moule, pp. 125, 176; Bauer, *s.v.* 3.

ἀρχισυναγώγων. The word is used (in addition to this
passage) in Lk. viii. 49, xiii. 14, Acts xiii. 15, xviii. 8, 17.
Cf. ἄρχων τῆς συναγωγῆς in Lk. viii. 41, and ἄρχων in
Mt. ix. 18, 23, Lk. xviii. 18. The ἀρχισυνάγωγος (Hebrew *rō'š
hakkᵉneset*) was the lay official responsible for the super-
vision of the synagogue building and the arrangements
for the services, but the designation was sometimes used
as an honorary title for distinguished members of the
synagogue.

ὀνόματι Ἰάειρος. Omitted by D *a d ff² i r¹* and not reproduced in Mt. Possibly, but by no means certainly, it should
be omitted.

The name Jair occurs in the O.T.: e.g. Num. xxxii. 41,
Judg. x. 3f. In Esth. ii. 5 the LXX uses the Hellenized form
that we have here. The suggestion that the name was chosen
for its symbolic appropriateness to this story (*Yā'îr*='he
enlightens' or *Yā'îr*='he awakes') is most unlikely, for it is
not Jairus who either awakens or is awakened!

πίπτει πρὸς τοὺς πόδας αὐτοῦ. See on i. 40 (γονυπετῶν). In
his anxiety for his daughter he forgets his dignity and takes
the position of a suppliant before Jesus.

23. παρακαλεῖ. παρεκάλει should perhaps be read with
B W Δ Θ f1 f13 *s*. A copyist would tend to assimilate this to
the neighbouring historic presents.

ἐσχάτως ἔχει. A colloquial expression for being 'at
death's door'.

ἵνα...ἐπιθῇς. An example of imperatival ἵνα (Moule,
pp. 144f.): 'please,...lay...'.

For Jesus' laying his hands on the person to be healed cf.

vi. 5, vii. 32, viii. 23, 25. The action is common in ancient stories of healings.

σωθῇ: Σώζω is quite often used in the sense 'heal'.

24. συνέθλιβον αὐτόν (cf. θλίβωσιν in iii. 9) prepares the way for the narrative in *vv.* 25–34.

25. This and the next two verses contain an example of something very rare in Mk, a long sentence built up by means of subordinate participial clauses. Cf. xiv. 66f., xv. 42f.

οὖσα ἐν ῥύσει αἵματος. See Lev. xv. 25–30, according to which this complaint renders a woman unclean so long as it lasts. For the ἐν see on i. 23. For a similar use in classical Greek see Sophocles, *Ajax*, 271.

26. ὑπό: here 'at the hands of'.

τὰ παρ' αὐτῆς: 'her wealth'; cf. Lk. x. 7, Phil. iv. 18 (also the masculine in Mk iii. 21).

27. τὰ περὶ τοῦ Ἰησοῦ. Either 'the reports concerning Jesus' (so Taylor—and this suits ἀκούσασα well), or else 'the deeds of Jesus' or 'the events in which Jesus had been concerned' (cf. Lk. xxiv. 19, 27, Acts i. 3, xviii. 25, Phil. ii. 20, in none of which can τὰ περί + genitive mean 'the report concerning'). If the latter alternative is right, we have an accusative with ἀκούω of the thing about which the person hears (cf. xiii. 7).

ἐν τῷ ὄχλῳ ὄπισθεν. Her desire for secrecy was dictated, not only by natural modesty, but by the fact that her complaint made her permanently ritually unclean so that she would be generally shunned.

28. ἔλεγεν. Here = 'she (had) thought' (so Mt. ix. 21: ἐν ἑαυτῇ). Cf. *'āmar* in Hebrew, e.g. Gen. xx. 11, xxvi. 9, Num. xxiv. 11. For her idea that if she touched Jesus she would be healed cf. iii. 10.

29. ἡ πηγὴ τοῦ αἵματος αὐτῆς. The phrase comes from Lev. xii. 7.

ἴαται. The perfect indicates that the consequences remain.

30. εὐθύς. As in *v.* 29 Mark stresses the immediacy.

τὴν ἐξ αὐτοῦ δύναμιν ἐξελθοῦσαν. The participle is dependent on the verb of perceiving (ἐπιγνούς). The words need careful translation. ἐξ αὐτοῦ qualifies δύναμιν; it does not go with ἐξελθοῦσαν. So trans. with R.V.: 'that the power *proceeding* from him had gone forth'.

At first sight it might seem as if the power here referred to is thought of as being something physical and impersonal—rather like an electric charge—which is transferred by contact automatically, independently of Jesus' will; for he apparently perceives only after the event and then does not know the person whom the power has affected. But there is nothing here inconsistent with the fact that the power residing in, and issuing from, Jesus is the personal power of the personal God. Though Jesus does not himself make a decision (at least so it seems) in this case, nevertheless God does. God controls his own power. He knows about the woman and wills to honour her faith in the efficacy of his power active in Jesus, even though her faith is no doubt very imperfect and indeed dangerously near to ideas of magic. The cure does not happen automatically, but by God's free and personal decision.

Τίς μου ἥψατο τῶν ἱματίων; A good many earlier commentators (including Calvin) think that Jesus knew all the time who had touched him, and asked simply to make her confess her faith. It is more likely that he did not know, and sought the information, not because he wished to make the miracle conspicuous—which would be inconsistent with his injunctions to secrecy—but because he desired to draw away from his clothes to himself an imperfect faith which was seeking his help apart from a personal relationship with himself.

31. The disciples' disrespectful protest (softened by Luke, and omitted in Mt.) is evidence of the reliability of the source Mark is using.

32. περιεβλέπετο. See on iii. 5.

τὴν τοῦτο ποιήσασαν. The use of the feminine does not imply that Jesus knew that it was a woman who had touched him, but reflects the viewpoint of the narrator.

33. φοβηθεῖσα καὶ τρέμουσα, εἰδυῖα ὃ γέγονεν αὐτῇ. Both participial clauses describe the circumstances of the actions denoted by ἦλθεν, προσέπεσεν, and εἶπεν. In Lk. viii. 47 the woman's realization that she had been found out is stressed: Mark does not mention it. Nor does he indicate why she was afraid (the words διὸ πεποιήκει (πεποίηκεν) λάθρα added after τρέμουσα in D Θ 28 pc a ff² i r¹ are clearly an insertion). The prospect of being discovered, the possibility that Jesus might be angry, and the nervous strain she had undergone, probably all contributed; but perhaps the words εἰδυῖα ὃ γέγονεν αὐτῇ provide a hint of what may have been an even more important cause of her fear—her realization that a miracle had been wrought upon her (cf. on i. 22, ἐξεπλήσσοντο).

34. Θυγάτηρ. So B D W: the great majority of MSS. have the vocative, but the nominative should no doubt be read. For the nominative used instead of vocative cf. vv. 8, 41, Lk. xviii. 11, etc.

πίστις. See concluding note on i. 29-31.

σέσωκεν. See on iii. 4. For Mark and his original readers there was probably here a *double entendre*: the religious sense of σώζω being suggested as well as the sense, 'heal'.

ὕπαγε εἰς εἰρήνην. Probably a Septuagintalism. It corresponds to the Hebrew *lᵉkî lᵉšālôm* (e.g. I Sam. i. 17), a formula of leave-taking. As such it 'is capable of bearing the meaning which the speaker puts into it' (Taylor). So on Jesus' lips it has a fullness of meaning derived from his person. (Cf. the openings and endings of N.T. letters, where traditional forms are explicitly filled out with Christian meaning. See Moule, *Colossians*, pp. 153-5.)

ἴσθι ὑγιὴς ἀπὸ τῆς μάστιγός σου. 'From this exhortation we infer that the benefit which she had obtained was fully ratified, when she heard from the lips of Christ what she had already learned from experience: for we do not truly, or with a safe conscience, enjoy God's benefits in any other way than by possessing them as contained in the treasury of His promises' (Calvin).

35. ἀπὸ τοῦ ἀρχισυναγώγου: 'from the ruler of the synagogue's *house*'—for they are actually addressing the ruler of the synagogue.

ἀπέθανεν. The aorist used where the perfect (as in Lk. viii. 49, but not in 52f.) would seem more natural; the meaning is not 'died', but 'is dead'. (See Moule, pp. 10ff.)

σκύλλεις is here used in the weakened sense that it came to have: so 'trouble'. Originally it meant 'flay'.

36. παρακούσας. The verb means 'to hear beside'; and so it comes to mean both 'overhear' and 'hear carelessly', so 'pay no need to'. The R.V. takes it here in the latter sense ('not heeding'), which is the sense the verb has in Mt. xviii. 17, the only other place where it occurs in the N.T.; but, while either meaning is possible here, it is better (*pace* Taylor) to accept the guidance of the Lk. parallel, which has ἀκούσας, and take it in the sense of 'overhear'.

Μὴ φοβοῦ. Generally, μή + the present imperative is used to tell someone to stop doing something he is already doing, μή + the aorist subjunctive to tell someone not to begin to do something. See Moule, pp. 135f., and M.H. i, pp. 122–6.

μόνον πίστευε. The present imperative is here used correctly to denote continued action. Not a single act, but a steady attitude, of faith is called for. It is perhaps rather suggested that the father has already shown faith by coming to Jesus—now he must go on believing.

37. See below on *v.* 40.

That the father also accompanied Jesus goes without saying, and is implied by the sequel.

For these disciples as the inner circle of the Twelve cf. ix. 2, xiv. 33, and (with the addition of Andrew) xiii. 3.

38. καὶ κλαίοντας καὶ ἀλαλάζοντας πολλά explains
θόρυβον, to which it is in apposition: '(people) both weeping
and wailing much' (this seems better than to take the καί
before κλαίοντας as = 'and'). The variant readings (substitution of genitive of the participles by D, and the omission of
the first καί by some MSS.) are attempts to make the sentence
smoother.

Many think that the people referred to are professional
mourners (cf. αὐλητάς in Mt.), but perhaps in view of the
shortness of the time since the child's death it is more likely
that members of the household are intended.

39. εἰσελθών. It is not clear whether it is the courtyard
or the actual house that Jesus enters at this point (Lk.
parallel is explicit: τὴν οἰκίαν), but at any rate this entering
is clearly distinguished from the further entering (presumably into the room where the girl lies) in v. 40.

οὐκ ἀπέθανεν ἀλλὰ καθεύδει. What did Jesus mean by
'sleeps'? C. H. Turner et al. maintain that, if Mark's
account is taken by itself, the natural interpretation is that
Jesus is saying that the girl is not dead, but in a coma. On
this view the miracle is reduced to a penetrating diagnosis
that saved the girl from being buried alive. But Taylor
rightly points out the objections to the view that Jesus
meant 'is in a coma': (i) Mark implies that Jesus has not yet
seen the girl; (ii) Jesus does not on other occasions state a
medical diagnosis. These objections—even though with
regard to (i) Mark's silence is not conclusive—are serious.

Then did Jesus mean simply that, though the child is
dead, yet, since God will one day raise her up, her death is
not without hope but is a sort of sleep? But, if Jesus meant
this, (i) one would have expected the hearers to understand
what was a quite ordinary idea for any who were influenced
by Pharisaic teaching (cf. Genesis Rabba on Gen. xlvii. 30:
'Thou shalt sleep, but thou shalt not die'): instead they
mocked (κατεγέλων); (ii) it is hard to see why he should put the

people forth and go into the girl's room accompanied only by the parents and the three disciples. It is more natural to take the words to mean that, though she is dead, yet, since he is going to raise her up, her death will be no more permanent than a sleep. See further on *v.* 42.

For Mark no doubt the words had also—besides their particular significance in this context—a general significance, as a reminder to Christians that death is not the last word but a sleep from which Christ will wake us at the last day, and therefore a rebuke to those who in the presence of death behave as those that have no hope.

40. κατεγέλων αὐτοῦ. Presumably because they understood his words in a literal sense but knew for a fact that she was dead. (This is more probable than that they understood him to mean that he would raise her, and disbelieved his power to do so.)

ἐκβαλὼν πάντας. With this and also *v.* 37 cf. the silencing of the demons and the injunctions to secrecy in connection with miracles (see on i. 25, and cf. *v.* 43 below; cf. also on iv. 11f.). Since the miracle Jesus was about to work was going to be a superlative one—one that actually pointed toward the final resurrection itself—it was particularly important to take such precautions. (His own resurrection was of course different, since in his case the final resurrection itself was accomplished—and no human eye at all was allowed to witness it.)

παραλαμβάνει τὸν πατέρα τοῦ παιδίου καὶ τὴν μητέρα καὶ τοὺς μετ᾽ αὐτοῦ. That there might be witnesses of the miracle, since, though the miracles are not meant to be compelling proofs, they are nevertheless signs to faith? Respect for Jewish sense of propriety (since the dead was a girl) is also a possible motive.[1]

εἰσπορεύεται ὅπου ἦν τὸ παιδίον. Apparently Jesus now sees her for the first time.

[1] Cf. A. Oepke in *T.W.N.T.* i, p. 784.

41. κρατήσας τῆς χειρός. Cf. i. 31.

Ταλιθα κουμ. A transliteration of Aramaic *ṭelîṭā' ḳûm*, of which the first word is the feminine of *ṭalyā'* (= 'lamb' or 'youth') and the second is the Mesopotamian form of the imperative 'arise'. A D Θ f 13 *pm* lat sy^p, h ς have the Palestinian form of the feminine imperative *ḳûmî*. It is not at all clear which form Mark wrote. (Lagrange, Taylor prefer κουμ; Lohmeyer κουμι.) The suggestion that this use of the Aramaic words has something to do with the fact that the use of foreign words is a feature of ancient miracle-stories is most unlikely—the fact that they are translated tells against it, and also the fact that Mark elsewhere retains original Aramaic words (iii. 17, vii. 11, 34, xi. 9f., xiv. 36, xv. 22, 34), but only on one occasion (vii. 34) in connection with a miracle. The explanation is rather that the original words were remembered and valued as being the actual words used by Jesus on a memorable occasion.

42. ἀνέστη...καὶ περιεπάτει: 'stood up and walked about' (note the correct use of tenses).

The specially strong expression used later in this verse to indicate the witnesses' amazement suggests strongly that Mark believed that the girl had been dead. That Mt. and Lk. imply that she was dead is clear. But was she really? An absolute proof either way is obviously impossible. But the evidence for Jesus' having raised the dead is rather stronger than Taylor indicates in his introduction to this narrative;[1] for in addition to this narrative and Lk. vii. 11–17 and Jn xi. 1–46 there is also the highly significant passage common to Mt. and Lk., Mt. xi. 4–6 = Lk. vii. 22–3, which has the words νεκροὶ ἐγείρονται, which are not found in the O.T. passages it recalls. Thus references to Jesus' raising the dead are contained not only in Mk and the material special to Lk.; there is a reference also in the material common to Mt. and Lk. Moreover, to be weighed against the diffi-

[1] P. 286.

culties of accepting the historicity of Jn xi. 1–46 is the not inconsiderable difficulty of believing that the Fourth Evangelist would call in question his own insistence on the importance of history by inventing such a narrative to illustrate a theological truth. See also the concluding note on i. 29–31.

ἦν γὰρ ἐτῶν δώδεκα looks like the sort of detail that someone who was present would remember: her age may well have been mentioned at the time.

ἐξέστησαν...ἐκστάσει. In the LXX the dative of a cognate noun is used with a verb to represent the infinitive absolute used with a finite verb in Hebrew (e.g. Gen. ii. 16f.). In the N.T. cf., e.g., Lk. xxii. 15, Jn iii. 29, Jas v. 17. (See Moule, pp. 177f.)

For the expression of amazement see on i. 22 (ἐξεπλήσσοντο).

43. For the injunction to secrecy see on i. 25. In reply to the often expressed view that this case shows the artificiality of Mark's motif of secrecy, since so remarkable a miracle could not be kept secret, it may be said that μηδείς should not be taken to imply that Jesus thought it was possible to keep the matter absolutely private, but simply that Jesus wanted it kept as private as possible—no one was to know about it who need not. There was at least a chance of avoiding unnecessary publicity. And if immediate publicity were avoided, the news when it was no longer fresh would cause less excitement when it did get round.

καὶ εἶπεν δοθῆναι αὐτῇ φαγεῖν. A vivid detail. The practical thoughtfulness of Jesus was remembered.

31. THE REJECTION AT NAZARETH (vi. 1–6a)
(Mt. xiii. 53–8; cf. Lk. iv. 16–30)

Bultmann's suggestion that the narrative is an ideal scene constructed by the primitive Palestinian community out of the saying which has come down to us in the Oxyrhynchus Papyri (see Huck, p. 18) is rightly rejected by Taylor. The section contains elements which it is particularly hard to imagine the early Church's inventing: the statement in *v.* 5, the reference to Jesus' kinsfolk in *v.* 4 which was discreditable to people who had come to be prominent in the Church, and probably also the designation of Jesus as 'son of Mary'. These guarantee that we have here reliable historical tradition.

1. ἐκεῖθεν with a verb of motion is used as a connecting-link between sections four times in Mk (here and vii. 24, ix. 30, x. 1). In view of this rareness and Mark's general restraint in introducing connections, it is probable that he at least had reason to suppose that the incident recorded in *vv.* 1–6a followed those recorded in v. 21–43, though other incidents may have intervened. The matter is particularly interesting, since in both Mt. and Lk. the rejection at Nazareth is placed in different contexts. The Mt. context does not differ so widely from the Markan; but Lk. has an independent account of a rejection at Nazareth at the very beginning of the Galilean ministry (iv. 16–30). On the whole it seems likely that Lk. iv. 16 ff. refers to the same incident as Mk vi. 1–6a = Mt. xiii. 53–8 (though it is strange that in Mk and Mt. there is no hint of the violence reported in Lk. iv. 28 f.). The Lk. context is clearly less probable. Lk. iv. 23 b betrays its artificiality. It was probably because it seemed a particularly significant frontis-piece for the account of the ministry of Jesus that Luke decided to place the narrative of the rejection in this setting.

τὴν πατρίδα αὐτοῦ. In neither Mk nor Mt. is Nazareth mentioned here, but presumably it is meant. That Nazareth is referred to as Jesus' πατρίς is not inconsistent with the tradition of his birth in Bethlehem; it was natural enough to use the term of the place where he was brought up.

καὶ ἀκολουθοῦσιν αὐτῷ οἱ μαθηταὶ αὐτοῦ. A detail dropped in Mt., but important for Mark, because in this part of the gospel he is concerned with their training. Their Master's rejection by his fellow townsmen was a valuable lesson for them, could they but grasp it.

2. For Jesus' teaching in the synagogue cf. i. 21 ff., 39, iii. 1 ff.

οἱ πολλοί. See on i. 34. Jeremias is probably right in thinking that the meaning here is 'all who were present' (cf. Lk. iv. 22: πάντες), though οἱ πολλοί can also mean 'the majority' (e.g. in Mt. xxiv. 12 the meaning 'all' is clearly impossible) and conceivably might here.

ἐξεπλήσσοντο. See on i. 22. The surprise here recorded was about to issue in incredulity and a σκανδαλίζεσθαι.

Πόθεν κ.τ.λ. While it is true that Lk. iv. 16 ff. appears to depict a developing crescendo of hostility, there is little justification in the text of Mk for the view that there is a perceptible change of tone between *vv.* 2 and 3, and surely not enough to warrant the suggestion that two different traditions have here been fused.[1] The passive participle δοθεῖσα is not necessarily an admission that the wisdom has been given by God: it is possible that some such dark suspicions as those mentioned in iii. 22 were not far away. On δυνάμεις see the concluding note on i. 29–31.

διὰ τῶν χειρῶν αὐτοῦ probably does not refer specially to the part played by his touch (e.g. i. 41), but simply reflects Semitic idiom.

3. The people of Nazareth know Jesus according to the flesh; but their very familiarity with him is a hindrance to knowing him truly, for it makes it all the more hard for them to see through the veil of his ordinariness.

[1] Schmidt, *Rahmen*, p. 155.

ὁ τέκτων, ὁ υἱὸς τῆς Μαρίας is read by all uncials, many minuscules, it (some MSS.) vg^w sy^{p,h} sa bo (most MSS.), except that some omit τῆς. But 𝔭^{45vid}, with support from f13 and also from it, attests ὁ τοῦ τέκτονος, ὁ υἱὸς τῆς Μαρίας, while some MSS. attest ὁ τοῦ τέκτονος, υἱὸς Μαρίας. Other authorities (including 33^{vid} 69 700 al it (a number of MSS.) vg (some MSS.) bo (some MSS.)) attest ὁ τοῦ τέκτονος υἱὸς καὶ (τῆς) Μαρίας. One of these readings with τοῦ τέκτονος is implied by Origen's statement in reply to Celsus that nowhere in the gospels current in the Churches is Jesus described as an artisan. Mt. here has ὁ τοῦ τέκτονος υἱός; οὐχ ἡ μήτηρ αὐτοῦ λέγεται Μαριαμ...; (while Lk. iv. 22 has οὐχὶ υἱός ἐστιν Ιωσηφ οὗτος;). We thus have a collection of textual evidence which it is extremely difficult to weigh. The crucial question is this: Is it easier to account for an original (A) ὁ τέκτων, ὁ υἱὸς τῆς Μαρίας in Mk being altered by Mt. to ὁ τοῦ τέκτονος υἱός; οὐχ ἡ μήτηρ αὐτοῦ λέγεται Μαριαμ...; (by Lk. to υἱός...Ιωσηφ), and by a copyist of Mk to ὁ τοῦ τέκτονος (ὁ) υἱὸς (καὶ) (τῆς) Μαρίας; or for an original (B) ὁ τοῦ τέκτονος (ὁ) υἱὸς (καὶ) (τῆς) Μαρίας in Mk being reproduced in Mt. as ὁ τοῦ τέκτονος υἱός; οὐχ ἡ μήτηρ αὐτοῦ λέγεται Μαριαμ...;, altered to υἱός...Ιωσηφ in Lk. and by a copyist of Mk to ὁ τέκτων, ὁ υἱὸς τῆς Μαρίας?

If (A) was original, then Mt. and Lk. might have altered it because they felt that the idea of Jesus himself being a carpenter might be offensive to Gentile readers (we know that Origen in replying to Celsus felt it important to show that Jesus was not himself a carpenter; and, before that, Lk. had dropped the word τέκτων altogether, whether of Jesus or of Joseph) and/or because ὁ υἱὸς τῆς Μαρίας seemed derogatory—tantamount to a charge of illegitimacy. And the alteration of Mk can be explained as assimilation to Mt., the καί before (τῆς) Μαρίας in some MSS. being due to conflation of Mt. with the original Mk reading. On the other hand, if (B) was original in Mk, the Mt. and Lk. texts present no difficulty; but what about the alteration of the

Mk text? Was it in the interests of the doctrine of the Virgin Birth? But, as both Mt. and Lk. (the gospels which clearly express that doctrine) are content that the people of Nazareth should call Jesus the son of the carpenter (of Joseph), this explanation seems unlikely. Besides, the altera-tion, if made with this motive, would be stupid; for anyway Jesus would have been the legal son of Joseph (cf. Lk. iii. 23: ὡς ἐνομίζετο), so that for the people of Nazareth to speak of Jesus as the son of Joseph would be in no way incompatible with the Virgin Birth's being historically true.   †

It seems therefore more probable that the original reading in Mk was ὁ τέκτων, ὁ υἱὸς τῆς Μαρίας and that Origen's denial is to be explained as due either to a lapse of memory on his part or, more probably, to his accepting a text of Mk that was assimilated to Mt. As to Taylor's objection that it was 'contrary to Jewish custom to describe a man as the son of his mother, even when the father is no longer living, except in insulting terms (cf. Judg. xi. 1 f.), and it is im-probable that Mark, and still less the Nazarenes, were familiar with the Virgin Birth tradition', it seems quite likely that rumours to the effect that Jesus was illegitimate did circulate and that Jn viii. 41, ix. 29, and the Jewish material given in S.-B. 1, pp. 39–43 (cf. Origen, *contra Cels.* 1. 28) reflect not just later Jewish polemic against the doctrine of the Virgin Birth but a charge actually made during Jesus' lifetime. It seems probable that what is after all the better attested reading in Mk reflects these rumours and accusa-tions and so is an important piece of evidence in support of the historicity of the Virgin Birth, though of a sort that the Church would naturally tend to avoid.

τέκτων. In the N.T. only here and in Mt. xiii. 55. Some-times used of masons and smiths (it is so understood by some of the Fathers in connection with Jesus or Joseph); but its proper meaning is 'carpenter' and it probably has that meaning here. The Jews (in striking contrast with the Greeks and Romans) had a high regard for manual work (cf. S.-B.

ii, pp. 10f.); and the Jewish attitude received its final confirmation in the fact that Jesus himself was a manual worker.

ἀδελφός. On the brothers of Jesus see on iii. 31. James is mentioned often in the N.T. (Acts xii. 17, xv. 13, xxi. 18, I Cor. xv. 7, Gal. i. 19, ii. 9, 12: Jas i. 1, Jude 1, are uncertain); the others (apart from Judas, if Jude 1 refers to him) are mentioned by name in the N.T. only here and in the Mt. parallel; but Paul refers to the brothers of Jesus in the plural in I Cor. ix. 5.

καὶ οὐκ εἰσὶν αἱ ἀδελφαὶ αὐτοῦ ὧδε πρὸς ἡμᾶς; might possibly suggest that Mary and the brothers were no longer resident in Nazareth, but the words need not imply this. The sisters are mentioned nowhere else in the N.T. except in the Mt. parallel. It may be that they never became Christians. By this time they were probably married women.

ἐσκανδαλίζοντο ἐν αὐτῷ. See on iv. 17. For σκανδαλίζεσθαι ἐν cf. Mt. xi. 6 = Lk. vii. 23, Mt. xxvi. 31, 33. Cf. also Rom. ix. 32 f., I Pet. ii. 6-8, Jn ix. 39. The meaning here is not just that they were provoked by him; there is also present the idea that to reject Jesus is to turn away from God.

4. The sentiment of this saying may be illustrated by numerous parallels both Jewish and Gentile; but, as these are not couched in terms of 'a prophet', we are hardly justified in calling the saying a 'common proverb' (Taylor), though it certainly is an aphorism. While it is by no means equivalent to a direct application of the title 'prophet' to himself, it perhaps does imply that he regarded the term as expressing a certain measure of the truth about himself.[1] That many of his contemporaries thought of him as a prophet is of course clear.

The reference to kinsfolk is omitted in Mt. xiii. 57, Lk. iv.

---

[1] But on the question of Jesus' attitude to the term 'prophet' as applied to himself see the interesting discussion in Barrett, *H.S.G.T.* pp. 94-9.

24, Jn iv. 44; its presence in Mk is perhaps one more sign of the priority of Mk, for the tendency would be to omit something discreditable to Jesus' family.

συγγενεῦσιν is used instead of the more regular συγγενέσιν —probably on the analogy of the dative of γονεύς.

5. οὐκ ἐδύνατο ἐκεῖ ποιῆσαι οὐδεμίαν δύναμιν. A bold statement, which, like xiii. 32, is unlikely to have been invented by the primitive community. It is toned down by Mt. (Lk. has no parallel to 5 f.). Mt. xiii. 58 rightly explains the οὐκ ἐδύνατο by reference to the ἀπιστία of the people. The point of οὐκ ἐδύνατο is not that Jesus was powerless apart from men's faith, but that in the absence of faith he could not work mighty works *in accordance with the purpose of his ministry*; for to have worked miracles where faith was absent would, in most cases anyway, have been merely to have aggravated men's guilt and hardened them against God.

εἰ μὴ ὀλίγοις ἀρρώστοις ἐπιθεὶς τὰς χεῖρας ἐθεράπευσεν states an exception to what has just been said. Did these few have faith? Or did Jesus sometimes in his freedom make exceptions to his normal practice of only working such miracles where there was at least *some* response of faith?

6a. ἐθαύμασεν. Only here and in Mt. viii. 10 = Lk. vii. 9 is θαυμάζειν used of Jesus. He marvels at the *Gentile* centurion's faith: here he marvels at the lack of faith of those who most of all ought to have had it. It does not necessarily imply that he expected something different—though he may have done so.

32. THE SENDING OUT OF THE TWELVE (vi. 6b–13)
(Mt. ix. 35, x. 1, 9–11, 14; Lk. ix. 1–6)

The narrative part of the section (i.e. *vv.* 6f. and 12f.) seems to be Mark's own construction, a framework for the two excerpts from the tradition of mission charge sayings. No doubt Mark thinks of these sayings as not only of historical interest but also relevant to the life of the post-Ascension church. On the historical question of the Mission of the Twelve see below.

6b. This can be taken either with *vv.* 1–6a or with what follows. If taken with *vv.* 1–6a, it describes the outcome of the rejection at Nazareth; if taken with what follows, it gives the background of the Mission of the Twelve. The latter alternative is probably to be preferred.

7. προσκαλεῖται. See on iii. 13.

ἤρξατο αὐτοὺς ἀποστέλλειν. The time of their preliminary training is over; further training will follow their return (related in *v.* 30).

δύο δύο: 'two by two', 'in pairs'. The repetition is perhaps due to Semitic influence (cf., e.g., Gen. vii. 9; and also the similar repetition in Mk vi. 39f.); but it is not necessarily un-Greek, as there is an example in a fragment of Sophocles (see Moule, p. 182). The normal Greek expression would be κατὰ δύο or, as in Lk. x. 1, ἀνὰ δύο.

The going in pairs reflects Jewish custom: cf. xi. 1, xiv. 13, Lk. vii. 18, Jn i. 35, the arrangement of the names of the apostles in pairs which is stressed by Mt. x. 2–4 alternating comma and καί, and in Acts Paul's working with Barnabas, and then with Silas. For Rabbinic examples see Schlatter,
* *Evang. Matt.* pp. 325 f. Cf. also Deut. xix. 15, Eccles. iv. 9–12.

ἐδίδου. It is unlikely that the imperfect is meant to imply that the authority was given to different pairs successively. Both Mt. and Lk. have the aorist.

The statement that he gave them authority over the unclean spirits Taylor finds difficult 'because in ix. 18 the disciples were not able to cast out a spirit, and in Lk. x. 17 the seventy speak of the casting out of demons in the name of Jesus as though it had been unexpected. Moreover, while M has δαιμόνια ἐκβάλλετε (Mt. x. 8), the Mission Charges in Q and L do not mention exorcism.' But (i) the implication of ix. 14–29 is not that they could not cast out the spirit because they had never been given authority, but that they tried to do it expecting to succeed because they had been given authority and had had successes, and then failed (see *in loc.*); (ii) Lk. x. 17 may equally well be explained on the assumption that they had been given authority, but were nevertheless excited at their successes; and (iii) too much weight should not be placed on the absence of a reference to exorcism in Lk. x. 1–16, particularly if (ii) is right and if x. 17–20 actually implies that they had been given such authority.

8. For ἵνα here see on iii. 9.

εἰ μὴ ῥάβδον μόνον. This exception is peculiar to Mk. In both Mt. x. 10 and Lk. ix. 3 the staff is expressly forbidden. See below on *v.* 9.

μὴ ἄρτον. They are not to take provisions with them, but to rely on hospitality.

πήραν. Perhaps a 'begging-wallet' (one was part of the equipment of a Cynic preacher) rather than just a 'knapsack'.

εἰς τὴν ζώνην. It was customary both in the east and the west to keep small change in one's girdle.

9. ἀλλὰ ὑποδεδεμένους σανδάλια. The construction changes to accusative and infinitive, the infinitive (perhaps πορεύεσθαι) having to be understood. σανδάλια is an internal accusative after ὑποδεδεμένους. In Mt. x. 10 and Lk. x. 4 ὑποδήματα, which are not to be distinguished from σανδάλια, are forbidden. As with the staff (in *v.* 8) the stricter version is probably original, Mark having modified it in view of western conditions.

μὴ ἐνδύσησθε δύο χιτῶνας. The *v.l.* ἐνδύσασθε (B* 33) should perhaps be read: both the subjunctive ἐνδύσησθε and the infinitive ἐνδύσασθαι being explicable as corrections of the unusual μή + aorist imperative. Whereas Mt. x. 10 and Lk. ix. 3 refer to taking a change of underwear, this apparently forbids wearing one χιτών over another, for which luxurious custom Bauer cites some references (Mk xiv. 63 is not an example, for there the plural denotes 'clothes' generally).

T. W. Manson has suggested, appealing to (*M*) *Ber.* ix. 5 ('He may not enter into the Temple Mount with his staff or his sandal or his wallet'), that perhaps the implication of the most primitive form of the charge is that the mission is a sacred undertaking comparable with worship in the Temple.[1] At any rate the rigour of these prohibitions implies that the mission was extremely urgent. The message the Twelve were charged with was (to judge from *v.* 12: cf. Mt. x. 7, Lk. x. 9) in essence the same as that which Jesus preached (i. 15: cf. Mt. ix. 35): it was a call to repentance in view of the nearness of the kingdom of God. Since God's kingdom was near, and indeed actually in the midst of the men of Israel of this generation, the summons to repent was extremely urgent; but this does not mean that Jesus necessarily expected the coming of the Son of Man in glory within a matter of weeks or months (see on xiii. 29, xiv. 7). The particular instructions apply literally only to this brief mission during Jesus' lifetime; but in principle, with the necessary modifications according to climate and other circumstances, they still hold for the continuing ministry of the Church. The service of the Word of God is still a matter of extreme urgency, calling for absolute self-dedication.

10. καὶ ἔλεγεν αὐτοῖς introduces a second excerpt from the tradition of mission charge sayings, dealing with matters which were of great importance for the Church at the time Mark was writing. The point of *v.* 10 is that, having once accepted a household's hospitality, they are not to dishonour it by moving elsewhere in the same village if more comfortable accommodation is offered. ἐκεῖ refers to the household, ἐκεῖθεν to the locality.

11. The dust of a heathen land was carefully removed from the feet and clothing by pious Jews before re-entering

[1] *Sayings*, p. 181.

Jewish territory, as something defiling (see S.–B. I, p. 571). So the significance of the action here enjoined is to declare the place which rejects them heathen. At the same time it is to give warning that the missionaries have fulfilled their responsibility toward the place and henceforth the inhabitants must answer for themselves. Cf. Acts xviii. 6, where the shaking off of the dust is accompanied by the words, 'Your blood be upon your own heads'.

εἰς μαρτύριον αὐτοῖς. It may be suggested that μαρτύριον here includes the ideas of (i) witness to God, to his grace and also to his judgement on those who reject his messengers; (ii) witness addressed to the people concerned—a warning and summons to repentance; (iii) evidence which will lie against them at the final Judgement—the fact that the warning has been delivered to them and not heeded will be produced against them. See further on xiii. 9 (cf. also i. 44).

12. See on *v.* 9 above.

13. καὶ δαιμόνια πολλὰ ἐξέβαλλον. Not only were they given authority (*v.* 7); they actually exercised it successfully. There is really no sufficient ground for doubting the truth of this statement. Cf. on *v.* 7.

ἤλειφον ἐλαίῳ. Oil was widely used in the ancient world as a medicament (Isa. i. 6, Lk. x. 34, Rabbinic literature, Josephus, Galen, etc.); but its use by the Twelve was probably symbolic rather than medical in intention (it seems likely that we are meant to infer that the cures followed the anointings immediately). Was the oil meant to be 'a visible token of spiritual grace, by which the healing that was administered by them was declared to proceed from the secret power of God' (Calvin)? Was it meant to direct attention away from their persons to God? And perhaps also 'to differentiate their miracles from those performed by the Master, who does not appear to have employed any symbol but His own hands or saliva' (Swete)?

On the value of this section (vi. 6b–13) as history opinions differ widely. At one extreme Wellhausen held that there was no historical tradition behind it—that there was no mission of the Twelve during Jesus' lifetime. More probable is the view of T. W. Manson: 'The mission of the disciples is one of the best-attested facts in the life of Jesus.' In support of the historicity of the mission three things may be mentioned: (i) it is attested by all four of the sources recognized by Streeter: Mk, Q, M and L (for details see Manson, *Sayings*, pp. 73 f.); (ii) there are a very large number of sayings of the mission charge sort; and (iii) while much in these sayings fits the conditions of the early Church, 'that which is characteristic of the early Christian missionary speech, the proclamation of the coming judgement and of the Messiahship of Jesus is missing' (Schniewind).

If then we accept as historical the mission of the disciples during Jesus' lifetime, what was its significance? According to Taylor[1] Jesus hoped when he sent the Twelve out that their mission would be the immediate prelude to the coming of the kingdom of God and the setting up of the messianic community of the Son of Man, but he was disappointed and this disappointment was a turning-point in his ministry. Thus, while not accepting Schweitzer's doctrine of 'consistent eschatology', Taylor agrees with Schweitzer in emphasizing 'the crucial importance of the mission and its decisive importance for Jesus Himself'. He thinks that the 'failure' of the mission was 'immensely fruitful': 'Through the failure of the mission, the fate of John the Baptist, and His own profound meditation on the Servant teaching of Isa. liii, Jesus was led to seek a deeper interpretation of the doctrine of the Son of Man.' But according to Taylor[2] Mark has no real appreciation of the importance of the mission in the ministry of Jesus; he 'does not tell us what the issue is. He records that the Twelve went out to preach,

[1] *The Life and Ministry of Jesus* (London, 1954), pp. 106–11.
[2] P. 302.

but does not relate their message apart from the phrase ἵνα μετανοῶσιν, and he has only vague ideas concerning their experiences and the results of the Mission. As Mark relates it, the incident is merely an extension of the teaching ministry of Jesus.'

But this interpretation of the mission of the Twelve reads too much into the scanty evidence we have. Rather than conclude that, because Mark does not give support to a modern hypothesis, he must have failed to see the significance of the mission, we should probably accept the picture he gives, which after all is intrinsically likely. Mark includes the mission because he knows that it occurred and because the charges given by Jesus in connection with it had a relevance for the later Christian mission. But he records it with a certain vagueness and lightness of touch, because he knows that it was indeed 'merely an extension of the teaching ministry of Jesus', a kind of appendage to Jesus' own preaching. Whereas after the Ascension the disciples' preaching would be *the* preaching, during Jesus' ministry it was altogether overshadowed by his, and therefore in a narrative of his ministry it is rightly given but little emphasis. The purpose of the mission was, we may assume, to bring the summons to repentance in view of the nearness of the kingdom of God to as many people as possible in Galilee. But no doubt there was the same indirectness about the kingdom of God in their preaching as in that of Jesus: indeed their preaching would probably be even more indirect since they themselves were not yet at all clear about the μυστήριον of the kingdom. The urgency of their mission was the urgency which in all circumstances appertains to the message of God. It seems also likely that Jesus intended this preliminary mission of the Twelve to be part of their training for their future mission, a period of practical experience which would be a valuable basis for the more concentrated teaching that he was soon to give them.

IV. JESUS GOES OUTSIDE GALILEE

(vi. 14–viii. 26)

The fourth main division begins with the account of Herod's fears (vi. 14–16) and the story of John the Baptist's execution (vi. 17–29), which is introduced at this point in explanation of the reference in vi. 16. There follows the closely-knit group of sections, vi. 30–56; and this in turn is followed by vii. 1–23, which consists for the most part of teaching. It is connected neither with vi. 30–56 nor with vii. 24–37, and has apparently been inserted here for convenience. According to Taylor it is a topical complex, but possibly it is a unit rather than a complex. We then have vii. 24–37, which relates the visit to the region of Tyre, the healing of the Syro-Phoenician woman's daughter, the journey from the region of Tyre to somewhere on the east side of the Lake of Galilee within the territory of the Decapolis, and finally the healing of the deaf-mute. It is perhaps the sequel to vi. 30–56. The conclusion to this division is formed by the complex viii. 1–26.

This division of the gospel shows Jesus seeking to withdraw from the crowds and directing his attention rather to his disciples. For the most part he is outside Galilee. But there is little justification in the text for the theory of a flight from Herod. Mark does not connect Jesus' withdrawal with what he has related in vi. 14–16, but indicates in vi. 31 that its motive was the disciples' need for rest.

The striking similarity of vi. 34–44 and viii. 1–9 gives rise to the question whether there really were two feedings of multitudes. Many scholars are convinced that viii. 1–9 is a doublet of vi. 34–44, Mark having received two traditions of the same incident. The parallelism actually extends further; for viii. 10 records a crossing and a landing which is parallel with the crossing and landing in vi. 45–56. Some go even further, pairing off vii. 1-23 and viii. 11-13, vii. 24-30 and viii. 14-21, vii. 31-7 and viii. 22-6; but this, as Taylor shows, is to go too far. That viii. 1-10 is a doublet of vi. 34-56, as Taylor himself thinks, is quite possible, but it is by no means an 'assured result'. It is not inconceivable that Jesus fed a crowd miraculously on two occasions, and the similarity of the two narratives would not be surprising, since the same liturgical and catechetical interests would be liable to affect both. The argument that the disciples' perplexity in viii. 4 would be impossible after they had witnessed the miracle of vi. 34-44 is hardly conclusive. In reply to it several things may be said:

(i) As a matter of fact, even mature Christians (which the disciples at this time certainly were not) do often doubt the power of God after they have had signal experience of it.

(ii) A considerable time may well have elapsed since the feeding of the five thousand.

(iii) It would anyway have been presumptuous for the disciples to have assumed that Jesus would meet the situation with a miracle, in view of his general reluctance to work miracles.

(iv) Allowance should be made at this point for the natural tendency to reproduce in the second narrative the pattern of the first.

(v) It is possible that Lagrange is right in thinking that viii. 4 reflects a rather different attitude from that reflected in vi. 37b, the disciples in vi. 37b having absolutely no thought of Jesus' being able to deal with the situation and asserting the impossibility of providing sufficient food in a rather disrespectful manner, while in viii. 4 'though it would be an exaggeration to say that they ask for the miracle albeit timidly, it is certain that their answer, in the form of a question, insists less on the impossibility than on their own embarrassment'.[1]

[1] P. 202.

33. HEROD'S FEARS (vi. 14–16)
(Mt. xiv. 1–2; Lk. ix. 7–9)

Mark seems not to have had any information about what
Jesus was doing during the period between the sending out
of the Twelve and their return. He has filled the gap with
this section about Herod's fears and popular opinions concerning Jesus, and with the following section which is an
explanation occasioned by the reference to John the Baptist
in *v.* 16. The connection between *vv.* 14–16 and what
precedes is not close—Mark simply joins by καί.

14. ὁ βασιλεὺς Ἡρῴδης. Herod Antipas, son of Herod
the Great and Malthace, tetrarch of Galilee and Peraea
from his father's death in 4 B.C. till A.D. 39. Mt. and Lk.
style him correctly here: Mark's βασιλεύς perhaps reflects
local custom. His ambition to have the title of 'king'
officially led to his downfall (Josephus, *Ant.* XVIII. 240–56).

φανερὸν γὰρ ἐγένετο τὸ ὄνομα αὐτοῦ. An explanatory
comment. ὄνομα here has the sense 'fame'.

καί is here used instead of ὅτι (cf. Rev. vi. 12: καὶ εἶδον... καὶ
σεισμὸς... ἐγένετο; and see further Bauer, *s.v.* I, 2, b), and
ἔλεγον... προφητῶν is what Herod heard. (The sentence is
better explained in this way than by supplying some such
object as τὴν ἀκοὴν Ἰησοῦ—cf. Mt. xiv. 1, Lk. ix. 7—for
ἤκουσεν.)

ἔλεγον. The third person plural read by B W (supported
by D which has a curious corrupt form but one that is
obviously plural in intention) is almost certainly right,
though the singular ἔλεγεν is very much better attested. The
singular is probably due to assimilation to ἤκουσεν. ἔλεγον
is an indefinite plural—'people were saying'. For these
popular notions cf. viii. 28.

Ἰωάννης ὁ Βαπτίζων. See on i. 4–8.

ἐκ νεκρῶν is regularly used without the article: cf. ix. 9f.,
xii. 25.

ἐνεργοῦσιν. Intransitive: 'are at work' (cf. Gal. ii. 8, Eph. ii. 2).

δυνάμεις. Here 'miraculous powers' rather than 'miracles'. John is not known to have worked any miracles in his lifetime (Jn x. 41 actually draws attention to the fact that he wrought no 'sign'); but it would be natural enough to expect John *redivivus* to do so.

15. 'Ηλείας. See on i. 6, ix. 9–13.

προφήτης ὡς εἷς τῶν προφητῶν: 'a prophet like one of the (old) prophets' (Taylor). Swete compares Judg. xvi. 7, 11 (LXX): ἔσομαι ὡς εἷς τῶν ἀνθρώπων, 'I shall be on a par with ordinary men'. According to this view Jesus is a prophet on a level with the ancient prophets—not *the* prophet foretold in Deut. xviii. 15 ff. In Lk. this has become an assertion that one of the old prophets has returned to life; but that is not the natural meaning of Mark's words.

It is significant, as Schniewind notes, that here among the popular opinions about Jesus there is no hint of his being the Messiah.

16. ὃν ἐγὼ ἀπεκεφάλισα 'Ιωάννην, οὗτος ἠγέρθη. The construction may be explained as an example of *casus pendens* followed by a resumptive pronoun. Here the *casus pendens* is drawn into the accusative by attraction to the relative. Cf. xii. 10. (See further M.H. II, pp. 423 f.)

Does Herod mean simply that Jesus is John the Baptist all over again? Or does he mean that Jesus is really John *redivivus*? We cannot be sure. It is by no means impossible that a guilty conscience working on a superstitious nature should have convinced him that John had really returned.

34. THE DEATH OF THE BAPTIST (vi. 17–29)
(Mt. xiv. 3–12; cf. Lk. iii. 19f.)

The historical value of this narrative has been questioned on several grounds.

(i) Alleged differences from Josephus: (a) there seems to be some contradiction about the name of Herodias' previous husband; (b) it is alleged that Mark implies that John was executed at Tiberias; (c) if αὐτοῦ is read in v. 22, there is a further difference from Josephus; (d) according to Josephus, *Ant.* xviii. 118, John's execution was due to political motives.

(ii) The presence of O.T. motifs—Jezebel, Esther.

(iii) The improbability of a princess's dancing at a banquet.

But on closer examination these objections are not so impressive. On (i) (a), (b) and (c) see the notes below. With regard to (i) (b), the only reason for assuming that Mark places the execution at Tiberias is that it seems a more natural place for the banquet; but there is no insuperable difficulty in supposing that the banquet took place at Machaerus. With regard to (i) (d) Taylor's remark that 'political ends and the anger of an insulted woman cannot be regarded as mutually exclusive' is thoroughly justified. It is likely that Mark's account takes us back to 'what was being darkly whispered in the bazaars or market-places of Palestine at the time' (Rawlinson). As to (ii), it is possible that these biblical analogies have coloured the narrative slightly, but most unlikely that the narrative is based on them. And (iii) is not an insuperable objection, when one makes allowance for the depraved morals of Herod's family.

The narrative is introduced as an explanation of the opinion about Jesus attributed to Herod in v. 16, and together with the previous section fills the interval between the sending out of the Twelve and their return to Jesus. Though not directly concerned with Jesus, it is yet relevant to the history of Jesus, the passion of the Forerunner being a pointer to the subsequent passion of the Messiah (cf. ii. 19 f.). The parallels between vi. 17–29 and xv. 1–47 are interesting: e.g. Herod's fear of John as ἀνὴρ δίκαιος καὶ ἅγιος (v. 20) and Pilate's attitude to Jesus (xv. 5, 14); Herodias' implacable hatred of John and the Jewish leaders' implacable hatred of Jesus; Herod's and Pilate's yielding to pressure; the details of the burials of John and Jesus.

17. Αὐτός is probably not emphatic ('himself') here. It is sometimes used in papyri in the unemphatic sense 'the aforesaid'; but here it is better explained as an Aramaism— a redundant pronoun anticipating a noun (cf. Mt. iii. 4; and see further Black, pp. 70 f.).

ἐκράτησεν, ἔδησεν, ἐγάμησεν should be translated as pluperfects.

φυλακῇ. According to Josephus, *Ant.* XVIII. 119, John was imprisoned and executed in the fortress of Machaerus (to the east of the Dead Sea in the southernmost part of Peraea).

Ἡρῳδιάδα τὴν γυναῖκα Φιλίππου τοῦ ἀδελφοῦ αὐτοῦ. Herodias was the daughter of Aristobulus, the son of Herod the Great and Mariamne, and so the niece of Herod Antipas. If by 'Philip' Philip the Tetrarch is meant, this contradicts Josephus who says (*Ant.* XVIII. 136) that Herodias was married to Herod the son of Herod the Great and Mariamne II. Philip the Tetrarch actually married Salome. It would seem that either Mark is mistaken, or the Herod to whom Herodias was married had also the name Philip, or Φιλίππου should be omitted with 47 (in the Mt. parallel it is *
omitted by D lat Augustine).

18. ἔλεγεν: 'had been saying' (Moule, pp. 9 f.).

'We behold in John an illustrious example of that moral courage, which all pious teachers ought to possess, not to hesitate to incur the wrath of the great and powerful, as often as it may be found necessary: for he, with whom there is acceptance of persons, does not honestly serve God' (Calvin).

19. ἐνεῖχεν. Ἐνέχειν + dative here means 'to have a grudge against'. It is an elliptical expression. The full χόλον ἐνέχειν τινί is used by Herodotus, I. 118. Cf. the ellipse of νοῦν with ἐπέχειν.

Mt. xiv. 5 alters the sense of this and the next verse of Mk considerably (but λυπηθείς in Mt. xiv. 9 seems rather to agree with the Mk account).

20. συνετήρει: i.e. against Herodias.

ἠπόρει. So א B L W (ἠπορεῖτο) Θ bo; but A C D and the great majority of Greek MSS. and also most versions support ἐποίει. The support for ἠπόρει, though numerically weak, is strong in quality, and intrinsically this reading is more likely (after ἐποίει the following words would be just a weak repetition, but after ἠπόρει they make good sense—καί meaning here 'and yet'). ἠπόρει vividly describes Herod's moral weakness.

21. Goes closely with v. 19, v. 20 being a parenthetic explanation of οὐκ ἠδύνατο.

γενομένης ἡμέρας εὐκαίρου. A temporal genitive absolute, to which the following ὅτε-clause adds more precise definition.

εὐκαίρου: 'opportune' (the suggestion that it here means 'festal' is not convincing). But is it opportune for Herod (i.e. for giving a banquet, his birthday being a suitable occasion) or opportune for Herodias? The latter is much better sense. Taking it this way, it is best to translate the καί at the beginning of v. 21 'But' (cf. καί with adversative force in v. 19 before οὐκ ἠδύνατο and in v. 20 after ἠπόρει). A further question arises: at what stage was the opportunity presented to Herodias? Does the narrator mean that it was the birthday feast which provided the opportunity and that Herodias seized it by sacrificing her daughter's respectability and deliberately sending her into the feast to dance, in order to win Herod's favour and put him into a frame of mind that would suit her purpose? Or was the opportunity pre-

sented to her only when Salome, having pleased the king,
came out to consult her? Or does the narrator mean that
the birthday feast was the time of opportunity for Herodias
without implying that she was aware of the opportunity
before Salome consulted her? Of these the second is the
least likely, for the structure of the sentence seems to require
us to take ὅτε... Γαλιλαίας as the explanation of εὐκαίρου.
In favour of the first is the fact that on this view we have
some explanation of the dance by Salome.

τοῖς γενεσίοις αὐτοῦ: 'on his birthday' (τὰ γενέσια
being used in late Greek for τὰ γενέθλια).

χιλιάρχοις. Properly the word denotes a commander of
1000 men, but here it is probably used loosely of military
officers of high rank.

τοῖς πρώτοις τῆς Γαλιλαίας: 'the leading men of
Galilee'; cf. Lk. xix. 47.

There was a palace as well as a prison in the fortress
of Machaerus, and presumably, though it was certainly
a long way from Galilee, if Herod was resident there, he
would be surrounded by his courtiers. It certainly seems
to be implied (vv. 27f.) that John was imprisoned close at
hand.

22. αὐτῆς. (i) αὐτῆς is read by A C W Θ and the
majority of Greek MSS. and supported by it (most MSS.)
vg syʰ. (ii) ℵ B D L Δ 238 565 have αὐτοῦ instead. (iii) The
word is omitted by f1 22 131 it (some MSS.) sysˢ, ᴾ co, etc.
According to (ii) the girl is herself named Herodias and
is described as Herod's daughter. But in v. 24 she is
Herodias' daughter. Herodias had a daughter called
Salome, but she was not Herod's daughter; and the narrative does not seem to allow for the union between Herod and
Herodias to have been long-standing enough for there to be
a daughter sufficiently old by it. So most commentators
accept the reading (i). We may then translate 'the daughter
of Herodias herself' (the nuance would be that it was

actually Herodias' own daughter who danced); or, perhaps more probably, αὐτῆς may be explained as a redundant pronoun anticipating a noun (an Aramaism: cf. on *v.* 17).

With the rest of the verse from ὁ δὲ βασιλεύς and also *v.* 23 cf. Esth. v. 3, 6. ἤρεσεν and the use of κοράσιον of a woman of marriageable age are perhaps also reminiscent of Esth. ii. 9. There is also a certain likeness between Esther's accomplishment of the destruction of Haman and Salome's of that of John. Perhaps the story of Salome reminded Mark of Esther, with the result that he used some of the language of LXX Esther.

23. After αὐτῇ 𝔓⁴⁵ D Θ 565 700 it (some MSS.) insert an adverbial πολλά: it should perhaps be read.

ἕως ἡμίσους τῆς βασιλείας μου. Cf. Esth. v. 3, 6, also I Kgs xiii. 8, Lk. xix. 8. To object that Herod was not in a position to give half his kingdom away, as he was dependent on Rome, is to take his words too prosaically.

24. αἰτήσωμαι. It is possible, though not certain, that a distinction is intended between the middle used here and the active in *vv.* 22 and 23. If so, the meaning here would be ' claim ', there being now a sort of business relationship since the king's promise.

25. μετὰ σπουδῆς and ἐξαυτῆς suggest eagerness on the part of Salome, and the grim ἐπὶ πίνακι seems to be her own idea.

26. περίλυπος. A strong word only used again in Mk in xiv. 34.

ἀθετῆσαι. For the verb cf. vii. 9, Lk. x. 16, Jn xii. 48, etc. Here it probably means 'disappoint', 'break one's word to'—a meaning it perhaps has in LXX Ps. xiv. 4 (M.T.: xv. 4).

27. σπεκουλάτορα. A transliteration of Lat. *speculator*, which properly means 'scout', but was used to denote a member of the headquarters' staff of a legionary commander in the Roman Imperial army or of a provincial governor, whose duties included the carrying out of executions: hence it came to be used as a loanword in Rabbinic Hebrew and Aramaic for an 'executioner'.

35. THE RETURN OF THE TWELVE AND THE ATTEMPT AT RETIREMENT (vi. 30–3)
(Mt. xiv. 13; Lk. ix. 10–11 a)

This section is closely knit together with the following one, and it is difficult to decide whether to regard it as a separate section or to regard *vv.* 30–44 as one section, as do Huck, Swete, Lagrange, *et al.* Those who do make a division differ as to where exactly it should be: thus *vv.* 31, 33, 34, 35 have all been suggested as the beginning of the new section. On the whole it seems best to make a division at the end of *v.* 33.

This narrative seems to have been constructed by Mark on the basis of definite tradition. The view that it is merely an artificial device for providing the setting required for *vv.* 34–44 fails to do justice to Mark's habitual abstinence from inventing details.

The section looks back to *vv.* 6b–13; and no connection is made with *vv.* 17–29, since that narrative is simply an explanatory note attached to *vv.* 14–16. In Mt. the addition of καὶ ἐλθόντες ἀπήγγειλαν τῷ Ἰησοῦ in xiv. 12 and the participle ἀκούσας in xiv. 13 do connect Jesus' withdrawal with his hearing the news of John's death; but it seems probable that this connection is artificial and due to a misunderstanding of Mk.

30. οἱ ἀπόστολοι. Ἀπόστολος occurs only here in Mk (in iii. 14 the clause containing it should almost certainly not be read). The N.T. use of the word derives, not from classical Greek in which it usually denotes the sending of a military or naval expedition, or the actual force sent, or a group of colonists, but from the use of the Hebrew šālîaḥ (derived from the verb šālaḥ, the equivalent of ἀποστέλλω). In

Rabbinic Hebrew *šālîaḥ* (Aramaic *šᵉlîḥāʾ*) denotes an authorized agent or representative, whether of a private person (e.g. a representative whom a husband appoints to deliver a writ of divorce to his wife) or of a corporation (e.g. a member of a synagogue appointed by it to lead its public worship, or the Rabbis sent by the Sanhedrin to carry out a visitation of the Jews of the Dispersion). *Šālîaḥ* is expressive of function rather than status: the agent was appointed to carry out a particular mission, and when it was accomplished his appointment lapsed. His authority was derived and dependent, and he was responsible to the one who had appointed him. In so far as he was loyally fulfilling his commission, it could be said of him that 'a man's agent is as himself' (cf. Mt. x. 40). That ἀπόστολος in the N.T. is in general the equivalent of *šālîaḥ* is clear (e.g. Mt. x. 40, Jn xiii. 16, II Cor. viii. 23). It is used sometimes quite generally, as in Jn xiii. 16; but it is also used as a technical term to denote (i) the Twelve; (ii) a larger number including Barnabas and Paul (Acts xiv. 14, etc.), Andronicus and Junias (Rom. xvi. 7). That Jesus actually used the Aramaic *šᵉlîḥāʾ* of the Twelve is uncertain, but extremely probable. (See further Moule, *Colossians*, pp. 155–9; K. H. Rengstorf, *Apostleship* (Eng. tr. of *T.W.N.T.* article, London, 1952).)

Taylor thinks that οἱ ἀπόστολοι is not used here as an official title but means simply 'the missionaries' with reference to the mission from which the Twelve return: he suggests that Mark uses ἀπόστολος here in preference to μαθητής because he has just used μαθητής of John's disciples. But, while it is probably right to see in the fact that Mark does not elsewhere refer to the Twelve as ἀπόστολοι an illustration of the primitive character of his gospel, it seems rather unlikely that on this one occasion when he does use the word he would use it of the Twelve without having in mind the technical sense which it commonly had by the time he was writing. The fact that here the sense 'missionaries' is close to hand does not mean that the word is used without its official connotation, but rather that the true significance of the official title is here being underlined: the significance of the Twelve lies in their being sent, commissioned, by Jesus. Cf. Bengel's comment: 'apta huic loco appellatio'. The true nature of their apostleship is further indicated by the reference to their gathering together to Jesus and reporting to him πάντα ὅσα ἐποίησαν καὶ ὅσα ἐδίδαξαν: they are dependent on, and accountable to, him who has commissioned them.

The general significance of this verse is well summed up by Calvin: '. . .having discharged a temporary commission, they went back to school to make greater advances in learning'.

31. αὐτοὶ κατ᾽ ἰδίαν: 'apart by yourselves'. See on iv. 34.

ἔρημον. Here and in *v.* 32 ἔρημος probably means 'lonely' rather than 'desert' (cf. i. 35).

οὐδὲ φαγεῖν εὐκαίρουν. Cf. iii. 20.

32. The site of this ἔρημος τόπος is not indicated. Various possibilities have been suggested. Somewhere on the N.E. shore of the lake seems most probable (cf. Dalman, *S.S.W.* pp. 161 ff.).

33. εἶδον is probably indefinite, πολλοί being the subject only of ἐπέγνωσαν.

πεζῇ. As often, 'by land'; here in contrast with ἐν τῷ πλοίῳ.

ἀπὸ πασῶν τῶν πόλεων: *sc.* in that area. Πόλεις is used loosely to cover towns and villages.

36. THE FEEDING OF THE FIVE THOUSAND
(vi. 34–44)

(Mt. xiv. 14–21; Lk. ix. 11b–17)

The close connection between this and the preceding section has already been noted. It seems probable that the connection is historical. As Taylor observes, the narrative 'has not yet attained the rounded form' of the typical orally transmitted miracle-story. The lively dialogue between Jesus and his disciples, especially their disrespectful question in *v.* 37, and the vivid description in *vv.* 39f. suggest the reminiscence of an eye-witness. The narrative may well be based on Petrine reminiscence.

The fact that we have six accounts of Jesus' feeding a multitude in the gospels (two in Mk, two parallels in Mt., one in Lk. and one in Jn) indicates that the early Church regarded the feeding(s) as being among the greatest and most luminous for faith of the mighty works of Jesus.

34. ἐξελθών: from the boat (cf. v. 2, vi. 54) rather than from retirement.

ὄχλον. The word has already occurred thirteen times in Mk. In all Mark uses it thirty-eight times. But the present verse is one of the key passages for the understanding of its N.T. significance. See below; and reference should also be made to the interesting article, 'The Multitude in the Synoptic Gospels', by B. Citron in *S.J.T.* vii, pp. 408–18.

ἐσπλαγχνίσθη. The multitude is the object of Jesus' compassion. Cf. viii. 2, Mt. ix. 36, xiv. 14, xv. 32. In the N.T. σπλαγχνίζομαι is only used of Jesus, apart from three occasions on which it occurs on his lips with reference to figures in parables that have a close connection with himself (Mt. xviii. 27, Lk. x. 33, xv. 20). It denotes not a mere sentiment, but a pity which expresses itself in active assistance.

ὅτι ἦσαν ὡς πρόβατα μὴ ἔχοντα ποιμένα. Cf. Num. xxvii.

17, I Kgs xxii. 17, II Chr. xviii. 16, Ezek. xxxiv. 5. The characteristic of the multitude which is stressed here as calling forth Jesus' pity is its helplessness and bewilderment, its likeness to shepherdless sheep. (On the sheep and shepherd metaphor in the Bible see further Cranfield, *The First Epistle of Peter* (London, 1950), pp. 109f.)   *

ἤρξατο διδάσκειν αὐτοὺς πολλά. The words indicate Jesus' response to the need and wretchedness of the multitude, the action springing from his pity. Their greatest need is to be taught. πολλά is used adverbially—'at length': the meaning is not that Jesus taught them a great number of different things, but that he taught the one message of the kingdom of God persistently.

Mt. and Lk. here mention his healing of the sick; the sequel tells of the feeding miracle. Jesus' compassion for the multitude leads him to teach, to heal the sick, to feed the hungry.

35. ὥρας πολλῆς and ὥρα πολλή. Πολύς = 'late' occurs also in Polybius, v. 8. 3, Dionysius of Halicarnassus, II. 54, Josephus, *Ant.* VIII. 118. Cf. Latin *ad multum diem* = 'till far into the day', *multo die* = 'when the day was far spent', *multa nocte* = 'late at night'.

36. κύκλῳ. See on iii. 34.

ἀγρούς. See on v. 14.

τί φάγωσιν: grammatically an indirect question, the subjunctive being used because the direct question would be deliberative. The parallels get rid of the expression.

37. ἀποκριθεὶς εἶπεν. See on iii. 33.

ὑμεῖς is here emphatic.

ἀγοράσωμεν: deliberative subjunctive.

δηναρίων διακοσίων: genitive of price. In Mt. xx. 2 a denarius is the wage for a day's work in a vineyard.

δώσομεν. The change to future indicative after the deliberative subjunctive is very harsh. It is not surprising that many MSS. read δώσωμεν—a natural improvement.

The tone of the question is 'characteristic of the boldness of Mark's narrative' (Taylor). As with iv. 38, in Mt. and Lk. the suggestion of disrespectfulness has been removed.

38. ὑπάγετε ἴδετε. Taylor notes that 'the two imperatives have a very decisive tone'.

γνόντες: 'when they had found out'.

39. συμπόσια συμπόσια. The word denotes a 'drinking-party', so a 'company of guests', a 'table-fellowship'. The underlying Aramaic is probably ḥᵃḇûrtā' (Hebrew ḥᵃḇûrāh), the word used to denote a group of people eating the Passover meal together. For the distributive force of the repetition see on vi. 7. The purpose of this breaking up of the crowd into companies was probably simply to secure order and to make the serving more easy.

ἐπὶ τῷ χλωρῷ χόρτῳ. The mention of the green grass may perhaps point to springtime; but near streams green grass might be found as late as July.

40. ἀνέπεσαν. Note the substitution of the weak for the strong aorist ending which is frequent in late Greek. The verb occurs again in viii. 6.

πρασιαί πρασιαί. For the repetition see on *v.* 39 above. The word πρασιά means 'garden-bed'. S.–B., II, p. 13, quote interesting examples from the Rabbinic literature of the arrangement of students sitting in rows before their Rabbis being likened to the rows of vines in a vineyard and to beds in a garden. Specially interesting is the interpretation of Song of Songs viii. 13 ('Thou that dwellest in the gardens'): 'When students sit arranged like garden-beds [Hebrew *ginnôniyyôṯ ginnôniyyôṯ* = πρασιαὶ πρασιαί] and are engaged in studying the Torah, then I come down to them and hearken to their voice and hear them—Song of Songs viii. 13: "Cause me to hear thy voice."' So doubtless here in Mk it is the regular arrangement in companies to which this expression refers, not (as has sometimes been suggested) the colours of the clothes of the crowd.

41. λαβών. Cf. Mt. xiv. 19 = Lk. ix. 16, Mk viii. 6 = Mt. xv. 36, Jn vi. 11, Mk xiv. 22 = Mt. xxvi. 26 = Lk. xxii. 19, I Cor. xi. 23, Lk. xxiv. 30, Jn xxi. 13, Acts xxvii. 35. According to Jewish custom at the beginning of a meal the head of the family or the host took the bread into his hands before saying the blessing.

ἀναβλέψας εἰς τὸν οὐρανόν. Cf. vii. 34, Jn xi. 41; also Job xxii. 26. It was an attitude of prayer. Possibly looking upward at this point rather than fixing his eyes on the bread was a characteristic of Jesus—Lk. xxiv. 35 might be an indication that he had a characteristic way of saying the blessing for the bread. But probably we should see in Jesus' prayer on this occasion not merely the usual prayer of thanksgiving but also his reliance on God for the power to work a miracle (cf. vii. 34, Jn xi. 41).

εὐλόγησεν represents the Hebrew *bērēk*, Aramaic *bārêk* = 'to bless', 'say the blessing (or *bᵉrākāh*)'. The object of *εὐλόγησεν* is not the loaves and fishes (in spite of *αὐτούς* in the great majority of MSS. in the Lk. parallel—see further on viii. 7), but 'the Lord' understood; for the *bᵉrākāh* was a blessing of the Name of God. The ancient *bᵉrākāh* for bread is: 'Blessed art Thou, O Lord our God, King of the world, who bringest forth bread from the earth.' (See *A.D.P.B.* p. 278.) On the various blessings see (*M*) *Ber.* *b Ber.* 35a says:. 'It is forbidden to man to taste of this world without saying a blessing: whoever tastes of this world without saying a blessing commits unfaithfulness.' This practice was based on Lev. xix. 24, Deut. viii. 10. (See further H. W. Beyer in *T.W.N.T.* II, pp. 751–63.)

κατέκλασεν. After the head of the family or host had said the *bᵉrākāh* holding the bread in his hands, he broke the bread, ate a piece of it himself and then distributed to those present. So Jesus here breaks the loaves.

ἐδίδου. The change to the imperfect is perhaps meant to suggest 'successive distributions of bread' (Taylor).

On this verse see further below.

42. ἐχορτάσθησαν shows that Mark regarded the meal as miraculous—not a sacramental meal in which the people received only a tiny fragment, but a meal in which their hunger was fully satisfied.

43. δώδεκα κοφίνων πληρώματα: 'twelve basketfuls', in apposition to κλάσματα. The κόφινος, a wicker basket, is mentioned by the satirist Juvenal as specially characteristic of Jews: 'Iudaeis quorum cophinus faenumque supellex' (iii. 14; cf. vi. 542). This verse confirms ἐχορτάσθησαν in the previous verse. Cf. Ruth ii. 14, II Kgs iv. 44, II Chr. xxxi. 10. Perhaps we should also see in it a reflection of the biblical respect for bread as God's gift and therefore not to be wasted.

That in this section Mark means to relate a miracle is clear. But various attempts have been made to explain the incident behind the narrative as non-miraculous. Thus it has been suggested that the numbers have been exaggerated in the oral tradition and that if this is allowed for the miracle disappears; that Jesus and his disciples shared their provisions with the crowd and thereupon others who had provisions with them followed their example ('a miracle of the awakening of fellowship in men's souls', as W. Barclay seems inclined to call the miracle of Jn vi. 1–14);[1] that it was simply a sacramental meal, each person receiving only a tiny fragment as a pledge of his share in the coming eschatological feast (Schweitzer); that it is a legend either based on O.T. narratives such as Exod. xvi, I Kgs xvii. 8–16, II Kgs iv. 42–4, or derived from pagan sources. Taylor gives it as his opinion that 'Much the best hypothesis is that of Schweitzer, coupled with the suggestion of Wellhausen that the numbers are exaggerated...'. But is there any really sufficient reason for setting aside Mark's account? On the general objections brought against the nature miracles see

[1] *And He had Compassion on them* (Edinburgh, 1955), p. 163.

the concluding note on i. 29–31. It is not easy to reconcile the presence of such an obviously primitive element as the disrespectful question in *v.* 37 (contrast Mt. and Lk.), which suggests the testimony of an eye-witness, with the suggestion that we have here a narrative in which a miraculous interpretation has been superimposed in the course of tradition upon an originally non-miraculous incident. It is unlikely that Mark, if he derived the story from Peter directly, would have misinterpreted the incident, and it is hardly conceivable that the apostles at the time misunderstood as a miracle something quite non-miraculous. If on the other hand the story has come to Mark through more indirect oral tradition, how is it that the question in *v.* 37 has remained unmodified?

We take it that the incident was a miracle. But it seems possible that the miracle was apparent only to the disciples and that the crowd accepted unthinkingly what was offered them. That would explain the absence of any reference to surprise on their part. If this view is right, then this miracle was not a spectacular public one as would rather seem to be the case if the multitude were aware of what was done. In this connection the simplicity of the fare Jesus provides should be noted. It is congruous with his reluctance to work miracles and his refusal to give 'signs'. The humble repast meets the crowd's real need, but its austerity is reminiscent of the manna in the wilderness (Num. xi. 6!) rather than the sumptuous fare of the eschatological feast of Isa. xxv. 6.

What significance did Mark see in this incident? Here a number of points should be mentioned. (i) Though ἐσπλαγχνίσθη in *v.* 34 is not actually connected with the miracle in the way that σπλαγχνίζομαι is in viii. 2, Mark probably regarded the feeding of the five thousand as the expression of Jesus' compassion on the multitude, his response to their physical hunger. (ii) But vi. 52, viii. 16–19, indicate that he thought of it as a pointer to the secret of the kingdom of God, the secret of the person of Jesus. (iii) The narrative should be seen against the background of the O.T., particularly of Exod. xvi, I Kgs xvii. 8–16, II Kgs iv. 42–4; possibly also Isa. xxv. 6, lv. 2, Prov. ix. 5. The first of these played a prominent part in Jewish thinking: e.g. *Qoheleth Rabba* on Eccles. i. 9: 'As the first Redeemer caused manna to descend, so shall also the last Redeemer cause manna to descend'; *Tanhuma, bᵉšallaḥ* 21: 'For whom has it [i.e. the manna] now been prepared? For the righteous in the age that is coming: everyone who believeth is worthy and eateth of it'; *Mekilta* on Exod. xvi. 25: 'Ye shall not find it [i.e. the manna] in this age, but ye shall find it in the age that is coming.' It may be that Mark's emphasis on the fact that the place is ἔρημος reflects a consciousness of the parallel with the manna in the desert. In the light of this O.T. background the miracle is a sign of the presence among men of the final Redeemer in whom God's promises are being fulfilled. (iv) Mark also surely has the Last Supper and the Eucharist in mind. Note the contacts between this narrative and Mk xiv. 22 ff.:

Mk vi. 40 ff.	Mk xiv. 22 ff.
vi. 40 ἀνέπεσαν	xiv. 18 ἀνακειμένων
	[Lk. xxii. 14 ἀνέπεσεν]
vi. 41 λαβών	xiv. 32 λαβών
τοὺς...ἄρτους	ἄρτον
εὐλόγησεν	εὐλογήσας
κατέκλασεν	ἔκλασεν
ἐδίδου	ἔδωκεν
ἐμέρισεν	[Lk. xxii. 17 (of the first cup) δια-μερίσατε]
vi. 42 καὶ ἔφαγον πάντες	[cf. xiv. 23 καὶ ἔπιον ἐξ αὐτοῦ πάντες]

Though these contacts may be explained as due to the fact that the same Jewish meal customs would be features alike of the feeding miracles, the Last Supper and the Eucharist,

Taylor's words are probably justified: 'Mark has conformed the vocabulary of the passage to that of the Supper in the belief that in some sense the fellowship meal in the wilderness was an anticipation of the Eucharist.' As the multitude had once enjoyed table-fellowship with Jesus as his guests by the Lake of Galilee, so now the Church enjoys table-fellowship with the exalted Jesus in the Eucharist. (v) Mark and the early Church probably also saw in this miracle a pointer to the final consummation, which is often likened to a banquet (e.g. Isa. xxv. 6ff., Lk. xiii. 29, xiv. 15, xxii. 16, 30, xiv. 16ff. = Mt. xxii. 1ff., Mt. xxvi. 29, Rev. xix. 9). Jesus may himself have had this significance in mind (his use of the feast metaphor for the final consummation makes this likely). (vi) Probably the thought of Jesus as the true bread of life, the true sustenance of men (cf. Jn vi), was also suggested to Mark by this miracle. (vii) Whether Mark also thought of the feedings of the five thousand and the four thousand (viii. 1ff.) as symbolizing the offering of the bread of life to the Jews and the Gentiles respectively is uncertain. This suggestion, which goes back to patristic times, has some support in the fact that the crowd in vi. 35ff. may plausibly be regarded as Jewish and the crowd in viii. 1ff. as Gentile, and in the rather curious stress on the distinction between κόφινος in vi. 43, viii. 19 and σπυρίς in viii. 8, 20 (there being some evidence that κόφινος was a characteristically Jewish article; see above on v. 43). (For the view that both narratives are meant to show that the gospel is to go to the Gentiles see G. H. Boobyer, 'The Miracles of the Loaves and the Gentiles', in *S.J.T.* vi, 77–87.)

37. JESUS WALKS ON THE WATER (vi. 45–52)
(Mt. xiv. 22–33)

The close connection between this section and the preceding makes the suggestion that we have here a displaced Resurrection appearance narrative most unlikely. The character of the detail with which the section abounds makes it also unlikely that the narrative is a pious legend or a symbolical story; it suggests rather the memory of an actual incident. When the third person plural is changed to the first person plural, the section reads like the vivid reminiscence of one of the Twelve. The sentence πάντες γὰρ αὐτὸν εἶδαν, which seems a little weak in Mark's narrative, becomes thoroughly natural when transposed into the first person. And v. 52 may well reflect Peter's humble confession as he looks back. It seems very likely that we have here Petrine reminiscence.

45. ἠνάγκασεν. Though the word is used in a weakened sense (see Bauer *s.v.*), it is still a strong expression and suggests a certain urgency. In Jn at this point (Jn vi. 14f.) the departure of Jesus εἰς τὸ ὄρος is connected with the excitement caused by the feeding of the five thousand. Jesus withdrew by himself because he perceived that 'they were about to come and take him by force, to make him king'. So from early times (e.g. Origen) people have sought to explain Mark's ἠνάγκασεν by reference to this dangerous situation indicated in Jn vi. 14f. Thus Latham wrote: 'He hurried the disciples on board that they might not catch the contagion of the idea.'[1] A more satisfactory explanation is that the crowd were not aware of the miraculous nature of the meal of which they had partaken (cf. p. 221: that Jn should make the miracle appear more public than it actually was would not be at all surprising), but were nevertheless dangerously enthusiastic after this meal in the desert, and so Jesus hustled the disciples away to prevent them from

[1] *Pastor Pastorum* (Cambridge, 1913), p. 307.

224

adding a spark to the tinder by revealing to the crowd the meal's miraculous character.

Βηθσαϊδάν. Probably the important Bethsaida Julias. Some older scholars were led by Mark's εἰς τὸ πέραν to conjecture the existence of another Bethsaida on the western shore of the lake, but this suggestion has now been generally given up. Others would get over the geographical difficulty by translating πρός 'opposite to', but Taylor rightly doubts the possibility of this when πρός is associated with a verb of motion. Taylor follows Burkitt in omitting εἰς τὸ πέραν with 𝔓⁴⁵ W f1 q sy⁵, regarding these words as an assimilation to Mt., though he admits the possibility that the omission should rather be explained as due to a sense of the geographical difficulty.

46. αὐτοῖς: i.e. the multitude (cf. Mt. xiv. 23: τοὺς ὄχλους); hardly the disciples.

προσεύξασθαι. See on i. 35.

47. ὀψίας γενομένης. In v. 35 we had ἤδη ὥρας πολλῆς γενομένης. If the time referred to there was late afternoon, the time indicated here would probably be quite late in the evening. Ὄψιος can refer to a time before or after sunset. So in i. 32 the less precise ὀψίας γενομένης is more exactly defined by ὅτε ἔδυσεν ὁ ἥλιος. In Judith xiii. 1 ὄψιος is used of the early night. Here it seems to be implied that it was light enough for Jesus on the high ground to see the disciples on the lake; but it was probably moonlight, for the general impression is that it must have been a good while after sunset since Jesus came to them in the fourth watch.

We should perhaps read πάλαι after ἦν with 𝔓⁴⁵ D f1 al it (some MSS.): cf. ἤδη in Mt. xiv. 24.

48. ἰδών. It seems more natural to suppose that Jesus was still on the high ground than that he had already come down to the shore.

βασανιζομένους. The verb was used in v. 7. Here the

participle could be either passive ('being buffeted') or middle ('toiling hard', 'exerting themselves').

περὶ τετάρτην φυλακήν. Mark follows the Roman custom of counting four night watches (cf. xiii. 35). The Jews divided the night into three watches.

περιπατῶν ἐπὶ τῆς θαλάσσης. Ἐπί+genitive can mean 'by' (cf. Jn xxi. 1, Acts v. 23, Exod. xiv. 2); but in view of the contrast with ἐπὶ τῆς γῆς in *v.* 47 and the amazement of the disciples it is clear that Mark means 'on'. (That it was so understood by Matthew is abundantly clear.) Taylor thinks that the shore was quite near, but that in the darkness it could not be seen and Jesus 'wading through the surf near the hidden shore' seemed to the disciples to be walking on the water: they misinterpreted the incident as miraculous. But would not Jesus quickly have discovered their mistake— and corrected it? The rationalization of the miracle is unsatisfactory. On Taylor's main objection that to accept the miracle would imply 'a docetic view of the person of Christ' see the concluding note on i. 29–31.

καὶ ἤθελεν παρελθεῖν αὐτούς. Only in Mk. Perhaps the words are to be explained as recording the impression the disciples had at the time: the impression they got was that he intended to pass by them. Or perhaps θέλω is here used as more or less equivalent to μέλλω. Some have suggested that his intention was to get to the other side before them, others that it was to test their faith. R. H. Lightfoot has suggested that though Jesus must needs go to help his disciples in distress, their lack of comprehension was so great a strain to him that 'He would have been glad to pass them by';[1] but this seems scarcely probable. Perhaps we should compare Lk. xxiv. 28, Jn xx. 15.

49. φάντασμα: 'an apparition', 'ghost'. According to S.–B. 1, p. 691, Jewish popular belief often recounted the appearance of unusual apparitions on the sea (examples

[1] *Gospel Message*, p. 114.

given in support). Cf. Wisdom xvii. 3 f., 15. Was it the fact that he ἤθελεν παρελθεῖν αὐτούς that made them think he was a φάντασμα?

ἀνέκραξαν. Cf. i. 23.

50. ἐταράχθησαν: 'were terrified', 'dismayed'. The verb occurs eighteen times in the N.T., but in Mk only here. Possibly we should compare the words expressive of amazement used in Mk referred to in the note on i. 22.

Θαρσεῖτε. The command θάρσει (or θαρσεῖτε) occurs seven times in the N.T.—always on the lips of Jesus (in Acts xxiii. 11 of the exalted Christ) except for Mk x. 49, where it is spoken by those who tell the blind man that Jesus is calling him.

ἐγώ εἰμι: the ordinary Greek for 'it is I'. It is conceivable that Mark intends his readers to be reminded of the O.T. use of the expression in Exod. iii. 14, Isa. xli. 4, xliii. 10, lii. 6.

μὴ φοβεῖσθε. See on v. 36.

51. καὶ ἐκόπασεν ὁ ἄνεμος. Cf. iv. 39. Does Mark regard this also as miraculous? Perhaps he regards it as natural, but feels its special appropriateness at this point and sees in this appropriateness a symbolical paraenetic significance.

λίαν ἐκ περισσοῦ ἐν ἑαυτοῖς. There are several unimportant variants: some authorities omit λίαν, others ἐκ περισσοῦ, while some transpose ἐκ περισσοῦ and ἐν ἑαυτοῖς.

ἐξίσταντο. See on i. 22 (ἐξεπλήσσοντο).

52 explains their utter astonishment. They had not understood about the loaves: though they must have realized that a miracle had been wrought, they had not grasped its significance as a pointer to the secret of Jesus' person. They had not believed, and so it had not been for them a luminous 'sign' (in the Johannine sense), but merely a 'marvel'. Thus their reaction was not joy and confidence, but faithless panic—an attitude that might have been

expected of those who did not know 'the mystery of the kingdom of God'.

οὐ...συνῆκαν. The same expression (μὴ συνιῶσιν) is used in iv. 12 with reference to οἱ ἔξω. Here the Twelve themselves come within its scope. Schniewind notes the striking contrast with all Hellenistic hero-worship and Jewish veneration of the pious. The Mt. parallel here departs radically from Mk—apparently in order to spare the Twelve and at the same time underline the doctrinal significance of the miracle.

ἦν αὐτῶν ἡ καρδία πεπωρωμένη. See on iii. 5.

With the whole verse cf. viii. 17. There is no need to see in the use of πεπωρωμένος here or in viii. 17 the influence of Paul. It is intrinsically likely that Jesus pondered on such passages of the O.T. as Isa. vi. 9-10, Jer. v. 21, Deut. xxix. 4, xxxii. 28. And, as far as the apostles were concerned, how else could they regard their slowness to understand, when after the Resurrection and Pentecost they looked back on it, but with amazement and penitence? (On Wrede's use of this feature see on i. 25.) Schlatter's comment here is to the point: 'It is part of the summons to repentance which the Gospel addresses to us, that alongside the riches of Jesus it shows us the poverty of the disciples and makes clear for all by their case how much kindness and patience He must show to us, before we will believe in Him.'

On this miracle generally see the concluding note on iv. 35-41. But this incident has some special features which must have seemed to Mark and his first readers to bear a message to the Church. (i) ἠνάγκασεν: if it is as a result of obedience to Christ's command that the Church or the individual Christian is in a situation of danger or distress, then there is no need for fear. (ii) This section shares with ix. 14-29 the feature of Jesus returning to his disciples after a period of separation. Mark and his readers in Rome will hardly have missed the parallel between the situation of the disciples separated from Jesus and that of the Church awaiting his Parousia. But the Church also expects him to come in the meantime in Word and Sacrament and also in the meantime to exercise his kingly power for the deliverance of his disciples. So the section contains a promise, 'Behold, I come', whose rich variety of meaning corresponds to the rich variety of meaning of the Church's prayer, *Marana tha*. (iii) But the Church will often have to cry 'How long?' with regard both to the Parousia and also to Christ's help in the meantime. Though he indeed comes quickly, yet the time of waiting is long. The Church which must expect him every moment (cf. xiii. 33–7) must also reckon with the fourth watch! (iv) When he comes, whether in his intermediate comings or his final coming, it is with fullness of divine power (cf. Job ix. 8, xxxviii. 16), the Lord of winds and waves.

38. HEALINGS IN THE NEIGHBOURHOOD OF GENNESARET (vi. 53–6)
(Mt. xiv. 34–6)

A summary statement composed by Mark on the basis of good historical tradition. Cf. iii. 7–12.

53. The addition of ἐκεῖθεν after διαπεράσαντες by D it (some MSS.) probably reflects the desire to allow for the fulfilment of the intention of Jesus recorded in *v.* 45, ἐκεῖθεν presumably being meant to refer to Bethsaida; but it is unlikely that it should be read. Probably the wind had driven the disciples out of their course.

Γεννησαρετ is either the fertile and populous plain to the S.W. of Capernaum or else a village or township in it. D it (some MSS.) vg (2) sy[s,p] bo (1) attest here the form Γεννησαρ, which is also attested by I Macc. xi. 67, Josephus, *B.J.* iii, 506. Lagrange maintains that Gennesaret is a village named after the plain, the feminine suffix being added

to the name of the plain. See further Dalman, *S.S.W.*
pp. 128, 130.

προσωρμίσθησαν: 'ran into shore', 'moored against the
shore'.

55. περιέδραμον. Indefinite plural.

ἐπὶ τοῖς κραβάττοις. The definite article here is rather
unexpected. Perhaps it should be rendered 'their'.

56. For ὅπου ἄν and ὅσοι ἄν with the indicative see on
iii. 11, and for ἵνα with the subjunctive to indicate the content of a request see on iii. 9.

κρασπέδου. Jesus, as a pious Jew, wears the fringes or
tassels commanded in Num. xv. 37 ff., Deut. xxii. 12. In the
former place the Hebrew is *ṣîṣiṯ*, in the latter *gᵉḏîlîm*.

For the healing of those who touched see on iii. 10, v. 28.

39. THE COMMANDMENT OF GOD AND THE
TRADITION OF MEN AND THE QUESTION OF
RITUAL CLEANNESS (vii. 1–23)
(Mt. xv. 1–20)

According to Taylor, *vv.* 1–2, 5–8 are an independent
pronouncement-story, to which Mark has attached *vv.* 9–13
and 14–23 as material dealing with similar topics. Others
regard *vv.* 1–2, 5, 14–15 as the original unit, *vv.* 14 f. containing the answer to the question asked in *v.* 5. On the
whole it is best to take *vv.* 1–23 as a single unit. Mark clearly
means his readers to do so; and Mt. xv. 20 b underlines the
unity of the parallel section. The order of Mt. is rather
easier, the Isa. quotation coming after, instead of before,
the *ḳorbān* example, but even in Mk the connection of
thought is fairly clear, *vv.* 9–13 being a counter-attack
(Jesus refuses to allow his adversaries to invoke against him
a tradition which itself is capable of violating the Divine
Law). Mt. xv. 11 perhaps gives a more original form of the
saying which Mark records in *v.* 15.

1. Mark apparently received the material of these verses unconnected with the preceding narratives and he has refrained from creating any artificial connection, introducing the section by a simple καί. He gives no indication of time or place—except that ἐλθόντες ἀπὸ Ἱεροσολύμων (for which see on iii. 22) rather suggests Galilee.

Taylor has no mark of punctuation after Ἱεροσολύμων and so makes καὶ ἰδόντες... ἄρτους in v. 2 parallel to ἐλθόντες ἀπὸ Ἱεροσολύμων in v. 1. (Cf. Souter and the R.V. which have a comma at the end of v. 1.) But it is better to put a full stop after Ἱεροσολύμων, as the Bible Society does. The words ἰδόντες... ἄρτους are then dependent on the verb which Mark intends to use, but which on account of the parenthesis of vv. 3 and 4 he does not express until v. 5 (ἐπερωτῶσιν), and vv. 2 and 5 form one sentence—though the structure is slightly anacoluthic, the καί at the beginning of v. 5 being unnecessary. This gives better sense than the other punctuation; for according to this both the Pharisees and the Jerusalem scribes see the disciples eating with unwashed hands, while the other punctuation would suggest that it was only the scribes from Jerusalem who saw them. There are variant readings in the next verse, which indicate both that from early times a full stop was read after Ἱεροσολύμων and also that the lack of a verb in v. 2 seemed awkward. Thus W Θ f1 f13 al latt sa(1) 𝔰 insert ἐμέμψαντο ('they blamed') after ἄρτους, while D inserts κατέγνωσαν and syp, h insert 'they complained'.

2. ἰδόντες τινὰς...ὅτι...ἐσθίουσιν might possibly be explained as a combination of two different constructions— ὁρᾶν τινά τι ποιοῦντα (cf. i. 10) and ὁρᾶν ὅτι τίς τι ποιεῖ (cf. ii. 16)—but is more probably an example of hyperbaton (i.e. displacement of the subject or object of a subordinate clause so that it becomes the subject or object of another clause, usually the main clause), for which cf. xi. 32, xii. 34, and see further Black, pp. 34–8. Hyperbaton is more

common in Aramaic than in Greek. The *v.l.* (supported by A D W Θ f1 f13 *s*) which omits ὅτι and substitutes ἐσθίοντας for ἐσθίουσιν is clearly an attempt to improve the grammar.

κοιναῖς. Κοινός is a theme-word of this whole section: it occurs again in *v.* 5, while the connected verb κοινοῦν occurs in *vv.* 15, 18, 20 and 23. In classical Greek κοινός means 'common' as opposed to 'private' (ἴδιος). In the LXX it is sometimes used in the classical sense; but in I Macc. i. 47, 62 it is used in the sense 'ritually unclean', for which the Hebrew would be *ṭāmē'*, and it has this sense in the N.T. in this passage and also in Acts x. 14, 28, xi. 8, Rev. xxi. 27. The explanation of this use would seem to be that first κοινός came to be used among Jews as an equivalent for *ḥōl* (which denotes 'that which is free for general use' as opposed to that which is *ḳāḏōš* ('holy'))—a not unnatural extension of the use of κοινός, as is illustrated by the fact that A.V., R.V. use 'common' to render *ḥōl*, e.g. in I Sam. xxi. 4f.—though this usage, which is seen in the N.T. in Heb. x. 29, is not found in the LXX, which renders *ḥōl* by βέβηλος, e.g. in I Sam. xxi. 4f. From this use of κοινός to translate *ḥōl* it was an easy step to use it for *ṭāmē'*, since the two pairs of opposites, *ḳāḏōš* ('holy') and *ḥōl* ('free for general use'), and *ṭāhôr* ('ritually clean') and *ṭāmē'* ('ritually unclean'), though they are quite clearly to be distinguished, are obviously closely related. The meaning of κοιναῖς here ('ritually unclean') would not be understood by Gentile readers: so Mark explains it first by τοῦτ' ἔστιν ἀνίπτοις and then by *vv.* 3f.

ἐσθίουσιν τοὺς ἄρτους. The expression is Jewish: cf. *leḥem 'āḵal* (e.g. Gen. xxxi. 54).

3. πάντες οἱ Ἰουδαῖοι. It has been objected that this phrase would come more naturally from a Gentile than from Mark; but, since in this parenthesis he is only addressing Gentile readers, it is not surprising that he should here adopt a non-Jewish point of view. πάντες is probably an exaggeration, but it seems likely that these rules of ritual purity were widely observed. (See further Taylor, pp. 338f. Interesting light has recently been thrown on the subject by the Dead Sea Scrolls, especially *The Manual of Discipline*.)

πυγμῇ. The difficulty of this word was felt early, as the *v.ll.* show. Δ sy⁵ sa omit πυγμῇ; א W read πυκνά (= 'often'), which is supported by it (some MSS.) vg; but πυγμῇ (= 'with a (the) fist') must clearly be read with A B D (πυκμῇ) L Θ and the great majority of MSS. C. C. Torrey suggested that an original Aramaic *ligmar* (לגמר) = 'at all' was misread as *ligmōd* (לגמד) = 'with the fist';[1] but Black has pointed out the linguistic difficulties in the way of this explanation (Torrey's *ligmōd* is a very dubious word).[2] The explanation is rather to be sought in the fact that according to Jewish custom different sorts of ritual washing were required for different degrees of impurity. In the Talmud a distinction is made between 'dipping (or lustrating) up to the wrist' (*neṭal* or *meśî 'ad happārak*), which is a minor ablution, and the more serious 'plunging up to the wrist' (*ṭebal 'ad happārak*), for which a large quantity of water was required (forty seahs). It seems likely that πυγμῇ νίψωνται is equivalent to the former of these and βαπτίσωνται in the next verse is equivalent to the latter. πυγμῇ might be explained as a not very felicitous way of saying 'up to the wrist'. Perhaps more probably it means 'with a fistful' with reference to the small amount of water necessary for the minor ablution. Other explanations have been suggested,[3] and the problem cannot be said to have been definitively settled.

τὴν παράδοσιν τῶν πρεσβυτέρων: equivalent to Hebrew *massôreṯ hazzeḳēnîm*. What is meant is the Jewish oral tradition or oral law, which was regarded as the 'fence for (preserving the integrity of) the Torah' ((*M*) *Ab.* iii. 14). Josephus, *Ant.* xiii. 297, speaks of τὰ ἐκ παραδόσεως τῶν

---

[1] *Our Translated Gospels* (London, n.d.), pp. 93f.   [2] P. 8.
[3] For a recent suggestion see P. R. Weis, 'A Note on πυγμῇ' in *N.T.S.* iii (1956–7), pp. 233ff.

πατέρων and, XIII. 408, of τῶν νομίμων...ὧν εἰσήνεγκαν οἱ
Φαρισαῖοι κατὰ τὴν πατρῴαν παράδοσιν.

4. ἀπ' ἀγορᾶς. Explained by Black, p. 37, as 'an example
of an emphasising hyperbaton along with a characteristic
Semitic use of the preposition ἀπό (=min), namely, in a
partitive sense': he translates 'anything from the market-
place'. Taking the phrase in this sense and reading ῥαντίσωνται, we get the meaning: 'they do not eat anything from
the market-place unless they sprinkle it'; and this is supported by the Arabic Diatessaron and by sa eth. But it is
probably better to take ἀπ' ἀγορᾶς to mean 'when they come
from the market-place' (cf. the insertion ὅταν ἔλθωσιν in
D W, supported by a number of it and vg MSS.).

ῥαντίσωνται is read by ℵ B, a few minuscules, and supported by sa. It is accepted by the Bible Society, as also by
W.H., Nestle, Huck, Taylor. But A D W Θ f1 f13 and the
great majority of other MSS. have βαπτίσωνται, and this is
supported by latt sy^{s, p} bo. Probably βαπτίσωνται should be
read; it is strongly attested and the alteration to ῥαντίσωνται
can perhaps be explained as due to the difficulty which
βαπτίσωνται would probably present to anyone who was
unfamiliar with the Jewish custom. The word βαπτίσωνται is
probably to be explained as denoting the more thorough
form of ritual washing, the plunging in a basin containing a
large quantity of water (see on *v.* 3 above), necessitated by
the defiling contacts of the market-place.

παρέλαβον. Παραλαμβάνω is the regular word in the N.T.
for 'receiving' tradition.

κρατεῖν. An epexegetic or explanatory infinitive.

ξεστῶν. The word is probably formed from the Latin
sextarius (which also appears in Rabbinic Hebrew as a loanword) and denotes a capacity measure, and so a vessel
holding about such a quantity, and so generally a 'jug',
'pitcher'.

5. After the parenthesis (3f.) the narrative is continued,

but Mark proceeds as though he had forgotten that he had already begun a sentence before his parenthesis—hence the καί which is properly not required.

After γραμματεῖς we should perhaps read λέγοντες with 𝔓⁴⁵ D W Δ Θ f13, some it and vg MSS., syˢ sa.

The question which follows, though ostensibly about the disciples, is really a challenge to Jesus himself.

περιπατοῦσιν. The use of περιπατῶ with reference to a person's way of life reflects Jewish usage (cf. hālak): it is frequent in Paul (e.g. Rom. vi. 4, viii. 4).

6 f. καλῶς: 'truly' (cf. xii. 32, Jn iv. 17).

ὑποκριτῶν. Ὑποκριτής means in classical Greek 'one who answers', so 'interpreter', 'expounder'; in Attic 'an actor'. In the LXX it occurs only twice in the canonical books (Job xxxiv. 30, xxxvi. 13) and represents Hebrew hānēp (= 'godless'). The meaning 'hypocrite' is biblical. The verb ὑποκρίνομαι in classical Greek means 'answer', 'expound', 'play a part (on stage)'; then it comes to have the sense 'exaggerate' (using theatrical style), and finally 'feign', 'pretend' (e.g. in Demosthenes). The thought here is probably not so much that the people concerned were consciously acting a part as that there was a radical inconsistency in their lives. Their outward appearance of piety was a lie, for inwardly they were godless. If they were themselves deceived as well as deceiving others, their situation was more, not less, serious. (See Schniewind, p. 103; *T.W.B.* pp. 109f.)

The quotation (from Isa. xxix. 13) differs from the LXX text slightly, the most significant difference being in the last four words, where the LXX has 'teaching the commandments and doctrines of men', which is more closely reproduced in Col. ii. 22 than here. A more serious difficulty is that the LXX differs from the M.T. From this Rawlinson argues that the quotation in Mk must be due to Mark or a source, and not to Jesus. But, while this is probably true as far as the form of the quotation is concerned, Taylor is probably right in maintaining that the M.T. could have served as a basis for the same charge (v. 8).

8. Jesus challenges the authority of the oral law radically. It pretended to be a fence to protect the Law from infringement, but in actual fact it tampered with the Law. Jesus charges the Pharisees and scribes with actually disobeying the Law of God through their exaggerated reverence for their oral law. For the Pharisees the oral law was equally binding with the written Law: Jesus rejects its authority— he calls it roundly 'tradition *of men*' (contrast παράδοσις τῶν πρεσβυτέρων—a name used by the Jews—in *v.* 3); cf. 'precepts *of men*' in the previous verse. His attitude to the written Law itself is expressed in the phrase τὴν ἐντολὴν τοῦ Θεοῦ: it confronts men with divine authority.

9. Καλῶς should probably be translated 'well enough', 'all right', the sense being: 'You are making a good job of rejecting the commandment of God....' To take the sentence as a question and render: 'Are you acting rightly in...?' seems less satisfactory.

ὑμῶν. Cf. ἀνθρώπων in *v.* 7 and τῶν ἀνθρώπων in *v.* 8.

τηρήσητε. The *v.l.* στήσητε (='establish') is strongly supported, and should perhaps be read. So Taylor.

10. Μωϋσῆς γὰρ εἶπεν. Mt. xv. 4 has ὁ γὰρ Θεὸς εἶπεν. Mark, of course, equally implies that the words are *God's* commandment.

Τίμα τὸν πατέρα σου καὶ τὴν μητέρα σου: an exact quotation of Exod. xx. 12a=Deut. v. 16a. The words Ὁ κακολογῶν...τελευτάτω are from Exod. xxi. 17 (LXX: 16) (cf. Lev. xx. 9). The LXX κακολογῶν here represents the Hebrew verb *ḳillēl*, which is usually rendered by καταρᾶσθαι.

θανάτῳ τελευτάτω. For the construction see on *v.* 42 (ἐξέστησαν ἐκστάσει).

11f. ὑμεῖς. Emphatic—contrasted with Μωϋσῆς. Note the difference between this contrast ('Moses' : 'you') and

that in Mt. v. 21–48 ('Ηκούσατε ὅτι ἐρρέθη τοῖς ἀρχαίοις...
ἐγὼ δὲ λέγω...): in the former case it is a matter of the
scribes and Pharisees tampering with God's Law, in the
latter case, of the Son elucidating its real significance.

Κορβαν is a transliteration of the Hebrew *ḳorbān* (= 'offering', 'oblation'), which occurs eighty times in the O.T., but
only in Lev., Num., and Ezek. The word is derived from
hiḳrîḇ = 'bring near' (Hiph. of *ḳāraḇ*) and denotes an offering
made to God: it is not used of a gift to a man (Mark's
explanatory note, ὅ ἐστιν δῶρον, is open to misunderstanding,
though he no doubt uses δῶρον as a technical term for
'oblation'). That which is offered to God as a *ḳorbān* becomes 'holy' and so is no longer available for ordinary use.
The (*M*) *Ned.* contains many examples of vows containing
the word *ḳorbān* or a substitute. To declare something *ḳorbān*
was to fix upon it the character of an offering dedicated to
God. It did not always mean that the thing concerned had
actually to be offered; rather, that it was withdrawn from
its originally intended use and was no longer available for a
particular person or persons. Usually it was the person
making the vow who was affected, but sometimes the
formula was used in order to prevent someone else from
using something. In the latter case the formula could be
'*Ḳorbān* (or *ḳônām*) be any benefit so-and-so has of me' or
'May such-and-such be *ḳorbān* to you'. In (*M*) *Ned.* viii. 7
we find a close parallel to κορβαν...ὃ ἐὰν ἐξ ἐμοῦ ὠφελήθης
here: '*Ḳônām* be the benefit thou hast from me....' Quite
often the *ḳorbān* formula was used hastily in anger and the
person who used it might afterwards be sorry. So the Rabbis
sought out ways of removing, or at least alleviating, the
effects of such hasty vows. It is not clear, however, whether
in the time of Jesus it was just one school of thought that
adopted the rigid attitude, or whether at that time the rigid
attitude was general, the more lenient view found in the
Rabbinic literature being a later development. Some

Jewish scholars have maintained that this passage is unfair
to the scribes, but it must be remembered that Mark is a
more nearly contemporary witness than is the Mishnah.
Jesus here has in mind a situation in which a man repents
of a harsh vow which would deprive his parents of all the
help which they would normally expect from their son, but
is told by the scribes to whose arbitration his case has been
submitted that he must abide by his vow.

13. ἀκυροῦντες τὸν λόγον τοῦ Θεοῦ τῇ παραδόσει ὑμῶν.
The scribes are actually setting at naught the Word of God
by means of their tradition. It is true that the scribes could
point to an absolute command concerning vows inside
scripture itself—Num. xxx. 1 f. (M.T.: 2 f.)—but it was their
interpretation, their tradition, which was at fault; for it
clung to the letter of the particular passage in such a way as
to miss the meaning of scripture as a whole.

ἣ παρεδώκατε is surprising. It is omitted by Mt. xv. 6 and
also by sy^s here in Mk. Moffatt and R.S.V. render by a
present tense, but that is questionable. Taylor suggests that
we have here a primitive corruption of the text due to the
close association between παράδοσις and παραδίδωμι, and
says that 'the sense requires παρελάβετε'. But perhaps
παρεδώκατε is used rather than παρελάβετε, because the
scribes are here thought of not just as passive recipients of a
tradition but as having had an active and responsible part
in the matter.

Jesus has not replied directly to the scribes' and Pharisees'
question (v. 5), but indirectly he has answered it; for by
showing that the tradition of the elders can lead men to
disregard the Law itself he has shown that it must not be
accepted without question as in all cases obligatory.

14. Καὶ προσκαλεσάμενος πάλιν τὸν ὄχλον. T. W.
Manson mentions these words as possible support for his
suggestion that in the conversation with the scribes and
Pharisees Jesus had used the Hebrew current in the

Rabbinic schools which the people would not understand;[1] but in view of Mark's frequent use of προσκαλεῖσθαι this support is very doubtful. Others see in this clause no more than an editorial link introducing independent material dealing with a similar topic; but it seems quite probable that the link is historical and that the teaching contained in *vv.* 14b–15 was actually called forth by the question in *v.* 5. Jesus' reply to the scribes and Pharisees was meant to silence them; but they had raised the question of cleanness and defilement, and it was a question on which it was desirable that the multitude should be given some instruction.

'Ακούσατέ μου πάντες καὶ σύνετε. Cf. the summons to attentive hearing in iv. 3. (Here the aorist imperatives are used appropriately, since the reference is to a single saying.) The words indicate that what follows is specially important and also that it calls for careful thought.

15. ἔξωθεν. Note that ἔξωθεν and ἔσωθεν, which had come to mean usually simply 'without' and 'within' (e.g. Lk. xi. 39f., II Cor. vii. 5, I Tim. iii. 7), here and also in *vv.* 18, 21 and 23 retain the proper significance of the ending -θεν and mean 'from without', 'from within'.

κοινῶσαι. The verb properly means 'make common', 'communicate', 'share'. Its meaning here ('defile') is determined by the special biblical sense of κοινός (see on *v.* 2). The verb occurs only once in the LXX (IV Macc. vii. 6) and then it means 'defile' (though there is a variant reading which has a different verb): in the N.T. it occurs (apart from this passage and the Mt. parallel) in Acts x. 15, xi. 9, xxi. 28, and Heb. ix. 13.

Rawlinson explains the two parts of the saying as equivalent to a comparison ('pollutions from within are more serious than pollutions from without') and compares Hosea vi. 6. If he is right, the saying is less revolutionary than it at first appears. But if the explanatory teaching in the follow-

[1] *Teaching*, p. 50.

ing verses is authentic or at least true to our Lord's intention, Rawlinson's explanation is inadequate. On the interpretation of the saying see further below. Of its genuineness there can be no doubt.

16. Omitted by ℵ B L Δ* 28 bo (most MSS.) geo¹, but read by A D W Θ f1 f13 *pl* latt sy sa (most MSS.) bo (some MSS.) ς. W.H., Nestle, Huck, Souter, the Bible Society, R.V., R.S.V., omit; but Moffatt, Lagrange, Taylor, and others prefer to read it. Taylor points to its special appropriateness here, but it must be said that that very appropriateness may have suggested its introduction from iv. 9. Perhaps the balance of probability is rather against the verse's authenticity here.

17. καὶ ὅτε εἰσῆλθεν εἰς οἶκον. Cf. ix. 28, 33, x. 10, and also iv. 10.

ἐπηρώτων αὐτὸν οἱ μαθηταὶ αὐτοῦ τὴν παραβολήν. Cf. iv. 10, ix. 11, 28, (32), x. 10, xiii. 3. For παραβολή see on iv. 2 and 11. In view of the nature of the saying in *v.* 15 an inquiry by the disciples would be quite natural and some such explanation as is given in *vv.* 18–23 is not intrinsically improbable—though there are features in it which suggest the influence of catechetical interests on its form.

18. Οὕτως καὶ ὑμεῖς ἀσύνετοί ἐστε; Cf. iv. 13, vi. 52, viii. 17, 21, and also iv. 12, vii. 14 (σύνετε). Οὕτως is here inferential ('then'). The second half of *v.* 18 repeats the substance of *v.* 15a, and then the explanation of *v.* 18b (and *v.* 15a) is given in *v.* 19. (Similarly, *v.* 20 repeats the substance of *v.* 15b, and then the explanation of *v.* 20 (and *v.* 15b) is given in *vv.* 21–3.)

For πᾶς...οὐ... used instead of οὐδείς see Moule, p. 182; M.H. II, pp. 433f. The construction is not un-Greek, but its frequency in the N.T. (cf., e.g., xiii. 20, Jn xi. 26, Acts x. 14, Eph. v. 5) probably reflects Semitic influence. (Cf. Hebrew *lō'*...*kol*....)

19. ἀφεδρῶνα. Ἀφεδρών = classical ἄφοδος or ἀπόπατος = 'a privy'. Instead of this word D reads ὀχετόν, which Wellhausen and Torrey accept and take to mean 'bowel', and, in spite of the breach of grammatical concord, take with καθαρίζων, translating 'the bowel which purifies all foods'. But such violence is unnecessary; for ὀχετόν in D probably means 'sewer' (as in Herodian v. 8. 9, etc.), and anyway ἀφεδρῶνα should surely be read. Here the natural process is spoken of with unselfconscious naturalness (cf. Schlatter, *Evang. Matt.* p. 486).

After ἐκπορεύεται it is best to put a question-mark and a dash (εἰς τὸν ἀφεδρῶνα ἐκπορεύεται being the end of what Jesus says). The words καθαρίζων πάντα τὰ βρώματα are best explained as the evangelist's own comment, drawing out the implications of Jesus' words with an eye on the contemporary problem of what was to be the Church's attitude to Jewish ideas about clean and unclean foods. Cf. our explanation of ii. 10, 28. This interpretation goes back to the Greek Fathers. The words are then grammatically dependent on καὶ λέγει αὐτοῖς at the beginning of *v.* 18, καθαρίζων agreeing with the subject of λέγει.

20. Τὸ ἐκ τοῦ ἀνθρώπου ἐκπορευόμενον. *Casus pendens*, ἐκεῖνο being resumptive.

21. οἱ διαλογισμοὶ οἱ κακοί. The evil thoughts, which are the origin of evil acts.

There follows a list of six nouns in the plural indicating evil acts and six nouns in the singular indicating moral defects or vices. πορνεῖαι is wider than μοιχεῖαι in *v.* 22, as it includes acts of sexual immorality generally. Κλοπαί, φόνοι and the first item of *v.* 22, μοιχεῖαι, occur together (in the singular) in Hos. iv. 2.

22. πλεονεξίαι: 'acts of coveting', or perhaps 'deeds of lustfulness'; for the word is quite often (as here) associated with words denoting sexual sin (e.g. Eph. iv. 19, v. 3, Col. iii. 5, II Pet. ii. 3).

πονηρίαι: 'a general term denoting acts of wickedness' (Taylor).

ἀσέλγεια: 'dissoluteness', 'debauchery'. ὀφθαλμὸς πονηρός probably denotes 'envy' or 'grudgingness', 'illiberality'; cf. Lk. xi. 34 = Mt. vi. 22f., Mt. xx. 15, and also Deut. xv. 9, Ecclus xiv. 10, xxxiv. 13 (LXX; E.VV.: xxxi. 13). Cf. also Deut. xxviii. 54, 56, Prov. xxiii. 6, xxviii. 22, where the LXX has misrepresented the M.T., and Ecclus xxxii (LXX; E.VV.: xxxv). 8, 10 where ἀγαθὸς ὀφθαλμός denotes 'generosity'. In view of this O.T. evidence it is unnecessary to seek to explain ὀφθαλμὸς πονηρός in the gospels by reference to the 'evil eye' of magic. For βλασφημία see on ii. 7. Taylor's view that the word here means 'slander' rather than 'blasphemy' is doubtful. ὑπερηφανία occurs only once in the N.T., though it is frequent in the LXX (where it represents several Hebrew words, most often those derived from the root g'h). The adjective ὑπερήφανος is found five times in the N.T. ἀφροσύνη is frequent in the LXX, usually representing 'iwwelet or nᵉbālāh. B.D.B. say of nābāl: 'foolish, senseless, esp. of the man who has no perception of ethical and religious claims...senseless, esp. of religious insensibility'. The 'fool' is the man who does not know God and does not want to know him.

Note the O.T. flavour of this list. Of the twelve items ten occur in the LXX in the canonical books, while another, ἀσέλγεια, occurs in the LXX in the Apocrypha and is used by two other translations (Aquila and Symmachus) in Hos. It is a thoroughly Jewish catalogue. Taylor argues that the vocabulary of the list is Pauline; but the evidence for Pauline influence, which at first looks impressive, is not nearly as impressive on examination. With regard to Taylor's table showing the distribution of these words in the different parts of the N.T. (p. 346) several points should be noted: (i) The simple comparison of the number of occurrences in Paul with the number of occurrences in Mk is misleading, since the Pauline corpus, even when the Pastorals are omitted, is more than two and a half times as long as Mk. (ii) In the case of πορνεία, κλοπή, μοιχεία, though these do not occur elsewhere in Mk, the cognate verbs do occur. (iii) Four of the expressions, κλοπή, μοιχεία, ὀφθαλμὸς πονηρός, and ὑπερηφανία, do not occur in Paul. (iv) Six of the ten occurrences of πορνεία in Paul are in I and II Cor., and there was apparently a special cause for references to the subject in writing to the Corinthian church. When these points are remembered, the case for Pauline influence in the Markan list appears less strong. It seems fair to say that the vocabulary by itself does not provide any adequate grounds for thinking that the list cannot go back to Jesus. Nor should we press the argument that such lists are not to be found elsewhere in the sayings-tradition; for the list of commandments in x. 19 is not so very dissimilar. At the same time the intrinsic probability that an original list would tend to get extended as a result of catechetical interests is to be admitted. The possibility that the whole of *vv.* 18b–23 is Christian interpretation of the saying in *v.* 15 and that *vv.* 17–18a is simply Mark's device for introducing it must be admitted—but it is no more than a *possibility*.

With regard to this section as a whole the following comments may be made in conclusion: (i) Jesus replies to the challenge of the scribes and Pharisees in *v.* 5 by challenging the authority of the oral law. (It was the oral law, not the written Law itself, that the disciples had infringed.) By the *ḳorbān* example he shows that the oral law can actually have the effect of leading men to violate the commandments of God. In view of this, it cannot claim to be accepted without question as sacrosanct. Thus in *vv.* 1–13 Jesus is taking his stand on the side of the written Law against the oral law. (ii) In the last resort the oral law or tradition was an attempt by men to get control of and to manipulate the Divine Law. It resulted from a false attitude to the Law.

Instead of allowing it to show them that they were sinners who could only live with God's Law on terms of the divine justification of sinners, the Jews were determined to establish their own righteousness. So they must needs attempt to render the Law something they could live with on other terms than the forgiveness of sins, something compatible with their self-righteousness and complacency. In so doing they substituted for the Law of God a human legalism. 'It is characteristic of all those who would find their justification in the Law', says H. Roux, 'that they always end by modifying it or perverting it, in order to escape from it and to make void its authority.'[1] Euthymius' comment on *v.* 13 (quoted by Swete) is in place: φοβηθῶμεν οὖν καὶ ἡμεῖς, ὁ τοῦ Χριστοῦ λαός, μὴ καὶ καθ' ἡμῶν ταῦτα ῥηθείη—for all human handling of the Word of God is continually beset by the temptation to try to turn the Word of God into a business of conventional piety and morals, something manageable and complimentary to human self-complacency. (iii) But Jesus is here not just the champion of the Law against the traditions of men. Verse 15 (unless it be understood as simply equivalent to a comparison—and Mark at any rate in *v.* 19 takes it as going further than that) actually implies the abrogation of the O.T. food laws. Is there then a contradiction between *v.* 15 on the one hand and *vv.* 8 and 10 ff. on the other? At first there seems to be. And the difficulty is not to be removed by saying that Jesus simply set aside the cultic law as unimportant but maintained the moral law, since elsewhere he shows himself conservative toward the cultic law (e.g. i. 44) and he regards the spirit rather than the letter of the moral law. The key is rather that Jesus speaks as the one who is, and knows himself to be, τέλος νόμου (Rom. x. 4)—the one to whom both Law and Prophets bear witness and in whom they find their fulfilment. As such a witness, the Law is that from which one jot

[1] *L'Évang. du Royaume*, p. 192.

or tittle shall in no wise pass away, till all things be accomplished (Mt. v. 18); but now that he has come, who fulfils the Law both by being the one to whom it bears witness and also by fully obeying its radical demands, some elements of it (e.g. laws concerning sacrifices, circumcision, foods), though still valid as witness to Christ, are no longer binding in the sense in which they were before his coming. The mystery of the 'parable' recorded in *v.* 15 is, then, no other than the mystery of the kingdom of God, which is the mystery of the person of Jesus.

40. THE SYRO-PHOENICIAN WOMAN (vii. 24–30)
(Mt. xv. 21–8)

We may agree with Taylor that this narrative contains 'details which stamp it as primitive' and that their evidence is supported by 'signs of Aramaic tradition reflected by the vocabulary and style'; but it is not clear that the Markan form is to be preferred to the Matthaean. (The relation of Mk and Mt. here is problematic, it being by no means obvious that Mk is basic to Mt. xv. 21–8.) In particular, it seems probable that the additional matter in Mt. xv. 23f. comes from a reliable tradition; for this is not the sort of thing that is likely to have been invented. It is conceivable that Mark knew the fuller tradition but omitted some things (and possibly at the same time added his *v.* 27a) in order to guard against the danger of misunderstanding by those for whom he wrote. The Mt. form of the narrative is liable to misunderstanding; but, when it is carefully examined, it clearly does not have the effect of supporting any exclusive Jewish-Christian viewpoint, for in Mt., no less than in Mk, the sequel is the granting of the woman's request, and in Mt. her faith is made to contrast all the more strikingly with the unbelief of Israel's religious leaders (depicted in the previous section) by the emphasis on the discouragement she met. The view that Mt. x. 5f. and xv. 24 'owe their rigour to exploitation by Jewish Christians in controversies regarding the Gentile Mission' (Taylor), which is widely held, seems to result from a failure to reckon seriously enough with the mystery of God's election of Israel.

On the questions raised by this section see further J. Jeremias, 'The Gentile World in the Thought of Jesus' in *B.S.N.T.S.* III (1952), pp. 18–28 and *Jesus' Promise to the* * *Nations* (London, 1958).

24. Ἐκεῖθεν may refer to the house (vii. 17) or to Gennesaret (vi. 53), or it may possibly have had some other reference originally, if it was actually in Mark's source, as the present setting of the narrative is not necessarily its historical setting. But see on vi. 1.

τὰ ὅρια Τύρου. Ὅριον in the singular means 'boundary', in the plural 'territory'. How far Jesus penetrated into this pagan area is not indicated. There is no mention of his entering any town in it (the same is true of his visits to the country of Decapolis and the neighbourhood of Caesarea Philippi—it looks as though he avoided having much contact with Gentiles during his ministry). The purpose of the journey is not recorded. It was not in order to preach, apparently, and there is no indication of a flight from Herod. It appears that Jesus wanted privacy. Was it in order to be better able to teach his disciples (though they are not mentioned by Mark in this section)? Or was it, as Taylor suggests, 'to reflect upon the scope and course of His ministry'? But privacy proved impossible: apparently his fame had spread across the frontier (cf. the mention of Tyre and Sidon in iii. 8).

The second καί is adversative (see Moule, p. 178; and cf. vi. 19, 20, 21).

ἠδυνάσθη. Ἠδυνάσθην is an Ionic form for the aorist of δύναμαι; the ordinary N.T. form is ἠδυνήθην, but ἠδυνάσθην is common in the LXX.

25. ἧς...αὐτῆς. See on i. 7.

προσέπεσεν πρὸς τοὺς πόδας αὐτοῦ. See on v. 22.

26. Ἑλληνίς. She is not Greek by nationality, as the next three words show. So the word must mean either Greek-speaking and Greek in culture or else 'Gentile', 'pagan'. In either case her non-Jewish character is stressed.

Συροφοινίκισσα. The term Συροφοῖνιξ was used to distinguish the Phoenicians of Syria from the Carthaginians (Λιβυφοῖνιξ). It is interesting to compare Elijah's miracle on behalf of a Phoenician woman (I Kgs xvii. 8ff., Lk. iv. 26).

For the ἵνα see on iii. 9.

27. Ἄφες πρῶτον χορτασθῆναι τὰ τέκνα. For τὰ τέκνα cf. Exod. iv. 22, Deut. xiv. 1, xxxii. 6, Isa. i. 2, Jer. xxxi. 9, Hos. xi. 1, Jubilees i. 24f., 28, Rom. ix. 4; and also (M) Ab. iii. 15: 'Beloved are Israel, for they were called children of God; still greater was the love in that it was made known to them that they were called children of God, as it is written: "Ye are the children of the Lord your God."' In πρῶτον... τὰ τέκνα we are up against the mystery of divine election. Cf. Rom. i. 16: Ἰουδαίῳ τε πρῶτον καὶ Ἕλληνι, and also Jn iv. 22, Acts iii. 26, xiii. 46. This priority of the Jews is implied in Isa. ii. 2–4, xlii. 1ff., lx. 1ff.: Israel is first to be gathered, and then afterwards the Gentiles. The Servant of the Lord is first 'to raise up the tribes of Jacob' and then to be 'for a light to the Gentiles' (Isa. xlix. 6). Jesus accepts this divinely appointed order and follows faithfully the path ordained for the Lord's Servant. So his whole earthly life was given to Israel. He was 'made a minister of the circumcision for the truth of God, that he might confirm the promises given unto the fathers' (Rom. xv. 8). For him during his ministry to conduct a mission to the Gentiles would have been to depart from the way of obedience. It is often suggested that πρῶτον is a Markan modification of the original tradition introduced with Gentile Christians in mind (Mt. has no parallel to this part of the verse), but this is by no means certain. As Taylor points out, it seems likely that some scrap of encouragement at least was 'given to the woman to prompt her witty reply'. But, even if πρῶτον or ἄφες πρῶτον χορτασθῆναι τὰ τέκνα is a Markan explanatory gloss added to forestall possible misunderstanding by Gentiles, it is clear that it brings out the true meaning of the attitude of Jesus. It is a mistake to regard the Mt. form of the story as narrow in outlook: Mt. xv. 24 simply indicates the actual limits of Jesus' earthly ministry in the purpose of God.

οὐ γάρ ἐστιν καλὸν λαβεῖν τὸν ἄρτον τῶν τέκνων καὶ τοῖς κυναρίοις βαλεῖν. The Jews called the heathen 'dogs' (examples in S.–B. I, pp. 724f.), but it is doubtful whether Jesus is following that Jewish usage here. The diminutive suggests that the reference is to the little dogs that were kept as pets (cf. b Ket. 61b; b Shab. 155b) and not to the dogs of the courtyard and the street. So, by means of the parable of the difference between the claims of the children of the house and those of the pet dogs, Jesus indicates the difference between the claims of Israel and those of the Gentiles. It is not fitting that he should for the sake of the Gentiles curtail his appointed mission to Israel. He recognizes the distinction between Jews and Gentiles and the historical privilege of the Jews as divinely appointed. At the same time it is no doubt true to say that Jesus intends 'not to extinguish the woman's faith' by his apparent coldness, 'but rather to whet her zeal and inflame her ardour' (Calvin).

28. Ναί is omitted by 𝔓⁴⁵ D W Θ 13 *pc* it (some MSS.) arm. It is perhaps an assimilation to the Mt. parallel.

Κύριε. Only here is Jesus addressed as κύριος in Mk (unless κύριε is read in i. 40, x. 51). It means here perhaps no more than 'sir' (cf. Jn xii. 21). See on i. 3.

καὶ τὰ κυνάρια ὑποκάτω τῆς τραπέζης ἐσθίουσιν ἀπὸ τῶν ψιχίων τῶν παιδίων. Her answer shows that she acknowledges Israel's privilege and does not rebel against

God's election. She does not want to diminish Israel's privileges, but desires only a superfluous crumb. She simply appeals to Jesus' kindness unconditionally. Calvin comments suggestively: 'The greatness of her faith appeared chiefly in this respect, that by the aid of nothing more than a feeble spark of doctrine, she not only recognized the actual office of Christ, and ascribed to him heavenly power, but pursued her course steadily through formidable opposition; suffered herself to be annihilated, provided that she held by her conviction that she would not fail to obtain Christ's assistance; and, in a word, so tempered her confidence with humility, that, while she advanced no unfounded claim, neither did she shut against herself the fountain of the grace of Christ, by a sense of her own unworthiness.... Though he appears to give a harsh refusal to her prayers, yet, convinced that God would grant the salvation which he had promised through the Messiah, she ceases not to entertain favourable hopes; and therefore she concludes that the door is shut against her, not for the purpose of excluding her altogether, but that, by a more strenuous effort of faith, she may force her way, as it were, through the chinks.'

29. Διά: 'in view of', 'because of'.

Jesus grants her request and heals her daughter. It is a healing from a distance: cf. Mt. viii. 5–13, Lk. vii. 1–10, Jn iv. 46–53. Taylor's arguments for thinking that it was rather a case of 'telepathic awareness' on the part of Jesus are only cogent if one starts from certain presuppositions about miracles.

The suggestion of B. W. Bacon that the woman's reply 'was to Him an intimation from the Father, opening His eyes to a wider extension of His Mission' seems to have little to commend it—for her reply does *not* in fact seem to have changed his course.

41. THE HEALING OF THE DEAF-MUTE (vii. 31–7)
(Cf. Mt. xv. 29–31)

The actual unit of tradition apparently begins with *v.* 32 and perhaps ends with *v.* 36. Its claim to be regarded as reliable is very strong, its details being of a sort more likely to be dropped than invented in the course of the development of the tradition.

31. The verse is editorial, connecting this section with the last. πάλιν refers back to *v.* 24. A journey northward from the neighbourhood of Tyre to Sidon and then south-eastward past Caesarea Philippi and through Philip's territory to a point on the eastern shore of the Lake of Galilee within the territory of the Decapolis is certainly roundabout, but there is no particular reason why Jesus should not have made it. It is not absolutely necessary to take διὰ Σιδῶνος to imply that Jesus actually entered the city of Sidon. The *v.l.* καὶ Σιδῶνος in 𝔭⁴⁵ A W f1 f13 *pl* sy sa (most MSS.) 𝔰 is of course easier, but is probably an early attempt to lessen the difficulty. Wellhausen's conjecture that διὰ Σιδῶνος represents a mistranslation of an original which should have been rendered εἰς Βηθσαιδαν (i.e. Bethsaida—it is so spelt in D at vi. 45) is hardly to be accepted—though it would certainly make a more obvious journey. ἀνὰ μέσον + genitive (= 'in the midst of') is rare in classical Greek, but is used in the LXX and is common in the papyri. If the neighbourhood of Hippos is intended, as it seems to be, the use of ἀνὰ μέσον is a little surprising. It is possible that this verse reflects a certain vagueness on Mark's part about the geography of northern Palestine.

32. The story of the cure of the deaf-mute begins with this verse. No note of time or place is contained in it, but Mark's editorial link (*v.* 31) suggests that it occurred in Decapolis.

φέρουσιν. For the indefinite plural cf. ii. 3, etc.

κωφόν. The word means 'blunt', 'dull': so it can mean both 'deaf' and 'dumb', and can also be used with regard to sight or intelligence. Here it means 'deaf'.

μογιλάλον. An extremely rare word. It occurs in the N.T. only here and in the LXX only in Isa. xxxv. 6; besides, it occurs in three other places in other Greek versions of the O.T. and (rarely) in late Greek writers. Strictly it should mean 'speaking with difficulty', 'having an impediment in speech'; this meaning is perhaps supported here by ἐλάλει ὀρθῶς in v. 35, but ἀλάλους in v. 37 supports the meaning 'dumb'. In view of the rareness of the word, it is almost certain that Isa. xxxv. 6 was in Mark's mind. (The v.l. μογγιλάλον ('hoarse of speech'), though found in a number of MSS., is hardly likely to be right: it is a word that is not given by L. & S. at all, but see Bauer s.v.)

33. καὶ ἀπολαβόμενος αὐτὸν ἀπὸ τοῦ ὄχλου κατ' ἰδίαν. Cf. viii. 23: ἐξήνεγκεν αὐτὸν ἔξω τῆς κώμης. Presumably to be connected with the injunction to tell no one in v. 36 (and also viii. 26?). See on i. 25. Is it perhaps also to be connected with the special difficulties which this cure seems to have presented? For the use of ἀπολαμβάνω of drawing a person aside privately cf. II Macc. vi. 21, Herodotus I. 209, etc.

ἔβαλεν τοὺς δακτύλους αὐτοῦ εἰς τὰ ὦτα αὐτοῦ καὶ πτύσας ἥψατο τῆς γλώσσης αὐτοῦ. 'Such actions are common to the technique of Greek and Jewish healers' (Taylor). For the touching of the part requiring healing cf. the example from j Ket. quoted in S.–B. II, p. 15; and see also on i. 41 (ἥψατο). For the use of spittle cf. viii. 22–6, Jn ix. 1–7; also Tacitus, Hist. IV. 81, Suetonius, Vesp. 7, and S.–B. II, pp. 15–17. Spittle was used in ancient magic along with incantations with a view to driving away the demon held responsible for the particular malady that needed curing. It was also used as a natural remedy. There is no question of the magical use here; but whether Jesus made use of spittle simply in order to indicate to the man that he was to expect a cure and so to awaken faith on his part, or whether he also had in mind any natural effect of the spittle, it is difficult to decide.

The variant readings in this verse seem to have originated from the wish to be less vague about the use of the spittle; but the text printed above is probably original.

34. ἀναβλέψας εἰς τὸν οὐρανόν. See on vi. 41.

ἐστέναξεν. In viii. 12 ἀναστενάζω is used. Taylor rightly rejects the suggestion that this sighing or groaning is connected with the technique of magic. Cf. Jn xi. 33, 38. Schniewind comments that στενάζω 'is a strong expression, which Paul uses for the inmost wrestling of the Christian (Rom. viii. 22f., 26; II Cor. v. 2, 4)', and sees its use here as congruous with the fact that the disablement is thought of as the result of demonic activity (as is indicated by Εφφαθα and δεσμός). It indicates the strong emotion of Jesus as he wages war against the power of Satan, and has to seek divine aid in urgent prayer.

Εφφαθα. For the use of the Aramaic word see on v. 41.

Εφφαθα represents 'etpattaḥ or contracted 'eppattaḥ, from the verb pᵉṭaḥ, and means 'be opened' or 'be released'. S.-B., II, pp. 17f., give examples of the verb being used in connection with the curing of blindness. The idea is not of the particular part of the person being opened, but of the whole person being opened or released. Cf. Lk. xiii. 16 and, in Mk, the use of δεσμός in the next verse, and also iii. 27. One whom Satan has kept shut up and bound is being released. To liken the command to the 'verbal encouragement' used in modern psychotherapy, as Taylor does, is not very helpful. It is rather the command that shatters the fetters by which Satan has held his victim bound.

Διανοίχθητι. Διανοίγω means 'open completely'.

35. ὁ δεσμὸς τῆς γλώσσης αὐτοῦ. See above on v. 34.

ἐλάλει: 'he began to speak'.

ὀρθῶς suggests that he had been suffering from a defect in

252

his speech rather than from dumbness. But contrast ἀλάλους in *v.* 37.

36. διεστείλατο...λέγωσιν. Cf. i. 25, 44, iii. 12, v. 43, viii. 26, and see note on i. 25. But it is noteworthy that the Gentile demoniac is not told to be silent (v. 19), and the implication of Mark's editorial link in *v.* 31 is that this healing also took place on Gentile soil.

μᾶλλον περισσότερον is pleonastic.

37. ὑπερπερισσῶς only occurs here: it must mean 'exceedingly'. Cf. ὑπερεκπερισσῶς, ὑπερεκπερισσοῦ.

ἐξεπλήσσοντο. See on i. 22.

Καλῶς πάντα πεποίηκεν. Perhaps an echo of Gen. i. 31: καὶ εἶδεν ὁ Θεὸς τὰ πάντα, ὅσα ἐποίησε· καὶ ἰδοὺ καλὰ λίαν. (Cf. also Ecclus xxxix. 16.) If so, we might compare Jn v. 17, where the working of the Son is associated with that of the Father.

It is better to place a colon after πεποίηκεν than a comma.

καὶ τοὺς κωφοὺς...λαλεῖν. Probably an echo of Isa. xxxv. 5 f. Perhaps these words and the preceding καλῶς πάντα πεποίηκεν reflect Christian meditation on the incident.

This narrative forms a pair with viii. 22-6, vii. 31-7 concluding the complex containing the Feeding of the Five Thousand, and viii. 22-6 the complex containing the Feeding of the Four Thousand. The two miracles have a notable feature in common. In both cases the narrative suggests that the cure was accomplished with difficulty and not instantaneously. So here Jesus prays (ἀναβλέψας εἰς τὸν οὐρανόν) and groans (ἐστέναξεν) and makes use of physical manipulations and spittle (*v.* 33), and it is implied that the cure took some time (εὐθύς in *v.* 35 only indicates that the loosing of the tongue followed immediately on the opening of the ears). This contrasts strikingly with such miracles as the healing of the leper (i. 41 f.) and that recorded in Mt. viii. 5 ff. = Lk. vii. 1 ff. It is noticeable that neither the healing of the deaf-mute nor the healing of the blind man of Bethsaida

is reproduced in Mt. and Lk. The later Synoptists apparently preferred to dwell on miracles which more obviously
illustrated the power of Jesus' word.

As the two miracles are closely similar and Mark seems to
underline their similarity—both concern healings that figure
in Isa. xxxv. 5 f., and he has placed them in parallel positions
in relation to the two feeding-miracles—it is probable that
Mark regarded them as a pair. He has placed the second
member of the pair immediately before Peter's Confession
(viii. 27 ff.). So it seems likely that he was aware of the
illuminating parallel between these two healings and Peter's
Confession, and that he intended his readers to see in these
healing miracles not only signs for faith that the promised
intervention of God of Isa. xxxv had taken place in the
ministry of Jesus (we saw above the evidence that he had
this chapter in mind—see on *v.* 32), but also an instructive
comment upon the apostles' recognition of Jesus as the
Christ. This is confirmed by the fact that in viii. 18 Jesus
refers to the blindness and deafness of the Twelve. The
Twelve had been deaf to the Word of God (it is interesting
to notice how often there are references to hearing in Mk:
e.g. iv. 3, 9, 12, 15, 18, 20, 23, 24, 33, vii. 14, [16], viii. 18,
ix. 7); but Jesus had taken them apart (did Mark see in
ἀπολαβόμενος αὐτὸν ἀπὸ τοῦ ὄχλου κατ᾽ ἰδίαν a picture of the
calling and training of the Twelve? Cf. i. 16–20, ii. 13 f.,
iii. 13–19, iv. 10–20, vi. 31, vii. 17–23, viii. 14–21, 27),
and at last he had opened their ears—by a miracle which
had been costly and gradual. They had been blind, but he
had opened their eyes, so that they recognized him as the
Christ. They had been dumb, but he had loosed their
tongues so that they were enabled at last to confess him.

If what has just been said is right, it is not improbable that
Mark also saw in these miracles a reminder for the contemporary Church that all true faith and all true confession
of Christ is miracle. We may well also see in the order here

(first ears, then tongue) a reminder that it is only as the Church hears the Word of God that it has anything worthwhile to say.

42. THE FEEDING OF THE FOUR THOUSAND (viii. 1–10)
(Mt. xv. 32–9)

See on vi. 34–44, and also the general introduction to vi. 14–viii. 26.

1. Note the absence of a connecting particle—unless δέ is read with D W Θ 28 700 and some versions.

ἐν ἐκείναις ταῖς ἡμέραις connects the episode loosely with vii. 24–37, but implies that Mark lacked precise information. The position of the narrative suggests that, since no fresh geographical detail is given, Mark thought of this incident as taking place in Decapolis—so on Gentile soil.

προσκαλεσάμενος. In contrast with vi. 35, it is Jesus who here takes the initiative.

2. σπλαγχνίζομαι. See on vi. 34; but note that, while there the ground of compassion is the fact that the people are like sheep without a shepherd, here it is the fact that they have been so long without food.

ἡμέραι τρεῖς: a parenthetic nominative or *nominativus pendens*. Cf. the Mt. parallel and Lk. ix. 28. As the parenthetic nominative occurs often in the papyri and can actually be traced back to the fifth century B.C. in popular Attic, there is no need to regard it as a Semitism.

Again contrast vi. 34–44, where only one day is involved.

3. εἰσίν. So B L Δ 892 bo. But it is better to read ἥκασιν with ℵ A D W Θ *al* f1 28 33 *pm* latt ς. ἥκασιν (the perfect sense of ἥκω sometimes causes it to be given a perfect form of conjugation) is, as Moulton says, 'a form which we might expect in Mk, and equally expect to find removed by revisers'.[1]

[1] *Proleg.* p. 53.

4. ὅτι is *recitativum*.

ἄρτων. The genitive of that with which one feeds someone is quite normal, though a dative or even a second accusative could also have been used.

5. εἶπαν. Note the ending. There was a tendency in late Greek to assimilate strong aorists to weak. Cf. viii. 28, εἶχαν in *v*. 7 below, ἐπέβαλαν in xiv. 45.

6. Much less vivid than vi. 39f.

εὐχαριστήσας. In vi. 41 εὐλογῶ was used, as here in *v*. 7 and in xiv. 22. Both εὐλογῶ and εὐχαριστῶ represent the Aramaic *bārēḵ* (Hebrew *bērēḵ*). Jeremias regards the substitution of εὐχαριστήσας for εὐλογήσας as a 'Graecizing of the Semitism'.[1] εὐχαριστήσας is also used in xiv. 23. See further on vi. 41.

7. καὶ εἶχαν ἰχθύδια ὀλίγα. Added rather awkwardly as an afterthought—probably because fish were not an element of the Eucharist (though they did of course become an important eucharistic symbol as a result of their part in the feeding miracles).

αὐτά is read by ℵ B C L W Δ Θ *al* f1 (exc. 118) f13 *al* it (most MSS.) vg. Some other MSS. have ταῦτα. But E G H S U V Ω 22 33 118 579 700 *pm* have εὐλογήσας without any object expressed, while D 472, with the support of it (1 MS.), have εὐχαριστήσας alone. The fact that there is a variation of order (between εὐλογήσας αὐτά and αὐτὰ εὐλογήσας) among those MSS. which do have αὐτά is possibly some support for its omission. Probably we should omit αὐτά (and also αὐτούς in Lk. ix. 16), and explain its presence in so many MSS. as due to Gentile scribes' ignorance of the Jewish usage.[2] On the other hand, if Mark did write εὐλογήσας αὐτά, his meaning would be 'having blessed (God's Name) for (or 'over') them', not 'having blessed them'. Cf. Paul's τὸ ποτήριον τῆς εὐλογίας ὃ

[1] *E.W.* p. 119.
[2] Cf. H. W. Beyer in *T.W N.T.* ii, p. 760; Jeremias, *E.W.* p. 119.

εὐλογοῦμεν (I Cor. x. 16), which surely means 'the cup of blessing for (or 'over') which we bless (God's Name)' and not 'the cup of blessing which we bless'.

8. σπυρίδας. Σπυρίς, which occurs in the N.T. also in viii. 20, Mt. xv. 37, xvi. 10, and Acts ix. 25, denotes 'a mat basket for provisions'. In Acts ix. 25 it is a basket large enough to carry a man. Another form, σφυρίς, is found here in many MSS.; even Attic Greek oscillates between the two forms.

9. Once again Mt. enhances the miracle by adding χωρὶς γυναικῶν καὶ παιδίων, as in the parallel to vi. 44.

10. The crossing is related in summary form. Contrast vi. 45 ff.

The name Δαλμανουθα here, together with the name Μαγαδαν in the Mt. parallel and also the various *v.ll.* in both Mk and Mt., presents a problem to which no really satisfactory solution has yet been found. The name Dalmanutha only occurs here. Most MSS. have Δαλμανουθα or a similar word; but D* has Μελεγαδα, Dᶜ Μαγαιδα, 𝔭⁴⁵ apparently Μαγεδαν, Θ f1 f13 Μαγδαλα. Various conjectures have been offered, but none is really convincing. It is best, as Lagrange points out, to retain Δαλμανουθα until a more satisfactory solution is reached.

43. THE PHARISEES REQUIRE A SIGN (viii. 11–13)
(Mt. xvi. 1–4; cf. Mt. xii. 38f., Lk. xi. 29)

The narrative is perhaps constructed by Mark; but it rests on a reliable tradition, though one which lacked details of time, place and circumstance.

11. No connection with the context is indicated. The section's position was probably dictated by topical considerations.

σημεῖον: the Synoptists use σημεῖον to denote an outward compelling proof of divine authority—something which unbelief demands but Jesus resolutely refuses to give. Cf.

Mt. xvi. 1–4, xii. 38f., Lk. xi. 16, 29, and also I Cor. i. 22. The request for such a sign is a temptation (πειράζοντες in Mt. xvi. 1, Lk. xi. 16 and here; cf. perhaps Mt. iv. 5–7 = Lk. iv. 9–12). To grant it would be to make faith impossible (for it would preclude a personal decision) and to abandon the path of messianic veiledness ordained by the Father. The miracles of Jesus are not signs in this sense. So the Synoptists call them not σημεῖα, but δυνάμεις. The Fourth Evangelist, on the other hand, though he does sometimes use the word σημεῖον in the Synoptists' sense (ii. 18, iv. 48, vi. 30), uses it characteristically of the miracles regarded as signs pointing to the secret of Jesus' Person, an effective manifestation of his glory for those who already believe, but for others unconvincing. This idea is present in the Synoptists, but the word σημεῖον is not used by them to convey it. (See concluding note on i. 29–31.) The Pharisees' request reflects their spiritual blindness: unable to recognize the signs which God gives them, they demand signs of their own choosing.

For the background of σημεῖον as used here reference should be made to Exod. iv. 8f., Deut. xiii. 1 (M.T.: xiii. 2), Isa. vii. 10–17, xxxviii. 7, in all of which the Hebrew 'ôth is represented in the LXX by σημεῖον. See further Schlatter, *Evang. Matt.* pp. 413–15.

ἀπὸ τοῦ οὐρανοῦ. Possibly simply a periphrasis for 'from God'; or possibly we should cf. Jer. x. 2 (M.T.: 'ôth; LXX: σημεῖον) and *Sifre Deut.* on Deut. xiii. 1 (M.T.: 2): 'sign in the heavens; wonder on earth' (perhaps cf. also Joel ii. 30f., Mk xiii. 24f., etc.).

12. ἀναστενάξας. The compound verb only occurs here in the N.T.: it is a strengthened form of στενάζω, which is itself properly a frequentative of στένω. The simple verb was used in vii. 34.

ἡ γενεὰ αὕτη. For γενεά cf. viii. 38, ix. 19, xiii. 30. In the LXX γενεά is used to translate several Hebrew words: most

frequently *dôr*, but also *zera'*, *môledet*, *mišpāḥāh*, and '*am*.
Perhaps here the phrase is best taken to mean 'this people',
i.e. the Jewish people (cf. Jer. viii. 3, where γενεά in the LXX
represents *mišpāḥāh*). But see further on the other passages
cited above.

αμην. See on iii. 28.

ὑμῖν. Omitted by B L 892 1342; but it should probably be
read. (𝔭⁴⁵ W omit λέγω ὑμῖν.)

εἰ δοθήσεται. A strong denial, the εἰ being the equivalent
of the Hebrew '*im* used in an imprecation. In II Kgs vi. 31
the full form is illustrated, while Ps. xcv (LXX: xciv). 11
provides an example of the usage with the apodosis omitted,
the isolated protasis remaining as a form of strong negation,
as here. In Aramaic it would be a Hebraism, reminiscent of
the O.T.

A sign such as they desire will not be given—though signs
of God's choosing are indeed being given.

In the Mt. parallel (xvi. 4) and also in Mt. xii. 39 =
Lk. xi. 29 the words εἰ μὴ τὸ σημεῖον Ἰωνᾶ are added.

13. πάλιν is better taken with ἐμβάς than with ἀφείς.

44. CONVERSATION IN THE BOAT (viii. 14–21)
(Mt. xvi. 5–12; cf. Lk. xii. 1)

The saying contained in *v.* 15 is commonly held to be an
isolated saying of Jesus which has been artificially inserted
into this context on the strength of the connection between
leaven and bread. But, as Taylor points out, 'it is not
Mark's habit to insert sayings into the body of a narrative,
as Matthew does...but to append them at the end'. Moreover, the saying is natural enough in this context (see below
on *v.* 15). We conclude that Mark has probably placed it in
its true historical setting. To the question 'Why then is
the saying not taken up in the rest of the section?' the
most likely answer seems to be that the disciples were so

preoccupied with their own problem and the resulting re-criminations among themselves that they failed to heed at the time what Jesus was saying to them.

If viii. 1 ff. is a doublet of vi. 34 ff., then we must conclude with Taylor that in the latter part of the section we are 'at a greater distance from' the original tradition 'than is usual in Mk'; but on the assumption that there really were two feeding miracles this conclusion is unnecessary.

14. The verse is closely linked with *v.* 13, ἐν τῷ πλοίῳ connecting with ἐμβὰς ἀπῆλθεν εἰς τὸ πέραν. As *v.* 13 is also linked with *vv.* 11 f. by αὐτούς, it is clear that the two sections are connected, even if *v.* 13 be regarded as the beginning of the new section.

ἐπελάθοντο. Translate by the pluperfect, 'they had for-gotten' (cf. Moule, pp. 11, 16).

εἰ μή: 'except': cf. ii. 26, v. 37, etc. (The smoother reading of 𝔭⁴⁵ W Θ f 13, etc.—ἕνα μόνον ἄρτον ἔχοντες instead of καὶ εἰ μὴ ἕνα ἄρτον οὐκ εἶχον—should probably be rejected as an improvement of a harsher original. So Taylor.)

15. Ὁρᾶτε. Here 'take care', 'take heed'. See on i. 44.

βλέπετε ἀπό. 'Beware of': cf. xii. 38, and also *B.G.U.* IV. 1079 (A.D. 41): βλέπε σατὸν ἀπὸ τῶν Ἰουδαίων.

τῆς ζύμης τῶν Φαρισαίων καὶ τῆς ζύμης Ἡρῴδου. In the N.T. (I Cor. v. 6–8, Gal. v. 9) and also in Rabbinic Judaism leaven is a common metaphor for the evil tendency in man which, though it may seem only a small thing, nevertheless corrupts the whole man. (In the N.T. it stands for something good only in Mt. xiii. 33 = Lk. xiii. 21.) Mt. xvi. 12 explains ζύμη by reference to teaching; Lk. xii. 1 glosses it by ἥτις ἐστὶν ὑπόκρισις: Mark, on the other hand, leaves the metaphor uninterpreted. The explanations are clearly secondary, but they are not inconsistent with each other or with the probabilities of the case. The disciples are to be on their guard against the hypocrisy of the Pharisees which spreads its influence by means of their teaching. The reference to the Pharisees is appropriate enough after *vv.* 11 f. The reference to Herod might possibly have been suggested by the proximity of Tiberias, but would be quite natural even apart from any such special reminder. Lagrange quotes Bede's comment: 'The leaven of Herod is adultery, murder, hastiness in swearing, affectation of piety, and hatred of Christ and His Forerunner.' It is apparently a warning against the godlessness of the man of the world, while the reference to the Pharisees is a warning against a false and inconsistent piety. Mt. xvi. 6 substitutes Σαδδουκαίων for τῆς ζύμης Ἡρῴδου; but this is probably secondary—Pharisees and Sadducees are associated together in Mt. iii. 7, xvi. 1, as well as in xvi. 6 and 11 f.

16. 𝔭⁴⁵ B W f1 (exc. 118) *al* it (some MSS.) co have ἔχουσιν; cf. εἶχαν read by D, supported by it (most MSS.). The great majority of Greek MSS., however, have ἔχομεν, and this reading is supported by it (some MSS.) vg syᵖ·ʰ, etc. Most of the authorities attesting ἔχομεν also insert λέγοντες before ὅτι. Probably we should prefer ἔχουσιν; for λέγοντες and ἔχομεν look like assimilation to Mt. If ἔχομεν is read, ὅτι can be either *recitativum* or else itself included in the quotation (with the meaning 'because'), an ellipse being understood: '(The Teacher says this,) because we have no bread.' If, however, we read ἔχουσιν, ὅτι cannot be *recitativum*, but must be translated either 'that' (introducing an indirect statement), or 'because' (giving the reason why διελογίζοντο πρὸς ἀλλήλους), or 'why' (introducing an indirect question, as in ix. 11, 28). Of these the last is perhaps the most satisfactory.

17. γνούς. There is no need to suppose that the perception here referred to was either supernatural or intuitive.

οὔπω νοεῖτε οὐδὲ συνίετε; Jesus rebukes the disciples for their slowness to understand (cf. iv. 13, 40, vi. 52, vii. 18).

πεπωρωμένην. See on iii. 5, vi. 52. Note how in the Mt.

parallel the rebuke is softened, the latter part of this verse
and all the next verse being omitted.

18. The first part of the verse is reminiscent of Jer. v. 21,
Ezek. xii. 2, and also Isa. vi. 9f. The last of these was quoted
in iv. 12, with reference to 'them that are without'. The last
three words of the verse introduce the direct allusions to the
miracles of vi. 34ff., viii. 1 ff., in *vv.* 19–20. On οὐ μνημονεύετε
Calvin's comment on Mt. xvi. 8 is apt: 'From these words
we infer that all who have once or twice experienced the
power of God, and distrust it for the future, are convicted of
unbelief; for it is faith that cherishes in our hearts the
remembrance of the gifts of God, and faith must have been
laid asleep, if we allow them to be forgotten.' But Jesus'
intention can hardly have been to suggest that the disciples
might always expect a miraculous meal, if they had forgotten the provisions. Rather, the point would seem to have
been that, had they remembered (and understood) the
miracles of vi. 34ff. and viii. 1 ff., they would not now have
been so wholly preoccupied with their own anxieties as to
be quite incapable of attending to what Jesus was trying to
say to them—they would rather have recognized the
authority of him who was speaking to them and therefore
given him their full attention.

19–20. The numbers are precise and a distinction is made
between the κόφινοι of the one story (vi. 43) and the
σπυρίδες of the other (viii. 8).

For εἰς used as equivalent to a dative cf. perhaps xiii. 10
(but see note *in loc.*); for other examples see Moule, p. 69.

σπυρίδων πληρώματα κλασμάτων. The first two words are
equivalent to a single noun, 'basketfuls' (cf. Euripides, *Ion*,
1051: κρατήρων πληρώματα), and κλασμάτων is a genitive of
content dependent on them.

45. THE HEALING OF THE BLIND MAN AT
BETHSAIDA (viii. 22–6)
(Mk only)

The similarities between this narrative and vii. 31–7 are striking: καὶ φέρουσιν αὐτῷ and καὶ παρακαλοῦσιν αὐτὸν ἵνα occur in both, while τυφλόν here corresponds with κωφὸν καὶ μογιλάλον, and αὐτοῦ ἅψηται with ἐπιθῇ αὐτῷ τὴν χεῖρα (ἐπιθεὶς τὰς χεῖρας αὐτῷ actually occurs later in this narrative, while ἥψατο occurs in vii. 33); with καὶ ἐπιλαβόμενος here cf. καὶ ἀπολαβόμενος in vii. 33; in both narratives Jesus works the cure in privacy or semi-privacy (cf. ἐξήνεγκεν αὐτὸν ἔξω τῆς κώμης here with ἀπολαβόμενος αὐτὸν ἀπὸ τοῦ ὄχλου κατ᾽ ἰδίαν in vii. 33); in both spittle is used (καὶ πτύσας, vii. 33, viii. 23); the words καὶ ἀναβλέψας occur in both (though in vii. 34 the subject is Jesus, in viii. 24 it is the blind man); τηλαυγῶς here corresponds with ὀρθῶς in vii. 35; and the command μηδὲ εἰς τὴν κώμην εἰσέλθῃς (or μηδενὶ εἴπῃς εἰς τὴν κώμην, if that reading be preferred) with ἵνα μηδενὶ λέγωσιν in vii. 36.

In view of the close similarity of the two sections Bultmann and others regard them as duplicate accounts of the same incident. But this explanation is rightly rejected by Taylor, who points out that 'the striking observation' in viii. 24 'is not the kind of variant which might arise in different accounts of the same story, but a highly distinctive detail which stamps the story as genuine'; that 'the reference to a second laying on of hands in *v.* 25 is without parallel in the Gospels and is not likely to have been invented'; and that 'to some extent the linguistic agreements may be explained by the admitted tendency of Mk to repeat himself and by the ease with which popular narratives assume fixed forms in oral tradition'. The true explanation is more probably that Mark had genuine historical traditions of two distinct incidents but regarded them as forming a pair and under-

lined this by similarity of treatment. See further on vii. 31–7.
The following notes should be supplemented by reference to
the notes on vii. 31 ff.

22. Καὶ ἔρχονται εἰς Βηθσαϊδάν. It is possible that this
sentence belongs to the previous section, but more probable
that it goes with what follows and that this incident was
already connected with Bethsaida in the tradition which
Mark received. The variant reading Βηθανίαν (D 262 it)
'may be a scribal correction influenced by κώμη in vv. 23
and 26' (Taylor).

23. κώμης with reference to Bethsaida seems odd; but
possibly it reflects some local usage such as could easily be
illustrated in modern England. Maybe the older fishing
village is meant. Bethsaida was a considerable town.

ἐπηρώτα αὐτόν, Εἴ τι βλέπεις; Only in this narrative does
Jesus ask such a question of someone he is healing. The use
of εἰ to introduce a direct question is not classical, but is
quite common in the N.T. (esp. in Lk. and Acts), though it
only occurs here in Mk: see Moule, pp. 151, 158.

24. ἀναβλέψας. In x. 51 ἀναβλέπειν means 'recover
one's sight'; but here it more probably means 'look up'.
'At the question the man involuntarily raised his eyes'
(Swete).

Βλέπω τοὺς ἀνθρώπους ὅτι ὡς δένδρα ὁρῶ περιπατοῦντας.
The words ὅτι and ὁρῶ are omitted by D W Θ and many
other Greek MSS. supported by the ancient versions; but
the more difficult reading of ℵ B, etc. is to be preferred. It
has been suggested that the difficulty is to be explained as
due to translation from Aramaic, an original *dᵉ* which
should have been translated οὕς having been wrongly
rendered by ὅτι,[1] or, alternatively, an original emphatic
hyperbaton ('I see men that like trees they are walking')
having confused a translator who took the Aramaic participial present to be a true participle and so put it into the

[1] W. C. Allen in *E.T.* xiii, p. 330.

accusative in agreement with 'men' and added a second verb (ὁρῶ).[1] But Taylor may well be right in thinking these suggestions unnecessary. The Greek as it stands vividly suggests the man's excitement.

There is a distinction between βλέπειν and ὁρᾶν: ' βλέπω... stresses more strongly than ὁράω the function of the eye. So it is often used absolutely as the opposite to being blind.'[2] We might translate: 'I can actually see people, for they look to me like trees—only they walk!'

At this stage the cure is apparently incomplete.

25. πάλιν refers back to ἐπιθεὶς τὰς χεῖρας αὐτῷ in v. 23. A gradual cure is implied here more plainly than anywhere else in the gospels, though vii. 32 ff. also suggests gradualness, as we saw above. The reference to a second laying on of hands is unique in the recorded miracles of Jesus.

διέβλεψεν: 'saw clearly'.

ἀπεκατέστη. Note the double augment (cf. iii. 5).

ἐνέβλεπεν. Ἐμβλέπειν is 'to look at'—to fix one's gaze on a particular object. Note the careful distinction of tenses: the aorist διέβλεψεν indicating the definite point at which the man achieved clear sight, and the imperfect ἐνέβλεπεν denoting continued action (or perhaps it is inceptive).

26. ἀπέστειλεν αὐτὸν εἰς οἶκον αὐτοῦ. Cf. ii. 11, v. 19.

Μηδὲ εἰς τὴν κώμην εἰσέλθῃς is read by ℵ B L W f1 (exc. 118) sy[s] sa bo (most MSS.) fa, and accepted by the Bible Society. But Taylor following C. H. Turner prefers, perhaps rightly, the reading implied by k (cf. c, and also D q): μηδενὶ εἴπῃς εἰς τὴν κώμην. Perhaps the εἰς for ἐν in this reading offended some people's grammatical strictness and so gave rise to the ℵ B reading. The later Byzantine text shows a conflation of the two readings—μηδὲ εἰς τὴν κώμην εἰσέλθῃς μηδὲ εἴπῃς τινὶ ἐν τῇ κώμῃ.

---

[1] Black, pp. 36f.   [2] W. Michaelis in *T.W.N.T.* v, p. 317.

V. THE WAY TO JERUSALEM

(viii. 27–x. 52)

With the account of Peter's confession of Jesus as the Messiah and the first prediction of the Passion the second half of the gospel begins. Henceforth Jesus addresses his teaching to the disciples rather than to the crowds. This division describes the journey from the neighbourhood of Caesarea Philippi to Jerusalem, and the main groups of material are introduced in turn by brief geographical notes (viii. 27, ix. 30, x. 1, 32).

46. PETER'S CONFESSION AND THE FIRST PREDICTION OF THE PASSION (viii. 27–33)
(Mt. xvi. 13–23: Lk. ix. 18–22)

For Bultmann *vv.* 27–30 are a 'faith-legend' expressing the Christian community's confession and *v.* 31 is similarly secondary, the creation of tne early Church. The original ending of the legend of Peter's confession is preserved, he thinks, in Mt. xvi. 17–19, and has been replaced by Mark by 'a polemic against the Jewish-Christian position represented by Peter from the standpoint of the Hellenistic Christianity of the Pauline sphere'.[1] Against this view it may fairly be pointed out that 'The reference to "the villages of Caesarea Philippi" by a writer who so rarely gives place-names commands respect' (Taylor) (Bultmann's attempt to separate the mention of Caesarea Philippi from *vv.* 27–30 and to fasten it to *vv.* 22–6 is unconvincing); the connection with the Transfiguration (ix. 2) seems to be pre-Markan and is precise; the picture of Peter in *vv.* 27–33 is life-like and suggests Peter's own reminiscence; the fact that Jesus does

[1] *G.S.T.* p. 277.

not confirm the confession is surely significant; and the
question asked by Holl: 'Who from the primitive community would have dared to call the revered Kephas
Satan?' 'stands, even when full justice has been done to the
conflicts between Pauline Christianity and Jerusalem,
which turned upon questions of circumcision and the eating
of Jews with Gentiles rather than soteriology' (Taylor).
Moreover, if the prediction in *v.* 31 were *ex eventu*, μετὰ τρεῖς
ἡμέρας would be rather surprising (see *in loc.*). That Jesus
should have foreseen for himself suffering and death is hardly
surprising: he had already experienced opposition from the
scribes and Pharisees, he had the example of John the
Baptist before him, and there were passages in the O.T. to
suggest suffering (see references *in loc.*). To the objection of
Loisy that it is surprising that the disciples should be so
unprepared for Jesus' death, if he had so clearly predicted
it, it may be replied that the disciples probably were quite
unable really to accept what he said about his death,
particularly perhaps about his dying rejected by the rulers
of Israel. That they should be taken by surprise in spite of
his teaching on the subject is surely not really surprising!

We conclude that in these verses we are near to the
personal reminiscence of Peter and have before us a section
based on sound historical tradition.

27. εἰς τὰς κώμας Καισαρίας τῆς Φιλίππου. For the
curious use of κῶμαι with the name of a town cf. the LXX of
Num. xxi. 32, xxxii. 42, Josh. x. 39, xv. 45, I Chron. ii. 23,
vii. 28, etc. The villages of the region of Caesarea Philippi
are meant. The town was named ἡ Φιλίππου to distinguish
it from Καισαρία ἡ παράλιος on the Mediterranean coast and
because it was rebuilt by Herod Philip and named by him
Caesarea. Its old name was Paneas. It was at the source of
the Jordan on the slopes of Hermon in the midst of very
beautiful and fertile country. (See further Smith, *Hist.
Geog.* pp. 473 f., Dalman, *S.S.W.* pp. 202 ff.) Mark does not

say that Jesus entered the town: cf. on vii. 24. Was his purpose in making this journey so far into Philip's territory to have an opportunity for instructing the disciples without interruption?

ἐν τῇ ὁδῷ. For another important conversation ἐν τῇ ὁδῷ cf. x. 32.

Τίνα με λέγουσιν οἱ ἄνθρωποι εἶναι; To argue that the content of the question and the fact that Jesus takes the initiative with it show that this material is secondary, since according to Jewish custom it was the disciple, not the Rabbi, who asked the questions, and since Jesus would not have asked a question concerning something about which he must have been as well informed as those whom he is supposed to question, is surely unimaginative. Jesus was not tied hand and foot to the forms and etiquette of Jewish Rabbis. It is quite possible that the disciples would have had chances of gathering information of this sort, which he would not have had himself—for they could mingle with the crowds unnoticed. But his chief purpose in asking this question was probably to lead up to the further question in v. 29.

28. λέγοντες. Redundant participle: cf. xii. 26. (Cf. Hebrew lē'mōr.) The construction which follows is abbreviated. After the first ὅτι, which is *recitativum*, οἱ ἄνθρωποι λέγουσίν σε εἶναι must be understood, similarly after the first ἄλλοι the words λέγουσίν σε εἶναι and after the second ἄλλοι the word λέγουσιν (a ὅτι-clause here replacing the accusative and infinitive), and, of course, after this second ὅτι the words σὺ εἶ.

With this verse cf. vi. 14f., and see notes thereon. It is significant that in neither passage is there any mention of a popular idea that Jesus is the Messiah. To the multitude he seemed to be a prophet (cf. Mt. xxi. 11): his Messiahship was concealed from them (see on xi. 1–10). When Peter in the next verse confesses that Jesus is the Messiah, his words do not echo popular opinion, but run counter to it.

29. αὐτός probably has no special emphasis here—it is actually omitted in both Mt. and Lk.—but is equivalent to ὁ δέ (cf. iv. 38, vi. 47, xiv. 15). Nevertheless, the fact that Jesus puts the question himself is important. He actually elicits a declaration from the Twelve. His purpose was perhaps to confirm them in their allegiance to him and to prepare them for the teaching he was going to give them about the necessity of his suffering. Schniewind suggestively draws attention to the connection between this leading question and Jesus' efforts to make his disciples understand referred to in i. 38f., iv. 13ff., iv. 40, vii. 17ff.; we may add viii. 17ff.

Ὑμεῖς is by its position (separated from the verb and placed at the beginning of the sentence) specially emphatic: 'you, the Twelve, in contrast with other men'.

ἀποκριθεὶς ὁ Πέτρος λέγει. Peter has not been mentioned since v. 37, but from now on is mentioned often. He now answers as the spokesman of the Twelve.

Σὺ εἶ ὁ Χριστός. In Peter's confession one of the themes of the gospel which was indicated in i. 1 (Χριστοῦ) is taken up. Behind the word Χριστός (= 'anointed') are the Hebrew māšîaḥ, which it often represents in the LXX, and the Aramaic mᵉšîḥā' (transliterated Μεσσίας in Jn i. 41, iv. 25, hence English 'Messiah'). The priests and the kings of Israel were anointed with oil (e.g. Exod. xxix. 7, 21, I Sam. x. 1) and māšîaḥ is used of both. It is also used metaphorically of the patriarchs, of the people of Israel as a whole, and of the Gentile ruler Cyrus. In I Kgs xix. 16 Elijah is ordered to anoint Elisha 'to be prophet in thy room'. The verb māšaḥ is also used metaphorically in connection with the prophetic ministry depicted in Isa. lxi. 1ff., and māšîaḥ itself is associated with the word for 'prophet' in Ps. cv. 15, though the people there referred to are actually the patriarchs (cf. Gen. xx. 6f.). Māšîaḥ carries with it the idea of consecration to God's service, of being specially chosen by him for a particular task and specially endowed by him with power (I Sam. x. 1, 6, xvi. 13, Isa. lxi. 1: with the Spirit of the LORD) to fulfil it.

In the time of Jesus the term was used particularly of the hoped-for ruler who was to restore the kingdom of David to more than its former glory and prosperity—see especially Pss. of Solomon xvii and xviii—though it is important to realize that there was a great variety of messianic expectation[1] (see further on viii. 31). Jesus' reluctance to use the title of himself was no doubt due, in part at least, to his recognition of the serious limitations and the objectionable features of the current messianic hopes. That he did, nevertheless, accept it when used of him by others (e.g. here and xiv. 61 f.) and knew himself to be the Messiah—albeit very different from the Messiah of popular expectation—is clear enough (*pace* Wrede, Bultmann, etc.). And this is hardly surprising; for the title, in spite of all the false and narrow hopes which had become attached to it, was peculiarly fitted to express his true relation both to the O.T. and to the people of God. O.T. Messiahship, like everything else in the O.T., is not properly understood simply by ascertaining what it meant to the ancient Hebrews or to the Jews of Jesus' time, but only as we look back at it in the light of its transformation and fulfilment by him. We can then see that all the time its real significance was that it was pointing forward to him, and that the title, applied to Jesus, designates him as the true meaning and fulfilment of the long successions of Israel's anointed kings and priests, the King and Priest, whom they but dimly and unworthily though nonetheless really foreshadowed; the Prophet anointed with the Spirit of God, who fulfils the long line of Israel's prophets; and the One in whom the life of the whole nation of Israel finds its fulfilment and meaning, in whom and for whose

[1] In the Dead Sea Scrolls there are frequent references to 'the Messiahs of Aaron and Israel', i.e. the future anointed high priest and anointed king (e.g. *Manual of Discipline*, ix. 11).

sake the people of Israel was, and the Church together with still unbelieving Israel is, the anointed people of God.

Peter's words expressed the truth of the gospel, but it is obvious that what he at the time meant by them was sadly inadequate. That the Twelve still thought of Messiahship along some such lines as Pss. of Solomon xvii and xviii seems to be indicated by viii. 32f., x. 35ff., Acts i. 6. Their understanding of Jesus and his ministry was as yet at the stage at which men look like trees walking rather than the stage of διαβλέπειν and ἐμβλέπειν τηλαυγῶς ἅπαντα (viii. 24f.). Even so Peter's confession is the watershed which divides the gospel in two.

See further T. W. Manson, *S.-M.* pp. 1–35 (esp. pp. 23–35), W. Manson, *Jesus the Messiah*, pp. 1–19, 94–120; and also J. Calvin, *Institutes*, II. xv (on the 'threefold office').   *

30. καὶ ἐπετίμησεν αὐτοῖς ἵνα μηδενὶ λέγωσιν περὶ αὐτοῦ. For ἐπετίμησεν see on i. 25. Perhaps here 'charged strictly'. Taylor explains this prohibition as 'a counsel of prudence in view of the political repercussions of such a confession'; but this explanation by itself hardly goes deep enough. While the desire to avoid rousing false political hopes was no doubt an important motive, it was surely not the only one. More fundamental was the will to obey the Father, who had purposed for his Son the path of messianic hiddenness (cf. on iv. 11f., also i. 25). Only when Jesus was a helpless prisoner in the hands of his enemies and his messianic claim must seem ridiculous was his Messiahship to be openly proclaimed.

Note that the charge given to the disciples here implies that Jesus did accept Peter's confession as true.

31. It is better to take this as closely connected with the preceding four verses (cf. Luke, who does not even start a new sentence here) than to regard *vv.* 31–3 as a new section, as some do. The first prediction of the Passion is the immediate sequel of Peter's confession.

δεῖ τὸν Υἱὸν τοῦ ἀνθρώπου πολλὰ παθεῖν. For δεῖ referring to a necessity beyond human comprehension, grounded in the will of God, a use highly characteristic of the N.T., cf. ix. 11, xiii. 7, 10, Lk. xxiv. 7, 26, Jn xx. 9, Acts iii. 21, I Cor. xv. 25, 53, II Cor. v. 10, etc. In Lk. especially is it emphasized that the whole life of Jesus moves under the constraint of this δεῖ of God's will. (See further W. Grundmann in *T.W.N.T.* II, pp. 21–5.)

The phrase ὁ υἱὸς τοῦ ἀνθρώπου (both nouns with articles) occurs in the singular 84 (83) times in the N.T.: 31 in Mt., 14 in Mk, 26 in Lk., 12 (11) in Jn, and once in Acts. Apart from Lk. xxiv. 7 and Jn xii. 34 (twice), which are not real exceptions since Jesus is being quoted, Acts vii. 56, and probably Mk ii. 10 with parallels and ii. 28, the use of the expression is always attributed to Jesus himself. The phrase used in the plural (Mk iii. 28, Eph. iii. 5) means simply 'men' in general. The indeterminate υἱὸς ἀνθρώπου occurs once in Jn, once in Heb., twice in Rev. Every instance of the phrase in the N.T., whether determinate or indeterminate, apart from the occurrences in the plural, refers, at any rate in the intention of the writers, to Jesus.

In the LXX the determinate ὁ υἱὸς τοῦ ἀνθρώπου never occurs in the singular; but υἱὸς ἀνθρώπου, υἱοὶ ἀνθρώπων, (οἱ) υἱοὶ τῶν ἀνθρώπων, all occur frequently (even υἱοὶ τοῦ ἀνθρώπου a few times), representing the Hebrew expressions, ben-'ādām, ben- 'enôš, benê-(hā)'ādām, benê-'îš, and the Aramaic bar-'enāš, benê-'anāšā', all of which would have been more correctly translated by (ὁ) ἄνθρωπος or (οἱ) ἄνθρωποι. From the O.T. material it is clear that the 'son(s) of' is simply Semitic idiom and that in both O.T. and N.T. all these phrases could be adequately rendered into English by 'man', 'a man', 'the man' or 'men' (occasionally the E.VV. do this—e.g. Eccles. iii. 21), though in some cases a capital 'm' would be required.

But, as we go on to ask what is the significance of ὁ υἱὸς

τοῦ ἀνθρώπου in the gospels, we enter a field that is full of complicated problems, about which many different opinions are held. The best we can do is to outline what seems to us the most satisfactory interpretation of the evidence and then give a relatively full bibliography to enable the reader to compare other views.

(i) It seems clear that the use of 'son of man' to designate Jesus must go back to Jesus himself; for, had it originated with the early Church, it would surely have appeared somewhere in the gospels on the lips of a disciple (see statistics above). The fact that the phrase was retained in the sayings of Jesus when the early Church preferred other titles for him also suggests that there was strong tradition that he had used it.

(ii) (a) It now seems clear that in the Aramaic spoken by Jesus bar-nāš(ā') meant 'a man', 'anyone', or 'one' (with reference to the speaker himself).

(b) It seems extremely probable that, on the basis of Dan. vii. 13, it was also fairly commonly used as a 'messianic' title. In support of this the following should be noted: (α) In the Similitudes of Enoch (i.e. I Enoch xxxvii–lxxi, probably first century B.C.) 'Son of Man' is used to designate a mysterious 'messianic' figure. (Cf. also IV Ezra xiii.) (β) In Rabbinic literature Dan. vii. 13 is always interpreted of the Messiah; and this interpretation must have been firmly established before the conflict with Christianity began, since otherwise it would hardly have continued to be held, in view of the place of 'Son of Man' in the Christian tradition. (γ) There is some evidence that the Rabbis could treat 'Son of Man' as a messianic title without reference to Dan. vii. 13: in Targ. Ps. lxxx bar-nāš is apparently synonymous with 'King Messiah'. It seems likely that the lack of more such evidence is to be explained as due to the effect of anti-Christian polemic.

(iii) In the sayings we have it seems clear that Jesus by 'the Son of Man' always means himself.

(*a*) The suggestion that he was referring to an apocalyptic figure other than himself must be rejected. Apart
from the sayings with reference to which the suggestion has
been made (e.g. Mk viii. 38) there is no scrap of evidence
that Jesus expected one greater than himself to come, and
there is much evidence to the contrary (e.g. Mt. xi. 2–6).
The fact, at first sight surprising, that Jesus never formally
identifies himself with the Son of Man, but refers to the Son
of Man in the third person, is rather to be explained by
reference to the messianic hiddenness or 'secret' (cf. below
(iv) (*d*)).

(*b*) The view that Jesus thought of 'the Son of Man'
collectively, as constituted by himself and his followers
together, is also, we believe, to be rejected. The Similitudes
of Enoch and the other evidence for the messianic interpretation of Dan. vii. 13 mentioned above weigh heavily
against it. In our opinion 'Son of Man' never has this sense
in the gospels. The Son of Man is a representative, not a
collective, figure. (To recognize this enables us to do justice
both to the close bond between Jesus and his disciples and
to the strong impression the gospels give of his standing over
against them.) And perhaps even in Dan. vii itself (on
which the collective theory largely rests) the representative
interpretation might after all be right. At any rate the
identification of the four beasts with four *kings*[1] according to
the M.T. in *v.* 17 suggests the possibility of interpreting 'one
like unto a son of man' in *v.* 13 as the ruler of 'the saints of
the Most High', who appears as their representative, rather
than as identical with them.

(iv) 'The Son of Man' is Jesus' characteristic self-
designation, the title he himself prefers to others. So in
Mk viii. 31 he substitutes it for the title Messiah which
Peter has just used (cf. xiv. 61 f.). The question why he chose
it is then obviously of the greatest importance for our under-

[1] *Pace* B.D.B. p. 1100.

standing of his own interpretation of his person and work. Here a number of suggestions may be made.

(a) It seems likely that he grew up among people who were deeply influenced by apocalyptic ideas and that he was familiar, in particular, with the Similitudes of Enoch or at any rate literature of the same tradition. Thus there was probably a certain natural tendency to regard himself as the Son of Man, when once he was conscious of his unique authority. (This is not, however, to suggest the sort of slavish dependence on the Enoch tradition visualized by R. Otto.)

(b) The title 'Messiah' (though, when rightly understood, it 'embraces all that is contained in our salvation')[1] was not adequate, as it was currently understood, to express the authority which Jesus was conscious of possessing. 'Son of Man' was a more majestic, and therefore more suitable title. (In Enoch the Son of Man's pre-existence is implied, and he is the final judge of men, a transcendent figure.)

(c) 'Son of Man' without much forcing could be made to carry the idea of suffering; for already in Enoch the figures of the Son of Man and the Servant of the Lord had been fused, and so, even if the sufferings were not one of the features of the Servant taken over in Enoch, the way was prepared for the idea of a suffering Son of Man. It is possible that that idea was actually already present in Dan. vii. 21. The fact that this title could hold together the ideas of transcendent majesty and vicarious suffering made it peculiarly suitable for Jesus' purpose: 'Servant of the Lord' would not adequately have suggested the former idea.

(d) The ambiguity of the term *bar-nāš(ā')* (see (ii) above) made it specially congruous with Jesus' messianic secret. This title, 'since it can denote both "the Man" with a capital letter and also "man" with a small letter, serves at the same time to indicate and to conceal with a discreet veil the secret

[1] Calvin, ii, p. 289.

of His person'.[1] The hearer could take it to be merely a common periphrasis for the first person singular pronoun (as in English a person may refer to himself as 'one'), or he could recognize it as the majestic title.

(e) This ambiguity also made *bar-nāš(ā')* a singularly appropriate self-designation for one whose mission was to identify himself with men, who was to give his life a ransom for many (Mk x. 45) and who after his exaltation would still continue to identify himself with the least of his brethren (Mt. xxv. 40, 45). Whatever nationalistic limitations may have adhered to the title in Dan. or in Enoch, as the everyday expression for 'man' it was well fitted to express the universal range of his work.

It remains to mention briefly two further points.

(v) The recognition that 'Son of' in this expression is merely Semitic idiom enables us to see a connection between ὁ υἱὸς τοῦ ἀνθρώπου in the gospels and such Pauline passages as Rom. v. 15, I Cor. xv. 21, 45–7.

(vi) On the question of the relation of 'Son of Man' in the N.T. to the widespread myth of the Heavenly or Primal Man the reader is referred to the excellent discussion in W. Manson's book mentioned below, pp. 7–11, 174–90. Suffice it to say here that, while Iranian ideas of the Primal Man may possibly have contributed to the thought of the Son of Man in Dan. and Enoch and so indirectly and remotely (after being thoroughly mastered and transformed by characteristically Hebrew ways of thinking) to the Son of Man sayings in the gospels, the suggestion that they had a direct and formative influence on those sayings seems to us altogether improbable.

See further: M. Black, in *E.T.* LX, pp. 11–15, 32–6, 321 f.; in *S.J.T.* VI, pp. 1–11; J. Bowman, in *E.T.* LIX, 283–8; R. Bultmann, *Theology*, I; J. Y. Campbell, in *J.T.S.* XLVIII (1947), pp. 145–55; in *T.W.B.* pp. 230–2; G. S.

[1] Preiss, *F. de l'H.* I, p. 45.

Duncan, *Jesus, Son of Man* (London, 1948); Farrer, *St Mark*, pp. 247–89; Zimmerli & Jeremias, *Servant*; T. W. Manson, *Teaching*, pp. 211–36; in *B.J.R.L.* xxxii, pp. 171–93; W. Manson, *Jesus the Messiah*, pp. 7–11, 98–103, 111–20, 173–90; in *S.J.T.* v, pp. 113–22; C. F. D. Moule, in *B.S.N.T.S.* iii (1952), pp. 40–53; S. Mowinckel, *He that Cometh* (Eng. tr., Oxford, 1956), pp. 346–450; R. Otto, *The Kingdom of God and the Son of Man* (Eng. tr., revised 1943), pp. 159–261; Preiss, *F. de l'H.*; also *Life in Christ* (Eng. tr., London, 1954), pp. 43–60; E. Sjöberg, *Der Menschensohn im Äthiopischen Henochbuch* (Lund, 1946); *Der verborgene Menschensohn in den Evangelien* (Lund, 1955); V. Taylor, *The Names of Jesus* (London, 1954), pp. 25–35; A. J. B. Higgins, 'Son of Man—*Forschung* since "The Teaching of Jesus"', in T. W. Manson Memorial Volume (Manchester, 1959).   *

πολλὰ παθεῖν. The Son of Man sayings fall into three main groups: those referring to the present; those referring to his sufferings and death; and those referring to his future glory. This saying clearly belongs to the second group. The question arises here: If δεῖ refers to God's will as revealed in scripture, what O.T. passages are in mind? The most obvious is Isa. lii. 13–liii. 12. *Pace* Bultmann, who says: 'The tradition of Jesus' sayings reveals no trace of a consciousness on his part of being the Servant of God of Isa. liii',[1] * it seems scarcely open to doubt that Jesus did apply Isa. liii to himself. (Cf. Zimmerli & Jeremias, *Servant*, pp. 98–104; and see also on ii. 20, ix. 12, x. 45, xiv. 24.) Other possible passages include Pss. xxii and cxviii. 10, 13, 18, 22, Dan. vii. 21, 25, Zech. xiii. 7.

The common assumption that Jesus was the first to associate suffering with Messiahship is questionable. Evidence for the idea of a suffering Messiah in Judaism exists (see Zimmerli & Jeremias, *Servant*, pp. 57–78): its rareness is probably the result of anti-Christian polemic.

[1] *Theology*, i, p. 31.

καὶ ἀποδοκιμασθῆναι ὑπὸ τῶν πρεσβυτέρων καὶ τῶν ἀρχιερέων καὶ τῶν γραμματέων. Probably a reminiscence of Ps. cxviii (LXX: cxvii). 22, which is quoted by Jesus in xii. 10. In the LXX ἀποδοκιμάζω is used there. Ps. cxviii. 22 is quoted in Acts iv. 11, and there the 'builders' are made to refer to the ἄρχοντες, πρεσβύτεροι and γραμματεῖς, and also the ἀρχιερεύς Annas and his kindred (in Acts iv. 11, however, ἀποδοκιμάζω is not used, but ἐξουθενῶ, a word that is used by Aquila, Symmachus and Theodotion to translate bāzāh in Isa. liii. 3). The πρεσβύτεροι here are the lay members of the Sanhedrin, as in xi. 27, xiv. 43, 53, xv. 1 (the use of πρεσβύτερος in vii. 3 was different). The ἀρχιερεῖς include not only the ruling High Priest, Caiaphas, and Annas, the emeritus, but also the members of the high-priestly families. For γραμματεῖς see on i. 22. Elders, high priests and scribes together make up the Sanhedrin.

ἀποκτανθῆναι. It is natural again to look to Isa. lii–liii.

καὶ μετὰ τρεῖς ἡμέρας ἀναστῆναι. Mk has μετὰ τρεῖς ἡμέρας in ix. 31 and x. 34 as well as here: Mt. and Lk. substitute τῇ τρίτῃ ἡμέρᾳ (τῇ ἡμέρᾳ τῇ τρίτῃ) every time (except in Lk. ix. 44 where the reference to the Resurrection is omitted altogether). While passages can be quoted to show that in late Greek the two phrases could be synonymous (see Schlatter, *Evang. Matt.* pp. 525 f.),[1] the fact that Mk's phrase is replaced in Mt. and Lk. supports the view that μετὰ τρεῖς ἡμέρας was not the most natural way of indicating in Greek the time which elapsed between the crucifixion of Jesus and his resurrection. The use of μετὰ τρεῖς ἡμέρας in Mk is perhaps a piece of evidence against the opinion that the prediction is a *vaticinium ex eventu*; for such *vaticinia* are generally accurate. 'After three days' on Jesus' lips would be an indefinite expression for a short time.

[1] The passages cited in Field, p. 13, fail to show that the two phrases are synonymous. If Hos. vi. 2 is an example of synonymous parallelism (as it probably is), it is evidence that the equivalent of τῇ τρίτῃ ἡμέρᾳ is μετὰ δύο ἡμέρας, not μετὰ τρεῖς ἡμέρας.

Such passages as Ps. xvi. 10, Ps. cxviii, Isa. lii. 13, liii. 10–12, may well have contributed to his expectation of a speedy resurrection.

32. καὶ παρρησίᾳ τὸν λόγον ἐλάλει. The reference is to the teaching recorded in the previous verse. With Peter's confession a new phase of Jesus' instruction of the Twelve had begun. While still maintaining his reserve as far as the crowds and the religious leaders were concerned (e.g. the command in *v.* 30), he now spoke to the Twelve with considerable plainness about the way he was to tread.

The MS. *k* reads *loqui*, thus connecting these words with the preceding infinitives so that the reference is to a speaking by Jesus after the Resurrection; and sy[s] and Tatian (with a future) support this. But the reading ἐλάλει must clearly be preferred.

προσλαβόμενος. For the use of the middle of προσλαμβάνω here cf. Acts xviii. 26. Peter draws Jesus aside, in order to give him advice. The motive of the drawing aside was possibly, as Bede suggests, 'in order that he might not appear to reprove the Master in the presence of his fellow-disciples': there is a suggestion of patronizing about it.

ἐπιτιμᾶν. See on i. 25. When used in the gospels with someone other than Jesus as subject ἐπιτιμᾶν usually denotes a rebuke which is presumptuous and is therefore not allowed to stand: so here and in x. 13f., 48. The rebuke recorded in Lk. xxiii. 40 is different, since it is delivered in a spirit not of superiority but of penitence, and similarly the brotherly rebuke referred to in Lk. xvii. 3.

Taylor is inclined to think that the variations in some it MSS. and in sy[s] which bear some resemblance to the extra words in the Mt. parallel represent the original text of Mk; for he thinks that the Mt. addition 'is not the kind of *addition* we should expect' in Mt., 'whereas it would be at home in Mk and accounts better for the rough reply of Jesus'. But the fact that these variants differ considerably among themselves (*c* has *rogare ne cui haec diceret*; *k* has *obsecrabat ne cui illa diceret*; while *a b n* and vg (2 MSS.) add *dicens, Domine propitius esto: nam hoc non erit*, and sy[s] has 'Then Simon Kepha, intending to spare him, said to him, Be it far from thee') rather suggests that they represent various attempts to soften the harshness of ἐπιτιμᾶν. The readings of *c* and *k* and sy[s] get rid of it altogether, and the additions of Mt. and *a b n* have the effect of softening it. The additional words in Mt. surely do not aggravate the roughness of Peter, as Taylor seems to think, but rather are designed to lessen it, and so are precisely the sort of addition we *should* expect in Mt.

It is often assumed that the suggestion that the Messiah would suffer must have been shocking to Peter. Perhaps it was rather the suggestion that he would suffer after rejection by the authorities of Israel that called forth Peter's rebuke. The idea of the Messiah suffering a glorious martyrdom at the hand of Israel's foes may not have been altogether strange to him (see on πολλὰ παθεῖν above).

33. ἐπιστραφείς. Cf. v. 30, Mt. ix. 22, Lk. vii. 9, 44, ix. 55, x. 23, xiv. 25, xxii. 61, xxiii. 28, Jn i. 38.

καὶ ἰδὼν τοὺς μαθητὰς αὐτοῦ. Only in Mk. For *their* sake a *public* rebuke of Peter was necessary.

Ὕπαγε ὀπίσω μου, Σατανᾶ. Cf. Mt. iv. 10 (though there the better reading is simply ὕπαγε, Σατανᾶ). Jesus regards Peter's attitude as a temptation, an attempt to draw him away from the path of obedience to his Father's will. Perhaps translate: 'Get out of my sight, Satan!' That seems preferable to the explanation of Schlatter that Jesus is ordering Peter back to his proper place as a disciple—i.e. following Jesus rather than trying to lead him. It is better to take the words as addressed to Peter himself than as addressed to Satan (thought of as acting through Peter), since the words that follow (including τὰ τῶν ἀνθρώπων) are applicable to Peter, but hardly to Satan.

ὅτι οὐ φρονεῖς τὰ τοῦ θεοῦ ἀλλὰ τὰ τῶν ἀνθρώπων. Τά

τινος φρονεῖν means 'to take someone's side', 'espouse someone's cause' (e.g. Demosthenes, in Phil. 3: οἱ τὰ Φιλίππου φρονοῦντες; and in the N.T. perhaps Rom. viii. 5), and it is better to translate here: 'for you are taking the side of men rather than the side of God', than to explain on the analogy of such expressions as τὰ ὑψηλὰ φρονεῖν (Rom. xii. 16). Schlatter notes that Jesus does not seek to justify the way of the Cross by showing the benefits it will bring, but simply indicates that it is God's will.

47. SAYINGS ON THE CONDITIONS OF
DISCIPLESHIP (viii. 34–ix. 1)
(Mt. xvi. 24–8; Lk. ix. 23–7)

A group of sayings about discipleship, some of which Mark may have found already joined together and some of which may possibly belong together historically. Mark probably had no information about their original context(s); but placed them at this point, because he recognized that there is a close connection between the need for the disciple to take up his cross and be ready to lose his life for his Master's sake and the fact that Jesus himself had to suffer many things and be rejected and killed. In so doing he showed true insight.

34. Καὶ προσκαλεσάμενος τὸν ὄχλον σὺν τοῖς μαθηταῖς αὐτοῦ appears to be Mark's editorial link. Mt. does not mention the ὄχλος, Lk. has ἔλεγεν δὲ πρὸς πάντας.

ὀπίσω τινὸς ἔρχεσθαι and ἀκολουθεῖν τινι are synonymous. What following Jesus involves is indicated in this and the following verses.

ἀπαρνησάσθω ἑαυτόν. The basic idea of (ἀπ)αρνεῖσθαι is 'to say "No"'. Cf. xiv. 30, 31, 72 and also 71, which expresses the meaning in other words. To deny oneself is to disown, not just one's sins, but one's self, to turn away from the idolatry of self-centredness. So it is something much more radical than any mere ascetic exercises or trivial 'self-denials'. The aorist imperative lays stress on the definite decision that has to be taken (cf. ἀράτω), but it does not rule out the idea that this is something which has to be repeated (so Lk. has the aorist ἀράτω in conjunction with καθ' ἡμέραν).

καὶ ἀράτω τὸν σταυρὸν αὐτοῦ. The expression αἴρειν (Mt. x. 38: λαμβάνειν; Lk. xiv. 27: βαστάζειν) τὸν σταυρὸν αὐτοῦ is explained by the fact that a criminal condemned to crucifixion was made to carry the cross-beam of his cross to the place of execution. The meaning here is that the disciple must be ready to face martyrdom—it is not to be explained by reference to Gal. ii. 19 (R.V.: ii. 20) or Rom. vi. 1 ff., nor yet to the later idea of 'cross-bearing', which is apparently in Luke's mind (Lk. ix. 23).

καὶ ἀκολουθείτω μοι. It is possible either to take this as a third requirement or—and this is perhaps more natural—to translate: 'And (so) let him follow me.' If the tense of ἀκολουθείτω is rightly pressed, the idea is that of the continuous relationship in contrast with the decisive acts.

35. Cf., besides the Mt. and Lk. parallels, Mt. x. 39 = Lk. xvii. 33, and Jn xii. 25. The saying is connected with the preceding by γάρ in Mk and in the parallels. In Mt. x. 38f. also it is joined with a saying on taking one's cross and following Jesus. The connection makes excellent sense—v. 35 following well on the reference to readiness to die in v. 34. The point of the verse is that the disciple who tries to save his life by denying his Master will lose eternal life, while he who loses his life for Jesus' sake will gain eternal life. (Cf. the similar double meanings of ζῶ and ἀποθνήσκω in Jn xi. 26.)

ἕνεκεν ἐμοῦ. (The omission of ἐμοῦ καί by 𝔭⁴⁵ D 28 it (some MSS.) sys is probably to be explained as originating in an accidental omission.) Jesus envisages his disciples dying for his sake. Note the absoluteness of his claim to their allegiance to his person.

καὶ τοῦ εὐαγγελίου. Only in Mk. Cf. x. 29. It is here probably equivalent to ἐμοῦ or τοῦ ἐμοῦ ὀνόματος (Mt. xix. 29) or τῆς βασιλείας τοῦ Θεοῦ (Lk. xviii. 29). Was it possibly added by Mark as a reminder to the contemporary persecuted Church that the apparently harsh and grievous demands of Christ are really all the time good news? Schlatter, on the other hand, takes εὐαγγέλιον here to mean the preaching of the gospel.

36. This and the following verse underline the incomparable value of one's ψυχη (the ψυχή denoted in v. 35 by αὐτήν rather than by ψυχήν). Perhaps, as Schniewind suggests, Jesus was here taking up a secular proverb, in which the reference was to that life which is lost at death, and filling it with a new meaning.

37. Cf. Ps. xlix (LXX: xlviii). 6 ff. The point here is that, if a man has forfeited his share in eternal life, he has nothing he can give to buy it back—even though he has gained the whole world.

δοῖ is a vernacular form of the third person singular aorist subjunctive of δίδωμι. The subjunctive is deliberative.

38. Mark links with the preceding by γάρ: the connection may well be editorial, but is certainly apt. If this saying is a variant of that contained in Mt. x. 33 = Lk. xii. 9, we should probably conclude that Lk. xii. 9 is more original than either Mk viii. 38 or Mt. x. 33 (the direct first person singular in Mt. x. 32 f. is less likely to be original than the indirect ambiguous forms of Lk. xii. 8 f. and Mk viii. 38); but it is not at all certain that Mk viii. 38 is not a different saying—in which case there seems to be nothing in it which could not be authentic.

ἐπαισχυνθῇ. It is an essential element in that messianic veiledness, to which we have had frequently to refer, that the Son of Man should in this age be one of whom men will often be tempted to be ashamed.

με καὶ τοὺς ἐμοὺς λόγους. W k* sa Tertullian(?) omit

λόγους, and this reading is preferred by C. H. Turner, T. W. Manson, Dodd, and Taylor. The meaning of τοὺς ἐμούς would then be 'my disciples'. The fact that D it (some MSS.) syᶜ Origen omit λόγους in the Lk. parallel supports the omission. But perhaps it is safer, in view of the ease with which λόγους could have been omitted accidentally by homoioteleuton, to follow the great weight of attestation and include it, though noting that there is a real possibility that the omission may be right. As in v. 35 note the implications of the place Jesus gives to his own person. Whereas the prophets stand aside so that their message, not their person, is everything, Jesus and his words are inseparable.

ἐν τῇ γενεᾷ ταύτῃ τῇ μοιχαλίδι καὶ ἁμαρτωλῷ. For γενεά see on viii. 12. Probably here it is best taken in the sense 'age', 'period of time', which is the primary meaning of the Hebrew dôr, the word it most often represents in the LXX, and a possible meaning of γενεά. The whole phrase is contrasted with ὅταν ἔλθῃ...ἁγίων, and so is roughly equivalent to ἐν τῷ καιρῷ τούτῳ in x. 30 which is contrasted with ἐν τῷ αἰῶνι τῷ ἐρχομένῳ. The time meant is the time before the Parousia. But it is not thought of simply as a period of time; the thought of the men living in it and of their character is also present and prominent—hence the adjectives μοιχαλίδι and ἁμαρτωλῷ. μοιχαλίδι has an O.T. flavour; cf. Hos. ii. 2, etc.

ὁ Υἱὸς τοῦ ἀνθρώπου. See on v. 31. Taylor says: 'If the saying is original, one of two possibilities must be true: either, at some time in His ministry, Jesus spoke of the coming of a supernatural Son of Man other than Himself, or by "the Son of Man" He meant the Elect Community of which He was to be the Head.' But we do not have to choose between these alternatives; for there is surely no reason why Jesus should not have used the simple and straightforward με of himself in his earthly life but the mysterious and ambiguous bar-nāš(ā') of himself at his

Parousia. See note on 'Son of Man' at viii. 31, sections iii and iv (*d*). To speak of himself directly as coming in the glory of his Father would be to lay aside his messianic veiledness: to speak of the Son of Man without expressly identifying him with himself was more consonant with the messianic secret—it revealed and yet at the same time concealed.

ἐπαισχυνθήσεται αὐτόν. For a man to be thus disowned by him is ζημιωθῆναι τὴν ψυχὴν αὐτοῦ (*v.* 36).

ὅταν ἔλθῃ ἐν τῇ δόξῃ τοῦ Πατρὸς αὐτοῦ. The first clear reference to a glorious Parousia in Mk. Veiled references there have been—e.g. iv. 21f., 30–2. See further on xiii. 26ff. Now he is one of whom men can be ashamed; then he will be manifest as the one who has the glory of God. On τοῦ Πατρὸς αὐτοῦ see on i. 11.

μετὰ τῶν ἀγγέλων τῶν ἁγίων. Angels are mentioned in connection with the Parousia frequently: e.g. xiii. 27, Mt. xiii. 39, 41, 49, xxv. 31, II Thess. i. 7. See further on xvi. 5.

ix. 1. καὶ ἔλεγεν αὐτοῖς. Often used in Mk as an editorial connecting-link, it seems to occur occasionally inside a unit (e.g. vii. 9). It is perhaps possible that the connection between ix. 1 and viii. 38 is historical—ix. 1 does (if understood in the way preferred below) make a tolerable contrast with viii. 38 (a contrast between those who are ashamed of Jesus and those of whom he can say that they will not taste death...), and this seems to be brought out by Luke's λέγω δὲ ὑμῖν ἀληθῶς—but it is more likely that the connection is editorial and that καὶ ἔλεγεν αὐτοῖς here introduces an independent saying.

Αμην. See on iii. 28.

The saying which follows is one of the most puzzling in the gospels. It is often cited (along with xiii. 30 and Mt. x. 23) as evidence that Jesus expected the Parousia within a very short time. But though this interpretation seems at first * sight the natural one, there are others, of which some at any rate deserve serious consideration.

(i) Dodd understands ἴδωσιν to refer to intellectual perception rather than physical sight, takes ἐληλυθυῖαν and the words that go with it as equivalent to a ὅτι-clause, and insists on the strictly past sense of ἐληλυθυῖαν as indicating an action already complete before the time of their perceiving it. He says: 'The meaning appears to be that some of those who heard Jesus speak would before their death awake to the fact that the Kingdom of God had come.'[1] But, while it is true that the perfect participle ἐληλυθυῖαν must indicate a coming that takes place before the action of the verb ἴδωσιν, the grammar does not require that the coming should have taken place at the time Jesus was speaking, or indeed any considerable time before the action of ἴδωσιν. So Mk ix. 1 seems to be a very doubtful support for the view that Jesus taught only a realized eschatology.

(ii) Another unlikely suggestion is that γεύσωνται θανάτου refers not to death in the ordinary sense but to a spiritual death from which faithful disciples will be exempt. It is true that Jn viii. 51 f. provides support for such a use of γεύεσθαι θανάτου, and that for the thought of a spiritual death from which believers will be exempt we may compare Jn xi. 26, and also that in this context (viii. 35) the idea of a life which can be retained even when one has lost one's life is present; but for this interpretation ἕως is difficult—would it be implied that after they have seen, they will 'taste death'?

(iii) Michaelis, noting that οἱ ἑστηκότες by itself can mean 'the bystanders', suggests[2] that the reading εἰσίν τινες ὧδε τῶν ἑστηκότων may represent a conflation of two alternative translations of the same Aramaic expression: εἰσίν τινες ὧδε and εἰσίν τινες τῶν ἑστηκότων. He then suggests that in εἰσίν τινες ὧδε the word ὧδε was not used in the sense 'here' but

[1] *Parables*, pp. 53 f.　　　　[2] *Verheissung*, pp. 34–9.

rather in the sense 'thus', 'so', and proposes as a possible original sense of the saying: 'Some are (or stand) in such a way that they will not taste death....' This, he thinks, would not necessarily refer to people present at the time that Jesus was speaking (in Aramaic the verb 'to be' would not have to be expressed). So he suggests that the meaning is that there will be some at least who will have the privilege of not dying before the Parousia, but that it is not said when these will live and not implied that they must belong to Jesus' contemporaries. This suggestion seems not very likely, but perhaps it is sufficiently plausible to encourage us to regard the question of the interpretation of this verse as still open.

(iv) The suggestion that 'the kingdom of God come with power' refers to the destruction of Jerusalem in A.D. 70 need not detain us.

(v) Others have thought of Pentecost and the spread of the gospel. But in that case the limitation to τινες is perplexing.

(vi) Taylor suggests: 'A visible manifestation of the Rule of God displayed in the life of an Elect Community is the most probable form of His expectation; but what this means cannot be described in detail because the hope was not fulfilled in the manner in which it presented itself to Him, although later it found expression in the life of the Church, as it still does in its life and its impact on human society. The Divine Rule was to come "in power", that is, in the manifested power of God and not by human effort and ingenuity.' He places the saying early in the Ministry—in the period between the limits indicated by Mk i. 15 and vi. 13, 'at a time when He still looked for the speedy inbreaking of the Divine Rule'.

(vii) The interpretation which (in our judgement) is most probable is one that goes back to the early Church—that which sees a reference to the Transfiguration. The careful noting of the number of days in ix. 2 suggests that the

Transfiguration is, at any rate according to the intention of the evangelist, to be understood as being in some sense the fulfilment of the promise contained in ix. 1 (cf. Barth, *K.D.* III/2, p. 574). With this interpretation ἴδωσιν fits well, for in the narrative ix. 2 ff. the fact that the disciples *saw* is emphasized (μετεμορφώθη ἔμπροσθεν αὐτῶν in *v.* 2, ὤφθη αὐτοῖς in *v.* 4, εἶδον in *vv.* 8 and 9). So also does τινες, for only three of the disciples were present at the Transfiguration. (The objection raised by Michaelis[1] and Beasley-Murray[2] that, if the reference is to the Transfiguration, τινες will imply that the majority, or at least a number, of the bystanders will die within the next few days is surely quite illogical; for, while ix. 1 implies that the majority will not live to see this thing themselves, it does not imply that they must necessarily die before the people denoted by τινες see it.) And τὴν βασιλείαν τοῦ θεοῦ ἐληλυθυῖαν ἐν δυνάμει is a not unfair description of what the three saw on the mount of Transfiguration. For the Transfiguration points forward to, and is as it were a foretaste of, the Resurrection, which in turn points forward to, and is a foretaste of, the Parousia; so that both the Resurrection and the Parousia may be said to have been proleptically present in the Transfiguration. Compare Barth's statement: 'In His Transfiguration they saw Him proleptically as the Risen One, in it they recognized transiently the Kingdom come in power, which afterwards in His Resurrection they recognized definitively, but thereby they recognized also already—*in parte pro toto* as ἀρραβών and ἀπαρχή—precisely that which in the Parousia as in its universal revelation will become recognizable and be recognized comprehensively and finally as His glory.'[3]

The reading of B, ὧδε τῶν ἑστηκότων, is fairly clearly to be preferred to the easier readings τῶν ἑστηκότων ὧδε and τῶν ὧδε ἑστηκότων (ἑστώτων) found in 𝔭⁴⁵ f1 and ℵ A C W

---

[1] *Verheissung*, p. 35.
[2] *Jesus and the Future*, p. 185.   [3] *K.D.* III/2, p. 600.

Θ etc. respectively. The addition of μετ᾽ ἐμοῦ in D 565 it is probably an attempt to make the words more readily intelligible. Translate as R.V.—though 'by' does not need to be put in italics, since οἱ ἑστηκότες by itself can mean 'the bystanders' (cf. Mt. xxvi. 73, Acts xxii. 25).

48. THE TRANSFIGURATION (ix. 2–8)
(Mt. xvii. 1–8; Lk. ix. 28–36)

In view of the special difficulties of this section it will be better to postpone general discussion of it until after the notes on the separate verses.

2. μετὰ ἡμέρας ἕξ. 'No other temporal statement in Mk outside the Passion Narrative is so precise' (Taylor). (Lk. has ὀκτώ, but his addition of ὡσεί indicates that he is giving a round number.) We have seen above that the fact that Mark has placed the saying contained in ix. 1 immediately before this precise dating suggests that he regards what follows as at any rate in some sense the fulfilment of the promise in that saying. The temporal note refers back to Peter's confession.

παραλαμβάνει. Cf. iv. 36, v. 40, x. 32, xiv. 33.

τὸν Πέτρον καὶ τὸν Ἰάκωβον καὶ Ἰωάννην. Cf. v. 37, xiv. 33 (in xiii. 3 the same three plus Andrew). The omission of the article before Ἰωάννην has the effect of grouping the two brothers together.

ἀναφέρει. The initiative of Jesus is indicated.

ὄρος ὑψηλόν. From early times identified with Mt Tabor, ten miles S.W. of the Sea of Galilee. But Mt Tabor is less than 2000 feet above sea level, and at this time it had a fortress on its summit. A spur of Mt Hermon (over 9000 feet and about twelve miles N.E. of Caesarea Philippi) or one of the three mountains over 4000 feet to the S.E. of Caesarea Philippi suggested by Dalman[1] is a more likely identification

[1] *S.S.W.* p. 205.

(though see L. H. Grollenberg, *Atlas of the Bible* (Eng. tr., 1956), pp. 122, 127). Any of these would provide the solitude which Jesus apparently desired (κατ' ἰδίαν μόνους).

μετεμορφώθη. The verb μεταμορφόω occurs in the N.T. only here, in the Mt. parallel, Rom. xii. 2, and II Cor. iii. 18. Elsewhere it is found mostly in writers later than the N.T., but it must have been in use in earlier times, for otherwise Ovid's use of the noun as a title of a poem would be inexplicable. In the Lk. parallel the word is avoided— probably because Luke did not like to use in this connection a word so much associated with pagan mythology and magic. The background of its use here is not to be sought in pagan ideas of metamorphosis but in Jewish apocalyptic. Cf. Dan. xii. 3, II Bar. li. 3, 5, 10, 12, Enoch xxxviii. 4, civ. 2, IV Ezra vii. 97. There is no need to see Pauline influence in Mark's use of the word.

3. In view of the parallels it is surprising that Mark does not mention Jesus' face. That a reference to it has dropped out of the text by mistake at a very early stage, as Streeter suggested,[1] is conceivable; but perhaps it is more likely that Mt. and Lk. have both introduced the reference independently under the influence of Exod. xxxiv. 29 ff.

For the brightness of the garments cf. Dan. vii. 9, Enoch lxii. 15 f., Rev. iii. 5, iv. 4, vii. 9. For λευκά cf. xvi. 5. The addition of ὡς χιών in many MSS. is perhaps to be explained as assimilation to Mt. xxviii. 3: clearly it should not be accepted.

οἷα γναφεὺς...λευκᾶναι. Only in Mk. A homely touch to indicate the heavenly (ἐπὶ τῆς γῆς is emphatic) origin of the whiteness.

4. ὤφθη. Cf. Lk. i. 11, xxii. 43, xxiv. 34, Acts ii. 3, vii. 2, 26, ix. 17, xiii. 31, xvi. 9, xxvi. 16, I Cor. xv. 5, 6, 7, 8. In the N.T. most often used of the sudden appearance of a heavenly form, whether real or in a vision.

αὐτοῖς: i.e. to the three disciples.

[1] *Four Gospels*, pp. 315 f.

'Ηλείας σὺν Μωϋσεῖ. The order of Mt. and Lk. (Moses mentioned first) seems more natural, Moses being the more important figure. Perhaps Mark's use of σύν has the same effect—making Elijah Moses' companion or attendant (so Lagrange); but contrast viii. 38 (the Son of Man μετὰ τῶν ἀγγέλων τῶν ἁγίων). More satisfactory perhaps is Lohmeyer's explanation that Elijah is put first as the forerunner *par excellence* of the End-time (Mal. iv. 5).

5. ὁ Πέτρος. As often, the spokesman of the disciples.

Ραββει. Used also in x. 51, xi. 21, xiv. 45. Literally, 'my great one'—the regular title of a teacher of the Law. (See also on i. 21 (ἐδίδασκεν).)

καλόν ἐστιν ἡμᾶς ὧδε εἶναι. Translate: 'It is a good thing that we are here' rather than as R.V. A good thing—probably because they can wait upon Jesus and his heavenly visitors; so preparing for the following suggestion.

ποιήσωμεν. Hortatory subjunctive. Possibly we should follow D W Θ f13 543 565 *b ff*² *i* in inserting θέλεις before ποιήσωμεν ('Do you wish us to make...?'). This reading would account for the Mt. εἰ θέλεις, and give a characteristic Markan construction (cf. x. 36, 51, xiv. 12, xv. 9, (12)). It is accepted by Taylor, following C. H. Turner. D W *b ff*² *i* read ποιήσω.

σκηνάς. Σκηνή is used in the LXX to translate *sukkāh* = 'booth' (e.g. Lev. xxiii. 42f., Neh. viii. 14ff.). Peter was perhaps thinking of shelters made of intertwined branches or twigs such as were used in the Feast of Tabernacles. But more frequently σκηνή represents '*ōhel* (= 'tent', 'dwelling' —used of the Tent of Meeting or Tabernacle, as well as of human dwellings) or *miškān* (= 'dwelling-place', also used of the Tabernacle, and of the Temple). So it is possible that Peter's idea was to provide more permanent dwelling-places. (See article by Michaelis referred to under iv. 32.)

6. οὐ γὰρ ᾔδει τί ἀποκριθῇ. So Mark excuses the incongruous remark.

ἔκφοβοι γὰρ ἐγένοντο. See on i. 22 (ἐξεπλήσσοντο).
Cf. especially xvi. 8, and note thereon.

7. καὶ ἐγένετο νεφέλη ἐπισκιάζουσα αὐτοῖς. The O.T.
background is here of the utmost importance. Cf. the
following groups of passages: Exod. xiii. 21f., xiv. 19f., 24,
xl. 36–8, Num. ix. 15–23; Exod. xxxiii. 9f., xl. 34f., Lev. xvi.
2; Exod. xvi. 10, xxxiv. 5; Exod. xix. 16, xxiv. 15–18,
Deut. v. 22; Ps. lxxviii. 14, xcix. 7, cv. 39; I Kgs viii. 10f.,
II Chr. v. 13f., Ezek. x. 3f.; Isa. iv. 5, (II Macc. ii. 8).
In Exod. xl. 35 the verb ἐπισκιάζειν is used in the LXX, as
here. In the N.T. cf. Acts i. 9; Mk xiii. 26, xiv. 62, I Thess.
iv. 17.

Oepke[1] is probably right in thinking that the meaning of
ἐπισκιάζειν here is not 'overshadow' but 'envelop', 'conceal', and that αὐτοῖς refers to Jesus, Moses and Elijah, and
does not include the disciples. (sy^s has the equivalent of
αὐτῷ here—i.e. Jesus—and similarly in Lk. 1604 has αὐτόν.)
It seems to be implied by ἐκ τῆς νεφέλης that the disciples
who are addressed are outside the cloud. (In Lk. ix. 34
Oepke takes the second αὐτούς as well as the first to refer to
Jesus, Moses and Elijah.)

καὶ ἐγένετο φωνὴ ἐκ τῆς νεφέλης. Cf. Exod. xxiv. 16.
For φωνή and for the first part of the message see on i. 11.
In i. 11 Jesus himself was addressed: here it is the disciples
who are addressed.

ἀκούετε αὐτοῦ. Cf. Deut. xviii. 15. The verb ἀκούειν here
has the strong meaning which Hebrew šāma' often has in the
O.T.—'hear and obey'.

8. οὐκέτι οὐδένα. For the double negative see on i. 44.

With regard to ix. 2–8 there are three main questions
which press for an answer.

(i) Is this a legend or a piece of theological symbolical
writing or is it historical? According to a good many scholars
it is a legendary development of a Resurrection-story which

[1] In T.W.N.T. IV, pp. 910f.

has been read back into the earthly life of Jesus. So Bultmann writes: 'That this legend is originally a Resurrection-
story has long been recognized.'[1] Against this theory it has
been pointed out[2] that all the accounts of Resurrection
appearances in the gospels begin with Jesus being absent,
whereas here he is present from the beginning; that in the
Resurrection appearance narratives something said by him
has an important place, whereas here he is silent throughout;
that the story is devoid of the features to be expected in an
appearance to Peter (see Jn xxi); that Moses and Elijah are
a surprising feature in a Resurrection appearance story (in
the Easter stories in the gospels the only figures from beyond
who feature are angels, and they are never said to be seen
at the same time as Jesus); that this theory leaves unexplained Peter's curious suggestion in *v.* 5.

According to others this is a symbolical narrative. So
Lohmeyer calls it an 'attempt to interpret the person and
work of Jesus as that of the eschatological Fulfiller'. For
him it has no historical basis, but is simply an expression of
theological conviction by means of imagery derived from
the O.T. and Jewish apocalyptic.[3]

There are, however, details in ix. 2–8 which suggest the
likelihood of some historical basis: the $\mu\epsilon\tau\grave{\alpha}$ $\dot{\eta}\mu\acute{\epsilon}\rho\alpha\varsigma$ $\ddot{\epsilon}\xi$, which
is hardly satisfactorily explained by reference to Exod. xxiv.
16, or by the fact that after six days comes the seventh—the
sabbath—or by reference to the days that a priest waited in
the Temple to cleanse himself; Peter's use of $\rho\alpha\beta\beta\epsilon\iota$, a title
never used in the N.T. outside the gospels and not likely to
have been used in a symbolical narrative created in the early

[1] *G.S.T.* p. 278.

[2] Cf. Boobyer, *Transfig.* pp. 11–16; Lightfoot, *Gospel Message*, pp. 43f.;
Dodd, 'Appearances', p. 25.

[3] H. Riesenfeld, *Jésus Transfiguré* (Copenhagen, 1947), while he
maintains that the background of the Transfiguration is the Feast of
Tabernacles and the motifs connected with it, rejects the idea that the
narrative was created in the Church on the basis of these motifs (see
especially p. 5, n. 13).

Church; perhaps also the homely reference to the fuller and Peter's suggestion in *v.* 5. Moreover, Mark gives no indication at all that he is not meaning to relate something that actually happened.

(ii) If then ix. 2–8 is in some sense a historical narrative, what was it that happened? There seem to be three main possibilities: to explain the whole as vision and audition; to explain the whole as factual; to explain as in part factual and in part vision and audition. The argument that Mt. xvii. 9 (the use of ὅραμα) shows that the writer thought of the incident as a vision must not be pressed; for, while ὅραμα does often denote a vision, it can also be used of what is seen in the ordinary way (e.g. Deut. xxviii. 34, 67, Eccles. vi. 9) and so can be simply equivalent to Mark's ἃ εἶδον and Luke's ὧν ἑώρακαν. The word ὤφθη is similarly neutral.

It seems clear that what is related, whether visionary or factual, was directed toward the three disciples rather than toward Jesus (ἔμπροσθεν αὐτῶν in *v.* 2, ὤφθη αὐτοῖς in *v.* 4, the third person used by the voice (contrast i. 11) and the command ἀκούετε αὐτοῦ in *v.* 7). If it was a vision and audition, then it was apparently shared by the three disciples. It was apparently also miraculous; for, though the O.T. and Jewish apocalyptic would provide the imagery, the implications with regard to the person of Jesus go much further than Peter's confession, so that such a vision would hardly have come naturally to the disciples during Jesus' ministry. On the whole, it seems rather more likely that the Transfiguration itself (*vv.* 2 b, 3) is factual. With regard to the content of *vv.* 4–7, we are inclined to think that we have here to do with the record of a vision and audition experienced by the three disciples (perhaps ἐξάπινα περιβλεψάμενοι κ.τ.λ. in *v.* 8 rather suggests people recovering from a vision?)—but a vision and audition which were miraculously brought about by God and were a real divine revelation to them.

(iii) What is the theological significance of what is recorded in ix. 2–8? We take it that the Transfiguration (*vv.* 2 b, 3) was an anticipation or prolepsis of the Resurrection and of the Parousia (see above on ix. 1 (vii)), so that those who saw it could not improperly be said to see τὴν βασιλείαν τοῦ Θεοῦ ἐληλυθυῖαν ἐν δυνάμει (ix. 1); but at the same time it was a revelation for a few moments of the glory which even then, before his Passion, belonged to Jesus. It was a 'temporary exhibition of his glory'—to use Calvin's words— which would enable the disciples after the Resurrection to realize for certain that 'even during the time that he emptied himself (Phil. ii. 7), he continued to retain his divinity entire, though it was concealed under the veil of the flesh'. This temporary exhibition of his glory, even while it lasted, was not complete; but 'under symbols which were adapted to the capacity of the flesh' (whiteness of clothes, shining of face (Mt.)) God enabled the disciples 'to taste in part what could not be fully comprehended' (Calvin).

The significance of the appearance of Moses and Elijah conversing with Jesus is well summed up by Victor of Antioch: δηλοῖ δὲ καὶ συνάφειαν παλαιᾶς διαθήκης καὶ νέας. Together they represent the Law and the prophets, that is, the O.T.; and their attendance on Jesus sets forth the relation of the O.T. to Jesus and of Jesus to the O.T. Cf. the κατὰ τὰς γραφάς of I Cor. xv. 3 f.; also I Pet. i. 10–12, Jn v. 46, Mt. v. 17, etc.

The cloud is at the same time the sign both of God's self-revelation and of his self-veiling (see above on *v.* 7). On the significance of the first part of the words spoken by the voice the reader is referred back to the note on i. 11; but, whereas at the Baptism the words were addressed to Jesus, confirming his consciousness of being the Son of God, here they are addressed to the disciples. The last two words, ἀκούετε αὐτοῦ, attest Jesus as the one in whom the prophecy of Deut. xviii. 15, 18 is fulfilled and underline his unique position. Moses and Elijah are not named alongside of him: he alone is to be heard and obeyed. Calvin comments: 'When he enjoins us to *hear him*, he appoints him to be the supreme and only Teacher of his Church...he alone is appointed to be our Teacher, that in him all authority may dwell....'

See further: Barth, *K.D.* III/2, pp. 574f., 578, 594, 600; Boobyer, *Transfig.*; A. M. Ramsey, *The Glory of God and the Transfiguration of Christ* (London, 1949).

49. THE CONVERSATION ON THE WAY DOWN
THE MOUNTAIN (ix. 9–13)
(Mt. xvii. 9–13)

It is clear that *vv.* 9f. are closely connected with the preceding section. Verses 11–13 could be detached from *vv.* 9f., and some regard them as a separate unit or connect them with ix. 1. So Bultmann, for instance, classifies *vv.* 12f. as an apocalyptic saying originating in the theological discussions of the community in connection with the saying recorded in ix. 1, which itself was, he thinks, a 'community-formation' due to the delay of the Parousia.[1] But it is not necessary to detach *vv.* 11 ff. from *vv.* 9f. The question about Elijah can be explained as suggested by his appearance in the vision (ix. 4ff.) (cf. Taylor); and we may agree with F. C. Burkitt's opinion that ix. 9–13 reads 'like the reminiscences of a real conversation'.[2]

9. καταβαινόντων αὐτῶν...αὐτοῖς. For the genitive absolute referring to persons otherwise mentioned in the sentence see on v. 2.

διεστείλατο αὐτοῖς ἵνα μηδενὶ ἃ εἶδον διηγήσωνται, εἰ μὴ ὅταν ὁ Υἱὸς τοῦ ἀνθρώπου ἐκ νεκρῶν ἀναστῇ. For the injunction to silence see on viii. 30. It is clear that the three themselves did not at the time grasp the significance of what they had experienced on the mountain; after the Resurrection they

[1] *G.S.T.* pp. 131f.   [2] *Christian Beginnings* (London, 1924), pp. 33f.

would understand it and it would in turn enable them better to understand the Resurrection. It would be time enough to tell the other disciples about this experience when they themselves had begun to understand it.

(For the radical critics the injunction is Mark's attempt to account for the fact that the Transfiguration was unknown to the earliest tradition.)

For the reference to the Resurrection see on viii. 31.

10. καὶ τὸν λόγον ἐκράτησαν πρὸς ἑαυτοὺς συνζητοῦντες. πρὸς ἑαυτούς can be taken either with ἐκράτησαν ('they kept the matter to themselves, questioning together...') or with συνζητοῦντες ('they kept the saying in mind, questioning together among themselves...'). Mark's use of συνζητεῖν elsewhere is not decisive; for, while he has συνζητεῖν πρός τινα in ix. 14, 16, he uses the verb absolutely in xii. 28 and (according to the ℵ B text) i. 27. Mark's use of κρατεῖν in vii. 3 f., 8, and the N.T. use of it generally, favour taking it to mean 'keep in mind', 'observe'. Victor takes πρὸς ἑαυτούς with συνζητοῦντες, as does sy[s], and this is probably right. The meaning of τὸν λόγον ἐκράτησαν will then be that they obeyed the injunction to silence—not that they kept in mind the reference to the Resurrection. (The suggested emendation of the text by inserting οὐκ before ἐκράτησαν, which would then be translated 'understood', is unnecessary.)

τὸ ἐκ νεκρῶν ἀναστῆναι. The reading of D W f1 f13, ὅταν ἐκ νεκρῶν ἀναστῇ, which has the support of lat sy[s, p], should possibly be preferred. It is rather more difficult. For the puzzledness of the disciples cf. ix. 31 f.

11. The first Ὅτι is best explained (with Taylor) as interrogative (= τί): cf. Mt. parallel which has τί. See on ii. 16, and cf. ix. 28 (perhaps also ii. 7). The scribes' teaching that Elijah would come back to prepare the way for the Messiah was based on Mal. iv. 5 f.: cf. IV Ezra vi. 26 (Elijah and Enoch together), Justin, *Dial.* 8 and 49, and Rabbinic examples in S.–B. IV, pp. 784–9, 792–8, and see on

i. 2. The most likely explanation of the disciples' question
would seem to be either that they are wondering how Jesus
can be what the Transfiguration has indicated that he is, in
view of the fact that Elijah has not yet come, or that they
are asking why the scribes maintain something which cannot
be true, since the Messiah has come, and Elijah has not yet
prepared his way.

12. Ἡλείας μὲν ἐλθὼν πρῶτον ἀποκαθιστάνει πάντα.
Jesus grants (μέν here means 'it is true') that the scribes are
right in saying that Elijah comes first (i.e. before the
Messiah) and restores all things. Cf. Mal. iv. 5f. (LXX),
and also Acts iii. 21. This sentence is better read as a statement than—as some prefer—as a question.

καὶ πῶς γέγραπται ἐπὶ τὸν Υἱὸν τοῦ ἀνθρώπου, ἵνα πολλὰ
πάθη καὶ ἐξουδενηθῇ; The καὶ πῶς...; is substituted for the
δέ that should normally follow μέν. Having admitted that
the scribes are correct in this that they say, Jesus goes on to
suggest that this 'restoring all things' cannot mean just
what on the surface it seems to mean, since scripture foretells
for the Son of Man much suffering and humiliation. On the
question of the O.T. passages referred to see on viii. 31. The
word ἐξουδενηθῇ here may provide a further clue. In the
LXX and other Greek versions of the O.T. ἐξουδ(θ)ενέ(ό)ω
and derivatives occur frequently. Symmachus and Theodotion use it to translate bāzāh ('despise') in Isa. xlix. 7, and
Symmachus uses it twice to translate that verb in Isa. liii. 3
(while Aquila and Theodotion use it once). This rather
suggests that behind it there may lie a reference to the
figure of the Servant. The noun ἐξουθένημα is used in
Ps. xxii (LXX: xxi). 6 and ἐξουδένωσις in Ps. cxxiii (LXX:
cxxii). 3, cxix (LXX. cxviii). 22; and, when Ps. cxviii (LXX:
cxvii). 22 is quoted in Acts iv. 11, the verb ἐξουθενῶ is
substituted for the LXX ἀποδοκιμάζω. Such passages might
perhaps also be in mind. In viii. 31, ix. 31, x. 33f., 45, there
is no explicit reference to scripture, as there is here. That

this question (*v.* 12 b) is a *vaticinium ex eventu* can hardly be maintained: it is too vague.

13. Ἠλείας ἐλήλυθεν: *sc.* in the person of John the Baptist: cf. Mt. xvii. 13, xi. 14, and also Mk i. 2–6 parallels.

ἐποίησαν αὐτῷ ὅσα ἤθελον. Mt. xvii. 12 b draws out the implication—the Forerunner's death is a pointer to what the Messiah himself must suffer.

καθὼς γέγραπται ἐπ᾽ αὐτόν. Is I Kgs xix. 2, 10 in mind? Possibly also traditions lying behind Rev. xi. 3–13? (See further Jeremias in *T.W.N.T.* II, pp. 930–43 (esp. 941–3).)

50. THE HEALING OF THE DEMONIAC BOY (ix. 14–29)
(Mt. xvii. 14–21; Lk. ix. 37–43a)

The wealth of detail and great vividness of the section strongly suggest that it is based directly on personal reminiscence—probably Peter's (it gives the impression of being told from the point of view of someone who came back with Jesus rather than of someone who was present when the disciples tried and failed to cure the boy). Suggestions of a combination of two separate miracle-stories (*vv.* 14–19 and 20–7, or *vv.* 14–20 and 21–7) or of two narratives about the same boy, in one of which the main interest was in the disciples' failure due to their neglect of prayer (*vv.* 14–19, 28 f.), while the other was the miracle-story proper, are surely unnecessary. It is also unnecessary to regard the private conversation (*vv.* 28 f.: cf. iv. 10, vii. 17, x. 10) as a mere device for introducing the early Church's interpretation; for it is intrinsically likely that the disciples would in the circumstances have asked this question at the earliest opportunity.

About the connection with ix. 2–8 we cannot be absolutely certain. We may perhaps regard it as probable. (The adoption of the reading ἐλθὼν...εἶδεν in *v.* 14 would not necessarily rule it out, since the singular could be used, even though the three were with Jesus, as he alone was to play a part in the sequel.)

On the feature shared with vi. 45–52 see the concluding paragraph on that section, points (ii), (iii) and (iv).

Another feature which must have made this narrative specially interesting to the early community is the light which it throws on the need for, and the nature of, faith.

14. ἐλθόντες...εἶδον. This reading (א B L W 892 1342 *k* sa) is probably to be preferred to the singular ἐλθών... εἶδεν (A C D Θ *al*, most cursives, it (except *k*) vg sy[p, h] bo). If the section is in its historical context, the subject of εἶδον will be Jesus, Peter, James and John.

γραμματεῖς. The only occasion that the word is used without the article in Mk. There is a noticeable vagueness about the reference. But Wellhausen's suggestion that γραμματεῖς here is a false *explicitum* for αὐτούς that has been wrongly introduced into the text can hardly be accepted in the absence of any MS. evidence in this verse (though the variations in the MSS. in *v.* 16 might be taken to support it). The presence of scribes in the neighbourhood of Mt Hermon (if that is the scene), while certainly surprising, is scarcely impossible. The cause of the questioning is apparently the disciples' unsuccessful attempt to exorcize the demon.

15. ἐξεθαμβήθησαν. See on i. 22 (ἐξεπλήσσοντο). Probably their astonishment was due to Jesus' unexpected and opportune arrival—the suggestion that it was because Jesus' face was still shining after the Transfiguration, like Moses' face (Exod. xxxiv. 29 ff.), is not very likely.

16. The first **αὐτούς** perhaps refers to the crowd, since one of the crowd replies, although in *v.* 14 it is the scribes who are represented as questioning with αὐτούς (i.e. the disciples). The ambiguity of the pronouns has caused several variant readings: A C *ς* have τοὺς γραμματεῖς instead of the first αὐτούς (thus making the verse consistent with *v.* 14), while for the second αὐτούς there are several variants, ἑαυτούς, ἀλλήλους and ἐν ὑμῖν. Reading αὐτούς in both places, we could take the second αὐτούς as reflexive, but it is better to take it to refer to the disciples.

17. εἷς. See on v. 22.

Διδάσκαλε. See on i. 21 (ἐδίδασκεν).

πρὸς σέ. It was his intention to bring his son to Jesus, but he had found the disciples without Jesus.

ἔχοντα πνεῦμα ἄλαλον. See on i. 23.

18. ῥήσσει. According to L. & S. this is not from ῥήσσω, the later form of ῥήγνυμι ('rend'), but from ῥήσσω, the Ionic form of ῥάσσω or ῥάττω ('dash', 'dash down').

ξηραίνεται. Perhaps 'becomes stiff' or 'becomes exhausted'. It is difficult to be sure of the meaning here. The verb occurs in Mk in iii. 1, iv. 6, v. 29, xi. 20f.

οὐκ ἴσχυσαν. The disciples had tried and failed.

19. Ὦ γενεὰ ἄπιστος. Possibly not exclusively directed at the disciples, but surely it is to them specially that the words are addressed. It is their lack of faith that has been brought to light by their failure to cure the lad (cf. Mt. xvii. 20: διὰ τὴν ὀλιγοπιστίαν ὑμῶν). Their lack of faith had not consisted in any failure to expect success; for apparently they had expected to be successful and had been disappointed (cf. v. 28). Apparently they had taken it for granted, on the strength of past success (cf. vi. 13, 30), that they would be successful again, and it seems that it was in this 'taking for granted' that their lack of faith lay (see further on v. 29).

After ἄπιστος 𝔭⁴⁵ W f13 pc add καὶ διεστραμμένη. Taylor accepts the addition; but perhaps we should reject it as an assimilation to Mt. and Lk., and explain the presence of the words in Mt. and Lk. as due to the influence of Deut. xxxii. 5 (cf. Phil. ii. 15).

With the first **πρός** cf. vi. 3.

ἀνέξομαι. Cf. II Cor. xi. 1, 4, 19f., II Tim. iv. 3.

20. ἰδών. The masculine is in agreement with τὸ πνεῦμα *ad sensum*.

συνεσπάραξεν. Cf. i. 26, ix. 26, where the simple verb is used.

πεσών. There is a change of subject; it is now the boy rather than the demon.

21. ὡς. Here 'since': cf. Sophocles, *Oed. Tyr.* 115; Thucydides, IV. 90. 3.

22. ἵνα ἀπολέσῃ αὐτόν. Cf. v. 13.

εἴ τι δύνῃ. Contrast the certainty of the leper in i. 40.

ἡμῖν. Taylor notes the vividness of the father's 'identification of himself, and perhaps his family also, with the lad, shown in his use of the plural'.

σπλαγχνισθείς. See on vi. 34.

23. Τὸ Εἰ δύνῃ. 𝔓⁴⁵ D Θ f13 *al* omit τό, but this difficult τό is much more likely to have been omitted than inserted by a scribe, and so should be read. A D Θ f13 *pm* lat syᴾ˒ʰ ς add πιστεῦσαι after δύνῃ, doubtless in order to make the sentence easier. Those who added πιστεῦσαι must have taken the subject of δύνῃ here to be the father. But then the τό is awkward, and moreover one would have expected in this case the pronoun σύ to be put in, seeing that the whole point would be in the fact that the subject of δύνῃ is now the father and not Jesus as in v. 22. τὸ εἰ δύνῃ without the addition must be read. The τό has the effect of making εἰ δύνῃ into a noun. Translate: 'As to your "If you can",....' Jesus quotes the father's words in order to challenge them.

πάντα δυνατὰ τῷ πιστεύοντι. Wellhausen pointed out that although, according to the sense of the passage so far, one would expect the faith here referred to to be the faith of the healer (the disciples failed because they lacked faith, but one who has perfect faith in his Father can do what they failed to do), the following verse shows that this is not the sense in which the boy's father understood Jesus' words (for he takes them to be a rebuke of his own unbelief). If then the faith referred to is not the faith of the healer (as Schniewind thinks), various interpretations are possible: 'There is nothing which a man who has faith cannot do'; 'There is nothing which cannot be done (*sc.* by Jesus or by God) for a man who has faith'; 'There is nothing which is impossible for (i.e. in the view of) a man who has faith' (in other words, 'A man who has faith will not set any limit to what I (Jesus) (or perhaps God?) can do'). Of these the last fits the context best. This father ought, instead of doubting the power of Jesus to help him, to have had a faith like that of the leper in i. 40.

24. Calvin comments: 'He declares that he *believes*, and yet acknowledges himself to have *unbelief*. These two statements appear to contradict each other, but there is none of us that does not experience both of them in himself. As our *faith* is never perfect, it follows that we are partly *unbelievers*; but God forgives us, and exercises such forbearance towards us, as to reckon us believers on account of a small portion of faith.'

25. ἰδών…ὅτι ἐπισυντρέχει ὄχλος. The approach of the crowd leads Jesus to carry out the exorcism at once— to avoid unnecessary publicity (cf. vii. 33, viii. 23). The verb ἐπισυντρέχω is not known to occur elsewhere. This reference to the crowd is puzzling. Is it a different crowd from that mentioned in *v.* 14? Or are we to suppose that Jesus and the boy and his father had withdrawn some distance from the crowd mentioned in *v.* 14, and that now that same crowd was approaching? Or is this reference a sign that the story as it stands is not a unity? (Or should we accept Black's suggestion (p. 85, note 3) that ἐπισυντρέχει represents an Aramaic word meaning 'to attack' and understand that the crowd were rushing upon the boy?)

ἐπετίμησεν. See on i. 25.

καὶ κωφόν. A new detail, but the difference is probably not significant.

26. τοὺς πολλούς. Perhaps, as in R.V., 'the more part', or, more probably, inclusively 'all', i.e. all who were present. See on i. 34.

27. κρατήσας τῆς χειρὸς αὐτοῦ. Cf. i. 31, v. 41.

28. On the relation of this and the next verse to the preceding narrative see the introduction to the section above.

"Ο τι. Here = τί, as in ii. 16, ix. 11.

29. γένος. Here = 'sort', as in Mt. xiii. 47, I Cor. xii. 10, 28, xiv. 10.

ἐξελθεῖν. Here 'used as the equivalent of the passive of ἐκβάλλω' (Taylor).

After ἐν προσευχῇ most MSS. add καὶ νηστείᾳ, but the authorities supporting omission (א* B k geo¹ Clement), though few, are important. Moreover, there was a tendency to add references to fasting, as is seen in Acts x. 30, I Cor. vii. 5 (though in both instances the MS. evidence for inclusion is weaker than in Mk ix. 29). We find also that this verse with the reference to fasting is added in the Byzantine and other authorities in the Mt. parallel. A motive for addition was near at hand in the interest of the early Church in fasting, indicated by such passages as Acts xiii. 2, xiv. 23, *Didache* vii and viii, Justin, *I Apol.* 61. It is more difficult to think of a possible motive for omission. Hauck's suggestion that it would be omitted because it seemed to contradict Mk ii. 18 ff. is not very likely; for there it is assumed that the disciples *will* fast after Jesus has left them. Hauck's point is surely a more weighty reason for thinking the words 'and fasting' intrinsically improbable than for thinking that a scribe would omit them, if he found them; for scribes' alterations are usually due to less subtle reasons than that which he suggests. The contemporary interest of the Church would be more likely to weigh with a scribe. Certainly the intrinsic probabilities are against the words being original; for there is no mention of Jesus' fasting except during the forty days, and (as Hauck argues with opposite purpose)

Jesus expressly sanctioned his disciples' not fasting so long as he was with them. We conclude that 'and fasting' is not part of the original text, and that behind this addition lies a radical misunderstanding of Jesus' point. Mt.'s form of Jesus' answer gives the true point. By 'prayer' he means not merely prayer as a pious exercise, but rather the sense of complete dependence on God from which sincere prayer springs. But it was early misunderstood in the sense of a meritorious human pious activity, as though what the disciples needed was a greater 'holiness' of an ascetic sort.

It would seem that the disciples had thought of the gift of vi. 7 as given to them in such a way that they had henceforth the disposing of it, and therein had lain their lack of faith. They had to learn that God's power is not given to men in that way. It has rather ever to be asked for afresh (ἐν προσευχῇ) and received afresh. To trust in God's power in the sense that we imagine that we have it in our control and at our disposal is tantamount to unbelief; for it is really to trust in ourselves instead of in God.

51. THE SECOND PREDICTION OF THE PASSION
(ix. 30–2)
(Mt. xvii. 22–3; Lk. ix. 43 b–45)

The three predictions of the Passion are held by many to be simply variant forms of the same saying; but, as Taylor says, 'each...is distinctive in its narrative setting, and it is inherently probable that Jesus made several attempts' to prepare his disciples for what was to happen. Moreover, the three sayings are by no means identical.

30. ἐκεῖθεν. That is, from the house mentioned in *v.* 28 or else, more generally, from the neighbourhood in which the healing of the demoniac boy took place. See on vi. 1.

οὐκ ἤθελεν ἵνα τις γνοῖ. 'Nothing is said of a desire to avoid the attentions of Herod and there is no need to assume this purpose' (Taylor). The motive for secrecy is indicated in the next verse.

31. The second prediction of the Passion is shorter than the first. There is no reference to suffering or rejection specifically.

παραδίδοται. The tense is explained by Taylor as 'a futuristic present which conveys a note of assurance' (both Mt. and Lk. have μέλλει παραδίδοσθαι). What has already been said on παραδίδωμι (see on i. 14) needs supplementing here. Παραδίδωμι (meaning 'hand over') can (like *māsar* in Rabbinic Hebrew) be used in a wide variety of connections: e.g. of transmitting a tradition, entrusting something to somebody, giving one's life, delivering a person into another person's hands (especially of delivering up for punishment), informing against someone, betraying someone. Here in the word παραδίδοται there is probably a reference to Jesus' being delivered by Judas into the power of the Sanhedrin, by the Sanhedrin into the power of Pilate, by Pilate into the power of the soldiers. But another idea is certainly present —that of Jesus being delivered by God into the power of men (cf. Rom. viii. 32, and also iv. 25). It is possibly because this idea was uppermost in the minds of the N.T. writers that the action of Judas is denoted by this verb, which can suggest such an overtone, rather than by the verb προδίδωμι, whose range is narrower. It was used of Judas in iii. 19.

For the rest of the verse see on viii. 31.

32. οἱ δὲ ἠγνόουν τὸ ῥῆμα. Cf. iv. 13, 40, vi. 52, vii. 18, viii. 17, ix. 10. There is nothing improbable in this picture of the disciples' failure to grasp the meaning of Jesus' warning.

ἐφοβοῦντο αὐτὸν ἐπερωτῆσαι. Possibly they understood enough to sense that to know more would be painful. Possibly they could see that the subject was painful to Jesus himself.

52. THE DISPUTE ABOUT PRECEDENCE (ix. 33-7)
(Mt. xviii. 1-5; Lk. ix. 46-8)

It seems clear that the elements making up ix. 38-50 have been arranged according to catchwords. It also seems clear that the connection between the first element of ix. 38-50 and the present section consists of such a catchword—ἐπὶ τῷ ὀνόματί μου and ἐν τῷ ὀνόματί σου. But it is not clear whether vv. 33-7 is similarly made up of independent units or is a unity. There are things which point to the former alternative (see notes below); on the other hand, if we were to confine our attention to this section itself, we could explain it fairly easily as a unity. The mention of Capernaum and 'the house' suggest that possibly vv. 33f. may go back to Peter's reminiscence. After v. 34 the connections between the verses (and in v. 37 between the two parts of the verse) are uncertain. But this uncertainty does not affect the genuineness of the sayings themselves.

33. ἦλθον εἰς Καφαρναουμ. In this context it would be natural to think of Jesus and his disciples as having just arrived at Capernaum on their return from the neighbourhood of Caesarea Philippi (viii. 27) and Mt Hermon, having passed through (northern) Galilee (ix. 30); but it is quite probable that the context is merely artificial. In the Mt. and Lk. parallels Capernaum is not mentioned, though it has been mentioned in Mt. xvii. 24.

τῇ οἰκίᾳ. Presumably Peter's: cf. i. 29.

34. μείζων. The comparative is here used for the superlative, as often in Hellenistic Greek. Schlatter points out that the question of precedence was specially important in Palestine and was incessantly arising, whether in the synagogue service or judicial proceedings or at meals.

35. καθίσας. Jesus normally sat to teach, like the Rabbis. Cf. Mt. v. 1.

ἐφώνησεν. That Jesus should be represented as calling the

Twelve when in the previous verse he was already talking to the disciples seems odd. The explanation may be that ἐφώνησεν simply marks his addressing them afresh after adopting the posture of a teacher, or that there is an interval between *vv.* 34 and 35, or that only some of the disciples were present before and Jesus wanted all the Twelve to hear what he was now going to say, or that *v.* 35 is an independent saying that has been associated with *vv.* 33 f. on account of its similar theme.

The saying which follows is not reproduced by Mt. here, and in Lk. it comes a little later in the same context (ix. 48 b). Mark himself has a similar (rather fuller) saying in x. 43 f. (= Mt. xx. 26 f.; in Lk. in a different context, xxii. 26). There is also another similar saying in Mt. xxiii. 11. This may well mean that the saying here in *v.* 35 is an independent saying; it certainly means that 'the primitive communities preserved a lively recollection of the way in which Jesus rebuked personal ambition' (Taylor). (See further on x. 43 f.)

36 f. The relation of *vv.* 36 and 37 a and 37 b both to each other and to *v.* 35 is problematic. It is possible to trace a connection of thought between them: Jesus, having declared that true greatness is a matter of humble service (*v.* 35), goes on to give an example of such humble service, underlining its real greatness by the explanation that service rendered to such a little child will be accepted as done to Jesus, and service done to Jesus will be accepted by God as rendered to God. But (i) there is a puzzling disagreement between Mk and Mt. here—Mt. places immediately after his parallel to Mk ix. 36 a saying similar to Mk x. 15, followed by a saying about the person who humbles himself being greatest in the kingdom of heaven (with which may be compared Mt. xxiii. 12, Lk. xiv. 11, xviii. 14), and then adds a parallel to Mk ix. 37 a, but not to Mk ix. 37 b; (ii) sayings similar to *v.* 37 b occur in Mt. x. 40 and Lk. x. 16 in connection with the sending out of the Twelve and Seventy respectively; (iii) the words ἕνα τῶν μικρῶν τούτων τῶν πιστευόντων in *v.* 42 seem very similar to ἐν τῶν τοιούτων παιδίων in *v.* 37 (this has led some to think that *vv.* 37 and 42 were originally a pair of sayings. The further question then arises whether the reference is to children or to humble believers. It has been suggested that *v.* 37 originally referred to humble believers and that Mark wrongly took it to refer to children and so connected it with *v.* 36). In view of these complications, while we may accept the connection of thought suggested above as probably intended by Mark, we cannot be sure that, historically, *v.* 37 a and *v.* 37 b are rightly connected with the action of Jesus recorded in *v.* 36, or that that action is rightly associated with the saying in *v.* 35.

ἐπὶ τῷ ὀνόματί μου. The meaning could be 'because the παιδίον belongs to me—as a believer' or 'because the παιδίον (in his human need and without necessarily being a believer) is my representative' (cf. Mt. xxv. 40, 45) or 'because this action is something I desire'.

With *v.* 37 b cf. the Jewish legal principle that a man's representative or agent (Hebrew: *šālîaḥ*) is as himself (see Rengstorf, *Apostleship*, pp. 14–16). For the idea of Jesus being sent by God cf. Mt. xv. 24, Lk. iv. 18, 43, (Mk xii. 6), Jn iii. 17, iv. 34, v. 23, 30, 36, 38, vi. 29, etc.

53. THE STRANGE EXORCIST (ix. 38–40)
(Lk. ix. 49f.)

The view that this is a community-product may be confidently rejected; for the creation of such a tolerant principle cannot credibly be attributed to the early Church, and the connection with a particular disciple supports the view that we have here genuine historical tradition. (The suggestion that the section is intended as a defence of Paul is fantastic: no partisan of Paul is likely to have been content with such a defence.) It is interesting to compare Num. xi. 26–9, though there is no reason to think that it has influenced the present narrative. The study by E. Wilhelms, 'Der fremde Exorzist', in *S.T.* III (1950–1), pp. 162–71, is interesting—though the close connection he sees between this section and the situation of persecution seems doubtful.

38. εἴδομέν τινα ἐν τῷ ὀνόματί σου ἐκβάλλοντα δαιμόνια, ὅς οὐκ ἀκολουθεῖ ἡμῖν. For the use of Jesus' name by unbelieving exorcists see Acts xix. 13 ff. There is no reason to doubt that even during his lifetime some who were not disciples used it. (Mt. vii. 22 is possibly relevant.)

ἐκωλύομεν. Translate: 'We tried to prevent him'—conative imperfect.

ὅτι οὐκ ἠκολούθει ἡμῖν. D W X f1 f13 *al* lat omit this clause, while ℵ B C L Θ sy co omit the ὅς-clause above. The Byzantine text retains both these clauses, though reading ἀκολουθεῖ instead of ἠκολούθει. Probably we should follow the Western text and omit the ὅτι-clause, which looks like assimilation to Lk.

39. Jesus' reply is a rebuke to the disciples' intolerance. The very fact of a man's having wrought a miracle in Jesus' name is at least some guarantee that he will not immediately bitterly revile Jesus. It is evidence that he is not altogether hostile, and, as such, it is a pointer to a certain openness toward Jesus, which, however exiguous it may be, is not to be despised. Cf. the spirit described in Isa. xlii. 3 (Mt. xii. 20).

40. A particularly interesting parallel to this saying and also to Mt. xii. 30 = Lk. xi. 23 occurs in Cicero, *Lig.* xi. In defending the Pompeiani Cicero says to Caesar: 'Let that maxim of yours, which won you your victory, hold good. For we have often heard you say that, while we considered all who were not with us as our enemies, you considered all who were not against you your friends.'[1] Jesus apparently

---

[1] 'Valeat tua vox illa, quae vicit. Te enim dicere audiebamus, nos omnes adversarios putare nisi qui nobiscum essent, te omnes, qui contra te non essent, tuos.' Quoted by Wilhelms in *S.T.* III, p. 165. Attention was earlier drawn to this parallel by W. Nestle in *Z.N.T.W.* XIII (1912), p. 85.

made use of a current proverb here, as he quite often did. There is no reason to question the saying's authenticity. It is best to take it with *vv.* 38f. closely (*pace* Bultmann and others). It states the general principle behind the μὴ κωλύετε αὐτόν of the previous verse, whereas *v.* 39 b is more limited in its application.

The saying is best interpreted in conjunction with Mt. xii. 30 = Lk. xi. 23, which on the surface seems to contradict it. The difficulty is probably not to be resolved either by contrasting the singular in Mt. xii. 30 = Lk. xi. 23 with the plural in Mk ix. 40 = Lk. ix. 50 (while there can be no neutrality as far as Jesus himself is concerned, the disciples must not be intolerant toward those who do not follow them), or by pointing out that there is no formal contradiction between the two sayings, but rather by relating these sayings to the messianic veiledness of Jesus (see on iv. 11 f., 33). Jesus avoided forcing men precipitously into a position in which they had to make a final decision about him and used delayed-action methods of teaching in order to give them as much time as possible in which to decide. So long as the critical point has not been reached the principle of Mk ix. 40 holds, and the attitude of the disciple toward those who have not yet decided is to be that of recognizing in the unbeliever of today the possible believer of tomorrow (cf. the Oxyrhynchus saying quoted by Huck in illustration of this verse). On the other hand, when the critical moment comes and the decision has to be made, it is the principle of Mt. xii. 30 that holds; to be neutral toward Jesus is to have decided against him. While the principle of Mk ix. 40 should govern the attitude of the Church toward those without, the principle of Mt. xii. 30 must be part of the Church's preaching both to those without and to those within.

54. FURTHER SAYINGS TO DISCIPLES (ix. 41–50)
(Mt. xviii. 6–9; cf. Lk. xvii. 1f., xiv. 34f., Mt. v. 13)

This section illustrates very clearly the way in which in the period before the gospels were written isolated sayings of Jesus were sometimes grouped together according to catchwords to make them more easily memorable. It looks as if *v.* 42 may first have been joined to *v.* 37 because of ἐν τῶν τοιούτων παιδίων and ἕνα τῶν μικρῶν τούτων, and afterwards *vv.* 38–40 may have been inserted after *v.* 37 because of another catchword, ἐπὶ τῷ ὀνόματί μου in *v.* 37 and ἐν τῷ ὀνόματί σου and ἐπὶ τῷ ὀνόματί μου in *vv.* 38–40, and *v.* 41 similarly inserted after *vv.* 38–40 because it contained ἐν ὀνόματι. The connection between *vv.* 42 and 43–8 is the word σκανδαλίζειν and also καλόν ἐστιν and βέβληται–βληθῆναι, and *v.* 49 seems to have been placed after *v.* 48 because both verses contained the word πῦρ. Similarly the connection between *vv.* 49 and 50 is ἁλισθήσεται–ἅλας.

41. ποτίσῃ . . . ποτήριον ὕδατος. An example of a very small and soon forgotten service.

ἐν ὀνόματι, ὅτι would probably strike copyists as strange— hence the variants, ἐν ὀνόματί μου, ὅτι and ἐν τῷ ὀνόματί μου, ὅτι; but, though rather unusual, it is a quite possible expression for 'on the ground that' (cf. Mt. x. 41f.: εἰς ὄνομα προφήτου, 'on the ground that he is a prophet' or 'as a prophet'; and the sentence βούλεται ὀνόματι ἐλευθέρου ('in virtue of its being freeborn') τὸ σωμάτιον ἀπενέγκασθαι in the report of a lawsuit for the recovery of a foundling in *P. Oxy.* 37, i, 17; and other examples in Bauer, *s.v.*).

Χριστοῦ. The use of the title in this way by Jesus would be very surprising, and, in view of Mark's sparing use of it and the fact that in the gospels and Acts, when it is used, it nearly always has an article, it seems probable that it was not written here by Mark. The suggestion of T. W. Manson[1]

[1] *Ap.* Taylor, p. 408.

that Mark wrote ἐμοί (א* has ἐμόν instead of Χριστοῦ) seems very likely. We should then translate ἐμοί ἐστε 'you are mine' (cf. Ps. Sol. ix. 16: ὅτι σοί ἐσμεν).

αμην. See on iii. 28. The use of αμην λέγω ὑμῖν and οὐ μή and the subjunctive make this statement very strong.

μισθόν. In Jesus' use of the term 'reward' the idea of deserving is not present; for he has rejected completely the Jewish notion of 'merit' (see, for example, Mt. xx. 1–16, Lk. xvii. 7–10). The giver of the cup of water will not receive 'his reward' because his trivial service has deserved it, but because God in his goodness values even the smallest token of faith and obedience. (See further the interesting article by H. Preisker and E. Würthwein in *T.W.N.T.* iv, pp. 699–736.)

42. σκανδαλίσῃ. See on iv. 17 and vi. 3. The verb here means to cause someone to stumble in his faith, to destroy someone's faith, to cause to fall away from God.

τῶν μικρῶν τούτων τῶν πιστευόντων. The humble members of the Christian community. Cf. perhaps the ἀσθενεῖς of Rom. xiv, I Cor. viii and ix? The addition of εἰς ἐμέ after πιστευόντων is strongly attested (A B W Θ f1 f13 *pm* lat sy *s*) and should perhaps be accepted.

καλόν ἐστιν αὐτῷ μᾶλλον: 'it would have been better for him'. For the positive followed by μᾶλλον cf. Acts xx. 35, Gal. iv. 27. The present indicative is used in the apodosis and the perfect indicative in the protasis for the sake of vividness, although the sentence is hypothetical. The dative αὐτῷ is to be taken strictly as meaning 'for him' (*not* 'better that he'): the punishment he will receive will be so severe that it would have been better for him had he been killed before he could do the wrong and so been saved from the punishment.

μύλος ὀνικός. A millstone turned by an ass in contrast with one turned by hand—so a large one.

Cf. Lk. xvii. 1 f. for the 'Q' version of the saying.

43–8. Whereas in *v.* 42 the thought is of causing someone

313

else to stumble, in these verses it is of causing oneself to
stumble. The general point of the verses is that it is worth
making the most costly sacrifices for the sake of not losing
eternal life. It would not be lost on the Roman Church in
the time of persecution.

καλόν...ἤ. The use of the positive instead of the comparative is Semitic—though Lagrange cites a parallel from
Herodotus, IX. 26. 7.

τὴν ζωήν. Ἡ ζωή here is equivalent to ζωὴ αἰώνιος in
x. 17, 30. In *v.* 47 ἡ βασιλεία τοῦ Θεοῦ is substituted for it.

γέενναν. The name of the valley to the south of Jerusalem
(Hebrew: *gê ḥinnōm* = 'valley of Hinnom') which had been
the scene of human sacrifices to Molech (Jer. vii. 31, xix. 5 f.,
xxxii. 35), but had been desecrated by Josiah (II Kgs xxiii.
10) and used for burning offal. It came to be used to denote
the place of divine punishment (e.g. Enoch xxvii. 2, xc. 26 f.,
IV Ezra vii. 36).

εἰς τὸ πῦρ τὸ ἄσβεστον. Possibly, as Taylor suggests,
Mark's own explanatory comment, based on Isa. lxvi. 24,
for the benefit of his Gentile readers.

Verses 44 and 46 (both identical with *v.* 48) are omitted by
א B C L W f1 *k* syˢ co fa, and should not be read.

Verse 48 is a quotation from Isa. lxvi. 24, a passage which
was important in the development of the idea of Gehenna.

The poetical form of these verses should be noted. The
picture of a destruction which continues endlessly is not to
be taken as a literal description, but as picture-language.
It should neither be explained away, nor thought of in
isolation from the whole record of Jesus' person, work and
words.

49. There are three main forms of the text of this verse:

(i) πᾶς γὰρ πυρὶ ἁλισθήσεται.

(ii) πᾶς γὰρ πυρὶ ἁλισθήσεται καὶ πᾶσα θυσία ἁλὶ ἁλισθήσεται.

(iii) πᾶσα γὰρ θυσία ἁλὶ ἁλισθήσεται.

(i) is supported by ℵ B L W (with ἀλισγηθήσεται = 'shall be polluted' instead of ἀλισθήσεται) f1 al syˢ sa; (ii) is supported by A C Θ (with ἀναλωθήσεται = 'shall be destroyed' instead of the first ἀλισθήσεται) f13 pm f l q r² vg ς; (iii) is supported by D a b c d ff² i, a variant being omnia [sic!] autem substantia consumitur, read by k.

The short text (i) should almost certainly be read; for, on the one hand, it is strongly attested, and, on the other hand, the extra clause in (ii) can be explained as a marginal gloss (someone having seen that Lev. ii. 13 gives a clue to the meaning) and the short text (iii) can be explained as due to the accidental omission of the first part of the long text (ii). (Couchoud's suggestion[1] that the Greek implied by k, πᾶσα δὲ οὐσία ἀναλωθήσεται (= 'and all their substance shall be destroyed'), which would be a continuation of v. 48, is the original is in some ways attractive. It has some support in Ψ, which reads ἀναλωθήσεται in place of the second ἀλισθή-σεται of the long reading; οὐσία could easily be misread as θυσία; the introduction of Lev. ii. 13 would be natural when once θυσία was read; and the first part of the long text could be explained as an explanatory gloss interpreting πᾶσα δὲ οὐσία ἀναλωθήσεται by the previous verses. But if this suggestion is accepted, it is difficult to see why the sayings which follow in v. 50 should ever have been placed in this context, whereas, if we accept short text (i), the presence of the word ἀλισθήσεται provides the reason.)

The connection with v. 48 is simply the presence of the catchword πῦρ (the γάρ is apparently a link inserted by the compiler): the connection with v. 50 appears to be similar. So we have to interpret v. 49 quite independently. The most probable clue is provided by the reader or copyist who inserted the quotation from Lev. ii. 13. The Jewish sacrifices had to be accompanied by salt (Lev. ii. 13, Ezek. xliii. 24; cf. Exod. xxx. 35). So the thought here seems to be that the

[1] In J.T.S. xxxiv, p. 124.

disciple ($\pi\hat{a}s$ we take to mean 'every disciple') is to be a sacrifice to God (cf. Rom. xii. 1) and that there is something which is as necessary an accompaniment of this sacrifice as salt was of the Temple sacrifices. This something is referred to as $\pi\hat{v}\rho$, which here (unlike $\pi\hat{v}\rho$ in v. 48) probably stands for the fires of trials and persecutions (cf. I Pet. i. 7, iv. 12). For the idea of the necessity of tribulation for the faithful disciple cf. viii. 34–7, Mt. v. 10–12.

50. The first and second parts of the verse, at any rate, belong together. Cf. Mt. v. 13, Lk. xiv. 34f. (Mark's $\H{a}\nu a\lambda o\nu$ $\gamma\acute{e}\nu\eta\tau a\iota$ and the Mt. and Lk. $\mu\omega\rho a\nu\theta\hat{\eta}$ appear to be variant translations of the same Aramaic word, which has both the sense of 'fool' and that of 'unsavoury'.) Here the associations of salt are not ritual, but domestic. Salt was a necessity of life in the ancient world (cf. *Sopherim*, xv. 8: 'The world cannot survive without salt'); it preserved from putrefaction food which without it would become putrid. So the disciples of Jesus are set, like salt, as a source of life and health in the midst of a world that left to itself must go bad. But they are warned of the possibility of their losing the very property which makes them precious, and so becoming futile like salt that has lost its saltness. It seems likely that the saltness of the salt stands for that for which the disciples are to be prepared to lose their lives (viii. 35), and of which they are not to be ashamed (viii. 38), i.e. the gospel, Jesus' words, Jesus himself.

The third part of the verse—$\H{e}\chi\epsilon\tau\epsilon$ $\acute{e}\nu$ $\acute{e}av\tau o\hat{\iota}s$ $\H{a}\lambda a$ $\kappa a\grave{\iota}$ $\epsilon\acute{\iota}\rho\eta\nu\epsilon\acute{v}\epsilon\tau\epsilon$ $\acute{e}\nu$ $\acute{a}\lambda\lambda\acute{\eta}\lambda o\iota s$—may be an independent saying: it could, for instance, belong to such a context as vv. 33f. or x. 41 ff. ('salt' perhaps referring to the attitude of humble service enjoined in v. 35 and x. 42 ff.). Or it may be closely connected with v. 50a and b, the sense being: Instead of allowing yourselves to become salt that has lost its saltness, take care to maintain in yourselves that which is the saltness of the salt, namely the gospel, the word of God (cf. Lk. xi.

28: τὸν λόγον τοῦ Θεοῦ...φυλάσσοντες; and see on iv. 20), and then you will be able to maintain peace with one another.

ἐν ἑαυτοῖς can mean the same as ἐν ἀλλήλοις (e.g. I Thess. v. 13), but here it is more natural to take it as contrasted with the following ἐν ἀλλήλοις, and so translate 'in yourselves'.

ἅλα. From ἅλς; in v. 50 a and b the later form ἅλας was used.

καί should probably here be translated 'and so' (taking the second imperative as conditional upon the first). If the disciples keep the word in their hearts, they will be able to live at peace among themselves; for it will destroy those things which would destroy true peace.

55. CONCERNING MARRIAGE AND DIVORCE
(x. 1–12)
(Mt. xix. 1–12; cf. Mt. v. 31 f., Lk. xvi. 18)

A summary statement (v. 1) is followed by a pronouncement-story (vv. 2–9), about which Taylor comments that 'the freshness of the original encounter is manifest'. The statement in v. 10 may well be based on tradition, though it is possible that in v. 12 the situation of a Gentile church may be reflected.

1. ἐκεῖθεν. See on vi. 1.

εἰς τὰ ὅρια τῆς Ἰουδαίας καὶ πέραν τοῦ Ἰορδάνου. The Byzantine reading, διὰ τοῦ instead of καί, is no doubt an attempt to get rid of a difficulty, but it probably gives the right sense. The fact that τὰ ὅρια τῆς Ἰουδαίας are mentioned before πέραν τοῦ Ἰορδάνου need not mean that Jesus reached Judea first and then crossed into Peraea; for in xi. 1 Jerusalem is mentioned before Bethphage and Bethany. The Western and Caesarean reading that omits καί, though strongly supported, is possibly an assimilation to Mt., and should probably be rejected in favour of the Alexandrian reading printed above. (If the reading without καί were accepted, the meaning would presumably be 'into that part of the territory of Peraea which though not politically part of Judea was Jewish in population'.)

Mark is probably describing Jesus' final journey up to Judea; though some scholars think that what is indicated here is not a journey from Galilee to Jerusalem, but rather a ministry in Judea and Peraea (see Lohmeyer, p. 198; T. W. Manson in *B.J.R.L.* xxxiii, p. 273).

The latter half of the verse indicates the resumption of Jesus' public teaching ministry.

The plural ὄχλοι (elsewhere it is always in the singular in Mk) is perhaps intended to suggest the different crowds which collected on different occasions.

2. προσελθόντες Φαρισαῖοι. Omitted by D *a b d k r*[1] sy[s], perhaps rightly (if so, ἐπηρώτων will be an indefinite plural).

εἰ...ἀπολῦσαι. Better taken as an indirect question than, with R.V., R.S.V., as a direct question.

If the Mt. addition, κατὰ πᾶσαν αἰτίαν (cf. μὴ ἐπὶ πορνείᾳ in Mt. xix. 9 and παρεκτὸς λόγου πορνείας in Mt. v. 32), correctly glosses Mk, then the issue was simply whether Jesus supported the stricter or the less strict of the Rabbinic opinions on the subject (that of Shammai who interpreted the 'unseemly thing' of Deut. xxiv. 1 as adultery or that of Hillel who allowed the divorce of a wife on quite trivial grounds, e.g. for letting her husband's food burn[1]); but it is much more probable that the question concerned divorce itself and that the exceptive clause in Mt. represents a later modification of the teaching of Jesus.

πειράζοντες αὐτόν. Their intention is presumably to see whether Jesus will say something which can be used against him—either to show him contradicting the Law or to compromise him in Herod's eyes (cf. vi. 17f.). Πειράζειν here means to 'test someone's defences', 'try to get someone off his guard'.

---

[1] See (*M*) *Gitt.* ix. 10.

3. Jesus directs them back to the Law. See on vii. 1–23 and also on x. 17–20.

4. The regulation about giving a certificate of divorce in Deut. xxiv. 1 assumes the practice of divorce and provides some protection for the woman.

In classical Greek and in the papyri ἀποστάσιον is a legal term containing the idea of giving up one's right to something. It was used in the LXX to translate the Hebrew *kᵉrîṯûṯ* in Deut. xxiv. 1, etc., and so gets the meaning 'divorce', which it has here.

The sense of the verse is that Moses permitted (ἐπιτρέπειν means 'permit', as in v. 13, rather than 'command') divorce provided that a certificate of divorce was given to the wife.

5. In this and the following verses Jesus is not setting the commandment of God against that of Moses, nor is he brushing aside the scripture.[1] Rather he is bringing out the real meaning of Deut. xxiv. 1. A distinction has to be made between that which sets forth the absolute will of God, and those provisions which take account of men's actual sinfulness and are designed to limit and control its consequences. Whereas the Ten Commandments (in this connection Exod. xx. 14) and such passages as the verses quoted in *vv.* 6–8 represent God's absolute command, Deut. xxiv. 1 is a divine provision to deal with situations brought about by men's σκληροκαρδία and to protect from its worst effects those who would suffer as a result of it. (Much that is contained in the O.T. falls within the category of such provisions.) The error of the Rabbis' interpretation lay in their losing sight of this distinction and so imagining that Deut. xxiv. 1 meant that God allowed divorce, in the sense that it had his approval and did not come under his judgement. This error lay beneath the form of the question (ἔξεστιν). So in *vv.* 11 f. Jesus directs his disciples back to the absolute command of God by his use of the word μοιχᾶται.

[1] *Pace* Manson, *Teaching*, p. 293.

Human conduct which falls short of the absolute command of God is sin and stands under the divine judgement. The provisions which God's mercy has designed for the limitation of the consequences of man's sin must not be interpreted as divine approval for sinning. When our sinfulness traps us in a position in which all the choices still open to us are evil, we are to choose that which is least evil, asking for God's forgiveness and comforted by it, but not pretending that the evil is good.

σκληροκαρδίαν. A LXX word, found also in the O.T. Pseudepigrapha, the N.T. and early Christian writers, but not in secular Greek. It means primarily man's stubborn rebelliousness against God. (See J. Behm in *T.W.N.T.* III, p. 616.)

6. Jesus directs their attention to the divine intention with regard to marriage as shown in the creation narrative in Gen. i and ii. The suggestion that ἀπὸ...ἀρχῆς κτίσεως means 'at the beginning of Genesis' or 'at the beginning of the creation narrative' is unnecessary, as is also the suggestion that there is a mistranslation from Aramaic here; for, although no other subject but Moses has been mentioned, it is perfectly possible to understand 'God'. The MSS. which add ὁ Θεός give the right sense, though the addition is probably an explanatory gloss. The quotation is from Gen. i. 27.

7. In the original context the ἕνεκεν τούτου in the second quotation refers back to Gen. ii. 21-3, but as it stands here in Jesus' adaptation it is natural to connect it with the words quoted in *v.* 6. The difference is unimportant; for, if Gen. i and ii are read as one story, it is natural to take ii. 21-3 as filling out the bare statement of i. 27b—and Jesus would be innocent of J and P.

The words added in the great majority of authorities after μητέρα are probably assimilation to Mt. (and Gen.).

8. εἰς σάρκα μίαν. A literal translation of *lᵉbāśār 'eḥāḏ*: in

Greek the εἰς is unnecessary, and the simple nominative would be more natural. The word σάρξ here is puzzling. Are we to take it as equivalent to σῶμα (cf. I Cor. vi. 16, Eph. v. 28–31), the meaning being that the two become one *person*? Or are we rather to understand it in the light of passages like Gen. xxix. 14, xxxvii. 27, Judg. ix. 2, Rom. xi. 14, the meaning being that a man and a woman by marriage cease to be merely members of two different families and become one *kindred*?

9. **ὃ οὖν ὁ Θεὸς συνέζευξεν.** The individual marriage union derives its sanctity from the fact that behind it stands the authority of God himself.

ἄνθρωπος μὴ χωριζέτω. The words repeat the absolute command of God. For man to dissolve such a union is something which inevitably stands under the divine judgement. It may nevertheless be proper for the state and also the Church to make provision for situations in which because of human sinfulness divorce may be the lesser evil.

10. Cf. iv. 10, vii. 17, etc.

11. To marry another after divorcing one's wife is to break the seventh commandment.

ἐπ' αὐτήν. According to Rabbinic law a man could be said to commit adultery against another married man, and a wife could be said to commit adultery against her husband, but a husband could not be said to commit adultery against his wife. So Jesus goes beyond Rabbinic teaching by speaking of a husband committing adultery against his wife. (Cf. Manson, *Sayings*, p. 136.)

Note the Mt. addition here.

12. Peculiar to Mk. There are three main forms of the text: (i) the text accepted by the Bible Society, which is Alexandrian (read by ℵ B, etc.); (ii) ἐὰν γυνὴ ἀπολύσῃ τὸν ἄνδρα αὐτῆς καὶ γαμηθῇ ἄλλῳ is supported (with slight variations) by A and the Byzantine text generally and also by f1 it (some MSS.) vg sy^{p, h}; (iii) D Θ f13 *al* it (most

MSS.) sy^s have (with slight variations) ἐὰν γυνὴ ἐξέλθῃ ἀπὸ τοῦ ἀνδρὸς καὶ γαμήσῃ ἄλλον μοιχᾶται. Of these (i) and (ii) do not differ substantially, but (iii) envisages the wife departing from her husband (without divorce) and marrying another —a possible allusion to Herodias. Taylor, following Wellhausen and Burkitt, accepts (iii); but it is perhaps rather more likely that (i) should be accepted. The support of I Cor. vii. 10 for (iii) cannot be pressed, since there χωρισθῆναι probably does not mean 'depart' but has a technical sense (cf. Bauer, *s.v.*). If (i) is original, the words in Mk may represent an adaptation of Jesus' teaching to the situation of a Gentile church (Jewish law did not allow a wife to divorce her husband[1]), or it may be that Jesus himself was looking beyond the custom of his own people (he can hardly have been altogether unaware of Gentile practice).

56. THE BLESSING OF THE CHILDREN (x. 13–16)
(Mt. xix. 13–15; Lk. xviii. 15–17; cf. Mt. xviii. 3)

A pronouncement-story, which in the course of tradition has lost all details of time and place. Its connection with the preceding section (it is introduced simply by καί) is probably topical—a story of Jesus blessing children seemed to follow suitably on a section concerned with marriage. It is possible that *v.* 15 is an independent saying (see below); but of its authenticity, as of that of the rest of the section, there is no doubt.

13. προσέφερον. Indefinite plural. The verb προσφέρειν can mean 'bring' without any idea of carrying (e.g. Mt. viii. 16, ix. 32, xii. 22, Lk. xxiii. 14; cf. the simple verb in Mk vii. 32, xi. 2, 7).

παιδία. The word is used in *v.* 39 of a girl of twelve years

---

[1] But see S.–B. ii, p. 23 for the possibility that this statement needs some modification. See also Manson, *Sayings*, pp. 136f.

(cf. v. 42), though usually it denotes a young child. The Lk. parallel has βρέφη, which means 'infants'.

ἵνα αὐτῶν ἅψηται. Jesus is often described as touching the sick or being touched by them (iii. 10, v. 27f., 30, vi. 56, vii. 33, viii. 22). Here the idea of those who bring the children is that Jesus should bless them. Cf. Gen. xlviii. 13ff. and examples in S.–B. I, pp. 807f.

ἐπετίμησαν. See on viii. 32 and i. 25. Presumably the disciples meant to save Jesus from being troubled.

αὐτοῖς. The variant τοῖς προσφέρουσιν is clearly due to the desire to get rid of the ambiguity of αὐτοῖς, which grammatically could refer to the children themselves. The masculine αὐτοῖς suggests that Mark did not think of those who brought the children as being necessarily the mothers.

14. ἠγανάκτησεν. Cf. iii. 5, the tone of ix. 19, and, if ὀργισθείς be read, i. 41. In both Mt. and Lk. the reference here to Jesus' indignation is omitted. Mark's use of asyndeton before μὴ κωλύετε has the effect of suggesting Jesus' impatience.

μὴ κωλύετε. The use of the verb κωλύειν, a word associated with baptism in the early Church (e.g. Acts viii. 36, x. 47, xi. 17; cf. Mt. iii. 14),[1] may possibly be an indication that this tradition had already been used as an argument in favour of child-baptism; in any case it would in the future encourage people reading the gospel to make that application.

τῶν γὰρ τοιούτων ἐστὶν ἡ βασιλεία τοῦ Θεοῦ. The genitive is possessive, the meaning being that the kingdom 'belongs to such' (cf. Mt. v. 3, 10)—not that it 'consists of such'. Taylor rightly notes that the implication of 'the concurrence of the statement that the Kingdom belongs to children with the command ἄφετε τὰ παιδία ἔρχεσθαι πρός με' is that 'in a true sense Jesus Himself is the Kingdom' (cf. on i. 15). The kingdom of God belongs to little children —and to other weak and insignificant ones—not because of

[1] See Cullmann, *Baptism*, pp. 71–80.

any merit of theirs, but because God has willed to give it to them (cf. Lk. xii. 32). To find the reason why the kingdom of God belongs to children in any subjective qualities of the children is surely to misunderstand: the reason is rather to be found in their objective humbleness, the fact that they are weak and helpless and unimportant, and in the fact that God has chosen 'the weak things of the world' (I Cor. i. 26 ff.; cf. Mt. xi. 25 f. = Lk. x. 21).

15. ἀμήν. See on iii. 28.

The reference in ὡς παιδίον again is not to the receptiveness or humility or imaginativeness or trustfulness or unselfconsciousness of children, but to their objective littleness and helplessness. To receive the kingdom as a little child is to allow oneself to be given it, because one knows one cannot claim it as one's right or attempt to earn it. (To think of any subjective qualities of children here is to turn faith into a work.) Jn iii. 3, 5 seem to be the Johannine version of this saying and provide an illuminating comment upon it. Nicodemus has to learn that he cannot enter the kingdom of God as a learned theologian and highly respected religious leader; if he is to enter it at all, it must be as one who is helpless and small, without claim or merit.

About the relation of this verse to *vv.* 13 f. and 16 we cannot be certain. It is not unsuited to this context, but neither is it indispensable to it, and in Mt. it is actually placed elsewhere (xviii. 3). It may be in its historical context here, or it may be an independent saying that has been appended to *vv.* 13 f.

16. ἐναγκαλισάμενος. Cf. ix. 36. Bengel comments: 'Plus fecit, quam rogatus erat.'

κατευλόγει: '...as in καταγελᾶν (v. 40), and καταφιλεῖν (xiv. 45), the force of κατά seems to be intensive—He blessed them fervently, in no perfunctory way...' (Swete).

57. RICHES AND THE KINGDOM OF GOD
(x. 17–31)
(Mt. xix. 16–30; Lk. xviii. 18–30)

The section is made up of three parts: (i) *vv.* 17–22; (ii) *vv.* 23–7; (iii) *vv.* 28–31. Though each of the three parts could be independent, it is probable that (i) and (ii) do belong together historically. Mark clearly means us to understand that the conversation in (ii) followed immediately on, and was occasioned by, the episode related in (i); and Luke has underlined the connection by the words 'seeing him' (xviii. 24). Verses 17–22 seem incomplete without some comment by Jesus on the man's sorrowful departure, and the words of Jesus in *vv.* 23–7, punctuated as they are by the disciples' surprise and bewilderment and culminating in *v.* 27, fit the context so well that it seems more reasonable to think that we have here a historical connection than to regard the two parts as originally separate units that have been brought together either at an early stage in the tradition for catechetical purposes or in the making of the gospel because Mark felt that it was unsatisfactory to end the pericope at *v.* 22.

The connection between (ii) and (iii) stands differently. Though (iii) certainly fits this context well, it is nevertheless easily detachable. It is noticeable that Mark, though clearly thinking of *vv.* 17–31 as a unit, does not link *vv.* 27 and 28 together with a conjunction of any sort—an indication maybe that he did not take over all three parts as a unit. Verse 31 is a floating logion, omitted here by Lk. and occurring elsewhere in the gospels. We conclude that (iii) may have been independent originally and have been attached to (i) and (ii) by Mark because of a similarity of theme. Placed here, it serves to provide a contrast to the man who valued his wealth above eternal life; for the disciples *had* given up all for Christ's sake and the gospel's.

325

The warning contained in *vv.* 17–27 is now matched by the promise in *vv.* 29 f.

Parts (i) and (ii) may well be Petrine. As to (iii), the sayings in *vv.* 29 f. and 31 are probably authentic, though they seem to have been remembered as isolated sayings. The connection of the whole section with x. 13–16 is probably topical.

17. ἐκπορευομένου αὐτοῦ εἰς ὁδόν: 'as he was setting out on his way' or, less probably, 'as he was coming out (from the house) on to the road'. The detail may well have been part of the tradition Mark received, though it is possible that it is editorial.

προσδραμών. A vivid detail, which suggests the man's eagerness.

εἷς. See on v. 22. Only in *v.* 22 are we told that he was rich. In Lk. xviii. 18 he is spoken of as τις ἄρχων, in Mt. xix. 20, 22 as ὁ νεανίσκος.

γονυπετήσας. See on i. 40.

Διδάσκαλε. See on i. 21 (ἐδίδασκεν).

ἀγαθέ. There is little justification for regarding this as 'a somewhat obsequious piece of conventional flattery, a *captatio benevolentiae*, from the unreality of which our Lord recoiled',[1] 'conventional effusiveness',[2] or 'irony'.[3] So far as it goes, his use of the epithet is surely sincere—a not insignificant tribute to the impression made by Jesus.

In Greek to address someone with ὦ ἀγαθέ or ὦ βέλτιστε was a common enough thing, but among the Jews this was not so. S.-B., II, p. 24, cites only one Jewish parallel to διδάσκαλε ἀγαθέ. In the O.T. only God is characteristically called 'good' (*ṭôb*), whether the word is used in the sense of 'morally good' or in the limited sense of 'kind' (the two senses cannot be rigidly separated). But we are not to infer either that the use of the epithet here implies that the

---

[1] Rawlinson, p. 138.   [2] Blunt, p. 217.
[3] I. Abrahams, quoted in Rawlinson, p. 138.

speaker regarded Jesus as more than man or that it is due
to a theological motive in the tradition or on the part of
Mark; for the word is occasionally used of men in the O.T.
(e.g. Prov. xii. 2, xiv. 14, Eccl. ix. 2) and Jesus himself
speaks of ὁ ἀγαθὸς ἄνθρωπος (Mt. xii. 35 par.). It is clear,
however, that ἀγαθέ here should not be described as
conventional.

τί ποιήσω ἵνα ζωὴν αἰώνιον κληρονομήσω; He at least
asks the question that really matters, even though the
sequel shows that he is not concerned deeply enough with
it. That he asks it at all shows that he is not altogether self-
complacent.

For ζωὴν αἰώνιον cf. τὴν ζωήν in ix. 43, 45. The phrase is
used in the LXX (Dan. xii. 2) and is the equivalent of the
Rabbinic expressions, ḥayyê ʿôlām ('eternal life') and ḥayyê
ʿôlām habbāʾ ('life of the age to come'). κληρονομήσω reflects
Jewish usage, which spoke of 'inheriting' eternal life. (On
κληρονομεῖν, etc. see further T.W.B. pp. 112–14.)

18. Jesus calls in question the man's use of ἀγαθέ. This is
difficult, and in Mt. both the man's question and Jesus'
answer have been altered—presumably because the author
felt that the latter as given by Mk was liable to be interpreted as a disclaimer both of absolute goodness and of oneness with God. But the words are not to be taken as
implying that Jesus was conscious of sin or of not being one
with God, nor yet as primarily intended as an assertion of
his divinity, as some have argued. Bengel points the way to
the true interpretation, when he comments: 'Jesus did not
rest in Himself, but referred Himself wholly to His Father.
He lived in the world as a pilgrim and stranger, and it was
in that condition in which the Psalms describe Him as *poor
and needy* that He wrestled toward that eternal good and
joy, about which this youth was inquiring.' The man's idea
of goodness is of a goodness that is man's achievement:
Jesus, on the other hand, confesses (here surely Jn v. 19

rightly interprets His mind), 'The Son can do nothing of himself'. So Jesus directs the young man's attention away from himself to his Father, who is the only source and only norm of goodness.

19. The second part of Jesus' answer also directs the inquirer's attention to God, this time by referring him to the Ten Commandments. They are the answer to his question, τί ποιήσω; And they are simple and plain enough—not that they are easy to obey, but the difficulty lies not in understanding them but in doing them. They are the answer to the question about eternal life, not because a man can keep them and so earn eternal life, but because, if he honestly tries to keep them, he will be brought to recognize his bankruptcy and prepared to receive the kingdom of God as a little child.

Only commandments of the Second Table are mentioned (cf. Mt. vii. 12, Gal. v. 14, Rom. xiii. 8–10), not because they are regarded as more important than those of the First Table, but because it is by a man's obedience to the former that his obedience to the latter must be outwardly demonstrated.[1]

There are textual variations here: (i) א^c B C *pc* sy^s co support Μὴ φονεύσῃς, Μὴ μοιχεύσῃς; A W Θ f 1 28 lat Clement ς have these in reverse order; D *k* Irenaeus support Μὴ μοιχεύσῃς, Μὴ πορνεύσῃς; (ii) B* W f 1 28 *al* sy^s Clement omit Μὴ ἀποστερήσῃς. With regard to (i), it may be argued, as by C. H. Turner, that the text that is different from Mt. and Lk. is more likely to be right, and that 'fornications' as well as 'adulteries' are mentioned in vii. 21 f.; but perhaps we should rather explain πορνεύσῃς as due to a slip (φονεύσῃς and πορνεύσῃς being very similar) and accept Μὴ φονεύσῃς, Μὴ μοιχεύσῃς. With regard to (ii), the balance of probability is on the side of retaining the phrase; for not only is there strong support of authorities for it, but there is also the con-

[1] Cf. the interesting discussion in Calvin, *Institutes*, II. viii. 52 f.

sideration that a scribe would be more likely to omit than to insert a commandment not included in the Ten. The verb ἀποστερεῖν is used in the LXX in Exod. xxi. 10, Deut. xxiv. 14 (A text), Ecclus iv. 1. It is usually explained here as representing the Tenth Commandment. The form μή + the subjunctive is used also in Lk. and in Jas ii. 11; Mt. follows the LXX in having οὐ + the future indicative.

20. The man's naïve reply makes it clear that he has not understood the Commandments nor ever really taken them seriously. But he was no more mistaken about the Law's real seriousness than were his Jewish contemporaries generally. (Cf. S.–B. 1, p. 814: 'That man possesses the ability to fulfil the Commandments of God perfectly was so firmly believed by the Rabbis, that they spoke in all seriousness of people who had kept the whole Law from A to Z.')

Mark's ἐφυλαξάμην is corrected to ἐφύλαξα in both Mt. and Lk. In the LXX φυλάσσειν is often used of 'keeping' commandments (e.g. Gen. xxvi. 5): in the N.T. cf. Lk. xi. 28 (τὸν λόγον τοῦ θεοῦ φυλάσσειν).

21. ἐμβλέψας αὐτῷ. See on iii. 5.

ἠγάπησεν αὐτόν is often taken to mean that Jesus felt attracted to him. It is perhaps more likely that ἀγαπᾶν here denotes, not a feeling of attraction, but the sort of love which, regardless of the worthiness or unworthiness of its object, shows itself by helping its object and goes out in self-giving toward it (cf. Gal. ii. 20, Lk. x. 30–7; and see further on xii. 28ff.).

Jesus' love for the man does not lead him to spare his feelings, but expresses itself in a challenge which is at the same time stern and gracious. The man must be made to see his need. In Jesus' words to him many things are combined, the sharp probe that will show the man his self-deception, the summons to repentance, the gracious offer of himself as the way, the command and the promise of that eternal life about which he had inquired.

Ἔν σε ὑστερεῖ. For the rather surprising accusative with ὑστερεῖν cf. Ps. xxiii (LXX: xxii). 1: οὐδέν με ὑστερήσει. Jesus is not, as Lohmeyer has suggested, inviting him to take a step beyond the Commandments to something higher than their requirements: the one thing lacking is the all-important thing, a single-hearted devotion to God, obedience to the first of the Ten Commandments. For the fact that the man goes away with darkened countenance is the sign that he has made his riches into an idol, from which it is too hard to part.

ὕπαγε, ὅσα ἔχεις πώλησον καὶ δὸς τοῖς πτωχοῖς. The counsel to sell all is given to a particular person: we are not to conclude that it applies equally to all. To recognize this is not to draw its sting, but rather to begin to see its full seriousness, for material wealth is not the only possible idol. At the same time Jesus' attitude to riches must not be glossed over (see further below). The command to give to the poor is here perhaps primarily an indication of the way to get rid of possessions which have become an idol—Jesus seems to be at this point particularly concerned with the First Commandment—but it is perhaps also an indication that the First and Second Tables of the Law cannot be separated.

καὶ ἕξεις θησαυρὸν ἐν οὐρανῷ does not mean that selling one's goods and giving the proceeds to the poor is a meritorious act that will *earn* treasure in heaven; for the reward is God's undeserved gift to those who are willing to receive it. But trust, willingness to accept God's gift as a gift, cannot help but show itself by outward tokens. Jesus by commanding the man to show the tokens which are the outward expression of faith is really appealing to him to have faith. (In 'treasure in heaven' Jesus is using a common Jewish expression (for examples see S.–B. 1, pp. 429 ff.), but without its associations of merit. Cf. Mt. vi. 19 f.)

δεῦρο ἀκολούθει μοι. Cf. i. 17 f. The command is at the same time a gift. Jesus offers himself to him: he is himself the answer to the man's question, the way to eternal life. To inherit eternal life one must lay hold on it where it is offered as a gift in the person of Jesus.

22. But the man loved his possessions too dearly, and went away apparently in silence.

στυγνάσας. Cf. in the LXX Isa. lvii. 17, Dan. ii. 12; and also Ezek. xxvii. 35, xxviii. 19 (A text), xxxii. 10, Wisd. xvii. 5, and Mt. xvi. 3.

λυπούμενος. His sorrow is a hopeful sign; for it means that Jesus, who loved him, has not let go his hold on him—the barb has stuck. Whether his sorrow was turned into repentance and faith we are not told.

23. περιβλεψάμενος. See on iii. 5.

In the O.T. there are two main attitudes toward riches: one regarding them as the sign of God's favour, a reward for goodness, the other identifying the poor with the pious, the rich with the ungodly. Jesus' attitude to the rich, as shown in this verse, is startlingly fresh. He neither covets their wealth, nor hates them. Instead he pities them—for the rich man is to be pitied because of his specially great temptations and the frightening handicap in relation to the kingdom of God under which he labours. It is so easy for him to feel a false security and rely on his possessions and become so taken up with them that he forgets what is infinitely more important.

The adverb δυσκόλως is very rare: in the N.T. it only occurs here and in the parallels. (The adjective δύσκολος occurs in *v.* 24, and nowhere else in the N.T.)

24. D it (some MSS.) place *v.* 25 before *v.* 24; and Taylor favours this order on the grounds that the astonishment of the disciples in *v.* 24 is more intelligible after *v.* 25, the return to the particular (*v.* 25) after the general statement (*v.* 24) is strange, and the intensification of the paradox in *v.* 24 would account well for the second and stronger expression of astonishment in *v.* 26. But it seems much more

likely that this Western order represents a scribe's attempt
to improve the sense, and that we should reject it. (Taylor's
last argument seems strange, for surely *v.* 25, implying that
it is *impossible* for the rich to enter the kingdom, is a more
intense paradox than *v.* 24, which speaks merely of the
difficulty of entering.)

There is little doubt that the words τοὺς πεποιθότας ἐπὶ
(τοῖς) χρήμασιν, which are added after ἐστιν in *v.* 24 by the
majority of MSS. and versions, should be omitted with
א B W *k* sa bo (some MSS.). They are apparently an attempt
to make the saying less drastic.

For the affectionate use of τέκνα cf. ii. 5; also Jn xiii. 33,
xxi. 5.

25. κάμηλον διὰ τῆς τρυμαλιᾶς τῆς ῥαφίδος διελθεῖν.
A humorous example of the impossible. A Rabbinic
reference to an elephant passing through the eye of a needle
is quoted in S.-B. i, p. 828. Cf. Mt. xxiii. 24, Lk. vi. 41 f.
Procrustean attempts to reduce the camel to a rope (reading
κάμιλον for κάμηλον) or to enlarge the needle's eye into a
postern gate need not be taken seriously.

26. Not unnaturally the disciples are more astonished
and bewildered than ever.

ἑαυτούς. א B C Δ Ψ co have αὐτόν, but ἑαυτούς should
probably be read. It is strongly attested and agrees with
Mark's usage.

καὶ τίς δύναται σωθῆναι; If this is the position, then can
anyone at all be saved?

27. ἐμβλέψας. Cf. *v.* 21.

The saying which follows is the key to the meaning of
vv. 17-27. To inherit eternal life, enter the kingdom of God,
be saved—this is outside the sphere of human possibilities
altogether, for the poor and the rich alike. But God can
bring about the impossible!

With πάντα γὰρ δυνατὰ παρὰ τῷ Θεῷ cf. Gen. xviii. 14,
Job x. 13 (LXX), xlii. 2, Zech. viii. 6 (LXX).

28. On the connection of *vv.* 28–31 with the preceding see the introduction to the section.

ὁ Πέτρος. For Peter acting as the spokesman of the disciples cf. viii. 29, 32, ix. 5, xi. 21.

On the distinction between the aorist ἀφήκαμεν and the perfect ἠκολουθήκαμεν Taylor comments: 'the decisive renunciation in Peter's mind stood out against the permanent following'.

Mt. at this point adds τί ἄρα ἔσται ἡμῖν; which quite probably expresses the thought behind Peter's question correctly, and also the saying about twelve thrones.

29f. Jesus does not at once rebuke the spirit of Peter's utterance. Instead he makes a quite general threefold promise. Everyone who forsakes house or kinsfolk or lands for his sake and the gospel's (i) shall in the present age receive back a hundredfold what he has given up; (ii) shall at the same time have to endure persecution; (iii) shall in the age to come inherit eternal life. The authenticity of the saying has been denied—unnecessarily, it would seem; for certainly neither (i) nor (ii) need be taken to reflect the experience of the early Church (with (i) cf. iii. 35, and with (ii) viii. 34ff.); and the objection to the linking of 'eternal life' with 'the age to come' in (iii), as uncharacteristic of Jesus, is only valid if the eschatological element in his teaching is very much less important than we take it to be.

For Ἀμήν see on iii. 28.

The words καὶ ἕνεκεν τοῦ εὐαγγελίου may be editorial. Cf. viii. 35.

It is noticeable that, while in *v.* 29 the items are joined by ἤ, in *v.* 30 they are joined by καί: the effect is to emphasize that what is gained will far outweigh what is lost.

31. A saying which occurs in other contexts also (Mt. xx. 16, Lk. xiii. 30) as well as in the Mt. parallel. We cannot be sure of its original context. It appears to be eschatological and to refer to the many surprises which the final judgement will bring and the fact that the values of this present age will be reversed. But within this general framework there are various possible references that immediately suggest themselves. Obvious possibilities are to refer the pair 'first' and 'last' to the rich and powerful on the one hand and the poor and unimportant in this world on the other; to the nation of Israel and the Gentiles (this is suggested by the context in which the saying is placed in Lk. (xiii. 22–30)); to the people with a reputation for piety (the Pharisees in particular) and the publicans and sinners (cf. Mt. xxi. 28–32); to the more and the less prominent among the disciples; but here it is perhaps most natural to understand the saying as a warning to Peter and the rest of the Twelve called forth by Peter's outburst in *v.* 28. The apostles must not become self-complacent because, unlike the rich man, they have left all to follow Jesus. Such self-complacence would be highly dangerous. Moreover, one who is at present a refuser may in the future by God's mercy accept the call and even in the age to come be preferred to them, while their having left all is not in itself a guarantee that they will remain faithful. (Judas was one of the Twelve, Paul was not!)

58. THE THIRD PREDICTION OF THE PASSION
(x. 32–4)
(Mt. xx. 17–19; Lk. xviii. 31–4)

The introductions to sections 46 and 51 and the notes on viii. 31 and ix. 31 should be consulted.

While it is of course possible that this last and most precise of the three predictions of the Passion reflects knowledge of the actual event, there are several considerations which should make us cautious about pronouncing a dogmatic verdict of *ex eventu*: (i) there is no feature which could not readily have been foreseen as likely to happen in the carrying out of a death sentence under the circumstances of the times; (ii) the details in *v.* 34 are not mentioned in the order in which they occur in Mk xv. 15–20; (iii) the more precise details in *v.* 34 are paralleled in two very obvious O.T. passages: μάστιγες and ἐμπτύσματα are mentioned in Isa. l. 6, and the idea of mocking is prominent in Ps. xxii.

32. ἀναβαίνοντες. It was usual to speak of going *up* to Jerusalem, to the Temple, to a feast: cf. the use of Hebrew *'ālāh.*

εἰς Ἱεροσόλυμα. The first mention of Jerusalem as their destination.

ἦν προάγων αὐτούς. The vivid picture of Jesus walking before his frightened disciples would no doubt have a special poignancy for Roman readers threatened by persecution.

καὶ ἐθαμβοῦντο, οἱ δὲ ἀκολουθοῦντες ἐφοβοῦντο. A distinction seems to be implied between οἱ ἀκολουθοῦντες and the subject of ἐθαμβοῦντο. This was apparently felt to be difficult from early times. Hence there are several variants, all of which get rid of this distinction. But the words printed above should certainly be read with ℵ B, etc. The most probable explanation is that two groups are distinguished—the subject of ἐθαμβοῦντο being the Twelve, while οἱ ἀκολουθοῦντες denotes other followers including perhaps the women mentioned in xv. 40f. The Twelve are specifically mentioned in *v.* 32 b, because the teaching in *vv.* 33 f. was given only to them and not to all who were following. This is preferable to taking this to be an example of clumsy redundancy of expression (Mark only meaning to describe one group) or to translating οἱ ἀκολουθοῦντες by 'they as they followed'. The emendation to ἐθαμβεῖτο is unnecessary. For ἐθαμβοῦντο and ἐφοβοῦντο see on i. 22 (ἐξεπλήσσοντο): here there is nothing surprising in this amazement and fear, which were obviously connected with the realization that Jesus was going into immediate peril.

παραλαβὼν πάλιν τοὺς δώδεκα. Cf. v. 40, ix. 2, xiv. 33. It seems better to take the two halves of this verse closely together (v. 32 a describing the vividly remembered circumstances in which Jesus had called the Twelve apart to tell them yet again about his approaching Passion) than to regard v. 32 a as an editorial sentence introducing the whole complex vv. 32-52, and v. 32 b as the beginning of a tradition-unit.

33. ὅτι is *recitativum*.

θανάτῳ. For the unusual dative after κατακρίνειν to denote the sentence cf. Dan. iv. 34 (LXX): τούτους κατακρινῶ θανάτῳ, Josephus, *Ant.* x. 124, Hermas, *Sim.* viii. 11. 3.

καὶ παραδώσουσιν αὐτὸν τοῖς ἔθνεσιν. Not paralleled in viii. 31 or ix. 31.

34. The subject of the plural verbs in this verse is presumably not the chief priests and the scribes, but the Gentiles. With ἐμπαίξουσιν αὐτῷ cf. xv. 20; with ἐμπτύσουσιν αὐτῷ cf. xv. 19; with μαστιγώσουσιν αὐτόν cf. xv. 15. These details are without parallel in viii. 31 and ix. 31.

59. THE REQUEST OF JAMES AND JOHN (X. 35-45)
(Mt. xx. 20-8; cf. Lk. xxii. 24-7)

That vv. 35-7 and v. 40 are based on sound tradition is hardly open to serious doubt; for the early Church is not likely to have invented anything so discreditable to two apostles as vv. 35-7 or a saying like v. 40, which indicates a limit to Jesus' prerogative. The extremely doubtful evidence for John's early martyrdom is not a sufficient ground for dismissing vv. 38f. as a *vaticinium ex eventu*. It is possible that v. 41 is an editorial link constructed for the purpose of appending vv. 42-5 to vv. 35-40; but on the whole it seems more likely that vv. 41-5 is the true historical sequel to the request of James and John. At least, a dispute about precedence seems much more probable in this context than in

that of Lk. xxii. 24 ff. On the question of the authenticity of
v. 45 see below. The only words linking *vv.* 35–45 as a whole
with its context are καί in *v.* 35 and another καί in *v.* 46; but,
if the section is Petrine, as it may well be, it is not unlikely
that its setting in the course of the journey to Jerusalem is
also derived from Peter's reminiscence.

35. δύο (B C *pc*) is omitted by most MSS. and should
probably not be read.

In the Mt. parallel it is the mother of James and John who
makes the request—the reputation of James and John being
'spared' presumably.

36. Τί θέλετέ με ποιήσω ὑμῖν; There are several variants:
D omitting τί θέλετέ με, so that the meaning is simply 'I will
do it for you', and others omitting με or θέλετέ με or adding
ἵνα before ποιήσω. If we read the text printed above with
ℵ^c B Ψ, we must explain it as a mixture of two constructions:
τί θέλετέ με ποιῆσαι and τί θέλετε ποιήσω.

37. They desire the chief places in the coming messianic
kingdom. Mark's ἐν τῇ δόξῃ σου is probably rightly interpreted by the Mt. ἐν τῇ βασιλείᾳ σου (which is to be distinguished carefully from 'in the kingdom of *God*'). They are
apparently thinking of the Messiah's rule (cf. Acts i. 6),
which was to be preliminary to the final kingdom of God.
Their request is, to use Calvin's words, 'a bright mirror of
human vanity'; for it shows that in following Jesus they
'have a different object in view from what they ought to
have'.

38. τὸ ποτήριον ὃ ἐγὼ πίνω. Jesus is apparently thinking
of the cup of God's wrath against sin (cf. Ps. lxxv. 8, Isa. li.
17–23, Jer. xxv. 15–28, xlix. 12, li. 7, Lam. iv. 21 f., Ezek.
xxiii. 31–4, Hab. ii. 16, Zech. xii. 2; also Ps. lx. 3, Job xxi.
20, Isa. lxiii. 6, Obad. 16) both here and in xiv. 36. For the
significance of this see further on xiv. 36. The use of the
present πίνω might possibly be taken to mean that he is
already drinking it (cf. Heidelberg Catechism, Quest. 37:

'during His whole life on earth'); but probably the tense should not be pressed; cf. παραδίδοται in ix. 31.

τὸ βάπτισμα ὃ ἐγὼ βαπτίζομαι. The thought underlying βάπτισμα and βαπτίζομαι here is that of being overwhelmed in trouble, in this case (in agreement with the use of ποτήριον) the trouble that is the burden of human sin and the judgement of God upon it. The verb βαπτίζω is used in extra-biblical Greek of calamities, etc. flooding or overwhelming someone (examples in Bauer, *s.v.*, 3. c, and *T.W.N.T.* 1, pp. 527f.). The nearest use of the actual verb in the LXX is in Isa. xxi. 4; but the same metaphor is found in Ps. xlii. 7, lxix. 2 (Aquila has βαπτίζω here), 15, Isa. xliii. 2, Jon. ii. 3-6. Jesus uses the same expression in Lk. xii. 50 with the same meaning, of the divinely appointed tribulation culminating in his death through which he must pass.

39. Δυνάμεθα. Their self-confident reply showed that they had not understood Jesus' meaning. That he was referring to sufferings which had to be endured they no doubt realized; but, whereas he was thinking of a shameful death under the curse of the Law and in abandonment by God (cf. xv. 34), they were thinking of heroic and glorious sufferings in the cause of the messianic kingdom, something which could be faced in the mood of the martyrs of Maccabean days.

Jesus' answer presumably means that, while in one sense his cup and his baptism are something that none can share (he alone is to die for the sin of the world), in another sense they are to be shared, and his followers will have to be ready to face suffering and death, if they are going to be faithful to him. We may compare I Pet. iv. 13: καθὸ κοινωνεῖτε τοῖς τοῦ Χριστοῦ παθήμασιν. The key to the interpretation of these two verses seems to be the recognition that, while in *v.* 38 Jesus means, by drinking the cup he has to drink and being baptized with the baptism that he has to be baptized with, an actual sharing in the burden which he as Son of Man is destined to bear (to his question in *v*. 38, then, the only true answer was, of course, 'No'), in *v*. 39 he means by the same terms simply a sharing in those sufferings which his followers will have to be ready to endure for his sake and which may indeed include martyrdom.

According to many commentators *vv*. 38f. are a *vaticinium ex eventu*, the brothers having been martyred before the tradition contained in these verses arose. But against this: (i) The evidence for the martyrdom of John the son of Zebedee is extremely doubtful. It consists of a statement by the late epitomist of the Chronicle by Philip of Side (*c*. 450) that 'Papias says in his second book that John the Theologian and James his brother were killed by the Jews'; a similar statement by a ninth-century writer, George the Sinner, which is probably not independent of Philip or his epitomist; and the precarious evidence of two martyrologies (one early fifth century, the other early sixth). It is perverse to prefer such evidence to the strong tradition that John lived to a peaceful old age in the province of Asia. (ii) It is by no means necessary to take *v*. 39 as a prediction of martyrdom—though it seems clear that from quite early times there was a tendency to read it that way (probably such a misunderstanding was the origin of the tradition mentioned by Philip of Side).

40. Taylor rightly regards this verse as belonging to the same category as xiii. 32—sayings that would never have been invented by the early Church, because they set limits to the knowledge and prerogatives of Jesus. The exact extent to which his prerogative is limited according to this saying is not absolutely clear. If we understand δοθήσεται after ἀλλ᾽, then the meaning is that the allotting of the chief places does not appertain to Jesus, but to God. If, however, we take ἀλλ᾽ as equivalent to εἰ μή (cf. iv. 22), the point will be that Jesus can only give the chief places to those for whom they have been prepared. Probably we should prefer the former interpretation. (The *v.l.* in some it and vg MSS. which inserts *vobis* after *dare* (= δοῦναι) looks like an attempt to counter Arian use of the saying. The reading ἄλλοις for ἀλλ᾽ οἷς is no doubt to be rejected—it is possibly of Marcionite origin.)

ἡτοίμασται. Cf. Mt. xxv. 34, 41, I Cor. ii. 9, (Jn xiv. 2f.). The addition of ὑπὸ τοῦ Πατρός μου is no doubt assimilation to Mt., but gives the sense intended.

42. προσκαλεσάμενος αὐτούς. Cf. iii. 13, 23, vi. 7, viii. 1, 34, xii. 43.

οἱ δοκοῦντες ἄρχειν. T. W. Manson objects to the usual interpretation ('they which are accounted to rule') on the grounds that (i) rulers of the first century did not merely seem to rule—they really ruled; (ii) the usual interpretation places the stress on what the rulers of the Gentiles do with their power, and this is irrelevant to the matter under discussion; (iii) it destroys the antithetic parallelism between *vv.* 42 and 43f., the latter verses being concerned with the question how greatness is to be achieved, not how it is to be used. So he prefers to translate 'those who aspire to rule', and appeals to various passages outside the N.T. in which δοκεῖν means 'to wish' or 'hope'.[1] Against this the following points should be noted: (i) a touch of irony would not be out of place, since the reality of power belongs to God (cf. Isa. x. 5, 15, Dan. iv. 17, etc.); (ii) on the other hand, δοκοῦντες might conceivably indicate the standing of the persons in question without any suggestion that it is merely appearance[2] (in which case οἱ δοκοῦντες ἄρχειν would mean about the same as the Mt. οἱ ἄρχοντες and the Lk. οἱ βασιλεῖς); (iii) Mt. and Lk. show no trace of the meaning Manson sees in δοκοῦντες. We conclude that the usual translation here is † preferable.

[1] *Teaching*, pp. 313–15.
[2] Cf. Gal. ii. 6 f., where according to G. Kittel, in *T.W.N.T.* II, p. 236, δοκεῖν does not suggest seeming without being (for the opposite view see C. K. Barrett in *Studia Paulina in Honorem Johannis de Zwaan*, ed. J. N. Sevenster, W. C. van Unnik (Haarlem, 1953), pp. 1–4).

κατακυριεύουσιν. In the LXX the verb is nearly always used of the rule of an alien. The κατα- gives it the sense of using lordship over people to their disadvantage and to one's own advantage. Cf. I Pet. v. 3.

οἱ μεγάλοι αὐτῶν: i.e. 'their (the Gentiles') great ones'. Those who have power and authority over others are meant.

κατεξουσιάζουσιν. Not used in the LXX. The verb can mean simply 'to exercise authority'; but here it clearly has the same nuance as κατακυριεύουσιν—of exploitation of the people over whom the authority is exercised.

43. οὐχ οὕτως δέ ἐστιν ἐν ὑμῖν. Cf. II Sam. xiii. 12. In the new Israel the worldly idea of greatness has no place.

43b, 44 repeat in more perfect form (in synonymous parallelism) the saying in ix. 35.

μέγας is apparently used for the superlative here, as it is parallel to πρῶτος: cf. the use of the positive for the comparative in ix. 43, 45, 47.

διάκονος particularly suggests the idea of personal service rendered to another: the διάκονος is one whose activities are not directed to his own interest but to that of another. To Greek ears the word had an ignoble ring (cf. the use of διακονικός in company with δουλοπρεπής and ἀνελεύθερος in Plato, *Gorg.* 518A). The Christian idea of service represents a 'transvaluation of values' effected by the gospel similar to that which E. G. Selwyn notes in the case of 'humility'.[1]

44. δοῦλος. 'By δοῦλος is expressed the truth that the apostle belongs to the congregation. It does not belong to him, but he to it; he owes it his life and work as his bounden duty' (Schlatter).

45 gives the ground for the peremptory statement in *v.* 43a. Worldly ideas of rank and privilege are out of order in the new Israel because they are inconsistent with the mission of the Son of Man.

καὶ γάρ. Here used in its more emphatic sense (= Latin

---

[1] *The First Epistle of St Peter* (London, 1947), p. 189.

nam etiam rather than *etenim*). The καί could be represented in translation by adding 'himself' after 'Son of Man'.

ἦλθεν. See on i. 38, iv. 21.

δοῦναι τὴν ψυχὴν αὐτοῦ. The expression 'give one's ψυχή or σῶμα or ἑαυτόν' was characteristically used by the Greeks of the death of soldiers, by the Jews of the death of martyrs.

λύτρον. In the N.T. only here and in Mt. parallel. Outside the Bible used of the ransom of a prisoner of war or a slave. In the LXX (almost always in the plural) it always (apart from Isa. xlv. 13) represents one of three roots, *kpr*, *pdh*, *g'l*. It denotes the half-shekel poll-tax, 'a ransom for his soul unto the LORD' (Exod. xxx. 12), the money a man paid to redeem his life which was forfeit because his ox had killed someone (Exod. xxi. 30), the price paid for the redemption of the firstborn (Num. xviii. 15), the money by which the next of kin ransomed an enslaved relative (Lev. xxv. 51 f.) or the payment for the redemption of a mortgaged property (Lev. xxv. 26).

But, while *kōper* (*pidyón*, *ge'ullāh*) may have contributed to the thought, another Hebrew word, never represented by λύτρον in the LXX, probably underlies the use of λύτρον here —'*āšām* (='guilt-offering': see Lev. v. 14–vi. 7, vii. 1–7, Num. v. 5–8). This word is used in Isa. liii. 10: 'when thou shalt make his soul an *offering for sin*'; and it seems likely that Jesus had this passage in mind (the use of διακονεῖν seems to point to a reference to the Servant, and ἀντὶ πολλῶν looks like an echo of the repeated *rabbîm* in Isa. liii. 11 f.), and was thinking of himself as the Servant who was to suffer

* vicariously for the sins of others. But the meaning of his vicarious suffering and his giving himself as a λύτρον to his Father cannot be read off from any O.T. passages, but must be understood (in so far as it can be understood at all by us) from the actual history of his Passion. (See further *inter alia* the notes on xiv. 36, xv. 34.)

ἀντί here means not 'on behalf of', but 'in the place of'.
As Büchsel (in *T.W.N.T.* I, p. 373) points out, ἀντὶ πολλῶν
is dependent on λύτρον, not on δοῦναι. ('Αντί is used only here
in Mk.)

πολλῶν probably means 'all' rather than 'many' (see on
i. 34, vi. 2). So in the Pauline or Deutero-Pauline version of
the saying (I Tim. ii. 6) πάντων is used. Cf. Calvin's comment: 'The word *many* (πολλῶν) is not put definitely for a
fixed number, but for a large number; for he contrasts himself with all others. And in this sense it is used in Rom. v. 15,
where Paul does not speak of any part of men, but embraces
the whole human race.'

The authenticity of *v.* 45 has been denied on various
grounds. It is alleged that (i) it is out of harmony with its
context which is concerned with service; (ii) the use of ἦλθεν
implies a date after the completion of Jesus' life and work;
(iii) λύτρον and the ideas associated with it are found nowhere else in his teaching; (iv) the original form of the
saying is preserved in Lk. xxii. 27, and Mk x. 45 is a 'dogmatic recast' of it made under the influence of Pauline
theology. But (i) is negligible; for if Jesus was going to refer
to his own serving as the ground of the rule which he had
just stated, it was only natural that he should refer to the
self-giving in which his serving was to culminate. As to (ii),
ἦλθεν can look back to his coming from God, which already
was in the past: it need not imply that his whole life was in
the past. With regard to (iii), though it is true that the word
λύτρον does not occur, there are other things which suggest
the same sort of idea, e.g. the saying about the cup in xiv. 36.
In answer to (iv), it must be pointed out that Lk. xxii. 24–7
bears the marks of Gentile-Christian influence, while Mk x.
45 is strongly Palestinian in expression (cf. Büchsel in
T.W.N.T. IV, p. 343; Jeremias in *T.W.N.T.* V, pp. 711 f.,
note 474). It is then by no means clear that Lk. xxii. 27, if
it is a variant form of this saying, is to be preferred (and it

may actually be an independent saying). Moreover, if
Mk x. 45 is due to Pauline influence, it is strange that λύτρον
never occurs in Paul (ἀντίλυτρον in I Tim. ii. 6 is not
certainly Pauline). The balance of probability is surely on
† the side of the authenticity of the saying.

60. THE HEALING OF BARTIMAEUS (x. 46-52)
(Mt. xx. 29-34; Lk. xviii. 35-43)

The last healing miracle recorded in Mk. Opinions about
it differ widely. Dibelius and Bultmann regard it as
legendary. More probable is the view that the narrative is
based on the reminiscence of an eye-witness.

46. Ιερειχω. See Smith, *Hist. Geog.* pp. 266-8; Dalman,
S.S.W. pp. 242-4.

ἐκπορευομένου. In Lk. the incident is placed before the
arrival of Jesus at Jericho, probably to make room at this
point for the Zacchaeus story.

ἱκανοῦ. Here 'considerable' (as often in Lk.–Acts).

ὁ υἱὸς Τιμαίου Βαρτιμαῖος. The fact that the explanatory phrase ὁ υἱὸς Τιμαίου, contrary to Mark's custom, is
placed before, instead of after, the Aramaic which it
explains suggests the possibility that it is a scribal gloss. The
Τιμαῖος is hardly likely to be the Greek name 'Timaeus';
probably it is *Ṭîmay* (a Rabbi Joshua bar Timay is mentioned in the Midrash on Eccles.). The mention of the name
here suggests that Bartimaeus may have been known in the
Church.

προσαίτης. A late word, occurring only here and in
Jn ix. 8 in the N.T., and never in the LXX.

47. ὁ Ναζαρηνός. See on i. 24.

Υἱὲ Δαυειδ. Jesus is addressed as 'son of David' in Mk
only here and in *v.* 48 (though see also xii. 35-7). If the title
was both intended by Bartimaeus as messianic and also sure
to be understood in that sense by the crowd, it is remarkable

that Jesus apparently did nothing to silence him—contrast viii. 30. There is of course an O.T. basis for the belief that the Messiah would be a descendant of David (e.g. Isa. xi. 1 ff., Jer. xxiii. 5f., Ezek. xxxiv. 23f.), and in post-Christian Jewish literature 'Son of David' is a common designation of the Messiah. But, as in pre-Christian times the only known occurrence of 'Son of David' as a messianic title is in Ps. Sol. xvii. 23 (21), it is perhaps possible that the use of the title by Bartimaeus was not an altogether unambiguous declaration of Jesus' Messiahship. Might it conceivably have been a polite way of addressing one who was known to be of Davidic descent, or even an acknowledgement that in the speaker's opinion Jesus was to a special degree a proper Israelite (cf. the references to David as 'our father' in Mk xi. 10, Acts iv. 25)? If any such explanation should be right, it would still of course be true that in the passing on of the Christian tradition the use of the title would be recognized as a confession of Jesus' Messiahship. Another possibility is that the words *υἱὲ Δαυειδ* in this verse and *v.* 48 have been inserted at some stage in the passing on of the tradition: that at a later stage there was a tendency to add them is to be seen from the occurrences of *υἱὸς Δαυειδ* in Mt.

48. ἐπετίμων. See on i. 25, viii. 32. The rebuke is hardly to be connected specially with his use of the title 'Son of David' (on the analogy of viii. 30), for such a rebuke would have been more likely to come from Jesus himself. The explanation is rather that they regarded his importunity as a nuisance. Cf. x. 13. It is a rebuke which, like those in viii. 32 and x. 13, is not allowed to stand; for in *v.* 49 Jesus calls for Bartimaeus. Even on his way to Jerusalem Jesus has time for the individual who needs his help.

49. Θάρσει. See on vi. 50.

50. Notice the vivid details in this verse, which are omitted in both Mt. and Lk.

ἀποβαλών. 565, supported by sy[s], reads *ἐπιβαλών*. Some prefer this reading on the ground that it fits oriental custom better. Lohmeyer goes so far as to assert that if ἀποβαλών is original, it betrays the Hellenistic origin of the narrative. But it is unwise to rule out the possibility that on such an occasion a blind beggar might react unconventionally, whether throwing off his outer garment (if he was wearing it) or throwing it aside (if it was spread in front of him to receive alms).

ἦλθεν. Apparently unaided.

51. Jesus is often depicted as asking questions in connection with his miracles (e.g. v. 9, 30, vi. 38, ix. 21, Jn v. 6). Here the question is probably designed to strengthen the man's faith by encouraging it to be articulate. In this case Jesus would hardly need information, as the man's trouble would be obvious.

Ραββουνει. A Jewish form of address which occurs in the N.T. only here and in Jn xx. 16. It is stronger than 'Rabbi', and means 'my lord', 'my master'. (See further Black, p. 21.)

ἵνα ἀναβλέψω. Grammatically dependent on θέλω understood after the question Τί σοι θέλεις ποιήσω; Ἀναβλέπω here means 'receive sight'.

52. In Mk no healing word or action of Jesus is mentioned: Lk. has ἀνάβλεψον and Mt. records that Jesus touched his eyes.

ἡ πίστις σου σέσωκέν σε. See on v. 34.

καὶ ἠκολούθει αὐτῷ ἐν τῇ ὁδῷ. A literal following of Jesus along the road toward Jerusalem is no doubt intended. Possibly Mark also had in mind the deeper significance of ἀκολουθεῖν (i. 18, ii. 14f., viii. 34, etc.), if Bartimaeus actually became a disciple, as seems likely from the fact that his name was remembered. The suggestiveness of the whole incident when thought of as a picture of the meaning of discipleship may well have struck Mark and those who related the story before him.

VI. MINISTRY IN JERUSALEM
(xi. 1–xiii. 37)

Three successive days are indicated by xi. 11f., 19f.; but whether all that is recorded in xi. 27–xiii. 37 occurred on the last of these is open to some doubt. It is noticeable that, while there are precise temporal connecting-links between the several sections of xi. 1–26, there are no such links in xi. 27–xii. 44. It is possible that xi. 27–33, xii. 13–37a, represent a pre-Markan complex of conflict-stories (cf. ii. 1–iii. 6), which Mark has inserted as a whole at the point where he judged (probably rightly) that its first member would be in its true historical context, only interpolating xii. 1–12 because he had strong historical reasons for so doing. Since the complex would be topical rather than historical, it is possible that xii. 13–17, 18–27, 28–34, 35–7a, may belong to an earlier period in the ministry (either in Galilee or in Jerusalem).

That John is correct in representing Jesus as spending more time in Jerusalem than is actually indicated by Mark is probable enough—Mk xiv. 49 might be a pointer in this direction.

For the view that the period covered by Mk x. 46–xvi. 8 was something like six months rather than a week see Manson, 'Cleansing'.

61. JESUS ENTERS JERUSALEM (xi. 1–11)
(Mt. xxi. 1–11; Lk. xix. 28–38)

The fact that the Markan account combines vividness of detail with the most notable restraint regarding messianic colour (e.g. *v.* 9 contrasted with both Mt. xxi. 9 and Lk. xix. 38, and the quiet ending of the section without any suggestion of a triumphal entry) is convincing evidence that it represents first-hand tradition of the greatest historical value. Quite probably it derives from Peter. A 'messianic legend' (Bultmann) or 'cultus-legend' (Dibelius) (the creation of the Church's messianic faith) would surely have been very much less restrained.

1. **εἰς Βηθφαγὴ καί.** D 700 it have simply καὶ εἰς, but the reference to Bethphage should probably be retained. It is often mentioned in Rabbinic literature in connection with the definition of the bounds within which sacred things can be prepared or used (e.g. (*M*) *Men.* xi. 2). It was a village or district close to Jerusalem (see further Dalman, *S.S.W.* pp. 251 ff., 315, 320; Lagrange, pp. 287 f.; Lohmeyer, pp. 228 f.). Bethany would be reached before Bethphage; but Bethphage is mentioned first, possibly because it was better known, or because, Jerusalem having been mentioned first, it was natural to mention next the place that was nearer to it.

Βηθανίαν. Usually identified with El Azariyeh (see further Dalman, *S.S.W.* pp. 249 ff.; K. Lake, *The Beginnings of Christianity* (London, 1920 ff.), v, pp. 475 f.).

τὸ ὄρος τῶν Ἐλαιῶν. The Mount of Olives is over 2600 feet high and lies on the east side of Jerusalem, stretching from north to south. Taylor, following Lohmeyer, speaks of its 'messianic associations'; but Lohmeyer's assertion that 'already by the time of Jesus there seems to have developed on the basis of these statements [i.e. II Sam. xv. 32, Ezek. xi. 23, Zech. xiv. 4 f.] the expectation that the Messiah would appear one day on the Mount of Olives' does not seem to be warranted by the passages (from Josephus and Rabbinic literature) which he cites.[1]

δύο. See on vi. 7.

2. **τὴν κώμην τὴν κατέναντι ὑμῶν.** Probably Bethphage, though it could just possibly be Bethany.

Cf. W. Foerster in *T.W.N.T.* v, p. 483, ll. 19 f. and n. 102.

εὑρήσετε. It is possible that Mark thought of this as an instance of supernatural knowledge on the part of Jesus—but it is not necessary to infer this. His narrative does not exclude the possibility of a previous arrangement or of the owner of the foal actually being with Jesus.

πῶλον. In classical Greek the word can denote the young of any animal, but is most often used of a horse's foal. There is no indication in Mk or Lk. that a foal of an ass is meant, though doubtless it is: Mt. and Jn are explicit.

ἐφ' ὃν οὐδεὶς οὔπω ἀνθρώπων ἐκάθισεν. While it is possible that this is an embellishment suggested by νέον in Zech. ix. 9 or by the belief that an animal or article that was to serve a sacred purpose should be one that had not already been put to ordinary use (cf. Num. xix. 2, Deut. xxi. 3, I Sam. vi. 7, II Sam. vi. 3), it is also possible that it is historical. If we assume a previous arrangement or the presence of the owner with Jesus, we may suppose that Jesus had been warned that the only available beast was one that had never been ridden, or that he had deliberately chosen the untrained foal. Such a detail would naturally have been remembered; for the appropriateness of the unbroken foal for such a sacred purpose would have struck the disciples afterwards. Swete compares Lk. i. 34, xxiii. 53.

3. Ὁ Κύριος. It is generally assumed that Jesus means himself; but it seems unlikely that he would refer to himself as 'the Lord'. While his disciples may sometimes have addressed him by the title mārî ('my lord') or māran(ā') ('our lord') (cf. Mt. vii. 21 = Lk. vi. 46: in the vocative it was a respectful form of address that need not mean more than 'teacher', 'sir'), it is doubtful whether he was referred to in the third person as 'the Lord' until after the Resurrection. In view of this difficulty it has been suggested that Jesus was referring to God, as in v. 19. Another possible explanation is that Ὁ Κύριος has been substituted in the course of tradition for some other expression. But it is more

satisfactory to translate ῾Ο κύριος 'his (i.e. the foal's) owner' (so Taylor) and to assume that the owner was with Jesus at the time. This explanation is supported by Mark's usage, by the fact that the message is not sent to the owner but to any-one who may intervene, and by the fact that it explains Jesus' knowledge of the foal.

καὶ εὐθὺς αὐτὸν ἀποστέλλει πάλιν ὧδε. This is most naturally taken to be part of the message—an assurance that the owner (or Jesus, if he means himself by ὁ Κύριος) will send the foal back without delay. ἀποστέλλει is a futuristic present (the v.l. ἀποστελεῖ is no doubt an assimilation to Mt.). ὧδε can refer either to the place where Jesus is waiting or to the village itself, which we may assume was close at hand. It is less satisfactory to understand the sen-tence as a statement that the person who intervenes (τις) will send the foal back with the two disciples.

4. ἐπὶ τοῦ ἀμφόδου. Probably 'in the street'.

5. τινες τῶν ἐκεῖ ἑστηκότων supports the view that the owner was not there. In Lk. it is altered to οἱ κύριοι αὐτοῦ.

7. ἐπιβάλλουσιν αὐτῷ τὰ ἱμάτια αὐτῶν. Instead of a saddle. (See further on next verse.)

ἐκάθισεν. The rather awkward change of subject is avoided here by Luke.

8. What is described is apparently a spontaneous expres-sion of respect. For the spreading of garments cf. II Kgs ix. 13. S.–B., I, pp. 844 f., gives parallels from Rabbinic litera-ture, and Lagrange cites Plutarch's description of Cato Minor's soldiers spreading their clothes at his feet when he was about to leave them (*Cat. Mi.* VII).

στιβάδας. The word στιβάς denotes a '*bed of straw, rushes,* or *leaves*, whether strewn loose or stuffed into a mattress' (L. & S.). So here perhaps translate 'foliage'.

9. οἱ προάγοντες καὶ οἱ ἀκολουθοῦντες simply denotes the crowd surrounding Jesus. Taylor rightly rejects the suggestion that two separate crowds (one from Jerusalem

and the other made up of those who had come up with Jesus) are distinguished.

Ὡσαννα. A transliteration of *hôša‘ nā’*, the Aramaic form of *hôšî‘āh-nnā’* (= 'save, we pray' or 'save now') in Ps. cxviii. 25. Perhaps the foliage that was being strewn to make a path of honour for Jesus reminded someone of the *lûlābîm* (bundles of palm, myrtle and willow) which were carried at the Feast of Tabernacles and shaken at the occurrence in the liturgy of the word *hôšî‘āh-nnā’* in Ps. cxviii (these *lûlābîm* were actually spoken of as 'hosannas'), and so called to his mind and lips the passage of the psalm, which once repeated would quite naturally be taken up by the crowd of pilgrims. This psalm was also used at Passover.

The rest of the verse is a quotation of Ps. cxviii. 26a (agreeing exactly with the LXX). In the psalm the sense is 'Blessed in the name of the Lord be he that cometh' (a blessing of the pilgrims who have come to the feast), and presumably the crowd used the words in this sense—whether with quite general intention or with a particular reference to the pilgrim whose way they were strewing with foliage is not clear. But Mark probably meant his readers to catch another meaning—taking ἐν ὀνόματι Κυρίου with ὁ ἐρχόμενος rather than with εὐλογημένος, and so to see the special appropriateness of the words on this occasion. Cf. Lk. xix. 38, where the addition of ὁ βασιλεύς makes this the plain meaning.

10. The words Εὐλογημένη . . . Δαυειδ are not a quotation from Ps. cxviii or any other psalm. Perhaps they are a patriotic shout called forth by the associations of Ps. cxviii and the Passover—a reference to the expected messianic kingdom. There is no need to take them to imply an identification of Jesus with the Messiah. For the use of πατήρ in connection with David cf. Acts iv. 25 (see also S.-B. II, p. 26 for a quotation from a late Talmudic tractate in which David is included among the 'Fathers').

Ὡσαννὰ ἐν τοῖς ὑψίστοις. The meaning is probably 'Save now (, O Thou that dwellest) in the highest'.

11. According to Mk Jesus enters Jerusalem, goes into the Temple and surveys 'all things', and then, as it is late afternoon, goes back again to Bethany with the Twelve for the night. In Mt. and Lk. it is not actually said that the cleansing of the Temple took place immediately on his entry into Jerusalem, but nothing is said about the intervention of a night. Mk is clearly to be preferred. 'A *dénouement* consisting of a survey of the Temple scene followed by a departure from the city is certainly not a product of imagination and invention' (Taylor).

περιβλεψάμενος. See on iii. 5.

εἰς Βηθανίαν. The statement in Lk. xxi. 37 that Jesus spent the nights (there is no need to translate Lk.'s ηὐλίζετο 'bivouacked') on the Mount of Olives does not contradict this, since Bethany could be regarded as on the Mount of Olives.

Though Mark has not allowed the messianic significance of the incident to colour his account of it (perhaps at all; certainly to the extent that that has happened in Mt. and Lk.), we may be quite certain that he had that significance in mind. He knew that what he was relating was the entry of the Messiah into Jerusalem, the riding on the foal was the fulfilment of Zech. ix. 9, and the spreading of the garments, whatever the disciples and those with them thought at the time, was in actual fact homage to the King of Israel (cf. II Kgs ix. 13).

But how far was this messianic significance apparent at the time? It is often assumed that Jesus was now at last unambiguously asserting his Messiahship (though many would add that by deliberately fulfilling Zech. ix. 9 he was making it as clear as he could that he was not the sort of Messiah that violent nationalism longed for), and that the demonstration by the people was a consciously messianic demonstration. But, in addition to the fact of Mark's restraint, there are several considerations which make this most unlikely: (i) The riding on the foal and the accompanying demonstration are not mentioned at the Jewish trial, though the authorities are apparently hard pressed to find an adequate charge, nor at the Roman trial; (ii) Had the demonstration been consciously messianic, the Romans would surely have got to know about it and themselves have arrested Jesus at once; (iii) The designation of Jesus as ὁ προφήτης in Mt. xxi. 11 (unless there is a reference to Deut. xviii. 15ff.) tells against it; (iv) Jn xii. 16 says explicitly: 'These things understood not his disciples at the first: but when Jesus was glorified, then remembered they that these things were written of him, and that they had done these things unto him' (the author seems to be reproducing an old and true tradition which actually conflicts with what he has said in xii. 13); and, if the disciples were unaware of the messianic significance of what was happening, it is most improbable that the crowd was aware of it; (v) What Mark relates in xi. 11 would be an incredibly quiet ending to a messianic demonstration. We conclude that Jesus' action in riding into Jerusalem was not an obvious and unambiguous assertion of his Messiahship and that neither the disciples nor the crowd were aware of its messianic meaning. It seems likely that the demonstration was a quite small affair (Mark does not speak of ὄχλοι, and his πολλοί in v. 8 need not imply a very large number), and v. 10 with its messianic flavour was either an expression of feelings aroused by Ps. cxviii and the approach to Jerusalem and the Passover, as suggested above, or else a reflection of the later Christian understanding of the incident which Mark has here allowed to creep in.

What then was Jesus' intention? In all four gospels his initiative in the matter of the foal is apparent. He made a deliberate choice, which, since it was not usual for a pilgrim to ride into the city, can hardly have been without special significance for him. It seems clear that he intended to fulfil the prophecy of Zech. ix. 9, but to do so in circumstances so paradoxical as to make the meaning of his action hidden. It was a veiled assertion of his Messiahship, which would not be recognized at the time, though it would afterwards be luminous for his disciples. To them it would then be a confirmation of the truth of his Messiahship—they would know that the scripture had been fulfilled, though the fact had been unnoticed at the time, and that he had indeed come to Jerusalem as the true Messiah. But it would also be a token of the nature of his Messiahship; for the Zech. passage told of a King who should 'speak peace unto the nations', not a conquering nationalist Messiah. Moreover, his royal entry into Jerusalem was to be of a piece with the rest of his ministry, his majesty hidden under an outward appearance that was far from kingly. So the King comes riding on a borrowed, untrained foal, and the acclamations and attentions of his followers are apparently so insignificant that the Roman authorities do not even notice them. The messianic hiddenness is still maintained.

62. THE CURSING OF THE FIG TREE (xi. 12–14)
(Mt. xxi. 18f.)

This narrative together with its sequel in the first two verses of section 64 bristles with difficulties. The most obvious is that the withering of the fig tree, alone[1] among the miracles attributed to Jesus in the gospels, is a miracle of destruction: the question is naturally asked whether it is not inconsistent with the rest of what we know about Jesus. A further difficulty is the juxtaposition in v. 13 of the two statements, ἦλθεν εἰ ἄρα τι εὑρήσει ἐν αὐτῇ and ὁ γὰρ καιρὸς οὐκ ἦν σύκων,

---

[1] The destruction of the swine in v. 1–20 is different in that it is *incidental* to the healing of the demoniac.

each of which renders the other problematic, while the latter seems to aggravate the moral difficulty. These problems give rise to a whole series of questions (besides those concerned with the habits of fig trees and the possibility of finding any edible fruit on a fig tree in the week before Passover in the neighbourhood of Jerusalem), e.g.: Has the incident been placed in what is not its proper historical setting? Ought we to allow for a much longer interval than is usually assumed between the entry into Jerusalem and the Feast of Passover? Did Jesus really work this miracle? If so, what was its purpose? Or, if he did not, how did this tradition arise?

One explanation, which is offered in various forms, is that the narrative is legendary. Sometimes it is said that a parable about a fig tree has been transformed in the course of tradition into a story of fact; sometimes that a popular legend grew up in connection with a particular withered tree on the road to Bethany. An objection (though not conclusive) to this is that the reference to Peter's remembering in *v.* 21 looks like personal reminiscence. The statement ὁ γὰρ καιρὸς οὐκ ἦν σύκων would be unlikely in a legend—but it would be explicable as an editorial comment inserted when the narrative was placed in its present setting.

Another explanation is suggested by T. W. Manson.[1] The incident, he thinks, took place not at Passover-time but in the autumn when the leaves would be beginning 'to change colour, but when one might still expect to find a few figs left over from the main crop'. Finding no fruit 'Jesus said something in Aramaic which could mean: "Let no one ever eat fruit from thee again" or "No one shall ever eat fruit from thee again" or "One will never eat fruit from thee again"'. According to Manson's suggestion Peter wrongly took the words in the first sense, but Jesus meant them either in the second (in which case he thinks the natural meaning

'Cleansing', pp. 279f.

would be that the Day of the Lord or the destruction of Jerusalem would occur before another fig harvest would be due) or in the third (i.e. Jesus would be put to death before the next harvest). Some combination of circumstances perhaps hastened the shedding of the leaves, so that the next day the tree was bare, and the disciples seeing it from a distance supposed that the words of Jesus which they had mistaken for a curse had taken effect.

There remains the possibility that Jesus really did work a destructive miracle. Before we accept Manson's verdict on the Markan narrative ('It is a tale of miraculous power wasted in the service of ill-temper (for the supernatural energy employed to blast the unfortunate tree might have been more usefully expended in forcing a crop of figs out of season); and as it stands it is simply incredible'), we ought to consider the possibility of the miracle's being an acted parable. The mention of Jesus' hunger (*v.* 12) need be no objection to this explanation; for Jesus may have used his hunger as an occasion for instructing his disciples. That is not to say that he expected to find edible figs. If the incident took place in the week before Passover, the final statement of *v.* 13 is incontrovertible.[1] But that Jesus should look for fruit on a fig tree at a season when there was no chance of there being any is exactly the sort of thing we should expect, if this was a parabolic action; for an element of the unexpected and incongruous, which would stimulate curiosity, was a characteristic feature of the symbolic actions of the O.T. prophets (e.g. Jer. xiii. 1 ff., xix. 1 ff.). The most satisfactory explanation of this difficult section is surely that which is given by the earliest extant commentary on Mk, that of Victor of Antioch, viz. that the withering of the fig tree was an acted parable in which Jesus 'used the fig tree to set forth the judgement that was about to fall on Jerusalem'. A people which honoured God with their lips but

[1] See Bishop, *Jesus of Pal.* pp. 217 f.

whose heart was all the time far from him (vii. 6) was like a tree with abundance of leaves but no fruit. The best commentary on *vv.* 12–14 and 20f. is to be found in the narrative which these verses enframe. 'That which happened in the Temple and Jesus' action against the tree explained each other' (Schlatter).

12. τῇ ἐπαύριον. In view of Mark's restraint with regard to the introduction of such links it seems probable that this incident was already connected with the preceding narrative in the tradition he received.

14. μή (here μηκέτι...μηδείς) + optative expresses a negative wish.

63. THE CLEANSING OF THE TEMPLE (xi. 15–19)
(Mt. xxi. 12f.; Lk. xix. 45–8)

The vividness of the story suggests the possibility of its being Petrine reminiscence. Verses 15a and 17f., while they may well be editorial (as many think), are not necessarily so. ἔρχονται (*v.* 15) and ἐξεπορεύοντο (*v.* 19) (but see on *v.* 19 below) could reflect Peter's first person plural.

15. ἐκβάλλειν. See on i. 43; but here some idea of compulsion is present: perhaps 'drive out'.

τοὺς πωλοῦντας καὶ τοὺς ἀγοράζοντας. The sale of animals and other requirements for the sacrifices was an established institution of the Temple. It was naturally much more convenient for the pilgrim to be able to buy within the precincts an animal already certified as suitable than to have to bring an animal with him which would then be subject to official inspection. This mart seems to have taken place in the Court of the Gentiles. (See further (*M*) *Shek.* iv. 7f., v. 3–5, Edersheim, I, pp. 114f., 369ff., Abrahams, *Studies*, I, pp. 82ff.)

κολλυβιστῶν. A late word. Temple dues had to be paid in the Tyrian coinage, the Tyrian shekel being the nearest available equivalent to the old Hebrew shekel. Facilities for changing ordinary Greek or Roman money into Tyrian were therefore required.

περιστεράς. See Lk. ii. 24, Lev. v. 7, 11, xii. 6, 8, xiv. 22, xv. 14, 29.

16. Peculiar to Mk. According to (*M*) *Ber*. ix. 5, a man 'may not enter into the Temple Mount with his staff or his sandal or his wallet, or with the dust upon his feet, nor may he make of it a short by-path; still less may he spit there'. Jesus may have been invoking an existing prohibition which had become a dead letter. In any case his action 'implies a respect for the holiness of the Temple and is thoroughly Jewish in spirit' (Taylor).

διενέγκη. Διαφέρω in the LXX and N.T. is usually intransitive, meaning 'differ', 'matter', 'excel'; here it is used transitively—'carry through' (cf. Acts xiii. 49, xxvii. 27).

17. The first quotation is from Isa. lvi. 7. In both Mt. and Lk. the words πᾶσιν τοῖς ἔθνεσιν are omitted. They are nevertheless an important part of the quotation; for the buying and selling in the Court of the Gentiles was effectually preventing the one area of the Temple that was open to the Gentiles from being a place of prayer.[1]

The last part of the verse is reminiscent of Jer. vii. 11. Instead of allowing the Temple to be what God wished it to be they had turned it into a robbers' lair. Λῃστής is a strong word meaning 'robber' or 'pirate' rather than 'thief'; and the Hebrew word used in Jer. vii. 11 is similarly strong (according to B.D.B. it means 'violent one (robber, murderer)'). The reference here is no doubt to the swindling and extortion practised in the Temple mart and by the money-changers.

18. Note the parataxis, καὶ ἤκουσαν...καὶ ἐζήτουν...,

[1] For a different view, according to which πᾶσιν τοῖς ἔθνεσιν is to be taken not with οἶκος προσευχῆς but with κληθήσεται, see Kilpatrick, 'Gentile Mission', p. 157.

where the meaning is, 'When they...heard, they began to seek...'. Note the definite connection made here between the cleansing of the Temple and the plot of the chief priests and scribes against Jesus. Mark has already mentioned the plotting of the Pharisees and Herodians in iii. 6.

πῶς is here used to introduce an indirect question, instead of ὅπως. It is sometimes so used in classical Greek (see L. & S., s.v., IV).

The latter half of the verse consists of two γάρ-clauses, one dependent on the other. ἐφοβοῦντο γὰρ αὐτόν explains why the chief priests and scribes went to work indirectly instead of taking immediate action. The second γάρ-clause explains why they feared Jesus. On ἐξεπλήσσετο see on i. 22; ἐφοβοῦντο here seems to denote an ordinary fear rather than awe.

19. ὅταν ὀψὲ ἐγένετο. Translate 'when it got late', and not as R.V. text or margin. For ὅταν + indicative = 'when' see on iii. 11.

ἐξεπορεύοντο. Taylor perhaps rightly prefers to read ἐξεπορεύετο with ℵ C D Θ f1 f13 pm lat ϛ, explaining the plural reading as probably an alteration made to harmonize with παραπορευόμενοι in v. 20.

The inner meaning of this incident is messianic, and this is doubtless in Mark's mind. In Calvin's words, 'He declared Himself to be both King and High Priest, who presided over the Temple and the worship of God'. Indeed, we may see here the fulfilment of the promise of Mal. iii. 1 ff. But outwardly the action did not go beyond the exercise of prophetic authority (cf. Jer. vii. 1 ff., xxvi. 1 ff.). Its messianic nature was veiled. Had there been anything openly messianic about it, the Romans would surely have taken action. At the same time the question may have arisen in the minds of the Jewish authorities whether possibly his action pointed to an assertion of more than prophetic authority.

On the question whether the Markan or the Johannine
(Jn ii. 13–22) date of the incident is more likely to be correct,
opinion is divided. (That there were two such occasions is
unlikely.) Taylor lists seven reasons for doubting the
Markan date; but none of them is very convincing. On the
whole, it seems more probable than the Johannine, which is
explicable as due to theological motives.

(See further Lightfoot, *Gospel Message*, pp. 60–79; also
J. A. Robinson, *The Historical Character of St John's Gospel*
(London, 2nd ed. 1929), pp. 29 ff.)

64. THE FIG TREE (*continued*) AND SAYINGS ON
FAITH, PRAYER AND FORGIVENESS (xi. 20–6)
(Mt. xxi. 20–2)

Verses 20 f. form the sequel to *vv.* 12–14. To them have been
appended some independent sayings probably already
collected together for catechetical purposes.

20 f. See on *vv.* 12–14.

ἐκ ῥιζῶν indicates the completeness of the destruction.
Cf. Job xviii. 16, xxviii. 9, xxxi. 12, Ezek. xvii. 9, Hos.
ix. 16.

22. It is possible to make out a connection with *vv.* 20 f.:
though the purpose of the fig tree miracle was something
quite different, the fulfilment of Jesus' word afforded
incidentally an occasion for some teaching on faith (teaching
on the lesson the miracle was intended to drive home having
presumably already been given at the time of the saying in
v. 14). But it seems more likely that *vv.* 22–5 are independent
sayings which have been appended to the conclusion of the
fig tree narrative. In either case it would appear that the
early Church was more interested in the fact that Jesus'
word was fulfilled than in the lesson about the judgement to
fall on Israel which the miracle was intended to teach, with
the result that the miracle, which apart from its significance

as an acted parable was pointless, has been liable to be misunderstood.

Ἔχετε. ℵ D Θ f13 28 it sy^s insert Εἰ before ἔχετε, thus making the last words of *v.* 22 part of the following sentence; but this is probably assimilation to Mt. xxi. 21 or Lk. xvii. 6.

πίστιν Θεοῦ: 'faith in God'. The suggestion that the genitive is subjective—'have the sort of faith God has'—is surely a monstrosity of exegesis. For the genitive after πίστις cf. Acts iii. 16, Rom. iii. 22, 26, Gal. ii. 16 (twice), iii. 22, Eph. iii. 12, Phil. i. 27, iii. 9, Col. ii. 12, II Thess. ii. 13, Rev. xiv. 12.

23. ἀμήν. See on iii. 28.

εἰς τὴν θάλασσαν. From the Mount of Olives the Dead Sea is visible.

διακριθῇ. In the N.T. the middle and passive of διακρίνω are used in the sense 'hesitate', 'doubt': cf. Acts x. 20, Rom. iv. 20, Jas i. 6, ii. 4.

πιστεύῃ ὅτι ὃ λαλεῖ γίνεται. Cf. πιστεύετε ὅτι ἐλάβετε in *v.* 24. What is here indicated by means of hyperbole is that one is to be absolutely confident in God's readiness to respond to faith. Cf. Isa. lxv. 24, Mt. vi. 8.

S.–B. 1, p. 759 illustrates the use of the expression 'mountain-remover' ('*ôḳēr hārîm*) in Rabbinic literature to denote a Rabbi who can remove difficulties of interpretation. Cf. Zech. iv. 7 for the figurative use of 'mountain' for an obstacle. Jesus means that God will, in response to faith, enable the disciple to do the impossible. Mt. xvii. 20 seems to be a different form of the same saying; Lk. xvii. 6 is perhaps a different saying. Cf. also I Cor. xiii. 2.

24. Probably an independent saying, which had already, before Mark received it, been attached to the saying preserved in *vv.* 22 f.

25. The connection with *v.* 24 is probably simply the occurrence of προσεύχεσθαι (see introduction to section 54).

στήκετε. For standing when praying cf. I Kgs viii. 14, 22,

Neh. ix. 4, Ps. cxxxiv. 1, Jer. xviii. 20, Mt. vi. 5, Lk. xviii. 11, 13.

For the teaching of this verse cf. Mt. vi. 14f., xviii. 23–35.

[26.] Omitted by ℵ B L W 565 700 *pc k l* sy^s. It is an addition from Mt. vi. 15.

65. 'BY WHAT AUTHORITY?' (xi. 27–33)
(Mt. xxi. 23–7; Lk. xx. 1–8)

A conflict-story, the connection of which with the Cleansing of the Temple is probably historical. The historical reliability of the narrative need not be doubted.

27. οἱ ἀρχιερεῖς καὶ οἱ γραμματεῖς καὶ οἱ πρεσβύτεροι. See on viii. 31. The three are mentioned together again in xiv. 43, 53, xv. 1. Presumably here it is not the whole Sanhedrin that is meant, but a few representatives of each group. The fact that all three groups were represented indicates the importance of the occasion.

28. ποίᾳ. It is doubtful whether it is right to press the strict meaning ('what sort of') here, though it would make good sense. The word is sometimes used as a synonym for τίς or ὅστις (e.g. xii. 28, Mt. xxiv. 42, Acts xxiii. 34).

ἐξουσίᾳ. See on i. 22. The reference is not to be limited to rabbinical authorization. They are asking quite generally what authority he claims to have, that he should do what he has done. They probably wondered whether he regarded himself as a prophet; the thought may also by this time have crossed their minds that he might possibly be thinking of himself as the Messiah.

ταῦτα. The substitution of διδάσκοντος...τὸν λαὸν...καὶ εὐαγγελιζομένου in the Lk. parallel to *v.* 27 for Mark's περιπατοῦντος suggests that in Lk. xx. 2 ταῦτα refers to Jesus' teaching and preaching; but in Mk ταῦτα is naturally taken to refer to the cleansing of the Temple. Cf. Jn ii. 18.

29. Jesus replies by asking them a question (cf. x. 3).

λόγον: 'matter', 'point'. ('Ἐπερωτᾶν + accusative means here 'ask about': cf. iv. 10, where the simple verb is used.)

ἀποκρίθητε. As in English, the imperative followed by 'and' can be used in the place of a conditional clause. Cf. v. 24 (πιστεύετε ὅτι ἐλάβετε, καί...).

30. τὸ βάπτισμα τὸ Ἰωάννου. The subject is placed first for the sake of emphasis.

ἐξ οὐρανοῦ: i.e. from God. Cf. the use of βασιλεία τῶν οὐρανῶν in Mt.; also Dan. iv. 26, Lk. xv. 18, 21, etc.

The question was no mere debating expedient, but thoroughly apposite; for the question whether John was a true prophet had a direct bearing on the question of Jesus' authority, their ministries being related as they were. Taylor rightly sees here a veiled and indirect claim to be the Messiah.

31. After λέγοντες D Θ Φ f13 28 pc it (most MSS.) insert τί εἴπωμεν; (or equivalent); this is accepted by C. H. Turner and Taylor, and should possibly be read.

αὐτῷ. Probably 'him' (i.e. John), though it could be 'it' (i.e. his baptism).

For this explanation of people's unspoken thoughts cf. ii. 6f. Their dilemma may have been written on their faces, but anyway could be inferred from their reply. (Actually ἑαυτούς could have the sense of ἀλλήλους, so that a whispered conversation among themselves is not absolutely ruled out.)

32. The second conditional sentence is broken off in the middle, the statement ἐφοβοῦντο τὸν ὄχλον followed by an explanatory sentence taking the place of the apodosis.

εἶχον. For this use of ἔχω (= 'hold', 'consider') cf. Mt. xiv. 5, xxi. 46, Phil. ii. 29. Here there is a mixture of constructions, a ὅτι-clause being substituted for ὡς (or εἰς) προφήτην.

ὄντως qualifies ἦν, not εἶχον; it has been put into the main clause for emphasis.

33. Calvin's comment is apt: 'They do not inquire what is true, nor do they put the question to their own conscience; and they are so base as to choose rather to shuffle than to acknowledge what they know to be true, that their tyranny may not be impaired. In this manner, all wicked men, though they pretend to be desirous of learning, shut the gate of truth, if they feel it to be opposed to their wicked desires.'

So Jesus leaves them in suspense, their question unanswered save by the veiled and indirect answer implicit in his counter-question.

66. THE PARABLE OF THE WICKED HUSBANDMEN
(xii. 1–12)
(Mt. xxi. 33–46; Lk. xx. 9–19)

On questions of authenticity see the notes below.

1. By αὐτοῖς Mark apparently means the chief priests, scribes and elders of xi. 27–33; for they are the most natural subject of ἐζήτουν, ἐφοβήθησαν, ἔγνωσαν and ἀπῆλθον in *v.* 12 (cf. xi. 18), and it is also natural to take αὐτοῖς here and αὐτούς in *v.* 12 to refer to the subject of those verbs. Similarly in Mt. it is implied that this parable was addressed to the people who had asked about Jesus' authority. Luke also, though he has πρὸς τὸν λαόν in xx. 9, implies that the scribes and chief priests, whom he mentions in xx. 19, had heard the parable.

ἐν παραβολαῖς indicates the manner of his speaking; it does not necessarily imply that there were a number of parables. Cf. the singular in Mt. and Lk. On παραβολή see on iv. 2.

The details are taken from Isa. v. 1 f., in the LXX text of which the words ἀμπελών, φυτεύω, περιτίθημι, φραγμός, ὀρύσσω, (προλήνιον—cf. ὑπολήνιον here in Mk), οἰκοδομῶ and πύργος all occur. (The ὑπολήνιον was the trough for the juice under the ληνός in which the grapes were crushed. The tower would be used for watching against thieves or animals and for shelter for the husbandmen.)

καὶ ἐξέδετο αὐτὸν γεωργοῖς, καὶ ἀπεδήμησεν. With these statements the parable strikes out in a different direction from Isa. v. Ἐκδίδωμι is occasionally used in the active in classical Greek in the sense 'let'; the middle is used in Polybius VI. xvii. 2, as here and in the parallels. For the spelling ἐξέδετο see Bauer, s.v., ἐκδίδωμι.

2. τῷ καιρῷ: 'at the appointed time', 'the proper time'.

δοῦλον. On the succession of slaves in vv. 2–5 see below.

3. ἔδειραν. Δέρειν originally meant 'to flay': here and in v. 5 (and also in xiii. 9) it means 'to beat'.

κενόν here means 'empty-handed': cf. in the LXX Gen. xxxi. 42, Deut. xv. 13, Job xxii. 9 (in each case τινὰ κενὸν ἐξαποστέλλειν).

4. ἐκεφαλίωσαν. So א B and a few other Alexandrian MSS.: most MSS. have ἐκεφαλαίωσαν. The meaning (whichever word Mark wrote) is probably 'wounded in the head' or 'smote on the head' (cf. *in capite vulneraverunt* in vg, and also δείραντες in the Lk. parallel), though κεφαλαιοῦν nowhere else has this meaning, and a verb κεφαλιοῦν is not otherwise known. The suggestion that what we have is a mistake for ἐκολάφισαν has no textual support and in any case is unlikely, since something more serious than ἔδειραν (or at least as serious) seems to be required.

5. ἀποκτέννοντες. Ἀποκτέννω is a late form of ἀποκτείνω, found in the LXX, Polybius, etc.

6. ἀγαπητόν here means 'only', as in LXX Gen. xxii. 2. (See on i. 11.)

7. ἐκεῖνοι has a disparaging sense here. It 'points back to the picture already drawn of the men: "those husbandmen, being such as we know they were"' (Swete).

δεῦτε ἀποκτείνωμεν αὐτόν. The same words are used by Joseph's brothers in LXX Gen. xxxvii. 20.

9. κύριος here means 'owner'.

In the latter half of the verse Jesus answers his own question. In Mt. xxi. 41 it is the audience which answers the question, and it is possible that the original parable ended with the question—though, as Dodd has pointed out,[1] apart from the fact that Jesus does not usually answer his own questions, there is nothing in 9b that is improbable on the lips of Jesus; for the details are feasible (for the destruction of the tenants Dodd refers to the example of Brutus collecting a debt by means of a force of cavalry (Cicero, *Att.* v. 21, vi. 1), and when the bad tenants had been destroyed it would be natural for the owner to let the vineyard to others), the general implication is consistent with Jesus' teaching elsewhere, and the details do not correspond so closely with subsequent historical events as to look like a clear *vaticinium ex eventu*.

According to Jeremias[2] the original parable was not allegorical. The part about the slaves is, he thinks, better preserved in Lk. xx. 10-12 than in Mk xii. 2-5. The killing of the third slave in Mk is 'a clumsy popular exaggeration, which weakens the point of the story by anticipating the fate which it was the lot of the son to undergo'; and 5b is an addition in the interests of allegorization, identifying the slaves with the prophets. The process of allegorizing is carried out most completely in Mt. Jeremias accepts Dodd's explanation of the naturalness and realism of the parable and agrees with him that the introduction of the son was due not to theological motives but to the inherent logic of the story. It was the Church, he thinks, that first interpreted the 'son' allegorically as standing for Jesus himself, and so was led to add 10f. as a reference to the Resurrection. The original point of the parable was to vindicate the offer of the gospel to the poor: the leaders of the people 'have multiplied rebellion against God.... Therefore shall the vineyard of God be given to "others".' In the 'others'

[1] *Parables*, pp. 126f.   [2] *Parables*, pp. 55ff.

Jeremias sees a reference to 'the poor' and compares Mt. v. 5.

But it is very doubtful whether this explanation, attractive though it undoubtedly is, can be maintained. Is it conceivable that Jesus could take up the O.T. figure of God's vineyard and then speak of the owner sending his slaves one after another without thinking of the prophets (cf. Jer. vii. 25 f.: καὶ ἐξαπέστειλα πρὸς ὑμᾶς πάντας τοὺς δούλους μου τοὺς προφήτας ἡμέρας καὶ ὄρθρου, καὶ ἀπέστειλα καὶ οὐκ εἰσήκουσάν μου καὶ οὐ προσέσχεν τὸ οὖς αὐτῶν, καὶ ἐσκλήρυναν τὸν τράχηλον αὐτῶν ὑπὲρ τοὺς πατέρας αὐτῶν—and also xxv. 4, Josh. xiv. 7, Amos iii. 7, Zech. i. 4)? (To the objection, mentioned by Taylor, that the O.T. prophet's function was 'to declare the will of God and not to gather His dues', it may be replied that the prophet's function was indeed to gather God's dues, to claim on God's behalf the loyalty and obedience owed to him by his people.) And, even if the other improbabilities in the story as a realistic story can be explained by appealing to the special circumstances of Galilean *latifundia* in unsettled times, is it possible to explain the owner's action related in *v*. 6 as a realistic feature of the story? Would a landlord whose slaves had been maltreated by rebellious tenants proceed to send his only son to them without taking precautions for his safety? It is surely more likely that this feature is due to an allegorical motive.

It seems probable that this parable was allegorical from the beginning—though that does not mean that every detail is allegorical any more than is the case in Isa. v—and that it was an earnest appeal to the consciences of those who were plotting Jesus' death. That Jesus should have warned them of the dreadfulness of what they were planning to do and of its consequences as clearly as was possible, short of dropping altogether the veiledness of his Sonship and Messiahship, is inherently likely. Such a warning, surely, we have here. That it is directed specifically to the leaders of the people and not to the people at large is indicated by the fact that, whereas in Isa. v the vineyard was at fault, here it is only the husbandmen. The centre of interest is the murder of the owner's son, in which the hearers are surely meant to see a reference to what they themselves are plotting. Their deed will be signally heinous and will be signally punished. But the veiledness is maintained; Jesus has made no direct claim (the relationship of the son to the owner *could* be taken as a non-allegorical detail like the winepress or the tower); what he has said is wholly ἐν παραβολαῖς. But he has gone as far as he possibly could, within those limits, to open their eyes to the truth. The form of the High Priest's question in xiv. 61 is possibly an indication that the hint was not altogether lost on the Jewish authorities.

10f. The quotation is from Ps. cxviii (LXX: cxvii). 22f., and follows the LXX exactly.

Λίθον. The nominative has been attracted into the accusative by the relative pronoun.

ἀπεδοκίμασαν. See on viii. 31.

The use of εἰς + the accusative instead of the simple nominative is due to the use of *l^e* in the original.

κεφαλὴν γωνίας. More probably the keystone, which holds together and completes the building, than the corner-stone (cf. Jeremias in *T.W.N.T.* I, pp. 792f., IV, p. 278). Cf. ἀκρογωνιαῖος in Eph. ii. 20.

αὕτη. The feminine (instead of the neuter) is a too literal reproduction of the Hebrew.

It is often maintained that *vv.* 10f. were added to the parable by the early Church in order to supply the missing reference to the Resurrection. But against this the following points should be noted: (i) In viii. 31, Lk. ix. 22, xvii. 25, Jesus applies this passage to the Son of Man (ἀποδοκιμάζω); (ii) The psalm is one of the Hallel psalms which Jesus used (xiv. 26) and upon which he must often have reflected; (iii) Rabbinic parables do sometimes end with a scriptural quotation to clinch the matter; (iv) The way the quotation is introduced is not characteristically Markan. For the identification of Jesus with the stone of Ps. cxviii. 22f. cf. Acts iv. 11, I Pet. ii. 7, (Eph. ii. 20). On the lips of Jesus the quotation is in line with what we have suggested was the meaning of the parable in *vv.* 1–9: it is as clear a warning to the leaders of Israel that the one whom they are rejecting will be exalted by God as Jesus could possibly give without dropping altogether his messianic veiledness.

12. With the first part of the verse cf. xi. 18. The second καί is adversative (see on vi. 21).

ἔγνωσαν γὰρ ὅτι πρὸς αὐτοὺς τὴν παραβολὴν εἶπεν. Better taken as explaining ἐζήτουν than ἐφοβήθησαν. The πρός here means 'with reference to', not 'to' (cf. Lk. xii. 41, Heb. i. 7f., xi. 18).

67. THE QUESTION ABOUT TRIBUTE (xii. 13–17)
(Mt. xxii. 15–22; Lk. xx. 20–6)

A pronouncement-story. The authenticity of the saying in *v.* 17 is not doubted—even by Bultmann. No statement of time or place is included; but the context in which Mark has set it seems intrinsically probable.

13. It is possible that Mark intends ἀποστέλλουσιν to be understood to have the same subject as the plural verbs in the previous verse (see on αὐτοῖς in *v.* 1); but it is perhaps better to take it as an indefinite plural used instead of the passive. In any case it is likely that it was either the Sanhedrin as such or else some members of it who sent the questioners.

Φαρισαίων. See on ii. 16.

Ἡρῳδιανῶν. See on iii. 6. The presence of partisans of Herod Antipas is no reason for thinking that this incident must have taken place in Galilee; for they would naturally be in Jerusalem for the feast (cf. Lk. xxiii. 7).

14. Διδάσκαλε. See on i. 21 (ἐδίδασκεν).

οὐ μέλει σοι περὶ οὐδενός. The expression μέλειν τινὶ περί is here used, not in the sense it has e.g. in Jn x. 13, xii. 6, but in a special sense, which is explained by the next sentence.

οὐ γὰρ βλέπεις εἰς πρόσωπον ἀνθρώπων. In the Hebrew O.T. there are several expressions for 'showing partiality' which include the word 'face': nāśā' pānîm, hikkîr pānîm, hādar pānîm. Of these the first is the most common. It can be used in a good sense, 'be gracious to', 'show consideration for' (e.g. Deut. xxviii. 50, II Kgs iii. 14, Job xlii. 8f., Lam. iv. 16); but is often used in a bad sense, 'be unduly influenced by', 'show partiality toward' (e.g. Deut. x. 17, Lev. xix. 15, Ps. lxxxii. 2, Prov. xviii. 5). It is rendered in the LXX sometimes by πρόσωπον λαμβάνειν (cf. the Lk. parallel here)—hence the N.T. words προσωποληµ-πτεῖν, -ψία, -πτης; sometimes by πρόσωπον θαυμάζειν. Βλέπειν εἰς πρόσωπον here might perhaps be explained as a variant of the LXX πρόσωπον θαυμάζειν or as reflecting rather the second or third of the Hebrew expressions mentioned above (hikkîr = 'regard', 'pay attention to'; hādar = 'honour'; βλέπειν εἰς here has the sense 'regard', 'pay attention to'), though it is never used in the LXX to translate them.[1]

ἐπ' ἀληθείας is better taken closely with διδάσκεις than as simply underlining the statement as a whole: not according to respect of persons but according to truth does Jesus teach God's way (cf. the use of ἀληθής earlier in the verse in combination with οὐ μέλει σοι περὶ οὐδενός).

τὴν ὁδὸν τοῦ Θεοῦ. 'The way of God' in the O.T. can mean either the way God himself takes, his acts and his dealings with men (e.g. Job xxvi. 14, Isa. lv. 8f., Ps. ciii. 7—usually the plural is used), or the way he ordains for man, the way of life he commands (e.g. Deut. viii. 6, x. 12f., Job xxiii. 11, Ps. xxvii. 11, cxix. 15). Here it is used in the latter sense.

[1] That it is to be explained thus, and not by I Sam. xvi. 7 (see LXX) is clear; a reference to respect of persons is apposite here, but not a reference to judging by appearance.

ἔξεστιν. 'Is it lawful', i.e. allowed by God's Law.

κῆνσον: Latin *census* transliterated; it occurs elsewhere in Greek (though rarely) and also in Aramaic. This poll-tax was particularly hated by the Jews as the sign of their subjection to Rome. The Pharisees, who were no friends of the tax, though they justified paying it, and the Herodians, who supported it, came together to ask Jesus, united by the desire to destroy him in one way or another.

The question was a trap; for, if Jesus said, 'Yes', he would be finished as far as the people were concerned, whereas if he said, 'No', he could at once be denounced to the Romans.

δῶμεν...δῶμεν. Deliberative subjunctives.

15. ὑπόκρισιν. See on vii. 6 (ὑποκριτῶν). Perhaps here the idea of conscious insincerity is intended. Their question was not a genuine question prompted by a desire for instruction.

πειράζετε. See on x. 2 (also i. 13, viii. 11).

φέρετέ μοι δηνάριον ἵνα ἴδω. He asks for the coin, not because he does not know what is on it, but because he wishes to show up their hypocrisy. If they can easily produce the coin, it will prove that they have already answered their own question—they are using Caesar's coinage. The *denarius* (the word had been taken into Greek and also Aramaic) was a small silver Roman coin, worth about a shilling. The most common type of *denarius* of Tiberius has on its obverse the Emperor's bust adorned with a laurel wreath and on its reverse a representation of his mother Livia. The legend, which is abbreviated, reads (in full): *Tiberius Caesar Divi Augusti Filius Augustus Pontifex Maximus.* Both legend and images set forth the mythology of the Imperial cult and so troubled the consciences of religious Jews.

17. Τὰ Καίσαρος. Jesus takes up their own admission. The image and inscription are Caesar's. According to ancient ways of thinking the coinage of a ruler was not only

guaranteed by him but actually belonged to him. If, therefore, the Jews used Caesar's coins, they could not object to
having to pay some of them to him as a tax.

ἀπόδοτε. Whereas the questioners had used the simple
verb 'give', Jesus uses the compound, which means to 'give
back or pay something which one owes as a debt'. They are
under an obligation. The attitude of Jesus to the Roman
Empire seems to have been similar to that of Jeremiah to the
Babylonian (cf. Jer. xxvii. 5 ff., xxviii. 14, xxix. 7, etc.).

But Jesus at the same time indicates the limits and rela-
tivity of the debt owed to Caesar: (ἀπόδοτε) τὰ τοῦ Θεοῦ τῷ
Θεῷ. Though the obligation to pay to Caesar some of his
own coinage in return for the amenities his rule provided is
affirmed, the idolatrous claims expressed on the coins are
rejected. God's rights are to be honoured. Here Jesus is not
saying that there are two quite separate independent
spheres, that of Caesar and that of God (for Caesar and all
that is his belong to God); but he is indicating that there are
obligations to Caesar which do not infringe the rights of God
but are indeed ordained by God. The answer of Jesus is of
far-reaching importance; but it is not by itself capable of
being the basis for a Christian doctrine of the state or of the
Christian's obligations to the state. The basis of such a
doctrine would have to include the Passion narratives,
Rom. xiii. 1–7, I Tim. ii. 1–6, I Pet. ii. 13–17, and passages
which deal with the present rule of the exalted Christ. See
further: on this Markan section, the chapter entitled, 'The
Story of the Tribute Money', in E. Stauffer, *Christ and the
Caesars* (Eng. tr., London, 1955), pp. 112–37; and on the
Christian understanding of the state, K. Barth, *Church and
State* (Eng. tr., London, 1939) and *Against the Stream* (London,
1954), pp. 13–50; W. A. Visser 't Hooft, *The Kingship of
Christ* (London, 1948); O. Cullmann, *The State in the New
Testament* (Eng. tr., London, 1957).

    *

ἐξεθαύμαζον. See on i. 22.

68. THE QUESTION ABOUT THE RESURRECTION
(xii. 18–27)
(Mt. xxii. 23–33; Lk. xx. 27–40)

Another pronouncement-story. The suggestion of Bultmann
that *vv.* 26f. are a later addition is quite unnecessary; for it
would be natural for Jesus to go on to deal with the real
question that lay behind the Sadducees' actual inquiry. The
whole section is thoroughly Jewish in content and manner.

18. Σαδδουκαῖοι. The Sadducees were the aristocratic
party, made up of the high priestly and leading lay families
of Jerusalem. They were wealthy and worldly. Their arro-
gance and their harshness in the administration of justice
were notorious. Conservative in doctrine, they rejected
what they regarded as Pharisaic innovations; but their main
concern was for the maintenance of their privileges, not for
doctrinal purity. The origin of the name is uncertain. It is
often explained as deriving from the Zadok mentioned in
II Sam. viii. 17, xv. 24, I Kgs i. 8, ii. 35, etc. (cf. Ezek. xl. 46,
xliii. 19, xliv. 15, xlviii. 11). A late Talmudic writing connects it with another Zadok, an alleged disciple of Anti-
gonus of Socho. Another explanation (put forward by
T. W. Manson) is that under the Hasmoneans the members
of the Jewish senate or council were sometimes called
σύνδικοι (the word was used in Athens in the fourth century
B.C. and was also used in Roman and Byzantine times) and
that the name Sadducee derives from an Aramaic transliteration of this word. See further J. W. Lightley, *Jewish
Sects and Parties in the Time of Jesus* (London, 1925); S.–B. IV,
pp. 334ff.; Manson, *S.-M.* pp. 12–16, and an article in
B.J.R.L. XXII, pp. 144ff.

οἵτινες λέγουσιν ἀνάστασιν μὴ εἶναι. Cf. Acts xxiii. 6–8.
On the Pharisaic belief in the resurrection see C. Guignebert,
The Jewish World in the Time of Jesus (Eng. tr., London, 1939),
pp. 117–21; A. Oepke in *T.W.N.T.* I, pp. 368–72.

19. διδάσκαλε. See on i. 21 (ἐδίδασκεν).

For levirate marriage see Deut. xxv. 5–10, the first two verses of which are here quoted freely and incompletely, Gen. xxxviii. 8, and (M) *Yeb.*

ὅτι...ἵνα.... A mixture of two constructions: ἔγραψεν ὅτι ἐὰν ἀποθάνῃ...λήμψεται and ἔγραψεν ἵνα ἐὰν ἀποθάνῃ... λάβῃ. In both Mt. and Lk. the sentence is made smoother.

20–3. The intention of the Sadducees is to ridicule the Pharisaic doctrine of the resurrection accepted by Jesus. The fact noted in *v.* 22a is important, since, if the last brother to marry the woman had had a son by her, he would naturally have had the preference. The words ὅταν ἀναστῶσιν in *v.* 23 are omitted by א B C D W *pc c d k r*[1] sy[p] sa bo (most MSS.), but should probably be retained; the tautology is in keeping with Mark's style (Taylor compares xiii. 19f.). For the second accusative after ἔχω in *v.* 23 cf. Mt. iii. 9, Lk. iii. 8, Phil. iii. 17, Heb. xii. 9.

24. διὰ τοῦτο anticipates μὴ εἰδότες...Θεοῦ.

μὴ εἰδότες: 'because you do not understand'.

τὰς γραφάς. In *v.* 10 the singular was used with reference to a particular scriptural passage; here the plural denotes the scriptures as a whole. Properly understood, the O.T. testifies eloquently to the truth of the resurrection (e.g. the passage quoted in *v.* 26).

μηδὲ τὴν δύναμιν τοῦ Θεοῦ. The resurrection is utterly incredible, if the power of God is not reckoned with. But the God revealed in scripture is a God of miracles. Those who understand the scriptures and therefore reckon with the power of God will not deny the resurrection because they cannot comprehend the 'how' of it. (For the suggestion that Jesus was thinking of the passage in the '*ᵃmîdāh* prayer which includes the words, 'Thou quickenest the dead with great mercy...and keepest thy faith to them that sleep in the dust', and which was known as *geḇûrôt*, i.e. 'powers' (*A.D.P.B.* pp. 44f.), see Barrett, *H.S.G.T.* pp. 74f.)

25. Had they understood the scriptures and the power of God, they would have reckoned with the otherness of the resurrection life.

The present tenses in this verse (γαμοῦσιν, γαμίζονται, εἰσίν), as also ἐγείρονται in *v.* 26, are not to be taken to imply that the resurrection life is already being lived. They either stand for the future (cf. ix. 31: παραδίδοται; Mt. xxvi. 18: ποιῶ; xxvii. 63: ἐγείρομαι; and see further Moule, p. 7), or, less probably, are to be explained as gnomic presents (Moule, p. 8). Cf. I Cor. xv. 12 ff.

For the resurrected dead being like the angels cf. I Enoch civ. 4, II Baruch li. 10. On ἄγγελοι see on xvi. 5. ἐν τοῖς οὐρανοῖς is to be taken closely with ἄγγελοι, not with εἰσίν. The point is not that the resurrected dead will be in heaven like the angels, but that they will have a life such as the heavenly angels have. The mention of the angels touches another point at which the Sadducees disagreed with the Pharisees (cf. Acts xxiii. 8).

26. In their question the Sadducees had actually assumed for the moment the fact of the resurrection and inquired about its manner. So Jesus deals first with its manner. Now he goes on to deal with the real question in their minds— that of the fact.

ἀνέγνωτε. Cf. ii. 25, xii. 10.

βίβλῳ. Both in biblical and non-biblical Greek the word tends to suggest special veneration or sacredness.

Μωϋσέως. Jesus appeals to the Law, the part of the scriptures on which the Sadducees specially relied.

ἐπὶ τοῦ Βάτου: 'at "the Bush"', i.e. in the passage relating the story of the burning bush. Cf. Rom. xi. 2: ἐν 'Ηλείᾳ. Other examples are given in S.–B. II, p. 28. (Βάτος is here treated as masculine, as in the LXX and in Attic; in the Lk. parallel it is treated as feminine, as is normal in Hellenistic Greek.)

The quotation is from Exod. iii. 6. Grammatically, the

words need mean no more than that the God who is speaking to Moses is the God who in the past revealed himself to, and was the God of, the patriarchs. But...

27. ...the fact that in Moses' time God could still call himself the God of Abraham, Isaac and Jacob implies that at that time he still remembered and cared for them, and, since he is the living, almighty and faithful God, those whom he remembers and cares for must be alive. (Cf. Origen, *Comment. in Matt.*, Tom. xvii. 36, quoted by Swete: 'It would be absurd to say that God, who said, "He which is, that is my name", is the God of men who have no existence at all....So then Abraham and Isaac and Jacob are alive and are conscious of God and of his grace.') And, if they were still alive with God (for this pre-resurrection life cf. Lk. xxiii. 43, xvi. 19–31, Phil. i. 23, IV Macc. vii. 18f., xvi. 25) in the time of Moses, we may be confident that at the last God will also raise up their bodies, so that they may share the final blessedness. The kernel of the argument is the faithfulness of God.

69. THE GREAT COMMANDMENT (xii. 28–34)
(Mt. xxii. 34–40)

The only significant feature common to this Mk section (and the Mt. parallel) and Lk. x. 25–8 is the combination of Deut. vi. 5 and Lev. xix. 18. The differences are more significant: the context; the initial inquiry; Jesus' concluding comment; the fact that, while in Mk and Mt. it is Jesus who brings the two O.T. texts together, in Lk. it is the lawyer; and the fact that, while in Mk and Mt. it is the summary of the Law, in Lk. it is what follows, that is the centre of interest. T. W. Manson is surely right in concluding that Lk. x. 25–8 is neither parallel to, nor a doublet of, this passage, but refers to a different occasion.[1]

The stress on the friendliness of the scribe strongly sup-

[1] *Sayings*, pp. 259f.

ports the view that the Mk narrative is based on reliable tradition.

28. The two participial clauses, ἀκούσας... αὐτοῖς, which connect this section with the preceding and at the same time prepare the way for the indication of the man's friendly attitude in *vv.* 32–4, are possibly editorial. The variant ἰδών (supported by ℵ* C D L W Θ fɪ fɪ3 *al* lat) is preferred to εἰδώς by C. H. Turner and Taylor.

Ποία. Here used in the sense of τίς (cf. Jn x. 32, and in LXX, e.g. II Sam. xv. 2).

πάντων. πασῶν might have been expected, as ἐντολή is feminine, and is actually read by some MSS.; but πάντων is to be explained as a stereotyped use of the neuter genitive plural to intensify the superlative (cf. Thucydides, ɪv. 52: πόλεις... καὶ πάντων μάλιστα τὴν ᾿Αντανδρον).

Attempts to distinguish between 'heavy' or 'great' and 'light' or 'little' commandments, and also to trace back the particular commandments of the Law to basic general principles, were often made by the Rabbis. Hillel, for instance, when challenged by a Gentile, 'Make me a proselyte on condition that you teach me the whole Law while I stand on one foot', replied: 'What you hate for yourself, do not do to your neighbour: this is the whole Law, the rest is commentary; go and learn.' (See further S.–B. ɪ, pp. 900–8.)

29f. In reply Jesus quotes the first part (Deut. vi. 4f.) of the Shema (šᵉma‘) or creed of Israel, which is recited daily by pious Jews (it consists of Deut. vi. 4–9, xi. 13–21, Num. xv. 37–41). The quotation agrees fairly closely with the LXX, though ἰσχύς is substituted for δύναμις, and the single Hebrew noun lēḇāḇ is represented by two nouns (καρδία and διάνοια) instead of by one.

Only in Mk is Deut. vi. 4 included here; but Taylor rightly says: 'The connexion of these words with those that follow is vital; for the command to love God is not simply a duty; it is an obligation arising out of the fact that He is One, in comparison with whom the gods of the heathen are idols, and that He has chosen Israel in covenant-love (κύριος ὁ θεὸς ἡμῶν).' The list of four nouns in v. 30 and the repetition of ὅλης stress the completeness of the response demanded. 'The love here commanded is the response of a man in the totality of his being to the prior love of God. The whole man is the object of the divine love and the whole man is thereby claimed by God for himself.'[1] On ἀγαπᾶν, the characteristic biblical verb for 'love', see the author's article on 'love' in *T.W.B.* pp. 131–6; and also G. Quell and E. Stauffer, *Love* (Eng. tr. by J. R. Coates of the article in *T.W.N.T.* I, London, 1949). For an extended exposition of Mk xii. 29–31 see Barth, *C.D.* I/2, pp. 381–454.

31. The scribe had asked which was the first commandment. Jesus adds a second, because he knows that these two are inseparable (cf. I Jn iv. 21). The quotation is from Lev. xix. 18 and agrees with the LXX exactly. The love which is here required, like God's own love to men and the love that men are commanded to have toward God, is a love which makes decisions and acts, not a mere feeling.

In Lev. xix. 18 the neighbour (ὁ πλησίον σου) is clearly the fellow-Israelite, as the first part of the verse shows, and it was in this sense that Jesus' contemporaries understood it— though they actually tended to interpret it more narrowly, for, whereas Lev. xix. 34 includes the resident alien, they tended to include only the full-proselyte (see S.–B. I, pp. 353 ff.) under the term 'the stranger that sojourneth with you', and so to limit the scope of 'neighbour' to fellow-Israelites and full-proselytes. That the term has a wider range for Jesus is clear from Lk. x. 25–37: if it can include the hated Samaritans, it must include all men. On the meaning of τὸν πλησίον σου here see further Cranfield, † 'The Good Samaritan' in *T.T.* XI, pp. 368–72, and 'Neighbour' in *T.W.B.* p. 158.

[1] *T.W.B.* p. 135.

ὡς σεαυτόν. Cf. Mt. vii. 12, Lk. vi. 31. The command to love one's neighbour as oneself does not in any way legitimize self-love (as has sometimes been thought); but in it God addresses us as the men that we actually are, sinners who love ourselves, and claims us *as such* for love to our neighbours. (See further Barth, *C.D.* 1/2, pp. 450f.)

The fact that in Lk. x. 27 it is the lawyer who combines Deut. vi. 5 and Lev. xix. 18 does not prove that others had made the combination before Jesus, as the lawyer may have known that Jesus had made it on other occasions; but it is quite likely that Jesus was not the first to bring the two texts together, as we find the two obligations of love to God and love to one's neighbour already connected in Test. Iss. v. 2: 'But love the Lord and your neighbour'; also in vii. 6 and Test. Dan v. 3. It may be that the combination of the two texts was well known in Judaism in the time of Jesus. In any case the newness of Jesus' teaching lies not so much in the originality of his ideas as in the fact that in him the Law was actually being fulfilled.

32. This and the next three verses are peculiar to Mk. They preserve the tradition of the scribe's friendly attitude.

Καλῶς may be taken with εἶπες: 'Truly, Master, thou hast well said...', but is perhaps better taken by itself as an exclamation.

εἷς ἐστιν. Note the omission of the divine name, which is typically Jewish.

καὶ οὐκ ἔστιν ἄλλος πλὴν αὐτοῦ. Cf. Deut. iv. 35, Isa. xlv. 21, Exod. viii. 10.

33. The substitution of σύνεσις for διάνοια in *v.* 30 introduces a little variety, but makes no appreciable difference to the sense.

Ὁλοκαύτωμα and θυσία often occur together in the LXX. The word ὁλοκαύτωμα represents the Hebrew *'ōlāh* and denotes a sacrifice in which the flesh was not eaten, but the whole victim was burnt. Θυσία generally represents *zebaḥ*,

which is the ordinary word for a sacrifice in which the flesh
was eaten by the worshippers.

For the sentiment of this verse cf. I Sam. xv. 22, Hos. vi. 6.

34. αὐτόν. See on vii. 2 (ἰδόντες τινὰς . . . ὅτι . . . ἐσθίουσιν).

νουνεχῶς: 'discreetly'. It occurs only here in the N.T.
and never in the LXX, but is used by Aristotle, Polybius, etc.

The scribe's unreserved acknowledgement of the demands
of God's Law without any attempt at evasion or at self-
justification (contrast the lawyer in Lk. x. 29) indicated a
certain openness and humility before God. So Jesus
encourages him—

Οὐ μακρὰν εἶ ἀπὸ τῆς βασιλείας τοῦ Θεοῦ. A hint of the
secret of the kingdom of God, calculated no doubt to
stimulate reflection. Could the scribe but come to realize it,
he was indeed not far from the kingdom of God; for he was
actually in the presence of, and apparently already to some
extent drawn toward, him in whose person and activity that
kingdom had come near to men, the one who is himself the
αὐτοβασιλεία (see on i. 15).

καὶ οὐδεὶς οὐκέτι ἐτόλμα αὐτὸν ἐπερωτῆσαι. In Mt.
placed at the end of the next section (Mt. xxii. 46), in Lk. at
the end of the previous section (Lk. xx. 40).

70. DAVID'S SON—DAVID'S LORD (xii. 35-7a)
(Mt. xxii. 41-6; Lk. xx. 41-4)

The authenticity of this saying has often been denied.
Bultmann, for instance, explains it as either the product of
the primitive community, originating in the desire to meet
the reproach that Jesus' Davidic descent could not be
proved or in the opposition of some circles to the dogma of
Davidic sonship in the interests of the Son of Man doctrine,
or else the product of the Hellenistic community, originating
in the desire to prove that Jesus was more than David's son
—in fact, the Son of God.

A more probable explanation is that of R. P. Gagg, 'Jesus und die Davidssohnfrage' in *T.Z.* VII, pp. 18–30. He maintains that it is the end of a conflict-story, the earlier part of which has been lost. (See further below.)

35. διδάσκων ἐν τῷ ἱερῷ. Mark only vaguely indicates the time and circumstances, and does not say who Jesus' interlocutors were (contrast Mt. xxii. 41). Once again the fact that he refrains from filling in missing details from imagination is to be noted.

Πῶς λέγουσιν οἱ γραμματεῖς ὅτι ὁ Χριστὸς υἱὸς Δαυείδ ἐστιν; As the section stands, it appears as if Jesus introduced the subject on his own initiative. But it seems unlikely that he would have done so; for he would hardly have introduced it as a merely academic question, and that he introduced it with a clear reference to himself is even more unlikely. Moreover, it is most improbable that he would have attacked a doctrine so firmly based on scripture as that of the Davidic descent of the Messiah (e.g. Isa. ix. 2–7, xi. 1–9, Jer. xxiii. 5f., xxxiii. 14–18, Ezek. xxxiv. 23f., xxxvii. 24); had he done so, the fact would surely have been brought up against him (but of this there is no trace) and this doctrine would hardly have been so established an element of the Church's faith as it was (e.g. Rom. i. 3, II Tim. ii. 8). On the other hand, the unanimity of early Christian tradition about Jesus' Davidic descent makes it most unlikely that this saying is the creation of the early Church.

The best explanation seems to be that of R. P. Gagg, that the section is the remains of an original conflict-story, the opening question of which has been lost in the course of tradition. A question whether he taught that Messiah would be David's son could have been part of his opponents' attack (cf. xii. 13ff., xii. 18ff.). It could have been asked in the hope that it might lead Jesus into saying something which could be used to incriminate him with the Romans or else possibly something which could be used to discredit him in the eyes of the people. Jesus then replies, as in other conflict-stories, not with a direct answer, but with a counter-question. His purpose is not to impart teaching but to escape a trap by breaking off the conversation.

Πῶς... could be translated: 'What do the scribes mean when they say...' and καὶ πόθεν in v. 37: 'In what sense then...'; but it is probably better to translate: 'How can the scribes say...' and 'How then can he be his son?' Cf. ix. 12.

36. Δαυειδ. Jesus assumes the Davidic authorship of Ps. cx. In this he shared the belief of his contemporaries. That he should be mistaken on such a matter is no difficulty.

ἐν τῷ Πνεύματι τῷ Ἁγίῳ. Cf. Acts i. 16, xxviii. 25, II Tim. iii. 16, II Pet. i. 21.

The quotation follows the LXX of Ps. cx (LXX: cix). 1 closely, though ὑποκάτω is substituted for ὑποπόδιον and the article is omitted before Κύριος (the majority of MSS. do however have a text assimilated to the LXX). The first Κύριος stands for the Name of God (the Tetragrammaton), but τῷ Κυρίῳ μου (so the Bible Society, but better τῷ κυρίῳ μου) stands for Hebrew la'ḏōnî (='to my lord'). Ps. cx is either from the Maccabean period, referring perhaps to Simon Maccabaeus, or else from the early days of the monarchy. That Jesus himself (and also his contemporaries) understood it as messianic is clear from his use of it here. The absence of Rabbinic evidence of the messianic interpretation before the second half of the third century A.D. is perhaps to be explained (with S.-B.) as due to the influence of anti-Christian polemic, Ps. cx. 1 being much used by Christians (it is more often quoted or referred to in the N.T. than any other O.T. verse).

37 a. For λέγειν + double accusative (='call') cf. x. 18. The usage is also found in classical Greek (L. & S., s.v., III. 4). A father does not refer to his own son as 'lord'; it is more natural for the son to call his father 'lord' (e.g. Mt.

xxi. 29). If then the Messiah is David's son, there is something problematic in David's referring to him as his lord.
How then do the scribes explain this difficulty?

We take it then that Jesus' primary purpose in propound-
ing this problem was not to convey instruction but to break
off a dangerous conversation. At the same time the fact that
Jesus propounds *this* problem suggests that he was conscious
both that he was the Messiah and also that the designation
'Son of David'—though true so far as it went—was not
an adequate description of his person. So the early Church
was not without justification when it fastened on the
christological implication of Jesus' words rather than their
immediate practical purpose as the centre of interest in the
story; but when once this had been done, it was very easy
for the original question asked by Jesus' opponents to be
forgotten.

71. BEWARE OF THE SCRIBES! (xii. 37b–40)
(Lk. xx. 45–7; cf. Mt. xxiii and Lk. xi. 37–xii. 1)

A saying or sayings apparently taken from a sayings-
collection (cf. the passages cited above) and introduced here
for topical reasons.

37b. Better taken with what follows than with *vv.* 35–
37a—a general statement introducing *vv.* 38–40.

ὁ πολὺς ὄχλος. Possibly 'the great crowd', but more
probably 'the mass of the people' (so Moffatt) or 'the
common people' (A.V., R.V.). Cf. the examples given in
L. & S. under πολύς, II.3.b. The determinate ὁ ὄχλος πολύς
should probably be read in Jn xii. 9, 12. The indeterminate
ὄχλος πολύς and πολὺς ὄχλος of course occur often and mean
'a great crowd'.

38. Καὶ ἐν τῇ διδαχῇ αὐτοῦ ἔλεγεν introduces the following saying (or sayings). Cf. iv. 2.

If *v.* 37b is rightly joined with what follows, it is implied

that Jesus' words are addressed to the multitude as well as to
the disciples (cf. Mt. xxiii. 1: Lk. xx. 45 has τοῖς μαθηταῖς
but precedes it by ἀκούοντος παντὸς τοῦ λαοῦ).

Βλέπετε ἀπό. See on viii. 15.

θελόντων. Θέλειν is here used in the sense of 'like', as
it frequently is in the papyri. The use of the accusative
ἀσπασμούς, etc. after it as well as the infinitive περιπατεῖν is
awkward. Luke improves by adding φιλούντων before
ἀσπασμούς.

ἐν στολαῖς (στοαῖς 'cloisters' should hardly be read, *pace*
Lohmeyer) **περιπατεῖν.** The word στολή here must denote
the *ṭallîṭ* or cloak. The word *ṭallîṭ* was used both of the cloak
worn by ordinary people and also of the cloak that was the
insignia of the learned. It is of course this latter which is
referred to here. The *ṭallîṭ* of the learned was apparently
specially long and flowing. (See further S.–B. II, pp. 31-3.)

ἀσπασμούς. Deferential salutations are no doubt meant
(cf. Mt. xxiii. 7, which adds καὶ καλεῖσθαι ὑπὸ τῶν ἀνθρώπων
Ραββει).

39. The πρωτοκαθεδρία was the bench in front of the ark
(containing the scriptures) and facing the people. For
πρωτοκλισίας cf. Lk. xiv. 7-11. The four things mentioned
in *vv.* 38f. as liked by the scribes indicate their love of being
shown deference, of receiving the glory of men (cf. Jn v. 44,
xii. 43).

40. We can either (i) put a comma at the end of *v.* 39 and
a colon or perhaps a dash after προσευχόμενοι and explain οἱ
κατέσθοντες as loosely substituted for the more correct τῶν
κατεσθόντων; or (ii) put a full stop or colon at the end of *v.* 39
and a comma after προσευχόμενοι and explain the first part
of *v.* 40 as a *casus pendens* followed by resumptive οὗτοι. If
(i) is chosen, *vv.* 38b-40 must all be one saying; but, if (ii) is
followed, *vv.* 38b-39 and *v.* 40 may be explained as separate
sayings. While Lk. xx. 47 is support for (i), the absence of a
parallel to *v.* 40 in Lk. xi. 43 and the fact that Mt. xxiii. 14

should probably be omitted with ℵ B D, etc. (it is anyway separated from xxiii. 6f.) tell in favour of (ii).

οἱ κατέσθοντες τὰς οἰκίας τῶν χηρῶν. Probably by abusing the generosity shown to them. Cf. Josephus, *Ant.* XVII. 41–2.

προφάσει. The word properly means an 'alleged motive or cause', and is specially used of a motive or cause that is falsely alleged. So it comes to mean 'pretext', 'pretence'. For its use here cf. Phil. i. 18, where προφάσει is contrasted with ἀληθείᾳ. For the charge προφάσει μακρὰ προσευχόμενοι cf. Mt. vi. 5. Jesus accuses them of making use of prayer ostensibly addressed to God for the purpose of winning the esteem of men. Taylor comments truly: 'Hypocrisy...is the standing peril of religious leaders....' Their situation is more, not less, serious, if they have actually deceived themselves as well as others, so that the pretence is not consciously pretence.

περισσότερον κρίμα. Because as the religious leaders of the people of God they of all men ought to have known better. Cf. Jas. iii. 1.

72. NOT AS MAN SEETH (xii. 41–4)
(Lk. xxi. 1–4)

A pronouncement-story. Its connection with the Temple (and possibly the fact that it is about a widow—cf. *v.* 40) could account for its being placed here; but it is quite likely that the episode belongs here historically (cf. Lagrange).

Its authenticity has been denied on the grounds that Jesus could not have known that the widow had given her whole living and that there are parallels to the story in Jewish and other traditions. But without thinking of supernatural knowledge on the part of Jesus it is perfectly reasonable to suppose that he would have been able to sense the situation from her manner, and the fact that similar stories are told of

others is no proof that this narrative is not historical. Moreover, as Taylor notes, it 'is in harmony with His teaching
elsewhere (cf. ix. 41, Lk. xii. 15) and the use of ἀμὴν λέγω
ὑμῖν is characteristic'.

41. τοῦ γαζοφυλακίου. What exactly is meant is not
certain: possibly the thirteen trumpet-shaped receptacles
which, according to the Mishnah, were placed against the
wall of the Court of the Women, or the Treasury itself, or
perhaps we should think of a receptacle for gifts placed in
the Treasury but having an opening on the outside of the
Treasury. The first or the last of these suggestions would
seem to fit the narrative better than the second.

χαλκόν. Properly 'copper' or 'bronze', so 'copper
money', then 'money' quite generally, as here.

42. μία. For εἷς = τις see on v. 22.

λεπτά. Λεπτός means 'husked' or 'peeled', so 'fine',
'small'. The neuter was used as a noun to denote a very
small coin.

κοδράντης. A transliteration of the Latin *quadrans*, a
quarter of an *as*, which itself at this time was of very little
value. Mark's use of κοδράντης supports the view that he
was writing in the west, as the *quadrans* was not in circulation
in the east.[1]

43. προσκαλεσάμενος. See on iii. 13.

Ἀμήν. See on iii. 28.

πλεῖον πάντων just possibly means 'more than any of
those who...'; more probably 'more than all of those put
together who...'.

44. ὑστερήσεως. Used also in Phil. iv. 11 in the sense of
'want', 'need'.

βίον. Here used in the sense of 'livelihood', as often in
classical Greek. Cf. Lk. xv. 12, 30, I Jn iii. 17.

It is natural to assume that large gifts are of more value to
God than small ones (cf. x. 26!)—after all more can be done

[1] See W. M. Ramsay in *E.T.* x (1898-9), pp. 232, 336.

with them. But Jesus here calls in question this complacent assumption of conventional piety. (Cf. the somewhat similar significance of xiii. 1–2.) The gifts of the rich, though large, were easy gifts: the widow's gift, though tiny, meant a real surrender of herself to God and trust in him, and therefore an honouring of God *as God*, as the one to whom we belong wholly and who is able to care for us. Calvin comments well: 'In two ways this doctrine is useful, for the poor, who appear not to have the power of doing good, are encouraged by our Lord not to hesitate to express their affections cheerfully out of their slender means; for if they consecrate themselves, their offering, which appears to men to be worthless, will not be less valuable than if they had presented all the treasures of Croesus. On the other hand, those who possess greater abundance...are reminded that it is not enough if in the amount of their beneficence they greatly surpass the poor and common people; because it is of less value in the sight of God that a rich man, out of a vast heap, should bestow a moderate sum, than that a poor man, by giving very little, should exhaust his store.'

73. THE PREDICTION OF THE DESTRUCTION OF THE TEMPLE, AND THE DISCOURSE ON THE MOUNT OF OLIVES (xiii. 1–37)
(Mt. xxiv. 1–36; Lk. xxi. 5–36)

Since T. Colani's *Jésus-Christ et les Croyances Messianiques de son Temps* appeared in 1864, the 'Little Apocalypse' theory has been very widely accepted, though attempts to reconstruct the original apocalypse have varied considerably in detail. A. M. Hunter wrote in 1950: 'It is now, as Moffatt says, "a *sententia recepta* of synoptic criticism" that this chapter contains a Jewish Christian apocalypse....' Even those scholars who reject or drastically modify the theory tend to agree with its supporters that the chapter, as it stands, does not give a true picture of the eschatological teaching of Jesus. (For the history of the 'Little Apocalypse' theory see G. R. Beasley-Murray, 'The Rise and Fall of the Little Apocalypse Theory' in *E.T.* LXIV, pp. 346–9, and his *Jesus and the Future*, which is a very full discussion of Mk xiii, including a full bibliography.)

One of the main objections to the authenticity of the discourse (*vv.* 5–37) is its alleged inconsistency. It is asserted that the idea of a sudden Parousia cannot be reconciled with that of a Parousia heralded by signs and that therefore *v.* 32 is 'out of harmony with the trend of 5–31'.[1] In reply it may be suggested that this view rests on two very questionable assumptions. The first is the assumption that *vv.* 5–31 contain precisely that sort of 'apocalyptic speculation, with its emphasis on an orderly succession of events preceding the End'[2] that the saying in *v.* 32 was meant to discourage. But this discourse differs radically from typical Jewish apocalyptic. While the language of apocalyptic is indeed used, the purpose for which it is used and even the form of the discourse are different. While it is characteristic of Jewish apocalypses that the seer is himself addressed or else relates in the first person what he has seen and heard, this discourse is marked throughout by its use of the second person plural imperative.[3] It is in fact exhortation, not ordinary apocalyptic. Its purpose is not to impart esoteric information but to sustain faith and obedience.

The second questionable assumption is the assumption that we need not reckon here with the possibility of intentional paradox. But paradox is highly characteristic of the N.T. (see, e.g., II Cor. iv. 7–11, vi. 8–10). There is a tension between, on the one hand, the absolutely clear warning against trying to know the date of the End in *v.* 32, and, on the other hand, *vv.* 28 f. and all that is said about the signs

[1] Taylor, p. 523.   [2] Taylor, *ibid.*
[3] Cf. Beasley-Murray, *Jesus and the Future*, pp. 212 f.

of the End in *vv.* 5–23. But both elements must be taken seriously. To ignore the warning of *v.* 32 is to make shipwreck of faith. But it is an equally false way to take account only of the fact that we cannot know the 'when' and pay no heed to the signs of the End. To disregard the signs of the End as a mere relic of Jewish apocalypticism is to be in danger of reducing eschatology to something purely academic and of losing sight of its relevance to the present. For the signs are reminders in the midst of history of the coming Lord. Again, there is a similar tension between 'the end is not yet' (*v.* 7) and 'the gospel must first be preached unto all the nations' (*v.* 10), on the one hand, and 'when ye see these things coming to pass, know ye that he is nigh, even at the doors' (*v.* 29), on the other. Once more the two elements of the paradox must be held together, so that each may control, and help to interpret, the other. When this is done, it becomes possible to recognize that the N.T. insistence on the nearness of the End is not exactly the same thing as an insistence that it is going to occur within a few years.

The second main objection to the authenticity of *vv.* 5–37 is its alleged inconsistency with Jesus' teaching elsewhere. This has been stated with emphasis by T. W. Manson: '...the picture of the times of the end given in the Little Apocalypse does not square with the account given by our other sources, notably Q....The Q account of the Day of the Son of Man is totally different....These two pictures are irreconcilable.'[1] But the inconsistency he alleges is precisely the same as the alleged inconsistency inside Mk xiii— the supposed incompatibility of the idea of a sudden coming with that of one heralded by signs—and what has been said above applies here equally.

The third main objection is that the discourse is incongruous with its immediate context: the disciples ask about

[1] *Teaching*, pp. 261 f.

the date of the destruction of the Temple and Jesus in reply
talks about the end of the world. For a reply to this see
notes below (especially on *vv.* 4 and 14–20).

Our tentative conclusion is that xiii. 5–37 does give us
substantially our Lord's teaching. That does not mean that
we can be certain that throughout the discourse we have his
exact words. It is intrinsically likely that his words have
suffered some modification in the course of transmission here
as elsewhere in the gospels. Nor is it implied that it was
uttered as a single discourse. That it is composite, just as
iv. 1–34 apparently is, seems likely from the fact that some
of the sayings in it occur in Mt. and Lk. in other contexts.
What we are suggesting is that these verses consist, substantially at any rate, of authentic sayings of Jesus which have
been brought together not unintelligently, so that the resulting discourse does not misrepresent the mind of Jesus. We do
not think that they are a mixture of authentic sayings with
extraneous material of an alien spirit, or that the chapter as
a whole gives 'a wrong impression of His eschatological
teaching'.[1]

It may well be asked whether the disparagement of this
chapter by much recent scholarship has not resulted in a
serious impoverishment and weakening of the Church's life.
Its insistence on the signs is perhaps a help to faith and
obedience that we cannot afford to dispense with; for the
recognition that the events of history are signs of the End and
pointers to the coming Lord rescues eschatology from the
realm of merely academic discussion and makes it relevant
for faith and obedience. As our faith recognizes the signs as
they occur, we are again and again put in remembrance of
our Hope, and our gaze, that is so easily distracted from the
Lord who is coming to us, is again and again directed back
to him. The events of the present become for us reasons for
lifting up our heads (Lk. xxi. 28) and so many summonses to

[1] Manson, *Teaching*, p. 262.

renewed penitence, obedience and joy. There is a sober recognition of the signs which is something altogether different from the stupid illusion that they enable us to predict the date of the End. (See further Barth, *K.D.* III/2, pp. 560–   ∗
616; Cranfield, 'St Mark xiii' in *S.J.T.* VI, pp. 189–96, 287–303, and VII, pp. 284–303; Beasley-Murray, *Jesus and the Future* and *Mark xiii*; Kümmel, *P. and F.*; Taylor, pp. 498–524 and 636–44; and the very important, but to the present writer unconvincing, discussion of N.T. eschatology by J. A. T. Robinson, *Jesus and His Coming: The Emergence of a Doctrine* (London, 1957).)   †

1. ἐκπορευομένου αὐτοῦ ἐκ τοῦ ἱεροῦ. For the genitive absolute see on v. 2. We have to turn back to xi. 27 for a reference to his entering the Temple; but it does not follow, of course, that all narrated between must have occurred during one visit. The phrase is possibly, but not necessarily, an editorial link.

ἴδε ποταποὶ λίθοι καὶ ποταπαὶ οἰκοδομαί. Lagrange sees here the reaction of 'a man of the people, who is more impressed by the size of the materials used in a building than by the style'. For a description of the Temple see Josephus, *B.J.* v. 184–247 and also *Ant.* xv. 380–425. It is possible that Jesus had already uttered some word of judgement against the Temple (cf. Mt. xxiii. 38: in Mt. Jesus' lament over Jerusalem (xxiii. 37–9) is placed immediately before the parallel to this verse), and that the disciple's words were meant as a rebuke.

2. Βλέπεις ταύτας τὰς μεγάλας οἰκοδομάς. The words are patient of various interpretations according to the weight we put on βλέπεις and the punctuation we put after οἰκο-δομάς. (i) If βλέπεις is not stressed, then (whether we read the words as question or statement) they are simply the equivalent of a gesture pointing to the Temple. But, if it is stressed, then the meaning could be either (ii) 'You see these great buildings [now; but the time is coming when] there shall

not...', or (iii) 'You are gazing at (i.e. letting your attention be occupied by) these great buildings; [but you should not, for] there shall not...'. In either case a question could be substituted for the statement without making much difference to the sense. Perhaps, in spite of the Mt. parallel, (iii) is the most probable, in view of *v.* 1.

οὐ μὴ ἀφεθῇ λίθος ἐπὶ λίθον ὃς οὐ μὴ καταλυθῇ. That Jesus did predict the destruction of the Temple is hardly to be doubted: cf. xiv. 58, xv. 29, Jn ii. 19, Mt. xxiii. 38. In so doing he was following in the steps of the prophets (cf. Jer. vii. 1–15, xxvi. 1–24, Mic. iii. 10–12). With regard to the significance of this prediction the following points may be suggested:

(i) Jesus, though he affirmed the real sanctity of the Temple (cf. xi. 15–17), as Schrenk rightly insists,[1] recognized nevertheless that it belonged to the old order that was even then being superseded. 'It is because "One greater than the Temple is here" (Mt. xii. 6), because He Himself is the Lord who is coming in His kingdom, that Jesus pronounces the downfall of the Temple.... The announcement of the destruction of the Temple is directly connected with the advent of the kingdom of God....'[2] The sacrificial system was being at once fulfilled and abrogated by Jesus. The sacrifices would no longer have any *raison d'être* when once the Sacrifice to which they had pointed had been offered.

(ii) It was not merely that the Temple would soon be obsolete; it had actually proved a stumbling-block. The people of Israel had imagined that God could not do without his Temple and that therefore they could sin in security; and now their sin was approaching its climax.

(iii) It was actually proving a stumbling-block to the disciples—they were apparently too much impressed by its size and beauty. 'As the vast size and wealth of the Temple',

[1] In *T.W.N.T.* iii, pp. 241–5.
[2] Roux, *L'Évang. du Royaume*, pp. 279 f.

says Calvin, 'like a veil hung before the eyes of the disciples, did not permit them to elevate their faith to the true reign of Christ, which was still future, so he affirms...that those things which occupy their attention will quickly perish.'

(iv) There is no reason to doubt that Jesus could also on the level of political insight see that, if his countrymen continued in their present mood, they would sooner or later bring on themselves the wrath of Rome.

3. καθημένου αὐτοῦ εἰς τὸ ὄρος τῶν Ἐλαιῶν. Between *vv.* 1f. and 3f. there is a change of scene. If Jesus was returning to Bethany (cf. xi. 11), his way would naturally be over the Mount of Olives.

κατέναντι τοῦ ἱεροῦ draws attention to the fact that the spot where the ensuing conversation took place commanded a view of the Temple across the Kedron valley. It was from the Mount of Olives that the full grandeur of the Temple could best be seen.

ἐπηρώτα αὐτὸν κατ' ἰδίαν. Cf. iv. 10, vii. 17, ix. 28, x. 10.

καὶ Ἀνδρέας. Andrew is not mentioned after his brother Peter, but at the end of the list, because the other three are closely associated together on other occasions.

4. The first ταῦτα must refer to the destruction of the Temple. Grammatically the second ταῦτα should have the same meaning. Taylor says: 'as the chapter now stands, ταῦτα πάντα appears to point forwards, and it is in this sense that it is commonly interpreted'; in other words, Mark has joined together things that did not originally belong together and so has made it natural for his readers to take the second ταῦτα to refer to what he has placed immediately after it. But Lagrange provides a better clue: 'After what precedes, [the second] ταῦτα can only mean the destruction of the Temple, but that cannot be (this goes without saying) an isolated event....' That it would be natural for the disciples to assume that the destruction of the Temple would be part of a complex of events leading to the End is likely (see Schrenk in *T.W.N.T.* III, pp. 238 ff.). So we take it that Mt. here gives the sense of Mk correctly. The disciples, excited and disturbed by Jesus' prediction, want to know when the Temple is to be destroyed and what is the sign by which they may know that the final consummation is approaching. Their question is one that pervades all biblical and extra-biblical apocalyptic. They want to be told what will be 'the sign'—that is, they want an infallible means of recognizing the approach of the End; they want in fact to be relieved from having to 'watch'. But instead of a single sign Jesus gives them a baffling multiplicity of signs. The purpose of his reply is not to impart esoteric information but to strengthen and sustain faith.

5–23. Jesus' answer, which takes up the rest of the chapter, falls into three divisions. Of these the first is *vv.* 5–23. We might call it *The End is not yet*; for Jesus is certainly warning his disciples that much has still to happen before the consummation of all things. They were, apparently, like people who 'wish to reap the harvest before the season arrives', inclined to 'confound the perfection of Christ's reign with the commencement of it' (Calvin). So they needed to be warned that 'the end is not yet' (*v.* 7) and that they must resist the deceivers who would be only too ready to play on their impatience. Or we might with equal fairness entitle this section *The Characteristics of the Last Times*, i.e., of the time between the Incarnation and the Parousia; for that is what we have here. Jesus warns his disciples what they are to expect during the time before the End. Or again, we might call it *The Signs of the End*; for these characteristic marks of the time before the End are also signs which point to the End. Though not to be mistaken for the End, they are nevertheless eloquent of it.

5. The first of these signs of the End is the presence of deceivers. Throughout the last times the disciples of Jesus will be liable to be led astray. So they must be on their guard.

6. The first part of the verse defines more closely the nature of this peril. The Greek is probably best taken to mean: 'Many shall come arrogating to themselves the name and prerogatives of Messiah, which by right are mine, and claiming to be Messiah.'

ἐπὶ τῷ ὀνόματί μου most naturally means (i) 'appealing to me as their authority', 'claiming to be sent by me', but it can also mean (ii) 'arrogating to themselves the title of Messiah which by right belongs to me'. According to (i) the many are false teachers claiming to speak in Jesus' name; according to (ii) they are false claimants to the Messiahship. The words λέγοντες ὅτι Ἐγώ εἰμι are also ambiguous. They could mean (a) 'saying, "I am"'—i.e. claiming to be Messiah (cf. Jn iv. 26 and the Mt. addition of ὁ Χριστός here), with possibly also the idea of claiming divine authority (cf. Exod. iii. 14; Deut. xxxii. 39; Isa. xli. 4, xliii. 10); (b) 'saying, "It is I"'—similar to above, but stress on idea of the Messiah's presence; (c) 'saying that it is I'—i.e. saying that I (Jesus) am come, or as W. Manson puts it, 'the Christ is come, the Parousia has arrived' ('The ΕΓΩ ΕΙΜΙ of the Messianic Presence in the New Testament' in *J.T.S.* XLVIII, pp. 137–45). Manson appeals to II Thess. ii. 2 for support; (d) 'saying that I (Jesus) am (the Christ)'—ruled out, because to say this would not be deceiving; (e) 'saying that it is I'—in the sense that the false ones will claim actually to be Jesus. Manson's combination of (i) and (c) should probably be rejected on the ground of the doubtful possibility of (c) and the presence of the Mt. gloss, ὁ Χριστός. Lohmeyer combines (i) and (a), explaining the words as meaning that the deceivers will preach themselves under cover of preaching Christ—an attractive suggestion but probably not as likely as the combination (ii) and (a). Taylor's conclusion 'that ἐπὶ τῷ ὀνόματί μου is a "Christian" addition to a Jewish or Jewish-Christian source' seems unnecessary.

7. The second characteristic of the last times is sufferings; and this and the next verse deal with sufferings common to all men. When the disciples hear news of war or of the threat of war, they are not to be inwardly disturbed; for these things fall within the eschatological purpose of God, a purpose which includes judgement as well as salvation. The phrase δεῖ γενέσθαι is characteristic of apocalyptic (cf. Dan. ii. 28, 29, 45, Rev. i. 1, iv. 1, xxii. 6). For δεῖ see on viii. 31.

ἀλλ' οὔπω τὸ τέλος. These things do not constitute a sign that the End is just round the corner; and the disciples of Jesus are warned against giving heed to sensational rumours that the Parousia is upon them. Christ wished, says Calvin, 'to restrain the apostles, who were disposed to fly with excessive eagerness to the possession of the heavenly glory, and to show them the necessity of patience'. These words must be set alongside those other N.T. passages which point to the nearness of the End. We then see the paradoxical nature of the N.T. expectation.

8. ἀρχὴ ὠδίνων ταῦτα. ἀρχή implies that there is plenty more to follow and that the sufferings will get worse—these things are only the beginning. But ὠδίνων points forward. Though these things do not mean that the End is come, they do point to it and are a pledge of it. To the eye of faith they are full of promise. 'To understand aright the significance of the metaphor, one must remember what motherhood meant for the Jewish woman. Without it her life was robbed of its goal and substance. The beginning of travail marked the end of the disgrace that rested on the childless woman, the approaching fulfilment of her strongest desire. It begins with grievous pains, but these pains are to her the promise of that for which she has waited with longing. Even so do the sufferings that come upon the disciples point to the end of the disgrace, which at present rests on them, through the fulfilment of the hope which gives their life its meaning.'[1]

[1] Schlatter, *Evang. Matt.* p. 699.

The Rabbinic expression 'the birth-pangs of the Messiah' (meaning not the sufferings of the Messiah but the sufferings expected to precede his coming) was probably already current in the time of Jesus (cf. S.-B. I, p. 950). The origin of the expression is perhaps to be seen in such passages as Isa. xxvi. 17, lxvi. 8, Jer. xxii. 23, Hos. xiii. 13, Mic. iv. 9f. For the use of the image in the N.T. cf. Jn xvi. 21, I Thess. v. 3, the first of which well illustrates the meaning here.

9. Βλέπετε...ὑμεῖς ἑαυτούς. For βλέπειν (in the sense of 'take heed') followed by the accusative cf. II Jn 8, though there it is followed by ἵνα μή + the subjunctive. The sufferings referred to in *vv.* 9–13 are sufferings peculiar to disciples—persecutions.

εἰς συναγωγάς is better taken with δαρήσεσθε (the εἰς being equivalent to ἐν) than with παραδώσουσιν.

The disciples of Jesus, regarded by their fellow-Jews as apostates, will be brought before the councils of synagogues and subjected to the public scourging that was the synagogue punishment for the disobedient and heretical; they will also have to appear on trial before governors and kings.

εἰς μαρτύριον αὐτοῖς. According to Strathmann (*T.W.N.T.* IV, pp. 477–520) εἰς μαρτύριον + dative here and in Mt. x. 18, xxiv. 14 means not 'for a witness to' (i.e. so that they may be given an opportunity to believe) but 'for an evidence against' (i.e. the fact that the disciples have been condemned by them will be an incriminating evidence against them at the Judgement). But it is surely better to allow for the various ideas which are involved in the witness-imagery rather than to insist on choosing between 'witness to' and 'evidence against'. We suggest that the meaning here is threefold: first, that the disciples' profession of Christ before the tribunals of governors and kings will be a piece of evidence for the truth of the gospel (cf. Calvin: '...Christ means that His gospel will be so much the more

397

fully attested, when they have defended it at the risk of their lives...their unshaken constancy...was...an authentic seal of the gospel...'); secondly, it will be a piece of evidence for the truth of the gospel offered to their persecutors (αὐτοῖς probably including both the governors and kings, who otherwise might not have heard the gospel, and also the disciples' Jewish persecutors); and thirdly, if the evidence for the truth of the gospel which this courageous profession of Christ's name presents is not accepted by the persecutors and judges, then at the final judgement it will be evidence against them (they will be without excuse, having witnessed such evidence for the truth of the gospel—and perhaps also because of the suffering they inflicted on the disciples).

10. Some MSS. connect καὶ εἰς πάντα τὰ ἔθνη with v. 9 (most of them inserting δέ after πρῶτον), and there is some support for this punctuation among the ancient versions. Kilpatrick[1] adduces in favour of it the fact that in Mk xiii the normal position for the verb is at the beginning of the clause (his actual figures are: forty-eight times at the beginning, sixteen in the middle, and nineteen at the end),[2] and proposes a punctuation of xiii. 9–10 according to which the words δαρήσεσθε, σταθήσεσθε, and δεῖ or πρῶτον (the Byzantine text has δεῖ before πρῶτον) introduce new clauses, and a comma is placed at the end of v. 10. But, as on Kilpatrick's figures there are thirty-five occasions in Mk xiii when the verb is not at the beginning of a clause, this argument is by no means conclusive. In view of the fact that πρῶτον δεῖ κηρυχθῆναι τὸ εὐαγγέλιον seems pointless in this context unless it is in some way qualified, it seems more probable that καὶ εἰς πάντα τὰ ἔθνη should be taken with what follows.

The words εἰς πάντα τὰ ἔθνη are perhaps more probably to

---

[1] 'Gentile Mission', pp. 149–53.
[2] He explains that he leaves vv. 9–10 out of account, and ignores introductory particles and adverbs and negatives which come before the verb, and also some v.ll. which affect the order of words.

be explained as indicating the *extent* of the preaching ($\epsilon\dot{\iota}s$ = 'unto', i.e. 'as far as') or else as meaning 'among all the nations' ($\epsilon\dot{\iota}s$ being used instead of $\dot{\epsilon}v$) than as an instance of $\kappa\eta\rho\acute{\upsilon}\sigma\sigma\epsilon\iota v$ $\epsilon\dot{\iota}s$ + the accusative meaning 'to preach to someone'.[1]

πρῶτον: i.e. before the End.

δεῖ. See on viii. 31.

κηρυχθῆναι. It has been suggested by Lohmeyer that the reference is not to missionary preaching but to an apocalyptic proclamation from heaven (cf. Rev. xiv. 6f.). But of the eleven other occurrences of $\kappa\eta\rho\acute{\upsilon}\sigma\sigma\epsilon\iota v$ in Mk (not counting the two in xvi. 9–20) two refer to the Baptist's preaching, three to Jesus' preaching, two to the preaching of the apostles during Jesus' ministry, and three to healed persons spreading the news of what Jesus had done for them. The remaining occurrence (xiv. 9) would support Lohmeyer's suggestion, if Jeremias' interpretation of it ('The Gentile World in the Thought of Jesus' in *B.S.N.T.S.* iii, pp. 21f.) were accepted, but see notes *in loc*. It seems more probable that $\kappa\eta\rho\acute{\upsilon}\sigma\sigma\epsilon\iota v$ here and also in xiv. 9 has its characteristic N.T. sense, and that the meaning of this verse is that it is part of God's eschatological purpose that before the End all nations shall have an opportunity to accept the gospel. The interval is the time of God's patience during which men are summoned to repentance and faith; it has for its content the Church's mission to the world. That does not mean that the world will necessarily get steadily more Christian or that the End will not come till all men are converted. It is a promise that the gospel will be preached, not that it will necessarily be believed. The disciples' witness is another characteristic of the last times.

That *v.* 10 is an insertion between *vv.* 9 and 11 is likely: it is parenthetic, *vv.* 9 and 11 being connected by thought and

[1] Of this there seems to be no absolutely clear example in the N.T. (Cf. Kilpatrick, 'Gentile Mission', pp. 146–9.)

by the repetition of παραδώσουσιν, παραδιδόντες. In Mt. the parallel has been placed a little later (xxiv. 14). But, while the possibility of its being an interpretative gloss by Mark may be allowed, the objections to its authenticity are inconclusive. Taylor argues that 'the problem faced by the primitive Church over the question of the evangelization of the Gentiles' would be difficult to explain on the assumption that so explicit a saying of Jesus was known; but the difference of opinion in the early Church was surely not so much about whether the Gentiles should be evangelized as about whether it was necessary for those of them who would be Christians to adhere to Judaism. The idea of a universal mission to the Gentiles may be traced back to the O.T. (e.g. Isa. xlii. 6, xlix. 6, 12, Ps. xcvi).

11. In their hour of need God (the passive is used to avoid mention of the Divine Name) will give them the word to speak (cf. Exod. iv. 12, Jer. i. 9).

On the question whether *v.* 11 b with its reference to the Holy Spirit is original or secondary see further Barrett, *H.S.G.T.* pp. 131f., and Taylor, pp. 508f. *Pace* Barrett, it seems likely that Lk. xxi. 15 is less primitive than Mk xiii. 11 b, Mt. x. 20, Lk. xii. 12; for the first person singular (ἐγὼ δώσω) suggests the post-Ascension faith of the Church, the relative clause (ᾗ οὐ…ὑμῖν) looks like Christian heightening (cf. Acts vi. 10, and also iv. 13, vi. 15, etc.), and the phrase διδόναι στόμα καὶ σοφίαν is at least as likely to be an instance of Luke's LXX colour (cf. Exod. iv. 11, Ezek. xxix. 21) as it is to reflect the original Aramaic saying. With 11 b cf. the use of παράκλητος of the Holy Spirit in Jn xiv. 16, 26, xv. 26, xvi. 7.

12. One of the hardest things disciples will have to face will be the breaking of the ties of natural affection. Such delivering up of kinsmen may be motivated by a fanatical hatred of the gospel or by a craven hope of saving oneself by betraying others or even by a sordid hope of gain.

θανατώσουσιν αὐτούς: 'will deliver them to death', 'bring about their death', rather than 'kill them'.

With this verse cf. Mt. x. 35f. = Lk. xii. 52f.; also Mic. vii. 6, IV Ezra v. 9, vi. 24.

13. καὶ ἔσεσθε μισούμενοι ὑπὸ πάντων διὰ τὸ ὄνομά μου. In addition to the parallels (Mt. xxiv. 9, Lk. xxi. 17) cf. Mt. x. 22; also Mt. v. 11, Jn xv. 18–20, I Jn iii. 13. Suggestive is W. Temple's comment on Jn xv. 18: 'Not all that the world hates is good Christianity; but it does hate good Christianity and always will.'[1]

ὁ δὲ ὑπομείνας εἰς τέλος, οὗτος σωθήσεται. The sufferings mentioned in *vv.* 9–13a (and also those referred to in *vv.* 7f. and the seducings referred to in *vv.* 5f.) will be a testing of the disciples. Testing is yet another characteristic of the last times.

εἰς τέλος here means not 'to the End' (τέλος does not mean the same as τὸ τέλος in *v.* 7), but 'to the end', 'right through', 'completely' (cf. Jn xiii. 1, I Thess. ii. 16, II Chron. xxxi. 1).

σωθήσεται. The verb is here used of final salvation, as in x. 26.

14–20. The disciples' question in *v.* 4 (if we understood it correctly) connected together two things—the destruction of the Temple and the End of all things. They were apparently thinking of the former as immediately preceding and heralding the latter. That Jesus refers to the End in *vv.* 24–7 is clear, and also that in *vv.* 5–8 he distinguishes between the End and various historical events. But what of *vv.* 14–20? Do they refer to an eschatological, or to an ordinary historical, event, or are the historical and eschatological here mingled together? Lk. xxi. 20–4 might encourage us to take these verses to refer simply to an approaching historical catastrophe; for Luke, writing after the events of A.D. 66–70, clearly regards them as a fulfilment of Jesus' words. Moreover, it can certainly be argued that, while there is nothing

[1] *Readings in St John's Gospel* (London, 1945), pp. 271f.

in *vv.* 14–20 that is absolutely incompatible with the reference to an approaching war, there is much here that fits such a reference well. On the other hand, II Thess. ii. 3–10 strongly supports the identification of 'the abomination of desolation' with Antichrist, and the curious masculine ἑστηκότα is perhaps further support for this interpretation, and *vv.* 19f. appear to be eschatological. It seems then that neither an exclusively historical nor an exclusively eschatological interpretation is satisfactory, and that we must allow for a double reference, for a mingling of historical and eschatological. Is Jesus then identifying an approaching historical event, a disaster threatening the Temple and Jerusalem, with the immediate prelude to the End? While the approaching disaster is being deliberately brought into relation to the End, there is also discernible a certain restraint, which leaves room for the possibility that the impending ruin of Jerusalem may be followed by other crises before the End comes.

14. τὸ βδέλυγμα τῆς ἐρημώσεως occurs in the LXX version of Dan. xii. 11, where it represents Hebrew *šikkûṣ šōmēm* (cf. Dan. ix. 27, xi. 31, I Macc. i. 54). The basic idea in *šikkûṣ* is that of being detestable to, and rejected by, God: it is particularly used of heathen gods and articles connected with them. The significance of the Hebrew participle *šōmēm* (rendered by τῆς ἐρημώσεως) is that the abominable thing causes the Temple to be deserted, the pious avoiding the Temple on its account. That in Dan. xii. 11 the reference is to the heathen altar set up by Antiochus Epiphanes over the altar of burnt-offering in the Temple in 168 B.C. is generally agreed (cf. I Macc. i. 54, 59, vi. 7). Jesus' use of the phrase implies that for him the meaning of the prophecy was not exhausted by the events of the Maccabean times; it still had a future reference. The Temple of God must yet suffer a fearful profanation by which its whole glory will perish.

ἑστηκότα. The masculine suggests that what is meant by βδέλυγμα is no mere idolatrous object but Antichrist himself.

ὅπου οὐ δεῖ. Mark's mysterious phrase is no doubt correctly glossed by Mt. xxiv. 15, ἐν τόπῳ ἁγίῳ.

ὁ ἀναγινώσκων νοείτω. The words have often been regarded as evidence that Mark was using a written apocalypse and not a tradition of Jesus' spoken words; but they more probably refer, not to the reading of the alleged apocalypse, but to the reading of Dan., and might possibly be Jesus' words but are more probably an insertion by Mark.

τότε οἱ ἐν τῇ Ἰουδαίᾳ φευγέτωσαν εἰς τὰ ὄρη. The words suggest a reference to a state of war, the mountainous regions being obvious places of refuge (cf. Gen. xiv. 10, I Kgs xxii. 17, Jer. xvi. 16, Nah. iii. 18, Zech. xiv. 5, Heb. xi. 38).

15f. These verses vividly depict the need for haste—not a moment is to be lost.

δώματος: i.e. the flat roof of a house (cf. I Sam. ix. 25, Jer. xix. 13, Acts x. 9).

μὴ καταβάτω goes closely with the following words. The man on the roof must of course descend in order to flee, but he is not to do so in order to enter his house. The roof would be reached by an outside staircase. The words εἰς τὴν οἰκίαν should possibly be read after καταβάτω with A D W Θ ς, though redundant.

ἱμάτιον. The outer garment that would not be required for work in the field, but would be highly desirable at night.

17. Cf. Lk. xxiii. 29.

18. χειμῶνος. When the heavy rains would have made the wadis difficult to cross.

19. ἔσονται...τοῦ νῦν. For the language cf. Dan. xii. 1; also Jer. xxx. 7, I Macc. ix. 27, Assumpt. Mos. viii. 1. The thought that the judgement of the people of God will be far more severe than that of the heathen (cf. Lk. xii. 48?) is perhaps present; but it seems likely that the thought here is eschatological, the final tribulation of history being in view. This is confirmed by the following words, καὶ οὐ μὴ γένηται. For the characteristically Semitic redundancy of ἣν ἔκτισεν ὁ Θεός cf. οὓς ἐξελέξατο in the next verse.

20. οὐκ...πᾶσα σάρξ. Two Semitic idioms are here combined: οὐ...πᾶς (cf. Hebrew *lō'*...*kol*) = 'no', 'no one', and πᾶσα σάρξ (cf. Hebrew *kol-bāśār*) = 'all men'.

ἀλλὰ διὰ τοὺς ἐκλεκτοὺς οὓς ἐξελέξατο ἐκολόβωσεν τὰς ἡμέρας. For the general idea of God curtailing afflictions for the sake of his chosen we might perhaps compare such passages as II Sam. xxiv. 16, Isa. lxv. 8. A few Rabbinic passages are cited by S.–B. I, p. 953. But the passages cited by Taylor, p. 514, hardly justify his reference to the idea 'that in His mercy and for the sake of the elect God has shortened the period of tribulation for mankind' as something 'found in many apocalyptic writings': they are not close parallels.

To sum up on *vv.* 14–20: Luke rightly recognized in the events of the years 66–70 a fulfilment of Jesus' words, but it was not a fulfilment without remainder. Antichrist was indeed present in the fierce nationalism of the Jews and the pride of Rome, and thus incarnate stood 'where he ought not'. But there was more to come. The new Israel like the old would be sinful and would again and again be menaced by divine judgement, and Antichrist would again and again embody himself in proud and sacrilegious men. Thus in the crises of history the eschatological is foreshadowed. The divine judgements in history are, so to speak, rehearsals of the last judgement, and the successive incarnations of Antichrist are foreshadowings of the last supreme concentration of the rebelliousness of the devil before the End. So for us the fulfilment of these verses is past, present and future, and they are rightly included under the heading 'Signs of the End' or 'Characteristics of the Last Times'. The key to their understanding is the recognition that there is here a double reference. The impending judgement on Jerusalem and the events connected with it are for Jesus as it were a transparent object in the foreground through which he sees the last events before the End, which they indeed foreshadow.[1]

21–3. Cf. *vv.* 5f., of which they are possibly but not necessarily a variant. Both the last supreme effort of the power of evil and also the various historical crises which foreshadow that final convulsion will be marked by the presence and activity of false messiahs and false prophets. One characteristic of these is specially mentioned. Unlike the true Messiah (see viii. 11f., xv. 32, Mt. iv. 5–7, xii. 39) they will not be at all reluctant to show signs and wonders. They will exploit to the full the natural craving of the disciples to escape from the painful paradoxes and tensions and indirectness of faith into the comfortable security of sight.

προείρηκα ὑμῖν πάντα is not necessarily a claim to have provided the disciples with a detailed map of the future (so an apocalyptic element): it may well mean simply: 'You have been adequately warned!'

24–7. The second part of Jesus' answer.

Verses 24f. speak of cosmic signs immediately heralding the Parousia. The ideas and language are derived from the O.T.

ἐν ἐκείναις ταῖς ἡμέραις. An O.T. stereotyped expression with eschatological associations (cf. Jer. iii. 16, 18, xxxi. 29, xxxiii. 15f., Joel iii. 1, Zech. viii. 23, etc.).

The words τὴν θλῖψιν ἐκείνην are perhaps best explained (with Calvin) as a 'general recapitulation of all the evils of which Christ had previously spoken': before the occurrence of these celestial signs the Church will have passed through the 'whole course of its tribulations'.

ὁ ἥλιος...σαλευθήσονται. Cf. Isa. xiii. 10, xxxiv. 4;

[1] Cf. K. Heim, *Die Königsherrschaft Gottes* (Stuttgart, 1948), pp. 55f.

also Isa. xxiv. 23, Joel ii. 30 f., iii. 15, Amos viii. 9, Ezek. xxxii. 7 f., Enoch lxxx. 2 ff., cii. 2, IV Ezra iv. 51 ff., etc. That this is picture-language which we must not seek to compress into a literal interpretation should go without saying.

26 f. These verses speak of the Parousia itself and the gathering of the elect.

τότε. The final eschatological 'then'—the End itself as opposed to the signs of the End.

ὄψονται. All men, not just disciples, are presumably included in this indefinite plural. It will be the end of that painful not-seeing which distinguishes the life of disciples during the time between the Ascension and the Parousia, throughout which they have to 'walk by faith, not by sight' (II Cor. v. 7); and the end of the veiledness which is the mark both of our Lord's earthly life and of the life of the Church.

τὸν Υἱὸν τοῦ ἀνθρώπου ἐρχόμενον ἐν νεφέλαις μετὰ δυνάμεως πολλῆς καὶ δόξης. The End-event will be the coming in glory of him 'who at that time was living on earth in the garb of a despised servant' (Calvin), the manifestation of that Kingship of Christ which from the time of his exaltation has all along been a reality. (Cf. viii. 38, xiv. 62.)

As in the two previous verses Jesus uses O.T. language. Cf. Dan. vii. 13 f. 'The description of the Parousia consists almost entirely of scriptural words. Jesus did not create His own images for the moment, in which He will manifest Himself to the world in the glory of God. He based the hopes of the disciples simply on the prophetic words, just as He strengthened Himself in the face of His cross by the realisation that Scripture connected together suffering and the divine commission' (Schlatter, on the Mt. parallel).[1]

With *v.* 27 cf. Deut. xxx. 3 f., Jer. xxxii. 37, Ezek. xxxiv. 13, xxxvi. 24, Zech. ii. 6. That *how* the elect will be gathered

[1] *Evang. Matt.* p. 710.

should be quite beyond our comprehension is not surprising: in fact, an event which we could neatly explain could hardly be *the* End. On the angels see xvi. 5. Eloquent and moving is Calvin's comment: 'Whenever, therefore, we perceive the Church scattered by the wiles of Satan, or torn in pieces by the cruelty of the ungodly, or disturbed by false doctrines, or tossed about by storms, let us learn to turn our eyes to this *gathering of the elect.* And if it appears to us a thing difficult to be believed, let us call to remembrance the power of *the angels*, which Christ holds out to us for the express purpose of raising our views above human means. For, though the Church be now tormented by the malice of men, or even broken by the violence of the billows, and miserably torn in pieces, so as to have no stability in the world, yet we ought always to cherish confident hope, because it will not be by human means, but by heavenly power, which will be far superior to every obstacle, that the Lord will *gather* his Church.'

28–37. The third part of Jesus' answer, to which we may give the general title *Watch therefore!*, falls naturally into three parts (*vv.* 28f., 30–2, 33–7) marked off by μάθετε, αμην λέγω ὑμῖν, and βλέπετε.

28. ἐκφύῃ. Better so accentuated (present subjunctive active) than ἐκφυῇ (second aorist subjunctive passive), since there is no reason to suppose a change of subject.

29. Strictly the reference of ταῦτα should include the coming of the Son of Man mentioned in *v.* 26; but, as the sense would then be, 'When you see the Son of Man coming, know that he is at hand', which would be pointless, it is better to take it to refer to the signs of the End described in *vv.* 5–23. (To take it to refer to the celestial signs of *vv.* 24f. would be no easier, as what was last mentioned would still not be included. Moreover, it is better to regard *vv.* 24–7 as describing a single event than a series of events.) It is unnecessary to conclude that *vv.* 28f. or 24–7 are out of their original context; for such a looseness of structure as is involved, if we take ταῦτα to refer to the signs of *vv.* 5–23, is natural enough, and something like *v.* 26 is actually needed here to provide a subject for ἐστιν in *v.* 29. We take the meaning of *vv.* 28f. to be that, when the disciples see the various things coming to pass that have been described in *vv.* 5–23, they are to know (γινώσκετε in *v.* 29 is better taken as imperative) that the Parousia is imminent.

This brings us up against the problem posed by the N.T. insistence on the nearness of the End (with this verse cf. Rom. xiii. 12, I Cor. vii. 29, Phil. iv. 5, Heb. x. 25, Jas v. 8f., I Pet. iv. 7, I Jn ii. 18, Rev. xxii. 20). Are we to say (with Dodd, Glasson, Taylor, *et al.*) that the primitive Church read into Jesus' teaching apocalyptic ideas that were alien to it? Or (with Schweitzer, Werner, T. W. Manson, Barrett, *et al.*) that Jesus was himself mistaken? Or is the solution to be found in a more theological understanding of what is meant by the nearness of the End? The paradoxical nature of the N.T. material (e.g. Mark can include *vv.* 7, 29, and 32 in one discourse) invites us to explore in this last direction. If we realize that the Incarnation–Crucifixion– Resurrection–Ascension, on the one hand, and the Parousia, on the other, belong essentially together and are in a real sense one Event, one divine Act, being held apart only by the mercy of God who desires to give men opportunity for faith and repentance, then we can see that in a very real sense the latter is always imminent now that the former has happened. It was, and still is, true to say that the Parousia is at hand—and indeed this, so far from being an embarrass- ing mistake on the part either of Jesus or of the early Church, is an essential part of the Church's faith. Ever † since the Incarnation men have been living in the last days.

30. Cf. on ix. 1. At first sight Jesus seems here to be saying that all the things described in *vv.* 5–27 (including his

Parousia) will come to pass before his contemporaries have all died. But this is not the only possible meaning. First may be mentioned four other possible meanings of ἡ γενεὰ αὕτη which have been suggested: (i) mankind in general; (ii) the Jewish people (both these go back as far as Jerome: the latter is accepted by a number of moderns, including Schniewind); (iii) disciples, Christians (so Chrysostom, Victor of Antioch and Theophylact); (iv) in a more general sense, 'this sort' (favoured by Michaelis,[1] who takes the meaning to be that there will be unbelievers till the end). There are also other ways of understanding ταῦτα πάντα: (v) some take the reference to be to the destruction of the Temple (so Bengel, Lagrange: Taylor thinks this was the original reference, though not the reference of the saying in its present context); (vi) Cullmann,[2] Barth,[3] Lightfoot[4] see a possible reference to Christ's Passion and Resurrection; (vii) ταῦτα πάντα can refer to the signs of the End in vv. 5–23 (cf. on ταῦτα in v. 29). The best explanation seems to be (vii). The meaning then is that the signs of the End which Jesus has described in vv. 5–23 will not be confined to a remote future: his hearers must themselves experience them, for they are characteristic of the whole period of the Last Times.

31. Cf. Ps. cii. 25–7, Isa. xl. 6–8, li. 6, which set God, his salvation, righteousness, word, over against created things. Here Jesus sets his words on God's side of this contrast. Judaism asserted the eternity of the Law (e.g. Ps. cxix. 160, Bar. iv. 1, Wisd. xviii. 4, IV Ezra ix. 36f., j Sanh. 2.20c (quoted in S.–B. 1, p. 244)). Cf. Mt. v. 18; but this only says of the Law that it will remain inviolate till heaven and earth pass away, while Mk xiii. 31 declares that Jesus' words unlike heaven and earth will never pass away.

---

[1] *Verheissung*, pp. 32f.
[2] *The Early Church* (London, 1956), pp. 152–4.
[3] *K.D.* iii/2, pp. 601–3.   [4] *Gospel Message*, p. 54.

*

We might perhaps suggest that *v.* 31, on the one hand, serves to underline the solemnity and authority of the preceding verse or verses and to reassure the disciples whose comfort and strength the Lord's words will be during the time before the Parousia, and, on the other hand, may be regarded as standing to *v.* 32 in the position of a concessive clause—although Jesus' words are of such authority, nevertheless even he does not know the day or hour of the End. But the connection of *v.* 31 with *vv.* 30 and 32 seems rather loose. Moreover, *v.* 32 would follow very well on *v.* 30. Perhaps *v.* 31 was originally an independent saying. (The fact that it contains the word παρελεύσονται might account for its insertion here after παρέλθῃ in *v.* 30.) In that case 'my words' might originally have meant Jesus' teaching as a whole. *Pace* Bultmann and Taylor, we do not see any convincing reason for doubting the authenticity of the saying.

32. Included with good reason by P. W. Schmiedel among his 'foundation-pillars for a truly scientific life of Jesus'.[1] Taylor rightly rejects as 'wholly improbable' the view of Bultmann that it is a Jewish saying to which a Christian redactor has added οὐδὲ ὁ Υἱός, εἰ μὴ ὁ Πατήρ. An assertion of Jesus' ignorance is unlikely to have been created by the Church. Even had the early community been as embarrassed by the so-called 'delay of the Parousia' as some allege, less uncongenial expedients for explaining away its embarrassment would surely have been available. That the saying was early an offence is indicated by its omission in Lk. and by the omission of the words οὐδὲ ὁ Υἱός by many ancient authorities in the Mt. parallel. At the time of the Arian controversy the saying was naturally an embarrassment for the orthodox. Ambrose actually declared that οὐδὲ ὁ Υἱός was an Arian interpolation.

By τῆς ἡμέρας ἐκείνης the day of the Parousia is clearly

[1] Art. on 'The Gospels' in *Encyclopaedia Biblica* (London, 1899–1903), II, col. 1881.

intended. In the O.T. 'that day' is an eschatological technical term. The addition of ἢ τῆς ὥρας possibly indicates, as Lohmeyer suggests, the suddenness and devastating force of the eschatological event (cf. Rev. xviii. 10).

In view of the particularly strong claim of this saying to be regarded as authentic the absolute use of ὁ υἱός is specially significant. It is an important piece of evidence against the view that Jesus could not have thought of himself as the unique Son of God. (Cf. Mt. xi. 27 = Lk. x. 22, and see on i. 11.)

The full reality of the Incarnation involved such ignorance on the part of Jesus during his earthly life. Calvin goes to the heart of the matter, when he speaks of the Son of God 'enduring' it 'on our account' and connects it with his 'discharging the office of Mediator'.

A clearer warning against all speculation about the *when* of the Parousia could hardly be imagined. Calvin comments with characteristic vigour: 'We ought therefore to be on our guard, lest our anxiety about the time be carried farther than the Lord allows; for the chief part of our wisdom lies in confining ourselves soberly within the limits of God's word. That men may not feel uneasy at *not knowing that day*, Christ represents *angels* as their associates in this matter; for it would be a proof of excessive pride and wicked covetousness, to desire that we who creep on the earth should know more than is permitted to the *angels* in heaven. Mark adds, *nor the Son himself*. And surely that man must be singularly mad, who would hesitate to submit to the ignorance which even *the Son of God himself* did not hesitate to endure on our account.'

33. The disciples' ignorance of the date of the Parousia is not an excuse for being unprepared, but a reason (γάρ) for unceasing vigilance.

34–6. The contacts of these verses with various passages in Mt. and Lk. are extremely complicated. Cf. Lk. xii. 35–8, Mt. xxiv. 42–4 = Lk. xii. 39f., Mt. xxiv. 45–51 = Lk. xii. 42–

6, Mt. xxv. 1–13 (particularly 13), Mt. xxv. 14–30 = Lk. xix. 12–27. Taylor is probably justified in regarding these verses as 'a homiletical echo of several parables'. Their general sense is anyway clear enough: it is the same as that of *v.* 33.

In *v.* 35 the four watches correspond with Roman usage (see on vi. 48).

37 sums up *vv.* 33–6 and also the whole discourse from *v.* 5 onwards. The command to watch is addressed not only to the four, but also to the rest of the Twelve, to Mark's readers in the Church of Rome, and to the whole Church throughout the Last Times. The meaning of this watching for the returning Lord, which may be said to be the whole duty of Christians, is drawn out by the three parables of Mt. xxv. To watch for him is to make sure that our faith is no counterfeit which at the last crisis will vanish, but that true faith that will enable us to take our place beside him. It is to use the time that remains before his coming in the work of winning others for him. It is to recognize him gratefully in his intermediate comings in the persons of the least of his brethren.

VII. THE PASSION

(xiv. 1–xv. 47)

It is generally agreed that a continuous narrative of the Passion must have been traditional from an early date. Mark has probably made use of the Roman form of this traditional narrative, inserting into it at appropriate points some independent tradition-units as well as material derived from Peter (and possibly from other eye-witnesses).

For a full and interesting discussion of the composition of the Markan Passion narrative, in the course of which it is

suggested that xiv. 1 f., 10 f., 17–21, 26–31, 43–6, 53 a, xv. 1,
3–5, 15, 21–4, 26, 29 f., 34–7, 39, 42–6 represent the
primitive Roman traditional narrative, see Taylor, pp. 653–
64. For the view that Mark was conflating a 'Twelve-
source' and a 'Disciples' source' see Knox, *Sources*, I,
pp. 115–47.

74. THE CHIEF PRIESTS' AND SCRIBES' PLOT
(xiv. 1–2)
(Mt. xxvi. 1–5; Lk. xxii. 1–2)

Not really an independent section. Mark probably received
vv. 1 f. + 10 f. as the tradition of Judas' offer to the chief
priests, and himself interpolated *vv.* 3–9. Verses 1 f. now
serve to date, and indicate the background of, the incidents
related in *vv.* 3–9 and 10 f., and also to introduce the Passion
narrative as a whole. What is said about the intention of the
chief priests and scribes may derive ultimately from members of the Sanhedrin (Nicodemus, Joseph of Arimathaea?);
but, if Jeremias' explanation of ἐν τῇ ἑορτῇ is accepted, there
is nothing here which could not have been readily inferred.

1. ἦν is really equivalent to ἤμελλεν εἶναι.

πασχα (cf. Aramaic *pisḥā'*, which in the time of Jesus was
probably vocalized *pasḥā'*) is used in the N.T. and often in
the LXX; φασεκ and φασεχ, which are nearer to the
Hebrew *pesaḥ*, are also quite often used in the LXX. The
word here denotes the passover meal (cf. the second occurrence in *v.* 12, and also *vv.* 14 and 16); in the first part of *v.* 12
it denotes the paschal lamb, while in Lk. xxii. 1 it denotes
the whole festival. The meal was eaten between sundown
and midnight on the 15th Nisan, i.e. early on the 15th, since
the Jewish day began at sunset. See further on *v.* 12.

τὰ ἄζυμα is the Feast of Unleavened Bread (Hebrew
maṣṣôṯ), which lasted from the 15th to the 21st Nisan. See
Exod. xii. 15–20, xxiii. 15, xxxiv. 18, Deut. xvi. 1–8.

Since the day on which the lambs were slain (i.e. the 14th) was sometimes referred to as the first day of Unleavened Bread (see on *v.* 12), there is some doubt whether we should reckon back two days from the 15th or the 14th. On the whole it is more likely that the combined phrase here indicates the 15th. Taking μετὰ δύο ἡμέρας as = τῇ τρίτῃ ἡμέρᾳ (see on viii. 31), we may suppose that some time on Nisan 13th is meant.

ἐζήτουν. The imperfect indicates 'a purpose entertained for some time' (Taylor).

ἐν δόλῳ: i.e. in a way that would be effective, but would not involve them in undue danger or embarrassment.

2 explains (γάρ) ἐν δόλῳ.

μή is elliptical: something like κρατήσωμεν αὐτόν is to be understood. If ἐν τῇ ἑορτῇ means 'during the feast', we may suppose that the plan to arrest Jesus after the feast was altered as a result of Judas' offer. But it is better (with Jeremias[1]) to translate 'in the presence of the festival crowd' (for ἑορτή = 'festival crowd' see L. & S., *s.v.*, 4, and cf. Jn ii. 23, vii. 11). We may then compare Lk. xxii. 6: ἄτερ ὄχλου. The future indicative ἔσται represents the danger 'as real and imminent' (Swete). (The *v.l.* μήποτε ἐν τῇ ἑορτῇ ἔσται θόρυβος τοῦ λαοῦ is exclusively Western and looks like an attempt to get rid of the difficulty which the verse presents when ἐν τῇ ἑορτῇ is taken to mean 'during the feast'.)

75. THE ANOINTING AT BETHANY (xiv. 3–9)
(Mt. xxvi. 6–13; cf. Jn xii. 1–8 and also Lk. vii. 36–50)

'A Story about Jesus which is on its way to become a Pronouncement-story' (Taylor). Even Bultmann accepts *vv.* 3–7 as historical.

The narrative in Jn xii. 1–8 is parallel to this and, though the two accounts are not easily harmonized, probably refers

[1] *E.W.* pp. 46–9.

to the same incident. In Jn the anointing is placed before
the entry into Jerusalem. As Mark seems to have interpolated *vv.* 3-9 between *vv.* 1 f. and 10 f., it may be that the
Johannine dating is more correct.

Though Jn xii. 1-8 seems to combine features of Mk xiv.
3-9 with features of Lk. vii. 36-50, it seems probable that
Lk. vii. 36 ff. records a different incident.

3. For **Βηθανίᾳ** see on xi. 1, for **κατακειμένου** on
ii. 15.

πιστικῆς. Variously explained: e.g. as = πιστῆς (= 'genuine') or πιστῆς (= 'liquid'), or as a scribal corruption of
σπικάτου (the name of an unguent: cf. vg *nardi spicati*); more
probably, as a transliteration of Aramaic *pĭstāķā*' which
denotes the ben or pistachio nut (cf. πιστάκιον), the oil of
which was used as a base for perfumes.

συντρίψασα. The asyndeton both here and before κατακειμένου may possibly point to the use of an Aramaic tradition. The breaking of the flask was perhaps the expression of
the wholeheartedness of her devotion. Having served this
purpose it would never be used again.　　　　　　　*

κατέχεεν αὐτοῦ τῆς κεφαλῆς. Cf. Exod. xxix. 7, I Sam.
x. 1, II Kgs ix. 3, 6, Ps. cxxxiii. 2. The anointing of the head
was not necessarily a royal or priestly anointing; in Lk. vii.
46 it is an ordinary courtesy (cf. Ps. cxli. 5). But the significant anointing *was* an anointing of the *head*. In Lk. vii. 38
and Jn xii. 3 it is the feet of Jesus that are anointed, but here
and in Mt. it is his head. It is not likely that the woman
thought of herself as anointing the Messiah, but Mark
doubtless intended his readers to recognize the messianic
significance of her action—though another significance of it
is indicated by Jesus in *v.* 8. He who had been anointed by
the Spirit at his baptism is now fittingly anointed with oil.
See also on viii. 29 (Σὺ εἶ ὁ Χριστός). That it was a woman
who anointed him is interesting (see on xvi. 1).

4. τινες. οἱ μαθηταί in the Mt. parallel probably gives

the right interpretation. The words of Jesus in *vv.* 6–9 are best understood as addressed to the disciples.

πρὸς ἑαυτούς. Perhaps to be explained as suggesting looks or remarks exchanged between them; or Black[1] may be right in thinking that it reflects an Aramaic ethic dative: 'were them vexed', 'were indeed vexed'.

5. ἐπάνω is here properly used as an adverb, not a preposition.

δηναρίων τριακοσίων is a genitive of price, it is not governed by ἐπάνω. Cf. I Cor. xv. 6. (The use of ὡσεί with numerals is similar, e.g. Mt. xiv. 21.) The fact that in Mt. xx. 2 a *denarius* is a day's wage is some indication of the value of the unguent.

δοθῆναι τοῖς πτωχοῖς. 'This interest in the poor is characteristic of the pious Jew' (Taylor).

ἐνεβριμῶντο. See on i. 43.

6. Ἄφετε. Ἀφίημι here means 'let someone alone'.

αὐτῇ κόπους παρέχετε. Cf. Lk. xi. 7, xviii. 5, Gal. vi. 17. The idiom is found in the papyri, but classical Greek prefers πράγματα or πόνον παρέχειν τινί.

καλόν. As an expression of generous, self-forgetting love, but also with reference to the action's special appropriateness in view of the uniqueness of its object and occasion— the Messiah about to die and be buried.

ἐν ἐμοί: 'upon me', 'to me' (cf. Hebrew *bî*).

7. This and the next verse give the reason for Jesus' approval. With *v.* 7a, c cf. Jn xii. 8 as well as Mt. xxvi. 11.

πάντοτε γὰρ τοὺς πτωχοὺς ἔχετε μεθ' ἑαυτῶν. The recognition that throughout history there will be men who will need the help of their fellows is of course no reason at all for not trying our utmost to establish social security.

καὶ ὅταν θέλητε δύνασθε αὐτοῖς εὖ ποιῆσαι does not imply that the care of the poor is unimportant and merely to be undertaken when we feel so disposed, but simply that

[1] P. 77.

it is not to be made a pretext for blaming the woman for seizing an altogether unique opportunity.

ἐμὲ δὲ οὐ πάντοτε ἔχετε, taken with the rest of the verse, is important evidence against the view of Barrett[1] *et al.* that Jesus did not envisage any significant interval between his death and his Parousia; for it is implied that there will be a time during which the disciples will be in a position to do good to the poor, but not to Jesus. Even Bultmann does not seem to question the authenticity of the saying. The words are also important as expressing a truth which has to be held alongside the promise in Mt. xxviii. 20.[2]

8. ἔσχεν: *sc. ποιῆσαι.* For ἔχειν = 'be able' cf. Lk. xii. 4 (see further L. & S., *s.v.*, (A) A. III).

προέλαβεν μυρίσαι. Though this is the only example of προλαμβάνω ('take beforehand', 'anticipate') with the infinitive given in L. & S., it can hardly be regarded as impossible Greek. There is the analogy of φθάνω, which, while it is normally used with the participle, is sometimes used with the infinitive. (For possible parallels in Josephus see Taylor *in loc.*)

εἰς τὸν ἐνταφιασμόν: 'to lay it out', 'to prepare it for burial' (ἐνταφιασμός means 'preparation for burial', 'laying out' rather than 'burial'). For the Jewish custom of anointing the dead cf. (*M*) *Shab.* xxiii. 5. The phrase indicates not her conscious intention, but the purpose which her action will actually serve. Taylor maintains (surely rightly) against Bultmann that there is no reason why Jesus should not have interpreted the woman's action in this way, especially if the incident occurred shortly before the Passion.

9. αμην. See on iii. 28.

ὅπου ἐὰν κηρυχθῇ τὸ εὐαγγέλιον εἰς ὅλον τὸν κόσμον is most naturally understood to refer to the missionary preaching of the disciples. Its authenticity is often denied, because (it is alleged) Jesus expected the immediate coming

---

[1] *E.T.* LXVII, pp. 143 f.　　　[2] See Barth, *Credo*, pp. 113–16.

of the Kingdom. But see on xiii. 10. Others accept the view of Jeremias[1] that ὅπου ἐάν has a temporal sense, that τὸ εὐαγγέλιον means 'the proclamation of the final victory of God', and that κηρυχθῇ refers to the final proclamation by God's angel (cf. Rev. xiv. 6). But see on xiii. 10 (κηρυχθῆναι). εἰς ὅλον τὸν κόσμον is probably equivalent to ἐν ὅλῳ τῷ κόσμῳ (cf. Mt. parallel).

εἰς μνημόσυνον αὐτῆς. Jeremias takes the meaning to be that her deed will be spoken of before God's throne in the last judgement in order that God may mercifully remember her (cf. Lohmeyer, pp. 295f.). But, while it is true that the idea of God's remembering people is often expressed in the O.T. (e.g. Gen. xxx. 22, Num. x. 9, Ps. xxv. 7, Jer. xv. 15; cf. Acts x. 4), the root *zkr* is more often used of remembrance by men. The noun μνημόσυνον when used in the LXX usually refers to remembrance by men; but normally, since it is a common and versatile word, if the context does not make the meaning clear, some precise indication of its sense is given. In the absence of any indication here that the reference is to God's remembering the woman, it seems clear that the ordinary meaning should be preferred.[2]

76. JUDAS GOES TO THE CHIEF PRIESTS (xiv. 10–11)
(Mt. xxvi. 14–16; Lk. xxii. 3–6)

Follows on from *vv.* 1f. The betrayal by one of the Twelve is a feature which would never have been created by the community. The historical worth of Mark's bald account is unquestionable.

10. Ἰούδας Ἰσκαριωθ. See on iii. 19.

ὁ εἷς τῶν δώδεκα. Ὁ εἷς is found in early papyri. It may be that the presence of the article here has no special signi-

---

[1] *B.S.N.T.S.* III (1952), pp. 21f.

[2] See further D. R. Jones, ''Ἀνάμνησις in the LXX and the Interpretation of I Cor. xi. 25' in *J.T.S.*, n.s. VI (1955), pp. 183–91.

ficance (so Lagrange); but perhaps it is meant to suggest the
contrast between the one traitor and the rest of the Twelve
or a reference to the use of the expression εἷς τῶν δώδεκα by
Jesus in *v.* 20, 'that "one of the Twelve"'.

That one of the Twelve had betrayed Jesus must have been
profoundly shocking to the early Church, and the reassur-
ance gained from Ps. xli. 9, cix. 8, Zech. xi. 12f. (the sense
that the horrible truth was not beyond the horizon of
prophecy) extremely welcome (cf. Mt. xxvi. 15, Jn xiii. 18,
Acts i. 16, 20).

παραδοῖ. See on i. 14, iii. 19, ix. 31. On the form see on
iv. 29. Exactly how Judas betrayed Jesus is not made
absolutely clear in the N.T.; but it seems to be implied that
the betrayal consisted in offering to inform the chief priests
of an opportunity to arrest Jesus quietly (cf. *v.* 11 and Lk.
xxii. 6), and then bringing those who were to carry out
the arrest to Gethsemane (cf. Jn xviii. 2) and preventing
a possible mistake in the darkness by greeting Jesus
(*v.* 45).

Mark gives no indication of Judas' motive. Mt. xxvi. 15a
hints at avarice (cf. Jn xii. 6); Lk. xxii. 3, Jn xiii. 2, 27 point
to the work of Satan. Various suggestions have been made
in modern times: e.g. as a Zealot he hoped to force Jesus'
hand and compel him to act and be the political messiah he
had hoped for, or he was embittered by Jesus' refusal to be
that sort of messiah; but these are merely speculation.   *

77. THE PREPARATIONS FOR THE PASSOVER
(xiv. 12–16)
(Mt. xxvi. 17–19; Lk. xxii. 7–13)

The parallels with xi. 1–7 are not such as to suggest that
one of the two narratives is a doublet of the other, but they
do rather suggest that either Mark derived both stories from
the same informant or he composed both himself on the

basis of tradition. The tendency to repeat the same patterns is of course a common feature of story-telling.

The comparison with I Sam. x. 1–9 has also been made; but it is small justification for labelling this section 'legendary'!

12. As τῇ πρώτῃ ἡμέρᾳ τῶν ἀζύμων properly denotes Nisan 15th and ὅτε τὸ πασχα ἔθυον clearly denotes the 14th, it has been suggested that the former is a mistranslation of an Aramaic phrase indicating the day before the feast; but, as there is some evidence (see S.–B. II, pp. 813–15) that the 14th was sometimes loosely referred to as 'the first day of Unleavened Bread', it is better to regard the first phrase here as ambiguous, its meaning being more exactly defined by the second. We may turn ἔθυον (indefinite plural and imperfect) by 'it was customary to kill'; the phrase need not imply that the killing had already begun when the disciples spoke. For πασχα see on *v.* 1.

This verse clearly implies that the Last Supper was a Passover meal and that the day (reckoned from sundown to sundown) on which Jesus was arrested, condemned and crucified was Nisan 15th. Jn xviii. 28 (cf. xix. 14, 31, 42), however, seems to imply that Nisan 15th did not begin till sundown on the Friday, and that therefore the Last Supper was not a Passover meal. It seems likely that the Synoptic dating is historically correct and that the Johannine is due to a desire to express the theological truth that Jesus is the true Paschal Lamb (cf. I Cor. v. 7, Jn i. 29, xix. 36); on Jn's dating he actually died at the time that the lambs were being killed.

In support of this view: (i) A number of features of the Last Supper suggest that it was a Passover meal: (*a*) it was eaten in Jerusalem, though Jesus and his disciples were apparently lodging in Bethany (xi. 11)—the Passover meal had to be eaten within the city; (*b*) it was eaten late at night (I Cor. xi. 23, Jn xiii. 30), whereas the normal time for the evening meal was late afternoon—the Passover meal had to be eaten at night; (c) the references to reclining (xiv. 18, Jn xiii. 23, 28: see on ii. 15) rather suggest a Passover meal— by this time it was obligatory for even the poorest to recline at the Passover meal; (d) xiv. 18, 22 indicate that the meal did not begin with the bread-breaking—this was a pecu- liarity of the Passover meal, in which the eating of bitter herbs preceded the breaking of the bread; (e) wine was drunk, whereas at ordinary meals water would be drunk by a Rabbi and his disciples; (f) ὑμνήσαντες in xiv. 26 suggests the Hallel, the Psalms sung at the Passover meal.

(ii) The objections urged against the Synoptic dating are not unanswerable: (a) the use of ἄρτος in xiv. 22 need not imply that the bread was leavened, for in ii. 26 it is used of the shewbread; (b) the absence of any reference to a lamb in vv. 18–26 may be due to a natural tendency to concen- trate on those features which belonged to the Eucharist; (c) with regard to the objection that Μὴ ἐν τῇ ἑορτῇ (xiv. 2) makes it unlikely that Jesus was arrested on Nisan 15th, see in loc.; (d) with regard to the alleged contraventions of Jewish law implied by the Synoptic dating, the following points may be made: it was permissible to spend the Pass- over night (though not to eat the meal) outside the walls, if one was within a certain area—which included Geth- semane; to carry arms on a festival was at this time per- mitted (cf. R. Eliezer's opinion in (M) Shab. vi. 4); while it is true that it was normally illegal to hold a trial on a festival (actually the prohibition applied also to the eve of a festival—so that the Johannine dating is on this score equally difficult), (M) Sanh. xi. 4 speaks of a rebellious teacher being executed on a festival day on the authority of Deut. xvii. 13 (only at a festival would 'all the people' be able to 'hear'); the various actions connected with the burial of Jesus seem to have been permissible on a festival (according to (M) Shab. xxiii. 5 one may do on the Sabbath all that is needful for the dead), though normally the actual burial would have had to wait till the next day; in this case, where (on the Synoptic dating) the first day of Unleavened Bread was followed by the Sabbath, the body could not in the climate of Palestine be left for two days.

(iii) Attempts (in the interests of the Johannine dating) to explain the Last Supper as a *ḳiddûš* or as a *ḥabûrāh* meal are unsatisfactory, since (*a*) the *ḳiddûš* was the sanctifying of a Sabbath or festival *as it began*, and the Last Supper was therefore twenty-four hours too soon to have anything to do with the *ḳiddûš* of the Sabbath or—on the Johannine dating —with the *ḳiddûš* of the Passover; and (*b*) there is no evidence for solemn meals celebrated by *ḥabûrôṯ* or religious fellow-ships apart from certain meals of legal obligation (e.g. those connected with circumcisions).

(iv) The suggestion that in this year some Jews were eating the Passover meal on the Thursday evening and some on the Friday evening, which has been made by various scholars on various grounds, seems unlikely.

* (See further Jeremias, *E.W.* pp. 1–60.)

13. δύο τῶν μαθητῶν αὐτοῦ. According to Lk., Peter and John.

ἀπαντήσει ὑμῖν ἄνθρωπος κεράμιον ὕδατος βαστάζων. More probably a pre-arranged sign than an instance of supernatural foresight. A man carrying a pitcher would be conspicuous, since normally only women carried water in pitchers: a man would carry it in a wineskin.

14. τὸ κατάλυμά μου: 'my guest-room', i.e. the one I have engaged.

φάγω. Subjunctive, on the analogy of a ἵνα-clause.

15. ἐστρωμένον. Doubtless with reference to the accommodation for reclining at the meal. How luxurious or how simple the accommodation was is not indicated. The verb is also used in xi. 8.

ἡμῖν. Swete notes that Jesus seldom uses this inclusive plural of himself and his disciples: cf. ix. 40.

78. JESUS FORETELLS THE BETRAYAL (xiv. 17–21)
(Mt. xxvi. 20–5; Lk. xxii. 14, 21–3)

It is possible that *vv.* 18–21 form an independent unit of tradition which has been inserted between *v.* 17 and *v.* 22 by Mark. There is no need to doubt its historical worth. Jesus' words may possibly have been intended as a last appeal to Judas; but the tradition was no doubt valued by the early Church chiefly as evidence that Jesus had not been taken by surprise.

17. ὀψίας. See on i. 32. The Passover meal would begin after sunset, when the new Jewish day (Nisan 15th) had begun.

τῶν δώδεκα. 'Either the term is used conventionally or Mark thinks that the two mentioned in 13 have returned' (Taylor).

18. On ἀνακειμένων and ἐσθιόντων see on *v.* 12 (i) (*c*) and (*d*). On παραδώσει see on ix. 31.

ὁ ἐσθίων μετ' ἐμοῦ. Apparently a reminiscence of Ps. xli. 9. Cf. Jn xiii. 18. B reads τῶν ἐσθιόντων instead of ὁ ἐσθίων. The fact that the whole phrase is omitted in Mt., which here follows Mk quite closely, suggests the possibility that it is a gloss in Mk.

19. Note the dramatic effect of the asyndeton.

εἷς κατὰ εἷς = 'one by one' (cf. Jn viii. 9) may either be explained as an expression 'formed backwards from the neuter' ἓν καθ' ἕν (L. & S., *s.v.* καθεῖς), or as an example of κατά used 'as an adverb distributively' (Moulton, *Proleg.* I, p. 105). Cf. also Rom. xii. 5, Rev. xxi. 21.

Μήτι ἐγώ; A question expecting a negative reply (cf. iv. 21).

20. Calvin rightly comments: 'Christ, by his reply, neither removes their doubt, nor points out the person of Judas, but only confirms what he said a little before....' (That ὁ ἐσθίων μετ' ἐμοῦ in *v.* 18 had not identified the traitor is, of course, clear from *v.* 19.)

ἕν should probably be read with B C*vid Θ 565 before τρύβλιον, though it is absent from most MSS. It stresses the baseness of the betrayal. It was probably omitted because it was assumed that Jesus was giving a sign to the Beloved Disciple.

The τρύβλιον is probably the dish containing the sauce (ḥᵃrôseṭ) of dried fruits, spices and wine or vinegar, in which the bitter herbs were dipped at the Passover meal.

21. ὑπάγει. Cf. Jn viii. 14, 21f., xiii. 3, 33, xiv. 4, 28, xvi. 5, 10, 17. Perhaps a characteristic expression of Jesus to denote his approaching death and return to his Father, which has been better preserved by the Fourth Gospel than by the Synoptics.

καθὼς γέγραπται περὶ αὐτοῦ. See on viii. 31, ix. 12.

οὐαί expresses sorrow and pity rather than a threat.

δι' οὗ (rather than ὑφ' οὗ) suggests the truth that the delivering up of Jesus is not simply an act of Judas, but part of a bigger purpose than his—he is in fact being used for the fulfilment of God's purpose. Nevertheless, it is his act, and he is responsible—hence the οὐαί and v. 21 c. The fact that God turns the wrath of man to his praise does not excuse the wrath of man. Note the μέν and δέ (the combination is rare in Mk) which emphasize the contrast between v. 21 a and 21 b.

καλὸν... ἐκεῖνος. The omission of ἄν in the apodosis and the substitution of οὐκ for the normal μή in the protasis enhance the poignancy of this unfulfilled conditional sentence by removing its contingent form (cf. Moulton, *Proleg.* I, p. 200). For the positive adjective καλόν used for the comparative cf. ix. 43, 45, 47.

79. THE INSTITUTION OF THE EUCHARIST (xiv. 22–5)
(Mt. xxvi. 26–9; Lk. xxii. 15–20; cf. I Cor. xi. 23–5)

The general historical reliability of our four primary sources for the institution of the Eucharist is not to be doubted. But when it comes to the attempt to determine which of the four sources is the most primitive, there is considerable difference of opinion. There is of course also great variety of opinion about the theological meaning of Jesus' actions and words. Since within the scope of this commentary it is impossible to deal at all adequately with the differing views, it has seemed best, as far as this section is concerned, to give in the main just one interpretation, indicating further reading below.

The most significant of the variations between the sources is that I Cor. and Lk. (if the longer text is read, as it probably should be) contain a command to repeat the observance, while Mk and Mt. do not. It is possible that Mark omitted this because he felt it could be taken for granted or, on the other hand, that the command, as given by Paul and Luke, interprets the intention of Jesus rather than preserving his actual words.

See further Jeremias, *E.W.*; A. J. B. Higgins, *The Lord's Supper in the New Testament* (London, 1952); J. Behm in *T.W.N.T.* III, pp. 726–43; Cranfield in *T.W.B.* pp. 254–7.

22. ἐσθιόντων αὐτῶν. See on *v.* 12 (i) (*d*). There is little doubt that αὐτῶν includes Judas: no hint is given in Mk that he has gone out before *v.* 22, and in Lk. the prediction of the betrayal follows the institution of the Eucharist.

On λαβὼν ἄρτον, εὐλογήσας and ἔκλασεν see on vi. 41. On the assumption that this was a Passover meal, the following items may be presumed to have preceded the taking of the bread: festal *ḳiddûš* and first cup (cf. Lk. xxii. 17), eating of bitter herbs, main meal brought in and second cup mixed, Paschal *haggāḏāh*, first part of *hallēl*, drinking of second cup.

τοῦτό ἐστιν τὸ σῶμά μου.   Since these words were separated from the cup-saying (v. 24) by the main part of the
meal, the assumption that Jesus used 'body' and 'blood' as
correlatives is questionable. It seems better to take the
bread-saying independently of the cup-saying. We may then
suppose that the Aramaic behind τὸ σῶμά μου is gûpî rather
than biśrî, and that the meaning was 'my person', 'myself'.
Jesus was about to leave his disciples; but henceforth bread
broken and distributed in the familiar way was to have a
new meaning for them—it was to be the pledge and the
means of his real personal presence with them, though unseen. According to this interpretation the primary gift of
the Eucharist is the real personal presence of the risen,
glorified Lord: the Supper is his appointed tryst with his
own. Confirmation of this is to be seen in the intimate
connection between the Eucharist and the Resurrection
(e.g. celebration on Sundays) and the use of the prayer 'Our
Lord, come!' (I Cor. xvi. 22) in the early Church at the
Eucharist. On this view, sacrificial ideas, while undoubtedly
of crucial importance in v. 24, are not the primary key to the
original meaning of the bread-saying.

23. ποτήριον: i.e. the third cup of the Passover meal.

εὐχαριστήσας. Over the third cup the prayer of thanksgiving was said. Hence the third cup came to be called 'the
cup of blessing'.

ἔπιον ἐξ αὐτοῦ πάντες makes it clear that the one cup
was passed round. It is likely that in the time of Jesus a
common cup was used at the Passover, though individual
cups became customary later.

24. Opinions differ as to whether Mk or I Cor. preserves
the more primitive form of the cup-saying. In favour of the
Pauline τοῦτο τὸ ποτήριον ἡ καινὴ διαθήκη ἐστὶν ἐν τῷ ἐμῷ
αἵματι, it may be argued that an assimilation of this form to
that of the bread-saying (so to something including τοῦτό
ἐστιν τὸ αἷμά μου) seems more likely than the alteration of

an original form that was parallel to the bread-saying into
the Pauline; and that the phrase τὸ αἷμά μου τῆς διαθήκης in   *
Mk, in which the reference to the covenant is introduced in
what seems—in view of its momentousness—a strangely incidental manner,[1] becomes explicable, on the hypothesis
that the Pauline form is the more primitive, as having
resulted from the attempt to combine an original reference
to the covenant with the form 'this is my blood'. But in any
case the Markan and the Pauline forms of the cup-saying
have essentially the same meaning. As the Old Covenant
had been ratified by the sprinkling of sacrificial blood (Exod.
xxiv. 6–8), so God's New Covenant with men is about to be
established by Jesus' death, and the cup (i.e. the wine it contains) makes those who share it partakers of the benefits and
the obligations of this New Covenant. The drinking of the
wine is analogous to being sprinkled with the blood in
Exod. xxiv.

With τὸ αἷμά μου τῆς διαθήκης cf. Exod. xxiv. 8 (in the
LXX: ἰδοὺ τὸ αἷμα τῆς διαθήκης ἧς διέθετο Κύριος πρὸς ὑμᾶς),
which it echoes. The word διαθήκη in classical Greek means
a 'will', 'testament', but was used in the LXX to represent
bᵉrît—probably because the more obvious equivalent συνθήκη
suggested an agreement between equals. In the I Cor. form
there is a direct reference to Jer. xxxi. 31. The addition of
καινῆς here in Mk in a good many authorities is no doubt an
assimilation to I Cor. The participle ἐκχυννόμενον, though
present, has a future sense (cf. Hebrew, Aramaic, in which
the present participle serves for the future; but cf. also ix.
31, where the present indicative has a future sense and see
note *in loc.*). For πολλοί meaning 'all' see on i. 34. Calvin
comments here: 'By the word *many* he means not a part of
the world only, but the whole human race.' In ὑπὲρ πολλῶν
there is probably an echo of Isa. liii. 12. Cf. x. 45.

25. The saying has a very Semitic flavour and every

[1] Contrast the emphatic way in which it is introduced in I Cor. xi. 25.

appearance of being authentic. 'The formula is, as regards its negative significance, that of a Nazirite vow. By making it, Jesus consecrates Himself for the imminent sacrificial offering of His life.'[1] Cf. Num. vi. 1–21. But the saying has also a positive significance: it looks forward to the end of the period of the vow, to the time when he will again taste wine —in the kingdom of God. This could be taken to refer to the final reunion with the disciples—the messianic feast (cf. Mt. viii. 11, Lk. xiv. 15, xxii. 29f., Rev. xix. 9); but perhaps it is better understood (with Barth) as referring to the period between the Resurrection and Ascension (cf. Acts x. 41; also see Lk. xxiv. 30f., 35, Acts i. 4). For the suitability of ἐν τῇ βασιλείᾳ τοῦ Θεοῦ on this interpretation see on ix. 1 (vii).

80. THE WAY TO GETHSEMANE; THE DENIAL BY PETER FORETOLD (xiv. 26–31)

(Mt. xxvi. 30–5; Lk. xxii. 39; cf. Lk. xxii. 31–4)

Probably Petrine.

26. ὑμνήσαντες refers (if the meal was a Passover meal) to the second part of the *hallēl*, i.e. Pss. cxiv (or cxv)–cxviii. C. H. Turner may be right in thinking that ἐξῆλθον reflects a first person plural in Mark's source.

27. σκανδαλισθήσεσθε. See on iv. 17, vi. 3, ix. 42.

Πατάξω...διασκορπισθήσονται. Quoted from Zech. xiii. 7. The future indicative πατάξω (as against the imperative in M.T., LXX) may be due to the use of the quotation as a *testimonium* in the early Church or it may go back to Jesus (it is even possible that it represents the original Hebrew text). In any case, there is no real difference of meaning; for to say that God commands the sword to smite is really the same as saying that God smites.

28. μετὰ τὸ ἐγερθῆναί με. See on viii. 31, ix. 9, 31, x. 34.

*

[1] Barth, *K.D.* iii/2, p. 603.

προάξω. The verb can denote a literal walking in front of someone (as in x. 32), and J. Weiss[1] took it here in that sense (an unfulfilled prediction that he would march at the head of his disciples back to Galilee). It can also be used metaphorically (e.g. Prov. iv. 27 LXX), and we could here understand that Jesus will lead the disciples in the sense that it will be in obedience to his instructions that they will go into Galilee. But it is best to take the meaning here to be 'go somewhere earlier than someone' (as in vi. 45). The saying looks forward to a Resurrection appearance in Galilee. The scattered flock will then be re-established. There seems to be no compelling reason for denying the authenticity of the saying. Peter's failure to refer to it in v. 29 is hardly surprising: it would be natural for him to be too taken up with the implied slur on his loyalty to pay much attention to anything else. See further on xvi. 7.

29. Εἰ καί: 'although'. On the difference between εἰ καί and καὶ εἰ see L. & S., s.v. καί, B. 8; Moule, p. 167.

30. Note the solemn αμην formula and the extremely emphatic σὺ σήμερον ταύτῃ τῇ νυκτί. The time is defined with ascending accuracy: 'to-day'—i.e. before sunset on Friday, 'this night', 'before the cock...'.

δίς is omitted by a good many authorities, but, as the corresponding ἐκ δευτέρου in v. 72 is only omitted by a few of these, the omission here is probably assimilation to Mt. or Lk. It has been suggested that the reference in ἀλέκτορα φωνῆσαι is to the bugle-call (*gallicinium*) which marked the beginning of the fourth watch; but more probably (especially in view of δίς) the ordinary meaning is intended.

The prediction cannot be explained as a *vaticinium ex eventu*: the early Church would hardly have created a prediction which aggravated the baseness of Peter's denial, even for the sake of showing that Jesus was not surprised.

31. ἐκπερισσῶς is not found in classical Greek or LXX,

[1] *Die Schriften des Neuen Testaments* (2nd ed.), I, p. 208.

and occurs only here in the N.T. Conceivably a Markan coinage.

For συναποθανεῖν cf. Herodotus, v. 47: συνέσπετο δὲ Δωριέϊ καὶ συναπέθανε Φίλιππος....

81. GETHSEMANE (xiv. 32–42)
(Mt. xxvi. 36–46; Lk. xxii. 40–6)

Probably Petrine. The historical value of the section is beyond serious doubt; for it is inconceivable that the early Church would ever have created such a picture of the Lord it worshipped or an episode so discreditable to its leading apostles. To regard this as legendary would be to go contrary to all historical probability. The objection that the disciples could not have known what Jesus prayed, as he was away from them and they were asleep, falls to the ground when it is realized that μικρόν in v. 35 probably denotes only a few yards and that the narrative need not imply that they had gone to sleep before Jesus had uttered the prayer recorded in vv. 35 f. (while the details in vv. 37–42 are only such as the three would become aware of when aroused by Jesus the three times).

32. ἔρχονται perhaps represents Peter's first person plural.

χωρίον: 'a piece of land', 'estate'. Jn xviii. 1 speaks of a κῆπος.

Γεθσημανει probably represents Hebrew *gaṯ šᵉmānîm* ('press of oils'). See on *v.* 12 (ii) (*d*), and also Dalman, *S.S.W.* pp. 321–7. Knowing that Judas knew he was likely to go there, he goes—'as if he had made an assignation with his enemies, he presented himself to death' (Calvin).

ἕως προσεύξωμαι. For ἕως (= 'while') followed by the subjunctive cf. Lk. xvii. 8. When used in this sense it usually takes the indicative (as in vi. 45, Jn ix. 4).

33. παραλαμβάνει...μετʼ αὐτοῦ. Cf. ix. 2. He takes the

three with him partly, no doubt, for his own sake, because in his anguish and loneliness he yearns for their company, for their presence as friends who care (so Luther speaks of him as 'seeking comfort from His disciples, whom previously He had comforted'[1])—though the effect of his taking them with him is actually to make more inescapably clear the fact of his aloneness; but surely also for their sakes and the world's, that they might be witnesses of his temptation and of his obedience, so that men might be in a position to understand better what had been done for them.

ἐκθαμβεῖσθαι here denotes a being in the grip of a shuddering horror in the face of the dreadful prospect before him. ἀδημονεῖν occurs in the N.T. only here, in the Mt. parallel and in Phil. ii. 26; but is found in classical Greek and the papyri. It means 'be sore troubled', 'be in anguish'. It denotes here 'an anxiety from which there was no escaping and in which He saw no help and no comfort'.[2]

34. Περίλυπός ἐστιν ἡ ψυχή μου ἕως θανάτου echoes several O.T. passages: Ps. xlii (LXX: xli). 5, 11, xliii (LXX: xlii). 5 (ἱνατί περίλυπος εἶ, ἡ ψυχή μου, καὶ ἱνατί συνταράσσεις με;); Jon. iv. 9 (σφόδρα λελύπημαι ἐγὼ ἕως θανάτου); cf. also Ps. xxii (LXX: xxi). 15, cxvi (LXX: cxiv). 3. Together with the phrase ἐκθαμβεῖσθαι καὶ ἀδημονεῖν in v. 33 and the content of vv. 35f., this saying makes clear the striking contrast between Jesus' frame of mind in the face of death and the joyful courage of Jewish and Christian martyrs or the gay serenity of a Socrates. Luther has the suggestive comment: 'No one ever feared death so much as this Man.'[3] One reason for this inexpressible fear and horror may be suggested here (the other—and even more important—reason is revealed in v. 36). Jn xii. 31 indicates the very special involvement of Satan in the events of the Passion (cf. Lk. xxii. 53?). In the wilderness Jesus had been

---

[1] W.A. xxxvii, p. 326.   [2] Barth, *K.D.* iv/1, p. 291.
[3] W.A. xxxvii, p. 326.

tempted by Satan to deviate from his appointed way as the
Servant and he had resisted and returned blow for blow.
Now in the garden Satan returns in force and in all his
majesty as the prince of this world, to avenge his earlier
defeat; and Jesus sees now in appalling immediacy the full
cost of his stedfast obedience. Now, to use Barth's phrase,
'the bill is being presented'.[1] In Gethsemane it became
plain that 'it was one thing to enter and continue on this
way, it was another to tread it to the end, and in this world
its necessarily bitter end. It was one thing to contradict and
withstand the tempter, it was another to see him actually
triumphant as he necessarily would be in this world, in the
humanity ruled by him, to be refuted by him in the hard
language of facts. From this we may gather something at
least of the convulsion of that hour.'[2]

The suggestion that γρηγορεῖτε means 'not that they
were not to go to sleep, but that they were to look out for
the *parousia*'[3]—though possibly not unnatural on the assumption that Jesus envisaged no significant interval between his
death and Parousia—is surely extremely improbable.

35. προελθὼν μικρόν. He separates himself only a little
from the three.

ἔπιπτεν ἐπὶ τῆς γῆς. The Mt. parallel (*ἔπεσεν ἐπὶ
πρόσωπον αὐτοῦ*: cf. Gen. xvii. 3, 17, etc.) probably expresses
Mark's meaning correctly. Luke's *θεὶς τὰ γόνατα* is more
restrained. It is possible that Swete is right in thinking that
the imperfect here 'describes the prostration as taking place
under the eyes of the narrator'.

προσηύχετο. To prepare the reader for the full impact of
v. 36, Mark gives first in indirect form the substance of the
prayer.

ὥρα is used more often in Dan. than in any other O.T.
book (e.g. viii. 17, 19, xi. 35, 40, 45). Cf. *v.* 41 and also xiii.

[1] *K.D.* IV/I, p. 292 (*C.D.* IV/I, p. 265).   [2] *C.D.* IV/I, p. 266.
[3] C. K. Barrett in *E.T.* LXVII, p. 144.

11, 32. In Jn ὥρα is specially prominent—e.g. ii. 4, v. 25, vii. 30, xii. 23, and esp. xii. 27.

36. Αββα. In the Aramaic of Jesus' time *'abbā'*, in origin †
an exclamation of small children, had replaced in ordinary
use *'ābî* ('my father'), both vocative and non-vocative, and
also the emphatic state *'ābā'*. It was not, however, used as
a form of address to God (its homely origin no doubt made
it seem unsuitable). So its use by Jesus is highly significant.
He seems to have used it regularly: it is to be discerned not
only where the actual Aramaic is quoted (as in Rom. viii.
15, Gal. iv. 6) but where ὁ πατήρ, πάτερ, ὁ πατήρ μου, πάτερ
μου and perhaps πάτερ ἡμῶν are used. It is significant that
Jesus calls God 'Father' at this moment—as he sees the cup
held out to him. He knows God as Father even in Gethsemane: to have failed to do so would have been to lose his battle.

παντα δυνατά σοι. Cf. x. 27.

παρένεγκε τὸ ποτήριον τοῦτο ἀπ' ἐμοῦ. For ποτήριον see
on x. 38. The other and more important reason for Jesus'
ἐκθαμβεῖσθαι καὶ ἀδημονεῖν is now indicated. In his identification with sinful men he is the object of the holy wrath of
God against sin, and in Gethsemane as the hour of the
Passion approaches the full horror of that wrath is disclosed.
(Of course, when we speak of God's wrath, we must remember that his wrath is not like ours: it contains no element of
spitefulness, pettiness, or hypocrisy, but is the reaction of the
altogether holy and loving God to sin. But any discussion of
the Cross which leaves out of account Christ's bearing of the
wrath of God is surely open to the charge: *Nondum con-
siderasti quanti ponderis sit peccatum.*) Isa. li. 22 speaks of the
cup of God's fury being taken away from Jerusalem. Now
Jesus prays that it may be taken away from him; but his
prayer is really a prayer, and not a demand, for he does not
set his will over against the will of his Father. He has not
actually made the removal of the cup his will; the wish he
expresses is conditional upon the will of God. That is the

significance of ἀλλ' οὐ τί ἐγὼ θέλω ἀλλὰ τί σύ and also of εἰ δυνατόν ἐστιν in v. 35. So his prayer does not call his obedience in question and Calvin is seriously misleading when he says that Christ 'corrects and recalls that wish that had suddenly escaped him'. The οὐ τί ἐγὼ θέλω ἀλλὰ τί σύ is indeed the heart of his prayer. Thereby in full awareness of the cost he embraces the will of God and sets his lips to the cup. (We should hardly supply γενηθήτω or γινέσθω, for then μή would be required, as in Lk.: it is probably best to explain the words as meaning, 'The question is not what I will...'.)

37. The only answer Jesus receives to his prayer is the hard answer of events. It begins with the failure of the three to watch with him, which drives home his utter loneliness.

38. The ἵνα-clause is better taken as expressing the content of the prayer than as final.

The noun πειρασμός occurs in Mk only here, but see on i. 13. Cf. Mt. vi. 13.

τὸ μὲν πνεῦμα πρόθυμον, ἡ δὲ σὰρξ ἀσθενής. The first phrase is perhaps an echo of *rûaḥ nᵉdîḇāh* ('a willing spirit') in Ps. li. 12 (M.T.: 14), which seems to be identified with 'thy holy spirit' in the previous verse. The meaning here would then be that God's Spirit which is imparted to them is willing, but their human nature is weak.[1] Or it may be that πνεῦμα is here used as in ii. 8, viii. 12, of the human spirit, and that Jesus praises their will to do right, 'in order that their weakness may not throw them into despair' (Calvin). The suggestion that Jesus is here speaking about himself is unlikely in view of the context (vv. 37, 38a). Rawlinson is no doubt right in thinking that the early Church would appreciate the value of this saying as a warning to those who had to face martyrdom not to forget the weakness of the flesh.

39. The words τὸν αὐτὸν λόγον εἰπών are omitted by D *a b c ff*² *k*, and are perhaps a gloss.

[1] So E. Schweizer in *T.W.N.T.* VI, p. 394.

40. With the last part of the verse cf. ix. 6.

41. It is possible to take Καθεύδετε τὸ λοιπὸν καὶ ἀνα-παύεσθε as a command, supposing either that by this time Jesus no longer feels the need of their watching with him, since he has placed the cup to his lips, or else that the command is ironical, a rebuke. (If we take the command to be seriously meant, we can explain the immediate change that follows by supposing that after Jesus has told his disciples to sleep on he suddenly sees Judas and his company approaching.) A perhaps better alternative is to take the words as a question (or possibly an exclamatory statement). The translation of τὸ λοιπόν will vary accordingly: it can mean 'henceforth', 'for the rest', 'then', 'so', 'now'.

ἀπέχει· ἦλθεν ἡ ὥρα. D W Θ Φ f13 al it (some MSS.) sy add τὸ τέλος after ἀπέχει; but this looks like an attempt to explain the difficult ἀπέχει and was perhaps originally a gloss suggested by Lk. xxii. 37. A great variety of explanations of ἀπέχει have been suggested: (i) 'it is sufficient', 'enough of this!', with reference to the disciples' sleeping; (ii) 'it is sufficient', with reference to the ironical rebuke (καθεύδετε...); (iii) in a technical commercial sense, 'he (i.e. Judas) has received it (i.e. the promised money)';[1] (iv) in a commercial sense but impersonally, 'it is paid up', so 'the time is up'; (v) 'he (i.e. Judas) is taking possession of (me)';[2] and, reading τὸ τέλος, (vi) ἀπέχει τὸ τέλος = 'it has its end', 'it is finished'; (vii) an Aramaic word meaning 'presses' has been wrongly read as another word meaning 'is far away'; the original sense would be: 'the end is pressing, the hour has come' or (substituting καί for ἦλθεν with D it (some MSS.)) 'the end and the hour are pressing';[3] (viii) 'the end is far away?' (ἀπέχει τὸ τέλος is then a third question, and what follows corrects the disciples' mistaken

---

[1] J. de Zwaan in *Exp.* vi, pp. 452 ff.
[2] G. H. Boobyer in *N.T.S.* ii, pp. 44–8.
[3] Black, pp. 161 f.

idea—'(On the contrary) the hour has come!')[1] Of these (i) seems on the whole the most probable.

42. ἄγωμεν may be translated 'Forward!' or 'Let us advance to meet them!' Ἄγειν was used intransitively as a military term (='to march', 'advance'), and ἄγωμεν is found as a loanword in *Genesis Rabba* meaning 'come on!' Cf. Euthymius: οὐ μόνον οὐκ ἔφυγεν, ἀλλὰ καὶ εἰς ἀπάντησιν αὐτῶν ἐξιέναι παρασκευάζεται, and Dodd, *The Interpretation of the Fourth Gospel* (Cambridge, 1953), pp. 406–9.

ἰδοὺ ὁ παραδιδούς με ἤγγικεν. Perhaps the three have not yet realized who it is who is approaching?

82. THE ARREST (xiv. 43–52)
(Mt. xxvi. 47–56; Lk. xxii. 47–53)

This section is less of a unity than the preceding one. After *vv.* 43–6 come various items loosely appended: *vv.* 47, 48f., 50, 51f. This is readily understandable; for, while Judas' arrival and his treacherous kiss would be indelibly stamped on the memories of the disciples, information about what followed immediately afterwards would tend to be scrappy and disjointed.

43. ἔτι αὐτοῦ λαλοῦντος links this section closely with the preceding.

ὄχλος μετὰ μαχαιρῶν καὶ ξύλων rather suggests a rabble collected for the purpose, though possibly it could denote some of the Temple police accompanied by slaves of the High Priest (στρατηγοὺς τοῦ ἱεροῦ in Lk. xxii. 52 suggests the presence of the former, while Mk xiv. 47 mentions a slave of the High Priest).

44. δεδώκει. For the omission of the augment see M.H. II, p. 190.

φιλήσω. The kiss was a customary greeting among the Rabbis and their disciples.

[1] J. T. Hudson in *E.T.* xlvi, p. 382.

ἀσφαλῶς. They were to take no chances.

45. ἐλθών, though it can be defended as referring to Judas' arrival at the place as opposed to his actually approaching Jesus, is probably to be regarded as redundant —perhaps a Semitism.

κατεφίλησεν. The compound perhaps indicates a prolonged kissing designed to give all the ὄχλος a chance to see which person is to be seized and to be ready to seize him at once.

46. The expression τὰς χεῖρας ἐπιβάλλειν τινί is frequent in the LXX, but is also found in Polybius, Lucian, etc.

47. Jn xviii. 10 identifies the assailant of the High Priest's slave as Peter. It is possible that εἷς τις here in Mk is meant to imply that the person's identity is known to the narrator (Lagrange cites Sophocles, *Oed. Rex*, 118, in support of this suggestion). The action was probably impulsive.

48 can be read either as a question or as a statement: in either case it is a protest against the manner of his arrest— perhaps rather against the blindness and stupidity that had deemed such force necessary than against the indignity done to himself as such.

49. καθ' ἡμέραν suggests a longer ministry in Jerusalem than Mark has recorded and is perhaps evidence in support of the Johannine tradition in this respect.   *

πρὸς ὑμᾶς. If the ὄχλος was only an *ad hoc* rabble, Jesus was hardly with (πρός) them when he was teaching in the Temple. But the ὄχλος may have included some of the Temple police, in which case πρὸς ὑμᾶς would be understandable; or it may be that some of the Sanhedrin had followed the ὄχλος to Gethsemane and by now were present (cf. Lk. xxii. 52); or we may suppose that Jesus' thought had passed beyond the actual company that was seizing him to those whose purpose they were fulfilling.

ἀλλ' ἵνα πληρωθῶσιν αἱ γραφαί could be explained as imperatival, but more probably γέγονεν should be understood (cf. Mt. xxvi. 56). For the γραφαί see on viii. 31, ix. 12.

50. ἀφέντες αὐτὸν ἔφυγον πάντες. The words drive home, as it were with hammer-blows, the failure of the disciples without exception (note the emphatic position of πάντες) and the complete forsakenness of Jesus.

51 f. It is hard to see why these two verses should be appended. Taylor is surely right in thinking that the attempt to explain them as inspired by Gen. xxxix. 12 or Amos ii. 16 is 'desperate in the extreme'. It is much more likely that we have here a genuine reminiscence. But why should Mark insert such a trivial detail in so solemn a narrative? Not unnaturally people have asked whether the unnamed young man is not Mark himself. If that were so, then these two verses would perhaps be a kind of modest signature to the gospel.

While γυμνός in v. 52 could, if v. 52 stood alone, mean 'clothed only in a χιτών', ἐπὶ γυμνοῦ in v. 51 must mean 'over his naked body', for there would be no point in saying that he had only a χιτών under his σινδών, as that would be perfectly normal. So, if ἐπὶ γυμνοῦ is read, γυμνός in v. 52 must mean 'naked'. But it is possible that ἐπὶ γυμνοῦ, which, though strongly attested, is omitted by W f1 c k sy^s sa(7), may be a correction of γυμνός, which is read here by Θ f13 (exc. 124) 543 565 sy^p eth, but must surely be due to a copyist's eye straying from σινδόνα in v. 51 to σινδόνα in v. 52. The view that ἐπὶ γυμνοῦ should be omitted is supported by the fact that ἐπὶ γυμνοῦ is an odd expression, the natural Greek for 'over his naked body' being ἐπὶ χρωτός or ἐν χρῷ; but the textual question cannot be regarded as settled beyond doubt. It is, therefore, impossible to be certain whether the young man was wearing nothing but his σινδών or whether he was wearing it over his χιτών.

The word σινδών denotes fine linen cloth or a garment made of it. Here it presumably denotes a linen ἱμάτιον or outer garment. (The ἱμάτιον was wrapped around one and so could more easily be discarded, if it had been seized, than

438

the χιτών, which had sleeves.) The use of σινδών is significant. The ἱμάτιον was normally of wool. This particular garment was apparently one of superior quality, which the owner would be specially sorry to lose.

Why the young man was following we are not told. Possibly he had heard of Judas' treachery and come (if ἐπὶ γυμνοῦ is read, one might guess that he had come straight from his bed without stopping to put on his χιτών) to warn Jesus, but arrived too late, and then followed the crowd as Jesus was led away. But here we are in the realm of speculation.

83. JESUS BEFORE THE SANHEDRIN (xiv. 53-65)
(Mt. xxvi. 57-68; Lk. xxii. 54f., 67-71, 63-5)

With regard to the ultimate source behind *vv.* 55-64, it seems reasonable to suppose that the tradition rests on the testimony of a member or members of the Sanhedrin. Some who were already well-disposed to Jesus may have been present (πάντες in *v.* 64 should perhaps not be insisted on too rigidly?), or the informant may have been someone who actually voted against Jesus but later came to believe in him (cf. Acts vi. 7, xv. 5?). The narrative seems too precise to be mere hearsay such as Peter might have heard in the court-yard; at the same time it is not as doctrinally coloured as it surely would have been, were it the free construction of the early community. (True, we are reminded of Isa. liii. 7 in *v.* 61a, but in a free creation there would surely have been more O.T. echoes.)

On the question whether the Sanhedrin had at this time the right to pronounce and execute a capital sentence reference may be made to Barrett, *John*, pp. 445f. Quite probably they did, and, had they wished, could have condemned and executed Jesus by stoning without reference to Pilate. But the leaders of the opposition to Jesus may well have felt that it suited their purpose better to make use of the Roman power—perhaps because they thought that in this way Pilate would bear the biggest share of the odium that the execution of Jesus might arouse among some elements of the people, perhaps because they wanted Jesus to die a death that was under the curse of the Law (Deut. xxi. 23), and perhaps because they felt that a political charge of treason before Pilate would be surer of success than a charge of blasphemy before the Sanhedrin.

The proceedings described in *vv.* 55–64 seem to have been not a trial but rather a preliminary inquiry held with a view to the formulation of a charge to bring before Pilate. (When this is recognized, the objections which have been made against the historicity of the narrative on the ground that the procedure described is not consistent with the rules for the conduct of trials laid down in (*M*) *Sanh.* iv–vii, are seen to be irrelevant.) The production of evidence with regard to the Temple (*vv.* 57f.) and the High Priest's concentration on 'blasphemy' in *v.* 64 are probably to be explained by the desire of the Jewish leaders to carry as many as possible of the Sanhedrin with them. Evidence of disrespect for the Temple or of blasphemy would be more likely to unite them than evidence of a possible threat to the Roman power. Having once got the members to agree that Jesus deserved to die as a blasphemer, the High Priest presumably then obtained agreement that they should actually proceed before Pilate with a political charge. It is of course clear that it was on a political charge—that of being a messianic pretender—that Jesus was actually condemned and executed by the Romans.

It seems probable that the meeting described in this section was informal, being held at night in the High Priest's house, and that the Sanhedrin had been summoned for the morning (xv. 1). If the morning meeting, though the more formal gathering, merely confirmed the decisions reached during the night, it was not unnatural that Mark should mention it only in passing.

See further Taylor's Additional Note, 'The Examination before the Priests', and the literature there cited, to which should be added G. D. Kilpatrick, *The Trial of Jesus* (Oxford, 1953). *

53. τὸν ἀρχιερέα: i.e. Caiaphas, who held office A.D. 18–36. The Synoptists do not mention Annas in connection with the Passion.

After συνέρχονται most authorities attest αὐτῷ, and it should probably be read. Its omission (ℵ D L Δ Θ f13 *al* lat) may have been due to a tendency to regard this as a formal meeting of the Sanhedrin.

54. ἕως ἔσω: 'right inside'. The palace would be built round the αὐλή or open courtyard, which would be entered through the προαύλιον mentioned in v. 68. Jn xviii. 15 f. explains how Peter was able to get so far. φῶς is used in the sense of πῦρ, as sometimes in classical Greek, but the idea of the light shed by the fire and illuminating Peter is in mind.

55. ὅλον τὸ συνέδριον is possibly a loose way of saying 'all the members of the Sanhedrin present'. The words ἐζήτουν κατὰ τοῦ Ἰησοῦ μαρτυρίαν support the view that this was an inquiry for the purpose of collecting evidence rather than a formal trial.

εἰς τό + infinitive occurs in Mk only here. It is frequent in Paul (e.g. Rom. i. 11, 20, iii. 26), but also occurs in Mt., Lk., Acts, Heb., I Pet. θανατῶσαι αὐτόν may be translated 'accomplish his death': it need not imply that they were expecting themselves to pronounce the effective sentence. (Cf. xiii. 12.)

56 explains οὐχ ηὕρισκον in v. 55. The agreement of two or three witnesses was required (cf. Num. xxxv. 30, Deut. xvii. 6, xix. 15).

58. Cf. xv. 29, Jn ii. 19–22, Acts vi. 14. There is little doubt that an actual saying of Jesus (probably distinct from

xiii. 2) lies behind this accusation. But, since the accusation is explicitly stated to be false (*v.* 57; cf. Acts vi. 13f.), and xv. 29 is the mockery of the passers-by, and Jn ii. 19 is quite probably not independent of Mk xiv. 58, xv. 29, it seems clear that the original form of the saying cannot be established with anything like certainty and that explanations of its original meaning should therefore be offered only tentatively and received with the utmost caution. It may perhaps have been a prediction of the destruction of the Temple and its replacement by the new Temple of the last times (cf., e.g., I Enoch xc. 28f.); or it may have been simply a prediction of the death and resurrection of Jesus, couched perhaps in the form of a *māšāl*.

It seems likely that χειροποίητον and ἀχειροποίητον are interpretative glosses added by the early Church. They have the effect of ruling out the mistaken interpretation of the Jews in Jn ii. 20. One might perhaps wonder whether a passive is not more likely to have been used than either the καταλύσω of Mk or the λύσατε of Jn. That false witnesses should have twisted a statement that the Temple would be destroyed into a statement that he himself would destroy it is quite possible. The phrase διὰ τριῶν ἡμερῶν ('after three days') is probably indefinite, 'three' standing for 'a few'.

On this verse see further: G. Schrenk in *T.W.N.T.* iii, pp. 243–5; O. Michel in *T.W.N.T.* iv, pp. 887–9.

60. εἰς μέσον. Perhaps to be explained as pregnant: 'arose (and stepped) into the midst (of the assembly)'; otherwise as meaning 'in the midst'.

Οὐκ ἀποκρίνῃ...καταμαρτυροῦσιν; is better taken as two questions (question mark after οὐδέν): to take it as a single question is unsatisfactory, for after ἀποκρίνεσθαι οὐδέν an indirect question introduced by τί would be very harsh— one would expect rather to have πρός.

61. Σὺ εἶ ὁ Χριστὸς ὁ Υἱὸς τοῦ Εὐλογητοῦ; That the

High Priest should thus attempt to make Jesus convict himself is hardly surprising in view of the earlier attempts to trap Jesus (xii. 13, ἵνα αὐτὸν ἀγρεύσωσιν λόγῳ); but in view of Rabbinic legal principles (see Barrett, *John*, p. 441) it is perhaps more likely to have occurred in a preliminary inquiry than in a formal trial. On ὁ Χριστός see on viii. 29. The fact that the High Priest asked this question implies that by this time the Jewish authorities had come either to suspect that Jesus might, or to know that he did, regard himself as the Messiah. It is conceivable that Judas had betrayed the secret which Jesus had bidden his disciples to keep to themselves (viii. 30); but, quite apart from that possibility, it is highly probable that, in spite of his injunctions to secrecy and his carefulness to avoid making any overt messianic claim, and in spite of the fact that many things about him were inconsistent with what was expected of the Messiah, some of the things which he had done and said would have raised in the minds of the chief priests and scribes the question whether perhaps behind his authoritative manner there might be an implicit claim to be the Messiah.

At first sight it looks as if ὁ Ὑιός τοῦ Εὐλογητοῦ (τοῦ Εὐλογητοῦ is of course a periphrasis for the Divine Name: cf. (*M*) *Ber.* vii. 3) is simply added as an obvious messianic title; but this is probably not the case, since it seems improbable that 'Son of God' was used as a messianic title in pre-Christian Palestinian Judaism (cf. Jeremias, *Parables*, p. 57; and see on i. 11). It is more likely that the words were added because the authorities were aware of some such utterance of Jesus as Mt. xi. 27 = Lk. x. 22 or had drawn conclusions from the parable of the Wicked Husbandmen (xii. 1–12).

62. Ἐγώ εἰμι. Θ f13 *pc* geo arm Origen attest σὺ εἶπας ὅτι ἐγώ εἰμι, which would account for Mt. xxvi. 64, Lk. xxii. 70 (it is not near enough to them to be easily explicable as

assimilation) and is intrinsically likely, being consistent with
Jesus' attitude toward the messianic title (cf. his immediate
substitution of 'Son of Man' in this verse). If ἐγώ εἰμι alone
is read, then we have here a clear affirmative answer, the
explanation of which must be that now at last, when he is
in the power of his foes and in such circumstances as make
the claim altogether paradoxical, it is consistent with his
mission to declare openly what hitherto he has had to veil.
But, if the Θ reading is accepted, the answer, though it is
still affirmative, is more guarded: 'it registers a difference
of interpretation...as if to indicate that the Speaker has
His own ideas about Messiahship' (Taylor). (For this σὺ
εἶπας Schlatter, *Evang. Matt.* pp. 740f., gives interesting
Rabbinic examples. In one of them the bearer of a piece of
bad news knows that it has been decided to kill the messenger
who brings this particular news. So he suggests the truth by
means of a parable, and then, when asked whether the
* matter is so, replies, 'You have said it'.)

καὶ ὄψεσθε κ.τ.λ. According to some interpreters (e.g.
Lagrange, T. F. Glasson,[1] Taylor, J. A. T. Robinson[2]) there
is here no reference at all to a second coming of Christ.
Both the O.T. passages echoed here (Ps. cx. 1, Dan. vii. 13),
it is argued, refer to exaltation, and ὄψεσθε does not refer to
a particular apocalyptic event, but 'more probably indicates that the priests will see facts and circumstances which
will show that Ps. cx. 1 and Dan. vii. 13 are fulfilled in the
person and work of Jesus' (Taylor). But, while it is true that
Dan. vii. 13 refers to a coming *to* God rather than from him
to the earth, the order of the two quotations rules out this
interpretation here; for in Mk the coming *follows* the sitting.
If then the reference in ὄψεσθε is to the Parousia, is it implied
that the Parousia is expected to occur during the lifetime of
the High Priest and his associates? Surely not! A more

---

[1] *The Second Advent* (London, 2nd ed. 1947), pp. 63–8.
[2] In *E.T.* LXVII, pp. 336–40.

probable explanation is that of J. P. Bercovitz:[1] they will see the Son of Man when he comes as Judge—possibly indeed during their lifetimes, but equally possibly after their deaths, when they are raised up for the last judgement. (The ἀπ' ἄρτι in Mt. xxvi. 64 is either to be understood as ἀπαρτί meaning 'surely', perhaps equivalent to αμην,[2] or as indicating that from henceforth (i.e. from the time of his death) they will not see him at all till they see him in his glory.)

For τῆς δυνάμεως as a periphrasis for the Divine Name cf. j Sanh. 28a.

63. τοὺς χιτῶνας αὐτοῦ. The plural is used in the sense 'clothes', 'clothing' (cf. τὰ ἱμάτια in the Mt. parallel and in xv. 24).

By rending his clothes the High Priest indicated that he regarded what he had just heard as blasphemy (cf. (M) Sanh. vii. 5).

64. τῆς βλασφημίας. See on ii. 7 (βλασφημεῖ). The High Priest probably has in mind Jesus' claim that they will see the Son of Man ἐκ δεξιῶν καθήμενον τῆς δυνάμεως; possibly also, if the direct ἐγώ εἰμι should be read, his claim to be the Son of the Blessed. A claim to be the Messiah was, of course, not in itself liable to be regarded as blasphemy.

κατέκριναν αὐτὸν ἔνοχον εἶναι θανάτου. Mark probably uses this form of expression rather than κατέκριναν αὐτὸν θανάτῳ (or ἀποθανεῖν), because he is aware that this was not a formal trial and that they were not pronouncing a sentence but rather giving a legal opinion.

65 seems to be a separate item which has been appended to the preceding narrative. In Lk. the parallel (xxii. 63 f.) is placed after Peter's denials and Mark's τινες are identified as οἱ ἄνδρες οἱ συνέχοντες αὐτόν. It is possible that we should

[1] In *The Parables of the Messiah*, an unpublished Edinburgh University doctoral thesis.
[2] Cf. A. Debrunner in *C.N.* xi, pp. 45–9.

read with D *a d f* τῷ προσώπῳ αὐτοῦ instead of αὐτῷ καὶ περικαλύπτειν αὐτοῦ τὸ πρόσωπον, and explain the majority reading as due to the influence of περικαλύψαντες αὐτόν in Lk. xxii. 64. Mt. xxvi. 67 provides support for the reading of D *a d f*.

κολαφίζειν. A word used several times in the N.T. and found in a pagan letter, but not attested in classical Greek or the LXX.

Προφήτευσον has in Mk (contrast Lk.) a general sense ('Play the prophet now!' perhaps with reference to the accusation mentioned in *v.* 58), for in Mk the words χριστέ, τίς ἐστιν ὁ παίσας σε; which are added in some MSS. are clearly not original. This is so, even if the longer reading with its reference to the covering of the head is preferred.

ῥαπίσμασιν...ἔλαβον seems to be a vulgarism, possibly due to Latin influence: cf. *verberibus accipere* (e.g. Cicero, *Tusc.* II. 14), and κονδύλοις ἔλαβεν, which occurs in a first-century papyrus.

84. PETER'S DENIALS (xiv. 66-72)
(Mt. xxvi. 69-75; Lk. xxii. 56-62)

Most probably Petrine.

66. If *v.* 54 was originally part of the story of the denial, ὄντος τοῦ Πέτρου κάτω ἐν τῇ αὐλῇ will be Mark's editorial adjustment on inserting *vv.* 55-65.

67. ἐμβλέψασα indicates that she looked straight at him, while ἰδοῦσα merely indicates that she noticed him.

The order τοῦ Ναζαρηνοῦ...τοῦ Ἰησοῦ is perhaps contemptuous.

68. ἠρνήσατο: 'denied (it)'; but possibly the reader is intended to think also of the meaning 'denied (him)'.

Οὔτε οἶδα οὔτε ἐπίσταμαι σὺ τί λέγεις may be variously interpreted according to whether we take the whole as one sentence or put a full stop after ἐπίσταμαι and a question-mark after λέγεις, and according to how we understand οἶδα and ἐπίσταμαι. Thus, (i) I neither know nor understand what you say (mean). (ii) I neither know him, nor do I understand what you say (mean). (iii) I neither know nor understand this that you say. What do you mean? (iv) I neither know nor am acquainted with him. What do you mean? A further suggestion is that there has been a mistranslation of an original Aramaic, which should have been rendered: (v) I neither know nor am I acquainted with him of whom you speak. We should perhaps choose (iii) or (i) on the ground that psychologically the first denial would more probably be indirect than direct.

ἐξῆλθεν ἔξω εἰς τὸ προαύλιον. Doubtless to escape unwelcome attention.

After προαύλιον the words καὶ ἀλέκτωρ ἐφώνησεν should probably be read, though omitted by ℵ B L W c syˢ. The omission of the words is probably to be explained as assimilation to Mt. and Lk., in which only one cock-crowing is mentioned—perhaps in order to make the denial seem a little less shameful. See on v. 30.

69. There is some variation between the four gospels as to who challenged Peter the second and third times, but Mark's account is simpler and to be preferred.

70. The imperfect ἠρνεῖτο suggests repeated denials.

Both the third challenge and the third denial are more emphatic than the others. The balance of probability seems to be in favour of reading καὶ ἡ λαλιά σου ὁμοιάζει after Γαλιλαῖος εἶ, in spite of the impressive witnesses for omission; for, if the words were an assimilation to Mt., the substitution of the rather odd ὁμοιάζει for the Mt. δῆλόν σε ποιεῖ would be difficult to explain, and the fact that D has ὁμοιάζει in the Mt. parallel favours the view that it was present in Mk.

71. ἀναθεματίζειν. Calling down curses perhaps both on himself, should he be lying, and also on those who say

* that he is a disciple of Jesus. It is noticeable that in Lk. there is no mention of Peter's cursing and swearing.

ὃν λέγετε: 'of whom you speak'. For this use of the accusative with λέγειν cf. Jn vi. 71, viii. 27, I Cor. x. 29.

72. On the question of ἐκ δευτέρου and δίς, both of which are omitted by some MSS., see on *vv.* 30 and 68.

ἐπιβαλών is difficult. Many different interpretations have been suggested: 'when he thought thereon'; 'covering his head'; 'drawing his cloak about his face'; 'dashing out'; 'throwing himself on the ground'; 'set to and'. The last, which is Moulton's suggestion,[1] is perhaps the most probable: it is accepted by Debrunner.[2]

85. THE TRIAL BEFORE PILATE (xv. 1–15)
(Mt. xxvii. 1 f., 11–26; Lk. xxiii. 1–5, 17–25)

The narrative is realistic and notably restrained, and clearly rests on primitive tradition.

1. For ἐτοιμάσαντες (א C L 892 1342) the better attested and also more difficult ποιήσαντες (A B W and the great majority of Greek MSS., also vg arm Aug.) should be read (cf. the Western reading ἐποίησαν, which looks like a mistake). While συμβούλιον ἐτοιμάσαντες would mean 'having prepared (reached) a decision', συμβούλιον ποιήσαντες must mean 'having held a council (consultation)'. The reading ἐτοιμάσαντες gets rid of the reference to a second meeting and so brings Mk in line with Mt. Taylor accepts ποιήσαντες and explains the reference to two meetings by the suggestion that Mark has inserted xiv. 55–65 into a narrative which originally only had this morning session. For what is surely a more probable explanation see the introduction to section 83.

δήσαντες. Jn xviii. 12 refers to a binding of Jesus at an earlier stage.

παρέδωκαν. See on ix. 31.

[1] *Proleg.* pp. 131 f.   [2] D.–B., §308.

Πειλάτῳ. Mark only gives his cognomen and assumes that his readers will know that he was the Procurator. He †
was Procurator of Judea A.D. 25/26–36. For information about him see, in addition to Lk. xiii. 1, Philo, *Leg. ad Gaium*, 38; Josephus, *Ant.* xviii. 35–89, *B.J.* ii. 169–77; Tacitus, *Ann.* xv. 44. Pilate would probably be resident in the fortress of Antonia (which overlooked the Temple area) during the Passover. Another view is that he would reside in Herod's palace.

2. **Σὺ εἶ ὁ Βασιλεὺς τῶν Ἰουδαίων;** Pilate perhaps has the charge in writing before him; at any rate he is using the terms of the Sanhedrin's accusation, and asking Jesus whether he admits its truth. The verse makes clear what the charge was (cf. *v.* 32).

For Σὺ λέγεις see on xiv. 62 (ἐγώ εἰμι).

3. πολλά is here more probably the direct object of κατηγόρουν (πόσα in *v.* 4 seems to support this) than used adverbially. τί τινος κατηγορεῖν is good Greek.

Though not in ℵ B D, etc., the words αὐτὸς δὲ οὐδὲν ἀπεκρίνατο (W Δ Θ *pc* f13 *al a c* sy^{s,h} geo eth arm) should probably be read after πολλά; *v.* 4 seems to presuppose some such statement.

5. οὐκέτι οὐδὲν ἀπεκρίθη. Cf. xiv. 61. It is not impossible that Jesus himself may have had Isa. liii. 7 in mind.

θαυμάζειν τὸν Πειλᾶτον. Cf. Isa. lii. 15 (LXX); and see on i. 22 (ἐξεπλήσσοντο).

6. There is no evidence of this custom outside the gospels. Perhaps the nearest parallel is *P. Flor.*, 61. 59 ff. (A.D. 85), in which a governor of Egypt says to a certain Phibion: 'Thou hadst been worthy of scourging... but I will give thee to the people.'

7. ὁ λεγόμενος Βαραββᾶς. The only other place in the N.T. where ὁ λεγόμενος is used in an exactly analogous way seems to be Lk. xxii. 47. Elsewhere it is used to attach a title or alternative name to a personal name already

mentioned (e.g. Mt. xxvii. 22) or to attach a name to a common noun or equivalent (e.g. Mt. xxvi. 3, Jn ix. 11). So, while (in view of Lk. xxii. 47) this expression cannot be called impossible, it is certainly unusual. Moreover, in Mt. xxvii. 16f. Θ f1 sy$^{s, pal}$ attest the addition of Ἰησοῦν, a reading which Origen mentions but rejects on theological grounds. It seems extremely probable that the addition should be read in Mt. xxvii. 16f., and, as this passage in Mt. is dependent on Mk, it is probable that Mk originally had Ἰησοῦς ὁ λεγ. B., and that Ἰησοῦς was omitted for the sake of reverence. (See further A. Deissmann in *Mysterium Christi*, ed. G. K. A. Bell and A. Deissmann, London, 1930, pp. 12–27.)

Βαραββᾶς (Aramaic *Bar 'Abbā'* = 'son of the father') is found as a surname of several Rabbis. The explanation that it represents *Bar-Rabbān* ('son of a Rabbi') is improbable.

στασιαστής is a late word meaning 'insurrectionist'. The insurrection is mentioned as something well known (ἐν τῇ στάσει simply), which it may well have been, although it is not mentioned outside the N.T. For the pluperfect without augment (πεποιήκεισαν) here and also in *v.* 10 (παραδεδώκεισαν) see on xiv. 44.

8. ἀναβάς should probably be preferred to the ἀναβοήσας of the majority of MSS. It has strong support in ℵ* B D latt co. It would be particularly appropriate, if Pilate was in the fortress of Antonia.

ὁ ὄχλος. Probably supporters of Barabbas who had come to ask for his release. The order of the verses supports this view; for the fact that *v.* 7 is placed before *v.* 8 rather than before *v.* 11 suggests that it is the explanation of *v.* 8 and not just of *v.* 11. There is no reason to think that *v.* 11 must mean that the priests suggested to the crowd something it had not already thought of; ἀνέσεισαν may equally well mean that they encouraged the crowd in its original purpose and sought to prevent it from being deflected by Pilate.

After αἰτεῖσθαι there is an ellipse: the meaning is 'asked (him to do) as...'.

9. Pilate's question perhaps reflects a misunderstanding on his part. Had he heard them asking for Jesus (i.e. Barabbas) and thought they meant Jesus of Nazareth?

10 may then be understood as explaining why it was that Pilate thought the crowd was asking for the release of Jesus of Nazareth—it was natural for him to think this, since he knew that Jesus was popular and that it was on account of their jealousy of his popularity and influence that the chief priests had delivered him up.

11. On the significance of ἀνέσεισαν see on v. 8 above.

ἵνα κ.τ.λ. There is an ellipse, the real meaning being 'that they should rather ask him to release...'.

12. The great majority of MSS. and versions read θέλετε before ποιήσω, but it is omitted by ℵ B C W Δ Ψ 1 13 al co geo, and should probably not be read. With regard to ὃν λέγετε, though there is strong support for its omission, the balance is perhaps in favour of retaining it.

That Pilate should have asked the crowd this question is surprising, but not incredible. Did he hope that the crowd would beg for the release of Jesus of Nazareth as well? Did he intend in that case to make a show of generosity by releasing two prisoners instead of one? Or did he hope to persuade them to alter their request?

13. πάλιν: here 'thereupon'.

14. Pilate's admission of Jesus' innocence which is implicit in his question (Τί γὰρ ἐποίησεν κακόν;) is made explicit in Lk. xxiii. 22 by the addition of οὐδὲν αἴτιον θανάτου εὗρον ἐν αὐτῷ (cf. Jn xviii. 38, xix. 4).

15. βουλόμενος is stronger than θέλων.

τῷ ὄχλῳ τὸ ἱκανὸν ποιῆσαι. Τινὶ τὸ ἱκανὸν ποιεῖν is a Latinism (= satis facere). It is used in the LXX in Jer. xxxi (R.V.: xlviii). 30 in a similar sense. In Polybius and Diogenes

Laertius it is used in the sense of 'giving security', which is another meaning of the Lat. *satis facere*.

φραγελλώσας. A Latin loanword. Φραγελλῶ is a transliteration of *flagello*. The fearful scourging it denotes was the normal prelude to crucifixion (cf. Josephus, *B.J.* II. 306, 308, v. 449; Livy, XXXIII. 36).

86. THE MOCKING BY THE SOLDIERS (XV. 16–20)
(Mt. xxvii. 27–31)

The parallel between ἵνα σταυρωθῇ in *v.* 15 and ἵνα σταυρώσωσιν αὐτόν in *v.* 20 is hardly sufficient reason for thinking that Mark has inserted *vv.* 16–20 into a narrative which did not originally include them, though the suggestion is not impossible. In any case, the section would seem to rest on primitive tradition.

That some of the actions of the soldiers may have been suggested by customs such as are described by J. G. Frazer, *The Golden Bough*, III, pp. 138 ff., is just conceivable. (On this see further the useful additional note in Taylor, pp. 646–8.)

On this section Calvin's comment is apt: 'But these matters call for secret meditation, rather than for the ornament of words.'

16. τῆς αὐλῆς. If αὐλή here means 'courtyard', then the explanatory ὅ ἐστιν Πραιτώριον is somewhat loosely attached (for πραιτώριον denotes the whole building, not just the courtyard); but perhaps here αὐλή means 'palace', as in I Macc. xi. 46.

Πραιτώριον. A Latin loanword, which was used of the official residence of a governor.

σπεῖραν. The word usually denotes a Roman cohort (about 600 men), but is also used of a maniple (200 men). It is here probably used quite loosely to denote the detachment of soldiers present in the Praetorium.

17. πορφύραν. The Mt. parallel probably interprets correctly by χλαμύδα κοκκίνην, i.e. 'a scarlet military cloak'. For *purpura* as the characteristic of kings cf., e.g., Virgil, *Georg.* II. 495 (*purpura regum*); of the Emperor, cf., e.g., Ammianus Marcellinus, XXI. 9. 8. The soldier's cloak was perhaps used as the nearest substitute for the *purpura* available.

ἀκάνθινον στέφανον. On the possible identification of the species of 'thorn' used see Dalman, *S.S.W.* pp. 246–8.[1] They probably had in mind the royal διάδημα.

18. Χαῖρε, Βασιλεῦ. Cf. the Latin greeting, *Ave, Caesar.*

19. προσεκύνουν αὐτῷ. Perhaps 'did homage to him'; but perhaps more than ordinary homage is meant, 'a mockery in terms of Caesar worship, or Oriental ideas of kingship' (Taylor).

20. The aorist ἐνέπαιξαν must be translated by the English pluperfect (cf. Jn xix. 30; see Moule, pp. 11, 16).

87. THE CRUCIFIXION (xv. 21–41)
(Mt. xxvii. 32–56; Lk. xxiii. 26–49)

These verses lack the sort of unity which may be expected in a narrative derived from the reminiscence of a single eyewitness; they give the impression of being rather the result of the piecing together of a number of eye-witness testimonies. But that is no reason to doubt their reliability. The suggestion that some of the details have been created on the basis of O.T. texts is improbable. If all the features containing O.T. echoes are removed, there are very few details left; and it is scarcely credible that the early Church should have preserved the memory of so few details of happenings so central to its life and so dramatic and which had been witnessed by so many people. But it was natural that the

[1] See also H. St J. Hart, 'The Crown of Thorns in John xix. 2–5', in *J.T.S.*, n.s. III (1952), pp. 66–75.

O.T. passages should influence the language in which the details were related.

21. It was normal for the condemned himself to carry the cross-beam of his cross to the place of execution. Presumably Jesus had carried it for a while, but had been physically unable to carry it further. Otherwise the impressing of someone to carry it for him would be surprising. (Contrast Jn xix. 17: John's omission of any reference to Simon was perhaps due to a desire to counter some Docetist idea that Simon had been crucified instead of Jesus.) This physical inability seems to call for explanation, since others who had also been scourged before crucifixion did carry their cross-beams themselves: it is reasonable to connect it (and perhaps also the fact that Jesus died more quickly than was usual (cf. xv. 44)) with the unique character of his sufferings (see on xiv. 33f., 36, xv. 34). The contrast between this picture and that of the effortless superiority of the ideal hero (e.g. *Odyssey*, XXI. 409: ἄτερ σπουδῆς!) is striking and significant.

ἀγγαρεύουσιν. Cf. Mt. v. 41. The word is said to be of Persian origin.

Κυρηναῖον does not tell us whether he was a Jew of the Diaspora or a Gentile.

ἐρχόμενον ἀπ' ἀγροῦ. Not necessarily from work on the land. He may have been coming from somewhere just outside the city. So this detail should not be regarded as evidence against the Synoptic chronology (see on xiv. 12); he may anyway have been a Gentile.

τὸν πατέρα 'Αλεξάνδρου καὶ 'Ρούφου. It is implied that the two names are well known to Mark's readers. Apparently Alexander and Rufus (perhaps Simon too) were Christians. Is this Rufus perhaps the same as the one mentioned in Rom. xvi. 13? The two sons are mentioned only by Mark. The account does not encourage any speculation on the feelings of Simon, but it is natural to wonder whether this experience led to his conversion.

ἵνα ἄρῃ τὸν σταυρὸν αὐτοῦ. The similarity of language to viii. 34 is noticeable.

22. φέρουσιν. For φέρειν meaning 'bring' cf. vii. 32, viii. 22, etc.

Γολγοθάν. In the Mt. parallel it is treated as indeclinable. It represents Aramaic *gulgaltā'* or *gólgóltā'* (=Hebrew *gulgôlet*), 'a skull'. It is not stated in the gospels that the place was a hill, but it is possible that it was and that its shape had suggested the name, or the name may have signified that the place was unclean (a reason for its being used for executions). Legend connects the place with the burial of Adam's skull. On the question of its identification see Dalman, *S.S.W.* pp. 346–56; Jeremias, *Golgotha* (1926); A. Parrot, *Golgotha and the Church of the Holy Sepulchre* (London, 1957).

23. It was a Jewish custom, based on Prov. xxxi. 6, to give wine drugged with myrrh to those who were about to be executed, in order to dull the senses. His refusal to drink may be explained as due to his vow recorded in xiv. 25. Another motive was probably also present—the will to avoid nothing of the cup which his Father had given him.

ἐδίδουν is best explained as conative.

24. καὶ σταυροῦσιν αὐτόν. The actual crucifixion is thus recorded with the utmost possible restraint. Crucifixion was the way in which slaves were executed. Cicero calls it *crudelissimum taeterrimumque supplicium.*

διαμερίζονται κ.τ.λ. It was customary for the condemned to be crucified naked, and his clothes were a recognized perquisite of his executioners. The words are reminiscent of Ps. xxii. 18; but there is no need to assume that the detail was suggested by the psalm. For the plural τὰ ἱμάτια meaning 'clothing' see on xiv. 63.

25. ὥρα τρίτη: i.e. about 9 a.m. Contrast Jn xix. 14. The most probable explanation of the disagreement between

Mk and Jn is that the later evangelist was influenced by the desire to represent Jesus as the true Paschal lamb—the killing of the lambs began at midday. But other explanations have been suggested: e.g. that there has been a confusion between a Γ (3) and a Ϝ (6).

The καί should here be translated 'when' (see Moule, p. 172).

26. It was the custom of the Romans to display a notice indicating the crime for which the person was being executed. In Jn xix. 19 a transliteration of the actual Latin term for this (*titulus*) is used. The words of the *titulus* make it clear that it was as a messianic pretender that Jesus had been condemned. The heathen governor unwittingly proclaimed the truth of Jesus' messianic Kingship and became 'a herald of Christ in the same sense that Caiaphas was a prophet (Jn xi. 51)' (Calvin). (Cf. Ἄλλους ἔσωσεν in *v.* 31, ὁ Χριστὸς ὁ Βασιλεὺς Ἰσραηλ in *v.* 32, and the centurion's declaration in *v.* 39.)

[28.] (καὶ ἐπληρώθη ἡ γραφὴ ἡ λέγουσα· Καὶ μετὰ ἀνόμων ἐλογίσθη) is added in many Greek MSS., and in lat syᵖ bo (a few MSS.), but it is not in ℵ A B C D *k* syˢ sa bo (most MSS.), and should not be read. Cf. Lk. xxii. 37.

29. That there should be passers-by is not surprising, since the place of crucifixion was quite probably close to a road out of the city, nor is their mockery at all unlikely. It is therefore quite unnecessary to suppose that this feature was suggested by Lam. ii. 15, though it is likely that the language in which it is related has been influenced by the O.T. (see also Jer. xviii. 16, Ps. xxii. 7). For the latter part of the verse see on xiv. 58.

31. The mockery of the chief priests and scribes is to the same effect as that of the passers-by, though not, like theirs, directly addressed to Jesus.

Ἄλλους ἔσωσεν. They are thinking of his healing miracles no doubt; but Mark will mean his readers to catch the unintentional *double entendre* (the full Christian significance of σώζειν). Cf. *v.* 26 and note.

ἑαυτὸν οὐ δύναται σῶσαι also has a double meaning. The speakers refer to the powerlessness of one nailed to a cross, and, in the sense in which they mean them, the words are untrue—he who had raised the dead could also have come down from the cross. On the other hand, he could not save himself if he was to remain true to his mission, if he was to save the world.

32. Ισραηλ. Whereas the Gentile Pilate had used the term οἱ Ἰουδαῖοι (*vv.* 2, 9, 12, 26; cf. *v.* 18, and also Mt. ii. 2, where it is used by the Magi), the chief priests and scribes use the term Ισραηλ, the proper designation of the people of God.

νῦν. Note the cruel sarcasm: 'now'—with reference to his helplessness.

ἵνα ἴδωμεν καὶ πιστεύσωμεν. Cf. Jn vi. 30; also Mk viii. 11 f. It was the same demand for a σημεῖον, a compelling proof, that Jesus had all along had to refuse. It had to be refused now, because the world's salvation depended on his staying on the cross and drinking the cup his Father had given him to the dregs. But, even apart from that reason, to give them in their unbelief the sort of 'seeing' they were demanding would have been to make impossible a real 'believing'. See on iv. 11 f.

καὶ οἱ συνεσταυρωμένοι σὺν αὐτῷ ὠνείδιζον αὐτόν. For ὠνείδιζον cf. Ps. xlii (LXX: xli). 10. Whatever it was they said, it is likely that their reproaches amounted to the challenge: 'Where is thy God?'

The silence with which Jesus meets this threefold chorus of mockery (*vv.* 29–32) is yet another step along the costly path of his messianic hiddenness.

33. The darkness which lasted from noon till 3 p.m. was possibly caused by a 'black sirocco' (cf. Bishop, *Jesus of Pal.* p. 250). Some see here in the coincidence of such a natural phenomenon with the last hours of Jesus' sufferings a miracle, others a legendary development.

γῆν. Here 'land' rather than 'earth'.

34 gives the only saying from the Cross recorded in Mk.

Ελωι Ελωι λαμα σαβαχθανει; A transliteration of *'elōhî 'elōhî lāmāh šᵉbaktanî*, which is a Hebrew-tinged Aramaic version of Ps. xxii. 1. Though repeated naturally in Aramaic in the earliest Church, the cry was probably originally uttered in Hebrew; for the Hebrew *'ēlî 'ēlî* would more easily be mistaken for the name of the prophet (or perhaps with Jeremias, *T.W.N.T.* II, p. 937, we should regard the Mt. form as original, in which the first two words are Hebrew, the others Aramaic).

The view of Bultmann that this saying is 'clearly[!] a secondary interpretation of the inarticulate cry of Jesus in *v.* 37, formed under the influence of Ps. xxii. 1' is most improbable; for the early Church is not likely to have invented Jesus' quotation of such words—that it was a source of embarrassment to the early Church is clear (cf. its omission by Lk. and Jn; and the variations in Mk in the textual tradition). We are on the firmest historical ground here. But what then does the saying mean? Various attempts have been made to get rid of its offence: e.g. it has been suggested that Jesus had the whole psalm in mind and that therefore the saying was really an expression of faith cut short by physical weakness which prevented him from quoting more; or that Jesus felt forsaken but was not really forsaken. But such softening explanations are unsatisfactory. Rather is the cry to be understood in the light of xiv. 36, II Cor. v. 21, Gal. iii. 13. The burden of the world's sin, his complete self-identification with sinners, involved not merely a felt, but a real, abandonment by his Father. It is in the cry of dereliction that the full horror of man's sin stands revealed. But the cry also marks the lowest depth of the hiddenness of the Son of God—and so the triumphant τετέλεσται of Jn xix. 30 is, paradoxically, its true interpretation. When this depth had been reached, the victory had been won. (It is, of course, theologically important to maintain the paradox that, while this God-forsakenness was utterly real, the unity of the Blessed Trinity was even then unbroken.)

35. τινες τῶν παρεστηκότων. Presumably Jews, since they think of Elijah.

'Hλείαν φωνεῖ. On the idea of Elijah as helper in time of need see Jeremias in *T.W.N.T.* II, pp. 932f. The present passage is the earliest evidence for it cited by Jeremias; but Elijah is often celebrated as helper in time of need in legends of a later date.

36. τις. Probably a soldier.

ὄξους probably denotes *posca* or sour wine, a supply of which the soldiers may be supposed to have brought for their own use. The incident apparently reminded the early Church of Ps. lxix. 21—hence perhaps the use of ἐπότιζεν.

"Αφετε is better taken closely with ἴδωμεν ('Let us see') than separately ('Let him alone; let us see'). Cf. Mt. vii. 4. In Mt. these words are represented as spoken, not by the soldier, but by οἱ λοιποί. It is possible that Mt. is correct in this, and that the attribution of the words to the soldier originated accidentally when Mark combined two separate items of tradition by inserting one (*v.* 36a) into the middle of the other (*vv.* 35, 36b).

37. ἀφείς: 'having uttered' (for this use of ἀφίημι cf. Demosthenes, XVIII. 218; Euripides, *Hipp.* 418, *Elect.* 59).

ἐξέπνευσεν. For ἐκπνέω used absolutely in the sense 'breathe one's last' cf. Sophocles, *Ajax*, 1026.

38. καταπέτασμα is used in the LXX sometimes of the curtain between the Holy Place and the Holy of Holies (e.g. Exod. xxvi. 31–5, xxvii. 21, xxx. 6, II Chron. iii. 14), sometimes of the curtain over the entrance to the Holy Place (e.g. Exod. xxvi. 37, Num. iii. 26). In the N.T. it is used in Heb. vi. 19, ix. 3, x. 20, of the former; and it seems probable that here in Mk it is also used in this sense, though a number of interpreters think rather of the latter curtain.

Is this verse Mark's statement of the theological significance (cf. καθαρίζων πάντα τὰ βρώματα in vii. 19; and see on ii. 10, 28) of what he has related in v. 37—the death of Jesus has opened the way into the presence of God? Or is it a legendary development with a doctrinal motive? Or does it record an actual occurrence in the Temple which coincided with the moment of Jesus' death? Some support for the last alternative is possibly to be found in the mention of various prodigies in Josephus, *B.J.* vi. 288-309; *b Yom.* 39b; *j Yom.* 43c; Tacitus, *Hist.* v. 13.

* 39. κεντυρίων. Latin *centurio*; Mt., Lk. have ἑκατόνταρχος, -ης.

ἐξ ἐναντίας αὐτοῦ: 'opposite him', 'facing him'.

There is strong textual evidence for the inclusion of κράξας before ἐξέπνευσεν, and it should perhaps be read. In any case it is, according to Mk (contrast Mt.), the manner of Jesus' death (not any accompanying event) that compels the centurion's exclamation.

Ἀληθῶς οὗτος ὁ ἄνθρωπος Υἱὸς Θεοῦ ἦν. What exactly *the centurion* meant by υἱὸς θεοῦ we cannot be sure. Quite possibly he used the term in a Gentile sense—'demi-god', 'hero'. If so, then this exclamation, like the use of Βασιλεὺς τῶν Ἰουδαίων in vv. 9, 12, 18, 26, and of ὁ Χριστὸς ὁ Βασιλεὺς Ἰσραηλ in v. 32, and the assertion Ἄλλους ἔσωσεν in v. 31, is an unwitting proclamation of the truth. For *Mark* it is clearly important that at this point, whether intentionally or unintentionally, the truth was publicly declared. A theme of the whole gospel (see on i. 1) here comes to its triumphant conclusion. The fact that Υἱός has no article does not at all necessitate the rendering 'a son', since 'definite predicate nouns which precede the verb usually lack the article' (Moule, p. 115, after E. C. Colwell).

40. This verse and the next give further information, the importance of which will appear in sections 88 and 89.

Μαρία ἡ Μαγδαληνή. Cf. *v.* 47, xvi. 1, [9], Lk. viii. 2, Jn xix. 25, xx. 1, 11–18. Magdala was a place on the west of the Lake of Galilee.

Μαρία ἡ ᾿Ιακώβου τοῦ μικροῦ καὶ ᾿Ιωσῆτος μήτηρ. She is referred to in *v.* 47 as M. ἡ ᾿Ιωσῆτος and in xvi. 1 as M. ἡ τοῦ ᾿Ιακώβου. Presumably both James and Joses were well known in the early Church. Cf. the designation of Simon as 'the father of Alexander and Rufus' in *v.* 21. It is possible that this James is the same as James the son of Alphaeus in iii. 18. Of Joses nothing is known.

Σαλώμη. Mt. xxvii. 56 has ἡ μήτηρ τῶν υἱῶν Ζεβεδαίου.

41 is interesting for the light it throws on Jesus' attitude to women. Cf. Lk. viii. 2 f.

88. THE BURIAL OF JESUS (xv. 42–7)
(Mt. xxvii. 57–61; Lk. xxiii. 50–6)

The striking vividness of this narrative combined with its obvious sobriety clearly stamp it as based on reliable information. Even Bultmann, though he needlessly excepts *vv.* 44 f. and 47 from this judgement, describes the section as 'an historical account, which...makes no legendary impression'.

42. ἐπεὶ...προσάββατον. This clause in conjunction with the genitive absolute preceding it explains why Joseph had to act when he did: there was only an hour or two left before the sabbath would be beginning. Παρασκευή was used to denote the day before a sabbath or festival—here the former. Mark explains it for the sake of his Gentile readers.

43. Ιωσηφ ὁ ἀπὸ ᾿Αριμαθαίας. Cf. Mt. xxvii. 57, Lk. xxiii. 50 f., Jn xix. 38. Arimathaea is probably to be identified with Ramathaim (I Sam. i. 1) some twenty miles N.W. of Jerusalem. (See Dalman, *S.S.W.* pp. 225 f.)

εὐσχήμων: properly 'graceful'; so comes to mean 'honourable', 'noble', as here.

βουλευτής: i.e. a member of the Sanhedrin.

ὃς καί...τοῦ Θεοῦ. Cf. Lk. ii. 25, 38. This does not go so far as Mt.'s ἐμαθητεύθη τῷ 'Ιησοῦ.

τολμήσας: 'plucked up courage and'.

44. ἐθαύμασεν: since death usually came much more slowly to the crucified. Θαυμάζω εἰ, though only found in one other place in the N.T., is the regular expression for 'be surprised that'.

Note the correct differentiation between the tenses in τέθνηκεν and ἀπέθανεν.

46. ἀγοράσας. See on xiv. 12 (ii) (d).

λελατομημένον ἐκ πέτρας. Rock-tombs of various types are to be found in the neighbourhood of Jerusalem. See Dalman, S.S.W. pp. 366 ff. for an interesting discussion of the subject; also (M) B.B. vi. 8, (M) Ohol. ii. 4, xv. 8f. See also on xvi. 5. That the tomb belonged to Joseph is not stated, but it is natural to assume that it did.

προσεκύλισεν...μνημείου. These rock-tombs were normally closed by means of a large stone rolled or pushed into position in front of the entrance.

47 looks forward to xvi. 1, explaining how the women knew where Jesus' body had been laid.

VIII. THE RESURRECTION

(xvi. 1-8 (9-20))

89. THE EMPTY TOMB (xvi. 1-8)
(Mt. xxviii. 1-10; Lk. xxiv. 1-11; cf. Jn xx. 1-10)

The existence of discrepancies (e.g. as to the number and names of the women concerned and their reaction to the angel's (or angels') words) between the several accounts of

the first Easter morning is well known; and, while the
various differences taken one by one can be more or less
satisfactorily reconciled (and there is no need to be either
unduly cavalier with such explanations or unduly pedantic
in discovering discrepancies!), the difficulties are nevertheless too numerous for this patient ironing away of them one
by one to be altogether satisfying. But it should be remembered that differences between eye-witness accounts of the
same events are by no means an unusual phenomenon. In
the gospels themselves there are often discrepancies elsewhere. It would in fact be suspicious, if just here everything
agreed exactly. The discrepancies are at least evidence that
we have not to do here with a piece of carefully concerted
deceit. Moreover, allowance should be made for the
uniqueness of the event the immediate sequel of which is
being recorded. It is not surprising that here the human
testimony should show signs of disturbance and strain. Here,
if anywhere, we should expect it to be a broken and
trembling testimony.

One feature of all four gospel accounts which goes a long
way towards authenticating the story as a whole is the
prominence of women; for this is a feature which the early
Church would not be likely to invent (see below on *v.* 1).

As far as the Markan pericope of the Empty Tomb is
concerned, the naturalness of the first part (esp. *v.* 3), the
simplicity and restraint of *vv.* 5–8, and the surprising feature
of the women's silence all point to its authenticity. It reads
like an eye-witness's account, not a dramatization of a
religious conviction.

See further Ramsey, *Resurrection*; Cranfield, in *S.J.T.* v,
pp. 282–98, 398–414.   †

1. διαγενομένου τοῦ σαββάτου: i.e. after sunset on the
Saturday, when the new Jewish day had begun. For the use
of διαγίνομαι cf. Acts xxv. 13, xxvii. 9.

Μαρία ἡ Μαγδαληνὴ καὶ Μαρία ἡ τοῦ Ἰακώβου καὶ Σαλώμη.

See on xv. 40. According to all four gospels women were the
first to receive the news of the Resurrection. It is significant
that none of the Twelve was the first. It is significant too, in
view of the attitude of Judaism to women (e.g. *j Sot.* 19a:
'Sooner let the words of the Law be burnt than delivered to
women'; *b Kidd.* 82b: 'Happy is he whose children are male,
and alas for him whose children are female'; and the prayer
in the Morning Service in *A.D.P.B.* p. 6, 'Blessed art thou,
O Lord our God, King of the universe, who hast not made
me a woman', which the men say after similarly thanking
God for not making them heathen or slaves), that those
who in the providence of God were given the precedence
over the apostles on this momentous occasion were women.
On this the proper comment seems to be I Cor. i.
26–9. (Cf. perhaps xiv. 3–9, the anointing of the Messiah
by a woman.)

ἵνα... ἀλείψωσιν αὐτόν. (Contrast Mt.: θεωρῆσαι τὸν
τάφον.) Neither this nor xiv. 8 need necessarily imply
(though they perhaps rather suggest) that the body was not
anointed at all; it would not be unnatural for the women to
wish to make their own offering of devotion, even if they
knew that someone else had already done what was required
(cf. Jn xix. 39f.). Their intention to anoint a body that by
the morning would have been dead two nights and a day
seems strange (in the climate of Palestine), but is not incredible, since love often prompts people to do what from a
practical point of view is useless.

The *v.l.* which omits from διαγενομένου to Σαλώμη, and
substitutes πορευθεῖσαι, is to be rejected as an attempt at
simplification.

2. λίαν πρωΐ is surprisingly qualified by ἀνατείλαντος
τοῦ ἡλίου, which seems inconsistent with it (Lk.'s ὄρθρου
βαθέως and Jn's σκοτίας ἔτι οὔσης fit λίαν πρωΐ much better).
D smoothes away the difficulty by reading ἀνατέλλοντος.
A. H. M'Neile's explanation that the aorist participle

(ἀνατείλαντος) is timeless[1] will hardly do. It seems best to take the combined expression as indicating the time immediately after sunrise. For the suggestion that ἀνατείλαντος τοῦ ἡλίου goes back to a misunderstanding of an Aramaic verb (nᵉgāh), which can refer either to the beginning of the Jewish day at sunset or to the drawing on of the next day any time after sunset, see Black, pp. 99f.

τῇ μιᾷ. The use of the cardinal numeral for the ordinal is often explained as a Semitism; but see Moulton, *Proleg.* pp. 95f. for a contrary opinion. See also Bauer, *s.v.* εἷς, 4.

3 suggests a vividly remembered anxiety.

4. ἦν γὰρ μέγας σφόδρα is placed at the end of *v.* 3 in D Θ 565 it (some MSS.) sy^{s, pal} Eus., but this is clearly an attempt to make a smoother text. The MS. *k* has here a quite extensive gloss of an obviously legendary character.

5. In front of the entrance to the sepulchre (θύρα τοῦ μνημείου in *v.* 3) there may have been a forecourt such as is mentioned in the Mishnah (e.g. *Ohol.* xv. 8). The entrance was probably small and low, so that one would have to stoop to look inside or to enter; the chamber itself perhaps six or seven feet square and the same height; the place where the body had rested a bench against one of the walls or a shelf or trough let into the wall.

νεανίσκον. Clearly an angel is meant (cf. Mt. xxviii. 2, 5, Lk. xxiv. 4, 23, Jn xx. 12; also II Macc. iii. 26, 33f.). Here a protest must be made against the widespread tendency to dismiss the angels as mere pious fancy, a tendency encouraged by the vain attempts of Christian artists to depict them. It may be suggested that the purpose of the angel's presence at the tomb was to be the link between the actual event of the Resurrection and the women. Human eyes were not permitted to see the event of the Resurrection itself. But the angels as the constant witnesses of God's action saw it. So the angel's word to the women, 'He is risen', is as it were

---

[1] *The Gospel according to St Matthew* (London, 1915), p. 430.

the mirror in which men were allowed to see the reflection
of this eschatological event. By means of the angel's testimony the event of the Resurrection in its infinite graciousness toward men and in its infinite mystery and majesty was
made known to men, and they were enabled to recognize
the risen Lord as what he really is. (The best discussion of
the angels known to the author is Barth, *K.D.* III/3, pp. 426-
* 608, a summary of which by W. A. Whitehouse is to be
found in *S.J.T.* IV, pp. 376-82.)

περιβεβλημένον στολὴν λευκήν. See on ix. 3.

ἐξεθαμβήθησαν. See on *v.* 8.

6. ἠγέρθη. While the mere use of the passive here must
not be pressed, since sometimes the passive of ἐγείρω is used
without any proper passive force (e.g. ii. 12), it is clear that
the N.T. characteristically refers to the Resurrection as
God's act (e.g. Acts iii. 15, iv. 10, Rom. iv. 24, viii. 11, x. 9,
I Cor. vi. 14, xv. 15, II Cor. iv. 14, I Pet. i. 21).

οὐκ ἔστιν ὧδε· ἴδε ὁ τόπος ὅπου ἔθηκαν αὐτόν. These
words, coming after ἠγέρθη, stress the evidence of the empty
tomb. It is sometimes said that, while all four gospels testify
to the fact that the tomb was empty, Paul knows nothing of
the evidence of the empty tomb. But, though it is true that
Paul does not mention it explicitly, the sequence ἀπέθανεν...
ἐτάφη...ἐγήγερται in I Cor. xv. 3f. clearly implies a belief
that the tomb was empty, and, as Paul is recounting what
he had 'received', we have here 'the proof that, long before
the composition of the Gospels, the certainty of the resurrection was grounded not only on the appearances, but equally
on the "empty tomb"'.[1] If then we accept the view that
the belief that the tomb had been found empty goes back to
the earliest days of the Church, how are we to account for
it? B. H. Streeter rejected the idea that the body of Jesus
was raised; but he thought that the evidence for the tomb's

[1] O. Cullmann, *The Earliest Christian Confessions* (Eng. tr., London,
1949), p. 32.

being empty was convincing. His explanation was that some unknown person had removed the body.[1] Kirsopp Lake, on the other hand, thought that the women went by mistake to the wrong tomb (a not very likely hypothesis quite apart from xv. 47) and a young man directed them to the right one with the words, 'He is not here: behold, there is the place where they laid him' (rejecting ἠγέρθη as a later addition and reading ἐκεῖ after ἴδε with D W Θ 565).[2] An obvious difficulty of both these explanations is that, if the empty tomb played any part in, or was implied by, the earliest preaching, one would have expected the truth to have emerged. Why did not the unknown person confess? Why did not the young man explain? That someone who knew where the body was should have kept his secret to himself seems equally improbable, whether he was friendly disposed toward the disciples, or hostile, or neutral. And, had the Jewish authorities been informed, they would have been in a position to destroy the new movement without difficulty, whereas, if any of the disciples had been told, it would mean that the Christian Church was founded upon a deliberate deception—a supposition not easy to reconcile with what we know of the early Church.

7. καὶ τῷ Πέτρῳ. The special mention of Peter is best explained as due to the fact that after his denials of Jesus he needed a special assurance that he had not been cast off. Had it been intended to mark him out as the chief of the apostles, he would probably have been mentioned before the others rather than after them.

The latter part of the verse contains a reference back to xiv. 28 (the note on which should be referred to). As in the case of xiv. 28, there does not seem to be any adequate reason for regarding this verse as secondary, though some do

---

[1] In *Foundations*, ed. B. H. Streeter (London, 1912), pp. 134f.
[2] *The Historical Evidence for the Resurrection of Jesus Christ* (London, 1907), pp. 68f., 250–2.

so regard it (e.g. it has been suggested that it is an interpolation intended to cover up the disgraceful flight of the disciples into Galilee and to serve as a transition to the idea which later became dominant that the disciples had remained in Jerusalem together, or to prepare the way for the introduction of an account of a Galilean appearance). The variant contained in D k, which implies that the speaker is the risen Lord ($\pi\rho o\acute{a}\gamma\omega$, $\mu\epsilon$ and $\epsilon\emph{ι}\rho\eta\kappa a$) is obviously improbable; it may perhaps have originated in an assimilation of $\epsilon\emph{ι}\pi\epsilon\nu$ to the $\epsilon\emph{ι}\pi o\nu$ in Mt. The meaning of $\pi\rho o\acute{a}\gamma\epsilon\iota$ can hardly be that Jesus is about to march at their head into Galilee, since $\emph{ε}\kappa\epsilon\emph{ι}$ $a\emph{ὐ}\tau\grave{o}\nu$ $\emph{ὄ}\psi\epsilon\sigma\theta\epsilon$ implies that they will not see him on the way. The $\pi\rho o$- refers to time, not place.

Lohmeyer, who thinks that the double tradition of the Resurrection appearances (Galilee and Jerusalem) is to be explained by the existence of two streams of primitive Christianity, for one of which the centre of interest was Galilee, which was regarded as *terra christiana*, the main scene of the Lord's earthly life and ministry and destined to be the land of eschatological fulfilment, while for the other the centre of interest was Jerusalem, argues that the reference in this verse must be, not to a Resurrection appearance, but to the Parousia itself. He maintains that $a\emph{ὐ}\tau\grave{o}\nu$ $\emph{ὄ}\psi\epsilon\sigma\theta\epsilon$ must refer to something which could only happen in Galilee; and, while a proof of the Resurrection could be given anywhere, according to the one primitive Christian view Galilee was to be the scene of the Parousia. But, although this interpretation has had considerable influence (cf., e.g., the statement of A. M. Ramsey: 'Mark seems to tell of the Resurrection as the Parousia: the day of the Son of Man'[1]), its foundations are insecure. There is little evidence for the idea that the Parousia was to happen in Galilee, and Lohmeyer's claim that the active of $\acute{o}\rho\emph{ᾶ}\nu$ is specially used in the N.T. with reference to the Parousia does not amount to much, since

[1] *Resurrection*, p. 88.

he himself has to admit that it is also used of seeing the risen Lord (I Cor. ix. 1, Jn xx. 18, 25, 29).

According to another view 'Galilee' here is a theological symbol. This line of interpretation, which goes back to early days (e.g. Augustine, Gregory the Great, Bede), has lately become popular again. So, for example, A. M. Ramsey writes: 'Perhaps the message about Galilee, and the saying of Jesus before the Passion to which it looks back, had a meaning symbolical rather than geographical and referred less to a place of meeting or journeying than to a Victory and a Mission that would follow the disaster of the Cross.'[1] (See also Lightfoot, *Gospel Message*, pp. 106–16.)   *

It seems best to understand the verse as a promise of a Resurrection appearance or appearances in Galilee, and to suppose that Jesus wished to meet his disciples in Galilee for some such reasons as those suggested by Calvin: 'When the angel sent the disciples into Galilee, he did so, I think, in order that Christ might make himself known to a greater number of persons; for we know that he lived a long time in Galilee. He intended also to give his followers greater liberty, that by the very circumstances of their retirement they might gradually acquire courage. Besides, by their being accustomed to the places, they were aided in recognising their Master with greater certainty....'

(On the tradition of Galilean Resurrection appearances see further C. F. D. Moule in *E.T.* LXVIII, p. 207.)

8 is specially interesting. The statement οὐδενὶ οὐδὲν εἶπαν—on the surface a very surprising sequel to the angel's command—is peculiar to Mk. Both Mt. and Lk. give the sort of sequel we should expect (Mt. xxviii. 8, Lk. xxiv. 9). Presumably Mark meant his words to be understood in a limited sense—their silence was only for a little while.[2] The

---

[1] *Resurrection*, p. 71.
[2] In this connection C. F. D. Moule's note in *N.T.S.* II, pp. 58f. may be mentioned.

reason he gives for it is ἐφοβοῦντο γάρ. It is unlikely that this was fear of the Jews or of not being believed or of being thought mad, as some have suggested; for Mark has already piled up words expressing fear and amazement, ἐξεθαμβήθησαν, μὴ ἐκθαμβεῖσθε, ἔφυγον, τρόμος, ἔκστασις, and, as these clearly refer to the fear aroused by their experience at the tomb, it is likely that ἐφοβοῦντο does too. Lightfoot rightly stresses its religious nature.[1] The women had seen the token, the traces, of God's direct intervention, indeed of God's eschatological action. The resurrection of which the angel had spoken was no mere resuscitation of a Lazarus or Jairus' daughter, though that was disturbing enough. Jairus' daughter and Lazarus had only been restored to a prolongation of natural life, which would once more succumb to death; but this was the final resurrection. Though it had actually happened at a particular moment and so in one sense was fully historical, it was also of an altogether different texture from the rest of history. It is not surprising that the women were afraid and rendered speechless for a while. Mark's account (more emphatically than any of the others) underlines the mystery and awe-fulness of the Resurrection and warns against all attempts to sentimentalize or domesticate or reduce to the measures of our mental capacity or emotional convenience the decisive intervention of God.

It is generally agreed that the following verses were not written by Mark (see introduction to xvi. 9–20 below). To the problem of the conclusion of the gospel there seem to be four possible solutions: (i) The gospel was never finished, Mark being in one way or another prevented from finishing it. (ii) The conclusion was lost or destroyed by some mischance. (iii) The conclusion was deliberately suppressed. (iv) xvi. 8 was intended to be the end of the gospel. Of these (iii) is unlikely; and (ii) is not very likely, since it involves

[1] *Gospel Message*, p. 97.

assuming both that Mark himself was dead or otherwise unavailable to rewrite the ending and at the same time that the gospel had not been in use long enough for someone else to be able to restore it from memory. In recent years (iv) has received considerable support (e.g. J. M. Creed in *J.T.S.* XXXI, pp. 175–80; Lohmeyer *in loc.*; A. M. Farrer, *The Glass of Vision* (London, 1948), pp. 136–46, and *St Mark*, pp. 172–81; Lightfoot, *Gospel Message*, pp. 80–97, 106–16), but should surely be rejected. Since the fact of Resurrection appearances was clearly an element of the primitive preaching (cf. I Cor. xv. 5 ff., and also Acts i. 22, ii. 32, iii. 15, x. 41, xiii. 31), it is highly improbable that Mark intended to conclude his gospel without at least one account of a Resurrection appearance. While absolute certainty is impossible, the most likely alternative is that Mark intended to include at least one such narrative, but for some reason never finished his work. (But it is not to be maintained that he broke off in the middle of a sentence. As far as the possibility of ending a sentence or paragraph—or possibly even a book—with γάρ and of using ἐφοβοῦντο without either a direct object or a completing infinitive or a μή-clause, Lightfoot may be said to have proved his case.)

THE LONGER ENDING (xvi. 9–20)

These verses, though found in the majority of Greek MSS., are omitted by ℵ B *k* sy[s] and by some MSS. of arm eth and geo. Both Eusebius and Jerome regarded them as unauthentic in view of their absence from almost all the Greek MSS. known to them. Eusebius omitted them from his 'canons'. The MS. *k* gives in their place a shorter ending, while L and a few other Greek MSS. and also some MSS. of co and eth give both this shorter ending and the longer as alternatives. One tenth-century Armenian MS., which has these verses, attributes them to 'the presbyter Ariston' (probably meaning the Aristion mentioned by Papias). There is a possible echo of xvi. 20 in Justin, *I Apol.* 45, but the earliest definite witness to these verses as a part of Mk is in Irenaeus (III. x. 6). They were probably attached to Mk some time before the middle of the second century, in order to fill the obvious gap. But the clumsy connection shows that they were not specially written for this purpose. Originally compiled, it would seem, as a catechetical summary, they may have been in existence for a considerable time before being appended to Mk. In style and vocabulary † they are obviously non-Markan.

9–11. Cf. Jn xx. 11–18. Note the clumsiness of the connection with *vv.* 1–8. The subject is not named, as though Jesus had just been mentioned, while Mary is described as though she were being newly introduced. With παρ᾽ ἧς ἐκβεβλήκει ἑπτὰ δαιμόνια cf. Lk. viii. 2. For the pluperfect without augment see on xiv. 44. With the statement that the disciples ἠπίστησαν cf. Mt. xxviii. 17 and Lk. xxiv. 11, Jn xx. 25. The unreadiness of the disciples to believe the news of the Resurrection is specially stressed in these verses (cf. *vv.* 13 and 14).

12f. Cf. Lk. xxiv. 13–35, but contrast *v.* 13b with Lk. xxiv. 33–5.

ἐν ἑτέρᾳ μορφῇ possibly means 'in a different form from that in which he had appeared to Mary' (with reference to the fact that the two took him for a traveller, while Mary had mistaken him for the gardener); but more probably it reflects Lk. xxiv. 16 and is to be explained as subjective to the two disciples (i.e., to them he appeared ἐν ἑτέρᾳ μορφῇ inasmuch as they did not recognize him).

14–18. Cf. Lk. xxiv. 36–49, Jn xx. 19–23, and also Mt. xxviii. 16–20. A homiletic motive is perhaps to be discerned in the emphasis on the unbelief of the apostles. At the end of *v.* 14 W has a lengthy gloss, which was apparently known to Jerome, since he quotes the first part of it as found in some

MSS., especially Greek (*contra Pelagianos*, ii. 15). Both the Greek gloss (which is often referred to as 'the Freer Logion') and Jerome's Latin version are printed in Huck, p. 213; the Greek gloss is in the Bible Society text, p. 163. The Greek may be rendered as follows: 'And they defended themselves, saying, This age of lawlessness and unbelief is under Satan, †who by means of unclean spirits allows not the true power of God to be understood† :[1] wherefore reveal thy righteousness now. They were speaking to Christ; and Christ replied to them: The limit of the years of Satan's authority has been fulfilled, but other dreadful things draw near, even for those for whom, because they had sinned, I was delivered up to death in order that they might return unto the truth and sin no more, in order that they might inherit the spiritual and incorruptible glory of righteousness which is in heaven.' It was apparently added with a view to softening the rebuke to the apostles in *v.* 14, probably at the end of the second or the beginning of the third century.

With *vv.* 15f. cf. Mt. xxviii. 18f. With εἰς τὸν κόσμον ἅπαντα and πάσῃ τῇ κτίσει cf. Lk. xxiv. 47. The argument that Jesus *cannot* have given such a clear directive as *v.* 15 and Mt. xxviii. 19 because, had he done so, the controversy between Paul and the Judaizers would have been impossible, is surely weak; for (i) the evangelization of the Gentiles was not in dispute, but rather their being admitted into the Church without being obliged to adhere to Judaism; and (ii) the argument does not take seriously enough the perverseness and disobedience which have from the beginning been an element in the life of the Church. (See on vii. 27, xiii. 10, xiv. 9.) Κτίσις is better taken to mean 'creature' here than 'creation'—so 'to every creature', i.e. 'to every man' (cf. the use of *bᵉrîʾāh* in the sense of 'man' in Rabbinic Hebrew). The point of *v.* 16 is that the apostolic message

[1] Between the two daggers Jerome is followed, the Greek here being corrupt.

brings either life or death for men; according as they respond
to it with faith or unbelief they will inherit salvation or be
condemned in the final judgement. Cf. Jn xx. 23. The
aorist is used (both πιστεύσας and βαπτισθείς), because the
thought is of the decision which has to be made in response
to the preaching (κηρύξατε in *v.* 15). The order, πιστεύσας
before βαπτισθείς, and perhaps also the absence of any μὴ
βαπτισθείς answering to ἀπιστήσας, rule out a magical,
mechanical conception of baptism.

For σημεῖα see below on *v.* 20. Calvin justifies the use of
τοῖς πιστεύσασιν (which indicates the whole community of
believers) on the ground that, though only some would have
the power to work miracles, 'that which was bestowed on a
few was common to the whole Church'. ἐν τῷ ὀνόματί μου
δαιμόνια ἐκβαλοῦσιν. Cf. iii. 15, vi. 7, 13, Acts viii. 7, xvi.
18, xix. 12. γλώσσαις λαλήσουσιν καιναῖς. Cf. Acts ii. 4,
x. 46, xix. 6, I Cor. xii. 10, 28, xiv. 2 ff. The word καιναῖς is
omitted in C* L Δ Ψ co arm, but is read by the great
majority of the authorities which contain the Longer
Ending, and should probably be accepted. It points to the
fact that these tongues are a fore-token of the age to come in
which God will make all things new. Cf. the use of καινός
in II Cor. v. 17, Gal. vi. 15, II Pet. iii. 13, Rev. ii. 17, iii. 12,
v. 9, xiv. 3, xxi. 1 f., 5.

For ὄφεις ἀροῦσιν cf. Acts xxviii. 3–6. There is no N.T.
instance of drinking poison without taking harm, but cf.
Eusebius, *H.E.* III. 39, and the apocryphal Acts of Jn xx.
For an example of healing by laying on of hands cf. Acts
xxviii. 8.

19–20 refer, on the one hand (μέν), to the Lord Jesus'
exaltation and, on the other (δέ), to the mission of the
apostles. μετὰ τὸ λαλῆσαι αὐτοῖς may refer to the conversation related in *vv.* 14–18, but it could quite well have a
more general reference, while μετά, anyway, need not mean
immediately after. The fact of the Ascension is stated in

language reminiscent of II Kgs ii. 11. For the use of ἀναλαμβάνω of the Ascension cf. Acts i. 2, 11, 22, I Tim. iii. 16. It is important here to distinguish between the event of the Ascension itself, which was surely unseen of mortal eyes just as were also the actual events of the Incarnation and Resurrection, and the accompanying miraculous sign with which the last Resurrection appearance ended, and which was seen by the apostles and is related in Acts i. 9–11, and with which we may compare the signs of the Virginal Conception and the angel's testimony in the tomb and the Resurrection appearances. The Ascension was both the transition to the glory referred to in the next clause and also the fulfilment of the words of Jesus in xiv. 7, ἐμὲ δὲ οὐ πάντοτε ἔχετε.

The words ἐκάθισεν ἐκ δεξιῶν τοῦ Θεοῦ (with which cf. xiv. 62) are an echo of Ps. cx. 1, the O.T. passage most frequently quoted or referred to in the N.T. That this language is picture-language is obvious. Calvin calls it 'a similitude borrowed from princes', and notes that 'the subject here considered is not the posture of His body, but the majesty of His empire' (*Institutes*, II. xvi. 15).

On the Ascension and *Sessio ad dexteram* see further: Barth, *Credo*, pp. 105–16; *Dogmatics in Outline* (Eng. tr., London, 1949), pp. 124–8; Whitehouse, *C.F.S.A.* pp. 84–9; Moule, 'Expository Problems: The Ascension', in *E.T.* LXVIII (1956–7), pp. 205–9; Cranfield, 'The Witness of the New Testament to Christ', in *Essays in Christology for Karl Barth* (ed. T. H. L. Parker (London, 1956)), pp. 76, 83–7.

ἐξελθόντες. From Jerusalem? From Galilee? Or is it simply 'having gone forth (i.e. into all the world)'? With τοῦ Κυρίου συνεργοῦντος καὶ τὸν λόγον βεβαιοῦντος διὰ τῶν ἐπακολουθούντων σημείων cf. Heb. ii. 3f., Acts xiv. 3; also Rom. xv. 19, II Cor. xii. 12. The exalted Christ, though in a real sense absent from his disciples (xiii. 34–6, xiv. 7), is also present with them (Mt. xxviii. 20) to help and support them (συνεργοῦντος). Fundamentally, the view of miracles implied here does not differ from that of Jesus or of Mark (see on i. 31). τὸν λόγον βεβαιοῦντος implies their subordination to the preaching of the gospel, to the truth of which they are pointers, but of which they are not compelling proofs.

THE SHORTER ENDING

The Greek is printed in the Bible Society edition, p. 164; Huck, p. 213; an English translation is to be found in the R.S.V. For its attestation see the introduction to the Longer Ending above. Unlike the Longer Ending it was specially written (apparently in the west) for the purpose of filling the gap left by Mark. From its language it is clear that it cannot † have been written by Mark.

SUPPLEMENTARY NOTES

The references are to the places in the Commentary
to which the notes refer

pp. ix–x

Several commentaries in English on Mark have appeared
since 1959:

CARRINGTON, P., *According to Mark* (Cambridge, 1960).

COLE, R. A., *The Gospel according to St Mark* (London, 1961).

JOHNSON, S. E., *The Gospel according to St Mark* (London, 1960).

WILSON, R. McL., in *Peake's Commentary on the Bible*, ed. M. Black and H. H. Rowley (London, 1962).   †

Mention may also be made here of four earlier commentaries not listed on pp. ix–x:

GRANT, F. C., in *The Interpreter's Bible*, VII (New York, 1951).

HUBY, J., *Évangile selon Saint Marc* (Paris, 43rd imp. 1948).

KLOSTERMANN, E., *Das Markus-Evangelium* (Tübingen, 4th ed. 1950).

SCHMID, J., *Das Evangelium nach Markus* (Regensburg, 4th ed. 1958). [Eng. tr. Cork, 1968].

pp. x–xiv

BULTMANN, *G.S.T.*—Eng. tr. by J. Marsh [2nd ed. 1968].

D.-B.—An Eng. tr. by R. W. Funk has been published: *A Greek Grammar of the New Testament and Other Early Christian Literature* (Cambridge, 1961).

Moule—Revised ed. 1959.

S.-B.—Two additional volumes, by J. Jeremias and K. Adolph, have been issued: V (Rabbinischer Index) and VI (Verzeichnis der Schriftgelehrten; Geographisches Register).

Two further books on Mark may be mentioned here: W. Marxsen, *Der Evangelist Markus* (Göttingen, 2nd ed.
† 1959; first published 1956) and J. M. Robinson, *The Problem of History in Mark* (London, 1957). They would have been referred to from time to time, had they been available before the commentary was at an advanced stage of preparation, though the views expressed in it would not have been materially modified. While both are books to be reckoned with, the amount of truth they contain will be
† variously estimated.

p. xv, line 12

Mention may also be made of a further book by Burrows, *More Light on the Dead Sea Scrolls* (London, 1958) and of M. Black, *The Scrolls and Christian Origins* (London, 1961); F. F. Bruce, *Biblical Exegesis in the Qumran Texts* (London, 1960). W. S. LaSor, 'Historical Framework: The Present State of Dead Sea Scrolls Study', in *Interp.* xvi (1962), pp. 259–79, is valuable both for general orientation and for the bibliographical information it provides. The same volume also contains (pp. 280–91) F. F. Bruce, 'Preparation in the Wilderness: At Qumran and in the New Testament' and (pp. 292–304) H. H. Rowley, 'Comparison and Contrast: Qumran and the Early Church'. A longer paper by Rowley, 'The Qumran Sect and Christian Origins', is to be found in *B.J.R.L.* xliv (1961), pp. 119–56. An important agreed summing-up on Qumran and the New Testament by a group of experts will be found in *N.T.S.* vii (1960–1), pp. 276–96: it was revised for publication by P. Benoit, and is in French. A most useful tool is K. G. Kuhn, *Konkordanz zu den Qumrantexten* (Göttingen, 1960).

For orientation in another field—that of the Gnostic Gospel of Thomas—reference may be made to H. E. W. Turner and H. W. Montefiore, *Thomas and the Evangelists*
† (London, 1962).

p. xv, line 28

Novum Testamentum Graece et Latine, ed. A. Merk (Rome, 8th ed. 1957) is another useful text with a valuable apparatus. *Novum Testamentum Graece: Evangelium secundum Marcum*, ed. S. C. E. Legg (Oxford, 1935), was constantly consulted in the preparation of the commentary, and should have been mentioned. †

p. 4, line 15

See A. Souter, *The Text and Canon of the New Testament* (London, 2nd ed. revised by C. S. C. Williams, 1954), p. 220; E. Haenchen, *Die Apostelgeschichte* (Göttingen, 3rd ed. 1959), pp. 8–10.

p. 8, line 20

For a recent statement of the case for a date later than A.D. 70 see S. G. F. Brandon, 'The Date of the Markan Gospel', in *N.T.S.* VII (1960–1), pp. 126–41.

p. 15, line 3

On the subject of section 4 see also C. F. D. Moule, 'The Intention of the Evangelists', in *New Testament Studies*, ed. A. J. B. Higgins (Manchester, 1959), pp. 165–79.

p. 16, lines 10–18

The intention of this paragraph, far from being to imply that Mark was not a theologian, was to suggest that he possessed, to an outstanding degree, that without which one cannot begin to be a true theologian, namely, a deep humility before God's self-revelation, and that he tried to state the facts of what he believed to be God's self-revelation as accurately as he could, refraining from all attempts at improving on them by artistry, precisely because he was a serious theologian—too good a theologian not to recognize the folly of trying to paint the lily or (to borrow an expression of B. L. Manning's) to varnish sunlight.

p. 17, n. 1

A considerable supplementary bibliography could be added here; but suffice it to mention the fresh stimulus given to research and discussion by H. Riesenfeld, *The Gospel Tradition and its Beginnings: A Study in the Limits of 'Formgeschichte'* (London, 1957) and B. Gerhardsson, *Memory and Manuscript: Oral Tradition and Written Transmission in Rabbinic Judaism and Early Christianity* (Uppsala, 1961). An interesting discussion of these works, both critical and appreciative, is W. D. Davies, 'Reflections on a Scandinavian approach to "The Gospel Tradition"', in *Neotestamentica et Patristica* (Cullmann *Festschrift*), ed. W. C. van Unnik (Leiden, 1962), pp. 14–34. See also now C. F. D. † Moule, *The Birth of the New Testament* (London, 1962).

p. 18, n. 1

Also XI (1960), pp. 253–64.

p. 20, n. 1

An Eng. tr. has now been published in *Kerygma and Myth* II, ed. H. W. Bartsch; tr. R. H. Fuller (London, 1962), pp. 83–132. Reference may also be made here to H. E. W. Turner, *Historicity and the Gospels* (to be published in London during 1963).

p. 22, line 26

A considerable amount has been written in the last decade or so on 'the theology of Mark'. E. Schweizer mentions some of the latest contributions in his 'Anmerkungen zur Theologie des Markus', in *Neotestamentica et Patristica* (Leiden, 1962), p. 35, n. 1. Mention may also be made of the work of A. M. Farrer, C. F. Evans, J. C. Fenton. A good deal of this output has been stimulated, directly or indirectly, by the works of R. H. Lightfoot. Much of value has been contributed. But the student who is about to engage in an exploration of this literature will be well advised to make sure that his equipment includes a considerable supply of *grana salis*.

p. 35, line 4

Though see E. Schweizer, *op. cit.* in previous note, p. 37, n. 2.

p. 37, lines 22–3

At any rate the name had come to be so explained. The question whether this etymology (in terms of *yāša'*) is strictly correct (see *T.W.N.T.* III, p. 290, n. 36) need not concern us here.

p. 41, n. 1

See also H. H. Rowley, 'The Baptism of John and the Qumran Sect', in *New Testament Essays*, ed. A. J. B. Higgins † (Manchester, 1959), pp. 218–29.

p. 52, line 9

K.D. IV/1, pp. 285 and 287 (cf. *C.D.* pp. 259 and 261).

p. 56, line 6

Also G. R. Beasley-Murray, *Baptism in the New Testament* (London, 1962). †

p. 59, line 25

This is being re-issued in a supplementary volume to *N.T.S.* by the Cambridge University Press.

p. 59, line 26

C.D. III/3, pp. 289–368, 519–31.

p. 63, line 6

See also *T.W.N.T.* VI, pp. 283 ff. (esp. p. 293).

p. 63, line 23

On the word καιρός reference should also be made to J. Barr, *The Semantics of Biblical Language* (Oxford, 1961), pp. 225 f. and *Biblical Words for Time* (London, 1962), pp. 20 ff. But the meaning of the word in this verse is in any case quite clear from the context.

p. 118, line 26

F. W. Beare, 'The Sabbath was made for man?', in *Journal of Biblical Literature*, LXXIX (1960), pp. 130–6, is a recent discussion of *vv.* 23–8.

p. 130, line 28

Revised ed. 1962.

p. 131, line 21

The discussion has recently been reopened by O. Betz, 'Donnersöhne, Menschenfischer und der davidische Messias', in *Revue de Qumran* III (1961), pp. 41–70.

p. 142, line 12

A different explanation is suggested by G. Bornkamm, in *The Background of the New Testament and its Eschatology*, ed. W. D. Davies and D. Daube (Cambridge, 1956), pp. 243 f.

p. 149, line 10

Among recent publications may be mentioned M. Black, 'The Parables as Allegory', in *B.J.R.L.* XLII (1959–60), pp. 273–87; G. H. Boobyer, 'The Redaction of Mark iv. 1–34', in *N.T.S.* VIII (1961–2), pp. 59–70; R. E. Brown, 'Parable and Allegory reconsidered', in *Novum Testamentum*, V (1962), pp. 36–45; J. Gnilka, *Die Verstockung Israels: Isaias 6. 9–10 in der Theologie der Synoptiker* (Munich, 1961); A. M. Hunter, *Interpreting the Parables* (London, 1960);

C. F. D. Moule, 'The Parables of the Jesus of History and the Lord of Faith', in *Religion in Education*, XXVIII (London, 1960–1), pp. 60–4.

p. 153, line 25

The word *rāz* occurs more than fifty times in the Dead Sea Scrolls. See Bruce, *Biblical Exegesis in the Qumran Texts*, pp. 8 ff., on its use, and also Benoit, in *N.T.S.* VII (1960–1), pp. 290 f.

p. 198, line 24

See also J. Jeremias, 'Paarweise Sendung im Neuen Testament', in *New Testament Essays*, ed. A. J. B. Higgins (Manchester, 1959), pp. 136–43.

p. 209, line 28

$\mathfrak{p}^{45}$ omits not only Φιλίππου but apparently τοῦ ἀδελφοῦ also.

p. 217, line 6

Now *I and II Peter and Jude* (London, 1960), pp. 126f.

p. 246, line 9

See also J. Munck, *Paul and the Salvation of Mankind* (1954; Eng. tr. by F. Clarke, London, 1959).

p. 271, line 15

Also H. J. Schoeps, *Paul: The Theology of the Apostle in the Light of Jewish Religious History* (1959; Eng. tr. by H. Knight, London, 1961), pp. 88–97; M. Black, *The Scrolls and Christian Origins*, pp. 145–63; Rowley, in *Interp.* XVI (1962), pp. 300f.; Benoit, in *N.T.S.* VII (1960–1), pp. 282f. †

p. 277, line 15

Also F. F. Bruce, *Biblical Exegesis in the Qumran Texts*, pp. 63–6; O. Cullmann, *The Christology of the New Testament*

(1957; Eng. tr. London, 1959), pp. 137–92; J. A. Emerton, 'The Origin of the Son of Man Imagery', in *J.T.S.* n.s. IX (1958), pp. 225–42; J. Muilenburg, 'The Son of Man in Daniel and the Ethiopic Apocalypse of Enoch', in *Journal of Biblical Literature*, LXXIX (1960), pp. 197–209; Schoeps, *op. cit.* in previous note, pp. 93–7; H. E. Tödt, *Der Menschensohn in der synoptischen Überlieferung* (Gütersloh,
† 1959); A.J.B. Higgins, *Jesus and the Son of Man* (London, 1964).

p. 277, line 24

Bultmann's view has recently received emphatic support in M. D. Hooker, *Jesus and the Servant* (London, 1959) and C. K. Barrett, 'The Background of Mark 10:45', in *New Testament Essays*, ed. A. J. B. Higgins (Manchester, 1959), pp. 1–18. On Miss Hooker's book the penetrating reviews by V. Taylor, in *E.T.* LXX (1958–9), pp. 300f., and J. Jeremias, in *J.T.S.* n.s. XI (1960), pp. 140–4, should be read. The reminder by A. J. B. Higgins that 'there is just as much danger in following uncritically, in the first flush of enthusiasm, suggested correctives of almost universally cherished assumptions, as there is in clinging uncritically to these assumptions' (*S.J.T.* XIII (1960), p. 95) is timely. See further the supplementary note to p. 342, line 30.

p. 285, last line

Both those who see in ix. 1 a genuine saying of Jesus and those who, like H. Conzelmann (*Die Mitte der Zeit* (3rd ed. Tübingen, 1960), p. 95, n. 1), regard it as a community-creation, tend to assume that the fact that Mark has placed it here is evidence that he himself was certain that the Parousia would occur within the lifetime of some of Jesus' contemporaries (so, e.g., W. Marxsen, *Der Evangelist Markus* (Göttingen, 1959), p. 140, n. 1; C. K. Barrett, *Luke the Historian in Recent Research* (London, 1961), pp. 53f.). While lack of space makes it impossible to discuss here the contributions to the understanding of Markan eschatology made by the scholars just named or by such books as E. Grässer, *Das Problem der Parusieverzögerung in den synoptischen Evangelien und in der Apostelgeschichte* (Berlin, 1957) and A. Strobel, *Untersuchungen zum eschatologischen Verzögerungsproblem auf Grund der spätjüdisch-urchristlichen Geschichte von Habakuk 2. 2ff.* (Leiden, 1961), it is perhaps worth while referring to just one possible objection to this common interpretation which seems to have received insufficient attention. If Mark himself, at any rate, understood xiii. 10 to refer to the Church's mission (as is surely highly probable in view of xiii. 9 and 11), is it really likely that he did not reckon with at least the possibility that this preaching εἰς πάντα τὰ ἔθνη might require a considerable period? More than half the time between the beginning of the Church's mission and the date beyond which no contemporary of Jesus could be expected to survive had already passed, when Mark was writing. Is he not likely to have reflected that much missionary work still remained to be done? When C. K. Barrett says (*The Epistle to the Romans*, London, 1957, p. 277) with reference to Rom. xv. 19ff., 'Since the eastern end of the Mediterranean had been dealt with and Paul "had no more scope in these parts" there remained for missionary work the north coast of Africa (from Alexandria to the province of Africa), Gaul, and Spain', he is giving the impression that the horizons of ancient geography were a good deal more confined than they in fact were. Not long before Paul was writing Claudius had conquered the southern part of Britain. Roman soldiers had good reason to be aware of the existence of the compatriots of Arminius. Parthia, the dreaded foe of Rome, is mentioned in Acts, as is also Ethiopia. Paul uses the name Scythian. Alexander the Great had penetrated to India, and Cicero, Catullus and Virgil mention it. And this list by no means completes the picture.

p. 339, line 19

Moreover, Gal. ii. 9 is evidence against the tradition that John was executed before the death of Herod, as J. A. T. Robinson has pointed out (in *N.T.S.* VI (1959–60), p. 126).

p. 342, line 30

See the supplementary note to p. 277, line 24. The following observations may be made here: (i) Miss Hooker's argument (pp. 74f.) that the Servant in Second Isaiah 'is primarily *Yahweh's* Servant' whereas the service envisaged in Mk x. 42 ff. is a service to men, will not bear much weight; for, while it is true that the word '*ebed* indicates the Servant's relation to God, it is clear that the actual content of the Servant's service of God is a service of men (see, e.g., Isa. xlix. 5 f., liii. 4–6, 11 f.) and also that the Son of Man's service of men is undertaken in obedience to God. (ii) It is true that neither διακονεῖν nor any of its cognates is used in the Servant Songs, and that (as far as the LXX is concerned, at any rate) '*Linguistically*, διακονεῖν does not recall Isa. 53, or any of the Servant passages' (Barrett, p. 4); but the force of the argument on the other side is *not* that διακονεῖν suggests the word '*ebed*, but that it recalls, and sums up in a word, the *whole picture* of the service to men which the Servant of Yahweh is to render. Is it not likely that behind the evangelist's use of διακονεῖν here and also in Lk. xxii. 27 lies the creative reflection of Jesus upon the Servant passages? (It should be noted that, on the one hand, the word παῖς could not be recalled, if a verb was to be used, as no cognate verb reflects the special use of παῖς in the sense of 'slave', and, on the other hand, the verb δουλεύειν, which might have recalled the δοῦλος of Isa. xlix, was unsuitable for expressing the manward aspect of Christ's service of God, since δοῦλος and δουλεύειν focus attention on the status of the slave in relation to his master, and a New

Testament writer would scarcely wish to imply that Christ was at any point the slave of men in the sense of being their chattel, wholly at their disposal. Phil. ii. 7 is the nearest the New Testament comes to using δοῦλος of Christ. Otherwise, neither δοῦλος nor δουλεύειν is ever used of Christ, whether in relation to men or to God. But διάκονος and διακονεῖν were suitable, since they focused attention not on the person's status, but on the service rendered, the work done.) (iii) With regard to the absence of any absolutely clear quotation of, or reference to, the Servant Songs in the sayings of Jesus, is it not true that, on the assumption that the thought of these passages had become an integral part of his own thinking and consciousness, it is indirect echoes rather than definite quotations that we should expect to find? (iv) It may be doubted whether any of the alternatives to the Servant passages which have been suggested (e.g. by Barrett, pp. 8 ff.) is really adequate to bear the weight of Mk viii. 31, ix. 31, x. 33 f., which seem to imply a definite 'scriptural pattern to be fulfilled' (cf. D. R. Jones, in *The Bishoprick*, xxxv (Durham, 1959–60), p. 12). (v) Barrett's argument (p. 8) that the fact that 'The οὐ—ἀλλά is intended to bring out a *contrast*...goes a long way towards removing the saying from the field of Isa. 53 and the Servant, for it would be more than a little precious to insist that the Servant did not come to be served' is a curious argument. The *form* of the saying surely in no way forbids us to assume that Jesus was here reminding his disciples of the truth he had already tried to teach them, namely, that the destiny of the Son of Man was not to be understood in the terms in which they were prone to think of it, but rather in terms of humble and costly service of men—an understanding of his own destiny which had to a large extent been moulded by his own deep reflection on the Servant passages.

p. 372, line 34

Also Cranfield, 'The Christian's Political Responsibility according to the New Testament', in *S.J.T.* xv (1962), pp. 176–92.

p. 391, lines 4 and 5
In *C.D.* iii/2, pp. 437–511.

p. 409, n. 3
In *C.D.* iii/2, pp. 500–2.

p. 415, line 20

Or perhaps the flask was of such a pattern that it had to be broken, if its contents were to be used.

p. 419, line 26

Another suggestion is made by E. Stauffer, *Jesus and His Story* (Eng. tr. London, 1960), p. 93.

p. 422, line 19

For Mlle A. Jaubert's theory, according to which the Last Supper took place on the Tuesday evening in Passion Week, see her book, *La Date de la Cène: Calendrier biblique et liturgie chrétienne* (Paris, 1957) and her article, 'Jésus et le calendrier de Qumrân', in *N.T.S.* vii (1960–1), pp. 1–30; and see also the reviews by G. Ogg in *Novum Testamentum* iii (1959), pp. 149–60, and by J. Jeremias in *J.T.S.* n.s. x (1959), pp. 131–3. Reference may also be made here to M. Black, 'The Arrest and Trial of Jesus and the Date of the Last Supper', in *New Testament Essays*, ed. A. J. B. Higgins
† (Manchester, 1959), pp. 19–33.

p. 427, line 2

The question of the possible Aramaic behind this phrase is debated by J. A. Emerton, *J.T.S.* n.s. vi (1955), pp. 238–40; xiii (1962), pp. 111–17, and Jeremias, *E.W.* (1966 translation), pp. 193–5.

p. 428, n. 1

In *C.D.* iii/2, p. 502.

p. 437, line 23

P. Winter's contention (*On the Trial of Jesus*, Berlin, 1961, p. 49) that καθ' ἡμέραν should be translated 'during day-time' rather than 'daily' seems most unlikely in view of Greek usage.

p. 441, line 6

Also J. Blinzler's learned and important work, *The Trial of Jesus* (Eng. tr. by I. and F. McHugh, Cork, 1959) and P. Winter, *op. cit.* in previous note. According to the latter the evangelists have seriously distorted the facts, being controlled by theological and apologetic motives, and desiring, in particular, to exonerate the Romans of responsibility for the death of Jesus and to fasten the blame upon the Jews. The book is deeply moving as a *cri de cœur* from one who, as his dedication indicates, has suffered grievously through the hideous evil of anti-semitism. It is also valuable both for the wealth of information it contains and for the stimulus to further research which it has provided. Nevertheless it must be said that it is a little ironical that the writer of this book should belabour the evangelists for tendentiousness. At a good many points Winter's statements and arguments need to be questioned; but the book requires, and deserves, a careful and detailed reply, such as cannot be undertaken here. †

p. 444, line 18

Stauffer's contention (*Jesus and His Story* (London, 1960), p. 150; but see also pp. 78f., 142–59, and cf. H. J. Schoeps, *Paul* (London, 1961), pp. 161f.) that the Ἐγώ εἰμι here is the theophanic formula '*ᵃnî hû*' is difficult to accept.

p. 448, line 1

G. Bornkamm, *Jesus of Nazareth* (Eng. tr. by I. and F. McLuskey and J. M. Robinson (London, 1960)), pp. 211 f., suggests that it was Jesus whom Peter cursed.

p. 460, line 13

The material in Josephus has recently been discussed by H. W. Montefiore in *Novum Testamentum*, IV (1960), pp. 148–54.

p. 466, lines 7 and 8

In *C.D.* III/3, pp. 369–519.

p. 469, line 12

Along with Lightfoot may be mentioned C. F. Evans, 'I will go before you into Galilee', in *J.T.S.* n.s. V (1954), pp. 3–18.

REVISED ADDITIONAL
SUPPLEMENTARY NOTES

p. x, line 6

A 2nd ed. of Taylor's commentary was published in 1966.

p. xii, line 6

A new translation of the thoroughly revised 3rd German ed. of Jeremias, *E.W.*, was published in London in 1966.

p. 23, line 13

B. M. Metzger, *The Text of the New Testament: its transmission, corruption and restoration* (Oxford, 2nd ed. 1968) may now be specially recommended.

p. 55, line 29

Also to I. H. Marshall, 'The Divine Sonship of Jesus', in *Interp.* XXI (1967), pp. 87–103, and 'Son of God or Servant

of Yahweh?—A Reconsideration of Mark i. 11', in *N.T.S.*
xv (1968–9), pp. 326–36, which contain much bibliographical information on recent work.

p. 67, line 26

Reference should now be made to G. E. Ladd, *Jesus and
the Kingdom: the Eschatology of Biblical Realism* (London, 1966)
and on the O.T. background, A. Gelston, 'A Note on
יהוה מלך', in *Vetus Testamentum* xvi (Leiden, 1966).

p. 121, line 22

I have changed my mind on this, and now think that
Armitage Robinson, while he succeeded in showing that
confusion between πωροῦν, πώρωσις and πηροῦν, πήρωσις was
extremely common among copyists and early translators,
never proved that they were not distinguished in the original
texts. Cf. my forthcoming I.C.C. commentary on Romans
on Rom. xi. 7.

p. 132, last line

On the Twelve, reference should now be made to R. P.
Meye, 'Messianic Secret and Messianic Didache in Mark's
Gospel', in F. Christ (ed.), *Oikonomia: Heilsgeschichte als
Thema der Theologie* (Cullmann *Festschrift*) (Hamburg, 1967),
pp. 57–68, and the same author's *Jesus and the Twelve:
Discipleship and Revelation in Mark's Gospel* (Grand Rapids,
1968).

p. 142, line 31

Cf. also Augustine, *Epistolae ad Romanos inchoata expositio*,
23 (in J. P. Migne, *Patrologia Latina*, xxxv, col. 2105).

p. 163, last line

On iv. 1–20 reference should now be made to B. Gerhardsson, 'The Parable of the Sower and its Interpretation',
in *N.T.S.* xiv (1967–8), pp. 165–93; and to C. F. D. Moule,
'Mark 4: 1–20 yet once more', in E. E. Ellis and M. Wilcox

(ed.), *Neotestamentica et Semitica: studies in honour of Matthew Black* (Edinburgh, 1969), pp. 95–113.

p. 195, line 9

For the fact that a man's acceptance of a child as his son conferred on him all the legal rights of legitimate sonship see S.-B. 1, p. 35: cf. E. Stauffer, *Jesus and His Story* (London, 1960), p. 25.

p. 195, line 29

On the first words of vi. 3 see further E. Stauffer, 'Jeschu ben Mirjam: Kontroversgeschichtliche Anmerkungen zu Mk 6:3', in *Neotestamentica et Semitica* (details in note to p. 163 above), pp. 119–28.

p. 340, line 31

There is an interesting parallel in Plutarch, *Aratus* 43.2: ἀλλὰ ὁρῶν ἀπαραίτητον ἐπικειμένην ἀνάγκην καὶ τὸν καιρόν, ᾧ δουλεύουσιν οἱ δοκοῦντες ἄρχειν, ἐχώρει πρὸς τὸ δεινόν. (B. Perrin's translation in the Loeb edition is as follows: 'But seeing how inexorable was the necessity laid upon him in the demands of the hour, to which those we call rulers are slaves, he went on towards the dread ordeal.').

p. 344, line 5

A study (in Afrikaans) of this verse by H. J. B. Combrink (*Die Diens van Jesus: 'n Eksegetiese Beskouing oor Markus 10.45*) was published in Groningen in 1968. It is also discussed briefly in D. Hill, *Greek Words and Hebrew Meanings: studies in the semantics of soteriological terms* (Cambridge, 1967), pp. 77–81.

p. 378, line 33

Reprinted in C. E. B. Cranfield, *The Service of God* (London, 1965), pp. 35–41.

p. 391, line 11

See also A. L. Moore, *The Parousia in the New Testament* (Leiden, 1966) and G. E. Ladd, *Jesus and the Kingdom: the Eschatology of Biblical Realism* (N.Y., '64; London, '66).

p. 408, line 33

I have stated the substance of this paragraph more fully in *A Commentary on Romans 12–13* (Edinburgh, 1965), pp. 90–93.

p. 433, lines 3–8

These lines are now revised (1971) in view of J. Jeremias, *The Prayers of Jesus* (London, 1967), pp. 54–65, to which reference should be made.

p. 449, lines 2 and 3

It now seems probable that Pilate's actual title was not *procurator* but *praefectus*. See C. H. Dodd, *Historical Tradition in the Fourth Gospel* (Cambridge, 1963), p. 96, n. 1, and literature there cited.

p. 463 line 31

In English, French and German, books on the Resurrection have been specially numerous in the last decade. Mention may be made here of just a few: D. P. Fuller, *Easter Faith and History* (Grand Rapids, 1964); W. Künneth, *The Theology of the Resurrection* (London, 1965); G. W. H. Lampe and D. M. Mackinnon, *The Resurrection: a dialogue arising from broadcasts* (London, 1966); C. F. D. Moule (ed.), *The Significance of the Message of the Resurrection for Faith in Jesus Christ* (London, 1968); N. Clark, *Interpreting the Resurrection* (London, 1969); C. F. Evans, *Resurrection and the New Testament* (London, 1970); and also of W. Pannenberg's essay, 'Did Jesus really rise from the dead?', in R. Batey (ed.), *New Testament Issues* (New York and London, 1970), pp. 102–17: and J. Moltmann, *Theology of Hope* (London, 1967), especially pp. 139–229.

p. 476, last line

For a recent discussion of the problems presented by the conclusion to Mark's Gospel see K. Aland, 'Bemerkungen zum Schluss des Markusevangeliums', in *Neotestamentica et Semitica* (details in note to p. 163 above), pp. 157–80.

p. 477, line 11

The following additional English commentaries may be mentioned:

JONES, A. *The Gospel according to St Mark* (London, 1963).

MOULE, C. F. D. *The Gospel according to Mark* (The Cambridge Bible Commentary, Cambridge, 1965).

NINEHAM, D. E. *The Gospel of St Mark* (The Pelican Gospel Commentaries, Harmondsworth, 1963).

Also SCHWEIZER, E. *Das Evangelium nach Markus* (Das N.T. Deutsch, Göttingen, 1967). [Eng. tr., London, 1971].

A commentary by Morna D. Hooker in The New Clarendon Bible series is to be expected soon.

p. 478, line 3

An English translation has now been published (*Mark the Evangelist: studies on the Redaction History of the Gospel*) by the Abingdon Press.

p. 478, line 10

The following additional books on Mark may be mentioned: E. Best, *The Temptation and the Passion: the Markan Soteriology* (Cambridge, 1965); J. Bowman, *The Gospel of Mark—the new Christian Jewish passover Haggadah* (Leiden, 1965); T. A. Burkill, *Mysterious Revelation: an examination of the philosophy of St Mark's Gospel* (New York, 1963; also London); E. Trocmé, *La Formation de l'Évangile selon Marc* (Paris, 1963); L. Hartman, *Prophecy Interpreted: the formation of some Jewish apocalyptic texts and of the Eschatological Discourse Mark 13 par.* (Lund, 1966); Morna D. Hooker, *The Son of Man in Mark* (London, 1967): also 'On the Composition of the Gospel of Mark', in H. Riesenfeld, *The Gospel*

494

Tradition (Philadelphia, 1970), pp. 51–74; R. S. Barbour, 'Recent Study of the Gospel according to St Mark', in *E.T.* LXXIX (1967–8), pp. 324–9; R. P. Martin, 'A Gospel in search of a Life-Setting', in *E.T.* LXXX (1968–9), pp. 361–4; O. Linton, 'Evidences of a second-century revised edition of St. Mark's Gospel', in *N.T.S.* XIV, pp. 321–55; C. Maurer, 'Das Messiasgeheimnis des Markusevangeliums', in *N.T.S.* XIV (1967–8), pp. 515–26.

p. 478 line 34

For the New Testament Apocrypha reference should now be made to E. Hennecke, *New Testament Apocrypha*, Eng. tr. ed. R. McL. Wilson, I (London, 1963), II (1965).

The excellent translation of the Qumran texts by G. Vermes, *The Dead Sea Scrolls in English* (Harmondsworth, 1962), appeared just too late to be included in the earlier supplementary notes.

p. 479, line 7

The Greek New Testament ed. by K. Aland, M. Black, B. M. Metzger and A. Wikgren, was published by the United Bible Societies in New York, London, Edinburgh, Amsterdam and Stuttgart in 1966.

p. 480, line 14

Two interesting recent articles may be mentioned here: E. Schweizer, 'Mark's Contribution to the Quest of the Historical Jesus', in *N.T.S.* X (1963–4), pp. 421–32; and A. W. Mosley, 'Historical Reporting in the Ancient World', in *N.T.S.* XII (1965–6), pp. 10–26. Also A. T. Hanson (ed.), *Vindications: essays on the historical basis of Christianity* (London, 1966); D. E. Nineham's rejoinder in W. R. Farmer, C. F. D. Moule and R. R. Niebuhr (ed.), *Christian History and Interpretation: studies presented to John Knox* (Cambridge, 1967), pp. 199–222; A. T. Hanson, 'The Great Form Critic', in *S.J.T.* XXII (1969), pp. 296–304.

p. 481, line 15

Also C. H. H. Scobie, *John the Baptist* (London, 1964).

p. 481, line 20

Also J. D. G. Dunn, *Baptism in the Holy Spirit* (London, 1970).

p. 483, line 3

Also I. H. Marshall, *Eschatology and the Parables* (London, 1963); G. V. Jones, *The Art and Truth of the Parables* (London, 1964); E. Linnemann, *The Parables of Jesus* (London, 1966).

p. 483, line 25

Also R. N. Longenecker, *The Christology of Early Jewish Christianity* (London, 1970), pp. 63–82.

p. 484, line 8

Also F. H. Borsch, *The Son of Man in Myth and History* (London, 1967); Morna D. Hooker, *The Son of Man in Mark* (London, 1967); F. Hahn, *The Titles of Jesus in Christology* (London, 1969), pp. 15–53; I. H. Marshall, 'The Synoptic Son of Man Sayings in Recent Discussion', in *N.T.S.* XII (1965–6), pp. 327–51; the appendix on *bar-nāš(ā')* in Jewish Aramaic by G. Vermes (with Black's comments), in the 3rd ed. (1967) of M. Black, *An Aramaic Approach to the Gospels and Acts*; A. Gelston, 'A Sidelight on the "Son of Man"', in *S.J.T.* XXII (1969), pp. 189–96; R. N. Longenecker, *The Christology of Early Jewish Christianity* (London, 1970), pp. 82–93. Tödt's book (mentioned on p. 484) is now available in English translation, *The Son of Man in the Synoptic Tradition* (London, 1965).

p. 488, line 26

Also to C. H. Dodd, *Historical Tradition in the Fourth Gospel* (Cambridge, 1963), pp. 109–12.

p. 489, line 26

See also A. N. Sherwin-White, *Roman Society and Roman Law in the New Testament* (Oxford, 1963).

INDEX

Only the main references are given